IFIP Advances in Information and Communication Technology

517

Editor-in-Chief

IFIP – The International Federation for Information Processing

IFIP was founded in 1960 under the auspices of UNESCO, following the first World Computer Congress held in Paris the previous year. A federation for societies working in information processing, IFIP's aim is two-fold: to support information processing in the countries of its members and to encourage technology transfer to developing nations. As its mission statement clearly states:

> *IFIP is the global non-profit federation of societies of ICT professionals that aims at achieving a worldwide professional and socially responsible development and application of information and communication technologies.*

IFIP is a non-profit-making organization, run almost solely by 2500 volunteers. It operates through a number of technical committees and working groups, which organize events and publications. IFIP's events range from large international open conferences to working conferences and local seminars.

The flagship event is the IFIP World Computer Congress, at which both invited and contributed papers are presented. Contributed papers are rigorously refereed and the rejection rate is high.

As with the Congress, participation in the open conferences is open to all and papers may be invited or submitted. Again, submitted papers are stringently refereed.

The working conferences are structured differently. They are usually run by a working group and attendance is generally smaller and occasionally by invitation only. Their purpose is to create an atmosphere conducive to innovation and development. Refereeing is also rigorous and papers are subjected to extensive group discussion.

Publications arising from IFIP events vary. The papers presented at the IFIP World Computer Congress and at open conferences are published as conference proceedings, while the results of the working conferences are often published as collections of selected and edited papers.

IFIP distinguishes three types of institutional membership: Country Representative Members, Members at Large, and Associate Members. The type of organization that can apply for membership is a wide variety and includes national or international societies of individual computer scientists/ICT professionals, associations or federations of such societies, government institutions/government related organizations, national or international research institutes or consortia, universities, academies of sciences, companies, national or international associations or federations of companies.

More information about this series at http://www.springer.com/series/6102

José Ríos · Alain Bernard
Abdelaziz Bouras · Sebti Foufou (Eds.)

Product Lifecycle Management and the Industry of the Future

14th IFIP WG 5.1 International Conference, PLM 2017
Seville, Spain, July 10–12, 2017
Revised Selected Papers

 Springer

Editors
José Ríos
Polytechnic University of Madrid
Madrid
Spain

Alain Bernard
École Centrale de Nantes
Nantes
France

Abdelaziz Bouras
Qatar University
Doha
Qatar

Sebti Foufou
University of Burgundy
Dijon
France

ISSN 1868-4238   ISSN 1868-422X   (electronic)
IFIP Advances in Information and Communication Technology
ISBN 978-3-319-89221-4   ISBN 978-3-319-72905-3   (eBook)
https://doi.org/10.1007/978-3-319-72905-3

Printed on acid-free paper

This Springer imprint is published by Springer Nature
The registered company is Springer International Publishing AG
The registered company address is: Gewerbestrasse 11, 6330 Cham, Switzerland

Preface

Product lifecycle management, also known as PLM, is an integrated business approach to the collaborative creation, management, and dissemination of engineering data throughout the extended enterprises that create, manufacture, and operate engineered products and systems. PLM is widely recognized as a key enabler for the industry of the future, since it plays two fundamental roles. Firstly, in the digital integration of processes along the industrial value chain, and secondly, as a source of true product-related data across the product entire lifecycle.

IFIP PLM 2017 marked the 14th anniversary of the conference, which continues its progress at an excellent rate both in terms of quality and quantity. The topics covered in the program include ontologies, knowledge and data models, product service systems approaches, new product development, modular design and products, cyber-physical systems, building information modelling (BIM), educational approaches to PLM, production process simulation, digital factory, CAX tools, knowledge creation and management, and studies on PLM maturity, adoption, and implementation.

The IFIP International Conference on Product Lifecycle Management (www.plm-conference.org) started in 2003 and since then it has been held yearly around the world and has facilitated the exchange and discussion of the most up-to-date information on product lifecycle management among professionals from academia and industry. This is the official conference of the IFIP Working Group WG 5.1 "Global product development for the whole lifecycle" (www.ifip-wg51.org), and IFIP PLM 2017 was held in Seville, Spain, during July 10–12, 2017.

One of the objectives of the conference is to provide a platform for experts to discuss and share their success in applying advanced concepts in their respective fields. The IFIP PLM 2017 conference included an outstanding technical program, with distinguished keynote speeches on current developments and future vision, with a special focus on the industry of the future, from Eratos Filos (European Commission), Prof. Rainer Stark (TU Berlin), Fernando Valdés (MINECO), Verónica Pascual (ASTI Technologies Group), Domingo Ureña (M&M), Víctor de la Torre (Fujitsu Lab. of Europe), and Andy Clark (Airbus), as well as two insightful visits to manufacturing facilities, AIRBUS A400M Final Assembly Line and RENAULT gearbox production line. The conference also offered a great opportunity to young and aspiring researchers to present their research proposals and ongoing work during a dedicated PhD Workshop on the preconference day. This regular workshop is designed to support students in their networking activities and help them build their future community.

In line with the conference scientific sessions, IFIP PLM 2017 aimed at encouraging innovation and exchange with industry and digital service providers. A full day was dedicated to industry applications, highlighting some efforts and initiatives related to industry digitalization, in particular, in the SME context (ASTI Technologies Group, M&M, TECNATOM, Integral PLM, Everis, Marlo Tech, Soltel, and Servinform).

This book, organized in 11 chapters, is composed of selected enhanced papers presented at the IFIP PLM 2017 conference. Submissions followed a double-blind peer-review process. From a total of 78 submissions, 64 of them were accepted to be presented at the conference. This book is part of the IFIP *Advances in Information and Communication Technology* (AICT) series that publishes state-of-the-art results in the sciences and technologies of information and communication.

In addition to this conference, the *International Journal of Product Lifecycle Management* (IJPLM) is the official journal of the WG5.1 (www.inderscience.com/ijplm).

On behalf of the conference, we thank all the authors, sessions' chairs, reviewers, and keynote speakers for their help and support in achieving a great conference. Our gratitude goes to the University of Seville (US), the AIRBUS factory at San Pablo, the RENAULT factory of Seville, the Computer Science Engineering School at US, the Department of Languages and Computer Systems at US, and our sponsors FIDETIA, FUJITSU, EVERIS, PRODETUR, and EXTENDA for their great support.

We hope this book serves as a step forward in this exciting area of PLM and we look forward to meeting you at the next PLM conference in Turin, Italy, during July 2–4, 2018 (www.plm-conference.org).

September 2017

José Ríos
Alain Bernard
Abdelaziz Bouras
Sebti Foufou

Organization

Program Chairs

J. Ríos   Polytechnic University of Madrid, Spain
A. Bernard   ECN Nantes, France
S. Foufou   Université de Bourgogne, France and New York University Abu Dhabi, UAE

Conference Chairs

F. Mas   Airbus, Spain
D. Dutta   Purdue University, USA

Steering Committee

K.-D. Thoben (Chair)   University of Bremen, Germany
A. Bouras   Qatar University, Qatar
B. Eynard   UTC Compiègne, France
C. McMahon   Technical University of Denmark, Denmark
S. Fukuda (Honorary Professor)   Keio University, Japan
S. Terzi   Politecnico di Milano, Italy
L. Rivest   ETS Montreal, Canada
B. Gurumoorthy   IISc Bangalore, India
L. Roucoules   Arts et Métiers Paris Tech, France
P. Chiabert   Politecnico di Torino, Italy
R. Bandinelli   University of Florence, Italy
F. Noël   University of Grenoble, France

Scientific Committee

A. Aoussat   Arts et Métiers ParisTech, France
R. Ahmad   University of Alberta, Canada
R. Bandinelli   University of Florence, Italy
A. Bernard   Ecole Centrale de Nantes, France
N. Bilalis   Technical University of Crete, Greece
A. Bouras   Qatar University, Qatar
N. Chakpitak   Chiang Mai University, Thailand
P. Chiabert   Politecnico di Torino, Italy
U. Cugini   Politecnico di Milano, Italy
C. Danjou   Ecole de Technologie Supérieure de Montréal, Canada
E. De Senzi Zancul   University of Sao Paulo, Brazil

L. Roucoules	University of Technology of Troyes, France
N. Sapidis	University of Western Macedonia, Greece
J. Sauza Bedolla	Politecnico di Torino, Italy
M. Schabacker	University of Magdeburg, Germany
F. Segonds	Arts et Métiers ParisTech, France
A. Silventoinen	Lappeenranta University of Technology, Finland
A. Smirnov	St. Petersburg IFI and A. R. Academy of Sciences, Russia
J. Tarbutton	Clemson University, USA
S. Terzi	Politecnico di Milano, Italy
S. Vajna	University of Magdeburg, Germany
D. Vieira	Université du Québec à Trois-Rivières, Canada
S. Vishal	Aalto University, Finland
R. Young	Loughborough University, UK

Doctoral Workshop Chairs

| Y. Ouzrout | University of Lyon, France |
| M. Rossi | Politecnico di Milano, Italy |

Local Committee

C. Del Valle (Chair)	University of Seville, Spain
M. J. Escalona	University of Seville, Spain
J. Racero	University of Seville, Spain
I. Eguía	University of Seville, Spain
Andrés Jiménez	University of Seville, Spain
Manuel Oliva	Airbus, Spain
Julián García	University of Seville, Spain

Contents

PLM and Process Simulation

PLM, CAX and Knowledge Management

PLM and Education

BIM

Cyber-Physical Systems

Modular Design and Products

New Product Development

Ontologies, Knowledge and Data Models

Product, Service, Systems (PSS)

PLM Maturity, Implementation and Adoption

Set Based PLM Implementation, a Modular Approach to PLM Process Knowledge, Management and Automation

Bas Koomen[(⊠)]

Cadmes B.V., 's-Hertogenbosch, The Netherlands
bas@cadmes.com

Abstract. In many cases PLM implementations are halted in the first phases of larger projects. On average, implementation projects take longer, cost more than planned and not all goals are achieved despite modern software implementation methods like Agile or Scrum. This paper proposes another approach, in which the implementation method is inspired by product development methods in general and set based concurrent engineering in particular. The method is structured in five major steps alongside a method of knowledge management and reuse to support the implementation method. The five steps deal with scope and maturity level, requirements analysis, process mapping, rationale based solution selection and system consolidation. The element of knowledge reuse makes this method also accessible for small and medium sized companies, generally reluctant to conduct a fundamental process analysis before starting a software implementation. From there this knowledge can evolve towards a product configuration framework for PLM implementation. The paper outlines the method in theory and proposes further steps to investigate each step in more detailed research and case studies.

Keywords: PLM implementation · Knowledge management
PLM process management · SME

1 Introduction

Over 15 years of field experience in industry have led to the realization that often organizations regard PLM mainly as software that should solve their business challenges. They rely on expertise from vendors or external experts from who they expect to explain to them what is the best software to select and how PLM should be implemented. First, they start with software implementation and then, during the project, they find out that they actually needed a definition of processes, procedures, structures, strategies, etc. after all and then need to retrace their steps in the project to save the investment made. This is especially the case with SME organizations where a high amount of time and money is lost on problematic implementations.

Research on PLM maturity level [1] shows that many organizations do not evolve beyond basic level of PDM (Product Data Management). In literature, different approaches have been laid out to overcome this problem. Section 2 elaborates more on this.

© IFIP International Federation for Information Processing 2017
Published by Springer International Publishing AG 2017. All Rights Reserved
J. Ríos et al. (Eds.): PLM 2017, IFIP AICT 517, pp. 3–12, 2017.
https://doi.org/10.1007/978-3-319-72905-3_1

A number of organizations that have been worked with are manufacturers of machinery. These organizations are working in an engineering-to-order structure, but are looking to change to a configure-to-order structure. At some point in time, around 2014, the idea came up that at a high level of abstraction, PDM/PLM software implementations could be regarded the same way. A first literature review was performed to look for existing research on this idea of which the most important findings are described in Sect. 2.

From literature review and insights from actual projects, a framework was defined for a new method to implement PLM, optimized for knowledge reuse and therefore suitable for SME. The framework is a middle way between a "blank canvas" PLM implementation and a fully standardized "off-the-shelf" or "industry template" implementation. The content of this framework is described in Sect. 3.

Before it can be confirmed or denied that this framework indeed can lead to a better world for PLM in SME, more research has to be performed, as further described in Sect. 4.

2 Background/Related Work

2.1 PLM

Holistic PLM. This paper builds on the concept of holistic PLM. In this concept, PLM is not just the software that is referred to as PLM software, but the combination of strategy, culture and people, structures, process and interaction patterns and IT architecture.

Processes and interaction patterns are defined by strategy, supported by (product and knowledge) structure and they use culture, people and IT architecture as a resource [2]. This implies that an implementation of PLM includes a transformation or at least some kind of assessment or formalization of all elements in the holistic concept of PLM. Also the IT infrastructure includes all software, hardware and network infrastructure relevant to the processes and interaction patterns.

The benefits of PLM are not discussed in this paper and assumed as significant for most organizations.

Implementation. Literature exists about different approaches to improve the implementation strategy for SME. Batenburg et al. [1] point out the importance of maturity level before implementing software and how to measure it with an alignment framework. Also they propose to do a step-wise implementation instead of a full scope implementation at once. What is not covered is how to achieve the desired maturity level.

Silventoinen et al. [3] propose a roadmap approach where the emphasis is on growing awareness of the benefits of PLM. From there a company derives motivation to implement processes and software. They also recognize the need for a certain process maturity level in order to be successful.

Schuh et al. [4] have defined a process framework with macro level process definitions for industries and the corresponding PLM software requirements. This research mainly looks for a match between macro level processes and reference models for IT-systems serving these processes.

Navarro et al. [5] have investigated the application of lean principles in PLM implementation projects. They suggest that when lean principles (customer value, creating flow, continuous improvement) are applied, PLM implementation challenges could be minimized.

Bokinge and Malmqvist have done a deeper review of existing literature on PLM implementation guidelines [6]. They have summarized it into twenty guidelines in four categories (Project process, goals, system and process design, organization). Main conclusion is that the pre-work before installing software is at least as or more important than the technical implementation.

Maturity Level. Another area of research that has been looked into is PLM maturity level [1–3] and organization capability level. Two conclusions can be drawn from this research: (1) Most surveyed companies do not evolve much beyond basic PDM processes when implementing PLM. (2) A solid PLM process definition is a critical success factor for a lasting PLM software implementation.

A question is whether conclusion 1 is a consequence of conclusion 2 and companies struggle to formalize and (re)define their processes. Apparently it is difficult for organizations which do not have in-house business process analysts to analyze their processes in a way that can be used effectively for a PLM software implementation.

2.2 Product Development

The main idea of this paper is to apply product development principles to the implementation of PLM. Therefore, literature has been reviewed about the following product development methods.

QFD. Quality Function Deployment [7] is a methodology in which different aspects of product development are related to each other. It offers a number of matrix diagrams in which product characteristics, customer requirements, process characteristics, competition characteristics, etc. can be checked for correlation.

SBCE. Set based concurrent engineering [8–11] is a modular design methodology in which different areas of a complex product can be developed in parallel. For each subsystem, a broad set of feasible solutions is defined based on proven technology.

2.3 Product Configuration and Modularization

Another area of product specification that has been reviewed is product configuration. Many companies are investigating product configuration as a mean to lower development costs but increase the flexibility to customize products for their customers. The most common way to do this is with a modular approach [12]. Modules are developed in variants. The final product is a combination of modules and parts based on customer requirements.

3   Proposed Implementation Approach

The main focus of this research is an implementation approach for holistic PLM with higher involvement of all stakeholders and lower investment needs for full business process analysis. The approach is structured in five major phases as pictured in Fig. 1. After defining the scope and process state, non-functional requirements are defined parallel to a three level process map. The operations in the lowest detail level of the process map serve as functional requirements. For each operation a set of possible PLM implementation alternatives is proposed. The alternative options are scored against the non-functional requirements and consolidated into a functional and technical specification of the entire PLM implementation. Solution sets are managed as knowledge in a knowledge base for later reuse.

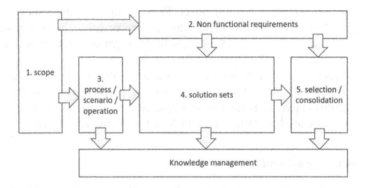

Fig. 1.   Schematic overview of steps in proposed set based PLM implementation method

In the following paragraphs, each phase is explained in more details.

3.1   Scope, State and Maturity Level

At the start of the method scope, state and maturity level must be made explicit for all stakeholders in the implementation process.

Scope.   The stakeholder must define which part of the organization or processes will be affected and involved in the PLM implementation. Interactions between this part and other parts of the organization need to be identified and described in terms of input and output of materials and information.

State.   The stakeholders must be able to answer whether the implementation of PLM affects the current state of the organization, future state or is a mean to transform from current to future state. This is important for process modeling in the third phase where process models need to be descriptive (describe what people are doing) or prescriptive (define what people should do) [13]. Bokinge and Malmqvist [6] found that the two main strategies for PLM implementation are: adopt the commercial software or adopt the business processes. This confirms the need to have a common awareness of state.

Maturity Level. Maturity level assessment is a way to determine if an organization is ready for a specific level of PLM implementation. To do this, the frameworks of Batenburg et al. [1] is selected to use for work units and processes.

VSM. A suitable method to assess scope and state may be value stream mapping, where stakeholders are offered a method to reach a collective understanding of current and potential future state as well as the scope boundaries. A value stream can be used to define a scope definition for a specific product or product family [14].

3.2 Requirements Analysis

Non-functional requirements are closely related to the business case of the implementation, since they deal with business aspects like legal constraints, economic constraints, safety, efficiency, capacity and performance.

Requirements analysis and requirements engineering (RE) are used in software development. RE distinguishes between functional and non-functional requirements, where non-functional requirements are requirements that cannot be defined as functional, data or process [15].

A framework of common requirements for companies in an industry segment needs to be defined for this paper's research. When starting RE with this framework, stakeholders can focus on the validation and negotiation phase and have better documented requirements sets at the end.

3.3 Process Modeling

The implementation methodology in this research aims to offer a framework of process modeling conventions that describes the tasks that the organization has to perform in a way that is usable for a PLM system design, can be understood by all stakeholders and can be reused in a modular way for future implementations in the same industry segment.

Three Detail Levels. Main concept of this process modeling framework is the definition for three detail levels:

- Process level. This is used to identify the main activity in the high level process chain of the organization.
- Scenario level. These are the user stories or what people have to do in their work.
- Operation level. These are specific tasks that a person or machine performs to do the work.

Processes and operations are sequential in most cases. Scenarios do not necessarily have to be sequential. This is one of the key elements in this approach. A process can be seen as a black box with input and output. Inside the black box certain "things" have to be done, which are represented by scenarios. Scenarios are composed of operations. In Fig. 2 an example is given to explain the principle.

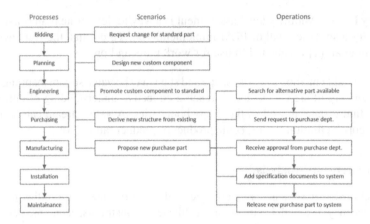

Fig. 2. Example of 3-tier process mapping for engineer-to-order company.

Reuse and Duplicity. Operations can appear in multiple scenarios and scenarios can be used in multiple processes. Also many operations are common in general or common for a specific industry segment.

Modeling Language. For this paper three methods have been reviewed to capture and model processes in the three different levels.

UML 2.0. Unified Modeling Language [16, 17] is a widely accepted framework of notations, used to develop software. It is very suitable for object oriented analysis and design and therefore can be used to model the interaction with data-objects. Since a PLM software implementation often uses already developed software, only a few diagram types are regularly used: mainly use-case diagrams, activity diagrams, use-case narrative and class diagrams.

BPMN 2.0. Business Process Model and Notation [18, 19] has many similarities to the UML Activity Diagram (AD). BPMN has more meaningful symbols for business processes and is automatically connected to Business Process Execution Language. Research has been done on difference in readability between UML AD and BPMN, but this was not significant [20, 21].

VSM. Value Stream Mapping [14] is a technique that originates in lean manufacturing. For this paper, VSM is useful because it focuses on the operation instead of the roles. It does not answer the question what a person does, but what is needed to be done in order to get a result. This leaves more room for alternative options for a given requirement.

After a review of different process modeling languages with a target group of PLM consultants, BPMN 2.0 has been named more suitable to model scenarios and operations. In Fig. 3, the previous example scenario is modeled in this language.

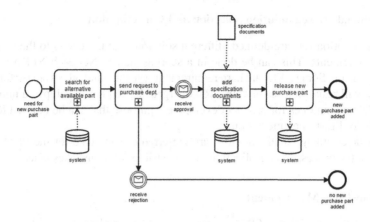

Fig. 3. A scenario modeled in BMPN 2.0.

To standardize the method of process modeling, the way BPMN is used needs to be narrowed down in purpose specific conventions for this implementation strategy. The detail levels must be right, not too detailed and not too course. Following conventions are proposed in this context:

- Scenario in the organization = process in BPMN
- Operation within a scenario = sub-process BPMN
- Definition when to use triggers, conditions, forks and states
- Start and end conditions must be compatible with connected processes

3.4   Solution Sets

The method to relate a finite number of possible solutions to an operation is inspired by SBCE [8]. The core principle is that more ways can be identified to perform an operation in a PLM environment. In the previous example, the scenario "propose new purchase part" includes an operation "send request to purchase department". A finite list of possible solutions could look like this:

1. Fill in a paper form and deliver it at purchase dept.
2. Write an email and send it to purchase dept.
3. Fill in a standardized digital form in a word processor and store it in a predefined location on the network.
4. Fill in a form in an ERP system.
5. Create a new item in a PLM software and start a "propose" workflow for approval.

The set of a single operation (functional requirement) and the list of possible solutions (function fulfillment options) is a module in the implementation strategy.

3.5 Rationale Based Solution Selection and Consolidation

When the solution sets are defined, different solutions can be related to the non-functional requirements. This can be done in a scoring matrix. Not each NFR requires a similar decision. Some NFRs are hard requirements (yes/no) and others are performance NFR that will result in a scalar value. Raudberget [22, 23] has developed a number of these selection matrices for product development purpose that can be tailored towards the needs for PLM implementation.

After determining which solutions are preferred or candidate for the PLM implementation, the process of consolidation of the feasible solutions takes place.

3.6 Knowledge Management

In line with the principles of SBCE (proven technology) and product configuration (no development in the specification process), the solution sets should be reused as much as possible. Therefore, a structure of knowledge management is needed.

Kennedy et al. [10] describe knowledge elicitation as a second value stream intersecting the primary value stream of the solution sets. Check sheets are used to capture design knowledge as the process is executed. With this method, capturing knowledge can be as accessible as possible for those involved in the implementation process.

4 Conclusion and Future Research

The literature review, performed for this research, did not reveal any similar approach to PLM implementation as proposed in this paper. So far, it can only be suspected that this method has a higher stakeholder involvement with less implementation time compared to other methods, since it has not been put to the test. Initial feedback from domain experts who have experience in PLM implementation has been positive.

Until now, individual elements of the proposed framework have been tested ad-hoc in running projects. The process modeling phase has been tried most thoroughly in a larger project as a second attempt after a "traditional" technical specification. The difference in involvement by the main stakeholder was significant and it laid a fundament under a successful implementation of software afterwards.

The next step to verify the proposed methodology is to perform case studies. A first case study is in progress at a Dutch SME company that develops waste recycling equipment. Phase 1 (scope) of the proposed method has been tested completely and confirms the benefits as expected. Stakeholders are more involved and there is a better common understanding of the project. Phase 2 and 3 are progressing in parallel, but it is too early for conclusions.

In parallel, a large number of finished PLM implementations are going to be analyzed in the three layered structure of processes, scenarios and operations. This will result in a better understanding of the commonality of scenarios and operations in a specific industry. The result will be used as input for a catalog of reusable solution sets.

To quantify the potential benefits of this proposed implementation methodology, an extensive survey is planned among PLM customers to unveil their initial motivations and expectation before they implemented the systems and what was realized at the end. Also, NFRs will be retrieved from this survey to build the framework of common requirements.

References

1. Batenburg, R., Helms, R., Versendaal, J.: PLM roadmap: stepwise PLM implementation based on the concepts of maturity and alignment. Int. J. Prod. Lifecycle Manage. 1(4), 333–351 (2006). https://doi.org/10.1504/IJPLM.2006.011053
2. Silventoinen, A., Pels, H., Kärkkäinen, L.H.: Towards future PLM maturity assessment dimensions. In: PLM11 – 8th International Conference on Product Lifecycle Management (2011)
3. Silventoinen, A., Papinniemi, J., Lampela, H.: A roadmap for product lifecycle management implementation in SMEs. In: The XX ISPIM Conference (2009)
4. Schuh, G., Rozenfeld, H., Assmus, D., Zancul, E.: Process oriented framework to support PLM implementation. Comput. Ind. 59(2008), 210–218 (2008). https://doi.org/10.1016/j.compind.2007.06.015
5. Navarro, R., Cloonan, J., Bubois, R., Tiwari, A.: Improving efficiency in Product Lifecycle Management implementation projects by applying lean principles. In: PLM11 – 8th International Conference on Product Lifecycle Management (2011). https://doi.org/10.1504/IJPLM.2013.063212
6. Bokinge, M., Malmqvist, J.: PLM implementation guidelines - relevance and application in practice: a discussion of findings from a retrospective case study. Int. J. Prod. Lifecycle Manage. 6(1), 79–98 (2012). https://doi.org/10.1504/IJPLM.2012.046442
7. Eureka, W., Ryan, N.: The Customer Driven Company, Managerial Perspectives on QFD. ASI Press, Dearborn (1988)
8. Ward, A., Sobek II, D.: Lean Product and Process Development, 2nd edn. Lean Enterprise Institute, Cambridge (2014)
9. Sobek, D., Ward, A., Liker, J.: Toyota's principles of set-based concurrent engineering. Sloan Manage. Rev. Winter 40(2), 67–83 (1999)
10. Kennedy, M., Harmon, K., Minnock, E.: Ready, Set, Dominate: Implement Toyota's Set-Based Learning for Developing Products and Nobody Can Catch You. The Oaklea Press, Richmond (2008)
11. Khan, M., Al-Ahaab, A., Doultsinou, A., Shehab, E., Ewers, P., Sulowski, R.: Set-based concurrent engineering process within the leanPPD environment. In: 2011 the 18th ISPE International Conference on Concurrent Engineering, Massachusetts (2011)
12. Hvam, L., Mortensen, N., Riis, J.: Product Customization. Springer, Heidelberg (2008). https://doi.org/10.1007/978-3-540-71449-1
13. Münch, J., Armbrust, O., Kowalczyk, M., Soto, M.: Software Process Definition and Management. Springer, Heidelberg (2012). https://doi.org/10.1007/978-3-642-24291-5
14. Martin, K., Osterling, M.: Value Stream Mapping: How to Visualize Work and Align Leadershop for Organizational Transformation. McGraw-Hill, New York (2014)
15. Mahalakshmi, K., Prabhakar, R.: Performance evaluation of non functional requirements. J. Comput. Sci. Technol. 13 (2013)
16. OMG: Unified Modeling Language Specification, version 2.5. Object Management Group (OMG) (2015)
17. Fowler, M., Scott, K.: UML Distilled: A Brief Guide to the Standard Object Modeling Language, 2nd edn. Addison Wesley Longman, Reading (2000)

18. OMG: Business Process Model and Notation (BPMN) Version 2.0. Object Management Group (OMG) (2011)
19. Freund, J., Rücker, B.: Real-Life BPMN: Using BPMN 2.0 to Analyze, Improve, and Automate Processes in Your Company. Camunda, Berlin (2014)
20. Geambasu, C.: BPMN vs. UML Activity Diagram for business process modeling. Account. Manage. Inf. Syst. 11(4), 637–651 (2012)
21. Peixoto, D., Batista, V., Atayde, A., Borges, E., Resende, R., Pádua, C.: A comparison of BPMN and UML 2.0 Activity Diagrams. In: Proceedings of VII Simpósio Brasileiro de Qualidade de Software (2008)
22. Raudberget, D.: Practical applications of set-based concurrent engineering in industry. J. Mech. Eng. 56(11), 685–695 (2010)
23. Raudberget, D.: Enabling set-based concurrent engineering in traditional product development. In: 2011 the International Conference on Engineering Design, Kopenhagen (2011)

PLM Adoption Model for SMEs

Mourad Messaadia[1(✉)], Fatah Benatia[2], David Baudry[1],
and Anne Louis[1]

[1] CESI/LINEACT, Rouen, France
{mmessaadia, dbaudry, alouis}@cesi.fr
[2] Laboratoire de Mathématiques Appliquées, Université M. Khider,
Biskra, Algérie
fatahbenatia@hotmail.com

Abstract. PLM adoption can be a source of competitiveness and sustainability for SMEs. In the other hand, the introduction of new ICT (Information and communication technologies) technologies, such PLM, is a complex process that involves challenging the existing organization, not only in terms of information flow but also the human resources management and OEM/Suppliers relationship level. As seen in literature review, there are a number of factors that facilitate the adoption of ICT technology, but we also identified a number of obstacles that will need to act as the adoption takes place. The paper focused on issues regarding the ICT adoption, especially PLM solutions by SMEs. Based on investigation, this paper proposes a mathematical model of PLM adoption.

Keywords: PLM · ICT adoption · SMEs · Data analysis

1 Introduction

The literature review has addressed the topic of PLM from different angles. However, the adoption aspect was only dealt by a few works such [1] where author proposes statistical tools to improve the organizational adoption of new PLM systems and highlights on the importance of survey early in the PLM introduction process; [2] provides a review of the main developments in the AHP (Analytical Hierarchy Process) methodology as a tool for decision makers to be able to do more informed decisions regarding their investment in PLM; [3] on the adoption of PLM IT solutions and discussed the relationship between "PLM adopter" and "lifecycle-oriented" companies in order to achieve the adoption aspect we have considered PLM as an innovate ICT for SMEs. Thus we integrated works on ICT and innovation adoptions.

ICT technology is one of the ways, at the disposal of a company to increase its productivity. ICT can reduce business costs, improve productivity and strengthen growth possibilities and the generation of competitive advantages [4]. Despite the work done and large companies evolution in terms of PLM, SMEs still have difficulties to understand all the potential of such technologies [5]. Their adoption of ICT is slow and late, primarily because they find that ICT adoption is difficult [6] and SMEs adoption is still lower than expected.

When implementing a PLM solution in a company, the implementation difficulties are directly dependent on the complexity of the organization, costs and the possible

J. Ríos et al. (Eds.): PLM 2017, IFIP AICT 517, pp. 13–22, 2017.
https://doi.org/10.1007/978-3-319-72905-3_2

opacity of the real behaviours in the field. Indeed, the implementation of PLM solution seems to scare SMEs in terms of resource costs and deployment.

The integration of the PLM solutions and its adoption by the SMEs has succeeded the interest of several research works. Among these research works we distinguish those on adoption process improving through statistical tools [1]. In the same way authors in [7] conducted an investigation around 1500 enterprises and analyse the process adoption. This investigation shows that size on enterprise, human capital of the workforce and the geographic proximity with large firms has an impact on ICT adoption. In another hand, we find investigation based on empirical analysis which highlights the role of management practices, especially the manager, and quality control on the ICT adoption.

Another investigation was conducted on a thousand firms in manufacturing in Brazil and India and examines the characteristics of firms adopting ICT and the consequences of adoption for performance [8]. In addition to previous results, they show the impact of educational system and the positive association between ICT adoption and education. Several barriers to IT adoption have been identified, including: lack of knowledge about the potential of IT, a shortage of resources such financial and expertise and lack of skills [6].

According to [9] the skill workers have an impact on ICT adoption. Workers with high (low) proportions of skill can have a comparative advantage (disadvantage) in minimizing the costs both of ICT adoption and of learning how to make best use of ICTs.

An investigation of works done on ICT adoption conclude on the importance to analyse the impact on ICT system implementation and adoption processes and how they do so, and how implementation and adoption processes could be supported on the organizational, group, and individual levels [10]. Based on previous works, we will consider that PLM is an innovative ICT solution for SMEs.

Next paragraph will introduce the problem statement and context of study. Third paragraph is on the proposed the model of PLM adoption based on quantitative KPIs. The fourth paragraph highlights the obtained results and their discussion. Finally, we conclude and discuss future work on how to improve and deploy our model.

2   Study Context

The first initiative of this work was conducted during the INTERREG project called "BENEFITS" where different adoption KPI's was identified [11].

On the basis of an analysis of the various studies carried out with several companies, it is possible to collect different indicators. These indicators have been classified according to 4 axes identified through PLM definitions analysis. The 4-axis structure (Strategy, Organisation, Process and Tools) seemed clear and gave a good visibility to the impact of the indicators on the different levels of enterprise [11].

For our work, Survey conducted followed different steps from questionnaire designing until data analysis [12]. One of problems faced during questionnaire design is the decision of what questions to ask, how to best word them and how to arrange the questions to yield the information required. For these questions were conducted on the basis of indicators, words were reviewed by experts and finally we reorganised questions according to new 4 axes: Human Factors, Organisational Factors, Technical Factors and Economic Factors. This new decomposition does not affect the indicators but brings a fluidity and easier understanding for the interviewees (SMEs) (Fig 1).

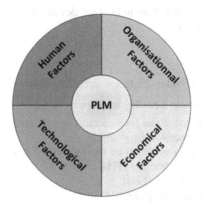

Fig. 1. PLM axis structuration

Also, the objective of the investigation is to understand the needs of SMEs according to the introduction of digital technology within the automotive sector and to anticipate the increase in competence needed to help these SMEs face the change by setting up the necessary services and training. The survey was conducted on a panel of 33 companies (14 with study activities and 19 with manufacturing activities) of which 50% are small structures as shown in Fig. 2.

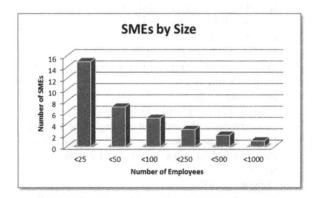

Fig. 2. Panel of SMEs interviewed

3 PLM Adoption Indicators

The concept of adoption may be defined as a process composed of a certain number of steps by which a potential adopter must pass before accepting the new product, new service or new idea [13]. Adoption can be seen as an individual adoption and organizational adoption. The individual one focuses on user behaviour according to new technology and have an impact on the investment in IT technology [14]. In the organisational adoption the organisation forms an opinion of the new technology and assesses it. Based on this, organisation makes the decision to purchase and use this new technology [14]. Based on work done in [11] we developed the questionnaire according to adoption factors (Table 1).

Table 1. Adoption factors according to the 4th axes

Axes	Questions according to adoption factors
Human factor	Ability to assess technological opportunities (FH1) Resistance to change (FH2) The learning effects on previous use of ICT technology (FH3) Relative advantage (FH4) Risk aversion (FH5) Emphasis on quality (FH6)
Organisational factor	Average size of effective of SME between 50 and 200 (FO1) Age of SMEs (FO2) Competitive environment (FO3) Rank of SME (FO4) Geographical proximity (FO5) Number of adopters (FO6) Interdependencies Collaboration (FO7) Existing leading firms (OEM) in your economic environment (FO8) Informal communication mode (FO9) Existing Innovation process (FO10) Knowledge Management (FO11) Process synchronization (FO12) Existing R&D activities (FO13) Existing certified (QM) system (FO14)
Technological factor	The position of SME related to ICT technologies (FT1) Interoperability (FT2) Ergonomic (FT3) Compatibility with similar technology (FT4) Compatibility with needs and existing process (FT5) How is evaluated before adopting technology (FT6) Have you had the opportunity to test the technology before its adoption (FT7) Complexity (FT8) The frequency of new technology integration (FT9) Level of skill and knowledge (FT10) Existing software (PDM, CAD/CAM, ERP) (FT11)
Economical factor	Indirect costs (FE1) Existing R&D process (FE2) Expected profitability (FE3) Merger-acquisition (M&A) Strategy (FE4)

4   Questionnaire Analysis

The previous step was the construction of the questionnaire by methodological tool with a set of questions that follow in a structured way (Fig. 3). It is presented in electronic form and was administered directly through face to face and by phone.

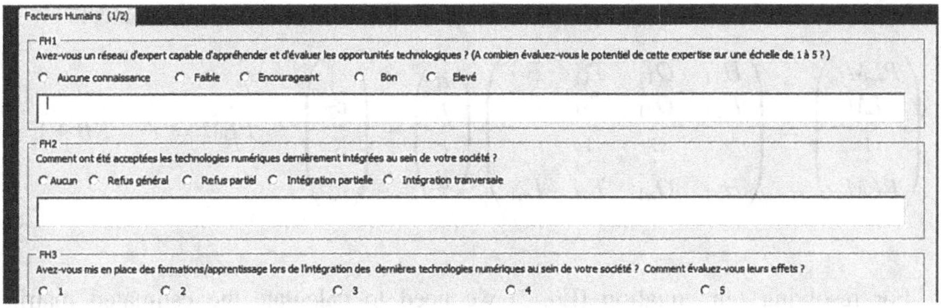

Fig. 3. PLM-Eval-Tool: questionnaire

The questions were asked by a PLM consultant with directors, engineers & technicians for increasing responses validity. The questions were design based on Likert scale and for five levels; in addition, a commentary frame has been added to question evaluation (from 1 to 5) which can be filled by the direct exchanges during the interview.

Once responses evaluated we need to describe the adoption model in mathematical way. Based on results we can write the dependencies equation which makes the link between the PLM Level (PLM_i) and adoption factors (O, H, T and E).

$$PLM_i = aH_i + bO_i + cT_i + dE_i + \varepsilon_i \qquad (1)$$

For: $i = 1, \ldots, n$, the hypothesis related to the model (Eq. 1) is the distribution of the error ε is independent and the error is centred with constant variance $\varepsilon_i \sim N(0, \sigma^2)$; $\sigma^2 = var(\varepsilon_i)$

In order to conclude that there is a significant relationship between PLM level and Adoption factors, the Regression (Eq. 1) is used during estimation and to improve the quality of the estimates. The first step is to calculate the adoption factors according to:

$$H_i = \frac{1}{n_H} \sum_{j=1}^{n_H} H_{ij}, n_H = \textit{number of questions related to the humain factor } H$$

$$O_i = \frac{1}{n_O} \sum_{j=1}^{n_O} O_{ij}, n_O, \text{ number of questions related to the Organisation factor } O$$

$$T_i = \frac{1}{n_T} \sum_{j=1}^{n_T} T_{ij}, n_T = \textit{number of questions related to the technogical factor } T$$

$$E_i = \frac{1}{n_E} \sum_{j=1}^{n_E} E_{ij}, n_E = \textit{number of questions related to the economical factor } E$$

Once the fourth factors calculated, the matrix form of our model becomes:

$$\begin{pmatrix} PLM_1 \\ PLM_2 \\ \vdots \\ PLM_n \end{pmatrix} = \begin{pmatrix} H_{11} & O_{11} & T_{11} & E_{11} \\ H_{21} & O_{21} & T_{21} & E_{21} \\ \vdots & \vdots & \vdots & \vdots \\ H_{n1} & O_{n1} & T_{n1} & E_{n1} \end{pmatrix} \begin{pmatrix} a \\ b \\ c \\ d \end{pmatrix} + \begin{pmatrix} \varepsilon_1 \\ \varepsilon_2 \\ \vdots \\ \varepsilon_n \end{pmatrix} \Leftrightarrow PLM = Y = XB + E \tag{2}$$

For resolving our equation (Eq. 2) we need to calculate the estimated matrix B. With estimated B called:

$$\hat{B} = (X^t X)^{-1} X^t Y \tag{3}$$

Through all these equations (observation) we can give the general regression equation of PLM.

$$PLM = aH + bO + cT + dE + \varepsilon \tag{4}$$

The methodology adopted started by determining (estimating) a, b, c, d parameters of the multiple-regression function. The result of estimation is defined by: $\hat{a}, \hat{b}, \hat{c}, \hat{d}$. For this, we choose the method of "mean square error" calculated through Matlab. In the second step, we calculate the dependency between PLM level (result of multiple-regression) and the adoption factors (H, O, T and E) by the regression coefficient (R), especially the Determination Coefficient (D).

Where:

$$D = R^2 = \frac{SSR}{SST}, SSR = \textit{Some square Regression}; SST = \textit{Total Some Square};$$

$$SSE = \textit{Some square Error}; SST = SSR + SSE$$

If $|R| \rightarrow 1$, We have a strong dependence and good regression.

4.1 Numerical Results

After the investigation the PLM-Eval-Tool generates a data table (Fig. 4) of evaluated responses that will be used to build our adoption model.

Once the data collected, we applied our approach for obtaining the estimated parameters $\hat{a}, \hat{b}, \hat{c}, \hat{d}$ through (Eq. 3).

Date de création	Secteur d'activités	Effectif	FH1	FH2	FH3	FH4	FH5	FH6		FO1
01/01/1905	l'ingénierie des métiers de l'automobile	100	5	3	3	4	3	5		3
01/01/1995	Fabrication de cartes électroniques assemblées	17	5	1	4	3	1	5		3
01/01/1984	l'automobile, l'aéronautique et la défense	15	4	4	3	4	1	4		3

Fig. 4. Brief view of collected data

$$\begin{pmatrix} \hat{a} \\ \hat{b} \\ \hat{c} \\ \hat{d} \end{pmatrix} = \begin{pmatrix} 0.0697 \\ 0.6053 \\ 0.1958 \\ 0.1137 \end{pmatrix} \tag{5}$$

With $R^2 = 0.9841$ which is considered as a very good regression, and validate the proposed equation (Eq. 1).

The numerical result equation is:

$$PLM_{Evaluation} = 0.0697H_i + 0.6053O_i + 0.1958T_i + 0.1137E_i \tag{6}$$

4.2   Result Discussion

Concerning the "Error" we will consider the highest one which is equal to $\frac{1}{n}\sum \varepsilon_i^2 = \frac{0.4217}{33} = 0.0128$. This means that all values of PLM_Evaluation will be considered with ± 0.0128. We can also determine confidence interval for the parameters a, b, c and d using the student law $t_{\alpha,k}$, where α is the Confidence threshold, or the Tolerance error rate, the choice of the value α in our case is $\alpha = 0.05$ and $k = 4$ is the degree of freedom (the number of parameters) $\hat{\sigma}_a$ is the standard deviation (the square root of the variance). In our case $t_{\alpha,k} = t_{0.05,4} = 2.132$ (Fig. 5).

Figure (5), shows Student's law with "k" degrees of latitude and different values of $\alpha = 0.0005; \ldots; 0.25$. The student test can be applied to a, b, c and d to determine the parameters influencing the PLM. By testing the null hypothesis $H_0 : a = 0$ against the alternative hypothesis $H_1 : a \neq 0$.

Using data from a sample, the probability that the observed values are the chance result of sampling, assuming the null hypothesis (H_0) is true, is calculated. If this probability turns out to be smaller than the significance level of the test, the null hypothesis is rejected.

k	0.25	0.20	0.15	0.10	0.05	0.025	0.010	0.005	0.0025	0.0010	0.0005
1	1.000	1.376	1.963	3.078	6.314	12.71	31.82	63.66	127.3	318.3	636.6
2	0.816	1.061	1.386	1.886	2.920	4.303	6.965	9.925	14.09	22.33	31.60
3	0.765	0.978	1.250	1.638	2.353	3.182	4.541	5.841	7.453	10.21	12.92
4	0.741	0.941	1.190	1.533	2.132	2.776	3.747	4.604	5.598	7.173	8.610

Fig. 5. Student table

$$\begin{cases} H_0 : a = 0 \\ H_1 : a \neq 0 \end{cases} \tag{7}$$

For this we will calculate: $T = \frac{|\hat{a}|}{\hat{\sigma}_a}$

Then we will compare it to the value of $t_{0,05;4} = 2,13$

If $T < t_{0,05;4} = 2,13$, we accept $H_0 : a = 0$, the H parameter does not influence the realization of PLM and we will then recreate another equation of regression without H. The same analysis was done for b, c, d.

5 Discussion

Once the model developed another aspect of the analysis was explored, that of the recommendations. Effectively, the PLM-Eval-Tool offer also a view (Fig. 6) the results according to such factors as change management, structured sharing, extended enterprise, evaluation capacity and willingness to integrate. These factors are seen as a numerical focus, and first returns on SMEs analysis are:

- 30% of companies consider themselves to be under-equipped regarding to information technology.
- Companies recognize that information technology is very much involved in the development process, but for the majority of them organizational aspects and informal exchanges are decisive.
- They believe that they have the in-house skills to anticipate and evaluate technological opportunities and are very "open" to the integration of new technologies.
- SMEs are pragmatic and are waiting for the opportunity of a project or a new client to introduce software and associated training: design or simulation tool, ENX link, digital models...

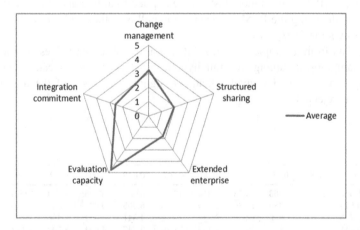

Fig. 6. Radar showing the average of the results obtained by the companies that responded to the questionnaire. Scaling from 0: Very low to 5: Very good

- Companies often note a gain when introducing a new technology but highlight compatibility issues with existing technologies, including ERP. (Systematic evaluation on demonstrator before implementation)
- **The adoption of digital technology by their partners and suppliers is not a concern today.**
- A concern to better structure their data and define their workflow in particular around knowledge management and collaborative innovation.
- A request for training on tools, existing gateways for data transfer, standards and standards to be used throughout the product lifecycle.
- A request for information on the potential of SaaS solutions and shared services. (Design, simulation, exchange platform)

According to obtained results, here is a list of first actions that we propose to implement:

- To make the players in the sector aware of the evolution of this increasingly digital environment.
- Diagnose the existing digital chaining in companies to promote the benefits of the PLM approach. (Processes, tools, skills, etc.)
- To propose levers of competitiveness by the identification of "Mutualized Services" and "Software as a Service" solutions.
- To propose devices to gain skills and accompany the change management of manufacturers, equipment manufacturers, to the SMEs in the region.

6 Conclusion

The statistical analysis allowed us to develop a mathematical model to evaluate the adoption of an SME in terms of PLM. Thus, SMEs will be able to carry out a first self-evaluation without calling on honest consultants. However, this model will have to improve with more SMEs results and taking into account the different activity sectors aspect.

As future work, we envisage to work on several cases studies (deployment on France) in order to improve the mathematical model. Also, another work will be carried out in order to generate recommendations automatically. The aim of this approach is to offer SMEs a tool for analysis and decision-making for the upstream stage in the introduction or adoption of PLM tools.

Acknowledgement. Acknowledgement is made to PFA automotive which has initiated this study around the technical information, processes and skills management system, which provides data structuring for the extended company with the support of the DIRECCTE IdF, the RAVI for the identification of companies and the CETIM to conduct the interviews.

References

1. Bergsjö, D.: PLM adoption through statistical analysis. In: Pels, J.H., et al. (eds.) The proceedings of 11th International Conference on Product Lifecycle Management, PLM, vol. 11, pp. 11–13, July 2011
2. Ristova, E., Gecevska, V.: AHP methodology and selection of an advanced information technology due to PLM software adoption. In: Proceedings of the 15th International Scientific Conference on Industrial Systems, September 2011
3. Rossi, M., Riboldi, D., Cerri, D., Terzi, S., Garetti, M.: Product lifecycle management adoption versus lifecycle orientation: evidences from Italian companies. In: Bernard, A., Rivest, L., Dutta, D. (eds.) PLM 2013. IAICT, vol. 409, pp. 346–355. Springer, Heidelberg (2013). https://doi.org/10.1007/978-3-642-41501-2_35
4. Barba-Sánchez, V., Martínez-Ruiz, M.D.P., Jiménez-Zarco, A.I.: Drivers, benefits and challenges of ICT adoption by small and medium sized enterprises (SMEs): a literature review. Problems and Perspectives in Management 5(1), 104–115 (2007)
5. Hollenstein, H.: The decision to adopt information and communication technologies (ICT): firm-level evidence for Switzerland. In: The Economic Impact of ICT, Measurement, Evidence and Implications, pp. 37–60. OECD, Paris, 2004 (2004)
6. Hashim, J.: Information communication technology (ICT) adoption among SME owners in Malaysia. Int. J. Bus. Inf. 2(2), 221–240 (2015)
7. Fabiani, S., Schivardi, F., Trento, S.: ICT adoption in Italian manufacturing: firm-level evidence. Ind. Corp. Change 14(2), 225–249 (2005)
8. Basant, R., Commander, S.J., Harrison, R., Menezes-Filho, N.: ICT Adoption and Productivity in Developing Countries: New Firm Level Evidence from Brazil and India (2006)
9. Forth, J., Mason, G.: Information and Communication Technology (ICT) Adoption and Utilisation, Skill Constraints and Firm Level Performance: Evidence from Uk Benchmarking Surveys. National Institute of Economic and Social Research (2004)
10. Korpelainen, E.: Theories of ICT system implementation and adoption–a critical. Aalto University publication ser., vol. 1, pp. 14–17 (2011)
11. Messaadia, M., Baudry, D., Louis, A., Mahdikhah, S., Evans, R., Gao, J., Mazari, B.: PLM adoption in SMEs context. Comput. Aided Des. Appl. 13(5), 618–627 (2016)
12. Franklin, S., Walker, C., (eds.): Survey methods and practices. In: Statics Canada, Social Survey Methods Division (2003)
13. Frambach, R.T., Schillewaert, N.: Organizational innovation adoption: a multi-level framework of determinants and opportunities for future research. J. Bus. Res. 55(2), 163–176 (2002)
14. Magni, M., Pennarola, F.: Intra-organizational relationships and technology acceptance. Int. J. Inf. Manage. 28(6), 517–523 (2008)

Maturity Models and Tools for Enabling Smart Manufacturing Systems: Comparison and Reflections for Future Developments

Anna De Carolis[1], Marco Macchi[1], Boonserm Kulvatunyou[2(✉)],
Michael P. Brundage[2], and Sergio Terzi[1]

[1] Politecnico di Milano, Via Lambruschini 4/b, Milan, Italy
[2] National Institute of Standards and Technology (NIST), Gaithersburg, MD, USA
serm@nist.gov

Abstract. One of the most exciting new capabilities in Smart Manufacturing (SM) and Cyber-Physical Production Systems (CPPS) is the provisioning of manufacturing services as unbundled "apps or services", which could be significantly more flexible and less expensive to use than the current generation of monolithic manufacturing applications. However, bundling and integrating heterogeneous services in the form of such apps or composite services is not a trivial job. There is a need for service vendors, cloud vendors, manufacturers, and other stakeholders to work collaboratively to simplify the effort to "mix-and-match" and compose the apps or services. In this regard, a workshop was organized by the National Institute of Standards and Technology (NIST) and the Open Applications Group Inc. (OAGi), with the purpose to identify – through parallel sessions – technology and standard needs for improving interoperability and composability between services. The workshop was organized into five working session. This paper documents evidences gathered during the "Smart Manufacturing Systems Characterization" (SMSC) session, which aims at establishing a roadmap for a unified framework for assessing a manufacturer's capability, maturity and readiness level to implement Smart Manufacturing. To that end, the technology maturity, information connectivity maturity, process maturity, organizational maturity, and personnel capability and maturity, have been identified as critical aspects for Smart Manufacturing adoptions. The workshop session culminated at providing a coherent model and method for assisting manufacturing companies in their journey to smart manufacturing realizations. This paper shows three different maturity models and tools that, thanks to their complementarity, enable one to reflect on the different perspectives required by SMSC. These models and tools are usable together for assessing a manufacturing company's ability to initiate the digital transformation of its processes towards Smart Manufacturing. Therefore, based on their comparison, the ultimate purpose of the research is to come up with a set of coherent guidelines for assessing a manufacturing system and its management practices for identifying improvement opportunities and for recommending SM technologies and standards for adoption by manufacturers.

Keywords: Smart manufacturing systems characterization · Maturity model
Manufacturer's capabilities · Industry 4.0 · Smart manufacturing readiness

© IFIP International Federation for Information Processing 2017
Published by Springer International Publishing AG 2017. All Rights Reserved
J. Ríos et al. (Eds.): PLM 2017, IFIP AICT 517, pp. 23–35, 2017.
https://doi.org/10.1007/978-3-319-72905-3_3

1 Introduction

With the introduction of Smart Manufacturing (SM), manufacturers are faced with new, advanced technologies that offer the potential to dramatically improve their manufacturing systems. Many definitions of SM have been proposed. Price Waterhouse Cooper identifies eleven digital technologies that are SM enablers [1]: mobile devices, IoT platforms, location detection technologies, advanced human-machine interfaces, advanced authentication and fraud detection, 3D printing, smart sensors, advanced algorithm for big data analytics, multilevel customer interaction, wearable augmented reality, and cloud computing. It is interesting to observe the wide scope of applications enabled by combining these technologies including supply chains, business models, and designs of products and services.

SM focuses on the end-to-end digitalization of all physical assets and integration into digital ecosystems with value chain partners [1]. A SM research project within the European union indicates that application of digital technologies in manufacturing will have three key impacts [2]: (i) full integration of product and asset life-cycle both within and outside the factory from cradle to grave; (ii) full integration of all the stakeholders in the value-network (i.e. suppliers and customers). The entire manufacturing system will be connected based on shared vision, standards, and service-oriented integration mechanisms that defy traditional, rigid functional hierarchies to create dynamic structures from their articulated functions; (iii) new business models based on new value-added services enabled by these technologies.

The application of new digital technologies in manufacturing leads to the rise of new, complex enterprise challenges [3–5]. Integrating so many different technologies inevitably leads to increased complexity of the whole manufacturing system, which might limit the obtainable advantages. For this reason, we assume that the impact of smart manufacturing technology introduction may differ depending on the maturity level of a company's capabilities. Before starting the transition towards SM or Industry 4.0, manufacturing companies should define their transformation roadmap according to the maturity level of their capabilities [6]. This requires proper methodologies for maturity or readiness assessment with respect to SM. The aim is to support companies in finding their own path to adopting SM technologies.

Even though such assessment methodologies are emerging, there is no established approach or framework. This paper describes three different, but complementary tools for analyzing the readiness of manufacturing systems and environments from an SM perspective. These are: DREAMY (Digital REadiness Assessment MaturitY model), SMSRL (Smart manufacturing readiness level), and MOM (Manufacturing Operations Management) Capability Maturity Model. Based on a comparison of these methods, we propose to establish a set of guidelines for maturity assessment to support the transition towards SM.

2   Smart Manufacturing Systems Characterization (SMSC) and Maturity Models

2.1   Smart Manufacturing Systems Characterization

Smart manufacturing systems rely on new information technologies in supply chains, in product development, in business to shop floor integration, in operations of smart products, and in production equipment [7]. SM is a convergence of new technologies and related capabilities brought from multiple areas and multiple business lifecycles. In order to guide manufacturers coping with the adoption of such complex systems, NIST and international researchers identified requirements for manufacturing systems characterization based on work carried out during the NIST/OAGi Workshop 2016 [8]. Smart manufacturing systems characterization will help identify and prioritize opportunities for improvement of manufacturing systems by providing recommendations on which SM technologies and standards to implement [8].

Manufacturers need to adopt a progressive introduction of SM applications, systems, and hardware based on a composition of different technologies [6]. The introduction of new technologies depends on understanding the actual readiness of the manufacturer to deploy the new technologies in its manufacturing system(s). Manufacturers should perform periodic assessments to monitor the maturation process towards SM. Manufacturing systems characterization is focused on the assessment of a manufacturer's capabilities, and readiness level to implement SM technologies and applications. The maturity of a company's manufacturing systems is a key indicator for success in adopting SM technologies. A maturity model is a critical tool to perform a characterization of existing manufacturing systems.

2.2   Maturity Models and Tools

It is appropriate to provide a definition of maturity for this paper since the understanding of maturity can vary even within the same field of expertise [9].

Maturity can be defined as *"the state of being complete, perfect or ready"* [10–12]. Another slightly different perspective on the concept of maturity is the one given by Maier et al. [9], who stated that the process of bringing something to maturity means bringing it to a state of full growth. In other words, maturity implies an evolutionary progress from an initial to a desired or normally occurring end stage [13]. This last definition, which stresses the process toward maturity, introduces another important concept, which is the one of *stages of growth* or *maturity levels*.

Before reaching a state of "full growth", an entity (an organization as well as a human being) must encounter different stages of growth or maturity levels. In particular, the stages an organization passes through have three main distinctive properties [14]: (i) they are sequential in nature; (ii) they occur in a hierarchical progression that is not easily reversible; and (iii) they involve a broad range of organizational activities and structures. We can state that maturity models can be used as tools for determining manufacturers' readiness level and capabilities within an SM perspective.

Maturity models in literature have different characteristics. Fraser et al. [16] presented a first clear classification per typology of maturity models. In particular, they distinguish three types of maturity models: (i) Maturity grids; (ii) Likert-like questionnaires; and (iii) CMM-like models.

The maturity grids typically illustrate maturity levels in a simple and textual manner, structured in a matrix or a grid. As Fraser et al. stated, maturity grids are of a moderate complexity and they do not specify what a particular process should look like. Maturity grids only identify some characteristics that any process and every enterprise should have in order to reach high performance processes [9]. On the other hand, the Likert-like questionnaires are constructed by "questions", which are no more than statements of good practices. A responder to the questionnaire has to score the related performance on a scale from 1 to n. A hybrid model can be defined as a combination of the questionnaire approach with the maturity grid definition [16]. Finally, the CMM-like models (Capability Maturity Model) identify the best practices for specific processes and measures the maturity of organizations in terms of how many practices are implemented [9]. Their architecture is more formal and complex compared to the first two. CMM models are composed of process areas organized by common features, which specify key practices to address a series of goals. Typically, the CMM-like models exploit Likert questionnaires to assess the maturity. The framework for defining maturity models have been improved successively by the Capability Maturity Model Integration (CMMI), which expands the scope of the original CMM beyond software development maturity [17].

Although a number of different types of maturity models have been proposed in literature, they share some common proprieties [6, 16]: (i) Maturity levels (typically from three to six); (ii) a "descriptor" for each level, which gives a meaningful name to each level; (iii) a generic description of the characteristics of each level; (iv) a number of dimensions or "process areas"; (v) a number of elements or activities for each process areas; and (vi) a description of each activity, that has to be performed at each maturity level.

The terms 'readiness' and 'maturity' are relative and related. We define the term 'smart manufacturing readiness' as the capability or maturity of a manufacturing company *to deploy* smart manufacturing concepts, and the term 'smart manufacturing maturity' as how well a manufacturing company *has employed* smart manufacturing concepts or its smart manufacturing capability. Following such definitions, certain maturity models can be viewed as part of smart manufacturing readiness assessment. For example, the manufacturing operation management (MOM) maturity model is a smart manufacturing readiness assessment. On the other hand, Industrie 4.0 Readiness [25], although calling itself readiness, is more of a smart manufacturing maturity. In the following section, three different tools for assessing manufacturers' readiness or maturity levels *to deploy* SM concepts are described.

2.3 DREAMY (Digital REadiness Assessment MaturitY Model)

The Digital REadiness Assessment MaturitY model is a tool with two objectives. The primary objective is to assess a manufacturing company's readiness level for starting the digital transitioning process, which is an aspect of smart manufacturing concepts

[10–12]. For this reason, DREAMY has the form of a maturity model based on the principles of the CMMI framework [18, 19] as shown in Table 1. The secondary objective is to identify a manufacturing company's strengths, weaknesses, opportunities, and create a roadmap for investments in digitalization and transitioning to smart manufacturing [6].

Table 1. Definition of DREAMY maturity levels (taken from [20])

ML 1 Initial	The process is poorly controlled or not controlled at all, process management is reactive and does not have the proper organizational and technological "tools" for building an infrastructure that will allow repeatability/ usability/extensibility of the utilized solutions
ML2 Managed	The process is partially planned and implemented. Process management is weak due to lacks in the organization and/or enabling technologies. The choices are driven by specific objectives of single projects of integration and/or by the experience of the planner, which demonstrates a partial maturity in managing the infrastructure development
ML3 Defined	The process is defined with the planning and the implementation of good practices and management procedures. The management of the process is limited by some constraints on the organizational responsibilities and/or on the enabling technologies. Therefore, the planning and the implementation of the process highlights some gaps/lacks of integration, information exchange, and ultimately interoperability between applications
ML4 Integrated and interoperable	The process is built on information exchange, integration, and interoperability across applications; and it is fully planned and implemented. The integration and the interoperability are based on common and shared standards within the company, borrowed from intra- and/ or cross-industry de facto standards, with respect to the best practices in industry in both perspectives of the organization and enabling technologies
ML5 Digital-oriented	The process is digitally-oriented and is based on a solid technology infrastructure and on a high potential growth organization, which supports – through pervasive integration and interoperability – speed, robustness and security in information exchange, in collaboration among the company functions and in the decision making

To define the DREAMY architecture, it was fundamental to identify the relevant manufacturing operational processes, within which value-added activities are performed, and that are strategic for the digital transition to SM [20]. To make the architecture as general as possible, manufacturing operational processes were grouped in five main areas: (1) Design and Engineering; (2) Production Management; (3) Quality Management; (4) Maintenance Management; (5) Logistics Management. Each process area can be considered as a self-contained module and therefore it is possible to add or remove areas as needed based on certain industrial situations. Cutting across the process areas is the Digital Backbone, within which all the information exchange processes across the process areas are considered [20]. The digital readiness of a manufacturing company is then defined through a scale of maturity levels. These levels provide a snapshot of the company's current abilities. The maturity levels are based on the principles from the CMMI framework [18, 19]. The CMMI maturity levels provide a generic staring point. These maturity levels have been adapted in order to gather the definitions, and so the semantic, of the digital readiness levels for the DREAMY model [20] (see Table 1).

According to the maturity level definitions in Table 2, a manufacturing company's digital readiness needs to be evaluated along the four dimensions as shown in Fig. 1: *Process, Monitoring and Control, Technology,* and *Organization* [20].

Table 2. MOM maturity level definitions

Level 0	There has been no evaluation performed
Level 1	Procedures for activities and their executions are at initial stage and not documented or formally managed
Level 2	Procedures of some activities are documented and executed with possibly repeatable results in the normal situation
Level 3	Procedures for activities are defined with documented standards for all activities whose executions are possibly supported by software tools and better handling of abnormal situations
Level 4	Procedures for activities are defined and documented across all organizational groups; and their executions are repeatable and monitored with software tools supports
Level 5	Procedures for activities are focused on continuous improvement and optimization

The DREAMY model in its current form can be used for descriptive purposes. That is, maturity indexes for each process can be calculated to reflect the as-is situation of a manufacturing company [20]. With further analysis, strengths, weaknesses, and opportunities (prescription [6]) for smart manufacturing adoption can be derived. Going forward, the model can be enhanced such that the strengths, weaknesses, and opportunities information can be automatically generated. The "factory" is the unit of the analysis considered by the model. However, thanks to the modular structure of the model, future work can be done to include other value-added process areas, such as Supply Chain Management, Sales, Marketing, Customer care, and Human Resource Management to extend the scope of the analysis. In addition, *Skills of Personnel* should be considered as another analysis dimension when assessing company capabilities, because specialized skills are needed to deploy smart manufacturing systems.

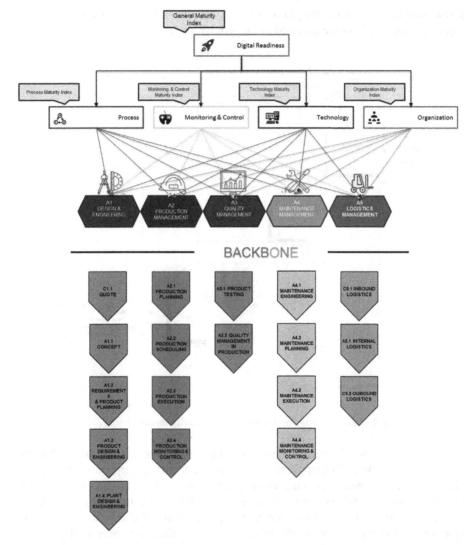

Fig. 1. DREAMY (Adapted from [20])

2.4 SMSRL

Smart Manufacturing System Readiness Level (SMSRL) is an index that measures a manufacturing company's readiness for employing smart manufacturing concepts with the assumption that smart manufacturing is essentially the intensive use of information and communication technologies to improve manufacturing system performance [21]. The SMSRL index bases its readiness model on the factory design and improvement (FDI) activity model [22, 23]. FDI consists of four high-level activities as shown in Fig. 2. Each activity has one further level of decomposition consisting of processes that should be regularly performed for continuously improving factory operational performances. The information flow between activities and the software functions supporting each activity are captured in the activity model.

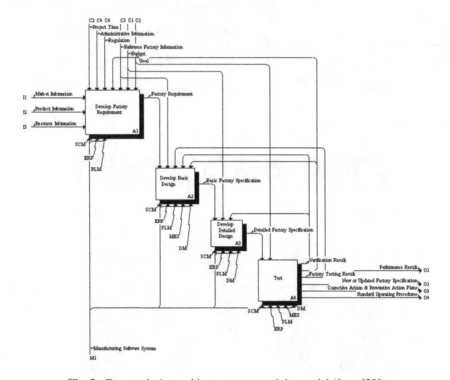

Fig. 2. Factory design and improvement activity model (from [23])

The figure shows software functions grouped into five categories entering the bottom of each activity box SCM (supply chain management), ERP (enterprise resource planning), DM (digital manufacturing), PLM (product life cycle management), and MES (manufacturing execution system). The more tasks performed, the more they are assigned with a responsible person, software functions deployed, and digital information used, the more ready a factory is for the deployment of smart manufacturing concepts. The contribution of these aspects and dimensions to the smart manufacturing readiness is illustrated Fig. 3. Differing ways of computing readiness index are used for C1 to C4. C1 uses the CMMI index qualification. C2 and C3 uses counting measures, while C4 uses incidence matrix-based similarity measure along with an incidence scoring scheme based on the technology used to enable the information flow. They are viewed independently or averaged into a single SMSRL index.

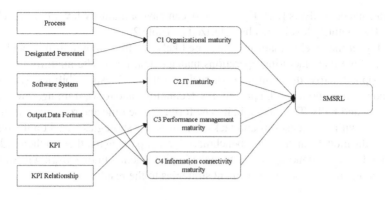

Fig. 3. SMSRL maturity dimensions [21]

Like other models, the output from an SMSRL assessment is largely descriptive. After an assessment, a company can use the model to prescribe goals to improve the readiness, but the model has not yet included guidelines for achieving those goals. The FDI activity model underlying the assessment focuses on factory improvement tasks, not day-to-day factory operation tasks, and has weaknesses on supply chain and logistics operations. The IT maturity dimension in the SMSRL assessment evaluates software functions utilized by a manufacturing companies as part of the *readiness* assessment. Some of these software functions may be considered smart manufacturing capabilities causing the SMSRL readiness index to overlap the smart manufacturing *maturity* assessment. Descoping of the FDI may be necessary to avoid this overlap. Consequently, the SMSRL assessment will benefit from alignment and harmonization with other assessment methods described in this paper.

2.5 MOM Maturity

MESA (Manufacturing Enterprise Systems Association) created the Manufacturing Operations Management Capability Maturity Model (MOM/CMM) to evaluate the maturity of manufacturing enterprises' manufacturing facilities [24]. The objective is to determine the policy, procedure, and execution of a manufacturing operation management to be organized, robust, and repeatable. In other words, MOM/CMM does not provide a measure of sophistication of the physical production, but a measure of the capability to streamline operations, particularly in response to abnormal events. The MOM/CMM focuses on four main *process areas*:

1. Production Operations Management
2. Inventory Management
3. Quality Test Operations Management
4. Maintenance Operations Management

Each *process area* consists of multiple *activities*: scheduling, dispatching, execution management, resource management, definition management, data collection, tracking, and performance analysis [24]. Each *activity* can have a maturity level from level 0 to level 5. The maturity levels are characterized in Table 2.

The higher the level of maturity, the more likely an efficient organization and fewer problems at the manufacturing operations management level. The maturity levels can be also applied across different aspects, such as roles and responsibilities, succession plans and backups, policies and procedures, technology and tools, training, information integration, and KPIs. The model, in its raw form, can be time and resource consuming to complete with 832 questions and lacks improvement strategies based on the results. However, the model can provide a benchmark for comparison to others in their industry and can aid in understanding where to make improvements. Future work will simplify the questionnaire and map improvement strategies to the results.

3   Models Comparison: Building a Framework for SMSC and Road-Mapping Its Development

From the review of the different methods described in the previous chapters (DREAMY, SMSRL, MOM maturity models), it is possible to state that they are complementarity in the overall scope of Smart Manufacturing. The MOM maturity model, which focuses on day-to-day factory operation tasks, can be complemented by SMSRL, which focuses more on assessing the maturity of factory improvement tasks. Neither MOM nor SMSRL includes product life cycle and business processes in their scope of analysis, so they can be complemented by DREAMY, which offers a business processes-oriented view also on product life cycles phases. According to their *different but complementary* objectives, DREAMY, SMSRL, and MOM models might be used by manufacturing companies with *different but complementary* purposes, i.e., descriptive and prescriptive, and descriptive and comparative respectively.

Table 3 summarizes the three models showing their objectives, clarifying their focus, and describing their structures.

Table 3. Comparison of DREAMY, SMSRL and MOM models

Element	DREAMY	SMSRL	MOM
Objective(s)	1. To assess a manufacturing company readiness level for starting the digital transformation process 2. To identify strengths and weaknesses and related opportunities manufacturers can gather from the digital transformation, with the final aim to help them in defining a roadmap for prioritizing investments	To assess a manufacturing company's readiness to employ data-intensive technologies for its performance management	To determine level of an organization's capability to have mature, robust, and repeatable manufacturing operations [24]
Focus	Manufacturing company/ Product and Factory Life Cycles	Maturity of performance improvement tasks/ processes, availability of software supports, maturity of information sharing capability, and availability of responsible personnel	Manufacturing Operations Management (MOM) processes
Analysis dimensions	Process/Execution, Monitoring and control, Organization, Technology	Organization, IT, Performance Management (process execution), and Information Connectivity	Process/Execution
Process areas	Product and asset design and engineering, Production management, Quality management, Maintenance management, Logistics management, Digital Backbone	(Change) Requirement developments, Basic (rough) design of a new or a change requirement, Detail design, and Test	Production Operations Management, Inventory Management, Quality Test Operations Management, Maintenance Operations Management
Maturity levels	5 (1–5)	6 (0–5)	6 (0–5)
Inspiring framework	CMMI	Factory design and improvement activity model	ISA-95 Enterprise control activities
Assessment methods	Interview/case study	Self-assessment	Self-assessment
Model purpose	Descriptive and prescriptive	Descriptive and comparative	Descriptive and comparative
Questions/Answers' type	Questions with normative answers	Yes/No question, Scoring question	Yes/No questions
Number of questions	About 200 scoring questions	242 scoring and at least ~123 Yes/No questions	832 Yes/No questions

4   Conclusions

The "recipe" for smart manufacturing involves combining different "ingredients" to obtain the best results in terms of performance improvements. Companies planning to build SM systems must possess basic capabilities. What are these capabilities and how can they be measured? This paper carries out some reflections of smart manufacturing system characterization (SMSC), showing three different tools for assessing manufacturing companies their ability to start the digital transitioning process. With this comparison, it is now possible to reflect on the different perspectives required by SMSC and on future developments expected for such type of tools.

First of all, the evidence from the literature and from the thoughts that emerged during the workshop organized by NIST and OAGi [8] show several perspectives on capabilities required in terms of organization, process execution and technology. Models and tools for assessing enterprise readiness to embrace SM should consider all these different perspectives to be effective. Therefore, we may expect that current and emerging models and tools may address additional perspectives. It is worth remarking that these models and tools should not be used solely during the assessment phase. Instead, they should be enhanced to support the prescription phase of improvements. In addition, with sufficient improvement data, benchmarks can be developed to provide evidence of return-on-investment for smart manufacturing systems adoption. This would accelerate overall industry adoption of SM. Finally, further studies should deal more with principles, providing an abstract view on the founding concepts to adequately address differences between other "readiness" and "maturity" models to suggest the most appropriate tool to use in each of the digitalization roadmapping phases.

References

1. P. GMIS: Industry 4.0: Building the Digital Industrial Enterprise (2016). https://www.pwc.com/m1/en/publications/documents/middle-east-industry-4-0-survey.pdf
2. E.R. for C. in M. SCorPiuS, Validated sCorPiuS Vision, pp. 1–17 (2016)
3. Jager, J., Schollhammer, O., Lickefett, M., Bauernhansl, T.: Advanced complexity management strategic recommendations of handling the "Industrie 4.0" complexity for small and medium enterprises. In: 49th CIRP Conference on Manufacturing Systems (CIRP-CMS 2016) (2016)
4. Elmaraghy, W., Elmaraghy, H., Tomiyama, T., Monostori, L.: Complexity in engineering design and manufacturing. CIRP Ann. Manuf. Technol. **61**, 793–814 (2012). https://doi.org/10.1016/j.cirp.2012.05.001
5. Jäger, J., Kluth, A., Schatz, A., Bauernhansl, T.: Complexity patterns in the advanced complexity management of value networks. In: Procedia CIRP, pp. 645–650 (2014). https://doi.org/10.1016/j.procir.2014.01.070
6. De Carolis, A., Macchi, M., Negri, E., Terzi, S.: Guiding manufacturing companies towards digitalization: a methodology for supporting manufacturing companies in defining their digitalization roadmap (2017)
7. Brandl, D.: Smart Manufacturing System Characterization Session (2016)
8. NIST/OAGi: Drilling down on Smart Manufacturing - Enabling Composable Apps (2016). https://www.nist.gov/news-events/events/2016/04/nistoagi-workshop-drilling-down-smart-manufacturing-enabling-composable. Accessed 18 Apr 2017
9. Maier, A.M., Moultrie, J., Clarkson, P.J.: Assessing organizational capabilities: reviewing and guiding the development of maturity grids. IEEE Trans. Eng. Manag. **59**, 138–159 (2012). https://doi.org/10.1109/TEM.2010.2077289
10. Simpson, J.A., Weiner, E.S.C.: The Oxford English Dictionary. Clarendon Press, Oxford (1989)

11. Mettler, T.: A design science research perspective on maturity models in information systems. Design **41**, 1–13 (2009). https://doi.org/10.2174/9781608050635110010

12. Kärkkäinen, H., Silventoinen, A.: Different approaches of the PLM maturity concept and their use domains – analysis of the state of the art. In: Bouras, A., Eynard, B., Foufou, S., Thoben, K.-D. (eds.) PLM 2015. IAICT, vol. 467, pp. 89–102. Springer, Cham (2016). https://doi.org/10.1007/978-3-319-33111-9_9

13. Mettler, T., Rohner, P.: Situational maturity models as instrumental artifacts for organizational design. Proceedings of the 4th International Conference on Design Science Research in Information Systems - DESRIST 2009, Article no. 22, pp. 1–9 (2009). https://doi.org/10.1145/1555619.1555649

14. Gottschalk, P.: Maturity levels for interoperability in digital government. Gov. Inf. Q. **26**, 75–81 (2009). https://doi.org/10.1016/j.giq.2008.03.003

15. van Steenbergen, M., Bos, R., Brinkkemper, S., van de Weerd, I., Bekkers, W.: The design of focus area maturity models. In: Winter, R., Zhao, J.L., Aier, S. (eds.) DESRIST 2010. LNCS, vol. 6105, pp. 317–332. Springer, Heidelberg (2010). https://doi.org/10.1007/978-3-642-13335-0_22

16. Fraser, P., Moultrie, J., Gregory, M.: The use of maturity models/grids as a tool in assessing product development capability. In: IEEE International Engineering Management Conference (2002)

17. Team, C.P.: Capability Maturity Model® Integration (CMMI SM), Version 1.1, C. Systems Engineering, Software Engineering, and Integrated. Product and Process Development/Supplier Sourcing (CMMI-SE/SW/IPPD/SS, V1. 1) (2002)

18. Macchi, M., Fumagalli, L., Pizzolante, S., Crespo, A., Marquez, J.F., Fernandez, G.: Towards eMaintenance: maturity assessment of maintenance services for new ICT introduction. In: International Conference - Advances in Production Management Systems-Tems, Cernobbio, Italy, 2010

19. Macchi, M., Fumagalli, L.: A maintenance maturity assessment method for the manufacturing industry. J. Qual. Maint. Eng. **19**, 295–315 (2013). https://doi.org/10.1108/JQME-05-2013-0027

20. De Carolis, A., Macchi, M., Negri, E., Terzi, S.: A maturity model for assessing the digital readiness of manufacturing companies. In: Lödding, H., Riedel, R., Thoben, K.-D., von Cieminski, G., Kiritsis, D. (eds.) APMS 2017. IAICT, vol. 513, pp. 13–20. Springer, Cham (2017). https://doi.org/10.1007/978-3-319-66923-6_2

21. Jung, K., Kulvatunyou, B., Choi, S., Brundage, M.P.: An overview of a smart manufacturing system readiness assessment. In: Nääs, I., Vendrametto, O., Reis, J.M., Gonçalves, R.F., Silva, M.T., von Cieminski, G., Kiritsis, D. (eds.) APMS 2016. IAICT, vol. 488, pp. 705–712. Springer, Cham (2016). https://doi.org/10.1007/978-3-319-51133-7_83

22. Jung, K., Choi, S., Kulvatunyou, B., Cho, H., Morris, K.C.: A reference activity model for smart factory design and improvement. Prod. Plan. Control (2016). https://doi.org/10.1080/09537287.2016.1237686

23. Kulvatunyou, B.: Factory Design and Improvement (FDI) Activity Model. https://www.nist.gov/services-resources/software/factory-design-and-improvement-fdi-activity-model. Accessed May 2017

24. Brandl, D.: MESA MOM Capability Maturity Model Version 1.0 (2016)

25. Lichtblau, K., et al.: Industrie 4.0 Readiness, VDMA. https://www.industrie40-readiness.de/?lang=en

A Federated Enterprise Architecture and MBSE Modeling Framework for Integrating Design Automation into a Global PLM Approach

Thomas Vosgien[1(✉)], Eugen Rigger[1,2], Martin Schwarz[3], and Kristina Shea[2]

[1] V-Research GmbH, Dornbirn, Austria
{thomas.vosgien,eugen.rigger}@v-research.at
[2] ETH Zürich, Zürich, Switzerland
kshea@ethz.ch
[3] Liebherr-Werk Nenzing GmbH, Nenzing, Austria
martin.schwarz@liebherr.com

Abstract. PLM and Design Automation (DA) are two interdependent and necessary approaches to increase the performance and efficiency of product development processes. Often, DA systems' usability suffers due to a lack of integration in industrial business environments stemming from the independent consideration of PLM and DA. This article proposes a methodological and modeling framework for developing and deploying DA solutions within a global PLM approach. This framework supports the identification of DA potentials and the definition of the DA task building blocks to support DA task formalization by practitioners. The aim is to make the specification and development of DA solutions more efficient and aligned with the business requirements and with the existing digital environments. This framework combines the usage of two standardized modeling languages to make the captured knowledge re-usable across heterogeneous PLM and DA applications. An industrial case study demonstrating the applicability of the framework is introduced and discussed.

Keywords: Design automation · Product Lifecycle Management
Enterprise architecture · Model-Based System Engineering · ArchiMate · SysML

1 Introduction

Product Lifecycle Management (PLM) has become a central management approach for managing product information, engineering processes and applications along the different phases of the product lifecycle [1]. Around 70% of costs for the market launch of new products are defined in the very early phases of the product lifecycle; i.e. product specification and development [2]. The engineering design departments of manufacturing companies are hence under increasing pressure to perform better in terms of low-time, high-quality and high value output that can provide competitive advantage for the organization [3]. Design Automation (DA) has already been identified as a key enabler for addressing these challenges [4] and is defined as the automatic running of a task or a sequence of tasks performed in an engineering design process [5] and can be divided

© IFIP International Federation for Information Processing 2017
Published by Springer International Publishing AG 2017. All Rights Reserved
J. Ríos et al. (Eds.): PLM 2017, IFIP AICT 517, pp. 36–48, 2017.
https://doi.org/10.1007/978-3-319-72905-3_4

into two types: information handling (acquisition, retrieval, and analysis) and knowledge processing [6]. That is why, on one hand, DA should be considered as a key enabler of a PLM approach increasing design process efficiency and supporting different types of concurrent engineering and Design-for-X approaches (anticipating and integrating downstream activities' constraints as early as possible in the product development phase). On the other hand, the acquisition, formalization and re-use of the engineering knowledge consumed or generated by DA applications strongly rely on the capabilities and the usage of PLM enabling technologies (CAX and IT systems as well as their interfaces). Therefore, companies developing mechanical products, have to consider the advantages of Engineering DA (EDA), its realization, implementation as well as its applicability and integration in their specific business environment. However, there is a discrepancy between availability of DA methods stemming from academia and their industrial application [7]. Reasons for that are uncertainties with respect to awareness of available opportunities, recognition of potential of applying DA and ability to define the automation task [7]. In order to overcome above mentioned shortcomings and pave the way for more systematic implementation of DA, this paper introduces a methodological and modeling framework supporting the identification of DA potential within the product development lifecycle and the specification of the required DA task building blocks to clearly define the context of a design task and thereby support DA task formalization by practitioners. The framework combines the usage of two standardized and neutral modeling languages to make the captured knowledge computational and platform independent and to enable the re-use of this knowledge across heterogeneous PLM and DA systems. Section 2 evaluates the current state of the art with respect to enterprise architecture (EA) modeling methods and approaches supporting the specification and development of PLM approaches as well as with respect to system engineering (SE) approaches and computational design task definition. Section 3 introduces the proposals for an EA and Model-Based System Engineering (MBSE) methodological framework including a DA task formalization methodology. Section 4 illustrates the application of the methodology on an industrial case study: the formalization of an optimization task for dimensioning box-type booms of maritime cranes designed and manufactured by Liebherr Werk Nenzing GmbH (LWN). Finally, the results and limitations of the proposed framework and methodology are discussed in Sect. 5 before concluding the paper and presenting lines of future work.

2 Background

DA, as part of a PLM strategy, is not only a technical solution for automating design tasks but also a strategic answer that has to consider many aspects of the company such as: the strategic business drivers, the specific business processes and related requirements; the different authoring and IT applications or platforms used for implementing and/or integrating DA methods; the interfaces between interdependent business processes, authoring applications and IT systems enabling all these elements to interoperate together; the IT infrastructures hosting and enabling these applications to be efficiently integrated and used within and outside the company; the complexity of the system to be designed, the formalization of the related engineering knowledge required for performing design tasks and finally the human factor, i.e. the user interaction, usability and user acceptance with respect to DA systems. One way to address and apprehend the complexity of such business digital environments is to use EA considering the different dimensions and elements listed above [8–10]. The second way is to evaluate methods and approaches for computational design task definition in order to enable practitioners to specify the required DA task building blocks.

2.1 EA Frameworks, SE Standards and PLM Applications

According to [9], "achieving alignment between business, application, information and technologies (IT) requires an integrated approach to all aspects of the enterprise" and EA is an important instrument to address this company-wide integration. Further, it provides "a coherent whole of principles, methods and models that are used in the design and realization of the enterprise's organizational structure, business processes, information systems, and infrastructure" [11]. However, as highlighted in [9], these domains are generally not approached in an integrated way; each domain speaks its own language, draws its own models, and uses its own techniques and tools. Therefore, it is important that the EA can be represented with relevant information and at the appropriate level of detail for all involved stakeholders [10]. For this purpose, several EA approaches, frameworks and methods have emerged since the 90's whether from the literature (e.g. Zachman, CIMOSA) or from standardization initiatives (e.g. IEEE-1471, ISO/IEC/ IEEE-42010, TOGAF). In literature, it is possible to distinguish between simple methods of representation (e.g. SADT, IDEFx) and reference architectures (e.g. CIMOSA, Zachmann, TOGAF). As highlighted in [12], most of these framework approaches aimed at representing business user's concerns with no direct link to IT implementation. Moreover, these frameworks and methods are generally complex to implement [10]. One reason of these difficulties is due to the existence and cohabitation, according to the viewpoints and domains, of different types of interrelated representations and modeling languages. The co-evolution and hence the consistency maintenance of these interrelated models across time as well as the interoperability between these models and the modeling tools implementing these languages represent major open-issues for efficiently implementing EA. The deployment of a PLM approach can only be achieved through the alignment between business processes, applications, information and technologies and should hence rely on EA modeling and monitoring. Nevertheless, few works can be found in the literature proposing and/or demonstrating the crucial role and contribution of EA for modeling, specifying and monitoring the architecture of the complex system of systems (considering simultaneously the system to be designed, its environment, its interfaces as well as the system for designing; i.e. resources such actors, CAx and IT systems) which is beyond a PLM approach. In [12], it is shown that most of the recent works in EA address the development of frameworks for interoperability, e.g. the IMAGINE and SIP projects. The latter focuses on interoperability through the implementation and evaluation of PLM standards, but also proposes to use EA and ArchiMate to model standards-based business collaboration scenarios and to model the test bed environment that will enable the execution/simulation of this scenario [13]. The SIP project also considers standards and practices of both PLM and SE communities, since PLM and SE are closely related. As stated in [13], although the scope of application of PLM is larger than the one covered by SE and a PLM strategy can be efficiently deployed being SE processes independent. Whereas ISO-15288, EIA-632 and IEEE-1220 are standards for SE process formalization, SysML has been established as a product data exchange standard for requirements and system architecture models. One goal of this work is to study and adapt EA frameworks to specify and model DA business scenarios.

2.2 Computational Design Task Definition

Generally, implementing DA requires a deep insight in the design process to be able to capture and formalize the principles in the design domain. This typically requires a set of building blocks (i.e. components/modules), which can be combined in certain ways to result in the product fulfilling the customer's requirements. Depending on the purpose of the automation task, the assembling procedure can be fixed yielding exactly one solution, or capable of exploring various assembling strategies resulting in a solution space. In [14, 15], building blocks for definition of conceptual design task are presented. However, the context of a task with regards to design process is not considered. With the intention of providing an easy-to-use categorization of DA tasks, in [4], authors introduce a categorization that puts design tasks that are suitable for automation into context with a generic design process, so to close the gap between product states and formalization. With a focus on reusability of task related knowledge, in [16, 17], authors propose a hierarchical decomposition of a design task to the level of granularity that enables re-use of templates that can be adapted and integrated for the given design task. In [18], authors address the formulation of process templates introducing an ontology-based approach including verification of inputs by means of rules. However, neither the usage of a standardized language that enables reuse of knowledge in a broader context, nor the context with EA is considered within these studies. MBSE "is the formalized application of modeling to support system requirements, design, analysis, verification and validation activities [...]" [19]. The SysML language supports such a MBSE approach by providing graphical representations and the semantic foundation for modeling system requirements, behavior, structure, and parametric system representations. With a focus on formalization of simulation-based design tasks, [20, 21] show the applicability of SysML for integrating design and analysis models. However, further analysis is needed to streamline and standardize modeling in SysML for the various design tasks and guide the designers for specifying a design task. In this paper it is proposed to use design task specific modeling templates and SysML stereotypes for modeling task specific knowledge according to given DA task categories.

3   The EA-MBSE Methodological Framework for Design Automation Task Formalization

In this section, a modeling framework and methodology based on the open, independent and standardized ArchiMate architectural framework and language [22], is proposed.

ArchiMate divides the EA into a business, applicative and technological layer and is partly based on the IEEE-1471. It permits to describe, analyze and visualize architectures within and across business domains with a restrictive number of artifacts and relationships. The easy-to-use implementation of ArchiMate in the free open source tool Archi®, as well as the possibility to define and re-use pre-defined models templates, were also determining. Further, it is proposed to combine the usage of ArchiMate EA models with SysML models for the definition and implementation of DA task specific building blocks.

3.1 The EA Modeling Framework

The methodology on which the proposed framework has been built is illustrated on the sketch of ArchiMate views of Fig. 1.

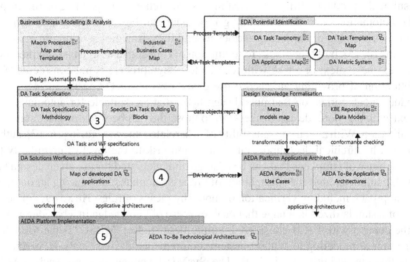

Fig. 1. Overview of the methodological modeling EA Framework for integrating DA into a global PLM approach – the blue framed area (steps 2 and 3) matches the focus of the paper. (Color figure online)

The first step of the methodology is dedicated to the business process models as well as models supporting the identification of DA potential within these processes. The "business process modeling and analysis" package encompasses a set of business process templates that can be re-used and adapted for modeling industrial business processes and DA business scenarios. The second step of the methodology is the "EDA potential identification" for which the framework provides a taxonomy and a map of DA tasks that have been derived from [4] and positioned according to their domain(s) of application. For each DA task category, the framework also provides a set of DA task templates to be re-used for specifying a DA task within an industrial DA business scenario instantiating and/or combining these templates (third step). Whereas Fig. 2 illustrates the generic design task templates, Fig. 3 illustrates the template of a specific design task category. Another package "Design Knowledge Formalization" comprises a set of meta-models for formalizing the engineering design knowledge required for performing the automated design task, as well as conceptual data models that intend to be implemented into knowledge-based repositories of DA systems. Finally, the instantiated and orchestrated DA task templates should provide all the information for fully specifying the DA solution workflows and architectures in the applicative layer (step 4) as well as the concrete implementation specifications (step 5). The focus of this paper is on steps 2 and 3, i.e. the specification of DA task building blocks through the re-use of identified DA task patterns and related ArchiMate templates.

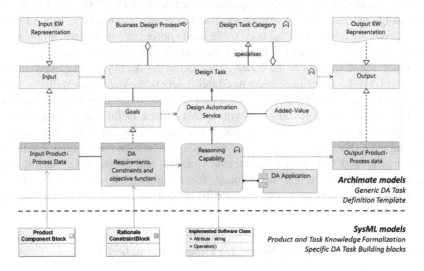

Fig. 2. Generic DA task definition template - Linking concept for integrating EA models in ArchiMate with product related system models in SysML.

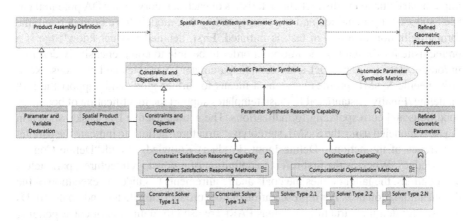

Fig. 3. Template for spatial product architecture parameter synthesis task

Input and output states as well as corresponding product knowledge are determining criteria for defining a design task. Further, the representations as well as problem solving strategy/reasoning technique, i.e. the reasoning capability, (Fig. 2) are key criteria for specifying the DA solution for a given task. Lastly, in analogy to [23], the goal of a task is investigated in order to account for the requirements, constraints and objectives. For reasons of "genericity" of the approach and for enabling re-use of formalized knowledge, the business and applicative elements of this DA task formalization should remain generic for each task category. In contrary, the reasoning capabilities vary according to the specific DA methods. This is illustrated in Fig. 3 that shows the DA task template defined for the design task category "Spatial Product Architecture Parameter Synthesis". The possible variations while instantiating such a template are related to the type of solver chosen for automating the task, for instance optimization methods or constraint solvers as well as the related knowledge representations for input and goals.

Further, Fig. 2 introduces the concept for linking the ArchiMate language with the SysML or UML language permitting to establish dependency and traceability relationships between the two. This work focuses on the specification of DA tasks and on modeling the related input and goals with SysML. Block Definition Diagram (BDD), constraint blocks as well as corresponding Parametric Diagrams (PD) are used for modeling the task knowledge, i.e. necessary equations and the corresponding relations to the product and task design parameters, variables and constraints. The following section introduces the generic methodology for formalizing a DA task in SysML and establishing the dependency and traceability relationships between ArchiMate and SysML models.

3.2   MBSE Methodology for Specifying Design Automation Tasks

Figure 4 shows the generic activity diagram relating the actions and inputs that are required for formally defining a DA task as well links to the specific activities that are implemented due to the distinct characteristics of each category. After DA potential has been successfully identified and the corresponding EA models have been defined, the formal definition of a design task is initiated. First, detailed product knowledge is a prerequisite for design task definition in order to be able to comprehensively describe in-/output states, e.g. product architectures, parameters, variables and relations. Next, task specific SysML profiles serve as a means to further guide and support the task modeling. Finally, instantiated EA task templates support the identification of boundary conditions and corresponding formalizations. The action "Define DA Task", shown in Fig. 4, is modeled using the SysML stereotype "structured action" to indicate the parallel occurrence of the actions "Define Input (Product) Knowledge" and "Define Control Knowledge". Whereas the first refers to definition of product architectures, parameters and relations, the latter defines the goals and requirements to guide the execution of the design automation task. For representation of both product knowledge and goals, BDDs are used for defining structures whereas PARs are used for definition of corresponding relations.

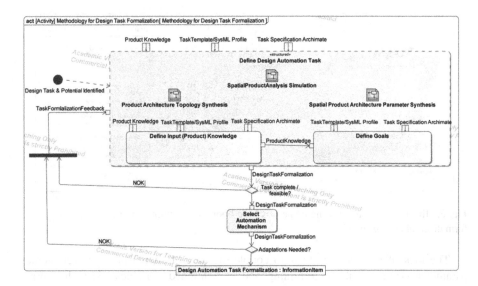

Fig. 4. SysML DA task formalization activity diagram.

After a task has been completely formalized, an appropriate automation mechanism has to be selected and translated from SysML to the corresponding formalization. Consequently, this translation has to be conducted for each DA method specifically.

4 Case Study: Design of Maritime Cranes' Box-Type Booms

The case study addresses the specification of an optimization task and related solution for the design of a box-type boom crane at Liebherr Werk Nenzing (LWN). Figure 5 provides a 3D illustration of the box-type boom, its components and design parameters. The objective is to minimize the costs of the middle section of the boom with respect to material of stiffeners and sheet metals as well as welding of stiffeners and sheet metals. As shown on Fig. 5, the boom is divided into multiple segments, each of which lies between two bulkheads or a bulkhead and the pivot- or end-section and is split into bottom plate, two (symmetric) side plates as well as a top plate. While the length of the boom, and the number and lengths of segments are given as input parameters, the thickness of each sheet metal as well as the number and type of stiffeners remain variables to be determined for each segment during the optimization procedure. Figure 5 shows the corresponding objective function and the complete formalization of the optimization problem, i.e. all constraints and variables. In order to satisfy the requirements stemming from the load case scenarios, the utilization within each segment has to be smaller than one. The utilization calculations are performed within all the plates of each segment with respect to stress, fatigue and buckling. Towards this end, LWN provides an external structural analysis tool.

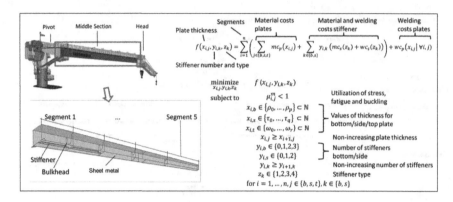

Fig. 5. Illustration of a maritime crane box type boom, cost optimization problem and related formalized objective function

The idea of this case study is to couple the task of spatial product architecture parameter synthesis (i.e. determining above mentioned variables) with the corresponding analysis. This is illustrated in Fig. 6, showing how two pre-defined DA task templates ("Spatial Product Architecture Parameter Synthesis" and "Spatial Product Analysis") are re-used, instantiated and combined to specify the automation of the business task "generate optimized design of the box-type boom".

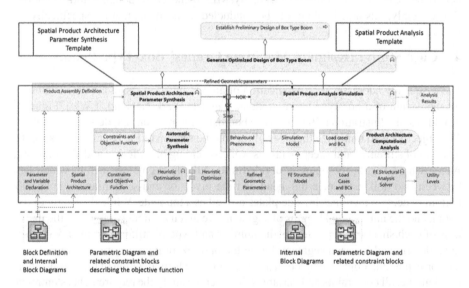

Fig. 6. Re-use and combination of two DA task templates for specifying the automated generation of optimized design of a box-type boom.

Figure 7 shows the BDD of the box-type boom for describing its architecture in terms of sub-components as well as related design parameters and variables. Figure 8 shows the PAR of the cost optimization function as introduced above. The constraint blocks that are illustrated within the PAR of Fig. 8 symbolize the rules for linking the specific parts and parameters of the text and include both the equations as well as parameters needed for relating the elements. Thus, design parameters, variables and constraints required for performing the cost optimization task and for implementing this objective function are interrelated.

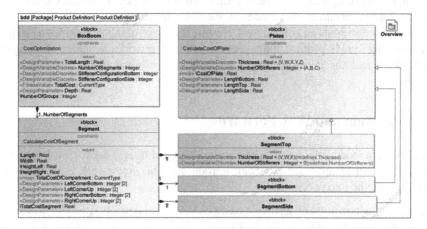

Fig. 7. SysML block definition diagram of the box-type boom.

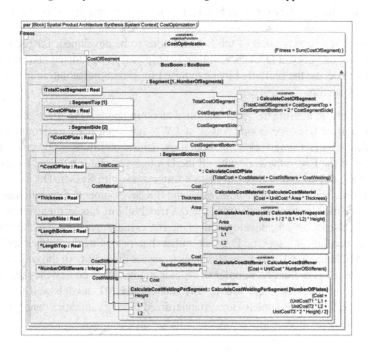

Fig. 8. SysML PAR of the cost optimization function and related constraint blocks.

This case study has permitted to demonstrate the applicability of the methodology on which the proposed EA and MBSE methodological framework for DA has been developed. The definition of the DA task building blocks has been performed based on predefined templates and is currently implemented for both heuristic and meta-heuristic solvers. Easy comparison of different solving strategies is hence enabled. For the shown case study, the design task has been formalized with respect to product knowledge describing the input (structure, parameters, variables, relations etc.) as well as the desired output state (constraints and objectives). Despite the usage of model libraries as well as corresponding SysML profiles, the expressivity SysML provides remains a challenge to the modeler and the corresponding interpretation for translation to a computable language.

5   Conclusion and Way Forward

In this paper, a federated EA and MBSE methodological framework for integrating DA into a global PLM approach has been introduced. This framework is built upon a systematic methodology for:

- ensuring the transition of academic methods to industrial practice through a comprehensible and comprehensive DA task categorization that allows practitioners to grasp the opportunities state-of-the-art DA offers;
- supporting the specification of industrial business cases and scenarios through business process modeling and re-use of business process templates;
- supporting the specification of the DA solutions to be developed: for each derived design task category, a DA task template is proposed to be re-used and instantiated in order to derive the building blocks required for the implementation of the appropriate DA method.

A case study addressing the specification of an optimization task and related solution for the design of box-type boom cranes at LWN has been used to demonstrate the applicability of the framework's methodology. Lines of future work comprise the completion of the EA framework with all the DA task templates required for each DA task category, the completion of the MBSE framework with SysML DA task profiles and stereotypes for each of these categories and the development of specific user interfaces to guide the designers for defining the DA task building blocks themselves. Future work should also include the development of interfaces that are restricted to the modeling capabilities needed for a specific DA task, rather than providing the entire expressivity of the SysML language. Further, mechanisms to assess the quality of the task definition need to be developed. Finally, in order to provide maintenance consistency and change propagation mechanisms while linking EA models, SysML models and the various platform-specific DA implementations, standardized linking semantics concepts should be investigated.

Acknowledgments. This work was supported by the K-Project 'Advanced Engineering Design Automation' (AEDA) that is financed under the COMET (COMpetence centers for Excellent Technologies) funding scheme of the Austrian Research Promotion Agency.

References

1. Abramovici, M.: Future trends in product lifecycle management (PLM). In: Krause, F.L. (ed.) The Future of Product Development, pp. 665–674. Springer, Heidelberg (2007). https://doi.org/10.1007/978-3-540-69820-3_64
2. Ehrlenspiel, K., Kiewert, A., Lindemann, U.: Cost-Efficient Design. Springer, Heidelberg, ASME Press, New York (2007)
3. Baxter, D., Gao, J., Case, K., et al.: A framework to integrate design knowledge reuse and requirements management in engineering design. Rob. Comput.-Integr. Manuf. **24**, 585–593 (2008)
4. Rigger, E., Münzer, C., Shea, K.: Estimating the potential of state of the art design automation - tasks, methods, and benefits. In: Proceedings of the DESIGN 2016 (2016)
5. Lund, J.G., Fife, N.L., Jensen, C.G.: PLM-based parametrics for design automation and optimization. Comput.-Aided Des. Appl. **2**, 37–45 (2005)
6. Cederfeldt, M., Elgh, F.: Design automation in SMEs - current state, potential, need and requirements. In: Proceedings ICED 2005, the 15th International Conference on Engineering Design: and Global Economics, p. 1507 (2005)
7. Cagan, J., Campbell, M.I., Finger, S., Tomiyama, T.: A framework for computational design synthesis: model and applications. J. Comput. Inf. Sci. Eng. **5**, 171 (2005). https://doi.org/10.1115/1.2013289
8. Whitman, L., Ramachandran, K., Ketkar, V.: A taxonomy of a living model of the enterprise. In: Proceedings of the 33rd Conference on Winter Simulation, pp. 848–855. IEEE Computer Society (2001)
9. Lankhorst, M.M.: Enterprise architecture modelling—the issue of integration. Adv. Eng. Inform. **18**, 205–216 (2004)
10. Moones, E., Vosgien, T., Kermad, L., Dafaoui, E.M., El Mhamedi, A., Figay, N.: PLM standards modelling for enterprise interoperability: a manufacturing case study for ERP and MES systems integration based on ISA-95. In: van Sinderen, M., Chapurlat, V. (eds.) IWEI 2015. LNBIP, vol. 213, pp. 157–170. Springer, Heidelberg (2015). https://doi.org/10.1007/978-3-662-47157-9_14
11. Bernus, P., Nemes, L., Schmidt, G.J.: Handbook on Enterprise Architecture. Springer Science & Business Media, Heidelberg (2012). https://doi.org/10.1007/978-3-540-24744-9
12. Chen, D., Doumeingts, G., Vernadat, F.: Architectures for enterprise integration and interoperability: past, present and future. Comput. Ind. **59**, 647–659 (2008)
13. Moones, E., Figay, N., Vosgien, T., et al.: Towards an extended interoperability systemic approach for dynamic manufacturing networks: role and assessment of PLMStandards. In: Boulanger, F., Krob, D., Morel, G., Roussel, J.C. (eds.) Complex Systems Design and Management, pp. 59–72. Springer, Cham (2015). https://doi.org/10.1007/978-3-319-11617-4_5
14. Dinar, M., Danielescu, A., MacLellan, C., et al.: Problem map: an ontological framework for a computational study of problem formulation in engineering design. J. Comput. Inf. Sci. Eng. **15**, 031007 (2015)

15. Dinar, M., Summers, J.D., Shah, J., Park, Y.-S.: Evaluation of empirical design studies and metrics. In: Cash, P., Stanković, T., Štorga, M. (eds.) Experimental Design Research, pp. 13–39. Springer, Cham (2016). https://doi.org/10.1007/978-3-319-33781-4_2

16. Yu, J., Cha, J., Lu, Y.: Design synthesis approach based on process decomposition to design reuse. J. Eng. Des. **23**, 526–543 (2012)

17. Panchal, J.H., Fernández, M.G., Paredis, C.J.J., et al.: A modular decision-centric approach for reusable design processes. Concurrent Eng. Res. Appl. **17**, 5–19 (2009)

18. Ming, Z., Yan, Y., Wang, G., et al.: Ontology-based executable design decision template representation and reuse. In: International Design Engineering Technical Conference and the Computer and Information in Engineering Conference. American Society of Mechanical Engineers (2015)

19. Friedenthal, S., Griego, R., Sampson, M.: INCOSE model based systems engineering (MBSE) initiative. In: INCOSE 2007 Symposium (2007)

20. Peak, R.S., Burkhart, R.M., Friedenthal, S.A., et al.: Simulation-based design using SysML part 1: a parametrics primer. In: INCOSE International Symposium, pp. 1516–1535. Wiley Online Library (2007)

21. Peak, R.S., Burkhart, R.M., Friedenthal, S.A., et al.: Simulation-based design using SysML part 2: celebrating diversity by example. In: INCOSE International Symposium, pp. 1536–1557. Wiley Online Library (2007)

22. The Open Group: ArchiMate 3.0 Specification. The Open Group, Reading, UK (2016)

23. Sim, S.K., Duffy, A.H.B.: Towards an ontology of generic engineering design activities. Res. Eng. Des. **14**, 200–223 (2003)

PLM Customizing: Results of a Qualitative Study with Industrial Experts

Ezgi Sucuoglu[1(✉)], Konrad Exner[2], and Rainer Stark[1,2]

[1] Technische Universität Berlin, Berlin, Germany
ezgi.sucuoglu@campus.tu-berlin.de, rainer.stark@tu-berlin.de
[2] Fraunhofer Institute for Production Systems and Design Technology, Berlin, Germany
{rainer.stark,konrad.exner}@ipk.fraunhofer.de

Abstract. The implementation and utilization of a product lifecycle management (PLM) system, including the continuously adoption to business processes, methods and functions, implies massive challenges and outlay for organizations. Despite the importance of customizing in PLM projects, there are no adequate models to support organizations in their customizing process. This paper focuses on the customizing process of PLM systems considering not only the technical IT view, but also the organizational and the human context. In order to identify the state of the art in industrial practice eleven qualitative interviews have been conducted. The results and implications are presented in this paper. The findings comprise five dimensions and an additional generic PLM customizing process.

Keywords: PLM customizing · Customizing process · PLM in industry

1 Introduction

The company specific adaption of PLM software is one of the major challenges during the PLM implementation process. Furthermore, configuration and customization is the main cost driver regarding PLM implementation, see Fig. 1. These initial investments will even be increased due to the need of continuous maintenance and support. Aggravating this effect is guaranteeing the release compatibly of the adapted PLM solution. However, PLM customizing is often indispensable due to a broad variety of constraints and demands. Firstly, from an IT system perspective company-specific information standards and security measures have to be observed and are often managed by a configuration of the PLM system. Secondly, the PLM IT solution needs to be optimally integrated in the overall IT deployment, thus interfaces needs to be considered and potentially configured or developed. Thirdly, from an organizational and user-centered perspective the PLM solution has to meet certain requirements regarding business processes and functionality. For instance, internal and external collaboration and communication is increasing and has to be optimally supported with PLM systems [1]. Therefore, the modification of the standard – out of the box (OOTB) or commercially over the shelf (COTS) – PLM solution is only avoidable with great limitations for these three considerations. Additionally, new frameworks which integrate the different perspectives such as organization, IT, data models, engineering activities etc. have to

© IFIP International Federation for Information Processing 2017
Published by Springer International Publishing AG 2017. All Rights Reserved
J. Ríos et al. (Eds.): PLM 2017, IFIP AICT 517, pp. 49–58, 2017.
https://doi.org/10.1007/978-3-319-72905-3_5

be utilized in order to conduct systematic change processes [2]. Eventually, the efficiency and effectivity of PLM customizing in reference to, for instance, business process can hardly be measured in practice.

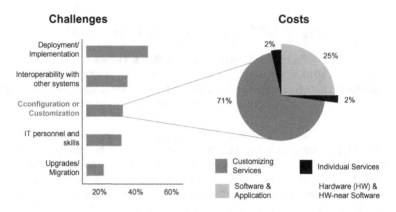

Fig. 1. Impact of customizing in PLM implementation (based on [3, 4])

In theory, product lifecycle management including strategies, software implementation and organizational background has been addressed intensively [5–7]. Customizing and configuration is addressed as an option to optimally suit PLM software to the customers' needs. Nevertheless, a discussion of differences between customizing and configuration as well as the advantages and disadvantages is rarely conducted. A rare exclusion is the quite extensive distinction between tailoring and customizing by [8]. Nevertheless, further approaches or guidelines regarding the adaption of an existing PLM system is missing. Therefore, in spite of this great affect, PLM implementation lacks certain PLM customizing specific methods and approaches which address these challenges. For this reason, many companies developed their own practices, which are often based on expert knowledge. In order to identify commonalities and differences and integrate them in a state of the art from an industrial point of view a qualitative study has been planned and conducted. The two main research questions are:

1. How is PLM customizing defined and conducted in industrial practice?
2. How can the added value of PLM customizing be measured?

The research approach including an extensive description of the procedure regarding the qualitative study is described in Sect. 2. The results of the case are presented in Sect. 3 and comprise a demographic overview of the participants as well as the findings of the study. In Sect. 4 the overall results will be discussed.

2   Research Approach

The research approach is based on the Design Research Methodology (DRM) [9] and covers a comprehensive research plan. The scope of this contribution covers step 1 and 2, marked green in Fig. 2.

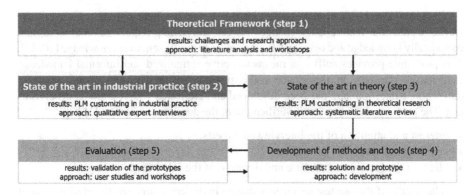

Fig. 2. Research approach (Color figure online)

Based on an initial literature analysis and workshops including discussions with industrial and research experts a lack of comprehensive description of PLM customizing has been identified. Therefore, the state of the art in industrial practice (step 2) as well as in theoretical research (step 3) need be assed. For this reason, a qualitative study has been planned and conducted.

2.1 Study Design

The study focuses three analyzing dimension with three clusters of questions each, which are given in Table 1.

Table 1. Study focus und questions

Dimension	Questions
Organization and processes	• How is the overall PLM strategy defined and communicated within the company? • How is PLM customizing defined, which phases are standardized and for what reason is PLM customizing conducted? • Which stakeholders with dedicated responsibilities are participating in the PLM customizing process and which criteria are defined for each phase?
IT systems and IT standards	• Which IT-systems are used for PLM? • How are IT-standards and guidelines as well as collaboration defined across different divisions and locations? • How is the performance and efficiency of PLM customizing measured?
Human, activities and methods	• How many users does the PLM system have and how is their usage intensity and purpose differentiated? • Are specific teams for PLM customizing responsible and do they use specific and formalized methods? • How are the user and their specific requirements integrated in the PLM customizing process?

Based on this clarification a specific interview type has been chosen: episodic interviews. A particular feature is the change between storytelling request in order to capture episodically knowledge and open questions in order to derive semantic knowledge [10, 11]. This procedure provides sufficient means to derive formalized and informal knowledge from the interviewers. In accordance to the method and the questions of the analyzing dimension, a questionnaire has been developed and pre-tested with a senior PLM consultant. The purpose of the pre-test is verification of the questions regarding [12]:

- interest and attention of the interviewed experts,
- continuity of interview procedure,
- effect of the interview structure and duration of the interview.

The results of the pre-test required a change in the procedure and the clarification of some questions. Overall, the interview has been rated as very interesting and of high relevance.

The target groups are medium-sized and large companies with at least 250 employers in order to ensure a certain amount of PLM users. The interview participants shall address different views on PLM customizing. According to these constraints eleven interview partners from seven companies participated in this study. A demographic overview and the results are discussed in Sect. 3.

3   Findings

The findings of the study are aggregated in three main sections. In the first section the demographic data of the study including information to the experts and their organization is given. The sustentative evaluation is analyzed separately in the second section to enable anonymity for participants. The last section represents the generic process of PLM customizing.

3.1   Demographic Evaluation

The demographic evaluation obtains information to organization (industry and number of employees), PLM IT systems (PLM software and number of users) and participants (PLM experience in years, position and education). Figure 3 illustrates the demographic data of the study.

One important aspect has been in acquiring participants of different branches and different size, which could be successfully achieved by integrating five different branches with companies ranging from 15.000 employees to over 200.000. Additionally, the interviewees represented experts with many years of experience in PLM.

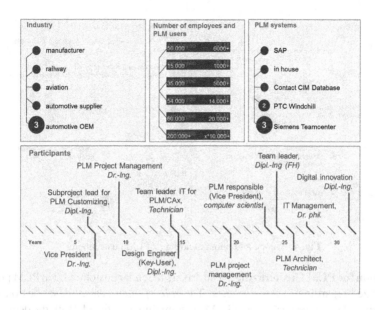

Fig. 3. Demographic data (The numbers dedicate the amount of nominations; no number refers to one nomination.)

3.2   Substantive Evaluation

In this paper the substantive evaluation focuses on five clusters which are derived from the three dimensions and belonging questions of the study given in Table 1.

Scope and Understanding of Customizing. Customizing can include not only configuration but also a complex system expansion. It is important to choose the adequate level of change considering the specific context. The initial step is to analyze the understanding of PLM customizing. Therefore three perspectives are considered:

- *Scope of Customizing* describes to what extent the systems is adapted
- *Prioritization of the scope* describes the preferred adoption variant
- *Strategic Focus* demonstrates two views for performing PLM customizing

Figure 4 summarizes the answers of the experts in these perspectives and clarifies the bride scope of different interpretations for customizing of PLM systems.

PLM Customizing comprises every deviation of an OOTB solution considering the level of individualization and the level of change. In house solutions, which are in our case a bundle of adopted systems from different vendors[1], have the highest level of individualization and change, since they are developed for and adopted to the special needs of the organization. There is no general way to perform PLM customizing. An in house solution can be the best way for one organization and the maximum use of OOTB functionalities for the other.

---

[1] Organization which develops or acquires software for selling.

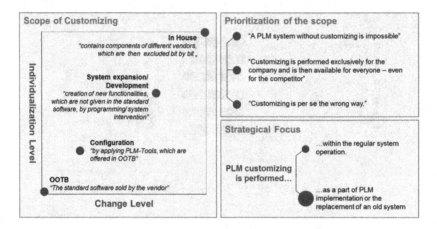

Fig. 4. Scope and understanding of PLM customizing

Motivation for PLM Customizing. The drivers to render customizing in PLM projects are analyzed regarding to three aspects. The *role of management* describes on which organizational level the necessity of PLM customizing is initiated. With the decision for performing the customizing the *focus* of proceeding the PLM customizing should also been set, which can be either the lead of the methods or the lead of the business processes. Besides this high level approach, specific *causes* are determined to execute the customizing of the PLM system. Figure 5 presents the state of the art for the motivation of PLM customizing according to the study considering the three aspects described above.

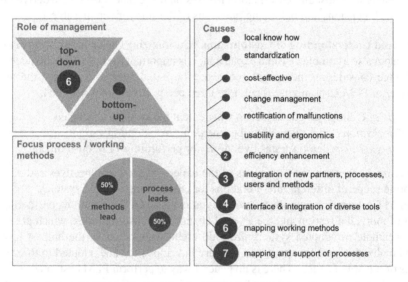

Fig. 5. Motivation for PLM customizing

The initiation is mostly top-down. Whereas the focus lies on both the methods and the business processes. The main reasons for customizing PLM are to adapt the working methods and the lived process to the software.

Challenges of PLM Customizing. The study analyzes PLM customizing by not only contemplating the IT and system view, but also the organizational und user-centered view. Therefore, the human context represents the biggest challenge for customizing PLM systems (see Fig. 6).

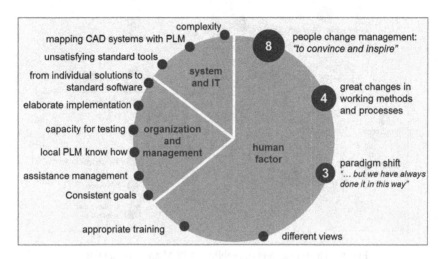

Fig. 6. Challenges of PLM customizing

Especially people change management and the inspiration as well as the conviction of the users for a change constitutes a significant issue for organizations.

Collaboration Model. The collaboration with external service providers and the vendor is a common practice for customizing PLM systems. However the collaboration model differs from strategic to operative level.

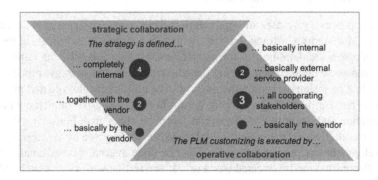

Fig. 7. Collaboration models for PLM customizing

Organizations mostly prefer to define their PLM customizing strategy internally, whereas, the operative execution is usually defined as an activity for external providers or cooperating stakeholders (see Fig. 7).

Impact and Traceability. Based on the results of the study only few or none models to measure the efficiency of PLM customizing by retracing could be identified.

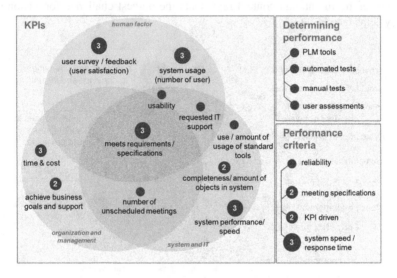

Fig. 8. The impact and traceability of PLM and customizing

It is hardly possible to make a statement about the impact of a customized part in a PLM system environment. Experts agreed on the necessity of such indicators and models which allow organization to measure and also ensure the success of PLM customizing. Nonetheless, organizations define KPIs and performance criteria to determine the performance of the PLM system and its customizing with different tools (see Fig. 8).

3.3   The Process of PLM Customizing

The generic process comprises all steps mentioned by the experts to perform the customizing of PLM systems. Customizing starts with taking up the requirements of the users in form of a specific definition or formulated wishes. Subsequently, the requirements are analyzed and evaluated considering the confirmation to the strategy, processes and methods. In a next step the requirements have to be clustered, analyzed and prioritized in order to release them in the steering group. For the operative implementation the documentation and the voting with partners has to be conducted. Following the specification, consultation and planning the final release has to be given by the steering board. The development and programming can either be done internally or externally despite to the collaboration model selected (see Fig. 7). The testing with key users, PLM team and IT can contain acceptance and usability test, consistency of process tests, system performance test, live-tests on system and tests with user cases on a test instance. The approval of customizing and the related documentation is usually done by the key user and the management of the specialist department. After implementing the customized part in the PLM environment and the official roll-out, the process ends with final documentation and adoption of methods and trainings. The generic process is represented in Fig. 9.

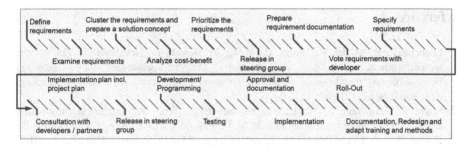

Fig. 9. The generic process of PLM customizing

Experts mentioned that besides this defined process small changes and customizing parts also are done separately with a small group of expert to shorten the time. Depending to the priority and urgency this work around can also be applied by bigger changes.

4 Conclusion and Outlook

This contribution comprises the extensive research results of qualitative study regarding PLM customizing. The results indicate a broad variety of strategies and perspectives addressing the challenges of adopting PLM systems to organizational needs. Besides specific findings discussed within chapter 3, three general statements could be derived. First of all is PLM customizing interpreted as a term differently, also within the same organization. Basically, only one company could certainly provide a specific differentiation between configuration, customization, modification etc. Nevertheless, in order to understand short-term and long-term costs and benefits a sound definition is strongly recommended. Secondly, PLM customizing should not only be addressed as an issue of IT. A user-centered approach including experts for PLM methods is a key success factor in order to overcome diverse challenges. Thirdly, the success of PLM customizing is almost exclusively measured by fulfilling the users' requirements and standard project KPIs. Nevertheless, the long term changes in affectivity and efficiency of the conducted changes are not analyzed at all. Considering the vast cost of PLM customizing, finally, tracking the customized modules and measuring its success is a great opportunity for companies.

In a next step a comprehensive and systematic literature review of PLM customizing will be conducted in order to complete these finding with the research perspective on PLM customizing. Eventually, a method will be developed which includes metrics to conduct and evaluate PLM customizing along the complete process, from the initial assessment to the long term tracking of the results.

Acknowledgments. The authors would like to express their sincere gratitude to the participants of the study. Their insights and expert knowledge based on years of experience provided invaluable information to this topic.

References

1. Lünnemann, P., Müller, P., Hayka, H., Wang, M., Kirsch, L., Neumeyer, S.: Zukunft der unternehmensübergreifenden Kollaboration.: Expertenmeinungen zu aktuellen Herausforderungen und zukunftsweisenden Trends in der kollaborativen Produktentwicklung, ed 1. Band., Berlin (2016)
2. Stark, R., Damerau, T., Hayka, H., Neumeyer, S., Woll, R.: Intelligent information technologies to enable next generation PLM. In: Fukuda, S., Bernard, A., Gurumoorthy, B., Bouras, A. (eds.) PLM 2014. IAICT, vol. 442, pp. 485–495. Springer, Heidelberg (2014). https://doi.org/10.1007/978-3-662-45937-9_48
3. Jackson, C.: The CIO's Role in PLM: Facilitation "Great Product" Development to Drive Economic Recovery (2009)
4. Eigner, M.: Out of the box oder doch customizing?: Product Lifecycle Management (PLM). Produktdaten J. **21**(2), 46–49 (2014)
5. Eigner, M., Stelzer, R.: Product Lifecycle Management: Ein Leitfaden für Product Development und Life Cycle Management, 2nd edn. Springer, Heidelberg (2009). https://doi.org/10.1007/b93672
6. Sendler, U.: Das PLM-Kompendium: Referenzbuch des Produkt-Lebenszyklus-Managements. Springer, Heidelberg (2009). https://doi.org/10.1007/978-3-540-87898-8
7. Feldhusen, J., Gebhardt, B.: Product Lifecycle Management für die Praxis: Ein Leitfaden zur modularen Einführung Umsetzung und Anwendung, 1st edn. Springer, Heidelberg (2008). https://doi.org/10.1007/978-3-540-34009-6
8. Best, O.: PLM: Configuration v Customization. Let's sort it out… (2015). http://beyondplm.com/2015/10/06/plm-configuration-v-customization-lets-sort-it-out/. Accessed 22 Feb 2017
9. Blessing, L.T.M., Chakrabarti, A.: DRM, A Design Research Methodology, 1st edn, p. 397. Springer, Dordrecht (2009). https://doi.org/10.1007/978-1-84882-587-1
10. Flick, U.: Das episodische interview. In: Oelerich, G., Otto, H.-U. (eds.) Empirische Forschung und Soziale Arbeit, pp. 273–280. VS Verlag für Sozialwissenschaften/Springer Fachmedien Wiesbaden, Wiesbaden, Wiesbaden, Ein Studienbuch (2011)
11. Kaiser, R.: Qualitative Experteninterviews: Konzeptionelle Grundlagen und praktische Durchführung. Springer VS, Wiesbaden, Online-Ressource (XIII, 157 S. 17 Abb, online resource) (2014). https://doi.org/10.1007/978-3-658-02479-6
12. Schnell, R., Hill, P.B., Esser, E.: Methoden der empirischen Sozialforschung, 9., aktualis. Auflage ed. Oldenbourg, R, München, 640 S (2011)

The Challenges of Adopting PLM Tools Involving Diversified Technologies in the Automotive Supply Chain

Joseph P. Zammit[1(✉)], James Gao[1(✉)], and Richard Evans[2]

[1] Faculty of Engineering and Science, University of Greenwich, London, UK
{J.Zammit,J.Gao}@greenwich.ac.uk
[2] Westminster Business School, University of Westminster, London, UK
R.Evans@westminster.ac.uk

Abstract. In order to reduce product development (PD) costs and duration, PD cycles are being accelerated in order to reduce the time to market and satisfy the end customer needs. Another key challenge in PD today, is product diversification in the technologies used, requiring improved collaboration amongst local and dispersed multi disciple PD teams. A main stream tool that aids and support engineers in PD to collaborate and share information/knowledge is Product Lifecycle Management (PLM). This research explores the benefits and requirements of implementing a PLM system for a PD and manufacturing company within the automotive supply chain. This paper first provides a brief background of the subject area, followed by an explanation of the initial industrial investigation for the implementation of a PLM system, from which investigation the resulting conclusions and recommendations are presented as the building blocks of the implementation project.

Keywords: Product Lifecycle Management · Product development
Automotive supply chain

1 Introduction

In today's fast moving engineering environment, accelerating product development (PD) is becoming the normal practice, in order to reduce the time to market, improve the quality, reduce costs and getting the PD process right the first time. Another critical challenge in PD today, is the required diversification in technologies used in the products and the way they are designed and manufactured. The main challenge to address these issues is to timely find PD information and reuse design information from past PD projects. There is also the challenge to improve collaboration between dispersed product development teams where companies form temporary partnerships in order to pool their mutual skills [1, 2], and engage with external engineering experts and institutes, forming dispersed PD teams.

A main stream tool that aids and support engineers in PD to collaborate and share information/knowledge is Product Lifecycle Management (PLM). PLM is defined as a strategic business approach that applies a consistent set of business solutions in support of the collaborative creation, management, dissemination and use of product definition

© IFIP International Federation for Information Processing 2017
Published by Springer International Publishing AG 2017. All Rights Reserved
J. Ríos et al. (Eds.): PLM 2017, IFIP AICT 517, pp. 59–68, 2017.
https://doi.org/10.1007/978-3-319-72905-3_6

information across the extended enterprise from concept to end of life - improving product quality, time-to-market and costs [3, 4]. While PLM tools are generally believed are for big OEM companies a lot of attentions from the PLM developers is now being addressed to smaller companies within the supply chain.

This research explores the benefits and requirements of implementing a PLM system for a PD and manufacturing company within the automotive supply chain, to improve the visibility and the information management of the various PD projects, in order to facilitate decision making and reduce the inefficiencies that lack of visibility and fragmented information bring with them. An extensive investigation has been conducted within a global industrial partner to explore their needs and requirements. Arising from the investigation are the identified main benefits and the recommended building blocks to implement such a system. This paper first provides a background of the subject area; this is followed by an explanation of the initial industrial investigation, from which the resulting conclusions and recommendations are presented and analysed.

2   Challenges in New Product Development

In business and engineering, New Product Development (NPD) refers to the development of a new product which is launched in the market place. Innovation and NPD are critical to the success and sustainable competitiveness of manufacturing enterprises. NPD projects require different engineering disciplines such as Design and Product Development (PD), Manufacturing Engineering and Electrical and Electronics engineers to combine and collaborate their efforts in order to achieve agreed goals [5].

A successful product is typically determined by five factors: good quality, low production cost, short development time, low development cost and effective development capability [6]. These key factors are normally managed by different departments or groups, such as R&D, testing, marketing, sales and finance within an organization. The success of a product may only be achieved if these departments and groups cooperate and work together in harmony to achieve the end NPD goal.

The effective management of communication, information and knowledge sharing activities in local or global NPD teams, between different departments like design, purchasing and testing, requires sensitivity to the uniqueness of product development. The capabilities of multiple types of communication mechanisms and an understanding of which of these mechanisms best meet a team's needs for information and knowledge dissemination is a huge undertaking [7, 8].

Getting communication right between the different NPD teams and re-using the knowledge that already exists within a company can determine whether a new product is launched on time and/or on budget. Recreating and re-collecting the same knowledge for different projects is both costly and time consuming, which shows the importance of capturing and managing pre-existing information and knowledge already available among employees, so that further knowledge can be built upon it, which constitutes innovation in your PD process.

NPD project should be carried out by a core team with extended team members. The core team normally consists of key people, such as team leaders and engineers from different disciplines, while the extended team members include the support personnel that aid the core team with the relevant knowledge and resources required for a project. A NPD core team will drive the project through different NPD phases in order to achieve their goal. The first phase is planning of the project which is followed by concept development, this then moves onto system level design and detail design, once the first sample is constructed this goes to the testing and refinement phase so that the final product can be finalized. Once the product is finalized the final NPD process is the production ramp up so that products can be distributed to the market place [9]. These NPD phases are the ideal theoretical development cycle, but as all things on this earth nothing is perfect.

Communication amongst NPD team members is another important factor that can directly influence the success of a NPD project. With the implementation of having a core team and extended members within a product development team brings to the table new problems. In global organizations these core teams and extended team members can be located at different offices within the same site or at different sites with the additional complication of having different time zones which further complicate people's availability, which only emphasize the fact that team member need to stay on top of communication and control it. Communication in project management comes in many shapes and forms, such as oral communication, meetings, telephone calls, emails, documents, specifications, instant messenger systems, teleconference calls, and video conference calls [10].

Communication plays a crucial role in information & knowledge sharing and the social dynamics of a team. Without adequate communication channels, the team would fail to produce new innovative ideas that could be transformed into new products [11, 12]. Therefore, the combination of effective communication, project management and knowledge management are critical to the success of NPD projects.

3   Benefits and Issues of Product Lifecycle Management

PLM emerged in the early twenty-first century to manage the knowledge intensive process consisting mainly of market analysis, product design and process development, product manufacturing, product distribution, product in use, post-sale service, and product recycling. As its name implies, PLM enables companies to manage their products across their lifecycles [13]. PLM is of great significance as it can improve the development of new products and reduce manufacturing costs by controlling the products through their lifecycle [14].

PLM expands Product Data Management's (PDM) scope to provide more product-related information to the extended enterprise. Product Data Management has been developed to improve the management of data and documented knowledge for the design of new products and focus on the design and production phases of a product [15] (Fig. 1).

Fig. 1. PLM defining elements

The management path of PD within PLM addresses the general product engineering process from the creation of a product idea to its delivery consisting of dedicated phases, incorporating workflows and link components to each other providing a complete picture of the product definition. Typical phases of the PD process within PLM is defined in the table below (Table 1).

Table 1. PLM phases [16]

Phase	Description
1. Conceive	Information is gathered from the marketplace, customer requirements are determined and the product is imagined and technical specifications based on this information are created
2. Design	The product's initial design is created, refined, tested and validated using tools such as CAD. This step involves a number of engineering disciplines including mechanical, electrical, electronic and software (embedded), as well as domain specific expertise i.e., automotive engineering
3. Realize	At this stage, the product design is complete and the manufacturing method is determined, with this phase addressing tool design, analysis, simulation, and ergonomic analysis
4. Service	In this final phase of the product lifecycle, we enter the service phase, which may involve repair and maintenance, waste management and end of life (disposal, destruction) of the product

Modern PLM systems are about sharing data instead of documents. Sharing data means information from documents is decomposed in pieces of information (metadata), in a database. Parts, related designs (3D models and drawings), Suppliers but also Tasks, Issues, Workflow processes and Requirements are handled in a connected database. This approach of integrated product data and document management has a massive advantage over a document-centric or a pure data centric approach as on-line status information becomes available for decision support and analysis providing the perfect balance for rigid and flexible data to be easily stored and shared. Figure 2 below shows the PLM architecture comparison of different data models.

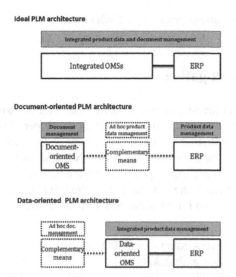

Fig. 2. PLM architecture comparison [17]

The benefits of implementing PLM systems is being driven by both internal and external needs; the internal needs are to improve the efficiency of innovation process and to speed up the innovation as well as improve or enable network collaboration [18], while the external needs come from increasing the use of PLM due to the globalization and competition which often lead to distributed cooperative product development, in order to save costs or gain access to resources, competencies and markets [19].

The critical component to enable this is the centralized single version of the truth that the PLM infrastructure provides so that the business can response more swiftly and decide on PD decisions correctly the first time because the required full and up-to-date information is available for them to use. This centralization of information is also crucial to support global PD operations by enabling live information updates communicated to stakeholders immediately when they become available for the whole team to consume and take decisions up on.

PLM also enables and supports engineers, the PLM users by providing up to date information across the PD lifecycle providing shared access and linked data greatly improving personal productivity in developing new products, re-using readily available information and communication amongst the PD team.

An important aspect of implementing PLM processes and tools is the cultural change required for the team to embrace. PLM enables collaboration but the users need to accept that collaboration requires them to work differently in handling information and knowledge because they are not working on a department level but intercompany along the PD chain which in some cases can involve global team members. Work done by users will have downstream benefits and later upstream benefits, for which PLM users need to be motivated for. The target is to convince the business and the users that the decision for a new practice requesting organizational change is required and works. Only then the organization can enable the full potential of the PLM methodology without remaining stuck in the current practice [20], which brings the required cultural change and system acceptance.

4 Industrial Investigation

An extensive industrial investigation was carried out with an industrial partner using multiple methods. The industrial partner is a global developer of costumed engineered products and solutions with manufacturing, design and testing facilities in several countries around the world. The main purpose of this investigate is to identify a tool that is able to support product development processes for the immediate and long term future, with the proposed solutions being faster and more efficient than the current environment, while also being scalable and future oriented. The methods chosen for this investigation included;

- Analysing current process going though PD quality manual,
- Investigative workshops with stakeholders,
- One on one interviews with key personnel and process owners, and
- Process walkthroughs.

The PD quality manual, consisted of a list of all the PD processes and relevant documentation describing procedures that need to be carried out during the entire PD cycle. All of these procedures where analysed, listed and ranked according to importance and impact towards PD as potential candidates for PLM implementations.

A considerable number of workshops with stakeholders were held in order to identify the benefits, PLM tools would bring to the business and highlight potential show stopper that current processes might bring with them. The stakeholders team consisted of two members from each and every department from the industrial partner. With one member being a seasoned person with multiple years of experience, while the second member from each department was recently joined with 1 year of experience. The purpose of this was to have a mix of opinions to balance out people set in there way with people with fresh ideas. This provided an extensive picture of current processes.

The one on one interviews were carried out with key personnel and process owners providing and extended understanding that was provided from the workshops. The interviews were carried out utilizing a structured questionnaire in order to obtain a consistent and balanced result from all the key personnel. While the final investigative method that of process walkthrough provided the researcher the opportunity to better understand each and every process and the possibility to question and challenge current thinking.

This investigation explored the benefits and requirements of implementing a PLM system for a PD and manufacturing company within the automotive supply chain, to improve the visibility and the information management of the various PD projects, in order to facilitate decision making and reduce the inefficiencies that lack of visibility and fragmented information bring with them.

4.1 Investigation Findings

The industrial partner worldwide employs over 6,000 people to serve a diversified group of customers in four market areas with automotive OEMs companies being their primary client base.

While extensive robust processes and procedures are already in place to support the PD process, it is heavily depended on a document-centric approach spread on over 150 IT systems, managing drawings, documents, product specifications, scheduling and ordering process to name a few. With their main PD file sharing storage area containing over 650,000 excel sheets, excluding documents on personal user laptops, and 1.4 million emails all containing vital PD information which is not revision controlled, easily searchable and could also be replicated in multiple locations creating the risk of out of date or obsolete information.

The current situation with information stored in different locations, with different interpretations lead to a complex environment in which an employee has to work. Highly experienced persons know where to find the proper information and how to interpret the data, although this is becoming harder over time. The lack of visibility and locked data are the main causes for inefficiencies, that could lead to fragmented information. The search ability and reusability of the information is also becoming an issue, and the larger the amount of disconnected data you have to search through the less likely users will re-use readily available data, that apart from data generation has a considerable impact on product development cost when the visibility to re-use parts for multiple project come into play. This situation increases the risk of taking the wrong decisions due to the use of wrong information, which leads to waste and mistakes. Which can have negative repercussions for the company from a financial, quality and reputation aspect.

The PD process follows the traditional path along the PD lifecycle shown in Fig. 3. The process is heavily document-centric with the only data-centric system along the lifecycle being the ERP system used for the production execution, but is completely disconnected from the product definition that takes place during the PD process.

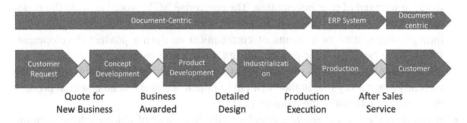

Fig. 3. PD process flow

The other clear observation throughout the PD process from the initial stages of quoting for new business right up to product servicing at the customer is bill of material (BOM) of the actual product, this is constant at each and every stage along the lifecycle implementing an integrated enterprise BOM system. The implementation should start around the BOM definition and can be expanded from there in different directions.

4.2   W/Shop Findings

The conducted w/shops involved participants from various departments covering the whole PD lifecycle from sale, engineering, project management right to operations staff. The stakeholders involved had different educational levels and positions within the organization of the industrial partner, this provided an extensive picture of the current PD processes in order to identify the existing gaps and the potential benefits PLM process and tools might provide. The main identified gaps of the current process were:

- *Improved linkage of PD information.* It is important to visually and physically access information which is linked to one another. A typical example identified was that of a component inside a BOM that will provide the user the accessibility to all related information pertaining to it as in drawings, manufacturing definition, purchasing and supplier quotes, etc. while also providing the links to the rest of the product both up and down stream providing the how product picture that is easily visualisable and understandable for the user.
- *Enhanced search ability of project/product information.* The disconnected information and multiple systems provide a massive issue to understand product and project definition. Engineering PD development project are executed over a long period of time, in the case of the industrial partner concept creation to start of production can take anywhere from 1–2 years of development. And in that time period the amount for data, information and knowledge generated is substantially large that is sometime with the best storage practices is hard to manage and retrieve especially if you are taking into consideration an older project. The importance of searching through Terabytes of information and within documents is vital tool to have in the future.
- *Better information reuse.* The reinventing the wheel situation, is a time consuming and costly process, when you consider that possible solutions are already available in the history of your previous product or projects.
- *BOM handling across the organization during the product lifetime.* Disconnected BOMs between departments creates the risk of errors and departments which are working with out of date information. The enterprise BOM would provide the structure and opportunity to communicate product definitions throughout the organization through shared data as a means of communication during product development. BOMs have been used for product design, production planning, procurement and maintenance as they contain the part list of a subassembly or assembly product. BOM currently plays a key role in the PLM environment because it is an essential product information platform in the industry [21].
- *Better link of project execution.* Similar to the first point of linking information the same was identified for project execution. The importance of providing status, information to team members, improved support of task execution and deliverables management providing a live and up-to-date picture of the project.

5   Conclusions

Implementing PLM has brought considerable benefits to other manufacturing companies. However, in parallel there is also the understanding that implementing PLM systems requires both the business and IT professionals to work together with equal priority to establish the PLM vision and system. The central vision supported by PLM is creating visibility for the whole organization and if needed the entire ecosystem to all product-related information in all phases of the product lifecycle. PLM provides information support not only in the bid or design phase but also provides support to the manufacturing planning and execution phase. Providing an environment where people share data, instead of owning data. A well-implemented PLM environment leads at the end to a "single version of the truth" for all product related information.

The investigation carried out provided real evidence for the industrial partner, highlighting the real tangible benefits that such a change to the organization can bring with it. Enhancing the linkage, search ability and improved BOM management of PD data provide a real tangible improvement that can have a significant cost reduction impact to the whole PD cycle, while also reducing the development time and therefore the time to market for NPD. These improvements would result in improved profits for the organization or more business by becoming more competitive. The improvements are not solely internal but throughout the supply chain, better control of information flow would bring benefits to the industrial partner's suppliers and customers effecting the entire supply chain.

The investigation has also highlight the feasibility of implementing such systems and provided a better understanding for the business where to go from here. PLM software's are vast complex systems that provide extensive tools and functionality for PD, it is not a plug and play package. Before implementing or even selecting a PLM tool, a business need to properly analyse and understand what their internal capabilities process before even thinking of implementing such tools

References

1. Trapp, A.C., et al.: Closing the Loop: Forging High-Quality Virtual Enterprises in a Reverse Supply Chain through Solution Portfolios (2015)
2. Panetto, H., Cecil, J.: Information systems for enterprise integration, interoperability and networking: theory and applications. Enterp. Inf. Syst. 7(1), 1–6 (2013)
3. Marchetta, M.G., Mayer, F., Forradellas, R.Q.: A reference framework following a proactive approach for Product Lifecycle Management. Comput. Ind. 62(7), 672–683 (2011)
4. Felic, A., König-Ries, B., Klein, M.: Process-oriented semantic knowledge management in Product Lifecycle Management. Procedia CIRP 25, 361–368 (2014)
5. Kratzer, J., Leenders, R.T.A.J., Van Engelen, J.M.L.: The social network among engineering design teams and their creativity: a case study among teams in two product development programs. Int. J. Proj. Manage. 28(5), 428–436 (2010)
6. Kidder, T.: The Soul of A New Machine. Little Brown, Boston (2011)
7. McDonough, E.F., Kahn, K.B., Griffin, A.: Managing communication in global product development teams. IEEE Trans. Eng. Manage. 46(4), 375–386 (1999)

8. Felekoglu, B., Maier, A.M., Moultrie, J.: Interactions in new product development: How the nature of the NPD process influences interaction between teams and management. J. Eng. Technol. Manage. **30**(4), 384–401 (2013)

9. Ulrich, K.T., Eppinger, S.D.: Product Design and Development. Irwin/McGraw-Hill, Boston (2000)

10. Roy, S.: Mastering the Art of Business Communication. Sterling Paperbacks, New Delhi (2008)

11. Crawford, L., Nahmias, A.H.: Competencies for managing change. Int. J. Proj. Manage. **28**(4), 405–412 (2010)

12. Leenders, R.T.A.J., van Engelen, J.M.L., Kratzer, J.: Virtuality, communication, and new product team creativity: a social network perspective. J. Eng. Technol. Manage. **20**(1–2), 69–92 (2003)

13. Stark, J.: Product lifecycle management. In: Product Lifecycle Management, pp. 1–29. Springer, Cham (2015)

14. Li, J., et al.: Big Data in product lifecycle management. Int. J. Adv. Manuf. Technol. **81**(1), 667–684 (2015)

15. Kiritsis, D.: Closed-loop PLM for intelligent products in the era of the Internet of things. Comput. Aided Des. **43**(5), 479–501 (2011)

16. Rizzo, S.: Why ALM and PLM Need Each Other (2014)

17. David, M., Rowe, F.: What does PLMS (product lifecycle management systems) manage: data or documents? Complementarity and contingency for SMEs. Comput. Ind. **75**, 140–150 (2016)

18. Ameri, F., Dutta, D.: Product lifecycle management: closing the knowledge loops. Comput. Aided Des. Appl. **2**(5), 577–590 (2005)

19. Silventoinen, A., Papinniemi, J., Lampela, H.: A roadmap for product lifecycle management implementation in SMEs. In: ISPIM Conference (2009)

20. Latta, G.F.: A process model of organizational change in cultural context (OC3 Model). J. Leadersh. Organ. Stud. **16**(1), 19–37 (2009)

21. Lee, J.H., Kim, S.H., Lee, K.: Integration of evolutional BOMs for design of ship outfitting equipment. Comput. Aided Des. **44**(3), 253–273 (2012)

Twenty Years of PLM – the Good, the Bad and the Ugly

Urs Meier[✉], Florian Fischli[✉], Anita Sohrweide[✉],
and Felix Nyffenegger[✉]

HSR, Rapperswil, Switzerland
{urs.meier,florian.fischli,anita.sohrweide,
felix.nyffenegger}@hsr.ch

Abstract. Looking back at the past 20 years of experience in implementation and customization of PLM applications, it can be observed that the technological complexity of the systems has increased dramatically, but it does not match the growing complexity of the business. These observations are discussed in research as well as in the PLM blogger community.

Vendors implement the new technologies primarily on the upper application levels, which produces on one side applications with the latest technology, that represent the latest research trends. On the other hand, on the lower levels of the architectures often use the same (old) technologies. The increasing number of integrated capabilities creates more diverse PLM-systems. And thus, creates a broader customer base. However, this brings the individual company and existing customers only a limited benefit. In contrast, systems increase in complexity, which is barely manageable - from the vendors and especially from the customer's perspective. The result is little added value and at the high price of lost flexibility.

This increase in system complexity, does not coincide with the increase of complexity of enterprises, which is mainly driven by growing organizational complexity (collaboration, decentralization) and increasing product complexity. Industrial companies require a deeper and better support of their existing processes and greater flexibility in adapting the tools to a changing business environment.

These findings result from a structured review of more than 30 PLM projects in various industries, from SME's to globally active large companies, 6 primary cases will be presented in this article.

Keywords: PLM · Case study mapping · Project experience · Trends
Organizational change · Tool complexity

1 Introduction

New topics such as Industry 4.0, closed loop PLM, digital twins, and others are discussed in research and strongly promoted by PLM vendors. Also, PLM vendors have invested into better flexibility and scalability and certainly moved from the toolbox approach to more out of the box functionality.

J. Ríos et al. (Eds.): PLM 2017, IFIP AICT 517, pp. 69–77, 2017.
https://doi.org/10.1007/978-3-319-72905-3_7

However, based on our experience, the scope of use cases in PLM implementations has not changed much during the past two decades. Yet, PLM Projects get more complex, time to production becomes longer, and the need for IT infrastructure has increased drastically.

This seems to be surprising and could lead to the conclusion, that either vendors do not meet the customer needs, or as some vendors say: the customers are ten years behind the tools. At least, this observation or sensation lead us, to have a closer look at the development of PLM during the past two decades.

In contrast to other studies, that analyze the elapsed development of PLM by literature reviews [1], knowledge from research experts [2] or quantitative analysis of literature [3, 4], the aim of this study is to share our personal experience (consultants and researchers). With a set of case studies, we created a structured look back on PLM projects we know in depth: what was the nature of the customer and its product, what was the scope in terms of processes and organizations, which tools and technologies were involved and how well the targets were achieved.

2   Related Research

Scientific work. Various authors discuss the history and future trends in PLM. Terzi et al. set a reference about the state of PLM for the research community in many ways [2]. It gives a detailed review of experts to PLM history and their vision for the future steps of the PLM in terms of emerging issues and topics that industrial practitioners and researchers need to address. Among others the concepts of closed loop lifecycle management and a new role of PLM in the age of digitization are discussed.

Bhatt et al. [4] as well as Nyffenegger et al. present large scale bibliometric studies of scientific literature in PLM. From their work, it can be concluded, that new topics such as BIM (building information modelling) or IoT (internet of things) are emerging. However, the later study also shows that the major topics mentioned by author keywords remain the same over the past 10 years [3].

Abramovici summarizes the current PLM state of the art and describes the main expected development directions in PLM and shows some results from PLM research projects in [5]. He sees the future of PLM in better integration of multidisciplinary products and special attention on "smart products" with embedded information devices on board. Each device will have a unique identification and will track and trace its own lifecycle. In this context, PLM will gain on importance in the next decade. However, missing industry standards and the complexity of current PLM solutions could be the bottleneck in this process.

PLM web community. In addition to scientific publications, there is also an active blogger community discussing the state of PLM. These discussions reflect a more subjective or even opinionated view, based on the personal expertise of the authors. However, longtime experience of these authors leads to a very differentiated view on current development in PLM.

Madjar mentions the cyclic trends in PLM, and asks if PLM is recycling itself [6]. During the last 20 years, he observes oscillating opinions about several topics such as customization or not, maintaining silos in best-in-bread systems vs. all-encompassing systems, cloud approach vs. on premise, model-based engineering, single BoM vs. multiple BoMs etc. As an example, there are times where customization is a bad word, while in other times it is natural way of improving efficiency.

In response, Shilovitsky compares in [7] the development of PLM technologies to startups. The success of new concepts depends on the right timing. Technologies or concepts (e.g. web base PLM) have been appearing in the past and dying again. 10 years later such a technology might suddenly be very attractive. Users and technology are ready. He sees cyclic behavior not as recycling, but rather as a necessity to choose the right time.

Complementary, he argued earlier, that old PLM ideas in people's minds are hard to escape [8]. Similar, also the limits of existing PLM architectures are hard to break. Most of them are 15 to 20 years old and completely server and database centric [9]. This does not fit the need for modern engineering and manufacturing environments, which are more likely a network of resources (see also, the "cobbler" model, mentioned in [2]). In some cases, PLM needs new inspiration to unlock future thinking.

One strategy to break out of these existing best practices is currently intensely discussed in industry as well as in research: the "bimodal" approach [10]. Adapting an established system and all its data and processes to a novel concept might involve a lot of work, resistance and risk. It is likely that this will result in a compromise between the old and the new concept. Instead, the bimodal approach suggests exploring new unpredictable concepts in a separate system without barriers (mode 2), while the existing system is optimized for the predictable and well-understood concepts (mode 1). Marrying a more predictable evolution of products and technologies (Mode 1) with the new and innovative (Mode 2) is the essence of an enterprise bimodal capability [11].

While these interesting inputs from PLM bloggers contribute on a substantial but personal level to the understanding of PLM, researcher do not widely share personal experience of implementation projects. None of them presents data to the history and the experience of real PLM implementations, and how these changed over time. We are aware that the selection of the samples is biased be the location and expertise of the authors. Still, we believe, this detailed, but subjective view on the history of PLM adds a new complementary perspective to the work described above.

3 Methodology

This study is a mapping of case studies into a standardized schema, to allow comparison and detection of trends along these cases. All case studies are based on consulting interventions executed by one or several of the authors. This ensures deep insight into these PLM projects, but of course the interpretation is a subject of individual judgment by the authors. However, the step of abstraction (mapping) allows an unbiased, or less biased, discussion of the evolution of PLM projects along the dimensions proposed. In addition, all cases which are selected for presentation in this publication are reviewed with the company to assure correctness of the data, particularly the timeline.

The interventions are characterized by different types of companies, different product types, and also by very different size of project scope. So, these factors must be respected in the interpretation of the case studies. Also, based on previous research and comments from bloggers, we were curious on how these PLM scenarios developed over time. The history of technology (servers, clients, upgrades, new tools, etc.) on one

Table 1. Dimensions of the case study mapping

Dimension	Description
Company name	Not shown in publication
Company size	Classification of the size into the following categories of total employees. Based on the classification suggested by the European Commission [12] 1: <50 2: <250 3: >250
Company domain	A rough categorization of the company domain, such as Plant-Engineering, Automotive or Building Technologies
Organization complexity	How complex the company was at the time of the intervention. 1: Local development and local manufacturing 2: Local development and global manufacturing 3: Global development and global manufacturing
Product complexity	To characterize the nature of the product complexity we decided to classify them by the product strategy or (strategy to connect sales with production). Since these strategies clearly influence the setup of PLM concepts. 1: MTS (Make to Stock) 2: ATO (Assemble to Order) 3: MTO (Make to Order) 4: ETO (Engineer to Order)
PLM tool	Not shown in publication
Main PLM capabilities	The most important use cases and functionalities that were implemented to achieve the customer's targets
Processes involved	The business processes that were primarily targeted by the project
Organizations involved	The organizational units that contributed to achieve the projects targets. These do not necessarily match with the processes. E.g. the service organization might be involved to add service relevant master data as part of the product development process
Year	Year, when the intervention of the authors started. The start of the PLM campaign might be earlier
Target history	The major targets of the company along the timeline of implementation
Timeline hardware requirements (server)	Simultaneous use of Server of the company for daily work, maintenance and updating
Timeline hardware clients	Number of users and working stations for PLM interaction as CAD-station (engineering), office-station (light) etc.

hand and the development of organizations on the other hand need to be understood. Therefore, the dimensions shown in Table 1 were chosen for the mapping.

As mentioned in Table 1, the name of the company and the vendor of the PLM tool will not be published, these are not considered relevant to the interpretation of the data and would probably cause damage to the involved actor. Furthermore, it is important to better understand the values of PLM capabilities. These were as far as possible aligned with the keywords preferably chosen by other authors [3], but bundled into clusters which are explained in Table 2.

Table 2. Values of PLM capabilities

PLM capability	Description
Engineering change management	Release workflows, ECR/ECO/ECN processes, business rules
MCAD integration	MCAD integration, configuration management for MCAD
ECAD integration	ECAD integration, configuration management for ECAD
Global collaboration	Replication, access rights and roles, concurrent engineering
Item and BOM management	Item centric principle, BOM management, BOM views, lifecycle status, configuration management, effectivities
Variant management	Overloaded BOMs including variants and options, configuration master data
Description catalogue	Standard terminology and schemas for texts such as names or descriptions
Mechatronics	Mechatronics structures and/or Software Integration
Requirements management	Management of requirements and/or functional structures in the PLM system, requirement tractability
ERP interface	Interface between PLM and ERP system, e.g. item, BOM, lifecycle status, etc.
Master data for service	Service relevant master data such as spare parts, spare part kits etc. and durability information, automatic generation of spare parts catalogs
Classification	Classifications of items for better management of items
Phase-out process	System supported phase-out process
Information and productivity apps	Application for easy and fast information access to PLM or ERP information (e.g. item information, paperless production, etc.)

4 Case Studies

A total of 39 case studies were considered. Since it is not possible to list all cases in this publication, a set of representative samples was selected to be presented in detail in Tables 3a, b of the appendix. The samples were chosen to show the typical variety of organizations and product strategies. Also, they give an idea of the typical steps in the timeline of PLM development. The table shows the evolution of PLM targets as well as the infrastructure used for different stages of the individual PLM journeys. A more detailed explanation of the listed PLM capabilities can be found in Table 1.

From the case studies the following observations can be captured:

  i. Looking at all 39 case studies, the scope of PLM stays within the range of traditional targets (as listed in Table 1). Only few exceptions look at more advanced topics such as mechatronic simulation or test management.
 ii. Typically, the steps of maturity include: first focus on MCAD integration and item and BOM management, next focus ERP integration and full engineering change management process and mechatronics structures, then optimization and minor enhancements, finally providing user specific information through app-like concepts.
iii. Companies that face a change organizational complexity (focus on global collaboration) tend to slow down PLM activities (case 1, 2, 3, 5).
 iv. Companies with constant organizations are able to keep constant pace in improvement (case 4, partially 6).
  v. Changes or upgrades of the PLM tool and/or CAD tool cause an interruption of several years (case 1, 2, 3, 5).
 vi. Scenarios with global collaboration tend to ask for remarkably more IT infrastructure (case 2, 5). Only one case achieved a reduction of IT complexity through global consolidation (case 3).
vii. Upgrades or replacement of legacy system almost all cases lead to more complex IT infrastructure (1, 2, 3, 5).
viii. Some small companies do not have a need to increase the scope of PLM (case 6).

5 Discussion

Observing these mapped case studies, the following hypothesis can be formulated.

Hypothesis I. PLM systems become more and more inflated and less flexible. This is the result of a continuous expansion of PLM capabilities by integrating a large number of sub-systems into current PLM platforms. This effect was increased by the acquisition strategy of PLM vendors to gain market share.

PLM Acquisitions of new technologies or competitors often follow the merging of the purchased tool landscape with the own architecture. This leads by nature to increase in complexity of the tool, but not to a quantifiable benefit to support of the needs of the end-user. For example, the growing number of available 3rd party tools integrations increase the number of potential customers for the system supplier, but often only creates limited added value for the existing clientele. In contrast, this leads to an ugly effect: System upgrades result in large scale projects, that might throw a company back for years instead of continuously developing their PLM maturity (observation v., vii.). Some companies don't even have a need to increase their PLM scope and are still forced to keep pace with the technology (observation viii.).

Another driver for the increasing complexity is the shift of technology from e.g. fat clients to web clients or apps, or as recently discuss form centralized databases to distributed organization of data. Such shifts in paradigm or new technologies are typically addressed by adding a new layer to the existing software architecture. The underlying basic functionality has not really much changed. At least, it is questionable if this vast mixture of technologies really supports the intention of the original paradigm.

Hypothesis II. Not just the PLM tools, also many companies have increased remarkably in complexity. The need for global collaboration and flexibility of PLM systems to continuously changing organizations is growing (observation iii., iv., vi.).

While ten years ago, the scope of many SMEs was to support the engineering team in the head quarter, recent company structures require true global engineering collaboration. Acquisition and merging has played an important role in the strategy of many enterprises (SMEs and large companies, observation iii.). Ten years ago, the focus was mostly on integration of mechanical CAD. Today it has shifted to the central platform for mechanic, electronic and software development (observation ii.). This trend might correlate in first place with the increasing complexity of the products. As a further driver for growing complexity, the growing decentralization can also be viewed. More and more companies have outsourced parts of their development sites to other countries.

Conclusion. While companies are rolling the same themes (observation i., [5, 6]) in increasingly complex and globally organized environments, the tools focused on the integration of more and more capabilities to grow market coverage. The suppliers and the companies have not developed in the same direction. Hence, the statement "customers are 10 years behind the tools" is not a surprise. They simply have another focus.

From hypothesis, II it can be concluded that it would be important for companies to solve their core problems (e.g. collaboration) efficiently and, above all, scalable and flexible towards changing organization, product strategies and business models. Then the willingness would certainly exist, to approach the next steps in the PLM maturity degree. However, based on hypothesis I, established PLM manufacturers might have a hard time to achieve this demand [8]. They aim of tools to cover more and more functionality was done on the price of flexibility (and sometimes usability).

A real exemption for the reduction of system complexity and the increase of flexibility would probably only succeed on the greenfield. This, of course, requires a lot of courage. Companies and consultants currently react to this dilemma with the bi-modal approach [10]. Eventually, it would not be surprising if a new disruptive PLM technology managed to shake the PLM world during the next decade.

Appendix

Table 3. Mapped case studies

(a)

Case No.	Size	Company Domain	Organization complexity	Product complexity	Main PLM capabilities	Processes Involved	Organizations Involved	Year	Target history	Timeline hardware requirements (server)	Timeline hardware clients
1	3	Machine building	3	3	- Engineering change management - MCAD/ECAD integration - ERP Interface - BOM management - Variant management - Masterdata for service (electronic spare parts catalog, 6 languages)	- Product development - Product documentation (Spare parts catalog) - Documentation - Service (Spare parts)	- Mechanical and electrical engineering - Documentation - Service	1998	- 1998: PLM evaluation - 1999: PLM implementation - 1999: PLM re-evaluation (because of PLM supplier merge / end of SW) - 1999/2000: PLM re-implementation - 2000: Data migration - 2000-2006: Several enhancements - 2006-2016 Operation/selective enhancements - 2016: Re-Work/upgrade ERP-interface - 2016-today: Operation/selective enhancements	- 1998-today: 1x server (PROD) 1x server (TEST)	- 1998: ~90 clients (engineering) ~20 clients (service, documentation, planning operation) today: ~5 clients(engineering) ~7 clients (service, documentation, planning operation)
2	3	Aerospace	3	4	- Engineering change management - MCAD (Multi-CAD) integration - BOM management - Global collaboration - Regulation conformity	- Product development - Product structuring - Purchase	- Mechanical and electrical engineering - Config control	2013	- 2013: PLM implementation - 2014/2015: Selective enhancements - 2016/2017: PLM-SW upgrade - 2017: Selective enhancements - 2018: ERP integration	- 2013-2018: 2x server (PROD) 2x server (TEST) - 2017-: 10x server (PROD) 2x server (TEST)	- 2013: ~14 clients (engineering) ~6 clients (config-control, planning operation) - today: ~90 clients (engineering/global) ~6 clients (config-control, planning operation)
3	3	Plant-Engineering	3	2,3,4	- Engineering change management - Global collaboration - BOM management - Variant management - Description catalogue - Global manufacturing masterdata (7 languages) - Classification (standardization) - Masterdata for service - ERP Interface	- Product development for plant components	- Mechanical engineering - Manufacturing - Standardization - Service	1998	- until 1999: Legacy PDM tool - 1999: Introduction of new PLM (due to CAD strategy), individual systems per site. - 2005: Attempt for global PLM (failure, due to poor acceptance) - 2010: Change of CAD system - 2010: Unifying PLM functionality: same configuration for all sites - 2011: Re-thinking the scope of PLM (because of PLM supplier merge / end of SW) - 2011: Evaluation of global PLM platform - 2012: Implementation and migration global PLM plattform (full capabilities) - 2013: Pilot with one BU and 2 sites - 2014-today: Global rollout (6 BUs, 14 Sites)	- HW legacy PLM systems - PROD: 24 server (4 per site) - TEST: 4 server - Hardware global PLM plattform - PROD: 6 server (application server) 10 (vault realization)	- 2010: ~400 (engineering) ~600 (light) clients (total of all engineering sites, in separate PLM systems) - today: ~550 (engineering) ~1000 (light clients)

(b)

Case No.	Size	Company Domain	Organization complexity	Product complexity	Main PLM capabilities	Processes Involved	Organizations Involved	Year	Target history	Timeline hardware requirements (server)	Timeline hardware clients
4	2	Subsystem supplier	1	2,3	- Engineering change management - MCAD/ECAD integration - BOM management - ERP interface	- Product development - Product structuring	- Mechanical and electrical Engineering - Manufacturing	2011	- 2009: Initiation of discussion about PLM (managing technical documents) - 2011: PLM evaluation - 2012: PLM implementation (full capabilities) - 2013: Engineering change management - 2014: ECAD integration - 2015: Minor enhancements - 2017: Upgrade project	- 2011-today: 1x server (PROD) 1x server (TEST)	- 2011-today: ~30 clients (engineering) ~90 clients (only document management)
5	2	Electronic component supplier	-1999: 1 > 2009: 3	1	- Engineering change management - MCAD/ECAD integration - BOM management - Global collaboration (advanced access rights) - Classification - ERP interface - Phase-Out process - Item information app	- Product development	- Mechanical electrical Engineering - Manufacturing	1996	- 1996: Item masterdata - 1998: BoM (mechatronic) management, change management, ERP interface - 2000: CAD-integration - 2002: Multi CAD (2D, 3D) - 2008: PLM item information client - 2008: One CAD for all - 2009: Advanced access rights and IP protection (due to aquisition strategy) - 2011: Major upgrade of PLM System - 2011: New ERP interface - 2011-today: Global rollout: integration of 11 new development sites (3 divisions) - 2013: Introduction of paperless production - 2013: Electronic workflow (change management)	- 1996-2011: 1x server (PROD) - 2010: Virtualisation - 2011: 2x server (PROD) + 4x DFM (replication), 2x server (TEST) - 2016: 3x server (PROD) 2x DFM (replication), 3x server (TEST),	- until 2010: 60 clients (engineering) - today: 90 clients (engineering) 40 additional clients (document, item)
6	2	Component and mechanical system supplier	<2005: 1 >2005: 3	1,2	- Engineering change management - MCAD integration - BOM management	- Product development - Equipment development	- Mechanical engineering - Equipment engineering	2005	- 2004: MCAD with PDM integration - 2004: MCAD change - 2005: PDM integration for new MCAD	1x server (PROD)	- 2004: ~10 clients (engineering) - 2005: ~14 clients (engineering) - today: ~20 clients (engineering)

References

1. Liu, W., Zeng, Y., Maletz, M., Brisson, D.: Product lifecycle management: a survey. In: Proceedings ASME 2009 International Design Engineering Technical Conferences and Computers and Information in Engineering Conference (IDETC/CIE 2009), no. 2007, pp. 1213–1225 (2009)
2. Terzi, S., Bouras, A., Dutta, D., Garetti, M., Kiritsis, D.: Product lifecycle management – from its history to its new role. Int. J. Prod. Lifecycle Manag. 4(4), 360 (2010)
3. Nyffenegger, F., Rivest, L., Braesch, C.: Identifying PLM themes, trends and clusters through ten years of scientific publications. In: International Conference on Product Lifecycle Management (2016)

4. Bhatt, S., Tseng, F.H., Maranzana, N., Segonds, F.: Scientometric study of product lifecycle management international conferences : a decade overview. In: International Conference on Product Lifecycle Management, pp. 1–8 (2010)
5. Abramovici, M.: Future trends in Product Lifecycle Management (PLM). In: Krause, F.L. (ed.) The Future of Product Development, pp. 665–674. Springer, Heidelberg (2007). https://doi.org/10.1007/978-3-540-69820-3_64
6. Madjar, I.: Cyclical Trends in PLM is PLM Recycling Itself Over and Over? LinkedIn (2017). https://www.linkedin.com/pulse/cyclical-trends-plm-recycling-itself-over-ilan-madjar
7. Shilovitsky, O.: PLM Waves – The History of the future. Blog Beyond PLM (2017). https://beyondplm.com/2017/02/04/plm-waves-history
8. Shilovitsky, O.: How to Escape from old PLM Ideas. Blog Beyond PLM (2016). http://beyondplm.com/2016/11/14/escape-old-plm-ideas/
9. Shilovitsky, O.: How to Break Limits of exisiting PLM Architectures. Blog Beyond PLM (2015). http://beyondplm.com/2015/03/13/how-break-limits-of-existing-plm-architectures/
10. Voskuil, J.: Best Practices or Next Practices? Jos Voskuil's Weblog (2016). https://virtualdutchman.com/2016/09/25/best-practices-or-next-practices/
11. Gartner Inc.: What is Bimodal IT? Gartner.Com (2015). http://www.gartner.com/it-glossary/bimodal. Accessed 28 Feb 2017
12. European Commission: What is an SME. Entrepreneurship and Small and Medium-Sized Enterprises (SMEs) (2016). http://ec.europa.eu/growth/smes/business-friendly-environment/sme-definition_de

PLM for Digital Factories

PLM 4.0 – Recalibrating Product Development and Management for the Era of Internet of Everything (IoE)

Julius Golovatchev[1(✉)], Prodip Chatterjee[1], Florian Kraus[2],
and Roger Schüssl[1]

[1] Detecon International GmbH – Deutsche Telekom Group, Cologne, Germany
{julius.golovatchev,prodip.chatterjee,
roger.schuessl}@detecon.com
[2] Detecon International GmbH – Deutsche Telekom Group, Munich, Germany
florian.kraus@detecon.com

Abstract. A rising complexity of products, the ongoing digitization and an accelerated shift of market demands lead to a rapidly rising number of uncertainties in business and technology environments. The Internet of Everything (IoE) offers many potential opportunities and benefits to both service providers and customers. This paper aims to integrate knowledge from diverse fields into a comprehensive, practical approach for development and implementation of products and services using IoE technologies. The research focused especially on the needs and challenges of innovation and product managers who have to find ways to cope with rising uncertainties and the problem of increasingly complex business environments and digitalization. Therefore, this paper presents first learnings that guides practitioners through implementation of industrial IoE and its impact on new product development and management. It gives them guidance on how the companies' IoE projects could be linked with its new product development initiatives.

Keywords: Internet of Things · IoT · Internet of Everything · IoE
Product lifecycle management · PLM · Product development · Digital economy
IoE platform

1 Motivation

The Internet of Everything (as next stage of Internet of Things) and related Smart Products offer companies and their customers many potential benefits. At first glance there may not seem to be much in common between new product development as well as product lifecycle management (PLM) and the Internet of Everything. However, the two subjects are closely related, as the "Things" are products and the devices are products, too.

Since a couple of years the topic of IoE has impact on new product development (NPD) as well as PLM which gains quite some attention from management science [1–5]. The detailed consideration and research on IoE and its impact on NPD and PLM are still missing.

© IFIP International Federation for Information Processing 2017
Published by Springer International Publishing AG 2017. All Rights Reserved
J. Ríos et al. (Eds.): PLM 2017, IFIP AICT 517, pp. 81–91, 2017.
https://doi.org/10.1007/978-3-319-72905-3_8

No doubt, IoE is one of the most important trend topics – the term is omnipresent and surprisingly hard to understand for many people in the technology industry and most importantly for many target customers across all verticals (e.g. Automotive, Pharma, FMCG, Energy etc.). Perhaps the most significant difference and one focus point of this paper is the importance and power of start-ups who are leveraging the IoE trend and building entirely new products, designed horizontally across industries or tailor made for a certain vertical. The pace of IoE start-ups emerging is significantly high and mainly driven by a dramatic drop in prices for sensors and computing power. In a nutshell, small IoE solutions can have big impact on customers – generating big opportunities but in case of wrong PLM, management will lead eventually to big risks as well [6]. By applying smart PLM for IoE solutions customers can leverage the potential of these new products without risks. Consequently, scholars as well as practitioners call for new perspectives that understand the challenges and opportunities of IoE for product development and management from a management perspective.

The key goals of this research is to understand hot product/service related topics and try to understand how these new emerging IoE players will change PLM especially customers, e.g. large enterprises. To do so, the paper aims at integrating knowledge from the diverse fields into a comprehensive, practical approach for the development and implementation of the products and services using IoE technologies. Furthermore, a more dedicated focus is being set across selected key sectors with strong impact of IoE and PLM in Healthcare, Automotive and the Energy sector.

2 Research Design

The research design was in cooperation with companies of Deutsche Telekom Group. In a first step practitioners' experiences were examined in order to assure practical perspectives and problem perceptions were considered sufficiently. Therefore, innovation managers of companies that had already implemented products and services in IoE fields have been inquired through structured expert interviews between June and September 2015 either on-site at the interviewee's office location or via teleconferencing. The interviewees belonged to big industrial companies as well as start-up in the IoE field (N = 22). All experts held a leading position in innovation departments or worked in comparable positions inside their organizations. The focus on members of innovation management departments was chosen to make sure that the interviewees can report from and share insights of different new product development projects in IoE field. Interviews were also conducted with experts from the Healthcare, Automotive and the Energy sector which led to new insights in those sectors. On average, the interviews lasted one hour and have been transcribed, codified and analyzed in order to extract central problems and challenges with IoE and product development.

The results have been consolidated in a second step to develop a comprehensive view that takes into account the identified criteria for the management and implementation of IoE as well as for practitioners' needs and problems. In order to validate the feasibility and practicability of the developed approach, an additional set of interviews with business consultants of Detecon Consulting (Member of Deutsche

Telekom Group) was conducted. This way of validation offered the chance to hypothetically check the developed approach with experiences from client projects.

Across all analyzed IoE sections, we found strong and clear evidence that start-ups market space is evolving very fast and market participants – analysts, incumbents and start-ups have no doubt that IoE adoption will come and be a big untapped and unleashed market for them. However, the different IoE sections do have different maturity levels.

Looking at customers and PLM we found the most surprising and definitely highest impact development that emerged with IoE solutions the radical shift of PLM amongst vendors (mostly start-ups) and customers (often midsize to large enterprises or cities). Key reason for this is on the one hand the innovativeness and focus of IoE vendors (focusing on a small niche) and on the other hand the impact of IoE generated software and services (especially data analytics) in customers' existing processes. In a nutshell this means that business customers are adopting more and more IoE solutions fitting to their specific needs, which they integrate into their IT infrastructure over time as well as into PLM step-by-step in order to generate more efficiency and improve their products. As these IoE solutions become essential to their business over time they are integrated into customers' PLM process – at this stage they are confronted with likely different PLM set-ups of themselves and their IoE vendors. Customers have to face complexity of managing various IoE vendors – each of them with their hardware, software and service – and have to manage them very carefully and slowly. IoE vendors on the other hand come from the technology sector and use to think in fast and agile environments framed by software releases, adoption to services, functionalities and hardware as well. They have to focus on their own product only and will eventually not be able to consider each of their customer' individual requirements while updating their product. These factors lead to a smart and adaptive PLM framework in order to master tomorrow's IoE landscape.

3   Internet of Everything and Product Lifecycle Management – Key Definitions and Status Quo

Detecon defines PLM as a strategic business approach for managing a company's products and services throughout their lifecycle in the most effective and efficient way: starting with the original idea, through the design, marketing and withdrawal phases. There's not an agreed definition of the Internet of Everything [5]. In this paper, we refer to the Internet of Everything (IoE). While IoT relates to the enablement and management of interconnected devices logically associated with physical things, IoE extends this concept beyond things to include people, processes and the data supporting them [7]. In order to proof the status quo of PLM and IoE, to evaluate the impact of IoE on the future product development and management and to develop the new framework and check its feasibility and practicability, an additional set of interviews with business consultants of Detecon Consulting (Member of Deutsche Telekom Group) was conducted alongside interviews with leading enterprises and start-ups across the highlighted four sectors of IoE. This way of validation offered the chance to hypothetically check the developed approach with experiences from client projects.

The key takeaways across several IoE categories are:

- IoE and IoT platforms are emerging, driven by large companies. There is a mutual consensus, that in the future customers will orchestrate their IoE solutions on a single platform but it is unclear which platforms will sustain or even dominate.
- Hardware and software need to interplay very well, with a stronger focus going into software and especially data analytics.
- Standardization is low in many areas of IoE due to conflicting consortia and overall the nascent stage of the entire sector.
- Smart factories are in the most advanced stage of that market.
- Artificial Intelligence is playing an increasing role in solution design.
- Enterprise customers start with solutions at small scale in sandbox environments before scaling up and integrating it deeply into existing systems.
- PLM may become a future important element as smart cities emerge [8].
- Digital Twins – designed to improve existing business models – digitally map the real world in the form of physical product instances over the entire product life cycle.
- Start-ups try to position themselves in some areas strongly by partnering with large companies (e.g. Industry 4.0) and others without (e.g. Smart Home).

4   PLM 4.0 in the Era of Internet of Everything (IoE): Management Framework and Application on Use Cases

In 2010 the authors composed a comprehensive study about PLM in the telecommunication industry for which they analyzed 50 communication service providers with regard to existing PLM structures [9]. In 2014 this PLM approach was adjusted to the Energy and Utilities industry [2]. The results show that an integrated product lifecycle management enables companies to control the increasing complexity such companies are facing. The companies in the Industry 4.0 and during the digital transformation are faced with similar challenges as a result of the increased complexity which makes both problem settings quite analogous [3]. The model proposed in the following section shows that through the structural similarity, problem-solving approaches can be adapted to the current challenges of the Industry 4.0 in the context of IoE implementation (see detailed description of the PLM Framework in) [9]. The dimensions of an integrated PLM and the related design elements were derived from the integrated management principles. The framework encompasses the four dimensions of PLM Strategy, PLM Process, Product Architecture, and PLM IT Architecture and should be used from companies as an orientation for their processes and products in the future (see Fig. 1). The developed PLM framework can serve as a basis for further evaluation of the impact of the IoE on the product development and management. We identified three exemplary use cases in the sectors of Automotive, Healthcare and Energy to outline and assess these challenges and risks.

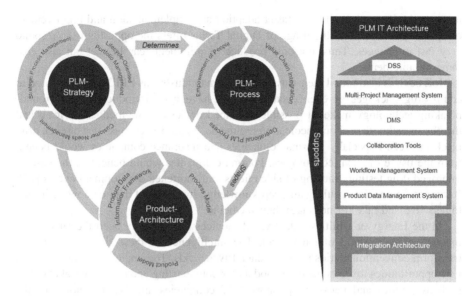

Fig. 1. Proposed next generation PLM Framework in the era of the IoE

4.1 PLM Strategy

PLM Strategy ensures alignment of products and portfolio with actual and potential market demands, and provides the guiding framework for PLM Process execution. For example, the development of an energy tariff, as incremental innovation, requires a completely different product development process design as the introduction of new innovation complex products and services in the context of e-mobility [10]. IoE brings more and more modules and devices into the game, product lifecycles change and interdependencies between all the components and network infrastructures need to be taken into consideration. Besides that, by designing a PLM Strategy, ever changing market needs have to be accounted. Feedback, demands and expectations are valuable to design individual solutions.

Original Equipment Manufacturer (OEM) in the Automotive industry for example face the challenge to integrate solutions like ProGlove in their smart factories and also in their product development cycles [11]. ProGlove is integrating technology into the natural movement of workers' hands. As a business intelligence solution for production management, it combines RFID, motion tracking, sensors and automated scanning. It is an almost perfect example for how to use IoE technology in the field of manufacturing and logistics. As the vendor's solution is integrated in the production at different OEMs, their requirements have an impact on product enhancements of the IoE device vendor, too. Another example how to use IoE technology in the field of manufacturing is via a Digital Twin. A Digital Twin depicts real products or systems digitally to constitute an application of its physical twin and predicts traits and performance over the whole lifecycle. By using live data (e.g. sensor data) it enables a realistic replication of the physical twin. A Digital Twin offers many opportunities, especially for the Automotive sector. For example, the abrasion of machines or unused capacity could be more easily detected. It allows a faster adaption and implementation and improvement of operations. Moreover, the usage of Digital Twins offers the opportunity to respond very fast to changes. Thus, not only producer requirements can be met but also customer requirements.

IoE devices also found their way in the Pharma industry, as RFID tags were used to equip drug packages or even eatable devices have been introduced. This groundbreaking technology makes it possible to embed devices in the medication itself and thereby to gather data about medication regiments, health issues, miss-use or even drug black markets. Especially pharma companies and insurance companies would benefit from the usage of such technologies. Pharma companies would benefit in the case of improved drug testing, tracking of side effects and shortened development cycles [12]. Insurance companies would gain deep knowledge by gathered data of how their customers live and take (or not take) their medicine.

In the Energy & Utilities industry, IoE devices have already been the enabler for innovation in the field of smart grid. The intelligence of these devices is able to transform conventional grids to smart, data driven, grids. The implementation opens up new opportunities towards business models for both existing and also new stakeholders such as utilities and network operators, ICT companies and last but not least the customers [13] (Fig. 2).

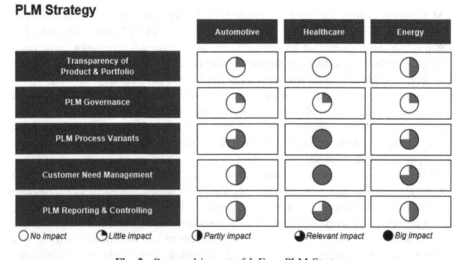

Fig. 2. Proposed impact of IoE on PLM Strategy

4.2 PLM Process

PLM Process facilitates execution of the collaborative process (efficiency goal) and the alignment of activities with the strategic PLM goals of the company (effectiveness goal). Integration and manageability of value-adding partners play a central role, as IoE broadens up opportunities to partner in any possible way. The challenge for the PLM

Process is to include all involved partners in the product development process. More and more complex products require standardized processes [10]. The bigger the size and scale of partners in the IoE era, the more challenging it is to align all of them. In times of social media, Big Data and the Internet of Everything, the management of information and innovations of value chain partners become two key success factors.

The interplay of all related parties, e.g. OEM and IoE vendor, becomes even more important in this context. The ProGlove case in the Automotive industry shows, that smart devices not only provide its users with useful information about products, processes and assembling instructions, but is also able to gather information, such as documentation about processes and workflow sequences, and send it back to a central server, in order to be circled back and made useful in the OEM's PLM processes. One of the main challenges for the OEM is to adapt to the fast iterations of the vendors [11].

If one considers a Health & Pharma industry with smart packages, it is very likely that useful information can be gathered along the product lifecycle and e.g. be used for improving inventory and drug counterfeiting. It also gives pharmacies and retailers a chance to store data (e.g. information for the patients on how to use the drugs) on the chips and provide useful information to the customers (Fig. 3).

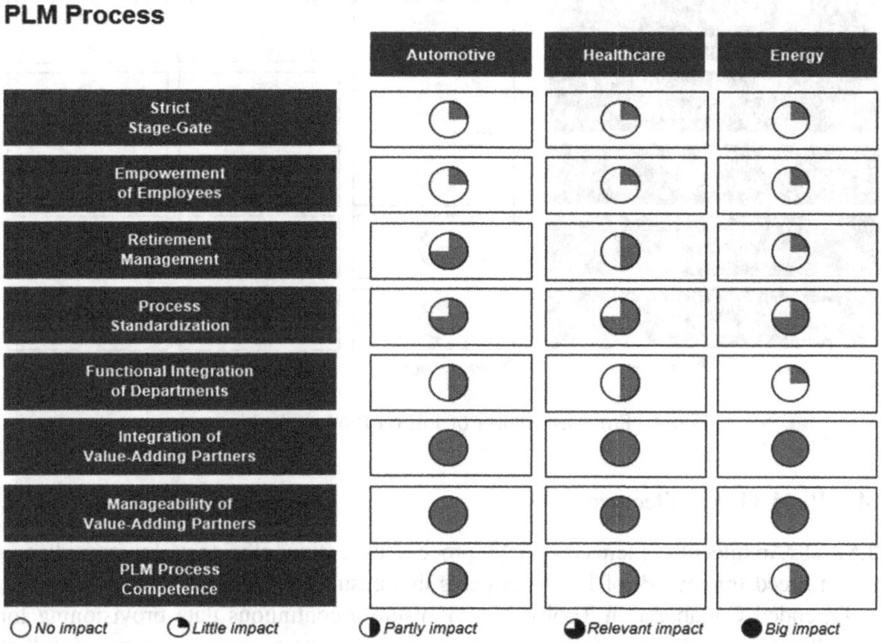

PLM Process

Fig. 3. Proposed impact of IoE on PLM Process

4.3 Product Architecture

Product Architecture enables product component reusability by defining constraints and rules for decomposing product functionality into modules with product data models. In an environment where products and services are becoming more and more virtualized, product model and product data have to be aligned carefully. Further integration needs be enabled upfront by creating a structured mode based on an information network. Implementing a Product Architecture that respects these aspects is a major challenge [1].

One of the most dramatic impact across all three analyzed sectors is the impact of product data to be aligned with product model. The core and heart of the IoE value addition lies in generation of data which was never measured before in real time, mainly complementing the core products. For an Automotive OEM it means that ProGlove's data will not change the car from the ground up, but rather influence the manufacturing process and certain car features. For Healthcare it means that data generated out of fitness bands influence the way obesity treatment is being done. Energy companies change their energy mix in real time due to smart meters. All follow same principles (Fig. 4).

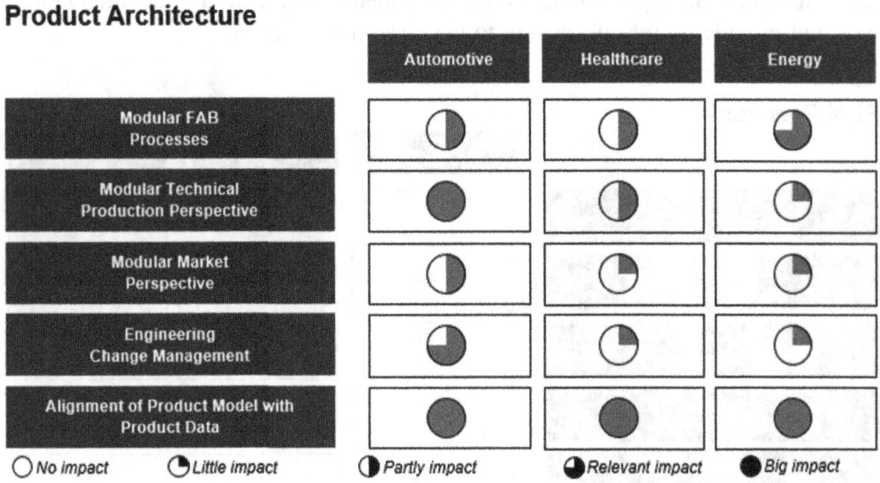

Product Architecture

	Automotive	Healthcare	Energy
Modular FAB Processes	◑	◑	◕
Modular Technical Production Perspective	●	◑	◔
Modular Market Perspective	◑	◔	◔
Engineering Change Management	◐	◔	◔
Alignment of Product Model with Product Data	●	●	●

○ No impact   ◔ Little impact   ◑ Partly impact   ◕ Relevant impact   ● Big impact

Fig. 4. Proposed impact of IoE on Product Architecture

4.4   PLM IT Architecture

PLM IT Architecture increases PLM process execution efficiency by providing a best-of-breed framework of IT components that ensures an optimal IT-to-process fit.

Extended Collaboration Tools need to ensure a continuous data provisioning for controlling and product portfolio purposes, both within the own organization, as well as with outside partners. Efficient and intelligent data management is a basic requirement to benefit from the power of IoT at all. Unstructured data is useless data, thus data management needs to cover data visibility and role-based access to information, harmonized data sources and data consistency, and versioning of product-related data to support availability, accuracy, timeliness and completeness of information towards achieving transparency for making the right decisions at the right time. Tracking and analyzing e.g. financial data from both, a customer-related and product-related point of view is only possible if there is an IT Architecture in place that supports application integration. Not only financial systems, but also Customer Relationship Management (CRM), Operation Support Systems (OSS) and Business Support Systems (BSS) need to be fully integrated [6].

Across all three verticals, PLM IT Architecture is probably one of the most challenging parts, mainly due to the strong implications and risks while implementing an IoE solution (e.g. from a start-up) at full scale especially in terms of data management. The key strategies here are piloting and sandboxing in the beginning and trial phase of the IoE product followed by a cautious step-by-step integration after successful pilot. In Automotive more data can lead to changed optimization processes in engineering but also after sales. Healthcare companies especially leverage IoE sensor data in its R&D phase when integrating additional data into their modelling and simulation tools. For utility companies, smart products can have major influence even on core elements of their ERP system (e.g. procurement and billing due to smart gateways and grids) [4].

The developed PLM Framework can serve as a basis for further evaluation of the impact of the IoE on the product development and management (Fig. 5).

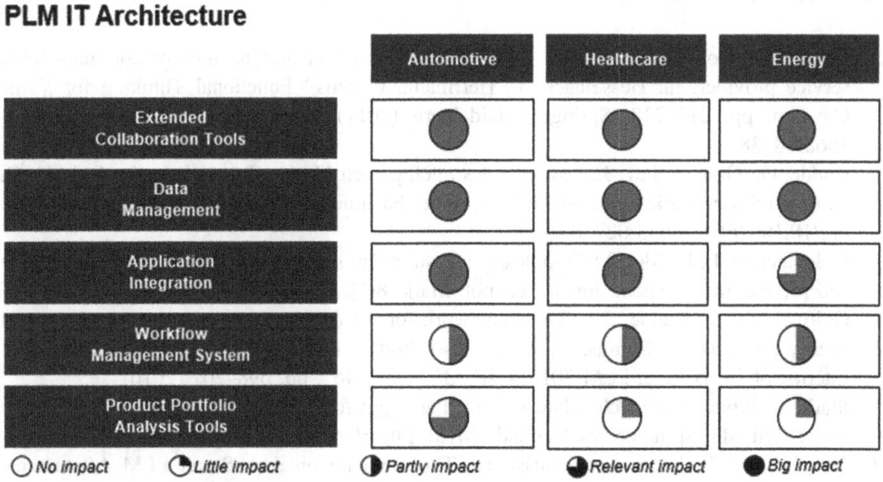

PLM IT Architecture

Fig. 5. Proposed impact of IoE on PLM IT Architecture

5 Conclusion and Outlook

The key goal of this paper is to understand hot product- and service-related topics, business- and go-to-market models of the participants inside the IoE market and trying to understand how these new emerging IoE players will change the PLM especially customers, e.g. large enterprises who are picking up to adapt and test these new IoE solutions - with many of these enterprises having not dealt with start-ups as suppliers for key product areas that have substantial effect on their business (processes).

The research results show that it is generally feasible to establish a general management perspective on development of products and services within IoE. Furthermore, new areas of research could have been identified by focusing on practitioners' challenges within IoE and new product development that have not been investigated by recent literature. Furthermore, a future outlook across selected key sectors (with IoE product related issues in Automotive, Healthcare, and Energy) is also a focus of this analysis.

The research focused especially on the needs and challenges of innovation and product managers who have to find ways to cope with rising uncertainties and the problem of increasingly complex business environments and digitalization. Therefore, this paper presents first learnings that guides practitioners through implementation of industrial IoE and its impact on new product development and management. It gives them guidance on how the company's IoE project could be linked with its new product development initiatives. Ideally, managers are able to achieve improved product market fit, save costs due to early problem identification and enjoy a wide range of communicative advantages by using the results of the paper.

References

1. Budde, O., Golovatchev, J.: Descriptive service product architecture for communication service provider. In: Hesselbach, J., Herrmann, C. (eds.) Functional Thinking for Value Creation, pp. 213–218. Springer, Heidelberg (2011). https://doi.org/10.1007/978-3-642-19689-8_38
2. Budde, O., Golovatchev, J.: Produkte des intelligenten Markts. In: Aichele, C., Doleski, O. D. (eds.) Smart Market, pp. 593–620. Springer Fachmedien, Wiesbaden (2014). https://doi.org/10.1007/978-3-658-02778-0_22
3. Golovatchev, J., Budde, O.: Complexity measurement metric for innovation implementation and product management. Int. J. Technol. Mark. **8**(1), 82–98 (2013)
4. Golovatchev, J., Budde, O.: PLM framework for the development and management smart energy products. In: Bouras, A., et al. (eds.) Product Lifecycle Management in the Era of Internet of Everything, PLM 2015, IFIP AICT, vol. 467, pp. 698–707 (2016)
5. Stark, J.: Product Lifecycle Management: Paradigm for 21st Century Product Realisation, vol. 1, 3rd edn. Springer, Switzerland (2015). https://doi.org/10.1007/978-3-319-17440-2
6. Golovatchev, J., Kraus, F., Schüssl, R.: The Tsunami breaker. Smart PLM 4.0 to tame Internet of Things. In: Detecon Management Report, no. 2, pp. 8–16 (2016)
7. IEEE: Towards a Definition of the Internet of Things (IoT) (2015)
8. Golovatchev, J., Felsmann, M.: Modulare und durchgängige Produktmodelle als Erfolgsfaktor zur Bedienung einer Omni-Channel-Architektur - PLM 4.0. In: Doleski, O.D. (ed.) Herausforderung Utility 4.0, pp. 199–210. Springer Fachmedien, Wiesbaden (2017). https://doi.org/10.1007/978-3-658-15737-1_11
9. Golovatchev, J., et al.: Next Generation Telco Product Lifecycle Management. How to Overcome Complexity in Product Management by Implementing Best-Practice PLM. Detecon, Bonn (2010). http://www.detecon.com/PLM
10. Golovatchev, J., Budde, O., Hong, C.: Integrated PLM-process-approach for the development and management of telecommunications products in a multi-lifecycle environment. Int. J. Manuf. Technol. Manag. **19**(3), 224–237 (2010)

11. ProGlove, as of 13th March 2017. http://www.proglove.de/
12. Connect webpage, as of 13th March 2017. http://www.connect.de/ratgeber/wearables-industrie-medizin-fallbespiele-bmw-sap-3120436.html
13. Jonker, W.: Smart Energy Systems in EIT ICT Labs - A European Perspective (2012)

Role of Openness in Industrial Internet Platform Providers' Strategy

Karan Menon[1(✉)], Hannu Kärkkäinen[1], and Thorsten Wuest[2]

[1] Tampere University of Technology, Tampere, Finland
{karan.menon,hannu.karkkainen}@tut.fi
[2] West Virginia University, Morgantown, USA
thwuest@mail.wvu.edu

Abstract. Industrial internet, Industry 4.0 and Cyber-Physical Systems (CPS) can be collectively defined as industrial systems that integrate computational and physical capabilities of machines in order to provide advanced analytics and interact with humans. Industrial internet platforms allow the industrial companies to manage data, information and knowledge effectively within and between product lifecycle phases. Industrial internet platform's openness plays a very important role in decision making related to platform selection for industrial companies. This paper focuses on various dimensions of openness and how it effects the strategy of platform owners or providers and how this strategy effects in short and long term to their end-users. In order to analyze the above Kaa IoT and PTC ThingWorx have been analyzed to understand the impact of openness dimensions on their strategy and business.

Keywords: Industrial internet · Platforms · PLM · Openness

1 Introduction

Industrial internet, Industry 4.0 and Cyber-Physical Systems (CPS) can be collectively defined as industrial systems that integrate computational and physical capabilities of machines in order to provide advanced analytics and interact with humans [1–4]. Industrial internet, or Industrial Internet of Things (IIoT) will go way beyond the traditional factory automation: the related applications will change the structure of various industries and even the structure and foundations of their competition (e.g. [5]), and can for e.g. significantly reduce the transaction costs for various industrial transactions in the value chain. It has also been found that industrial internet and the related rather lately matured technologies (e.g. sensors, data analytics and various types of industrial internet platforms) can bring significant benefits and possibilities to the management of product lifecycle information, for instance joining various types of data, information and knowledge from different lifecycle phases in a more efficient manner, and facilitating the so-called Closed-Loop PLM (e.g. [6]).

© IFIP International Federation for Information Processing 2017
Published by Springer International Publishing AG 2017. All Rights Reserved
J. Ríos et al. (Eds.): PLM 2017, IFIP AICT 517, pp. 92–105, 2017.
https://doi.org/10.1007/978-3-319-72905-3_9

The significance of various types of platforms has grown increasingly in various industries (e.g. [7]) as well as in industrial internet (e.g. [8]). Importantly, platforms and platform-like digital services can provide new ways to access and accelerate the capturing of data and converting it into insightful information and knowledge. Access to data, information and knowledge across the life cycle phases and within the different phases is the key to the value creation from product related lifecycle data, information and knowledge [9]. Platform openness has been an interesting topic both academically and for companies – openness has been found to be one of the key concepts in the design and governance of platform ecosystems (e.g. [10]). There are various strategies related to openness of platforms, and platform openness can provide both significant benefits and risks or disadvantages for both platform providers and platform users alike. For instance, according to [11], opening a platform can increase platform adoption by network effects, reduce users' concerns about lock-in, stimulate the creation of differentiated goods that meet better the user needs, as well as reduce users' switching costs and increase platform provider competition.

Currently, there are significant differences in the degree of platforms' openness, i.e. how 'open' the platforms are for example in letting third party developers and companies to make applications over the platform using the data and information from the platform [7,11]. The benefits of various types of platform openness, especially the long-term ones, as well as the potential downsides of openness, are often difficult to be understood, and thus, the selection of most suitable platforms can be challenging for platform users. Furthermore, according to a recent review [10], openness has been mostly discussed from a technology-oriented perspective, while openness is closely related to how access is granted to technology. Finally, the long-term benefits and downsides of platform openness have been very little studied in the more specific context of industrial internet, and we have not been able to find related studies especially from the perspective of industrial internet platform users.

Accordingly, we have derived the following research questions to address the existing research gaps related to platform openness, as well as its importance to platform users especially in the context of industrial internet platforms:

1. What is the current status and future plans of the industrial internet platforms towards openness with respect to different types of platform openness?
2. What is the overall strategy regarding platform openness for the industrial internet platform providers?
3. What kinds of short and long-term impacts (Benefits and Risks) of the different types of platform providers' openness strategy are there for the industrial internet platform users?

The rest of the paper is divided into theoretical background, research methodology and design, results and findings, discussion and conclusions.

2   Theoretical Background

2.1   Industrial Internet Platforms

Platforms on a very broad level can be divided into 'internal' or firm level platforms and 'external' or ecosystem level (industry wide) platforms. We follow the definition of Industry Platform by [7]. According to them, "industry platforms are defined as products, services, or technologies developed by one or more firms, that serve as foundations upon which a larger number of firms can build further complementary innovations and potentially generate network effects." External or industry platforms are probably the most relevant forms of platforms in the context of PLM, because they can enhance the management of data, information and knowledge not only internally, but also amongst the various organizational actors (stakeholders) throughout the lifecycle phases (BOL, MOL, EOL). In case of industry or external platforms, there are differences in the degree of platforms' openness meaning how 'open' the platform is in order to let third party developers and companies while develop applications for the platform using the data and information from the platform [7, 11].

Industrial Internet, Industry 4.0 and CPS can be collectively defined as industrial systems that integrate computational and physical capabilities of machines in order to provide advanced analytics and interactions with humans [1–4, 12]. Industrial internet platforms can access data from different sensors, actuators, enterprise systems, social media and other novel data sources [13, 14]. The industrial internet platform is able to aggregate data into a single database which can be stored, either in dedicated in-house servers or with other third party cloud storage providers [2, 3].

In the context of PLM, there has been a marked shift in its vision, which would ideally mean the ability to access, manage and control product related information across all phases of the lifecycle [15]. In case of PLM, industrial internet platforms can provide the real time management of data and information flows as well as help in the data-information-knowledge (D-I-K) transformations along all phases of the product lifecycle.

2.2   Industrial Internet Platforms' Openness and PLM

Industrial companies need to select the platforms based on optimal levels of openness because of their requirement to use the platforms with various different actors (for example: suppliers, customers, designers). Furthermore, in PLM context industrial internet platform openness can provide variety of benefits, possibilities and restrictions considering the management of D-I-K both within and between lifecycle phases. As defined by Eisenmann et al. 2009 [18], *A platform is "open", as long as, (1) no restrictions are placed on participation in its development, commercialization or use; or (2) any restrictions-for example, requirements to conform with technical standards or pay licensing gees-are reasonable and non-discriminatory, that is, they are applies to all the potential platform participants.* This definition is applicable to variety of actors that participate in the creation, usage and propagation of the platform. These actors are distributed in four categories; (1) demand-side platform users, basically end-users (2) supply-side platform users, complementors or 3rd party developers (3) platform providers (4) platform sponsors.

In this study we have used the analytical framework presenting the dimensions of platform openness and their detailed sub-dimensions developed in our previous study [16]. The conceptual analytical frame work can be found in Table 1.

Table 1. Dimensions and sub-dimensions of platform openness [16]

Dimensions of openness	Detailed sub-dimensions of openness	Definitions
Demand-side user (end user)	Access to information	Level of access to information on interfaces to link to the platform or utilize its capabilities [7]
	Cost of access	Cost of access as in patent or licensing fees [7]
	Control in terms of rules to use the platform	Types of rules governing use of the platform [7]
Supply-side user (application developer)	Core developers	They are developers employed by the platform management company itself. They develop tools and applications which allows the users to use the platform effectively [17]
	Extension developers	They are outside parties or 3rd party developers who add features (applications) and value to the platform to enhance the functionality of the platform [17]
	Data aggregators	Data aggregators collect different interaction based data and re-sell it to the companies (as per the platform laws), who then can target advertisements etc. to the users [17]
Platform provider and sponsor related openness	Proprietary model	A single firm plays both provider and sponsor role [18]
	Licensing model	A single firm sponsors the platform then licences to multiple providers [18]
	Joint venture model	Multiple sponsors jointly sponsor the platform but a single firm serves as its sole provider [18]
	Shared model	Multiple sponsors collaborate to develop the platform's technology and then compete with each other to provide differentiated but compatible versions to the users [18]

Openness Within Lifecycle Phases. In this paragraph the value and characteristic of openness within the different lifecycle phases (BOL, MOL and EOL) is discussed. The general structure is based on the three main 'openness criteria' identified previously (see Table 1).

The openness from demand-side (end-user) can generally be understood to be essential during the BOL and EOL phase and in most cases also during the MOL phase. During BOL and MOL, the end users are relatively clearly defined and their openness requirements are also well understood. When investigating the openness requirement from the supplier-side (application developer), the different phases are more homogeneous than the previously discussed demand-side. In terms of the openness criteria platform provider and platform sponsor, the implications on the different lifecycle phases are mostly related to interoperability issues.

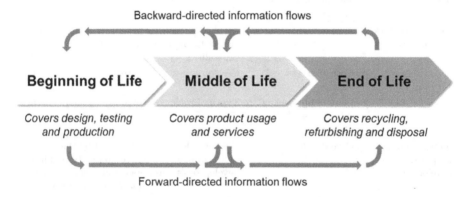

Fig. 1. Product lifecycle management phases and information flows within and between phases [19]

Openness Between the Lifecycle Phases. The following structure presents a simplified view on the interfaces of the three main lifecycle phases. There might be more complex constellations that require taking all phases in a more networked structure into account to replicate interdependencies between all phases. However, this needs to be studied in detail and is not in the focus of this manuscript. More information regarding the information flows between different phases themselves can be found in [19, 20].

The demand side (end user) openness requirements at the interface between BOL – MOL are expected to be high. Information access over lifecycle phase borders is essential for many applications. A rather common application of such cross-border information exchange that demands openness is design based on usage data [21]. The same high requirements towards openness stand true for BOL – MOL and MOL – EOL interfaces. From the supplier side (application developer) openness criteria, the interfaces are rather important as well. Designing an application to collect usage data for use during the beginning of live requires a high degree of openness regarding the interface between BOL – MOL for example. And this certainly stands true for other cross platform applications. With regard to the openness criteria platform provider and platform sponsor, the same arguments can be used for the interfaces between phases as for the phases themselves.

2.3 Short and Long Term Benefits and Risks

When an industrial company selects a particular industrial internet platform, it has to take into account various benefits and risks, both short and long term ones. In this study we focus specifically on the short and long term benefits and risks of platform openness from the viewpoint of the end-user or customer. There are a few studies that discuss the long and short term benefits and risks of Internet of Things (IoT) or Industrial internet platforms. The immediate or short term benefits, such as the fastened implementation of industrial internet or industry 4.0 for the company, fast access to various types of data, information and knowledge, aggregation of various types of different data into a single database for analytics, and potential at least short-term cost savings (provided that the platform purchasing and/or usage is free or nearly free) and others have been discussed in the literature [2,3,8]. Long term benefits, such as interoperability between companies and different software at a large scale, facilitating the "closed-loop PLM" (facilitating the linking of data, information and knowledge between and within the lifecycle phases), and stimulation of the creation of differentiated goods to better user needs, have been noted as important, as well [11,16]. Short term downsides and risks, such as security risks, heavy investments play an important role while selecting a platform. Long term risks are not that easy to point out because the technology is so new, but still risks like lockin and security risks are very important to take into consideration. However, as a summary, the aforementioned papers on benefits and risks of industrial internet platforms are largely non-empirical and conceptual, and actual empirical studies in the recognition and analyses of industrial internet platforms' short and long-term benefits and risks, especially the benefits and risks of platform openness from the viewpoint of end-users and customers are lacking.

3 Research Methodology and Design

In this article we focus on impact of openness and related dimensions on industrial internet platforms. The underlying idea of platform openness and its effect on the strategy of platform companies is assessed using the framework developed in our previous papers [16]. Qualitative approach is used in this research because of the novelty of industrial internet platforms and related openness [16]. In this article the interest is to understand the strategy related to platform openness that creates long term and short term benefits and risks for user companies from the platform company's perspective. "Why?" questions offer a deeper understanding and explanation of strategies selected by platform companies. The qualitative approach has different underlying methods for collecting primary data [22], including interviews, group discussions, ethnography, participating observations, and experiments. We use semi-structured interviews to gain detailed insights because they allow a structured approach while leaving room for in-depth analysis. In the questionnaire, there are open and closed, simple and complex, and direct and indirect questions. The questions were created based on the findings in the theoretical section and with regard to the interviewee type [22]. The basic structure of the questionnaire is discussed in Sect. 3.1 in detail.

The selection of the interview partners was undertaken under the premise of selecting cases which are typical for the process. In this article, we selected cases which had maximum variation between them but also were representatives of major industrial internet platforms. Kaa-IoT is a completely open source platform with limited personnel managing the platform's development and maintenance. PTC ThingWorx is a one of the most popular and one of the largest revenue generating (100 Million USD in 2016 fiscal year[1]) industrial internet platforms. If platform openness was put in a continuum then Kaa IoT would be at one end of the continuum (almost completely open) and PTC Thing-Worx would be closer to the other end of the continuum. Hence, discussing their strategic views on openness provides a large variation to the research. All the interviewees are in high positions in their respective platforms, with the position of CEO, CTO or something similar. All interviews, ranging from 45 min to one hour, were carried out via phone, Skype, or in a face-to-face meeting. The qualitative interviews were conducted in the beginning of 2017. The interviews were recorded, hence data was prepared by transcribing the recordings. The answers were analyzed by their type and depth to identify the underlying meaning.

3.1   Components of the Questionnaire

The qualitative semi-structured interview was basically divided into the following components: Strategy component, Openness dimensions related component, PLM component, Long term and short term benefits and risks component.

Strategy Component. Questions in this particular component address the overall strategy of the industrial internet platform related to openness. Long term and short term strategies were also discussed in this component.

Openness Dimensions Related Component. This component addresses questions related to the strategies for openness dimensions and sub-dimensions in Table 1.

PLM Component. This component brings out the information regarding the respective platform's strategies when it comes to sharing data, information and knowledge within and in between lifecycle phases. Section 2.2 points towards the

---

[1] http://www.ptc.com/news/2016/ptc-announces-q4-fy16-results.

impact of openness in industrial internet platform within and between lifecycle phases in case of PLM from existing literature.

Long Term and Short Term Benefits and Risks of Platform Openness Related Component. This component brings out the long term and short term benefits and risks of platform openness for platform end-users that might effect the selection of industrial internet platforms for the end-users. Section 2.3 brings out certain long and short term benefits and risks of platform openness for platform end-users from the literature.

4 Results and Findings

Based on the interviews conducted with Kaa-IoT and PTC ThingWorx personnel, we present the results and the findings in this section.

Strategy Component. For Kaa-IoT the overall strategy of their industrial internet platform is to move from a services company to a product centric company. Kaa IoT - *"The services business model has restrictions, growth related. Hence Kaa will have an enterprise cloud which will make Kaa a PAAS (Platform-as-a-service). Reason for this strategy is that it is easier to sell products than engineering hours."* For PTC Thingworx, moving towards shared model from the existing licensing model using partnerships (with other industrial internet platforms) is the overall strategy. PTC ThingWorx - *"Leverage partners to grow PTC's industrial internet business is the overall growth strategy"*. For Kaa-IoT Robotics and sophisticated as well as complex manufacturing industries are the target industries for their industrial internet platforms. PTC ThingWorx is focusing on Oil and Gas, Mining, Smart Cities, solutions related to tracking and logistics as part of their industrial internet strategy.

Openness Dimensions Related Component. Table 2 summarizes the findings based on openness dimensions. Both Kaa-IoT and PTC Thingworx consider the supply-side user openness (marked in green in Table 2.) dimension as the priority when it comes to investment out of the three dimensions. Kaa-IoT - *"Application developers are the real end user of the platform. Application developers should develop unique and useful applications for industries to use and make value from."* Whereas, for PTC Thingworx, *"Platform is an application developer tool"*, i.e. even if the industrial customers are the real end users of the platform, applications contribute maximum to the value creation. When asked to rate from 1–5 (1-not very open and 5-very open) the three dimensions, Kaa-IoT rated all the dimensions as 5. PTC ThingWorx rated the dimensions as 5, 4 and 4. For the access to information sub-dimension, Kaa-IoT uses Apache 2.0 protocol (the most open protocol), latest industry protocols (related to interoperability) and security standards. PTC ThingWorx is a java application working on any browser, uses apache libraries, connectivity agnostic and also can work as

Table 2. Findings from Kaa IoT and PTC ThingWorx based on openness dimensions

Openness Criteria	Detailed Criteria	Investment Priority (green color) and level of openness (Scale 1-not very open 5- very open)		Details of openness for every dimension	
		Kaa IoT	PTC ThingWorx	Kaa IoT	PTC ThingWorx
Demand-side user openness (Platform User)	Access to information (Openness standards)	5	5	Apache 2.0 protocols, various latest industry protocols, security standards	Java application working on a browser, Apache libraries, Connectivity agnostic, works as middleware
	Cost of access			No cost of access	Three payment models: Standard, Enterprise and Professional
	Control in terms of rules to use the platform			User decides the rules	User decides the rules
Supply-side user openness (Application Developer)	Core developers Extension (3rd Party) developers Data aggregators	5 (Application developers are real end-users of Kaa IoT)	4 (For PTC ThingWorx, platform is an application developer tool)	There is no difference in terms of access to data for core or 3rd party developers. Data aggregation is not allowed	No core developers for application development, applications are made only by 3rd-party developers. Data aggregation is allowed
Platform provider and sponsor related openness	Proprietary model Licensing model Joint venture model Shared model	5 (Shared model-mostly hardware partners-no platform partners)	4 (With more platform partners moving towards shared model)	Currently under shared model and would continue to be shared model	Currently in between licensing and shared model, would move to shared model

a middleware with wrappers around. In case of the cost of access dimension, Kaa IoT is completely free at all stages and for all kinds of industries whereas PTC ThingWorx has three payment models, Standard, Enterprise and Professional models. For the control in terms of rules to use the platform, for both the platforms, users decide the rules. As far as the application developers are concerned, for Kaa-IoT there is no difference in the access to data between core developers and 3rd party developers. Kaa-IoT does not allow Data Aggregators to access the platform. Whereas for PTC ThingWorx, they don't have core developers for application development, applications are made only by 3rd party developers and there is no restriction with respect to data for them. Data aggregation is allowed but the control is given to the end-user. For the final dimensions both the platforms have similar strategy of being very open by adopting sharing model but the difference lies in the kind of partnerships for both the platforms. Kaa-IoT is not going to partner with any other industrial internet platform. Partnership with complementors, hardware suppliers is what drives Kaa-IoT's sharing model. For PTC ThingWorx, its very different. All kinds of partnerships, i.e., with competing industrial internet platforms, hardware suppliers, system integrators etc. is the key driving force for their sharing model.

PLM Component. As depicted in Table 3, the focal IIoT platform providers have different ambitions when it comes to the different product lifecycle phases.

PTC's strategic goals align with the potential offered by their sophisticated and comprehensive set of legacy systems spanning all phases of the lifecycle (design to disposing). Kaa, as an open source IIoT platform provider, allows and encourages end-users to customize their system to a large extent, which brings forth the possibility of solutions for the different lifecycle phases. However, they are not natively build in and/or connected to the platform itself. Most of the customers of Kaa use the platform for managing their MOL and EOL phases. This focus on MOL/EOL seems to stand true for most IIoT platforms today, while some start to include the later part of the BOL, manufacturing, assembly and logistics, in their core offering. With regard to full BOL support and inclusion, PTC stands out within the IIoT platform landscape due to their own PTC CREO solution. This access to an product design solution allows them to provide full support for closed-loop lifecycle management. With such a comprehensive coverage, the previously theorized option of incorporating MOL/EOL (IoT) data directly in the design of the next generation of products is coming within reach for industry/manufacturers. This functionality is also possible with other platforms, e.g., Kaa's, through developing the required apps and interoperability standards/interfaces, and thus providing the MOL/EOL data to the CAD solution (BOL).

Table 3. Usage of industrial internet platforms within & between lifecycle phases

	BOL	MOL	EOL
PTC-ThingWorx			
Kaa-IoT			

Long Term and Short Term Benefits and Risks of Platform Openness Related Component. Table 4 shows the platform end-user or platform customer short and long term risks and benefits of platform openness from the platform provider's perspective. For short term benefits category Kaa-IoT considers the platform to be production and implementation ready. The platform is completely free, so for smaller companies it will save costs. Being open source, Kaa IoT allows any developer to develop applications. For PTC ThingWorx, the short term benefits include the fact that platform is ready to use and has a very low entry barrier for the end-user. Although the platform is not completely free but with very low internal resources the end-users can start development without any other technological investments. In case of long term benefits for Kaa-IoT, their strategy is centered around open source model. Because of being open source, over time, large pool of engineers would be available to custom make solutions for the industries using the capabilities of Kaa IoT. The platform end-user or the customer was the one who customized and engineered the platforms as per their company's requirement. Hence, over years the end-user becomes an expert with the technology that they developed using Kaa-IoT. With industrial internet becoming the central focus of all future business models, this is a big advantage. As the end-user matures and deploys many more devices

Table 4. Short & long term - benefits & risks of platform openness for end-users

	Short Term		Long Term	
	Kaa-IoT	PTC-ThingWorx	Kaa-IoT	PTC-ThingWorx
Benefits	-Platform is production & implementation ready	-Platform users have a low barrier to entry. Platform is ready to use	-Larger pool of engineers would be available to custom make the solutions for industries	-Platform would allow people to join you later - work with partners, 3rd parties, even competitors etc.
	-Being free, for small companies it would save costs	-Not completely free, but with small internal resources companies can start development quickly, without any technological investments	-Because it was customized by the end-user, end-user becomes an advanced expert in the technology. With industrial internet becoming part of the core business, this is an advantage	-ThingWorx is a widely used platform, considering the number of companies and the revenue, which means in long term it will be more sustainable to use ThingWorx as a platform
	-Open source allows any kind of developer to develop applications		-As the end-user matures, it will have many devices connected to the platform, and because the platform is free, end-user company will save lot of costs	
Risks	-Platform is complicated and complex, hence it is not a plug-n-play kind of platform	-Requires maturity and experience in the end-user organization	-Platform is open source and if the open source community stops the development then the platform will cease to exist	-Security risks
	-Platform requires sophisticated programming for implementation	-Scalability risks	-Lack of a big investor/sponsor might effect the future development of the platform	-Data management related risks, for example, data storage, data integrity
	-Platform requires to be customized by the end-user in order to use it in their business	-Security risks		

that are now connected using Kaa-IoT saves a lot of costs, because Kaa-IoT would be still free for them. For PTC Thingworx, the long term benefits include the fact that the platform allows other firms, 3rd parties, even competitors to join in the en-user's platform instance at any given point of time. Currently, PTC ThingWorx is one of the most widely used platforms in terms of user base and revenue generated. This makes PTC Thingworx a very sustainable platform as the time progresses. Short term risks for Kaa-IoT include the fact that the platform is complicated and complex, hence it requires implementation skills. It is not a plug-n-play kind of platform like other commercial platforms. Kaa-IoT requires sophisticated programming skills to implement the platform before the end-user can actually use it. Platform needs to be customized by the end-user as per their business requirements. In case of PTC ThingWorx, short term risks include lack of maturity and experience from the end-user leading to under-usage of the platform initially. Other short term risks for PTC thingworx are scalability and security risks. In case of long term risks for Kaa-IoT, it being open source, it is heavily reliant on the open source community to further develop in the future or else it would cease to exist. Lack of a big investor/sponsor might also effect the future development of Kaa-IoT which would effect the end-user in long term. In case of PTC Thingworx, long term risks are around security and data management related risks.

5 Discussion and Conclusions

Our purpose was to analyze strategy of platform provider's towards openness and related dimensions as well as short and long term benefits and risks of the aforementioned strategy.

For both the industrial internet platforms, Kaa-IoT and PTC ThingWorx, openness plays a very important role in their current as well future strategies related to the growth of the platform. Kaa-IoT, is primarily a services company where they provide engineering services around the implementation of the platform. They will become a more product oriented company by releasing their enterprise cloud built around the open source Kaa-IoT platform. This strategy will be useful for scaling up the business of Kaa-IoT. For PTC ThingWorx, openness, allows them create more partnerships with other industrial internet platforms like, Azure, GE Predix, Amazon AWS and others. Partnerships of these kind will allow them to grow the platform business using network effects as well as interoperability resulting from openness.

The above mentioned openness related overall strategy resulted in prioritizing the supply-side user openness dimension (as shown in Table 2) over the other two for both the platform companies for similar reasons. For both the platforms, application developers create the solutions that industrial end-users will create value and grow business. Hence, investing into developing applications is very important.

Although Kaa-IoT is free to use and open source, but being complex for implementation makes it difficult to adopt for industrial customers who are not mature in industrial internet technologies. PTC Thingworx, on the other hand, has a payment model for every kind of user group but implementing the platform is simple because of the plug-n-play mechanism (Table 4). In long term, the complex implementation of Kaa-IoT would actually be a benefit for industrial customers because they would be experts of their own unique technology platform which will lead to better security practices when compare to commercial platforms like PTC Thingworx. On the other hand if the open source community stops developing Kaa-IoT's platform technology, it would cease to exist and cause a long term risk for their industrial customers, unlike PTC ThingWorx, that has a big brand like PTC to sustain the development of the platform. PTC's historical expertise in PLM related issues allows ThingWorx to accommodate all the PLM challenges [16] effectively within and between lifecycle phases. Kaa-IoT's focus on MOL-EOL data, information and knowledge exchange creates a limitation for the industrial companies to facilitate the BOL phase, but being open source this can be solved by developing an additional module to the existing platform stack. Both options have their advantages and disadvantages, e.g., while PTC's comprehensive solution offers native integration, it also forces companies to constrain themselves to one provider. For supplier's which are required to work with the OEM's CAD system, this might present a problem. Other providers, who focus on MOL/EOL (IoT) data might not offer the native support of the whole product lifecycle, but due to that lack of BOL coverage, they might be forced to think more in terms of interoperability and offering interfaces to interact with BOL (CAD) solutions of other providers. In the end, it depends on the individual company and their strategic goal, customer/supplier base and existing infrastructure which approach might be more suited for their needs.

The studied platforms consider openness as high priority (Table 2) despite difference in their strategy and different positioning in the continuum of openness. This is also reflected in the manner that the platforms have rated (Very High) the various dimensions of openness in order to provide maximum value to industrial end-users. (RQ1)

Supply-side user (application developer) openness is a dimension where both companies plan to invest significantly. This helps to customize and add features as per customers needs which in turn enhances the value of the platform for the end-users. Both companies (PTC and Kaa) make use of enhanced openness (in some respect) in order to improve the data, information and knowledge exchange within and between the lifecycle phases. Industrial internet platforms allow to close the loop in the true meaning of the word with respect to data information and knowledge in case of PLM. (RQ2)

Both the platforms explicated different types of both short and long terms impacts of openness (as in Table 4) which were related mainly to quick and low barrier implementation of platforms as well as cost of usage and access (low cost on investment means the platform can be easily tested and experimented by SME's). (RQ3)

The purpose of this study was also to allow managers of platforms and industrial end-users to get an insight into the strategy of industrial internet platforms like Kaa-IoT and PTC ThingWorx. It allows them to select a platform based on their needs as well as keeping in mind the long term and short term benefits as well as risks of industrial internet platform selection. The limitation of this study was the limited number of industrial internet platform cases that were presented. The future studies will include other leading industrial internet platforms as well as industrial end-user viewpoints on the issue of different types of openness and their impacts to the business.

References

1. Hermann, M., Pentek, T., Otto, B.: Design principles for Industrie 4.0 scenarios. In: 2016 49th Hawaii International Conference on System Sciences (HICSS), pp. 3928–3937. IEEE, January 2016
2. Lee, I., Lee, K.: The Internet of Things (IoT): applications, investments, and challenges for enterprises. Bus. Horiz. **58**(4), 431–440 (2015)

3. Evans, P.C., Annunziata, M.: Industrial internet: pushing the boundaries of minds and machines (2012)
4. Iansiti, M., Lakhani, K.: Digital ubiquity. How connections, sensors, and data are revolutionizing business. Harvard Bus. Rev. **92**(11), 90–99 (2014)
5. Porter, M.E., Heppelmann, J.: Managing the Internet of Things: how smart, connected products are changing the competitive landscape. Harvard Bus. Rev. 2014–2016 (2014)
6. Kiritsis, D.: Closed-loop PLM for intelligent products in the era of the Internet of Things. Comput.-Aided Des. **43**(5), 479–501 (2011)
7. Gawer, A., Cusumano, M.A.: Industry platforms and ecosystem innovation. J. Prod. Innov. Manag. **31**(3), 417–433 (2014)
8. Golovatchev, J., Chatterjee, P., Kraus, F., Schüssl, R.: The impact of the IoT on product development and management. In: ISPIM Innovation (2016)
9. Jun, H.B., Kiritsis, D., Xirouchakis, P.: Research issues on closed-loop PLM. Comput. Ind. **58**(8–9), 855–868 (2007)
10. Schreieck, M.: Design and governance of platform ecosystems – key concepts and issues for future research. In: ECIS 2016 (2016)
11. Eisenmann, T.R.: Managing proprietary and shared platforms. Calif. Manag. Rev. **50**(4), 31–53 (2008)
12. Agarwal, N., Brem, A.: Strategic business transformation through technology convergence: implications from general electric's industrial internet initiative. Int. J. Technol. Manag. **67**(2–4), 196–214 (2015)
13. Heppelmann, J., Porter, M.E., Heppelmann, J.E.: How smart, connected products are transforming competition. Harvard Bus. Rev. **92**(11), 64–88 (2014)
14. Porter, M.E., Heppelmann, J.E.: How smart, connected products are transforming companies. Harvard Bus. Rev. **93**(10), 96–114 (2015)
15. Terzi, S., Bouras, A., Dutta, D., Garetti, M., Kiritsis, D.: Product lifecycle management - from its history to its new role. Int. J. Prod. Lifecycle Manag. **4**(4), 360 (2010)
16. Menon, K., Kärkkäinen, H., Gupta, J.P.: Role of industrial internet platforms in the management of product lifecycle related information and knowledge. In: Harik, R., Rivest, L., Bernard, A., Eynard, B., Bouras, A. (eds.) PLM 2016. IFIP AICT, vol. 492, pp. 549–558. Springer, Cham (2016). https://doi.org/10.1007/978-3-319-54660-5_49
17. Parker, G.G., Van Alstyne, M.W., Choudary, S.P.: Platform Revolution: How Networked Markets are Transforming the Economy and How to Make Them Work for You. Norton, New York (2016)
18. Eisenmann, T.R., Parker, G., Van Alstyne, M.: Opening Platforms: How, When and Why? In: Platforms, Markets and Innovation, pp. 131–162. Edward Elgar Publishing (2009)
19. Wuest, T., Wellsandt, S., Thoben, K.-D.: Information quality in PLM: a production process perspective. In: Bouras, A., Eynard, B., Foufou, S., Thoben, K.-D. (eds.) PLM 2015. IAICT, vol. 467, pp. 826–834. Springer, Cham (2016). https://doi.org/10.1007/978-3-319-33111-9_75
20. Wellsandt, S., Nabati, E., Wuest, T., Hribernik, K., Thoben, K.D.: A survey of product lifecycle models: towards complex products and service offers. Int. J. Prod. Lifecycle Manag. **9**(4), 353–390 (2016)
21. Lehmhus, D., Wuest, T., Wellsandt, S., Bosse, S., Kaihara, T., Thoben, K.D., Busse, M.: Cloud-based automated design and additive manufacturing: a usage data-enabled paradigm shift. Sensors **15**(12), 32079–32122 (2015)
22. Eriksson, P., Kovalainen, A.: Qualitative methods in business research. Oxford Univ. Press **3**, 675 (2008)

Value Chain: From iDMU to Shopfloor Documentation of Aeronautical Assemblies

Manuel Oliva[1(✉)], Jesús Racero[2], Domingo Morales-Palma[3], Carmelo del Valle[4], and Fernando Mas[1]

[1] AIRBUS. PLM Methods, Process and Tools, Seville, Spain
{manuel.oliva,fernando.mas}@airbus.com
[2] Department of Industrial Management, Universidad de Sevilla, Seville, Spain
jre@us.es
[3] Department of Mechanical Engineering and Manufacturing, Universidad de Sevilla, Seville, Spain
dmpalma@us.es
[4] Department of Computer Languages and Systems, Universidad de Sevilla, Seville, Spain
carmelo@us.es

Abstract. Competition in the aerospace manufacturing companies has led them to continuously improve the efficiency of their processes from the conceptual phase to the start of production and during operation phase, providing services to clients. PLM (Product Lifecycle Management) is an end-to-end business solution which aims to provide an environment of information about the product and related processes available to the whole enterprise throughout the product's lifecycle.

Airbus designs and industrializes aircrafts using Concurrent Engineering methods since decades. The introduction of new PLM methods, procedures and tools, and the need to improve processes efficiency and reduce time-to-market, led Airbus to pursue the Collaborative Engineering method. Processes efficiency is also impacted by the variety of systems existing within Airbus. Interoperability rises as a solution to eliminate inefficiencies due to information exchange and transformations and it also provides a way to discover and reuse existing information.

The ARIADNE project (Value chain: from iDMU to shopfloor documentation of aeronautical assemblies) was launched to support the industrialization process of an aerostructure by implementing the industrial Digital Mock-Up (iDMU) concept in a Collaborative Engineering framework. Interoperability becomes an important research workpackage in ARIADNE to exploit and reuse the information contained in the iDMU and to create the shop floor documentation. This paper presents the context, the conceptual approach, the methodology adopted and preliminary results of the project.

Keywords: PLM · iDMU · Interoperability · Collaborative Engineering
Assembly

© IFIP International Federation for Information Processing 2017
Published by Springer International Publishing AG 2017. All Rights Reserved
J. Ríos et al. (Eds.): PLM 2017, IFIP AICT 517, pp. 106–115, 2017.
https://doi.org/10.1007/978-3-319-72905-3_10

1   Introduction

PLM systems integrate all phases in the product development. The full product lifecycle, from the initial idea to the end-of-life, generates a lot of valuable information related to the product [1].

In aerospace industry, the long lifecycle (about 50 years), the number of parts (over 700.000 as average in a short range aircraft) and the modifications, make the aircraft a high complex product. Such complexity is drawn both from the complexity of the product and from the amount of resources and multidisciplinary work teams involved.

A complexity of multidisciplinary is found during the interaction between functional and industrial designers which brings inefficiencies in developing time, errors, etc. Research studies propose the necessity to evolve from the concurrent way of working to a more efficient one with the objective to deliver faster, better and cheaper products [2–4]. One proposal to comply with such challenge is the Collaborative Engineering concept [5, 6].

Collaborative Engineering involves a lot of changes in terms of organization, teams, relationships, skills, methods, procedures, standards, processes, tools, and interfaces: it is a business transformation process. The main deliverable of a collaborative team is the iDMU [7]. The iDMU concept is the approach defined by Airbus to facilitate the integration of the aircraft development on a common platform throughout all their service life. An iDMU gathers all the product, processes and resources data, both geometrical and technological to model a virtual assembly line. An iDMU provides a single environment, in which the assembly line industrial design is defined and validated.

To cover the bridge between the complexity of product information and the different PLM software tools to manage it, interoperability has raised as a must nowadays to improve the use of existing data stored in different formats and systems [8]. Interoperability foundation is the Model Base System Engineering (MBSE), as a starting point for organizing a formal way of communicating and building knowledge [9] from data and information.

The development of solutions, to facilitate the implementation of both the concurrent engineering and the Collaborative Engineering in the aerospace industry, was the objective of some projects since the end of the 1990's decade. Two of the most relevant ones are the European projects ENHANCE [10, 11] and VIVACE [12].

In the last decade, different research projects have been conducted for a complete integration of the iDMU and all the elements in the different stages of the life cycle (from design to manufacturing). The CALIPSOneo project [13] was launched by Airbus to promote the Collaborative Engineering. It implements the iDMU as a way to help in making the functional and the industrial designs evolving jointly and collaboratively. The project synchronizes, integrates and configures different software applications that promote the harmonization of common set of PLM and CAD tools.

EOLO (Factories of the future. Industrial development) project was developed as an initiative to achieve a better integration between information created in the industrialization phases and the information created in the operation and maintenance phases.

The ARIADNE project emerges as an evolution of both, CALIPSOneo and EOLO projects, which incorporates the integrated management of the iDMU life cycle (product, processes and resources), the Collaborative Engineering and interoperability between software systems (independent vendor). These characteristics will provide an improvement of data integration, knowledge base and quality of the final product.

2 ARIADNE Project

2.1 ARIADNE Project Organization

ARIADNE is organized around three work packages: MINOS, HELIOS and ORION. The relationship between work packages is shown in Fig. 1.

- MINOS (coMpetItive New PLM systems interOperability Scenario). Main target in this work package is to analyze the functionalities provided by a commercial PLM, 3DExperience by Dassault Systèmes [18], to build an iDMU and support Collaborative Engineering. A second target is to study interoperability between CATIA v5 by Dassault Systèmes [18], the PLM platform currently running in most of the aerospace companies, and 3DExperience. An analysis of the 3DExperience platform is been performed in ARIADNE with the objective of checking the main functionalities needed for the industrial design, that represents an improvement over CATIA v5. It is not an exhaustive analysis of all functionalities of 3DExperience, but it is a study of the characteristics provided by 3DExperience that covers the main requirements of manufacturing engineering activities for the industrialization of an aerospace assembly product.
- HELIOS (new sHopfloor assEmbLy documentatIon mOdelS). HELIOS proposes research on a solution to extract information from an iDMU independently of the software provider. The conceptual solution is based on developing the models and transformations needed to explode the iDMU for any other external system. Currently, any system that needs to exploit the iDMU would have to develop its own interfaces. In case the iDMU is migrated to a different PLM, those interfaces must be changed also. To help with those inefficiencies and to be independent from any existing PLM, HELIOS will generate a standardized software code (EXPRESS-i) that any external system can use to communicate and obtain the required information from the iDMU.
- ORION (laser authOring shop flooR documentatION). ORION aims to develop a system to exploit assembly process information contained in the iDMU with Augmented Reality (AR) technics using laser projection technology. This system will get any data from the iDMU needed for the assembly, verification or maintenance process. ORION is based on the SAMBAlaser project [14], an 'AR by laser' technology developed by Airbus. ORION will analyze new ways for laser programming besides numerical control and will provide a 3D simulation tool. Also it will propose a data model to integrate the iDMU with the AR laser system and to facilitate the laser programming and execution.

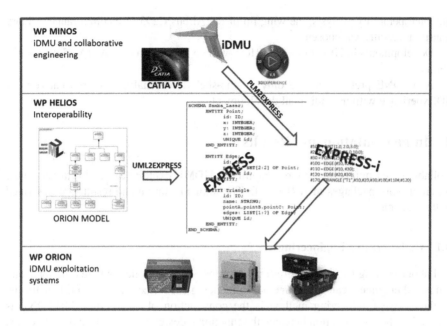

Fig. 1. ARIADNE project organization

2.2 ARIADNE Project Functional Architecture

ARIADNE architecture is a consequence of the conclusions and the proposed future work in CALIPSOneo project in 2013. CALIPSOneo architecture for a collaborative environment was CATIA v5 in conjunction with DPE (DELMIA Process Engineering) to hold the process definition in a database (also called Manufacturing Hub by Dassault Systèmes). The architecture in CALIPSOneo, although still in production in Airbus and available in the market, is not and architecture ready to support the requirements from Industry 4.0 and is quite out of phase in technology to connect or communicate with today's technology.

To develop MINOS, the decision on the tool to support it was 3DExperience a natural evolution of CATIA v5. Data used in MINOS, the Airbus military transport aircraft A400M Empennage shown in Fig. 2a, are in CATIA v5 format. To keep the 3DExperience infrastructure simple, and thanks to the relative low volume of data of the A400M empennage, a single virtual machine with all the required servers were deployed for the project.

For the interoperability between CATIA v5 and 3DExperience, CATIA v5 the input data are stored in file based folders containing the geometry in CATPart and the product structure in CATProduct as Fig. 3. FBDI (File Based Data Import) is the process provided by Dassault Systèmes that reads and or imports information (geometry and product structure) into 3DExperience. The option 'Import as Native', selected in FBDI will read the CATIA v5 as a reference, meaning, creating a 3D representation in 3DExperience as in CATIA v5, but will not allow it to be modified. Resources and assembly processes will be designed in 3DExperience based on the product (in CATIA v5) previously imported. For the interoperability analysis, the wing tip of the Airbus C295 (a medium range military transport aircraft) was chosen.

Developments in HELIOS and ORION will be based also on CATIA v5 data availability.

ARIADNE pretends to use only off-the-shelf functionalities offered natively by 3DExperience with no additional development.

3   Implementation and Results

Collaborative Engineering, interoperability and iDMU exploitation are the targets in the different work packages of ARIADNE. The implementation and results are described in this section.

3.1   Collaborative Engineering

Collaborative Engineering requires an integrated 3D environment where functional and industrial engineers can work together influencing each other. The main driver for the Collaborative Engineering method is the construction of the iDMU. ARIADNE is focused in the collaboration between the functional design and industrial design teams. ARIADNE will check if 3DExperience provides such environment to build the iDMU where Collaborative Engineering can be accomplish.

To analyze 3DExperience collaborative environment a few use cases were defined and tested with the Airbus A400M empennage product represented in Fig. 2a.

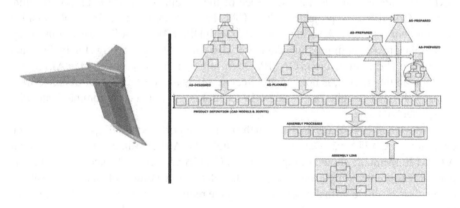

Fig. 2.   (a) Empennage A400M. (b) Airbus product views

One of the bases to integrate the information in a PLM is to be able to hold the different ways or views (As-Design, As-Planned, As-Prepared) [15], shown in Fig. 2b, for defining the product in Airbus. Keeping these views connected is basic to the Collaborative Engineering [7]. In the work performed it was possible to build the As-Design view. Following, the As-Planned view was built from the As-Designed view while sharing the same 3D geometry for each of the structures. This is represented in Fig. 3b.

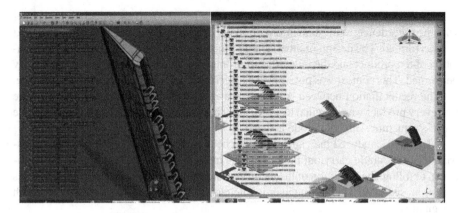

Fig. 3. (a) As-Design view. (b) As-Planned view

A set of additional functionalities were performed in the As-Planned view such as the possibility of navigating through the structure as well as in the As-Design or filtering of product nodes in the product tree. Reconciliation in 3DExperience has proven to be an important functionality to assure a fully connection As-Design and As-Planned. This functionality indicates in the tree with a color code the issues found when comparing both structures.

3.2 Building the iDMU

The third structure created in ARIADNE, which is the main one used for the industrialization of a product, is the As-Prepared. This structure is also a product structure rearranged as a result of the different assembly processes needed to build the product. The As-Prepared tree organization shown in Fig. 4a is a consequence of the network of assembly processes. To build such network, precedence between assembly processes and operations must be assigned as in Fig. 4b. Also tools like Gantt representation in Fig. 4c helps deciding the precedence based on constrains (resources and times). Additional functionality for balancing constrains is too basic in 3DExperience for Airbus product complexity. Optimization tool is not offered by 3DExperience. Additional development would be needed to cover these last two functionalities [16].

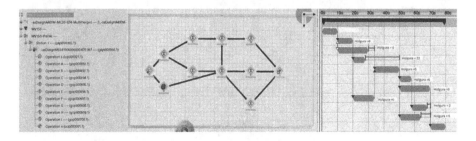

Fig. 4. (a) As-Prepared. (b) Precedence between operations. (c) Operations Gantt chart

The iDMU was built by assigning product and resources to each operation together with the precedence. With such information in the iDMU, the use case design in context was performed. The design of an assembly process or a resource requires the representation of the product and the industrial environment based on the operations previously performed. This context was possible to be calculated and represented in 3DExperience.

The reconciliation between As-Planned and As-Prepared was tested to make sure that every product was assigned to a process. This functionality is also shown in the tree process structure with color code nodes.

ARIADNE analyzed the capabilities to check how functional designers and industrial designers could carry out their activities influencing each other. For this, a mechanism to follow the evolution of the maturity states of the product, process and resources was proposed [19]. This mechanism is intended to foster an interaction between both design areas.

3.3   Interoperability CATIA v5 and 3DExperience

Recent developed aircrafts (A380, A350 and A400M) in Airbus have been designed in CATIA v5. Migration of a complete product design of an aircraft requires a high effort in resources and cost. Finding a solution where the product design can be kept in CATIA v5 while downstream product lifecycle uses a more adequate environment to cover their activities becomes a target for MINOS work package.

MINOS analyzed the degree of interoperability between 3DExperience and CATIA v5. Interoperability in this use case is understood as the set of required characteristics to develop the industrialization activities performed by manufacturing engineering in 3DExperience without affecting the product design activities (functional design) of the design office performed in CATIA v5.

Initially a reading of product design (product structure and product design) in CATIA v5 was carried out in 3DExperience, step 1 in Fig. 5. Checking the result of such work

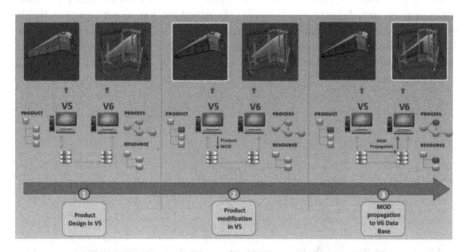

Fig. 5.   Interoperability CATIA v5 (functional design) and 3DExperience (industrial design)

in 3DExperience demonstrated a successful import of the information for the product structure and for the 3D geometry. Following, a modification was introduced in the CATIA v5 product, step 2 in Fig. 5. FBDI process did detect such change of the product and propagated it in 3DExperience, step 3 in Fig. 5. Also 3DExperience sent a warning to update the product structure with the modified product. An impact on the process and resources related to the modified product was performed based on functionalities provided by 3DExperience.

3.4   Interoperability and iDMU Exploitation

Due to the increasing added value that the iDMU provides, it becomes an important asset to a company. Once assembly processes are designed and stored in the iDMU, information to production lines to perform the tasks can be extracted with an automatic application system.

As the current production environment in Airbus is CATIA v5, extracting information from the iDMU is constrained to such environment. HELIOS has developed an interoperable framework based in a set of transformations to exploit the iDMU independently from the PLM vendor and STEP is the tool selected. The use case HELIOS is based on is the ORION UML (Universal Model Language) model. The ORION UML model is transformed (UML2EXPRESS) into a schema defined in a standard language such as EXPRESS [17]. The schema is the input to any PLM (CATIA v5 or 3DExperience) to extract the information from the iDMU with a second set of transformations (PLM2EXPRESS). This last transformation will generate the instantiated code (EXPRESS-i) with the required information. This standardized code will be the same input to the different laser vendors.

Currently, in Airbus, the SAMBAlaser [14] is in production for projection of work instructions. To enhance the SAMBAlaser functionalities, ORION work package has developed an integrated user interface with the laser system control, optimized the quantity of information to project without flickering and built a simulation tool to check the capabilities of projecting within an industrial environment without occlusion.

4   Conclusions

Main conclusion is the successful proof of concept of the existing PLM technology in an industrial environment.

As mentioned, first test of interoperability CATIA v5 and 3DExperience was successfully. As preliminary conclusions it would be possible for industrialization engineers to work in a more advanced environment, 3dExperience, while functional designers can keep working in CATIA v5. Additional in-depth use cases (annotations, kinematics, and tolerances) need to be performed to check the degree of interoperability.

The introduction of HELIOS as the framework that 'separates' or make any iDMU exploitation system independent of the PLM that support it, is an important step for interoperability between different PLM systems and vendor independency and also enhances the necessity to have a model based definition for the iDMU. Thus, once

3DExperience becomes the production environment in Airbus, ORION will not need to be modified. HELIOS will be able to support any other iDMU exploitation system just by expanding the UML model.

The three views interconnected (As-Design, As-Planned, As-Prepared) together with the capability of creating a network of processes and operations have proven to build an iDMU to support the collaboration engineering and the facilitation of the interaction between functional an industrial engineers.

3DExperience has demonstrated to provide an interoperable collaborative 3D PLM environment to the industrialization of aeronautical assemblies. However an enterprise organizational model must be put in place to bring together functional and industrial engineering as one team with the iDMU as the unique deliverable.

Since ARIADNE is a proof of concept, no direct estimates on cost, time or other benefits are measured. However, based on previous experiences, significant benefits (time, costs, and reduction of errors) are expected after the deployment phase.

5 Future Work

The current status of ARIADNE project suggests some improvements and future work after the proof of concept of the technology.

ARIADNE project has tested some basic 3DExperience capabilities. The need to explore the 3DExperience capabilities to support the industrialization of an aircraft requires launching additional industrial use cases to cover industrialization activities.

ARIADNE project avoids developing IT interfaces. Connection and interfaces from other tools that provide solutions not fully covered by 3DExperience such as line or station balancing and optimization might need to be analyzed.

ARIADNE objective was not to test computing performances. Performing stress test with high volume of data (metadata, 3D geometry) is another important point to study, mainly for the aerospace industry.

Acknowledgments. Authors wish to thanks to Andres Soto, Gonzalo Monguió and Andres Padillo for their contributions. ARIADNE is partially funded by CTA (Corporación Tecnológica Andaluza) with support from the Regional and National Government.

References

1. Ameri, F., Deba, D.: Product lifecycle management: closing the knowledge loops. Comput. Aided Des. Appl. **2**, 577–590 (2005)
2. Pardessus, T.: Concurrent engineering development and practices for aircraft design at airbus. In: Proceedings of the 24th International Congress of the Aeronautical Sciences (ISCAS 2004) (2004)
3. Haas, R., Sinha, M.: Concurrent engineering at airbus - a case study. Int. J. Manuf. Technol. Manage. **6**(3/4), 241–253 (2004)
4. Mas, F., Ríos, J., Menéndez, J.L., Hernández, J.C., Vizán, A.: Concurrent conceptual design of aero-structure assembly lines. In: Proceedings of the 14th International Conference on Concurrent Enterprising (ICE), Lisbon (2008)

5. Lu, S.C.-Y., Elmaraghy, W., Schuh, G., Wilhelm, R.: A scientific foundation of collaborative engineering. CIRP Ann. Manuf. Technol. **56**(2), 605–634 (2007)
6. Mas, F., Menéndez, J.L., Oliva, M., Gómez, A., Ríos, J.: Collaborative engineering paradigm applied to the aerospace industry. In: Bernard, A., Rivest, L., Dutta, D. (eds.) PLM 2013. IAICT, vol. 409, pp. 675–684. Springer, Heidelberg (2013). https://doi.org/ 10.1007/978-3-642-41501-2_66
7. Mas, F., et al.: iDMU as the collaborative engineering engine: research experiences in airbus. In: 2014 International ICE Conference on Engineering, Technology and Innovation (ICE). IEEE (2014)
8. Penciuc, D., et al.: Towards a PLM interoperability for a collaborative design support system. Procedia CIRP **25**, 369–376 (2014)
9. Liao, Y., et al.: Semantic annotations for semantic interoperability in a product lifecycle management context. Int. J. Prod. Res. **54**, 5534–5553 (2016)
10. Braudel, H., Nicot, M., Dunyach, J.-C.: Overall presentation of the ENHANCE project. Air Space Europe **3**(3–4), 49–52 (2001)
11. VIVACE Project. http://ec.europa.eu/research/transport/projects/items/vivace_en.htm. Accessed March 2017
12. Nguyen Van, T., Féru, F., et al.: Engineering data management for extended enterprise - context of the European VIVACE project. In: International Conference on Product Lifecycle Management, Bangalore, India (2006)
13. Mas, F., et al.: PLM based approach to the industrialization of aeronautical assemblies. Procedia Eng. **132**, 1045–1052 (2015)
14. Serván, J., et al.: Augmented reality using laser projection for the airbus A400M wing assembly. In: Proceedings of the 29th International Manufacturing Conference (2011)
15. Mas, F., Gómez, A., Menéndez, J.L., Ríos, J.: Proposal for the conceptual design of aeronautical final assembly lines based on the industrial digital mock-up concept. In: Bernard, A., Rivest, L., Dutta, D. (eds.) PLM 2013. IAICT, vol. 409, pp. 10–19. Springer, Heidelberg (2013). https://doi.org/10.1007/978-3-642-41501-2_2
16. Rios, J., Mas, F., Menéndez, J.L.: A review of the A400M final assembly line balancing methodology. In: AIP Conference Proceedings, vol. 1431, no. 1, AIP (2012)
17. ISO 10303-21:1994: Industrial automation systems and integration – Product data representation and exchange. International Organization for Standardization (1994)
18. https://www.3ds.com/. Accessed March 2017
19. Morales-Palma, D., Eguía, I.: Managing maturity states in a collaborative platform for the iDMU of aeronautical assembly lines. In: IFIP 14th International Conference on Product Lifecycle Management, 9–12 July 2007, Seville, Spain (2007)

Agent Based Framework to Support Manufacturing Problem Solving Integrating Product Lifecycle Management and Case-Based Reasoning

Alvaro Camarillo[1,2(✉)], José Ríos[2], and Klaus-Dieter Althoff[3,4]

[1] Exide Technologies GmbH, Odertal 35, 37431 Bad Lauterberg, Germany
alvaro.camarillo@eu.exide.com
[2] Mechanical Engineering Department, Universidad Politécnica de Madrid,
Jose Gutierrez Abascal 2, 2800 Madrid, Spain
a.camarillo@alumnos.upm.es, jose.rios@upm.es
[3] German Research Center for Artificial Intelligence (DFKI),
Trippstadter Straße 122, 67663 Kaiserslautern, Germany
klaus-dieter.althoff@dfki.de
[4] University of Hildesheim, Universitätsplatz 1, 31141 Hildesheim, Germany

Abstract. During the execution of manufacturing processes, problems arise and they have to be solved systematically to reach and exceed production targets. Normally, a production team analyzes and solves these problems, with the support of different methodologies and working directly on the shop floor. This paper presents an ontology-based approach to easily capture and reuse the knowledge generated in such a process of Manufacturing Problem Solving (MPS). The proposed ontology is used as basis in an ad-hoc MPS software system. The architecture of the MPS system is based on the integration of three technologies: PLM (Product Lifecycle Management), CBR (Case-Based Reasoning) and software agents. The PLM system is used as an automatic source of the problem context information. The CBR system is used as repository of cases and artificial intelligence tool to support the efficient reuse of knowledge during the resolution of new problems. A software agent platform allows developing an integrated prototype of an ad-hoc software system. This paper shows the architecture of the MPS system prototype.

Keywords: Ontology · Product Lifecycle Management (PLM)
Case-Based Reasoning (CBR)
Process Failure Mode and Effect Analysis (PFMEA)
Manufacturing Problem Solving (MPS)

1 Introduction

Analytical methods are applied to prevent failures during the design phase of manufacturing processes and facilities, but the reality shows that the defined production targets are often not reached due to the arise of problems. Aiming to solve them in a systematic way, different methods have been developed. Continuous Improvement Process (CIP)

© IFIP International Federation for Information Processing 2017
Published by Springer International Publishing AG 2017. All Rights Reserved
J. Ríos et al. (Eds.): PLM 2017, IFIP AICT 517, pp. 116–128, 2017.
https://doi.org/10.1007/978-3-319-72905-3_11

and Manufacturing Problem Solving (MPS) embrace these methods [1]. A relevant example of them is the 8D methodology, which is quite spread and known in manufacturing since nowadays it is the standard method used to analyze and present quality claims in important industrial sectors such as the automotive one [2]. The 8D method, similarly to other CIP or MPS methods, provides a structured process to facilitate finding and improving solutions, but it only brings results when actors with enough experience and knowledge drive it [3]. This paper proposes a software system to compensate the possible lack of experience and knowledge of some team members. One of the key requirements for such a system is the capability to collect and reuse knowledge created during the application of the 8D method in the resolution of production problems at the shop floor level. In that way, the system would be linked to the daily MPS activity of the manufacturing plant. To address this global aim, the proposed approach is structured into:

1. Manufacturing problems have to be described in a consistent and systematic way to allow a common understanding by the MPS personnel and their processing by means of a software system. The definition of an ontology is the alternative to address this aspect [4]. This requires reviewing two main methods. Firstly, how the 8D method allows defining a manufacturing problem. Secondly, how Process Failure Mode and Effect Analysis (PFMEA) [2], as preventive method, allows defining manufacturing problems, effects and solutions and how this method could be used to create an initial set of cases of potential problems.

2. The ontological approach is the basis to create two repositories of manufacturing-related knowledge. Manufacturing is an extremely wide context. Therefore, it is necessary to distinguish among different problems and to connect them with previously found solutions; this can be achieved by means of context data. A PLM (Product Lifecycle Management) application [5] can be used as a logical source of extended information of Product-Process-Resource (PPR) related to each problem, and therefore, to describe the context of each manufacturing problem. This will allow enriching automatically the initial problem description given by the MPS personnel. A CBR system [6] can be used as the logical source of manufacturing problems and solutions, where the initial PFMEA case base of potential problems is stored and extended continuously with the resolution of new problems.

3. To assist the MPS personnel, it is needed a systematic reasoning method to connect each problem with similar cases already solved. Case-Based Reasoning (CBR) [6] is proposed as an artificial intelligence tool to support the efficient reuse of collected knowledge in new problems and to assist in the problem solving process.

The paper starts with a general introduction to the main topics and a review of existing similar research works. Section 3 shows the developed ontology to represent a manufacturing problem. Section 4 presents the ontological model implementation in a MPS process flow and the MPS system architecture of the prototype application. The prototype application is implemented as case study in the company Exide Technologies, a multinational company that produces stored electrical energy solutions. The paper ends with some results, conclusions and future work proposals.

2 State of the Art

2.1 Knowledge Representation Based on Ontology

A fundamental aspect of this work is the representation of manufacturing knowledge and problems. One way to address it is by means of an ontology. In the literature, there are examples of ontologies applied to the context of MPS. Foguem et al. [7] create an ontology based on conceptual graphs for Feedback Experience Systems (FES). This approach relates to the topic MPS, however its structure it is not compatible with the PFMEA method, which is considered as the main initial source of solved cases. Dittmann et al. [8] and Ebrahimipour et al. [9] present two examples of ontologies for the FMEA environment developed to ensure the easy reuse of the information stored in the FMEA analyses. The work of Dittmann et al. is selected as basis for the knowledge representation model of this work due to its focus on FMEA and the clarity and simplicity of its model. It proposes a ROOT_CONCEPT class that has as subclasses FMEA, Component, Function, Failure_mode, Control_method, Risk_priority_number, and Containment_action. It also defines relationships among the different concepts, for example "fulfills_a_function" that relates Component to Function, or "has_failure_mode" that relates Function to Failure_mode. In parallel, the classes Component and Function have associated taxonomies. The associated taxonomies allow limiting the possible values to be used when instantiating the model classes, in that sense, it could be seen as a taxonomic approach to natural language processing [10]. An approach based on free text would be an alternative, but in that case a domain specific dictionary and free-text natural language processing techniques would be required to search for relevant text. That line of research is out of the scope of this work.

Having introduced the way of representing knowledge, the next subsection presents PLM systems as the logical source of extended PPR information related to the manufacturing problem under analysis.

2.2 Product Lifecycle Management Systems

As explained in the introduction, the application domain of manufacturing is extremely wide. The ontology selected above allows representing a problem following the PFMEA method. However, it has to be taken into account that the document resulting from applying the PFMEA method is a detailed analysis of a specific process, therefore the specified information is restricted to the scope of the components of that process. In the approach of this work, that limited scope must be cut, the proposed framework should allow dealing with problems coming from any type of manufacturing processes at any place. To do so, it is needed an additional input of information that sets clear differences among problems, and that is the context of the problem. A PLM system [5] arises here as the natural and logical source of this context, since it aims facilitating the storage of all the PPR information of a company.

The work of Bertin et al. [11, 12] is very relevant for this work because they also proposes the use of a PLM system as central repository of data for a Lessons Learned System (LLS). They focus on the capture and reuse of knowledge along the Engineering

Change Request (ECR) process of the company. This approach sets the focus on the technical staff of the company, which is the typical group of users leading ECR. By contrast, the framework presented in this paper sets the focus on the operators working directly on the line, being this group much less used to computer system, and with less technical background. This puts some additional requirements for developing intuitive and simple interfaces. Additionally, it is proposed the use of the PFMEA method as an initial set of possible problems, so the system should be able to provide the users with some solutions from the very beginning.

Having defined the way of representing knowledge, and the system to retrieve structured information needed to describe the context of the manufacturing problem, the next section introduces CBR as the artificial intelligence tool to support the storage of cases and the finding of solutions during the MPS activity.

2.3 Case-Based Reasoning

CBR is useful when the reality under analysis is too complex and difficult to be represented in a model [6]. This is the case of manufacturing, the application domain of this work, with a huge variety of production processes being influenced by many types of machines, environments, materials, methods or persons. CBR is particularly applicable to problems where earlier cases are available, even when the domain is not understood well enough to create a deep domain model. The approach adopted in this work focuses on CBR as the artificial intelligence tool to support the storage of cases and the reasoning to find solutions during the MPS activity.

Manufacturing, as application domain, represents a big challenge for CBR due to its vast extension and complexity. A single case base, containing information related to failures from hundreds of different types of processes, coming from many different manufacturing lines and plants would create serious problems of retrieval speed, and maintainability. Multi-case base reasoning systems were created years ago to tackle this type of issues. Among the different research paths available in the literature related to this type of systems, and due to its flexible approach to knowledge modularization, this work focuses on SEASALT (Shared Experience using an Agent-based System Architecture LayouT). SEASALT is a domain-independent architecture for extracting, analyzing, sharing, and providing experiences [13]. The work of Reuss et al. [14] is an application example of SEASALT linked to Problem Solving in aircraft diagnosis and maintenance, where the system provides maintenance solutions to known failures.

Based on the introduced theoretical background, the next section presents a concrete proposal of ontology to represent manufacturing problems in a generic way.

3 Manufacturing Problem Solving Ontology

This section presents a proposal of ontology to represent any kind of manufacturing problem from any process at any manufacturing place. This ontology has also the additional requirement of being compatible with the information structure of the PFMEA method. As it was previously mentioned, PFMEA can provide the first set of possible problems to a computer system based on this ontology.

As mentioned in Sect. 2, this ontology uses the model of Dittmann et al. [8] as basis. The classes Component, Function, and Failure with all its interrelationships are taken from that model (see Fig. 1), but additional classes were added to create the proposed ontology. These three initial classes allow defining the core description of the problem with the same structure of a PFMEA analysis. In a PFMEA analysis, each component has different functions, and each function may have different failure modes, aiming to find all possible failures in the process. It should keep in mind that when aiming to find the resolution of a problem, a single and concrete issue is addressed. This creates the need for extending the initial set of classes with the class Problem (Fig. 1) that will have the link to the specific and unique threefold structure: component-function-failure. This threefold structure contains the core definition of the problem under analysis.

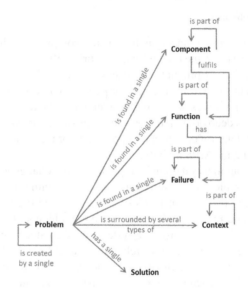

Fig. 1. Manufacturing Problem Solving main concepts ontology

Figure 1 shows that the three classes (Component, Function, and Failure) have a relationship of type "is part of" pointing to themselves. This means that these classes have their own subclasses forming a taxonomy, which could be used by a CBR system to calculate similarity among cases.

As previously stated, the proposed ontology defines a problem as a specific threefold structure of component-function-failure. However, the same exact threefold structure can be found in different scenarios or contexts. This issue is not found in the PFMEA method because each analysis is linked with a specific process in a specific machine, so the context is clearly defined. Therefore, the ontology needs an additional class to add information related to the surroundings of the problem: the class Context. This class has also a relationship of type "is part of" pointing to itself. Therefore, as Component,

Function and Failure it has a taxonomy that has been developed under similarity criteria to allow the later finding of similar problems by a CBR system.

Finally, a last class is needed, to contain the information of the solution to the manufacturing problem: the class Solution. This class will comprise the information related to containment actions, corrective actions, and preventing actions that should be applied to solve a problem.

Each defined class has different associated attributes, and these attributes have sets of allowed values and restrictions. The attributes of the class Problem must be defined by the MPS personnel and they create a basic definition of the problem following the recommendations of the MPS method Kepner-Tregoe [15] (i.e. to answer to the questions "How often?", "What?", "When?", "Where?", "Who?", and "Why is a problem?"). The attributes of the classes Component, Function and Failure are their corresponding type within the defined taxonomies, and they should be also defined by the MPS personnel. The class Context has the attribute of its position within the taxonomy, and all its associated subclasses have a big variety of attributes attending to their nature (e.g. max. casting temperature, min. pressure, or brand of a machine component). These attributes should be defined with data stored in the PLM system.

In order to perform a preliminary validation of the proposed ontology, several problems from different manufacturing environments (machining, stamping, casting and assembly) were collected and represented with this ontology. Table 1 shows an example.

Table 1. Example of problem description with the proposed ontology

Class	Attribute	Allowed values	Value
Problem	Problem ID	ID Number from 0 to 9999	253
	What Problem?	String	Plate with burrs
	Where Product?	Section from set of values	Product A
	Where Machine?	Section from set of values	Line 1 - Station 40
	Who?	Section from set of values	Mr. Smith
	When?	Date from 01.01.00 on	28.05.2016
	How often?	Section from set of values	Every minute
	Why Problem?	String	Product NOK, risk of shortcircuit
	Problem created by	ID Number from 0 to 9999	254
Component	Taxonomy position	Value from Taxonomy	Material
Function	Taxonomy position	Value from Taxonomy	Be within specification/Shape
Failure	Taxonomy position	Value from Taxonomy	50% fulfilment
Context	Taxonomy position	Value from Taxonomy	Process/Casting
	Temperature	From 300 to 400 °C	350
	Taxonomy position	Value from Taxonomy	Man/Operator
	Experience	From 0 to 99 years	3
Solution	Containment	String	Stop production and control produced units since last inspection
	Corrective	String	Not defined
	Preventive	String	Not defined

4   Ontological Model Implementation: MPS Process Flow and MPS System Architecture

The presented ontology is used as basis to define the main data structure to be managed by a prototype MPS software system, with the aim of providing production operators with an MPS tool based on the 8D method to be used during their daily MPS activities. The system must allow capturing and reusing knowledge directly at the shop floor level. A first prototype of the MPS system was developed to support an MPS process flow based on the 8D method (Fig. 2). The system is currently under implementation as case study in the company Exide Technologies, a global provider of stored electrical energy solutions (i.e. batteries and associated equipment and services) for transportation and industrial markets, with several production plants in Europe and USA running similar processes, which could benefit from this work.

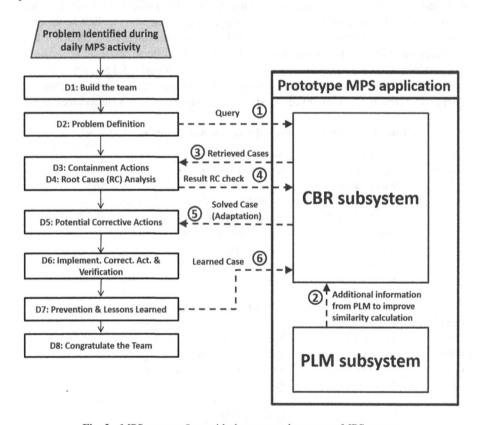

Fig. 2. MPS process flow with the proposed prototype MPS system

The case study considers that during the MPS activity, the MPS personnel must identify a problem that prevents from reaching the defined production targets. The MPS personnel start the analysis following the eight steps of the 8D method. The objective is, instead of carrying out the method in a paper-based way, the MPS personnel must use the prototype MPS system.

The main characteristic of the targeted users for this software system (i.e. operators) is their lack of deep knowledge about the processes and products. In some cases, the operators are temporary workers, due to seasonal increases of production volumes, and they have no knowledge at all about the production process and/or resources. This profile of the future users of the prototype MPS system means that the application must be able to provide automatically as much information as possible to compensate their lack of knowledge. The user must be able to create a problem query, input the data associated to it (i.e. component-function-failure plus some additional basic information such as date, line, or product, where the problem is found), and the system should connect with the PLM system to extract automatically all existing context information of the problem.

The PLM solution selected for the development of the prototype was Aras Innovator. This PLM application provides an Application Programming Interface named AML (Aras Markup Language) that allows extracting data from the PLM database.

The PLM system has to be customized to fit into the defined ontological model, and it has to be configured to retrieve the requested information in a format understandable by the CBR system. According to the PFMEA methodology [2], used as basis in the proposed ontology, there are six types of components: process, machine, material, man environment and method. The initial configuration of Aras Innovator provides an item type called "Parts" to contain any mechanical design element, so the components of type material and machine can be of that type. The PLM main types has to be extended with four additional items called "Manufacturing Process", "Manufacturing Man", "Manufacturing Method", and "Manufacturing Environment" to contain the rest of component types. Both the part type and the new types need to be created or extended with the following general attributes:

- Name.
- Component number. It represents the reference number in the PLM system.
- Revision number.
- State. It has two alternatives 'released' or 'not released'.
- Effective date. From which date on the item has the state released.
- Classification. Represents the position of the component in the Context taxonomy.
- List of Methods. It contains links to items of type Manufacturing Method.
- Item Nature. It is an attribute to indicate if the component where the problem occur is real or abstract. The 'abstract' alternative allows indicating a general family of products or production lines instead of a specific one. Therefore, specific elements will be tagged with "Real", and general ones with "Abstract". This attribute is used when searching for the problem context data in the PLM application.

The item Manufacturing Method is associated to the PFMEA component Method, which represents the defined procedures or standards. In the proposed model, Manufacturing Method contains the technical specification associated to an item (e.g. Part or Manufacturing Process). Part of this technical information can be common for a whole family of components (e.g. a family of hex bolts with a specific diameter and thread where each one distinguishes from the others in the length). Since the Manufacturing

Method is the container of technical data, each of the other five items (component, machine, process, man and environment) have the attribute called "List of Methods". This attribute allows specifying the links to several Manufacturing Methods containing technical information from multiple levels within the family structure of the component (e.g. Manufacturing Method for all hex bolts made of stainless steel, Manufacturing Method for all hex bolts with standard thread and diameter 5/8″-11, and Manufacturing Method for the hex bolt with length 6″).

The definition of a Manufacturing Method is based on the attribute "List of Manufacturing Parameters". A "Manufacturing Parameter" is the smallest data unit. It contains the type of a single attribute (e.g. pressure, temperature, or experience years), its limit type (i.e. max, min, nominal, or not applicable), its value (either numerical or a selection from a set of possible values), and its measurement unit. The attribute "List of Manufacturing Parameters" contains an open list where an unlimited number of items of Manufacturing Parameter type can be indexed. For example, an instance of the item Manufacturing Process "Casting" will have a link to an instance of an item Manufacturing Method "Casting method", and "Casting method" will contain a list of instances of the item type Manufacturing Parameter, such as "Pressure/10/bar", or "Temperature/300/°C".

Back to MPS process flow (Fig. 2), based on the information introduced by the user, the MPS system must search for the involved components in the PLM subsystem. Once the components are identified, the value of attributes to be used as context information of the problem should be extracted. For example, in a problem related to a component of type Man (i.e. operator) the MPS system should get, from the PLM subsystem, the experience of the operator, but also the type of process and machine where the operator works. In the case of a problem related to a component of type Process, the MPS system should get, from the PLM subsystem, data contained in the associated "Manufacturing Method", for instance the parameters that define the nominal pressure or temperatures at which the process has to run, and but also the type of material that is processed.

The input for the CBR subsystem is the problem description introduced by the MPS system user together with the context information extracted from the PLM subsystem. The CBR subsystem is responsible for providing to the MPS personnel with a list of similar solved problems identified in the case base. The similarity calculation makes use of the problem description and the context information. The open source software myCBR was selected for the CBR subsystem.

As it was previously mentioned, the initial set of manufacturing problems to fill the case base of the CBR subsystem is derived from the PFMEA analysis of the production lines. The PFMEA analysis is conducted during the development phase of the manufacturing processes, and therefore it is available prior to the start of the production. This represents a quite significant set of possible failures that allows having similarity results from the start. As soon as the production starts and the MPS personnel start reporting problems by using the MPS system, the case base will increase. The use of proposed MPS system requires not only the report of problems, but also, the report of the solution to such problems (i.e. the feedback step of the 8D method).

Once the MPS process flow and the main subsystems of the proposed MPS system are discussed, it is then time to introduce the MPS system architecture. As it was previously mentioned (Sect. 2.3), this work takes as reference the SEASALT architecture. Figure 3 shows the architecture of the proposed MPS system.

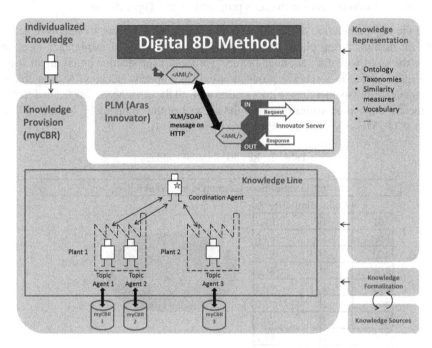

Fig. 3. SEASALT architecture adapted to the proposed MPS system

In this work, the SEASALT architecture was simplified. The SEASALT architecture includes also the modules Knowledge Formalization and Knowledge sources, which are not included as such in this work. The Knowledge Representation module corresponds with the ontological model (Sect. 3). The implementation is made of three different types of agents [16] (see Fig. 3):

- Individualized Knowledge Agent. It is located in the SEASALT Individualized Knowledge module. It is responsible for capturing and showing information to the MPS system user through the Graphical User Interface (GUI). In the prototype, the GUI is developed to represent a digital form of the 8D method. It also includes the needed interface to collect the problem context information from the PLM subsystem. The number of Individualized Knowledge Agents corresponds with the number of the MPS system users. Such agents are hosted in the devices located directly at the production lines where the users are located (e.g. PC, smart touchscreen, or even a smart phone).
- Topic Agent. It is located in the SEASALT Knowledge Provision module. It is responsible for calculating similarities through the CBR subsystem, and proposing the best solution from its specific case base. The number of Topic Agents correspond with the number of production units. Each Topic Agent is hosted in a central device of its corresponding production unit (e.g. PC or Server).

- Coordination Agent. It is located in the SEASALT Knowledge Provision module. It is responsible for the communication coordination among agents, and the selection of the best solution among the ones proposed by the Topic Agents.

In the implementation of the MPS system, the different agents are deployed across different manufacturing plants of the company (locations), and inside each location, across the areas with different manufacturing processes (production units). In this way, each agent hosted in a specific production unit of a specific location will be able to communicate and to interchange information with all the other agents hosted in different production units and locations through the intranet of the company by sending HTTP-based MTP (Message Transport Protocol) messages [14].

Table 2. Results of initial validation

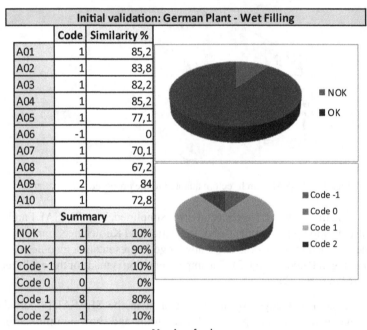

Initial validation: German Plant - Wet Filling			
	Code	Similarity %	
A01	1	85,2	
A02	1	83,8	
A03	1	82,2	
A04	1	85,2	
A05	1	77,1	
A06	-1	0	
A07	1	70,1	
A08	1	67,2	
A09	2	84	
A10	1	72,8	
Summary			
NOK	1	10%	
OK	9	90%	
Code -1	1	10%	
Code 0	0	0%	
Code 1	8	80%	
Code 2	1	10%	

Meaning of codes

-1 = No solution useful out of system proposals but no similar case in case base

0 = No solution useful out of system proposals even though there are similar cases in case base

1 = One solution directly useful out of system proposals

2 = One solution useful out of system proposals with adaptation by user

5   Results, Conclusions and Future Work

The proposed ontological model was applied in the development of a prototype MPS system, which integrates a PLM subsystem and a CBR subsystem. The system follows the 8D method and takes results from PFMEA analyses as initial case base.

The developed prototype has been tested in the company Exide Technologies with an initial case base containing 72 cases. A single process and a single production plant have been selected for this first validation step, which represents the easiest level of complexity for the system, since the cases in the prototype were all collected in the same process and plant. 10 problems found on the shop floor have been analyzed in parallel by the system and experts. As it is showed in the Table 2, 80% of the results obtained for the queries were similar to the answer provided by experts, and an additional 10% could guide to the solution by adapting the proposal of the system to the context of the problem under analysis. The results obtained showed the importance of the problem context information, defined in the PLM subsystem, in the case similarity calculation. A second version of the prototype MPS system is currently under development to be tested in different processes and production plants in parallel.

An advantage of the proposed MPS system, which has been realized during the execution of the tests, is the access and reuse by operators of solutions to problems already identified in the PFMEA analyses of their lines. This is significant, because without the support of the prototype MPS system, such reuse rarely happens, mainly because of the difficulties in finding and analyzing information in the complex document of a PFMEA analysis. The population and maintenance of the system is conducted by a role named Knowledge Engineer. The current version of the application allows uploading cases by means of a csv format file.

Two possible barriers were identified during the implementation of the first prototype of the MPS system. The first one is the requirement of having a PLM system, where information of the products, their processes and resources (PPR) of the company should be stored. The second one is the need of having access to the MPS system at the shop floor level. Nevertheless, the current trend of digitalization in the industry (e.g. Industry 4.0 initiative) [17] should help to overcome these possible barriers.

A possible future work is the development of the Knowledge Source and the Knowledge Formalization modules, defined in the SEASALT architecture, to extract automatically knowledge from PFMEA analyses. In that direction, some research works propose the use of SysML, to create a system model, where artifacts contain FMEA information, and the use of Prolog engine to query the created model to derive FMEA results [18].

References

1. Bhuiyan, N., Baghel, A.: An overview of continuous improvement: from the past to the present. Manage. Decis. **43**(5), 761–771 (2005). https://doi.org/10.1108/00251740510597761

2. VDA: Qualitätsmanagement in der Automobilindustrie – Qualitätsmanagement-Methoden Assessments. Verband der Autoindustrie (VDA) (2015)

3. Liu, D.R., Ke, C.K.: Knowledge support for problem-solving in a production process: a hybrid of knowledge discovery and case-based reasoning. Expert Syst. Appl. **33**, 147–161 (2007). https://doi.org/10.1016/j.eswa.2006.04.026

4. Sowa, J.F.: Knowledge Representation - Logical, Philosophical and Computational Foundations. Brooks Cole Publishing Co., Pacific Grove (2000). ISBN 0 534-94965-7

5. Stark, J.: Product Lifecycle Management. Springer International Publishing, Switzerland (2015). https://doi.org/10.1007/978-3-319-17440-2. ISBN 978-3-319-17440-2

6. Richter, M.M., Weber, R.: Case-Based Reasoning: A Textbook. Springer, Heidelberg (2013). https://doi.org/10.1007/978-3-642-40167-1. ISBN 978-3-642-40167-1
7. Foguem, B.K., Coudert, T., Béler, C., Geneste, L.: Knowledge formalization in experience feedback processes: an ontology-based approach. Comput. Ind. **59**(7), 694–710 (2008). https://doi.org/10.1016/j.compind.2007.12.014
8. Dittmann, L., Rademacher, T., Zelewski, S.: Performing FMEA using ontologies. In: 18th International Workshop on Qualitative Reasoning, Evanston, USA, pp. 209–216 (2004)
9. Ebrahimipour, V., Rezaie, K., Shokravi, S.: An ontology approach to support FMEA studies. Expert Syst. Appl. **37**(1), 671–677 (2010). https://doi.org/10.1109/RAMS.2009.4914711
10. Cambria, E., White, B.: Jumping NLP curves: a review of natural language processing research. IEEE Comput. Intell. Magaz. **9**(2), 48–57 (2014)
11. Bertin, A.: Intégration d'un système de Retour d'Expériences à un PLM. Doctoral dissertation - Laboratoire Génie Production (LGP) - Ecole Nationale d'Ingénieurs deTarbes - Université de Toulouse (2012)
12. Bertin, A., Noyes, D., Clermont, P.: Problem solving methods as lessons learned system instrumentation into a PLM tool. In: 14th IFAC Symposium on Information Control Problems in Manufacturing, Bucarest, Roumanie, 23–25 May 2012 (2012). ISBN: hal-01005542
13. Bach, K.: Knowledge acquisition for case-based reasoning systems. Ph.D. thesis, University of Hildesheim (2012)
14. Reuss, P., Althoff, K.D., Hundt, A., Henkel, W., Pfeiffer, M.: Multi-agent case-based diagnosis in the aircraft domain. In: Workshop Proceedings - 23rd International Conference on Case-Based Reasoning (ICCBR 2015), pp. 43–52 (2015)
15. Kepner, C.H., Tregoe, B.B.: The New Rational Manager - An Updated Edition for a New World. Princeton Research Press, Princeton (2008). ISBN 978-0-9715627-1-4
16. Bellifemine, F.L., Caire, G., Greenwood, D.: Developing multi-agent systems with JADE. Wiley Series in Agent Technology. Wiley, England (2007)
17. Cearley, D.W., Walker, M.J., Burke, B.: Top 10 Strategic Technology Trends for 2016: At a Glance. Gartner (2015)
18. Scippacercola, F., Pietrantuono, R., Russo, S., Silva, N.P.: SysML-based and prolog-supported FMEA. In: 2015 IEEE International Symposium on Software Reliability Engineering Workshops (ISSREW), pp. 174–181. IEEE (2015)

PLM-MES Integration to Support Industry 4.0

Gianluca D'Antonio[1(✉)], Lisa Macheda[2], Joel Sauza Bedolla[1], and Paolo Chiabert[1]

[1] Politecnico di Torino, corso Duca degli Abruzzi 24, 10129 Turin, Italy
{gianluca.dantonio,joel.sauza,paolo.chiabert}@polito.it
[2] AEC Soluzioni, corso Unione Sovietica 612/3A, 10135 Turin, Italy
aec@aecsoluzioni.it

Abstract. In order to effectively deal with the Industry 4.0 paradigm, companies need accurate strategies to manage data collected on both the real world and its virtual counterpart. Proper information systems need to be implemented; Product Lifecycle Management (PLM) and Manufacturing Execution Systems (MES) play a key role in this task. A primary issue is the mutual integration of such systems, with the aim of reducing time and cost for data management, as well as risks of errors and data redundancy. The present paper aims to present the results of a survey submitted to a set of Italian companies to measure their digital maturity and their proneness in implementing further information systems and in enabling their integration.

Keywords: Product Lifecycle Management · Manufacturing Execution Systems Information systems · Industry 4.0

1 Introduction

Today, one of the most popular keywords in the field of manufacturing is "Industry 4.0". Despite a wide variety of scientific, technical and business literature, a shared definition of Industry 4.0 has not yet been achieved. However, the most of authors agree in stating that this paradigm relies on the implementation of the Internet of Things (IoT) technology in manufacturing environment [1]. The wide-scale deployment of IoT will promote enhanced communication between humans and machines and support the implementation of the so-called Cyber-Physical Systems (CPS) [2], i.e. systems consisting in a real entity (for example, a machine) and its corresponding virtual model – embedding all the models for mimicking the behavior of the real counterpart – capable to communicate with each other.

In order to implement a CPS, two complementary and parallel approaches are necessary: (i) cyberizing the physical, and (ii) physicalizing the cyber [3]. To deal with the first task, a virtual model of each entity in the physical factory must be realized. Then, simulation models must be implemented to transform the static models in dynamic systems. An integration between the virtual and the physical worlds is necessary to feed virtual models with data acquired in field, aiming to simulate future scenarios without

J. Ríos et al. (Eds.): PLM 2017, IFIP AICT 517, pp. 129–137, 2017.
https://doi.org/10.1007/978-3-319-72905-3_12

the need to input data manually [4]. Next, all the communication between machine and network, machine-to-machine and machine-to-human should be flawlessly designed.

This approach can be extended from company resources to products: physical products should be transformed in uniquely identifiable information carriers, which may be whenever located to know their history, status and alternative routes to achieve their target state [5].

Hence, machines need to be equipped with enough computing and communication capabilities to have the ability to act independently, without direct human intervention. Further, a structured approach to manage the wide quantity of data that can be collected is necessary and information systems should be properly integrated.

In previous work [6], a roadmap to achieve the smart factory has been depicted. The present paper aims to focus on the role that Product Lifecycle Management (PLM) and Manufacturing Execution Systems (MES) – as well as their integration – can play in supporting the Industry 4.0 paradigm. An analysis of possible benefits is provided; moreover, the results of a survey made to measure the interest of manufacturing companies in this topic are presented.

The remainder of the paper is organized as follows. In Sect. 2, the state of the art is depicted and the role of PLM-MES integration in supporting the Industry 4.0 paradigm is presented. The structure of the survey is presented in Sect. 3; the results are provided in Sect. 4. Conclusive remarks and hints for future work are discussed in Sect. 5.

2   Information Systems Supporting Industry 4.0

2.1   Product Lifecycle Management

Over the last decade PLM has become one of the key technological and organizational approaches and enablers for the effective management of product development and product creation processes [7]. Product information is generated when the product is first conceived, then it continues to evolve with the addition of Computer-Aided Design (CAD) models and drawings detailed specifications, user manuals, manufacturing instructions, service manuals, disposal and recycling instructions [8]. The management of the life cycle of products and related services has become a central factor in the manufacturing industry.

Manufacturing is the function that has the greatest benefit from the application of PLM technology [9]. The manufacturing objective is to fabricate a product with precisely defined specifications and tolerances utilizing the least amount of resources. In order to reduce the time to market, manufacturing companies have relied more and more on simulations to early (and digitally) test and optimize the manufacturing process. Simulations are used in both long-term decisions, such as facility layout and system capacity configuration, and short-term decision-making, as for example CNC simulation [10]. The term that resume this concept is Digital Manufacturing (DM). It represents the production data management systems and simulation technologies that are jointly used for optimizing manufacturing before starting the production and supporting the ramp-up phases [11]. DM is considered as one of the main technologies to enable the next frontier in manufacturing, the so-called Cyber Physical Production System (CPPS) [12].

CPPS are defined as systems of collaborating computational entities in constant connection with the surrounding physical world with its on-going processes, providing and using (at the same time) data-accessing and data-processing services available on the internet [13]. CPPS are a core element of Industry 4.0; hence, the integration of the DM and the CPPS would be a milestone for this paradigm.

In this background, PLM is the backbone of the digitalization, simulation and integration of systems. CPPS require a digital model of all the equipment in the factory along with the product itself. PLM connects and maintains the integrity of the systems and plays a fundamental role in the management of product and process changes. However, the PLM structure will need to be adapted to the growing amount of information that will received from the shop floor and from the product at use stage.

2.2   Manufacturing Execution Systems

Manufacturing Execution Systems are IT tools that enable information exchange between the organizational level of a company – commonly supported by an ERP – and the control systems for the shop-floor, usually consisting in several, different, very customized software applications [14].

A MES has two principal purposes. First, the system has to identify the optimal sequence planning taking into account the constraints of the process, such as the times for processing and setup, and the capacity of the workstations, taking into account the requirements and the necessities given by the organizational level. The system also has to manage and allocate resources such as the staff and the material necessary for the manufacturing process.

The second aim of a MES is to manage the bottom-up data flow. The data collection necessary for feeding the CPS is triggered by the recent development of low-cost, small, easily available sensors. MES is in charge of collecting the data gathered on the shop-floor, analyze it through proper mathematical techniques, and extract the information necessary to provide an exhaustive picture of the current state of the process. Possibly, the analysis should be performed in real-time, in order to make decisions to control the process with the necessary rapidity.

Given this background, MES plays a strategic role in supporting Industry 4.0: it is a platform for transforming data collected on the shop-floor into information, which can feed the simulation models and, in turn, enable DM.

2.3   Integration Between PLM and MES

Up-to-date, few work in the field of PLM-MES integration has been done. A first attempt has been made by Ben Khedher et al. [15]: they analyze the data exchange between the PLM and MES systems and propose a model for this integration. Nevertheless, this general model lacks of validation, since no evidence of application is shown. This is the only work in which a methodological approach is proposed.

In previous work, D'Antonio et al. [16] identified the benefits resulting from the integration between PLM and MES through a case-study in the manufacturing of aeronautics components. In [17], a case-study in the field of automotive has been analyzed.

In both the two works, the main benefit deriving from the integration between the two systems could be the reduction of errors in information management and the improved reactivity in taking decisions.

The integration between PLM and MES would allow to realize a synchronized system where product design and production are strictly tied. In the flow from design to production, the PLM contains the information necessary to define the properties of the finite part to be manufactured. The MES contains the information necessary to transform the product defined in the PLM into a physical object, such as the routings and the process parameters. The PLM also contains data concerning the features necessary to ensure a proper product quality, while the MES contains the operative steps required to evaluate product quality. In summary, MES should only contain process information, while product information should be stored in the PLM; however, in many cases, MES also contain product information. This may lead to duplicate information (i.e. information contained both in the PLM and in the MES), with possible risks for errors.

In the opposite flow (i.e. from production to design), MES is the repository of the in-field information collected on the shop-floor. This role is enhanced by the Industry 4.0 paradigm: resources will be increasingly equipped with sensors and devices for data acquisition, and a structured approach for their analysis and collection is necessary. A connection between PLM and MES enables product managers and designers to identify at any time possible criticalities, evaluate their impact and develop possible solutions. This can lead to an overall product quality improvement: as soon as a criticality is found, designers can take decisions to solve it, based on the data collected on the shop-floor and stored in the MES. Further, when a new product is released, the ramp-up production phase can be tightly monitored through the MES, and the necessary adjustments to product features or to the control plans can be quickly done.

3 Structure of the Survey

The survey used to measure the proneness of manufacturing companies in integrating information systems has been implemented through the free tool made available by Google. The structure of the survey is made of five steps.

Step 1. Introduction. The name of the company in which the recipient is employed is required, and a short description about the aim of the survey is provided. However, to guarantee anonymity, the reply to this question was not mandatory.

Step 2. Digital maturity. The recipient is asked to select from a given list the information systems that are currently used in his company. The possible answers are: CAD; PDM; ERP; PLM; MES; SCM; Other. In a further question, the recipient is asked whether any of these information systems are mutually integrated, with particular concern for: ERP-MES; CAD-PLM; ERP-PLM; SCM-MES.

Step 3. Focus on PLM. Here, a short definition of PLM and its aims is provided; then, the recipient is asked whether he is interested in integrating a PLM system in his company, and which are the expected benefits, among: (i) Time and cost reduction for product development; (ii) Improvement in product information management and sharing; (iii) Improved traceability of new product releases; (iv) Overall product quality improvement, due to updated and shared product specifications; (v) Improved product management due to detailed BOM. In case the company is already equipped with a PLM system, the name of the deployed software is requested.

Step 4. Focus on MES. The structure of this section is similar to the previous one. A short definition of MES and its role is provided. Then, the recipient is asked whether his company is interested in using a MES and which would be the expected benefits, among: (i) Improved process management and monitoring; (ii) Improved cost management and monitoring; (iii) Acquisition of data collected on-field from the machines; (iv) Improved management of criticalities, such as non-conformities, breaks, failures; (v) Integrated management of the flow of materials and information flowing through the process; (vi) Improved production planning. In case the company is already equipped with a MES, the name of the deployed software is requested.

Step 5. Focus on PLM-MES integration. A set of possible advantages resulting from the integration between PLM and MES is provided. Then, the recipient is asked whether his company could be interested in a possible integration the PLM system with a MES and which would be the expected benefits, among: (i) Time-to-market reduction; (ii) Integration between design and production activities; (iii) Improvement in information traceability; (iv) Improvement of the quality level provided to the customer.

4   Results

The invitation to submit the survey described in Sect. 3 has been sent to 400 companies settled in the Piemonte region (Italy). Small, Medium and Large companies involved in different manufacturing areas have been contacted; a detailed description of the sample is provided in Table 1. 33 replies were obtained, corresponding to the 8% of the initial sample; although a low value, it is in line with the results commonly obtained by surveys. Among the respondents, 21 people also stated the name of the company for which they are employed. In the following, the results for each survey section are shown; a graphical representation is provided in Fig. 1.

Digital maturity. The companies that state to deploy CAD software are 30; the only companies that do not deploy such tool are involved in Food & Beverage and in Logistics. The second most popular information tool is the ERP: this kind of software is used in 21 companies among the ones that replied to the survey, while 9 companies deploy a PDM tool. SCM is used by three companies. MES is used by 8 companies; among them, 7 state that the software is directly integrated with an ERP, and in three cases the integration with a SCM has also been implemented. PLM is used in 6 companies. Among them, in three cases PLM is integrated with the ERP and in two cases it is also integrated with the CAD software; conversely, in the other three cases, there is no integration between PLM and other information systems. No companies own both a PLM and a MES.

Focus on PLM. As said, among the 33 companies that replied to the survey, 6 ones already have a PLM system. 15 companies state to be not interested in implementing such solution, while 12 companies are interested. All of them would appreciate a solution enabling to improve management and sharing of product information; 9 of them are interested in improving the traceability of product changes, while 7 companies aim to reduce time and cost for new product development.

Table 1. Synthesis of the companies involved in the survey, organized by manufacturing field and by company size.

Manufacturing field	Invited companies	Submitted surveys
Mechanics	205	9
Automotive	51	2
Textile	39	2
Food & Beverage	30	3
Building components	21	–
Chemistry	14	1
Electronics	12	–
Aerospace	7	–
Glass/Wood	6	–
Logistics	6	1
Consumer products	9	3
Unknown	–	12
Total	400	33
Company size	Invited companies	Submitted surveys
Small companies (10–50 employees)	18	3
Medium companies (50–250 employees)	294	12
Large companies (250 + employees)	88	6
Unknown	–	12
Total	400	33

Finally, 4 companies would adopt a PLM system to have an overall product quality improvement, and three companies aim to be supported in having complete and exhaustive BOMs and thus improve the management of new product configurations.

Focus on MES. Eight companies that replied to the survey already use a MES. Among the other ones, 9 would be interested in a MES, while 16 are not. The most popular advantages expected from the deployment of a MES are: the improved cost management and monitoring (8 preferences), the improved process management and monitoring, and the integrated management of the flow of materials and information flowing through the process (7 preferences each). The capability to acquire process data in real-time from the shop-floor and an improved management of failures and non-conformities are also appreciated (5 preferences each).

Focus on PLM-MES integration. According to the results obtained in the second section, none of the companies that replied to the survey own both a PLM and a MES. In this section, an overview of the possible benefits coming from such integration was

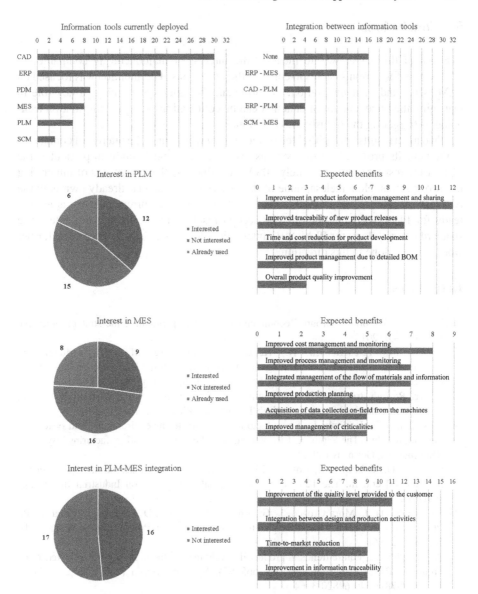

Fig. 1. Results of the survey.

provided. After reading this list, 16 companies stated that such advantages could be interesting, while 17 declared to be not interested in a PLM-MES integration.

5 Conclusions

The aim of this paper was to measure the interest of manufacturing companies in deploying information systems to enhance their activities. The attention was focused on PLM, MES and their integration; in particular, the latter system plays a key role in managing the huge amount of data that can be collected through the information technologies triggering the Industry 4.0 paradigm.

Two main results are highlighted by the present work. First, the interest of companies in the benefits provided by the systems taken into account is high; in particular, the highest interest rate (approximately 50%) is obtained by the advantages of integrating the two systems. Nonetheless, none of the interested companies already own both the two systems. Hence, although the interest rate is high, the current industry is not yet ready for PLM-MES integration. The second result is that, although this interest, a standard methodology for PLM-MES integration does not exist yet. Therefore, further work must be done in this direction.

References

1. Industrie 4.0 Working Group, Recommendations for implementing the strategic initiative Industrie 4.0 (2013)
2. Brettel, M., Friederichsen, N., Keller, M., Rosenberg, M.: How virtualization, decentralization and network building change the manufacturing landscape: an industry 4.0 perspective. Int. J. Mech. Aerosp. Ind. Mechatron. Manufact. Eng. **8**, 37–44 (2014)
3. Anderl, R.: Industrie 4.0 - advanced engineering of smart products and smart production. In: The 19th International Seminar on High Technology, Piracicaba, Brasil (2014)
4. Westkämper, E., Jendoubi, L.: Smart factories - manufacturing environments and systems of the future. In: The 36th CIRP-International Seminar on Manufacturing Systems, Saarbruecken, Germany (2003)
5. Gorecky, D., Schmitt, M., Loskyll, M., Zühlke, D.: Human-machine-interaction in the industry 4.0 era. In: The 12th IEEE International Conference on Industrial Informatics (INDIN), Porto Alegre (2014)
6. Sauza Bedolla, J., Mora Orozco, J., Guarín Grisales, A.D.J., D'Antonio, G., Chiabert, P.: PLM in a didactic environment: the path to smart factory. Int J. Prod. Lifecycle Manag. 9(4), 333–352 (2016)
7. Abramovici, M.: Future trends in product lifecycle management. In: Krause, F.L. (ed.) The Future of Product Development, pp. 665–674. Springer, Berlin (2007). https://doi.org/10.1007/978-3-540-69820-3_64
8. Framling, K., Kubler, S., Buda, A.: Universal messaging standards for the IoT from a lifecycle management perspective. IEEE Internet. Things J. **1**(4), 319–327 (2014)
9. Grieves, M.: Product Lifecycle Management: Driving the Next Generation of Lean Thinking. McGraw Hill Professional, New York (2005)
10. Mourtzis, D., Papakostas, N., Mavrikios, D., Makris, S., Alexopoulos, K.: The role of simulation in digital manufacturing: applications and outlook. Int. J. Comput. Integr. Manufact. **28**(1), 3–24 (2015)
11. Westkämper, E.: Strategic development of factories under the influence of emergent technologies. In: CIRP Annals - Manufacturing Technology, pp. 419–422 (2007)

12. Jackson, K., Efthymiou, K., Borton, J.: Digital manufacturing and flexible assembly technologies for reconfigurable aerospace production systems. In: The Sixth International Conference on Changeable, Agile, Reconfigurable and Virtual Production (CARV2016) (2016)
13. Monostori, L.: Cyber-physical production systems: roots, expectations and R&D challenges. In: Proceedings of the 47th CIRP Conference on Manufacturing (2014)
14. Meyer, H., Fuchs, F., Thiesl, K.: Manufacturing Execution Systems (MES): Optimal Design, Planning, and Deployment. McGraw-Hill Professional, New York (2009)
15. Ben Khedher, A., Henry, S., Bouras, A.: Integration between MES and product lifecycle management. In: IEEE International Conference on Emerging Technologies and Factory Automation (ETFA 2011), Toulouse (2011)
16. D'Antonio, G., Sauza Bedolla, J., Chiabert, P., Lombardi, F.: PLM-MES integration to support collaborative design. In: International Conference on Engineering Design (ICED 2015), Milano, Italy (2015)
17. D'Antonio, G., Sauza Bedolla, J., Genta, G., Ruffa, S., Barbato, G., Chiabert, P., Pasquettaz, G.: PLM-MES integration: a case-study in automotive manufacturing. In: Bouras, A., Eynard, B., Foufou, S., Thoben, K.D. (eds.) PLM 2015. IAICT, vol. 467, pp. 780–789. Springer, Cham (2016). https://doi.org/10.1007/978-3-319-33111-9_71

PLM and Process Simulation

Towards Cloud in a PLM Context: A Proposal of Cloud Based Design and Manufacturing Methodology

Hussein Khlifi[1,2(✉)], Abhro Choudhury[1(✉)], Siddharth Sharma[1(✉)],
Frédéric Segonds[1(✉)], Nicolas Maranzana[1(✉)], Damien Chasset[2(✉)],
and Vincent Frerebeau[2(✉)]

[1] Arts et Métiers, ParisTech, LCPI, 151 Boulevard de l'Hôpital, 75013 Paris, France
{Hussein.khlifi,abhro.choudhury,siddharth.sharma,
Frederic.segonds,Nicolas.maranzana}@ensam.eu
[2] Dassault Systèmes, 10 Rue Marcel Dassault, 78140 Vélizy Villacoublay, France
{Damien.chasset,Vincent.frerebeau}@3ds.com

Abstract. Product Lifecycle Management (PLM) integrates all the phases a product goes through from inception to its disposal but generally, the entire process of the product development and manufacturing is time-consuming even with the advent of Cloud-Based Design and Manufacturing (CBDM). With enormous growth in Information Technology (IT) and extensive growth in cloud infrastructure the option of design and manufacturing within a cloud service is a viable option for future. This paper proposes a cloud based collaborative atmosphere with real-time interaction between the product development and the realization phases making the experience of design and manufacturing more efficient. A much-optimized data flow among various stages of a Product Lifecycle has also been proposed reducing the complexity of the overall cycle. A case study using Additive Manufacturing (AM) has also been demonstrated which proves the feasibility of the proposed methodology. The findings of this paper will aid the adoption of CBDM in PLM industrial activities with reduced overall cost. It also aims at providing a paradigm shift to the present design and manufacturing methodology through a real-time collaborative space.

Keywords: Cloud · Collaborative design · PLM · Additive manufacturing
Manufacturing

1 Introduction

With the emergence of new advanced technologies and rapidly increasing competition for efficient product development, researchers and industry professionals are constantly looking for new innovations in the field of design and manufacturing. It has become a challenge to meet the dynamics of today's Marketplace in the manufacturing field as the product development processes are geographically spread out. In the research community of Cloud Based Design and Manufacturing ongoing debate constantly takes place on the key characteristics like cloud based design, communication among users,

© IFIP International Federation for Information Processing 2017
Published by Springer International Publishing AG 2017. All Rights Reserved
J. Ríos et al. (Eds.): PLM 2017, IFIP AICT 517, pp. 141–151, 2017.
https://doi.org/10.1007/978-3-319-72905-3_13

safety of data, data storage, and data management among others. Such discussions have now been answered with the developments of cloud based design and manufacturing. Efforts are now directed towards making advancements in the field of design and manufacturing by using IT tools & PLM concepts. Few researchers are advancing in the field of developing a PLM paradigm in linking modular products between supplier and product developers [1], few others have extended their PLM research in the domains of Building information modeling by taking motivation and best practices from PLM by emphasizing more on information centric management approach in construction projects [2]. A revolutionary advancement of cloud services which now offers distributed network access, flexibility, availability on demand and pay per use services has certainly given push for applying cloud computing technology in the field of manufacturing. The intended idea of performing manufacturing on cloud has reached to such an extent that industries are forced to carry out operations in cloud rather than using the traditional methods.

Today's world is moving faster and is more connected than ever before due to globalization which has created new opportunities & risks. Traditional methods lack the ability to allow users, who are geographically spread out to work in a collaborative environment to perform design & manufacturing operations. Traditional Design processes have a one-way process that consists of four main phases: customer, market analysis, designer and manufacturing engineers followed in the same order where each phase was a standalone centralized system with minimum cross functional interaction. With the time technologies like CAD, internet services and client server model evolved drastically but overall the advantages provided by these systems were limited in nature as it was still following the same one-way methodology [3]. Moreover, there exists a rigid and costly system of supply chain till now whereas in Cloud-based Supply Chain, the supply chain is customer centric and the users with specific needs are linked with the service providers while meeting the cost, time and quality requirements of the user.

This is where adoption of Cloud Based Design and Manufacturing (CBDM) becomes essential as it is based on a cloud platform that allows users to collaborate and use the resources on demand and on a self-service basis. This provides flexibility and agility, which is required to reconfigure the resources to minimize the down-time, also called Rapid scalability. CBDM is designed to allow collaboration and communication between various actors involved from design to delivery phase in the cross-disciplinary teams to work in a collaborative way in real time from anywhere in the world with access to internet. Cloud manufacturing allows to produce variety of products of varying complexity and helps in mass customization. Using the CBDM system, the prototypes of the part can be manufactured without buying costly manufacturing equipment. Users can pay a subscription fee to acquire software licenses and use manufacturing equipment instead of purchasing them. Finally, usage of cloud-based environment leads to saving of opportunities as the tasks that were not economically viable earlier can be done using the cloud services.

2 State of the Art

2.1 Cloud Based Collaborative Atmosphere

With the coming & advancement of Web 2.0, social collaborative platforms provided a wonderful way to exchange information and data [4]. The internet based information and communication technologies are now allowing to exchange information in real time and are providing means to put into practice the concepts of mass collaboration, distributed design & manufacturing processes [5]. Collaboration-based Design & Manufacturing comprises all the activities that revolve around the manufacture of a product and leads to significant economies of scale, reduced time to market, improvement in quality, reduced costs etc. In a cloud manufacturing system, manufacturing resources & capabilities, software etc. are interconnected to provide a pool of shared resources and services like Design as a Service, Simulation as a Service, and Fabrication as a Service to the consumers [6]. Current researches have emphasized a lot on the connectivity of products or in other words smart connected products via cloud environment for better collaboration of various operations of manufacturing being carried out on a product [7] and hence this acted as a first motivation of going into cloud domain for design and manufacturing. Also many larger scale enterprises have formed decentralized and complex network of their operations in the field of design and manufacturing where constant interaction with small scale enterprise is becoming a challenge. However, with the emergence of cloud computing there is an observation that more and more enterprises have shifted their work into cloud domain and have saved millions of dollars [8, 9] and hence this forms our second motivation behind implementing manufacturing which in our case is AM on "Cloud" which is backed by the fact that the currently automobile and aeronautics giants have been shifting wide portion of their work into cloud platform by implementing cloud computing technology into many business lines pertaining to engineering domain. This also reaffirms our belief that cloud computing is envisaged to transform enterprise both small and big to profit from moving their design and manufacturing task into the cloud. Hence this forms the first pillar of the proposed CBDM.

2.2 Rapid Manufacturing Scalability

The idea of providing manufacturing services on the internet was in fact developed a long time ago when researchers envisaged the propagation of IOT (Internet of Things) in the production. Recent research has showcased the importance to have continuous process flow in lean product development which gave rise to an idea of having scalability in manufacturing process to have more liquidity in the manufacturing process.

In a world of rapid competition, scalability of rapid manufacturing is more important than ever. In the alignment to the statement made by Koren et al. [10] regarding importance of reconfigurable manufacturing systems (RMSs) for quick adjustment in production capacity and functionality, CBDM allows users to purchase services like manufacturing equipment, software licences with reconfiguration module which in turns allow scalability of the manufacturing process and prevents over purchasing of computing and manufacturing capacities. This digital manufacturing productivity greatly enhances the scalability of the manufacturing capacity in comparison to the traditional manufacturing paradigm and this has been evident from the recent research work carried out by Lechevalier et al. [11] and Moones et al. [12] who have show-cased efficient interoperability in a collaborative and dynamic manufacturing frame-work. As stated by Wua et al. [13], from the perspective of manufacturing scala-bility, CBDM allows the product development team to leverage more cost-effective manufacturing services from global suppliers to rapidly scale up and down the manu-facturing capacity during production. Hence, Rapid manufacturing scalability forms our second pillar of the proposed methodology.

2.3 Design and Additive Manufacturing Methodology Model

In this section, the flow of information in the digital chain has been studied to optimize the quality of AM which remains our focus in the experiment to test proposed method-ology. This information management system interacts with the support infrastructure [14] (The standards, methods, techniques and software). The table whose phase 3 to 6 are represented in Fig. 1, provides an overview of the eight distinct stages and transitions. With a clear understanding of the various phases of additive manufacturing and transi-tions of information between each phase, we were able to identify optimization oppor-tunities of additive manufacturing and establish mechanisms and tools to achieve them. In the current research phase 3 and 4 have been considered as represented by dotted line region in Fig. 1. This transition is an important preparedness activity to AM that is essential to the achievement of the final product [15]. It includes activities like journal of 3D model, generation of the carrier around the 3D model, decomposition in successive layers of a 3D model and generating a code which contains the manufacturing

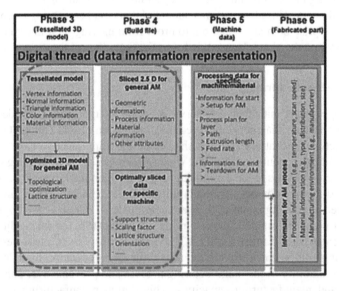

Fig. 1. Extract of digital channel information flow for AM as proposed by Kim D [14]

instructions for the machine. It is this transition stage "Activities for AM process" which is dealt later in this research project where AM process is optimized in the proposed methodology making this model a fourth pillar to the methodology.

2.4 Real-Time Business Model

One of the major advantages of using CBDM is that we are always linked to the outer world and this lets us know the real-time scenario. So as one of the pillars of our methodology we propose Real-time Business model to execute the entire process in the most efficient way in terms of quality and cost. The Real-Time Request for Quotation (RT-RFQ) is an interesting feature which increases the utility of the system. This basically utilizes the Knowledge Management System (KMS) which are an integral part of Cloud based design and manufacturing systems [16]. The selection of candidate KSPs is done based on the abilities and the capacities of the KSP to produce the product within stipulated time, cost and quality.

The entire process of generating a request for quotation, finalising the service provider and delivery of the final product is in real-time thus creating collaboration between the sellers and the buyers, which we name it as "Market Place". The entire Material Management and the Supply Chain of the product in a collaborative platform is an integral part of our proposed methodology thus forming one of the pillars.

3 Proposal of a Methodology

3.1 Synthesis

Synthesis of the proposed methodology is supported by four foundation pillars: Cloud environment, Rapid manufacturing scalability, Design and additive manufacturing methodology model and real-time business model. As discussed in the Sect. 2.3, optimization process involved in AM workflow is rich in research opportunities and thus important to reduce the number phases involved in the manufacturing process. In the construction of methodology, a centralized system has been considered which controls all the process i.e. cloud domain and forms a platform where all actions will take place. Thus "Cloud" atmosphere forms heart of the methodology which starts with inputs that are decided during the RFQ and award acknowledgement process of a project. 3D design (phase-1) followed by two new functionalities such as Preparation for manufacturing (phase-2) and the Marketplace (phase-4). Then comes generic processes manufacturing (phase 4) which in combination with phase-1, phase-2 and phase-3 gives the power of rapid manufacturing scalability as discussed in the Sect. 2.2. Last two phases represent packaging (phase-5) and delivery (phase-6) that constitutes the supply chain network of the process and are interconnected to phase-3 "Marketplace" in cloud by the means of interactions. Phase-3, phase-5 and phase-6 along with inputs given to the process is inspired form the real-time business model as discussed in the Sect. 2.4. This way four pillars forms the backbone of the methodology. Collaboration at each phase in form of propagation of design, consultation, evaluation and notification happens in parallel or simultaneously during the process which forms a distributed and connected network in the methodology.

In addition to defining pillars, the existing methodologies workflow was simplified. The methodology process has been scaled down to six phases, instead of eight as mentioned by Kim D [14]. For that, some sub-stages were regrouped into phases to optimize the process and simplify the methodology Indeed, it was noticed that by reducing phases and regrouping linked sub-stages to a single phase, we can minimize the interactions that could happen during transitions between the different phases that aided us in achieving 6 phase methodology process with multiple parallel interactions. By grouping sub steps to main steps, we proposed a 6-phase methodology. This approach of grouping sub steps represents our idea of moving for a "task to do" vision to a "defined role" vision. Instead of thinking as a task of 3D scanning, 3D modelling or a triangulation together, it would be a better to think as a task of a function such as 3D designer or a mechanical engineer. Following this approach, we group several tasks to a specific role. That's how we simplified our methodology, which is checked and validated in the case study applied to AM.

3.2   Methodology

From the 3D design to the product delivery, this methodology describes six phases including five transitions with tractability on the cloud as outlined in the Fig. 2.

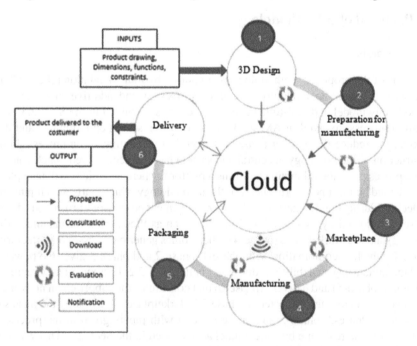

Fig. 2. Proposal of a CBDM methodology

As shown on Fig. 2, the methodology process starts with a 3D design phase (1) which involves designing the product in a 3D environment, produce 3D CAD File and save it on the Cloud by allowing collaborative work with someone who has the access. This file is then sent to be prepared for manufacturing (2). A preparation of the 3D model before manufacturing is basically deciding the manufacturing process that will be used to produce the designed part. Sub steps such as repair geometry, meshing, weight optimization and finite elements simulations are grouped in a single manufacturing preparation phase (2). Once the file prepared for manufacturing, it's uploaded to a Marketplace (3) platform where the product will be evaluated and reviewed by service providers. It an online collaborative platform which brings together buyers (designers, engineers and product developers) and sellers the key service providers (KSPs) who manufacture and bring the design and the concept to realization. Here phase 2 and 3 works in parallel to double check whether the 3D file is ready for manufacturing or requires a further preparation or optimization for manufacturing process to be used. At this stage, the product design has been optimized, prepared for manufacturing and the most efficient service provider has been awarded the order by the designer. Those service providers will lead the customer to the appropriate manufacturing process and will start the manufacturing phase (4). A validation and evaluation product loop occurs after manufacturing to make sure the product matches the requirement specifications. Once the product is manufactured and validates the requirements, the service provider proceeds to the packaging (5) then the delivery (6). The service provider selected in the Market place also has the responsibility of providing packaging and delivery service.

The methodology proposed here, is the result of a conceptual and theoretical work. However, it must be applied at a practical level to evaluate its efficiency. We have implemented the proposed thermotical model on a case study to enlighten the benefits of this model in a real-world scenario. The following section describes a case study of the proposed methodology, applied to Additive Manufacturing.

4   Case Study: Additive Manufacturing

This research is conducted in a partnership between the LCPI, a research lab in the Engineering School Arts et Métiers ParisTech, and Dassault Systèmes company. Collaborate to unify an academic research entity and an industrial Leader is one of our main purposes to point out merits of CBDM such as distributive & collaborative network as a solution to today's design & manufacturing activities. The proposed model in this paper, is tested by carrying out designing, manufacturing, trading on Marketplace and finally packaging for a very common industrial product called "joiner" in a collaborative & distributed environment on a cloud platform to demonstrate the feasibility of the proposed solutions by experimental tests.

Additive manufacturing (AM) has become a new way to realize objects from a 3D model [17] as it provides a cost-effective and time-efficient way to produce low-volume, customized products with complex geometries and advanced material properties and functionalities.

From 3D design to product delivery, step by step the proposed methodology discussed in the Sect. 3 has been applied in AM context and thus changing the step (2) from "Preparation for manufacturing" to "Preparation to Additive Manufacturing" and the rest remains the same. As the project was conducted in a partnership with Dassault Systèmes, and the fact that we want to use a unique platform for the whole CBDM process, the "3DEXPERIENCE" solution by enterprise was used to test the proposed methodology. The focus was on optimizing the methodology dataflow, which impacts directly the product quality.

Step 1: 3D design
In the first phase, the user will use a 3D design app on the cloud and work collaboratively. Once the product is designed and converted into an appropriate format, we proceed to the preparation process for manufacturing.

Step 2: Preparation for manufacturing
We have a 3D model file at this stage which requires preparation for the 3D printing. The Fig. 3 describes the fundamental AM processes and operations followed during preparation for manufacturing the CAD model in an AM environment. During the process Pre-context setting, Meshing were also carried out.

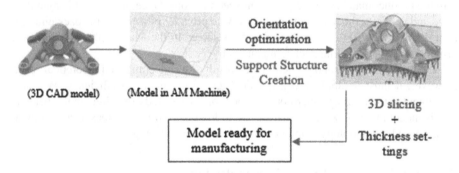

Fig. 3. Preparation for manufacturing steps

Step 3: The 3DMarketplace
The 3DMarketplace is a platform for additive manufacturing. It addresses the end-to-end process of upstream material design, downstream manufacturing processes and testing to provide a single flow of data for engineering parameters. The objective here as a buyer is to select the most efficient key service provider possessing the required capabilities and skill sets on the Marketplace to proceed to the manufacturing phase (Fig. 4). The Marketplace shows up a list of service providers that can process the product manufacturing. A printing request was sent to the laboratory where a back and forth transition between the buyer and the service provider is necessary to make assure the printability of the 3D model and the use of the right manufacturing technology. This phase is done by confirmation of the order and starting of the AM process.

Step 4-5-6: Manufacturing, Packaging and delivery
As defined in the proposed methodology section, the service provider from the Marketplace takes care of the manufacturing, packaging and delivery service. For the delivery,

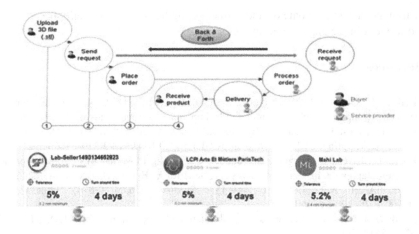

Fig. 4. The 3D marketplace procees with used service providers during experiment

we chose to pick up the part. The customer can rate their experience and raise complaints on the 3DMarketPlace if required, and thus allowing improvement in the services provided.

5   Conclusion and Future Work

The successful implementation of Cloud based additive manufacturing demonstrated that Collaborative and distributed design and manufacturing task as complex as AM can be performed with ease by using cloud based service. This research points towards a centralized user interface i.e. cloud platform which forms the heart of the proposed methodology thus allowing its users to aggregate data and facilitate coordination, communication and collaboration among its various players of design, development, delivery and business segments.

We optimized the digital workflow while applying the proposed methodology, which helped in obtaining better quality products, shorter machining time, less material use and reduced AM costs. One of the main gains from study was the use of 3D market place in the methodology which offers a collaborative atmosphere for discussing subjects such 3D model design, geometry preparation and the appropriate manufacturing and also aides in the evaluation and validation of the two previous phases of the proposed methodology which is great from the outlook of the optimization and accuracy point of view in product development and delivery. The prototype of the CBDM system presented in this work will help to develop confidence in the functioning of a CBDM system especially in the domain of AM and will serve an ideal framework for developing it better for the near future.

Future work can consist of an adapted version of the proposed methodology CBAM (Cloud Based Additive Manufacturing) with more optimized process for AM. Overall the proposed methodology based on the work performed in the case study offers: a simplified, optimized, collaborative and AM applied solution that could be used in industrial and academic contexts and further strengthens the idea of adoption of cloud based services in the manufacturing sector soon.

References

1. Belkadi, F., Gupta, R.K., Vlachou, E., Bernard, A., Mourtis, D.: Linking modular product structure to suppliers' selection through PLM approach: a frugal innovation perspective. In: Harik, R., Rivest, L., Bernard, A., Eynard, B., Bouras, A. (eds.) PLM 2016. IAICT, vol. 492, pp. 227–237. Springer, Cham (2016). https://doi.org/10.1007/978-3-319-54660-5_21
2. Boton, C., Rivest, L., Forgues, D., Jupp, J.: Comparing PLM and BIM from the product structure standpoint. In: Harik, R., Rivest, L., Bernard, A., Eynard, B., Bouras, A. (eds.) PLM 2016. IAICT, vol. 492, pp. 443–453. Springer, Cham (2016). https://doi.org/10.1007/978-3-319-54660-5_40
3. Abadi, D.: Data management in the cloud: limitations and opportunities. IEEE Data Eng. Bull 32(1), 3–12 (2009). 312
4. Wu, D., Schaefer, D., Rosen, D.: Cloud-based design and manufacturing systems: a social network analysis. In: Proceedings International Conference on Engineering Design (ICED 2013) (2013)
5. Schaefer, D., Thames, J., Wellman, R., Wu, D.: Distributed collaborative design and manufacture in the cloud-motivation, infrastructure, and education. In: ASEE (2012)
6. Ren, L., Zhang, L., Tao, F., Zhao, C., Chai, X., Zhao, X.: Cloud manufacturing: from concept to practice. Enterp. Inf. Syst. 9(2), 186–209 (2015)
7. Goto, S., Trolio, E., Yoshie, O., Tamaki, K.: Multi-party interactive visioneering workshop for smart connected products in global manufacturing industry considering PLM. In: Harik, R., Rivest, L., Bernard, A., Eynard, B., Bouras, A. (eds.) PLM 2016. IAICT, vol. 492, pp. 501–511. Springer, Cham (2016). https://doi.org/10.1007/978-3-319-54660-5_45
8. Wu, D., Rosen, D.W., Schaefer, D.: Cloud-based design and manufacturing: status and promise. In: Schaefer, D. (ed.) A Service-Oriented Product Development Paradigm for the 21st Century, pp. 1–24. Springer, London (2014). https://doi.org/10.1007/978-3-319-07398-9_1. ISBN 978-3-319-07398-9
9. Wu, D., Rosen, D.W., Wang, L., Schaefer, D.: Cloud-based manufacturing: old wine in new bottles?. In: Proceedings of the 47th CIRP Conference on Manufacturing Systems, Windsor, Canada, pp. 94–99 (2014)
10. Yoram, K., Moshe, S.: Design of reconfigurable manufacturing systems. J. Manufact. Syst. 29, 130–141 (2010)
11. Lechevalier, D., Narayanan, A., Rachuri, S., Foufou, S., Lee, Y.T.: Model-based engineering for the integration of manufacturing systems with advanced analytics. In: Harik, R., Rivest, L., Bernard, A., Eynard, B., Bouras, A. (eds.) PLM 2016. IAICT, vol. 492, pp. 146–157. Springer, Cham (2016). https://doi.org/10.1007/978-3-319-54660-5_14
12. Moones, E., Dafaoui, E.M., Abderrahman, E.M., Figay, N., Koudri, A.: Interoperability improvement in a collaborative dynamic manufacturing network. In: Harik, R., Rivest, L., Bernard, A., Eynard, B., Bouras, A. (eds.) PLM 2016. IAICT, vol. 492, pp. 286–295. Springer, Cham (2016). https://doi.org/10.1007/978-3-319-54660-5_26
13. Wua, D., Rosena, D., Wangb, L., Schaefer, D.: Cloud-based design and manufacturing: a new paradigm in digital manufacturing and design innovation. CAD 59(2015), 1–14 (2015)
14. Kim, D.B., Witherell, P., Lipman, R., Feng, S.C.: Streamlining the additive manufacturing digital spectrum: a systems approach. Addit. Manufact. 5, 20–30 (2015)

15. Fenves, S.: A core product model for representing design information. 2001 National Institute of Standards and Technology, Gaithersburg, MD (2001)
16. Li, Y., Linke, B.S., Voet, H., Falk, B., Schmitt, R., Lam, M.: Cost, sustainability and surface roughness quality–a comprehensive analysis of products made with personal 3D printers. CIRP J. Manufact. Sci. Technol. **16**, 1–11 (2017)
17. Thompson, M., et al.: Design for additive manufacturing: trends, opportunities, considerations, and constraints. CIRP Ann. Manuf. Technol. **65**(2), 737–760 (2016)

Flexible Best Fit Assembly of Large Aircraft Components. Airbus A350 XWB Case Study

Rebeca Arista[✉] and Hugo Falgarone

Airbus, 12, Rue Pasteur, 92150 Suresnes, France
{rebeca.arista,hugo.falgarone}@airbus.com

Abstract. The need for assembly parts and structures where the perfect fitting is not guaranteed due to manufacturing/assembly tolerances and/or the influence of several physical effects, i.e. gravity, is increasing constantly in different industrial sectors and in particular in the aerospace industry.

Some techniques have been developed to deal with it. In the field of large aero structures, custom-made parts using reverse engineering techniques are used to machine parts whose geometry requires to be customized for each produced aircraft. In the field of aircraft shells, a technique based on the characteristics of non-rigid components that can be slightly deformed to clear geometrical conditions by controlled forces to strain within its stress limits.

FITFLEX project exploit this last technique and was carried out by Airbus Group Innovations and Airbus. The objective is supporting the Airbus A350 XWB ramp-up and the current manual positioning process of the shell by force control, defining a measurement based assembly including a flexible best-fit system.

The case subject of study on FITFLEX project is the A350 XWB rear fuselage, a 14 m by 5 m side shell positioning process.

Keywords: Flexible best-fit · Assembly simulation · Flexible assembly
Tolerancing

1 Introduction

In the aerospace industry, large non-rigid and rigid components are assembled respecting defined functional requirements, such as geometric conditions or stress in the joints. This compliance to reach the final assembled part leads to non-value operations such as loads control, shimming, and rigging or ad-hoc parts manufacturing [1].

Non-rigid components can be slightly deformed to clear geometrical conditions by controlled forces to strain the part within its stress limits; these limits are more constrained for composite materials. This is the case of Airbus A350 XWB rear fuselage assembly, conformed by composite non-rigid shells held at the assembly station by an over constrained tooling to maintain its form.

Airbus A350 XWB benefits from being built with over 70% advanced materials; combining carbon composites (53%), titanium and modern aluminium alloys, to create a lighter and more cost-efficient aircraft while also reducing maintenance requirements.

© IFIP International Federation for Information Processing 2017
Published by Springer International Publishing AG 2017. All Rights Reserved
J. Ríos et al. (Eds.): PLM 2017, IFIP AICT 517, pp. 152–161, 2017.
https://doi.org/10.1007/978-3-319-72905-3_14

Physical models generated during conceptual and design phase of the aircraft, to analyze the stress propagation during flight and define the assembly requirements could be reused to describe the part behavior of flexible parts during assembly.

FITFLEX project was carried out by Airbus Group Innovations and Airbus, with the objective of supporting A350 XWB ramp-up and the current manual positioning process of the shell by force control, defining a measurement based assembly including a flexible best-fit system.

The novelty of this approach is to re-use the physical model description made during the aircraft design phase, to adjust a real part during its assembly with no need of FEA computation or expertise, solving an optimization problem to find the best part positioning, that fulfills the requirements while controls and minimizes the constrains introduced to the part.

This paper is structured into six sections. Section 2 presents the background research which leads to the work made on FITFLEX project. Section 3 shows the project methodology and the contributions to the existing process. Section 4 presents the case study used to validate the development. Results obtained in this use case are described in Sect. 5. Finally, Sect. 6 presents the conclusions of the work. For confidentiality reasons of the use case subject of this paper, images and results information do not reflect the exact reality.

2 Background Research Base of This Work

Research works performed in partnership between Airbus Group and ENS Cachan have been conducted for twenty years on several research topics, which are basis of the work performed in FITFLEX project. Best fit assembly considering behavior of components was studied using a helicopter door assembly use case [2]. Also, the assembly sequence influence on geometric deviations of parts was studied using a hydraulic system assembly case [3].

Research made in the frame of LOCOMACHS (Low Cost Manufacturing and Assembly of Composite and Hybrid Structures) EU project [4], on geometrical defects transfer in rigid and non-rigid components assemblies, lead to ANATOLE and ANATO-LEFLEX software tools developments [5], which are used in FITFLEX project to define the use case assembly process and criteria. Also in LOCOMACHS framework, research on assembly process generation for composite structures [6], and measurement geometric characterization of flexible assembly [7] supported the project development.

Additional research made by Airbus Defence and Space on MISTRAL project [1], using reverse engineering techniques to manufacture customized parts for each aircraft to cope with discrepancies remaining after a rigid best-fit process, helped to analyze the scope and benefits of a flexible best fit process usage.

3 Methodology

The methodology proposes considering only small component displacements and a linear system model; therefore we can rely on a linear static analysis to simulate forces and displacements, for each point of a discrete geometry [2].

In certain cases, linear behavior is not realistic enough, especially when there are clearances in the linkages and contact uncertainties. In these cases it is necessary to consider the assembly process as a nonlinear problem. Indeed, computing contact behavior involves using a nonlinear solver, and the use of finite element software is justified for the simulation. A prediction of gap between components is a case for which a non-linear model is needed [7, 8].

Research found in the bibliography [9–11], consider parts contact during assembly to simulate and find the best assembly process, generating flexible assembly simulations with rigid and non-rigid parts by using a Finite Element Analysis (FEA) with computation tools (i.e. ABAQUS-SIMULIA by Dassault Systèmes).

In order to avoid the need of FEA computation and be able to have a quick and light computation on a shop floor tool, we approach the assembly process during the parts positioning stage, before the contact phase between the parts for its final assembly. Therefore, a reduced stiffness matrix of the part can be used as sensitivity matrix for computation of the optimal part positioning.

Thanks to the knowledge of the sensitivity matrix and assembly criteria, an optimization on the part positioning can be made within boundaries of the tolerance regions [12]. The next points describe the optimization problem solved using developed mathematical algorithms, how the sensitivity matrix is generated, and the process to follow in order to obtain the part optimal positioning, through a flexible best fit process for each aircraft.

3.1 Linear System and Optimization Problem

The mathematical method used relies on a linear system equation solving, using a sensitivity matrix that describes the system behavior. The equations are solved inside an optimization problem, to obtain the best setting of the component to fulfill the imposed characteristic requirements.

To describe the problem, we define the series of required characteristics as C_i, that need to be fulfilled within a given range during the assembly process, in order to reach the final assembled part functional requirement. These characteristics can be either displacements, on contact or non-contact points, or forces on contact points.

$$C_i \in \left[C_{i,min}, C_{i,max} \right] \forall i = (1, \infty) \tag{1}$$

We define positioning contact points as D_j, in which adjustable imposed displacements can be made within limits (small displacement assumption) (Fig. 1).

$$D_j \in \left[D_{j,min}, D_{j,max} \right] \forall j = (1, \infty) \tag{2}$$

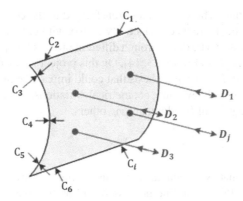

Fig. 1. Problem description

Describing the behavior of the assembly as a multi-input/multi-output linear function depending on the displacement of the positioning contact points, the component characteristics and the assembly process defined, we describe:

$$\delta C_i = f\left(\delta D_j\right) \tag{3}$$

Given the characteristics initial state $C_{i,init}$, the best fit problem is defined as: to find δD_j so that

$$C_{i,init} - \delta C_i \in \left[C_{i,min}, C_{i,max}\right] \qquad \forall i = (1, \infty) \tag{4}$$

The function f is defined by the sensitivity matrix or behavior model, described next point.

3.2   Sensitivity Matrix

The sensitivity matrix or behavior model of the part can be generated following different methods (i.e. empirical, mathematical). In our case, we reused the Finite Element Model (FEM) created by Airbus Stress Department, used for full aircraft flight simulation during the aircraft design phase.

This FEM mesh needs to be split into section or component meshes, to keep only the corresponding part of the aircraft belonging to the case of study. As it was designed to analyze large in-flight loads and displacements, one task of the project will be validating its behavior on small displacements, which will be the case during the part assembly positioning.

On a second step, the mesh needs to be updated to the exact assembly condition of the assembly process stage of the case study. This means that the reused mesh might not be compliant to the real part status on assembly process stage under study.

The system characteristics (i.e. degrees of freedom) are defined as points in the part CAD model, kinematic links of the jig to the part, requirements on the part and degrees of freedom in each point. These points are transformed to the corresponding nodes of the FEM model, to extract a reduced sensitivity matrix with only the points of interest.

This CAD-CAE link can be done through different process (i.e. point to closest node or point to set of neighbor nodes) [5, 13, 14]. On this project we made the link by point to closest node method. Further hypothesis that could impact the model are, the manufactured composite material deviation, geometrical variations, jigs knowledge on operation direction and degrees of freedom, among others.

3.3 Process

Once the sensitivity matrix is generated on an off-line process as described in the previous point, the following on-line process would be followed at the shopfloor for each Manufacturing Serial Number (MSN) or individual aircraft:

1. Load assembly definition and sensitivity matrix (K on Eq. 5) of the case of use in FITFLEX software interface.
2. Get from the measurement system (i.e. laser tracker) and jig force sensors in the kinematic links, the initial state of the part position and forces, and import the values (C_i and F on Eq. 5).
3. Execute the optimization mathematic algorithm, solving the matrix system to obtain D_j:

$$[K]\begin{bmatrix} C_i \\ D_j \end{bmatrix} = \begin{bmatrix} 0 \\ F \end{bmatrix} \tag{5}$$

making as first step a function minimization without constrains and a second step considering the tolerance domains.

A so called virtual test is also possible to generate, simulating the result of the part constrains and requirements when making a set of displacements in the jig actuators.

4   Use Case

The case subject of study on FITFLEX project is the A350 XWB rear fuselage Section 16 assembly, carried out at Airbus facilities in Hamburg, Germany. This assembly process comprises four shells and one grid floor; all made from carbon fiber reinforced plastic material (CFRP). Figure 2 shows the five components during assembly process, conforming Section 16. The project was focused only in the left side shell positioning process.

The CFRP material has stronger restrictions on gaps at interfaces. This is the reason why a specific jig was designed for this parts positioning, giving the possibility to adapt the form of the part by introducing small constrains.

The Left Side Shell (LSS) have approximate 14 meters long and 5 meters of cord on the frontal frame, and it is positioned at the assembly station by 12 hoisting points, that can generate a rigid body translation and rotation to the part or that can be independently

Fig. 2. Image of Airbus A350 XWB rear fuselage Section 16 at the assembly station

activated, moving each actuator at a time on a flexible movement. These hoisting points are the positioning control points of our problem definition, as shown on the Fig. 3. The requirement points are position characteristics, in the points of the part contour and along selected frames, and force characteristics, at the actuators location.

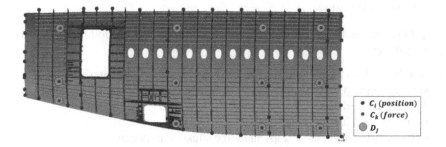

Fig. 3. Variables defined for the Left side shell case study

The system characteristics (i.e. degrees of freedom) are defined as points in the CAD, mapped to the corresponding nodes of the FEM model, to extract a reduced stiffness matrix, behavior model of our system. This process is made only one time on a preparation phase, and for this project it was made using ANATOLE and ABAQUS tools [5].

On the shop floor, for each MSN Left Side Shell positioning process, FITFLEX software will be executed loading the assembly definition and behavior model on a new project. Figure 4 shows the work flow of the software interface, being the first image the new project generated.

After measuring the initial forces and initial position of the part at the assembly station, the values are imported using an excel template file, showing in the software interface the state of compliance of the requirements using a color code, which can be seen on Fig. 4 second image. Then, an optimization function should be executed, to obtaining the rigid body move and flexible move that should be applied on the jig actuators to get a LSS position compliant to the requirements, shown on Fig. 4 third image.

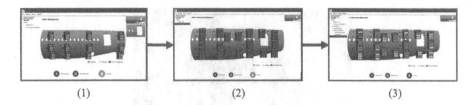

|(1)|(2)|(3)|

Fig. 4. FITFLEX software workflow (Color figure online)

5   Results and Discussion

The use case objective was to introduce a behavior model that could help to find more quickly a convenient situation for the shell according to gaps specifications and force limitation on actuators. As presented in the previous chapter, our approach is based on a FEM model and on the capture of an initial state with force and dimensional data. The validation of FITFLEX approach on the use case is proposed through an overall process validation and justifications based on elementary tests.

5.1   Process Validation

Using FITFLEX solution with the appropriate model loaded, the following validation has been done:

1. Introduce a LSS panel on the jig (without any specific conditions)
2. Measure target points position and force in actuators (to obtain initial state)
3. By using FIFLEX:
   - Introduce values of initial state
   - Get an overall status on gaps and force situation to targets
   - Run optimization
   - Identify rigid movement + smaller flexible displacement of actuators
   - Get an overall status of final state where all requirements are met (Gap and force).
4. Execute displacement on actuators (rigid + flexible).

This process with FITFLEX is almost immediate compared to current iterative and manual setting process. However, even if the predicted final situation deviates from the final real situation in meeting all requirements, a second FITFLEX optimization can be made using the first setting result as a new initial state, leading to an acceptable situation.

5.2   Part Geometrical Variability

A part geometrical deviation from its nominal geometry can be caused by several reasons (i.e. manufacturing process). A geometrical variability analysis was made on the LSS, to assess an order of magnitude of the part variability, as well as a process quality indicator for the behavior model to comply with, using historical measurements of several MSN.

5.3 MSN Experiences versus Behavior Model Simulations

Two Measurement Campaigns were carried out in different MSN, to analyze the real LSS behavior on interface edge points. The complete set of points were measured during 12 load cases (activating each one of the 12 jig actuators for each load case), recording the actuators displacements and initial-final force.

The load cases were simulated with several boundary condition options, and the results were compared to the measurement campaign experience, analyzing:

- the FEM model used from Airbus Design Office (definition, usability and simplification)
- Simulation vs MSN global results, identifying a correct behavior (within the quality indicator given by the LSS geometrical variability) and correct definition of simulation conditions.

In a real MSN positioning process of the LSS, after the LSS is located in datum position on the station, the initial state of the position requirements have deviations in the order of centimeters on all directions. From this initial state, the displacements that have to be applied on each actuator are also in the order of magnitude of centimeters in the corresponding actuator degree of freedom. In this initial state, after simulating the displacements applied on the actuators, the standard deviation between the experiences versus simulation results is in the order of millimeters.

On following loops for the real MSN positioning, the requirements deviations are smaller (order of millimeters). Simulating the real displacements made on these loops (also in the order of millimeters), the experiences versus simulation standard deviation is lower than half of a millimeter.

The prediction model shows therefore consistent results for all tested MSN, meaning also this model is not a dedicated model for one MSN. The simulation results shown a force deviation compared to the experiences, and possible causes are under investigation: the decimal numbers considered on linear equation solver, the point where the force is measured vs. point defined on the simulation, and elasticity on the kinematic links.

5.4 Optimizations

Analyzing the result of these simulations, and in order to maintain the problem within the small displacement assumption and system linearity, to calculate the optimum actuator displacements, we incorporated as first step a rigid body move, to minimize the deviations without introducing any constrains, and as second step, use a flexible body move best fit.

Several optimization scenarios can be generated varying weight on overall gaps (requirements), overall forces, gaps on each point independently (i.e. to give priority to interface points), or force on each actuator independently. An optimization final test in the assembly station was not possible due to ramp-up constrains, but optimization show promising results.

6   Conclusion

In this paper, a new approach for a flexible best fit positioning of parts to respect defined functional requirements, was presented. Its originality resides on the re-use of a physical model description made during aircraft design phase to adjust a real part during its assembly, considering a system linear behavior within small displacements.

The tool developed for shop floor usage need no FEA computation, solving an optimization problem in short time to find the best part positioning, that fulfills the requirements while controls and minimizes the constrains introduced to the part.

The new solution was applied to a use case (left side shell of A350 XWB rear fuselage) to evaluate the developments and their implementation under industrial conditions. Different aircrafts historical records were used to test and validate the developed applications, the prediction model shown consistent results for all tested MSN and optimization simulations shown promising results. Although the results were correct and demonstrated the suitability of the developments, additional testing of optimization algorithms on real part positioning is needed to validate full capabilities.

When compare to the current approach, the new flexible best fit could conduct to an increase on control of constrains introduced to the part, reduced positioning time for assembly, and creates new possibilities for new assembly process with flexible jigs usage to comply with requirements while controlling constrains.

A future work is to test and adapt the developed applications to a multi-part positioning problem. This is a different approach to the one used in this work, as it would consider overall assembly deviations and tolerance zones, to achieve the full part compliance to the ultimate requirement of the assembled part.

Acknowledgment.   FITFLEX project was partially funded by LOCOMACHS EU project. Authors want to thank to their colleagues from Airbus Hamburg, IMACS and DPS for their contributions and kind collaboration.

References

1. Gomez, A., Olmos, V., Racero, J., Rios, J., Arista, R., Mas, F.: Development based on reverse engineering to manufacture aircraft custom-made parts. Int. J. Mechatron. Manuf. Syst. **10**(1), 40–58 (2017)
2. Chevassus, N., et al.: A new approach for best fit assembly based on the behavior of components. SAE Technical Paper (2006)
3. Mounaud, M., Thiébaut, F., Bourdet, P., Falgarone, H., Chevassus, N.: Assembly sequence influence on geometric deviations of compliant parts. Int. J. Prod. Res. **49**(4), 1021–1043 (2011)
4. LOCOMACHS: LOw COst Manufacturing and Assembly of Composite and Hybrid Structures. http://www.locomachs.eu/. Accessed May 2017
5. Falgarone, H., Thiébaut, F., Coloos, J., Mathieu, L.: Variation simulation during assembly of non-rigid components. Realistic assembly simulation with ANATOLEFLEX software. In: 14th CIRP CAT 2016 - CIRP Conference on Computer Aided Tolerancing (2016)
6. Andolfatto, L.: Assistance à l'élaboration de gammes d'assemblage innovantes de structures composites. Autre. École normale supérieure de Cachan - ENS Cachan (2013)

7. Lacroix, C.: Caractérisation géométrique des assemblages flexibles par la mesure. Autre. École normale supérieure de Cachan - ENS Cachan, Français (2015)
8. Liu, G., Huan, H., Ke, Y.: Study on analysis and prediction of riveting assembly variation of aircraft fuselage panel. Int. J. Adv. Manuf. Technol. **75**(5–8), 991–1003 (2014)
9. Ghandi, S., Masehian, E.: Assembly sequence planning of rigid and flexible parts. J. Manuf. Syst. **36**, 128–146 (2015)
10. Gouyou, D., Ledoux, Y., Teissandier, D., et al.: Tolerance analysis of overconstrained and flexible assemblies by polytopes and finite element computations: application to a flange. Res. Eng. Des. **28**, 1–12 (2017)
11. Cheng, H., Li, Y., Zhang, K.F., Mu, W.Q., Liu, B.F.: Variation modeling of aeronautical thin-walled structures with multi-state riveting. J. Manuf. Syst. **30**(2), 101–115 (2011)
12. Liao, X., Wang, G.G.: Simultaneous optimization of fixture and joint positions for non-rigid sheet metal assembly. Int. J. Adv. Manuf. Technol. **36**(3–4), 386–394 (2008)
13. Paroissien, E., Sartor, M., Huet, J., Lachaud, F.: Hybrid (bolted/bonded) joints applied to aeronautic parts: analytical two-dimensional model of a single-lap joint. J. Aircr. **4**(2), 573–582 (2007)
14. Gonze, A.P., Verstuyft, J.: Associative sizing of aeronautical structures from catia v5 to samcef: applications to static and bird impact analyses. In: 9th SAMTECH Users Conference (2005)

An Integrated Framework for Simulation and Analysis of Manual Assembly Process

Kyung-Hee Lee[1], Jong Youl Lee[2], Kyoung-Yun Kim[2], Sang-Do Noh[1(✉)],
Sung-Jun Kang[3], and Doo-Myun Lee[3]

[1] Department of Industrial Engineering, SungKyunKwan University, 300 Cheoncheon-dong,
Suwon, Gyeonggi-do 400-746, Korea
{schnlui,sdnoh}@skku.edu
[2] Department of Industrial and Systems Engineering, Wayne State University, 4815 Fourth St.,
Detroit, MI 48202, USA
{jong.youl.lee,kykim}@wayne.edu
[3] 675-3 84B, Gojin-dong, Namdong-du, Incheon-si, South Korea
{ksj98364002,ldm}@segos.com

Abstract. This research aims to build an integrated framework to analyze the production flow efficiency (in terms of worker utilization) of the manual machine component assembly process. Problems related to spontaneous decision making among the workers in the manual assembly processes which cause inconsistency in the manufacturing speed, productivity, and quality. Often it is difficult to simulate all the possible situations to reduce such inconsistencies. This study aims to suggest an alternative way by introducing a prediction framework that is integrated with Modeling and Simulation (M&S) and a CART algorithm. M&S is used to create different scenarios out of the original layout for comparison. The CART algorithm is utilized to extract decision rules from the simulation results. These decision rules provide an understanding of patterns that affect workers' utilization rate. The research goal is to adopt the rules on the simulation models, and to offer guidelines on improved alternatives for building simulation models of manual assembly process.

Keywords: Manual assembly · Modeling and simulation · Production flow
Integrated simulation · Analysis framework · Decision rule

1 Introduction

Manufacturing industries, in modern days, have been flourished with advanced technology on robotics and automation in production. However, manual assembly still takes a notable proportion in todays' industries and its manufacturing process. Due to difficult assemblage of unevenly shaped parts and the needs of exquisite work, many problems arise from the spontaneous decision making by workers during the assembly process [1]. This problem leads to defective products, irregular quality, fluctuations in productivity and confusion at the work site by the unorganized assembly order. The most prominent problem this research focuses on is the unorganized decision making process among

© IFIP International Federation for Information Processing 2017
Published by Springer International Publishing AG 2017. All Rights Reserved
J. Ríos et al. (Eds.): PLM 2017, IFIP AICT 517, pp. 162–173, 2017.
https://doi.org/10.1007/978-3-319-72905-3_15

workers on the shop floor. [2]. The current manual assembly process, a worker proceeds defective check by spreading the assembled parts before the next assembly process; however, another worker later also proceeds defective check with the same routine. This overlap of the same process reduces productivity and working speed. To prevent such problems the unnecessary double-check of defectiveness should be avoided. Rather than checking defectiveness on each phase. Checking at the final point of assembly can be one of multiple recommended alternatives. To gauge these problems, this research constructs an integrated decision support framework to analyze the production flow efficiency (in terms of worker utilization) of the manual assembly process. The integrated decision support framework works on the configuration level. An alternative way is by introducing a prediction framework, which is based on the simulation data of the assembly process. A CART algorithm that is utilized to extract decision rules from the QUEST simulation. These decision rules provide an opportunity to understand patterns that effect the workers' utilization rate. With the presented case study, we confirm that the presented framework provides comprehensive understanding of a wide number of variables. From total required time, to inefficient factors such as uneven labor utilization occurred during the manual assembly process. That also reflects those factors to simulation, so that more precise and accurate prediction within the decision making guidelines are enabled on the manual assembly shop floor.

2 Background

Shop floor operation can be reconfigured and experimented in practice, however, this can be too expensive, or impractical to do in the system it represents. In a broader sense, simulation is a tool to evaluate the performance of a system, existing or proposed, under different configurations of interest and over long periods of real time [4]. Simulation is defined as techniques of initiating the behavior of a situation or system by means of an analogous situation, model or apparatus, either to gain information conveniently or to personnel [5]. As to evaluate the performance of a system existing or proposed, under different configurations of interest and over long periods of real time. Simulation is the methodology robust enough to systematically examine the role and impact of product complexity and other key variables on factory performance. This is especially true because simulation models can capture many of the requirements and attributes of real life problems that are difficult to consider using analytical model for the layout optimization problems. Computer simulation can provide an operational assessment of the performance objectives and can be examined to see if achieving those objectives is possible through modification to the existing facility.

There are many researches working on solving problems related to manual assembly. Many research suggests Modeling and Simulation (M&S) as a methodology; however, there is not much progress in adopting more than two research methodology with the case. Previous studies mainly focused on variation in productivity due to manual work process design. One of the studies [5] presents an application of simulation modelling within a facility layout of a handwork area. This study is to analyze and optimize the production flow efficiency at the handwork area using QUEST simulation analysis. To address the problem, simulation modelling is employed. Simulation modeling is used in this research since it allows verification of the flow design without having to rearrange the actual physical layout. The outcomes of the simulation model can be used as benchmarks for the efficiency of the new layout. Another study [6] is on problem detection in production lines using simulation. It suggests changing production lines and balancing work efficiency for improving productivity. The study is confined to comparing productivity due to different labor allocation on each machine. Moreover, the study includes manual assembly lines but it only reflects on inefficiency during manual assembly process.

3 Model Construction for the Integrated Simulation and Analysis Framework

Before building simulation models. We design a framework for creating simulation models of the manual assembly process. This step is essential since the given manual assembly has many variables related to labors on the shop floor and many decision variables to decide which phase of work to proceed, when to start/switch work and to move the finished parts to the next procedure. The unorganized decision process among labors occurs significantly different work scenarios even though they proceed the same assembly process under the same work manual, and work condition [7].

3.1 General Model Construction Process

The general model construction process for modeling & simulation applied in manual assembly process follows the steps below (Fig. 1):

1. *Define the current system and project objective:* one of the objectives of this project is to optimize labor utilization in a manual assembly shop floor. Developing the thought process, we considered the parameters that have some effects on simulation results. The machines used for the assembly procedure were manually operated. Moreover, no automated material handling system was adopted for shop floor logistics, the material movement was performed by the labors using trolleys. As the machines' production rate, material handling time, etc., were all dependent on the labor deployed on each machine, the effect of the labor element on the system got bigger. As the machines' production rate, material handling time, etc., are all dependent to the labor deployed on each machine, the effect of the labor element on the simulation model gets bigger.
2. *Data collection:* for data collection the known and unknown parameters were specified. The known parameters include the machine and labor specifications, raw material and final product specifications. While the unknown parameters include the utilization time of machines and labors, the idle times for each labor and machines, the average distance travelled by each labor per day.
3. *Defining decision variables:* the labor utilization parameter depends on the state times (specifically idle time) and the total working time. The objective was not only to increase each labor utilization, but also to have uniform distribution in labor

utilization. The total working time for each labor is constant, (10.5 h in this case), the only variable is the idle time. The idle time of each labor varies with the amount of work allocated to the labor. The more the work, the less the idle time. But this is not always the optimal solution. High utilization of one worker may lead to low utilization of other workers, creating imbalance in the system. Thus, the decision variables were; idle time and labor utilization (percentage as well as its distribution).

4. *Pre-requisites for simulation model:* before preparing the simulation model, a layout of the existing system was prepared. Which depicted the machine placements, labor placements, the raw material source, finished products sink and buffer storages. A spaghetti diagram was constructed to map the material flow and the labor movement. This layout was then used as a reference to create the simulation model.

5. *Preparation of existing system simulation model:* the existing system simulation model was constructed. This model generated raw data which was refined and then classified into relevant and non-relevant data. The relevant data in this case was the labor utilization percentage, state times of the each labor, distance travelled by each worker, number of assemblies performed, production rate of the machines. This data was analyzed and the results were documented.

6. *Modifying the existing model:* the labor utilization was not uniform, thus modifications were performed to improve the existing model. The aim of the modification was to create more simulation models of the system by allocating workers to various tasks, discretely or simultaneously. The labor allocations were performed by considering all possible and feasible permutations and combinations.

7. *Data analysis:* this relevant data was then analyzed and the results were displayed. The models with uniform distribution of utilization were separated. The models with maximum production were selected to be optimal.

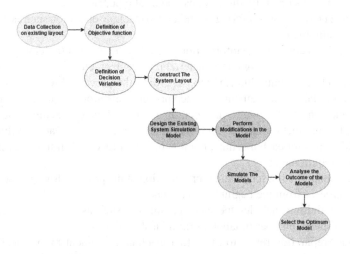

Fig. 1. Process map for shop floor simulation model construction

3.2 Simulation Scenario Generation

To create meaningful and realistic simulation models, we designed a simulation scenario based on the process as illustrated in Fig. 2. This formal process helps by building simulation scenarios that are based on a previous model. It increases a chance to assuage previous problems and stepping forward to optimal scenario. The algorithm consists of 19 factors.

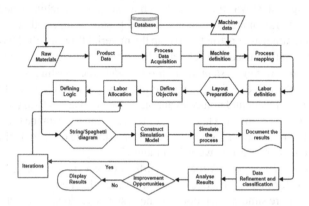

Fig. 2. Simulation scenario generation process

1. Database contains historical data of machines, parts, raw materials, labor, manu-facturing process, etc.
2. Raw Material Data is the information of the raw material for producing the final product such as quantity, dimensions, material type, etc.
3. Machine Data contains information related to machine operation such as cycle time, labor requirement, etc.
4. Product Data contains the information related to the product (assembly or sub-part assembly), like, the design, raw material requirement, etc.
5. Process Data contains Information, regarding the process flow, process types in shop floor, labor requirements for each process, rejection rate for each machine.
6. Machine definition provides information about the type of machines used in shop floor, the production rate of each machine, process(es) on each machine, labor specifications for each machine, number of parts processed simultaneously, buffer storage requirements.
7. Process mapping is a schematic representation of the process flow and the elements in the process from the beginning to the end.
8. Labor Definition includes the labor parameters such as labor movement speed, rotation speed, number of labor working in shop floor.
9. Layout Preparation refers to the actual machine placement by physical distance between machines, material handling systems (if any), labor placements, buffer stocks, source of raw material, sink of finished products.
10. Labor Allocation refers to Assignments of the labor to respective machine(s). It also assures that every worker is assigned and no worker is free of work.

11. Defining logic is one of the most important element. Logics are specified with which the labor works in the system. Moreover, logics are also specified for the process each machine performs; the logics may include sequence of operation, time offset for a machine to start working, operation time for elements in the system.

12. String/Spaghetti Diagram represents the material flow in the system. It also depicts the labor movement, amount of rework.

13. Prepare simulation model, Simulation model is the replication of the physical system. Simulation models are useful when testing plans, modifications without physically changing the actual object.

14. Define objectives and specifying objectives is very important to get expected outcome from simulation. The outcomes depend on decision variables due to your objectives.

15. Simulate the process, Each Simulation model will generate data. This obtained data are used as a standard when planning for designing next simulation scenario.

16. Data collection of the raw data is carried out and documented for extracting the specific data.

17. Data refinement & classification, the data is refined, and those meaningful data are classified according to the objectives. For example, labor utilization, and labor idle time if you are focused on labor efficiency.

18. Result Analysis is conducted to see if there's any hindrance in the production flow and labor utilization. If there is any chance of improvement, the process is iterated by changing the parameters related to the hindrance (Refer to Table 2).

19. Display Result records and displays the result which showcases the decision variables, the number of iterations required to attain optimization and the optimization values.

3.3   CART Algorithm Rule Extraction

In this paper, we employ a Decision Tree algorithm for data classification and rule extraction from the QUEST simulation dataset. A decision tree is a hierarchical structure of combination of nodes and links. Each node has a predictive condition and a link represents a value of each condition. In our research, Classification and Regression Trees (CART) algorithm is used. The CART is a nonparametric decision tree algorithm that used to generate regression tree or classification, depends on whether the response variable is continuous or categorical. By using surrogate splits, CART can handle missing values of the dataset. The data is obtained by the QUEST simulation. The following equation is a basic concept of the CART algorithm.

$$Y_p = \bar{r}(X_t) = \left[r(X_t, \lambda, D)\right],$$

where, Y_p = final predicted value, $\bar{r}$ = average regression function, X_t = observation from test set, λ = random parameter of partition, D = Total data.

By using this equation, we made up a model for accurate prediction of the utilization for each labor. X_t is the value from the test set which is from dataset D. λ is a random parameter of partition, which represents m values from the n variables in the test set, where $m < n$. Bootstrap aggregating is a common method in the decision tree that machine learning ensemble meta-algorithm devised to ameliorate both accuracy and stability of the algorithm. A random sample of m predictors is chosen as split candidates from the full set of n predictors while constructing the decision trees. The split should use one of those m predictors. The output of expected values is given as the final predicted value. The predicted value is Y, a leaf node of each branch of the tree. The following section describes a case study and how the simulation data are generated and analyzed with the CART algorithm.

4   Case Study: Slide Rail Assembly Process Simulation and Analysis

The case study is conducted on the slide rail assembly process. To build simulation models with different scenarios, our research team gathered data for simulation and analyzed present condition of both physical layout of the slide rail assembly line as well as refining the collected data to a certain type of form process flow of slide rail assembly, and process cycle time for building simulation models. The entire assembly process is segmented into modules that have each function on individual levels. By the data collected from the physical slide rail assembly line, a virtual factory similar with the real factory is constructed using QUEST. The simulation model is modified on the module level to create various scenarios on the work shop. The scenarios constructed with this process is used to compare and see if there's any improvement with the modi-fication. In order to generate different scenarios out of the original model, we decided independent variables and dependent variables to thoughtfully compare each model. Independent variables are; simulation time, assembly inputs, pre-set cycle times and layout that are already given.

4.1   Slide Rail Manufacturing Shop Floor

The assembly requires nine steps of the production process in order to produce one finished slide rail. There are twelve workers deployed on the shop floor. While eleven workers assemble the slide rails, the one proceeds sub-part assembly and takes a charge of the shop floor inflow logistics. Each worker decides whether to do inflow logistics, preparation, and packaging in idle time. However, decision making in the manual

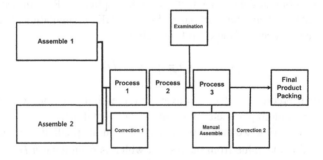

Fig. 3. Process flow of slide rail assembly

assembly process based on the worker's subjective observation leads to disorganization, confusion, and fluctuation in both quality and productivity on the work shop.

In order to organize scenarios in simulation, the process flow is thoughtfully divided into nine main parts as shown on Fig. 3. Those segmented module units are analyzed to find out which data should be independent variables and which should be dependent variables. Figure 4 Shows the virtual model of the shop floor and Table 1 includes the cycle time of the nine phases of the job shop, which is obtained from the QUEST Current Run Summary Report.

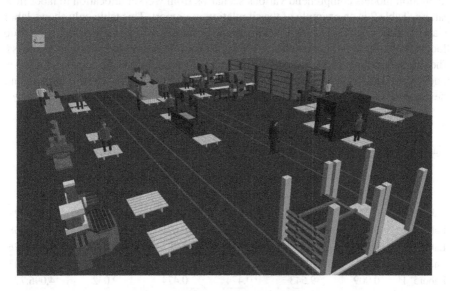

Fig. 4. Virtual model of the shop floor

Table 1. Cycle time of the slide rail assembly

	Phase of order		Cycle time per unit	
1	Part 1 – Part 2	Pre-work 1	8 s	33 s
		Part 1 – Part 2 assembly	25 s	
2	Part 1 – Part 2 – Part 3	Pre-work 2	8 s	33 s
		Part 1 – Part 2 – Part 3 assembly	25 s	
3	Correction 1		20 s	
4	Process 1		8 s	
5	Process 2		8 s	
6	Examination		15 s	
7	Process 3		25 s	
8	Sub-part assembly		12 s	
9	Correction 2		20 s	

4.2   QUEST Simulation Results

To get the best result and compare as many scenarios as possible, our research team created 50 different simulation models out of the original model. First, we simulated the original model. In the simulation run report, we found that there are multiple values indicating inefficiencies in the process. For example, we assumed that uneven values in the labor report section refer to unfairly distributed work. By modifying work distribution in the simulation model, we wanted to see if there was any improvement. The 50 simulation models comprehend various scenarios from worker allocation to labor flow pattern. Table 2 is an example of the simulation run report. This table only shows labor analysis section. In Table 2, 'Idle' indicates idle time of each labor allocated in the shop floor and , 'Utilization' indicated how efficiently each labor is used in the whole process. The simulation run report is used to see if there's any hindrance in the current simulation model's production flow and labor utilization. If there is any chance of improvement, the process is iterated by changing the parameters related to the hindrance.

Table 2. Labor analysis by QUEST Current Run Report

Name	State times				Utilization (%)	Distance travelled
	Idle	Idle - parked	Busy - loaded travel	Busy – empty travel		
Labor1_1	0.003	6.986	1.065	2.445	33.432	15,164,928
Labor2_1	0.02	9.219	0.631	0.631	12.016	5,450,458
Labor3_1	0.019	4.033	2.725	3.723	61.412	27,856,676
Labor4_1	0.009	9.541	0.475	0.475	9.044	4,102,443
Labor5_1	0.009	9.543	0.474	0.474	9.032	4,096,778
Labor6_1	0.02	9.332	0.574	0.574	10.935	4,960,183
Labor7_1	0.019	9.589	0.446	0.446	8.495	3,853,170
Labor8_1	0.009	9.613	0.439	0.439	8.361	3,792,360
Labor9_1	0.009	9.532	0.479	0.479	9.129	4,140,884
Labor10_1	0.114	7.019	1.684	1.684	32.071	14,547,564
Labor11_1	0.168	5.606	2.106	2.62	45.009	20,416,178
Labor12_1	0.327	9.336	0.418	0.418	7.969	3,614,694

4.3   Labor Utilization Prediction and Rule Extraction

Table 3 shows the regression rules that are extracted by the Classification and Regression Trees (CART) algorithm. In this study, the CART algorithm is utilized to understand the patterns of factors that affect workers' utilization. Labor utilization is assessed from labor idle, idle-parked, busy-loaded travel, busy empty travel and so forth. The entire assembly process via the equipment and the shop floor logistics are performed by labor. The simulation result elements related to labor, such as machines and parts processed in each phase of the assembly, are affected by the labor utilization. Thus, the shop floor performance (assessed with the elements' utilization, idle, busy-processing, average process time, number of products, average cycle time, production rate, average part residence time etc.) depend on labor utilization. Obtaining evenly distributed labor utilization indicates the entire process is well organized and has less likelihood for having a bottleneck problem.

Table 3. Rule examples extracted from QUEST simulation

Labor (worker)	Rule condition	MSE	Utilization
1	Labor1_1_Busy_Empty Travel < 3.1365, Machine10_1_Idle < 5.2265	25.00	33.34
	Labor1_1_Busy_Empty Travel < 3.1365, Machine10_1_Idle > 5.2265		8.27
	Labor1_1_Busy_Empty Travel > 3.1365		69.81
2	Labor2_1_Idle_Parked < 7.161	0.22	60.33
	Labor2_1_Idle_Parked > 7.161, Labor2_1_Busy_Loaded Travel > 0.8675		26.22
	Labor2_1_Idle_Parked > 7.161, Labor2_1_Busy_Loaded Travel < 0.8675		12.02
4	Labor4_1_Busy_Loaded Travel < 1.443, Labor4_1_Idle_Parked < 3.8435	16.804	0.00
	Labor4_1_Busy_Loaded Travel < 1.443, Labor4_1_Idle_Parked > 3.8435		10.42
	Labor4_1_Busy_Loaded Travel > 1.443		62.65
6	Labor6_1_Busy_Loaded Travel < 0.786, Labor6_1_Idle_Parked < 9.1425	19.067	1.594
	Labor6_1_Busy_Loaded Travel < 0.786, Labor6_1_Idle_Parked > 9.1425		10.630
	Labor6_1_Busy_Loaded Travel > 0.786, Labor7_1_Idle_Parked < 7.7495		26.620
	Labor6_1_Busy_Loaded Travel > 0.786, Labor7_1_Idle_Parked > 7.7495		46.390
12	Labor12_1_Idle_Parked Travel < 7.8025, Labor12_1_Idle_Parked < 7.144	1.96	36.320
	Labor12_1_Idle_Parked Travel < 7.8025, Labor12_1_Idle_Parked > 7.144		27.950
	Labor12_1_Idle_Parked Travel > 7.8025, Labor12_1_Busy_Loaded Travel < 0.637		7.937
	Labor12_1_Idle_Parked Travel > 7.8025, Labor12_1_Busy_Loaded Travel < 0.637		18.070

The parameters of the data are selected from the QUEST simulation dataset based on the potential factors which can affect the utilization of each labor. Those parameters are extracted from machine, labor and sink data, which seems highly related to the utilization of each labor. In the machine data, the following data features are included: 'idle time,' 'busy processing time,' 'blocked unload block time,' 'blocked wait block time,' 'average process time,' 'added parts,' 'the number of products,' 'average cycle

172 K.-H. Lee et al.

time,' 'production rate,' 'average part residence time,' and 'machine utilization'. Also, in the labor data, 'idle time', 'parked idle time', 'busy loaded travel time', 'busy empty travel time', 'the number of parts added', 'distance travelled', and 'utilization of labor'. 'Finished parts' parameter is selected from the sink data. Before implementing the CART algorithm, we clean and find out missing data in the preprocessing step. Then CART is applied to extract the decision rules (i.e., regression trees) for each labor. The objective of the regression model is to minimize Mean Squared Error (MSE) of the model output.

$$MSE = \frac{1}{n} \sum_{i=1}^{n} \left(y_i - f(y_i) \right)^2$$

y_i = actual value, $f(y_i)$ = model prediction value, n = number of observations.

Table 3, shows five extracted decision rule examples, which have relatively low MSE among the twelve labors. Based on the CART result, the rule condition and predicted utilization of each labor is derived. These rules provide various information. For example, the utilization of Labor 2 is related to 'parked idle time' and 'busy loaded travel time'. For Labor 6, it is interesting to know that the utilization of Labor 6 is related to 'busy loaded travel time' of Labor 6, 'parked idle time' of Labor 6, as well as 'parked idle time' of Labor 7. The predicted utilization of selected labors (workers) is also indicated. The right column shows the predicted labor utilization when the corresponding rule condition is satisfied.

5 Conclusions

This paper presents a concept of the integrated simulation and analysis framework for slide rail assembly process. Simulation model construction and scenario generation process were used to analyze the manual assembly process and productivity. The QUEST simulation provided a comprehensive analysis of labor utilization. The CART analysis from the QUEST Current Run Report enhanced the simulation by providing the prediction capability and rule pattern analysis. In the future research, the team will continue to validate the prediction algorithm to enhance with random forest algorithm. Also, the framework concept will be implemented as a unified modeling and simulation research environment.

Acknowledgement. This research was supported by grants from BK21 Research & HRD Team for Smart Factory Design, Operation and Optimization based on Industrial Data Analytics (Program No.: 22A20154613485), and WC300 Project for Smart Rail & Smart Manufacturing System Development (Program No.: S2367439). These supports are gratefully acknowledged.

References

1. Bäckstrand, G., De Vin, L. J., Högberg, D., Case, K.: Attention, interpreting, decision-making and acting in manual assembly. In: Innovations in Manufacturing (2006)
2. Gonzalez, C., Lerch, J.F., Lebiere, C.: Instance-based learning in dynamic decision making. Cogn. Sci. **27**(4), 591–635 (2003)
3. Frazzon, E.M., Albrecht, A., Hurtado, P.A.: Simulation-based optimization for the integrated scheduling of production and logistic systems. IFAC-PapersOnLine **49**(12), 1050–1055 (2016)
4. Maria, A.: Introduction to modeling and simulation. In: Proceedings of the 29th Conference on Winter Simulation, pp. 7–13. IEEE Computer Society, December 1997
5. Alia, M., Omara, A.R., Samana, A.M., Othmanb, I., Halima, I., Rahima, A.H.: QUEST® Simulation Analysis for Facility Layout Redesign of Handwork Area (2010)
6. Yun, Y.-S.: An methodology for improving worker utilization and productivity of part assembly line by 3D simulation analysis. Rev. Bus. Econ. **21**(6), 2803–2822 (2008)
7. Battini, D., Faccio, M., Persona, A., Sgarbossa, F.: New methodological framework to improve productivity and ergonomics in assembly system design. Int. J. Ind. Ergon. **41**(1), 30–42 (2011)

Analysis of the Robustness of Production Scheduling in Aeronautical Manufacturing Using Simulation: A Case Study

R. Pulido[1(✉)], T. Borreguero-Sanchidrián[2], A. García-Sánchez[1], and M. Ortega-Mier[1]

[1] Universidad Politécnica de Madrid, José Gutiérrez Abascal, 2, 28006 Madrid, Spain
{raul.pulido,alvaro.garcia,miguel.ortega.mier}@upm.es
[2] Airbus Group, John Lennon S/N, 28906 Getafe, Madrid, Spain
tamara.Borreguero@airbus.com

Abstract. The use of PLM tools is widely spread in the aeronautical industry. Although scheduling and line balancing have remained aside these tools for long, they are being developed in the recent years. They need to tackle with complex resource constrained scheduling problems. In this work we present a simulation model we have developed for evaluating the robustness of a baseline scheduling for an aero structure assembly line. To begin with, we have identified and quantified the main causes of the disruptions. Then we have created a discrete event simulation model of the production line to take everything into consideration, and then run several experiments to evaluate different production planning obtained with the different methodologies and the impact of failures in the deliveries of finished products. Also, different scenarios in terms of failure quantity and typology have been studied.

Keywords: Simulation · Aeronautical industry · Flexible job shop with operators
Case study

1 Introduction

The use of PLM tools is widely spread in the aeronautical industry. Mas et al. (2015a) provided a detailed review on the impact that PLM tools have had on this industry. They stated it has been a major enabler for shortening development timeframes in spite of the increasing aircraft complexity. According to them, one of the current challenges of PLM tools is to allow the simulation of the whole manufacturing of the aircraft.

During the define phase of an assembly line, the conceptual design is tested against a set of what if scenarios (Mas et al. 2013). Discrete event simulation models can contribute to the evaluation of the expected performance, providing additional information to that on the industrial Digital Mock Up (iDMU) (Mas et al. 2015b). Moreover, although process simulation has been used more often in that early design phase (Jahangirian et al. 2010) it can also provide valuable inputs later in the lifecycle. As stated by Murphy and Perera (2002), it can provide quicker response time for decision making and evaluation of those decisions.

J. Ríos et al. (Eds.): PLM 2017, IFIP AICT 517, pp. 174–183, 2017.
https://doi.org/10.1007/978-3-319-72905-3_16

In this work, we have used simulation as part of the scheduling and line balancing system, in order to test the robustness of different production scheduling solutions in a set of what if scenarios. It uses the detailed process definition from the industrial iDMU and, once validated, provides information to the Manufacturing Execution System (MES) see Fig. 1.

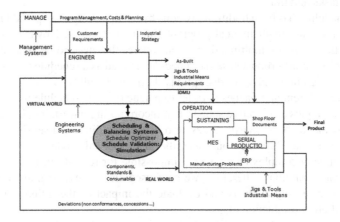

Fig. 1. Context of the scheduling and line balancing system

The model uses two kinds of inputs: on the one hand, it uses the detailed process definition coming from the previous. On the other, we have worked on the identification and quantification of the main causes of disruptions.

Afterwards, it has been used to run several experiments to evaluate different production schedules and risk avoidance strategies in terms of resource management. For each of them, several scenarios in terms of disruption rates have been studied.

Using this simulation model, it is possible to compare the delivery rate of the finished products. This comparison between different schedules in the face of multiple objectives is not straightforward. For example a production planning that minimizes the number of operators may be less robust to any failure or absence of workers but perform better in terms of work in progress.

We believe that this simulation tool can provide a wider understanding on the assembly line expected behavior. Together with a scheduling tool or on its own it can provide useful information for preventive risk management as it helps to evaluate the results of different production schedules or line designs.

This paper is organized as follows: In the next section, we present a Literature Review. In Sect. 3 we present the Method and briefly discuss its validation. Section 4 is dedicated to the simulation results. Finally, in Sect. 5 we draw the final discussion and future research.

2 Literature Review

Scheduling in the aeronautical industry is a complex resource constrained scheduling problem. For example, in the aero structure part manufacturing it is necessary to schedule within the same assembly line, several parts that share resources, and have different production tasks and times.

This scheduling has been traditionally done by hand, relying on experts' knowledge. Nowadays, there are mathematical programming tools to do it. However, during the tasks execution there are multiple disruption sources that need to be tackled. There is an interest of defining a robust baseline schedule, defined as a schedule whose performance remains high in the place of disruptions (Leon et al. 1994).

There are different approaches in order to pursue or asses schedule robustness. The three main strategies are reactive scheduling, incorporating uncertainty in the baseline schedule (by means of stochastic, fuzzy or robust scheduling) and sensitivity analysis (Herroelen and Leus 2005). In our case, the mathematical model of the scheduling baseline is already complex and makes it impossible for real life instances to add the complexity of disruptions. Therefore, we have used discrete event simulation in order to provide a sensitivity analysis and evaluate the impact of the different unforeseen events on different production plans.

Discrete event simulation is a form of computer-based modeling that provides an intuitive and flexible approach to representing complex systems. It models the operation of the factory as a sequence of events that occur in a particular part of the time. The state of the system changes only when an event occurs. It has proven a useful technique for manufacturing systems analysis. (Cunha and Mesquita 1996; Kadar et al. 2004). In the case of the aeronautical industry, Scott (1994) provided an early overview of the most relevant aspects for aeronautical assembly line simulations. Most of the later references have dealt with problems related to final assembly lines. Heike et al. (2001) published a case study to compare the use of constant or variable cycle times within a flow shop. Ziarnetzky (2014) used discrete-event simulation for analysing different inventory policies during a station of a final assembly line. It considers supplier and production disruptions. Lu et al. (2012) used simulation to identify bottlenecks and Noack and Rose (2008) proposed simulation optimization for workforce balancing.

Nonetheless, the literature is still surprisingly lacking of contributions discussing the utilization of simulation in the aero structure production. Neither has it been used to test operator management strategies, as is the case of our study. This can serve for a dual purpose: as a support in the design of the aeronautic production line and during the short and long term planning of the aero structure production.

3   Method

The object of our case study is an aero structure assembly line that produces two aero structures (FCA and FCB), each of them in their right hand (RH) and the left hand (LH) version. In all, 4 products are delivered by the line, called: FC-A LH, FC-A RH, FC-B LH and FC-B RH. Each product goes through nine different steps.

The production times per step and product, could be considered constant. At the same time, the problem is that the circumstances for the production change from one week to another. The holidays or programed maintenance are taken in consideration in the baseline schedule, but other disruptions such as break downs, absence of workers, and product rejections are not taken into consideration when the production schedule is done using the current methods based on mathematical modeling.

Once the range of availability of workers for the scheduling period and the delivery rate are defined, different detailed schedule options are generated for each aero structure using a MILP based software, that provides the optimal schedule for that input data. In Table 1, we presented two production options given by the software using 22 and 24 operators.

Table 1. Options of the production schedule.

Option	Early shift	Late shift	Test operators
A	11	10	1
B	12	11	1

Associated to these options we have detailed the bar charts of the production for each aero structure. The decision maker has to decide which of the generated production schedules is better (see Table 2). The option A uses fewer workers and led to a higher occupancy but also it is a tight solution to deal with any contingency. The option B uses more workers with lower occupancy but it is a loose solution that helps us to deal with contingencies.

Table 2. Scenarios for the Simulation.

Scenario	Absence	Test rejection
L-L	Low	Low
L-H	Low	High
H-L	High	Low
H-H	High	High

We cannot simply minimize the operators cost. The robustness of the solutions against the disruptions is equally relevant. It is useless to have a perfect schedule that would fail at the first setback.

The simulation model we have developed is key to evaluate the trade-off between the different scheduling options (Option A and Option B) and between different risk avoidance resource management strategies (include extra workers in some shifts). It helps the decision makers to know the expected delay in the case of disruptions for each option.

The discrete simulation model of the plant takes into consideration the production times of each part, the movements of the aero structures, different types of workers, programed maintenance and programed absences. Beside of this, four types of disruptions are modeled: machine failures, errors that require extra work, absence of operators and final test rejection (High and Low).

The machine failures and errors that require extra work are steady along the year but the absence of operators and the rejection rate vary from one week to another. Therefore, we are going to evaluate four scenarios for each instance. The final test could have three outcomes, the first one is that everything is fine, the second is that minor corrections are needed, and the last one that mayor corrections are required.

A simulation was modeled in Simio Enterprise (2017) to develop a visual interface tool for the decision maker. To simulate this factory, an entity is represented as each aero structure part. Each part has to visit the different workstation spending a production time based on its type. Each operation requires a type worker with an attached shift. In Fig. 2, a snapshot of the 2D simulation model is presented, the FC-A are presented in light grey and the FC-B in dark grey. The operator is working in a FC-B-RH. There are three aero structure waiting in the buffer to be processed, and the work station in the left is idle.

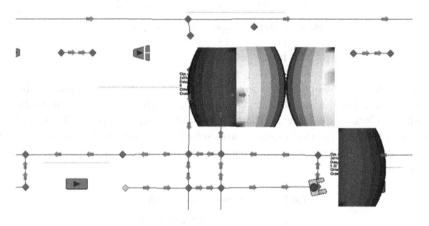

Fig. 2. Snapshot of part of the 2D model.

The backbone of this simulation are the job orders. A job order implied that a task should be performed at a certain moment. This job orders can be created from different sources:

1. As an input from the baseline bar chart (see Fig. 3). All the working requirements are transformed into job orders.
2. Due to an extra work requirement for a process.
3. Due to an unfinished job (the shift ends and the work is not finished).
4. Due to the correction work after the final test.

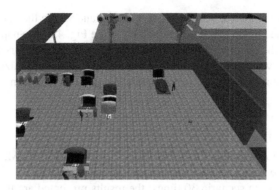

Fig. 3. Snapshot of part of the 3D model.

The job order is launched at determined time, but sometimes it cannot be executed because the server is busy/damaged, there is not aero structure to perform the job, the resources are not idle or there is no available worker. All the order launched that are not attended remain in stand by waiting to be attended.

An aero structure is only processed if the station is available, the required resources are ready and there are worker in the station. A worker can be in a station only if there is a job order that required him to go there.

When there is no problem all the job orders created in the input state (source 1) run smoothly because they always find workers and resources to perform their tasks. The problem occurs when sources 2, 3 and 4 start to create job orders that cannibalize the resources. Additionally, the availability of resources could decrease due break downs or programed maintenance, the same for the workers due to programed day-off and absences.

The simulation model includes a 3D view where the decision maker could follow the behavior of the system at different speeds and see how delivery delays begin to arise.

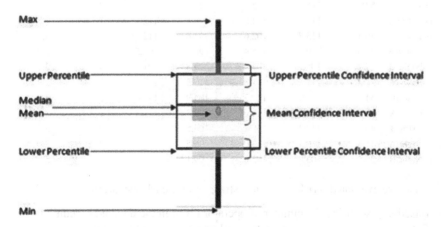

Fig. 4. SMORE plot layout explanation.

He can see how the required variables are updating and where the aero structures, the transporter and the workers are in each moment. (See Fig. 4 for a Snapshot)

Validation of the simulation model has occurred at two levels. Firstly, validation of the output results without any disruption or error against the optimization model and secondly, validation of the entire system model against real data from the plant.

4 Results

The experimentation was done in an Intel Core 7 with 8 GB of RAM, using Windows 10 and the discrete simulation software Simio Enterprise (2017).

We replicated each scenario 30 times; the results presented are the average of the replications. We tested the each option with the four scenarios described in Table 3.

Table 3. Simulation Results for Options A (11 + 10 + 1 Operators) and B (12 + 11 + 1 Operators)

Scenario	Cumulated delay (h)	Deliver time (h) FCA-LH	Deliver time (h) FCA-RH	Deliver time (h) FCB-LH	Deliver time (h) FCB-RH	Units on time	Failures
H-H-Base-A	92.8	122.4	118.1	111.4	125.0	0	3.0
H-H-Base-B	52.5	115.7	103.8	103.8	113.2	2	3.1
H-H-Extra-A	50.5	115.7	102.6	103.8	112.5	2	3.1
H-H-Extra-B	57.1	115.7	114.6	98.3	112.5	1	2.8
H-H-Night-A	46.6	110.7	115.8	97.0	107.1	2	2.9
H-H-Night-B	27.2	105.1	104.9	99.8	101.3	4	2.9
H-L-Base-A	83.1	119.4	115.7	110.3	121.8	0	2.9
H-L-Base-B	54.9	113.4	106.7	105.9	112.9	2	3.5
H-L-Extra-A	58.5	117.0	114.6	98.3	112.5	1	2.9
H-L-Extra-B	45.3	113.4	100.1	103.5	112.2	2	3.5
H-L-Night-A	42.9	110.6	113.3	96.8	106.2	2	3.0
H-L-Night-B	25.3	103.8	105.0	99.1	101.5	4	3.1
L-H-Base-A	92.0	120.3	120.1	111.2	124.4	0	2.9
L-H-Base-B	52.2	115.7	103.8	103.8	112.9	2	3.1
L-H-Extra-A	57.1	115.7	114.6	98.3	112.5	1	2.8
L-H-Extra-B	50.5	115.7	102.6	103.8	112.5	2	3.1
L-H-Night-A	45.0	110.3	115.4	96.8	106.5	2	2.9
L-H-Night-B	27.2	105.1	104.9	99.8	101.3	4	2.9
L-L-Base-A	81.2	117.3	117.8	110.3	119.9	0	2.9
L-L-Base-B	54.6	113.4	106.7	105.9	112.6	2	3.5
L-L-Extra-A	58.5	117.0	114.6	98.3	112.5	1	3.0
L-L-Extra-B	45.3	113.4	100.1	103.5	112.2	2	3.5
L-L-Night-A	41.8	110.1	113.0	96.5	106.2	2	3.0
L-L-Night-B	25.3	103.8	105.0	99.1	101.5	4	3.1

Also, we evaluated 3 risk avoidance strategies for each scenario:

- Baseline case, using the number of operator given in the detailed schedule.
- Extra workers case, using one extra worker per early and late shift

- Night workers case, using two extra operators per night shift.

In the results tables (Table 3), the first column is the scenario name that is composed of (Absence rate – Test Rejection – Type of risk avoidance strategy-Option A or B). The second column is the sum of all the delays (delivery hour – expected end). From the 3rd to the 6th column are the delivery hour of each aero structure. In the 7th column the on time deliver is the number of aero structures delivered before mid-day of the due day (96 + 12 = 108 h for this example). Finally, the 8th column is the mean number of failures that was caused due to machine failures and errors that require extra work.

The results have also been plotted using a SMORE (Simio Measure of Risk and Error) diagram. The layout of the plot is explained in Fig. 4. The SMORE plots (Fig. 4) have been built using a confidence interval of 95%, with a lower percentile of 25% and an upper percentile of 75%.

In option A, it is interesting that the baseline case does not deliver more than one aero structure on time and zero in the more severe situation. The use of extra workers decreases the delay. It can be observed that the solution with extra workers presents better results as it can see in Fig. 5. The schedule is more robust against the variation of absence rate. In all the cases putting the extra workers during the night shift presents better results.

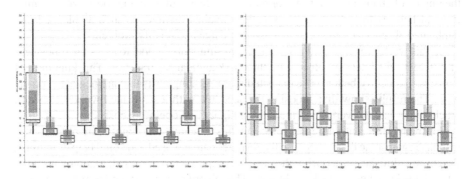

Fig. 5. Confidence interval of Option A (Left) and Option B (Right)

In a high rejection rate scenario, despite the improvement of the performance, neither adding operators during the early and late shift nor adding a night shift do we obtain a good performance. No option delivers more than 50% of the products on time in this scenario.

The baseline case of option B and the extra workers of option A, use the same number of workers and the option B delivers the double of units on time. The behavior of this schedule against the different scenarios was more stable due the extra number of workers. Not in all the cases the extra workers during the early and late shifts improve the result. The use of extra works during the night could deliver in the majority of the cases on time (incurring in the extra cost of the number of workers).

The effect of the failures is hard when the problems occur in certain process and moments. Analyzing the processing times, if we have 4 days, with 2 shifts we have 64 working hours. The time of the process equipping for FC-A-LH needs 60 h. Any problem or delay in this process will severely impact in the solution. Also, the number of workers during the week is constant, but when the absence of operators coincides with the day with a peak of work, its impact is higher.

Even though the rate of machine failures and errors that require extra work do not change from one scenario to another, they is not constant in all the runs due to the stochasticity of the model. The number of failures has an impact on the severity of the run. The difference of number of failures among the scenarios will decrease as we make more runs of each scenario.

5   Discussion

The deployment of PLM tools has provided relevant improvements in the aeronautical industry. One of its main aims is to enable the simulation of the whole manufacturing of the aircraft.

In this sense, discrete event simulation is an efficient tool for validating the production process design. It allows the identification of possible production process pitfalls at an early stage. It is also a useful tool not only for the preliminary design of the line but also for operative decision making during the production stage, for example, to asses the impact of changing for a faster or more reliable machine. In the short term planning it could help us to test contingency actions against disruptions such as planned and unplanned absences of workers, machine breakage and quality problems.

In this work, we have used a discrete event simulation model to asses the robustness of different schedules combined with three risk avoidance strategies. This kind of tests helps us to quantify better those expected real operating costs that are neglected otherwise. The results show that choosing the schedule with less planned workers leads to much higher late deliveries and therefore a higher real operating cost.

From the different strategies tested in this research, the night shift offers better response against the delays because the resources are not used and could help us to finish the entire unfinished task during the day. It is important to highlight, that only until the job order is launched the task could start. The job orders are launched as it was planned or to solve any problems, then they cannot advance work.

The importance of testing the robustness of the solution is better exemplified if we compare the Baseline Option A to Option B with extra workers. Baseline Option A delivers the double of units of time than Option B with extra workers. This is interesting since both use the same amount of workers during the shifts. The only difference is that in the Option B all the workers have assigned tasks, and help to solve the incidences when they can. In Option A, the original workers are over saturated with task, and the extra workers try to solve the incidences, which turns out to be a better policy.

As a future work we would like to extend the use of simulation to test the production process together with another processes of the plant, evaluating which option is better for each case. Another future research direction is to make further experimentation to create learned lessons such as the fact that the production scheduling with the minimum cost is not always the best solution.

References

Cunha, P.F., Mesquita, R.M.: The role of discrete event simulation in the improvement of manufacturing systems performance. In: Camarinha-Matos, L.M., Afsarmanesh, H. (eds.) Balanced Automation Systems II. IAICT, pp. 137–145. Springer, Boston, MA (1996). https://doi.org/10.1007/978-0-387-35065-3_13

Heike, G., Ramulu, M., Sorenson, E., Shanahan, P., Moinzadeh, K.: Mixed model assembly alternatives for low-volume manufacturing: the case of the aerospace industry. Int. J. Prod. Econ. **72**(2), 103–120 (2001)

Herroelen, W., Leus, R.: Project scheduling under uncertainty: survey and research potentials. Eur. J. Oper. Res. **165**, 289–306 (2005)

Jahangirian, M., Eldabi, T., Naseer, A., Stergioulas, L.K., Young, T.: Simulation in manufacturing and business: a review. Eur. J. Oper. Res. **203**, 1–13 (2010)

Mas, F., Gómez, A., Menéndez, J.L., Ríos, J.: Proposal for the conceptual design of aeronautical final assembly lines based on the industrial digital mock-up concept. In: Bernard, A., Rivest, L., Dutta, D. (eds.) PLM 2013. IAICT, vol. 409, pp. 10–19. Springer, Heidelberg (2013). https://doi.org/10.1007/978-3-642-41501-2_2

Mas, F., Arista, R., Oliva, M., Hiebert, B., Gilkerson, I., Ríos, J.: A review of PLM impact on US and EU aerospace industry. Procedia Eng. **132**, 1053–1060 (2015a)

Mas, F., Oliva, M., Ríos, J., Gómez, A., Olmos, V., García, J.A.: PLM based approach to the industrialization of aeronautical assemblies. Procedia Eng. **132**, 1045–1052 (2015b)

Murphy, C.A., Perera, T.: The definition of simulation and its role within an aerospace company. Simul. Pract. Theory **9**, 273–291 (2002)

Kadar, B., Pfeiffer, A., Monostori, L.: Discrete event simulation for supporting production planning and scheduling decisions in digital factories. In: Proceedings of the 37th CIRP International Seminar on Manufacturing Systems, pp. 444–448 (2004)

Leon, V.J., Wu, S.D., Storer, R.H.: Robustness measures and robust scheduling for job shops. IIE Trans. **26**(5), 32–43 (1994)

Lu, H., Liu, X., Pang, W., Ye, W., Wei, B.: Modeling and simulation of aircraft assembly line based on quest. Adv. Mater. Res. **569**, 666–669 (2012)

Noack, D., Rose, O.: A simulation based optimization algorithm for slack reduction and workforce scheduling. In: Proceedings of the 2008 Winter Simulation Conference, pp. 1989–1994 (2008)

Scott, H.A.: Modelling aircraft assembly operations. In: Proceedings of the 26th Conference on Winter Simulation, pp. 920–927 (1994)

Simio Enterprise [Computer software] Version 8.136. PA, USA: Simio LLC (2017)

Ziarnetzky, T., Mönch, L., Biele, A.: Simulation of low-volume mixed model assembly lines: modeling aspects and case study. In: Proceedings of the Winter Simulation Conference 2014 IEEE, pp. 2101–2112 (2014)

Development of a Part Criticality Index in Inventory Management

Clint Saidy[1]([⊠]), Liudas Panavas[1], Ramy Harik[1],
Abdel-Moez Bayoumi[1], and Joseph Khoury[2]

[1] Department of Mechanical Engineering, College of Engineering and Computing,
University of South Carolina, Columbia, SC, USA
{csaidy,lpanavas}@email.sc.edu, {harik,bayoumi}@cec.sc.edu
[2] Methode Electronics Middle East S.A.L.,
Mega Mall, Lower Level, Damascus Road, Furn El Chebbak, Beirut, Lebanon
Joseph.khoury@methodemideast.com

Abstract. Due to uncertainties in demand, some parts might go out of stock during the manufacturing process leading to backorders if an out-of-stock part is critical. In order to reduce additional cost it is important to optimize restocking processes. To do so, the concept of Part Criticality is used to rank and prioritize parts involved in the production of different products. In this paper, we develop an algorithm to get the Compound Global Index which represents the part criticality.

Keywords: Supply chain · Inventory control · Uncertainty · Criticality

1 Introduction

As businesses grow in size, inventory management analysis is becoming more important to increase efficiency and profits by reducing backorders and surpluses. Part of this change is a result of limited in house production of parts and a focus on final assembly, which creates a need to evaluate part criticality in the supply chain. The two fundamental problems that arise from a poor supply chain are a large backlog and surplus. The percentage of items backordered and the number of backorder days are important measures of the quality of a company's customer service and the effectiveness of its inventory management. On the other hand, if the business has an inventory surplus it will incur costs to store, track and insure inventory. Therefore, creating an inventory management system that ranks part criticality based on their creation of backorders and surpluses can create significant financial and customer service improvements for a business.

Two common inventory-management strategies are the just-in-time (JIT) method, where companies plan to receive items as they are needed rather than maintaining high inventory levels, and materials requirement planning (MRP), which schedules material deliveries based on sales forecasts. JIT means that manufacturers and retailers keep only what they need to produce and sell products in inventory, which reduces storage and insurance costs, as well as the cost of liquidating or discarding unused, unwanted inventory. To balance this style of inventory management, manufacturers and retailers must

Published by Springer International Publishing AG 2017. All Rights Reserved
J. Ríos et al. (Eds.): PLM 2017, IFIP AICT 517, pp. 184–195, 2017.
https://doi.org/10.1007/978-3-319-72905-3_17

work together to monitor the availability of resources on the manufacturer's end and consumer demand on the retailer's. The MRP inventory management method is sales-forecast dependent. This means that manufacturers must have accurate sales records to enable accurate planning of inventory needs and to communicate those needs with materials suppliers in a timely manner. These methods are geared towards supply chain management and are concerned with when certain products are to be ordered but do not incorporate in what order and whether they should be ordered. Overall, these methods view all parts as having equal importance and miss the part criticality tier that helps account for imperfections and differentiation between different parts that affect production time.

To achieve a balance between efficient customer service and low inventory cost, an optimization model should be set in place that finds a part that is most critical amongst the bills of material. Companies cannot spread their recourses equally amongst all the products and inventory management. By defining the most important parts companies will be able to more efficiently delegate their resources. In order to do this, an algorithm will be created using different components of existing part criticality models found through a literature review. Then the part criticality index will be generated in order to target critical parts on the inventory floor and will be simulated through randomly generated number tests. Finally, the system will be placed in a real world application to test its effectiveness.

2   Literature Review

As business and production facilities grow in size and complexity, inventory and supply chain management have grown increasingly important to gain an upper edge. Today's environment is no longer brand vs brand but instead involves entire supply chains [4]. A large part of this supply chain is material requirement planning and safety stock decisions. With the cost of holding inventory as high as 40% of the inventory value, it is important to maintain the optimal amount [8].

Modeling and determining the optimal amount of inventory depends on several factors. Depending on the company size, either a single or a multi-echelon system should be put in place. If the model represents a single entity, such as a warehouse, a single echelon model is used. Multi-echelon, composed of many single-echelon systems, models are used most often due to current companies size [3]. Finally, event occurrences can be assigned numbers, deterministic or stochastic, when creating inventory models. All these variables create a variety of inventory management policies.

The first part criticality inventory system investigated is the spare parts theory, which involves the assignment of criticality to the parts that make up the manufacturing equipment. Due to the high uncertainty of the requirement of the spare parts and small amount of suppliers, spare parts are inherently difficult to manage. This generally causes a large amount of overstocking [7]. In order to deal with these issues, spare parts are generally put into categories in order help create proper stocking. Drekker began this by allowing equipment criticality to determine the stock of spare parts by assigning each piece of equipment a status of either "critical and non-critical" [2].

In order to determine the optimal order quantity and reorder point for aircraft spare parts, Aisyati et al. [1] used a continuous review model. The suggested model resulted in smaller total cost compared with existing policy. An ABC classification system was used to categorize the parts based on their dollar contribution. Focus was on class A and B which commonly known as important classes. The result from the research indicates that the continuous review policy gives a significant amount of saving compared to the pre-existing policy. Finally, in order to expand on the ABC model, Stoll [9] used a three dimensional approach allowing for the predictability of demand and importance of the part to be calculated in. The spare part inventory theories lay the groundwork for determining the criticality of different parts of a production facility.

Another way to examine the importance of a part is to investigate the intricate web of the interactions among the units of related systems. One of the most successful recent approaches to capturing the fundamental features of the structure and dynamics of complex systems has been the investigation of the networks associated with the units (nodes) together with their relations (edges). Mones et al. [6] developed an approach and proposed a measure capable of capturing the essential features of the structure and the degree of hierarchy in a complex network. The measure introduced is based on a generalization of the m-reach centrality, which is first extending to directed/partially directed graphs. Then, a global reaching centrality (GRC) was defined, which is the difference between the maximum and the average value of the generalized reach centralities over the network. Results for real networks show that the hierarchy measure is related to the controllability of the given system (Fig. 1).

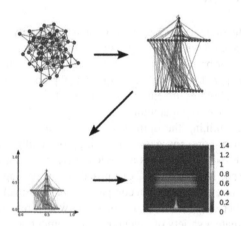

Fig. 1. Diagram illustrating the process of visualizing an ensemble of networks [6].

Manzini et al. [5] uses the method of nodes and edges to create a system to deal with manufacturing-to-order and assembly-to-order processes. Since each product is unique there is no large part inventory to pick from. To formalize the utilization of the part in the production, Manzini lets the source node be when the part is introduced and the sink node be the milestone before the production operation requiring the component. Then to evaluate the criticality of the part, Manzini finds the overlap of the probability that the component is needed in the production operation and the probability that component has not arrived. An overlap of these provides a risk that determines the criticality of the part. The system of edges and nodes works well in production lines because of the step-by-step nature of manufacturing facilities.

3 Defining the Part Criticality Index

The solution employed in this paper focuses on the idea on part Criticality in Inventory Management. This idea stems from:

- The spare parts inventory management technique where equipment spare parts are assigned a value due to their criticalness to the production line [2].
- The system of nodes and edges Mones et al. put forward to describe the fundamental features and hierarchies of a structure and dynamics of complex systems [6].

Combining these two systems gave a unique approach to determining the part criticality. The spare parts inventory management system introduced the concept of backlogs and order demand to part criticality while the system of nodes and edges allowed for the complex system of a product and production line to be simplified and quantified.

The system of nodes and edges can be applied to a production line if the nodes are looked at as parts and edges being the assembly links. If a part is out of stock, this cuts off connections not allowing the production to flow through the map to the final assembly. The most critical parts of a product then become the parts with the most connections due to their ability to cut off more of the production line and are therefore given preference in stocking systems. The spare part inventory technique was used to rank the product criticality by including the demand and backlog. This way the most important part could be found by combining the most important parts and products of a production line. This will helps envision the bigger supply chain later in order tackle criticality not only on the factory floor but by reaching suppliers and enhancing the cooperation between all the supply chain entities. A general approach for the creation of each factor in the methodology is listed below followed by a more detailed approach.

3.1 Local Influence

The first step is to define the local influence of a certain node i (nodes in this case represent parts, sub-parts, and the final product) in an unweighted directed graph. The studied network is a directed network since only parts lead to sub-parts which lead to final product and not the other way around. The local influence, LI(i), is defined as the proportion of all nodes in the graph that can be reached from node i via incoming edges to i.

$$LI(i) = \frac{\# \, of \, direct \, child \, links}{Total \, \# \, of \, links} \tag{1}$$

A child link is a link that connects the parent node to the child node i.

3.2   Maximum Local Influence

After calculating local influence at all nodes, we designate LI^{max} as the highest Local Influence. LI^{max} will be used in the following step in order to normalize the Local Influence to compare LI of a certain part between different products.

$$LI^{max} = \max_{i \leq N-1} LI(i) \tag{2}$$

3.3   Part to Product Influence

Thus, we can calculate the Part to Product Influence (PPI):

$$PPI = \frac{\sum_{i \in V(j)} [LI^{max} - LI(i)]}{N - 1} \tag{3}$$

Note that V(j) denotes the set of nodes in the network composing Product j.

Calculating the PPI allows us compare the influence of the parts on different products.

3.4   Global Influence

The Global Influence of a Part in a Product can be calculated as follows:

$$GI(i) = \sum_{V(j)} [LI(i)] \tag{4}$$

In other words GI(i) represents the weight of each part in a product, bigger GI(i) shows that part i is a major component of the product.

3.5   Product Influence and Backlog History

Calculate Product Influence and Backlog History of each product. This is an important criterion to relate each product to the larger picture of the entire production facility.

a. PD(j) is the weighted average of Demand over a 40 week horizon for product j.
b. BH(j) is the weighted average backlog over a 40 week horizon for product j.
c. Calculate the product Index PI which is the product of PPI, PD, and BH.

3.6 Compound Global Index

The last step is to find the Compound Global Index (CGI) that represents the part criticality among all products. The CGI brings together the most important parts and products to find the most critical parts to the production line. To calculate CGI for each part, we use the following equation representing the sum-product of parts Global Influence in each product and the Product Influence:

$$CGI(i) = \sum_j GI(i) * PI(j) \tag{5}$$

The higher the parts CGI the more critical it is.

4 Inventory Model

4.1 Products

Six fictional products where created in order to apply the above-mentioned algorithm. Each product consists of a set of parts, subsets, and sets. Note that subsets are subassemblies of parts, and sets are subassemblies of parts and subsets. Creating multiple products helps create a more realistic representation of a large final assembly production facility.

4.2 Supply and Demand

In this model, both supply and demand are set as constant stochastic variables. The distribution used is the uniform distribution. Furthermore, a finite planning horizon of 40 weeks is used.

4.3 Inventory and Backlog

In order to perform accurate long run simulations a model was created to help us simulate a realistic scenario where inventory is not scrapped from period to another and unmet demand is met in the upcoming periods. In create this model inventory from one period to another is kept and unmet demand from one period to another is backlogged.

Inventory, $I(n)$, and shortage, $S(n)$, for a typical period n is calculated as follows:

$$I(n) = I(n-1) + Max[Q(n) - D(n), 0]$$
$$I(0) = 0 \tag{6}$$

$$S(n) = S(n-1) + Max[D(n) - Q(n), 0]$$
$$S(0) = 0 \tag{7}$$

Note that $D(n)$ and $Q(n)$ represent Demand and Supply during a period n respectively.

5 Discussion of Results

5.1 Primitive Model

A first model was developed with the following assumptions: surplus inventory from one term to another is scrapped and backlog is not allowed, i.e., unmet demand during a certain period is disregarded in the next period. For this model, all random simulation led to same result, the same part was found to be critical. But, this model is not logical since inventory can be kept from one period to another and unmet demand is usually met in the upcoming periods. Hence, a more realistic model was developed in order to take into consideration surplus inventory and backlog. The integration of these parameters was already discussed in Sect. 3.3.

5.2 Short Run Results

After embedding surplus inventory and backlog in the model, short run simulation were run based on a 40-week horizon, and then long run results were calculated. The long run results were based on a series of 10 short runs.

Many short run simulations were run, and every time a different part was found to be critical. This randomization was boosted by the introduction of the 2 assumptions discussed above. 5 runs are documented in the table below. For the first run, part N was the most critical, for the second and fourth run, part D was the most critical, and followed by part A. And for the third and fifth runs, Part A was the most critical followed by part D. this can be explained by the probabilistic distributions used to represent both supply and demand and their involvement in the calculation of the Product Index PI (Sect. 3.5). The short run simulations did not provide definitive results so the long-term model was though of and put in place to see if a more consistent results could be obtained.

5.3 Long Run Results

In order to develop the long run results, ten short run simulations were run and a weighted average of the CGI for every part was calculated. This procedure was repeated three times, and the same part was found to be critical. This shows that regardless of the variations on the short term, on the long term, the same part will be critical. Table 1 shows that the most critical part on the long run is A followed by the part D. The long run simulation amortized the effect of the stochastic distribution of the demand and supply leading to one part being critical on the long run.

Table 1. Global compound index calculation

Part	Run 1	Run 2	Run 3	Run 4	Run 5	Long Run
Set 1	0.00377075	0.01551306	0.00278513	0.01262664	0.00974517	0.00762882
Set 2	0.01476691	0.00870292	0.00638843	0.01012183	0.01360051	0.01741808
Set 6	0.0147669	0.0004902	0.00369514	0	0.01181458	0.00638000
Set 7	0.0147669	0.0004902	0.00369514	0	0.01181458	0.00638000
Subset1	0.0037707	0.0155130	0.00547842	0.01473918	0.01065167	0.01095505
A	0.0336402	0.0340810	0.02179057	0.03309916	0.03720555	0.04400146
B	0.0037707	0.0237257	0.00278513	0.02063593	0.01062458	0.01534066
D	0.0223084	0.0479417	0.01465198	0.04549695	0.03487678	0.04371381
E	0.0037707	0.0155130	0.00547842	0.01473918	0.01065167	0.01095505
F	0.0076533	0.0314087	0.00763605	0.02532956	0.01957679	0.01576854
G	0.0147669	0.0087029	0.00908172	0.01223438	0.01450702	0.02074432
H	0.0148787	0.0090855	0.00845421	0.01019812	0.01368696	0.01792899
J	0.0147669	0.0087029	0.00369514	0.00800929	0.01269400	0.01409185
L	0.0148787	0.0008728	0.00576092	7.63E-05	0.01190104	0.00689090
M	0.0334164	0.0168612	0.00954791	0.0105903	0.0325542	0.01757349
N	0.0443007	0.0014706	0.01108543	0	0.03544376	0.019140008
O	0.0223084	0.03151636	0.00387883	0.02102819	0.02949191	0.01498517

5.4 Pareto Analysis

Ideally, management wants to focus its attention on fixing the most important problems. But how do they decide which problems they need to deal with first? Pareto Analysis helps prioritize the most critical parts by finding the 20% of parts that generate 80% of the criticality.

In this simulation, 80% of the criticality is caused by more than 20% of the parts (Figs. 2 and 3), thus violating the 80/20 rule. Pareto charts are extremely useful for analyzing what problems need attention first because the taller bars on the chart, clearly illustrate which parts have the greatest cumulative effect on a given system (Figs. 4 and 5).

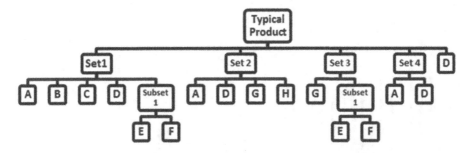

Fig. 2. Typical product

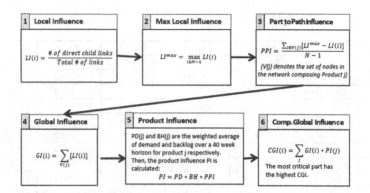

Fig. 3. Path to find part criticality

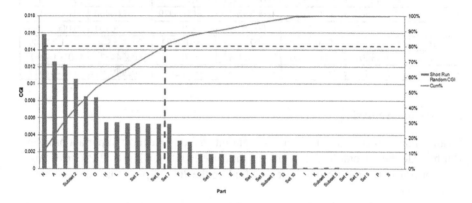

Fig. 4. Random Short Run Pareto Chart

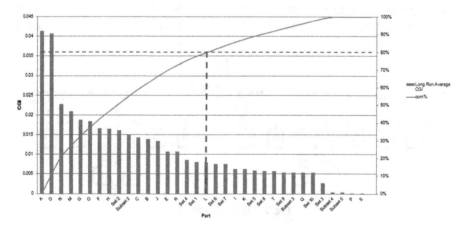

Fig. 5. Long Run Pareto Chart

6 Industry Significance

Our next step is to create a program that optimizes inventory management by identifying the criticality of parts to a company's production. The program will allow a company to insert data from their production line and the most important parts will then be determined using a part criticality algorithm. These parts will then be given priority in the pre-existing inventory management system.

The long-term goal for this project will be to create a wiki-like database for local manufacturers that can create parts used in the aerospace industry. Many large companies such as Boeing outsource many of the parts that go into their planes first from outside the USA and second from outside of South Carolina. Therefore, if a part is defective there are long shipping times and delays that may occur. Determining both the criticality of the parts used on the assembly line and the parts in the products delivered could help reduce these issues because local manufacturers could be identified in order to get the part quickly. This would be a part of the actions taken in order to help engage local suppliers in the advancement of the aerospace market in South Carolina. The figure below shows the breakdown of the Boeing 787 airplane along with the origin of each part.

The figure below shows the breakdown and origin of major parts of the Boeing 787 manufactured in Charleston, SC.

The below image shows the spread of first tier suppliers hired by Boeing.

Figure 6 shows the available aerospace related companies in South Carolina. These companies can be beneficial for Boeing since they are close to the plant in Charleston leading to easier cooperation and less variability (Fig. 7).

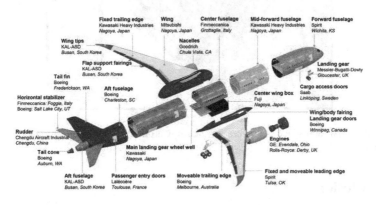

Fig. 6. Boeing 787 breakdown (Boeing 787 Dreamliner structure: parts from around the globe. Retrieved May 10, 2017, from http://www.aeronewstv.com/en/industry/commercial-aviation/3707-boeing-787-dreamliner-structure-parts-from-around-the-globe.html).

Fig. 7. Countries supplying parts for Boeing Charleston

Our goal is to create a multi-echelon cooperative supply chain network within South Carolina in order to increase the involvement of local aerospace related companies in the manufacturing of the Dreamliner and hence decreasing the criticality among the parts since suppliers will be more within reach (Fig. 8).

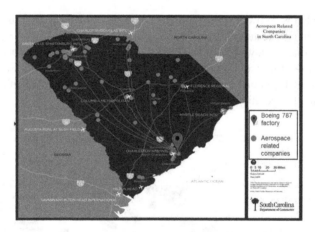

Fig. 8. Potential aerospace suppliers in South Carolina (South Carolina Department of Commerce)

7   Conclusion

In this paper, we determined the Part Criticality defined as Compound Global Index. This index defined part criticality by utilizing the interdependence of different parts as well as backorder and surplus quantities. A set of simple products having common parts was employed in order to validate the algorithm. Results showed that on the short term, criticality might vary form one term to another. This is mainly caused by the variability of demand and supply. Furthermore, this criticality was affected by the inventory policy set in place for this simulation.

A further step would be to simulate other inventory policies in order to study their effect on the part criticality. As for the long run results, it was realized that one part was the most critical. This short run/long run differentiation helps the management have a plan to tackle parts that are critical on the short term as well as creating long term improvement policies to decrease the long term part criticality.

References

1. Aisyati, A., Jauhari, W.A., Rosyidi, C.N.: Determination inventory level for aircraft spare parts using continuous review model. Int. J. Bus. Res. Manage. (IJBRM) **4**(1), 1–12 (2013)
2. Dekker, R., Kleijn, M., Rooij, P.D.: A spare parts stocking policy based on equipment criticality. Int. J. Prod. Econ. **56-57**, 69–77 (1998). https://doi.org/10.1016/s0925-5273(97)00050-9
3. Hausman, W.H., Erkip, N.K.: Multi-Echelon vs. Single-Echelon inventory control policies for low-demand items. Manage. Sci. **40**(5), 597–602 (1994). https://doi.org/10.1287/mnsc.40.5.597
4. Lambert, D.M., Cooper, M.C.: Issues in supply chain management. Ind. Mark. Manage. **29**(1), 65–83 (2000). https://doi.org/10.1016/s0019-8501(99)00113-3
5. Manzini, M., Urgo, M.: Critical components evaluation in manufacturing-to-order processes. Procedia CIRP **37**, 146–151 (2015). https://doi.org/10.1016/j.procir.2015.08.046
6. Mones, E., Vicsek, L., Vicsek, T.: Hierarchy measure for complex networks. PLoS ONE **7**(3), e33799 (2012). https://doi.org/10.1371/journal.pone.0033799
7. Roda, I., Macchi, M., Fumagalli, L., Viveros, P.: A review of multi-criteria classification of spare parts. J. Manuf. Technol. Manage. **25**(4), 528–549 (2014). https://doi.org/10.1108/jmtm-04-2013-0038
8. Sandvig, C., Reistad, A.: Safety stock decision support tool. Prod. Inventory Manage. J. **41**(4), 7–10 (2000)
9. Stoll, J., Kopf, R., Schneider, J., Lanza, G.: Criticality analysis of spare parts management: a multi-criteria classification regarding a cross-plant central warehouse strategy. Prod. Eng. **9**(2), 225–235 (2015). https://doi.org/10.1007/s11740-015-0602-2

PLM, CAX and Knowledge Management

Cost Estimation Aided Software for Machined Parts: An Hybrid Model Based on PLM Tools and Data

Marc-Antoine Michaud[✉] and Roland Maranzana

École de technologie Supérieure, Montréal, Canada
marc-antoine.michaud.1@ens.etsmtl.ca,
roland.maranzana@etsmtl.ca

Abstract. For each manufacturer, exact cost estimation is both a major priority and a challenge. This routine task is far from being optimized and depends on a very large number of parameters both strategic and technical. To help estimate a cost, applications have been developed but estimation is a task that would greatly benefit from the re-use of knowledge and data found in alphanumeric and geometric documents. Every manufacturing company has switched to numerical data with CAD, CAM, or ERP systems but one of the main drawbacks is the low usage of all these information that contain valuable knowledge and expertise. This paper describes the current state of cost estimation and proposes a new hybrid approach whose purpose is to maximize the re-use of information for machined parts. Our approach is based on a parameterized and customized cost model, an extractor of semantic descriptors in geometric documents (Model Based Definition files) and related textual documents and finally correlations to adjust the cost of machined parts.

Keywords: Knowledge reuse · PLM tools · Model based definition
Case-base reasoning · Semantic search · Machining part · Cost estimation

1 Introduction

As the competition is fiercer, companies have to stay competing while also being able to deliver and produce high quality products in a fair time. Having a reliable and precise cost estimation is crucial for this, it will limit the risks of overheads, allow a better production and budget management and help making better strategic decisions. As the use of CAD software has allowed enormous time savings for design [10], cost estimation represents a task which would greatly profit from a computer application to produce faster and more accurate quoting for both the clients and the contractors. This task is often entrusted to one or two experts who will rely on both tacit knowledge acquired from experience and explicit parameters or standard guidelines [18]. Software applications such as Apriori or Techniquote are sometimes used but they present limitations, their database has to be up to date, they need to be adapted to the different processes of the company and they often require a lot of time to estimate. However, companies struggle to obtain repeatable price for the same type of machined parts through time because it is the combination of knowledges being both tacit and explicit

J. Ríos et al. (Eds.): PLM 2017, IFIP AICT 517, pp. 199–211, 2017.
https://doi.org/10.1007/978-3-319-72905-3_18

regrouping the capacity of the company, the type of part and their features as well as the human and financial aspects.

The main objective of this paper is to propose a methodology for the cost estimation which can adapt to the resources and capacity of the company. Tacit knowledge remains a master piece in the machined part cost estimation process that we need to understand and integrate. Therefore, we suggest an innovative approach based on similarity based-knowledge in order to develop models of customized costs which rely on the massive re-use of former data related to similar parts as an alternative to this tacit knowledge.

The rest of the paper is organized as follows: Sect. 2 focus on the literature review in cost estimation, model based definition and part similarity assessment. The Sect. 3 will present the observations that have been made in the industry as well as our hypothesis for the model. In Sect. 4, we describe our proposed methodology, present our contribution and illustrate the model with a simple example. In Sect. 5 we will discuss some perspectives of work and conclude the paper.

2 Literature Review

Cost estimation has been an alive nerve of industry for almost a century because it is a primordial stage in a product life cycle [5]. Thus, one can find a broad panoply of methods and techniques, each one depending on available information, type of parts, materials or industrialization stage for example [8]. As described by Niazi et al. [15] and Ben-Arieh [2], all of these methods can be divided into two groups, the quantitative and the qualitative ones. Each of them is then separated in two classes, and inside those subdivisions other categories can be made. This is also described in [16]. However, every method has its advantages, its field of predilection, its limits and is better suited for a specific time in the product life cycle, as illustrated in [8].

2.1 Quantitative Approaches

Parametric techniques
These cost estimation techniques were widely used because they often produce accurate estimation, and are easy to implement, but cost drivers needed to be correctly identified, limiting each method to one type of parts and making it prone to errors when parts were changing too much. Even if [6] show that these techniques have been improved, some limitations are still present and are innate to the parametric approach.

Analytical techniques
They regroup models based on cost-tolerance, activities, features or operations. Cost-tolerance models are almost all based on the quality-loss function proposed by Taguchi [21] and curve fitting techniques [20]. Machining or form features based models such as presented by Feng and al. [7] or Xu et al. [24] tends not to take into account all the processes and does not consider the impact of tolerances for example. Moreover, the enormous data requirements for these techniques restrict their use for the final phases of industrialization process.

2.2   Qualitative Approaches

Analogical techniques
These methods rely more on regression analysis or neural networks in order to find relationships between cost and a selected set of variables. They are good to deal with non-linear problems and to adapt but they are data-dependent and more difficult to develop or implement [16].

Intuitive techniques
On the other hand, intuitive techniques, such as rule-based or knowledge-based system [19] are often quicker and handles very well uncertainty. However, they are also hard to keep updated, limited to a sort of design and the implementation often requires too much effort as well. Case based reasoning address some of these issues and is one of the most used techniques nowadays [8]. The main drawbacks of all the CBR techniques are the necessity to abstract features or parameters in order to compare parts, resulting in techniques that are applicable to one type of design and the need for past designs.

As you can see a large number of models have been developed for various kinds of applications, each one having its advantages and the limitations as shown in [15]. But the existing models often rely too much on mathematical models and are not prone to be customized to the needs of a given company. Recent research papers show a new trend to get quicker and more precise results by combining several approaches as shown in [11]. As studied in [9], theses new methods provide more promising results and are also increasingly based on the new capabilities of data treatments, semantic researches or machine learning for instance [6–18]. In deed, the last decade has shown some interesting projections for the treatment of great volumes of non-structured data. Digital systems like, computer-aided design (CAD), or ERP (enterprise Resources Planning) have become widely used [1]. But the interoperability between these applications is almost none existent, information is dispersed in innumerable files resulting in duplicates and inconsistency. The problem is even acuter on the level of mechanical engineering where a significant portion of information is locked up in the 3D geometry. The MBD including the 3D model as well as the PMI makes it possible to have a complete representation of the part in a single file. Moreover, these crucial data are complex to retrieve from the design drawings and the extraction would be easier from a MDB. According to Quintana and Venne [17–22], companies in aeronautics, automobiles or software preach this practice aiming to decrease design times and gather numerically all information at the same place.

This proliferation of digital information created the need for search engines and there exist nearly fifty company search engines made by Oracle, SAP, Dassault for example. However, they are limited to the indexing of alphanumeric items. Several approaches for indexing 3D models were proposed in scientific articles [3], but few applications crossed the stage of the university research. Yet some software like 3DPartFinder are able to index parts directly by the boundaries representation [14], characterized by a higher degree of accuracy, an index much more concise and improved performances. As pointed out in [14–24], similarity and reuse of knowledge are an under-exploited domain, over 70% of the customized product can be made out from the existing product design resources for example, which comfort the interest to invoke similarity.

3 Industrial Observations and Hypotheses

3.1 Observations

In order to verify and put to the test what the literature taught us, several meetings and discussions were conducted with the different companies involved in the project. Therefore, after multiple visits and cost estimations, we could make several reports, some of them matching what was seen in the research studies and some not:

- There exist *at least two methods* and the choice of the methods *depends essentially on the available time*, the overall complexity or the added-value of the part.
- The model is always *affected by strategic factors* and selling cost is not the same as pricing cost
- It always *remains a significant proportion of tacit knowledge* inversely proportional to the allocated time
- Historical data and reuse of knowledge are *underused*
- They only have *few options to reduce specific costs*

We also made some observations concerning the models. As shown in the Eq. (1), the majority divide the cost into 3 or 4 distinct categories: material cost, machining cost, post-processing cost and various cost like margins, tools, hardware, assembly. This is an approach [5–13] brought up in their studies. The practices are also often based on the same approaches but with some variations:

- Using a volumetric approach to raw material cost and machining time
- Submitting tenders in order to know the exact prices
- Estimating the machining time according to the operations and the machines used
- Sorting of the parts and using historical data when possible

$$C_{part} = C_{material} + C_{machining} + C_{post-process} + C_{others} \tag{1}$$

From what we observe there are some gaps between research models and the industry how-to and thus the need to come up with a different approach. The companies seek to maximize their productivity, estimating as fast as possible in order to process a maximum of requests for quote. Moreover, even if the time granted to quote a part should depend on its added-value, companies often allows the minimum necessary to estimate. Therefore, an adequate model should be presented being both simple enough, quick and putting the emphasis on the reuse of valid knowledge and the reliability of the cost. The objective would be to reduce the potential error and make it possible to better understand from which parameters the estimation comes while offering a variable level of detail depending on what the user is looking for. The Fig. 1 tend to show the contribution of our final model.

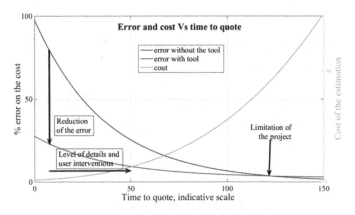

Fig. 1. The contribution of the project

3.2   Hypothesis

Based on our observations and the state of the art we can draw some hypothesis for our current work listed below [12–14]:

- Cost depends on several parameters with different levels of influence.
- Geometric similarity implies other correlations such as similar machining, material, or processes and parts with similar information tend to converge towards the same cost value.
- The more similar part we have, the higher degree of confidence we get on a cost estimation.

4   Proposed Methodology

4.1   Overview

The complete methodology has been designed to answer the research questions. It composed 4 groups and 6 steps (see Fig. 2). The first one aim to understand the environment of the company, to identify the key parameters, the way of proceeding, and to quantify the tacit knowledge. The second one is the design of a generalized model which will be detailed in the present section. The third one consists in merging all the information obtained during the first step with the model. Finally, the last group is for evaluating the final model and validating the benefit of the geometrical similarity.

4.2   The Generalized Model

Problem Description

Based on our observations, companies estimate costs using comparable methods, some parameters are common between them, others are specific to the enterprise. We can

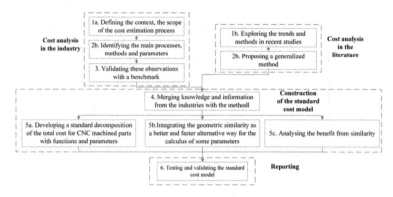

Fig. 2. Methodology steps

then divide each problem into two entities: *An object P* (in costing, it represents the part) and *its environment E* (illustrated by the company).

The parameters and functions
Each of these entities will also be defined by a number of parameters x_i (see Eqs. (2) and (3)) and a set of functions:

$$P = (x_i) \, with \, i \in \{1, \ldots, n\} \tag{2}$$

$$E = (x_j) \, with \, j \in \{n, \ldots, m\} \tag{3}$$

We can then classify the parameters and the functions used to calculate the costs into two categories as illustrated in Table 1. Nevertheless, the functions can be anything from a sum, to linear regression and are either exact functions or approximation depending on the company. They are used to break-down a parameter into other ones, more detailed. The number of parameters will be determined by the necessary levels of decomposition to obtain an acceptable result and by the process of the enterprise specifying the prevalence of certain parameters. The more parameters there are, the more precise the refinement can be. We then have a tree with K_i—Layers of decomposition depending on the top parameter. In theory, each parameter can be refined until it is exact or coming from a database, but in practice it might not be possible or necessary. The decomposition stops when no function is found to break down the

Table 1. Function and parameter types with example

	Type of function or parameters	Example
Parameter	Part-related, robust	*A length is part-related*
	Environment-related, variable	The hourly rate depends on the company
Function	Part-related, robust	$V_{Boudingbox} = L * l * h$
	Environment-related, variable	$Cost = time * Hourly_{rate}$

considered parameter or when it is not considered profitable. As an example, a length or a density cannot be further decomposed, whereas features machining time can but it might be too complicated to implement. The challenge is to find a suitable balance between the level of decomposition, its practicability and its benefit.

The Notion of source of the parameters
Decomposing a parameter is not the only way of obtaining a value for it. As a consequence, we have decided that the provenance of a parameter is almost as much important as its value and have distinguished five different possible sources: exact, database, tacit, similar or calculus.

Exact: Parameter is taken from the MDB or databases that are not prone to change in time. A density or an area extracted from the 3D model are examples of exact source.

Database: Parameter is coming from a database, but the value can fluctuate over time like a price of material.

Tacit: The value is entered by the user depending totally on his personal knowledge.

Calculus: A parameter x_i can be broken down into x_j, x_v using a specific function.

Similar: The value is predicted either by finding a relationship between two or more correlated parameters with a regression for example or by using a set of rules. Data used to build the model are only taken from geometrically similar parts and a similarity index is defined between the new part and old ones allowing to keep the most similar and to weigh the influence of each part within the relationship.

The Reliability and Precision
Another major point is that an estimation has to be reliable and precise. To address this matter, we propose to attribute a reliability coefficient scaling from 0 to 1 to each parameter depending on its source and an absolute error. The reliability coefficient represents the confidence we have in the value, and the absolute error represents the potential error we made on the value. The reliability coefficient for the calculus or similarity provenances will vary depending on the RC of the parameters used and on their correlation. In case of a simple multiplication or fraction calculus, the reliability coefficient will behave as combined probability of two independent events. For similarity, we will use the Wang and Stanley composite reliability formula between two parameters [23] in order to determine the composite RC that will be adjusted depending on the number of similar parts used, their seniority and the difference of batch size. The absolute error is taken from the computer tools or the measurement methods. For the calculi and the similarities, we will use partial differential method and weighted mean absolute error.

Geometric similarity and priority
The model allows to emphasize some sources depending on the reliability coefficient or where the data is available. The source with the highest reliability is prioritized if possible, even if the user has always the decisive verdict and can overwrite any value using his knowledge. The model allows us to get values from different origins for the

same parameter. The Fig. 3 shows an example of decision tree about these choices that can change from parameter to parameter. The other main contribution is the possibility to use the geometric similarity between parts as an alternative way to obtain parameters which are too complicated to decompose or depend too much on tacit knowledge [4]. By finding similar parts we can then adapt any given parameter. This allows us to transcribe the tacit knowledge to be able to reuse it. The model rests on the assumption that geometrically similar parts will likely serve the same function, leading to similar characteristics, letting us determine analogically some variables and costs which are not calculable with a parametric technique. Furthermore, to refine the similarity search we can filter the parts by material for example, in order to have fewer chances of exceptions.

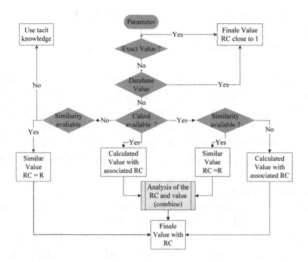

Fig. 3. Decision tree depending on the source

4.3   An Example with the Cost of the Raw Material

In order to illustrate the process of the generalized model, we decide to take a simple example to calculate the cost of the raw material for a CNC part. Let's say enterprise 1 machine aluminum part for motorcycle market. Here is the list of parameters for the part and the enterprise, Eqs. (4) and (5):

$$P = \left(C_{raw}, W, V_{raw}, V_{boundingbox}, \rho, material \right) \tag{4}$$

$$E = \left(Price_{material}, K \right) \tag{5}$$

The fictive enterprise has a database linking material, density and price as shown in Table 2 below (densities are correct but prices are fictive):

Table 2. Density and price database example

Material specification	Density (kg/m^3)	Price ($/kg)
Al 7050	2800	3.56
Al 7178	2830	4.35

Using our previously described method, a possible decomposition scheme is detailed in Fig. 4. We decide to use as much as possible exact data and use similarity to interpolate the raw volume. Indeed, we suppose that the raw volume depends on many other parameters like the volume of the bounding box, the type of machine, machining strategy like near net shape or picture frame. We then expect to find these relations encapsulated inside the past machined similar parts. As a comparison, the company has its own function to calculate the raw volume where K is a tacit factor going from 1.05 up to 1.15 (to add 5 to 15% of the volume) with a reliability factor of 0.7.

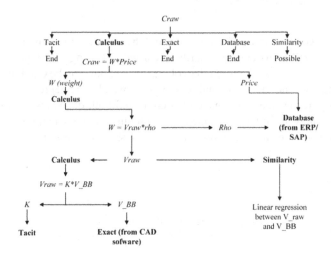

Fig. 4. Decomposition scheme for the example

We have to find the cost of the raw material of the part 4, represented as the blue part. The Table 3 shows the results of the similarity query and the values of the different parameters as well as their origin and reliability coefficient. The RC of the different volume is assumed to be close to 1 as it is taken from the MBD itself. The volume of the raw is the real value measured by operators, thus we assume the RC to be 0.99 with a negligible absolute error depending on the measurement tools. The RC of the price is set to 0.95 as it is a parameter fluctuating in time, and we assume an absolute error of 0.1 if the database has not been updated recently.

Table 3. Parameters of the similar parts and results of the similarity query (ref in blue)

Part		1	2	3	4
C_{raw} ($)	Value	$ 30,323	$ 24,621	$ 22,511	
	Origin	Calcul	Calcul	Calcul	
	RC	0,9405	0,9405	0,9405	
W (kg)	Value	8,518	5,660	5,817	
	Origin	Calcul	Calcul	Calcul	To be
	RC	0,99	0,99	0,99	determined
V_{raw} (m³)	Value	3,042E-03	2,000E-03	2,070E-03	
	Origin	Exact (real)	Exact (real)	Exact (real)	
	RC	0,99	0,99	0,99	
$V_{boundingbox}$(m³)	Value	2,667E-03	1,639E-03	1,813E-03	
	Origin	Exact (MBD)	Exact (MBD)	Exact (MBD)	Exact (MBD)
	RC	1	1	1	1
Material	Value	Al 7050	Al 7178	Al 7075	Al 7050
	Origin	Exact (MBD)	Exact (MBD)	Exact (MBD)	Exact (MBD)
	RC	1	1	1	1
ρ (kg/m³)	Value	2800	2830	2810	2800
	Origin	Database	Database	Database	Database
	RC	1	1	1	1
Price ($/kg)	Value	$ 3,56	$ 4,35	$ 3,87	$ 3,56
	Origin	Database	Database	Database	Database
	RC	0,95	0,95	0,95	0,95
Similarity Index	Value	0,941	0,853	0,76	REF

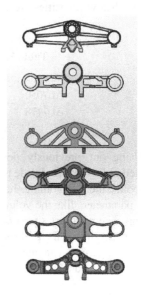

We have used similarity and calculus to find the volume of the raw material for the new part 4, as well as its cost. Similarity is carried out using a weighted linear least squares regression analysis between the volume of the bounding box and the volume of the raw material. The similarity index serves to weight the regression in order to minimize the error estimate. We have then compared both of the results with the real cost that we know in order to evaluate the potential of our methodology. Figure 5 display the outcome of the regression and Table 4 show the resulting comparison.

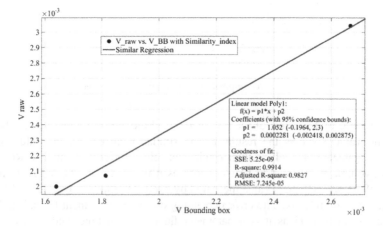

Fig. 5. Results of the weighted least square regression

Our approach shows promising result when used for the cost of the raw material which is already a consistent part of the total cost for a CNC machined part. We manage to reduce the absolute error from $2 to $1.18 on a $28 price, but more important we manage to have a really higher reliability coefficient on that estimation. The tacit factor K is depending on the experts, whereas, using similarity we are able to estimate the raw volume more precisely with a RC up to 0.897 against 0.7. Thus, this allows us to be both closer to the real price ($28.2 estimated with similarity versus $28 real) and more confident with an RC of 0.85. Furthermore, this reliability can be easily increased if we choose parts with a higher similarity index. The methodology helps to evaluate and measure the quality and the confidence of the estimation which both are key factors for the quotation process. The first results obtained with our methodology are very encouraging, therefore more experiments and estimations will be conducted in order to suggest a complete cost estimation model for the different companies and to enhance our possible outcomes.

Table 4. Comparison between the similar method and the approximate calculus of entreprise 1

Part 4	Value	Origin	RC	Absolute error	Error from real value
$V_{boundingbox}$ (m^3)	2,477E−03	Exact (MBD)	1		
K	1,10	Tacit	0,7	0,05	
$V_{raw} = K*V_{boudingbox}$ (m^3)	2,725E−03	Calcul	0,7	0,000123875	3,1%
V_{raw} similar (m^3)	2,831E−03	Similar	0,89776	3,83926E-05	0,7%
V_{raw} (m^3)	2,812E−03	Exact(Real)	0,99		
Price ($/kg)	$ 3,56	Database	0,95	0,1	
ρ (kg/m^3)	2800	Database	1		
C_{raw} calcul ($)	$ 27,17	Calcul	0,665	$2,00	3,1%
C_{raw} similar ($)	$ 28,221	Similar	0,85287	$1,18	0,7%
C_{raw} ($)	$ 28,026	Exact(Real)	0,9405		

5 Conclusion and Future Work

5.1 Conclusion

In this paper, we proposed a new generalized methodology for cost estimation in the case of CNC machined parts. We identified the different models in circulation in the industry and suggested a new approach to deal with the tacit knowledge that is always a major factor during the estimation process. Similarity can be used as an alternative method to obtain precise and valuable information about the cost of a product. It allows to reduce considerably the risk of errors, and increase the fidelity. Accordingly, this proposal shows the importance of knowledge contained within the companies and how many aspects derive from a part's geometry. Hence, the advantages of similarity, for some specific tasks, clearly appears, as stated in this paper.

5.2 Future Work

Our future work concerns the development of a standardized cost estimation model for each aspect of a machined part price (material, machining, post processing, and so on). By talking more with the experts, tracking and benchmarking some parts, we aim to refine further the parameters, functions and models used for the different calculi and better integrate and use the geometrical similarity. We also plan to test further our model in some real-world scenarios to extend its validity and address any potential issues.

Acknowledgement. This work was financed by the Canadian program MITACS, Techniprodec, Conception Genik, Arconic and Stelia North America.

References

1. Alemanni, M., Destefanis, F., Vezzetti, E.: Model-based definition design in the product life cycle management scenario. Int. J. Adv. Manuf. Technol. **52**, 1–14 (2010)
2. Ben-Arieh, D.: Cost estimation system for machined parts. Int. J. Prod. Res. **38**, 4481–4494 (2000)
3. Brière-Côté, A., Rivest, L.: Vers une nouvelle approche pour la mesure et la représentation des différences entre modèles géométriques. In: Communication lors de la conférence: 4e Édition du Colloque sur les Technologies CAO/FAO au Québec, Sherbrooke, Canada, 19 mai 2010
4. Brière-Côté, A., Rivest, L., Maranzana, R.: 3D CAD model comparison: an evaluation of model difference identification technologies. Comput. Aid. Des. Appl. **10**, 173–195 (2013)
5. Boothroyd, G., Radovanovic, P.: Estimating the cost of machined components during the conceptual design of a product. CIRP Ann. Manuf. Technol. **38**(1), 157–160 (1989). Web
6. Chougule, R., Ravi, B.: Casting cost estimation in an integrated product and process design environment. Int. J. Comput. Integr. Manuf. **19**, 676–688 (2006)
7. Feng, C., Kusiak, A., Huang, C.: Cost evaluation in design with form features. Comput. Aid. Des. **28**, 879–885 (1996)
8. Ficko, M., Drstvenšek, I., Brezočnik, M., Balič, J., Vaupotic, B.: Prediction of total manufacturing costs for stamping tool on the basis of CAD-model of finished product. J. Mater. Process. Technol. **164–165**, 1327–1335 (2005)
9. Layer, A., Brinke, E., Houten, F., Kals, H., Haasis, S.: Recent and future trends in cost estimation. Int. J. Comput. Integr. Manuf. **15**, 499–510 (2002)
10. Liu, F., Qiao, L.: Product information modeling and organization with MBD. Appl. Mech. Mater. **163**, 221–225 (2012)
11. Ma, Y., Sajadfar, N., Campos Triana, L.: A feature-based semantic model for automatic product cost estimation. Int. J. Eng. Technol. **6**, 109–113 (2014)
12. Maranzana, R., Msaaf, O., Rivest, L.: Interprétation des modèles géométriques 3D: application à la recherche de pièces et à la comparaison de leurs représentations géométriques. In: Communication lors de la conférence: 75e Congrès de l'Association Francophone pour le Savoir (ACFAS), Trois-Rivières, QC, Canada, 7–11 mai 2007

13. Molcho, G., Cristal, A., Shpitalni, M.: Part cost estimation at early design phase. CIRP Ann. Manuf. Technol. **63**, 153–156 (2014)
14. Msaaf, O., Maranzana, R., Rivest, L.: Part data mining for information re-use in a PLM context. In: Turbo Expo 2007, vol. 1, 13 March 2017. n. pag. Web
15. Niazi, A., Dai, J., Balabani, S., Seneviratne, L.: Product cost estimation: technique classification and methodology review. J. Manuf. Sci. Eng. **128**, 563 (2006)
16. Özcan, B., Fıglalı, A.: Artificial neural networks for the cost estimation of stamping dies. Neural Comput. Appl. **25**(3–4), 717–726 (2014). https://doi.org/10.1007/s00521-014-1546-8. Springer Nature
17. Quintana, V., Rivest, L., Pellerin, R., Venne, F., Kheddouci, F.: Will model-based definition replace engineering drawings throughout the product life cycle? a global perspective from aerospace industry. Comput. Ind. **61**(5), 497–508 (2010). https://doi.org/10.1016/j.compind.2010.01.005. Elsevier BV
18. Estimating Roy, R., Kelvesjo, S., Forsberg, S., Rush, C.: Quantitative and qualitative cost estimating for engineering design. J. Eng. Des. **12**, 147–162 (2001)
19. Shehab, E., Abdalla, H.: Manufacturing cost modeling for concurrent product development. Robot. Comput. Integr. Manuf. **17**, 341–353 (2001)
20. Sutherland, G.H., Roth, B.: Mechanism design: accounting for manufacturing tolerances and costs in function generating problems. J. Eng. Ind. **97**(1), 283 (1975). https://doi.org/10.1115/13,438,551. ASME International
21. Taguchi, G.: Introduction to Quality Engineering. Asian Productivity Organization, Tokyo (2001)
22. Venne, F.: Capture des Annotations au sein de la Maquette numérique en Développement de Produits aéronautiques (2009)
23. Webb, N.M., Shavelson, R.J., Haertel, E.H.: 4 reliability coefficients and generalizability theory. Handb. Stat. **26**, 81–124 (2006). Web. 13 Mar 2017
24. Xu, X., Fang, S., Gu, X.: A model for manufacturing cost estimation based on machining feature. In: International Technology and Innovation Conference, IET 2006, pp. 273–278, Hangzhou (2006). http://ieeexplore.ieee.org/xpl/mostRecentIssue.jsp?filter%3DAND%28p_IS_Number%3A4751946%29%26rowsPerPage%3D100&refinements=4225444339&pageNumber=1&resultAction=REFINE. Accessed 22 Feb 2017

Transformable Product Formal Definition with Its Implementation in CAD Tools

Elise Gruhier[1([⊠])], Robin Kromer[2], Frédéric Demoly[3], Nicolas Perry[1], and Samuel Gomes[3]

[1] Arts et Métiers ParisTech, I2M, CNRS UMR 5295, 33405 Talence, France
elise.gruhier@ensam.eu
[2] IRT Saint Exupéry, I2M, CNRS UMR 5295, 33405 Talence, France
[3] ICB, UMR 6303, CNRS, Univ. Bourgogne Franche-Comté, UTBM, 90010 Belfort, France

Abstract. Nowadays products extend their capabilities towards changing their configurations in order to cover multiple usage needs. They may be named transformable products and have not been taken into consideration in early design stages yet. In this paper, a proactive definition of the product is provided with transformation intrinsic properties. The formalization leads to an architecture. This enables developing a transformable product from two ordinary non-evolving objects. Different configurations and transformation processes have been set and implemented within a CAD tool to design a transformable product. A new paradigm is thus initiated, which will lead to efficient and dynamic design of transformable product.

Keywords: Configuration management · Formal definition · Transformation
Evolving product · Skeleton-based design

1 Introduction

Current design methodologies have been developed to support designer's activities in the definition of "static" product. Product is considered as static in the use phase, when no major evolution is undergone. However, static products are limited in performance [1], leading to the emergence of other kinds of product, such as mechatronical or transformable products. The paper focuses on transformable products, which are characterized by different configurations in the use phase. The transformable product is nowadays under investigation. In literature, few methodologies consider the evolutions related to the transformation stages [2]. Besides, tools are not currently suited to design transformable product [3]. Indeed kinematic scheme, part-to-part relationships graph and CAD tool do not give any information on the different states/configurations of the product during the design process. Therefore, a proactive design methodology taking into account the specific properties and constraints of transformable products needs to be developed, in order to design them efficiently. One of the requirement of this research work is to clearly state what are the transformations encountered by the product and how they could be formalized. Then, a dynamic CAD application taking into consideration the product evolution at the early design stages could be developed. Further investigations,

J. Ríos et al. (Eds.): PLM 2017, IFIP AICT 517, pp. 212–222, 2017.
https://doi.org/10.1007/978-3-319-72905-3_19

such as augmented reality, could be developed based on this work. In this paper, the objective is to propose a transformable product definition considering its evolution during the use phase. First, a brief literature survey presents transformation research works in design process. Then, formal mereotopological and skeletal definitions of transformable product are proposed and lead to an architecture implemented within CAD tools. Finally, in the context of collaborative and proactive design, the interest of these definitions is discussed in the case study.

2   Review on Transformable Product Design Methodologies

With the idea that transformable product will be commonly developed in the future, few research works have been undergone in the domain of design methodologies. Son and Shu [4] have compared the benefits of transformable products and standard products. Transformable products are seen as more efficient to overcome obstacles to "environment significant behavior". Moreover, Camburn et al. [5] have developed indicators to decide when a transformable design is applicable depending on the category of transformer capacity (e.g. store, adjust and so on). Thus, the design of transformable products is justified by those advantages. Besides, Kuhr et al. [6] have created a methodology to determine the opportunities for transformation within each state based on concept opportunity diagrams. The idea was to facilitate the creation of transformable concepts. In addition, transformation principles and facilitators have been observed by Singh et al. [3]. They have listed existing embodiments, such as the expansion, exposition and fusion of products. Finally, Huang et al. [7] have also developed transformable 3D models. However, the product was more regarded as a puzzle, because they did not consider kinematic pairs.

The positioning of the proposed idea regarding other research works is detailed in Fig. 1. All these previous works have been developed at the early product development phase and sometimes even before the design phase. Besides, they have no link with CAD tools for direct application. This paper focuses on the understanding of the transformation and its formal definition to promote the design of evolving products (e.g. transformable products). Besides, a proper architecture has been proposed in order to give specific information to designers. The authors planned to define the architecture of transformable products during the design process in a dynamic way as they are perceived in the real world by users. Indeed, as stated by the CEO of Solidworks "large assemblies open and simulations complete in real-time as perceived by humans" is the next future of CAD tools [8].

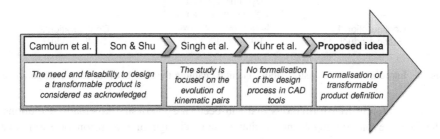

Fig. 1. Positioning of the proposed idea regarding to our literature review

3   Transformable Product Definition

3.1   Transformation Principles

Transformable products are currently part of our everyday life and our dreams. For instance, every day Mary uses her cabriolet (transformed into a car with a roof if it is raining), her sofa (transformed into sofa-bed when a friend visits), wears her leggings (extended depending on her weight) and dreams to have a "Transformer" robot like in the Hollywood movie. Here, a transformable product is defined as being able to adapt to the environment, having multiple functionalities and being able to reversibly transform. Besides, it changes from one configuration related to one environment, to another configuration related to another environment (cf. Fig. 2). So, a transformation, including a change of primary functions, occurs from one configuration to another. During the transformation process, the product is evolving and can be considered as dynamic. On the contrary, during a configuration the product is fully single-state static. As such, transformable products cater to different user needs by performing more than one primary function [9]. Compared to single-state products, transformable products must meet several technical functions and make the link between parts, which are only useful for one configuration. So, the product architect and the designer must take into account more information and make more decisions in the early design stages [10].

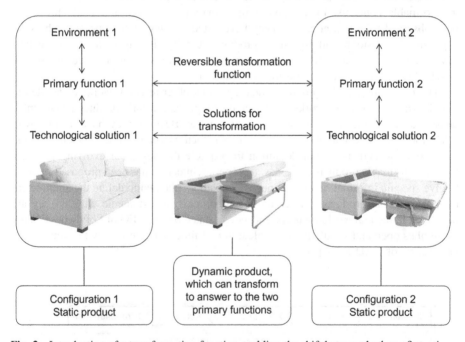

Fig. 2. Introduction of a transformation function enabling the shift between both configurations

Two different transformations that can occur are intern and kinematic evolutions. The intern evolution represents a change (e.g. change of dimension or form) that impacts just one component. The kinematic evolution represents a change of kinematic pairs between two components. Here, the product definition is focused on kinematic evolution during the use phase.

3.2 Transformable Product Architecture

This section explains how from two different static products (based on routine design) the product architect can propose an architecture defining the novel transformable product. Figure 3 introduces the transformation diagram composed of four columns. The first and third columns list parts, which are only used in one configuration. The second one represents parts belonging to both configurations. The last column gives the proposed technological solutions (e.g. kinematic pairs) chosen between two parts or the transformation technological solutions (e.g. transformation relationships described later). The product architect proposes an initial structure with parts and kinematic pairs corresponding to product evolution encountered in the use phase. A design process strategy is determined to aid the designer in configurations 1 and 2. The difficulty will be to implement this transformation diagram for a complex product. In this case, a design methodology will be required.

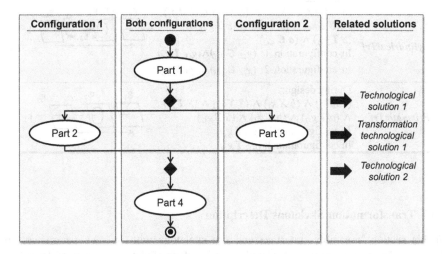

Fig. 3. Transformation diagram showing the link between both configurations and related technological solutions

3.3 Transformation Mereotopological Definition

Transformable products evolve during the use phase when the user wants a specific function. This evolution needs to be formally described, so as to be later applied in information or Computer-Aided Design (CAD) system. Therefore, mereotopological theory has been used to describe the evolution into spatiotemporal relationships (i.e. primitives). Mereotopology is a region-based theory enabling the formalization of two predicates (i.e. parthood and connection) with mathematical descriptions.

The primitives have been named upon *Trf* (referring to Transformation) adding to the kinematic pair name. Table 1 shows some examples of mereotopological descriptions and their related representations. *a* and *b* are two parts in relation and *S* is the sketch to design *a* and *b* (*b* is the base part, which does not evolve). This enables designing in a top-down manner where parts are designing from a common relationship. *X*, *C* and *T* respectively stand for *Cross*, *Coincident* and *Tangent* mereotopological primitives. The skeletons *k*, *f* and *g* are described in the section below.

Table 1. Examples of some mereotopological descriptions of transformation primitives

Primitive name	Mereotopological description in the use phase	Representation
RevoluteTrf	During design: $(a\,X\,k_1) \wedge (b\,X\,k_1) \wedge (S\,X\,k_1) \wedge (S\,T\,f_1)$ $\wedge\,(S\,T\,k_2) \wedge (a\,C\,g_{i2})$ In configuration 1: $(g_{i2}\,C\,g_1)$ In configuration 2: $(g_{i2}\,C\,g_3)$	
CylindricalTrf	During design: $(a\,X\,k_1) \wedge (b\,X\,k_1) \wedge (S\,X\,k_1) \wedge (S\,T\,f_1)$ $\wedge\,(S\,T\,k_2) \wedge (a\,T\,g_{i5}) \wedge (b\,T\,g_4) \wedge$ $(S\,T\,g_{i5}) \wedge (a\,C\,g_{i2})$ In configuration 1: $(g_{i2}\,C\,g_1)\wedge(g_{i5}\,T\,g_4)$ In configuration 2: $(g_{i2}\,C\,g_3)\wedge(g_{i5}\,T\,g_6)$	
PrismaticTrf	During design: $(a\,X\,k_1) \wedge (b\,X\,k_1) \wedge (S\,X\,k_1) \wedge (S\,T\,f_1)$ $\wedge\,(a\,T\,g_{i2}) \wedge (b\,T\,g_1) \wedge (S\,T\,g_{i2})$ In configuration 1: $(g_{i2}\,T\,g_1)$ In configuration 2: $(g_{i2}\,T\,g_3)$	

3.4   Transformation Skeletons Description

In this section, assembly, interface and use skeletons with its own parameters are described for each primitive. Assembly and interface skeletons are reused from previous works achieved in the assembly process [11]. Assembly skeleton (i.e. named *k*) ensures assembly positioning and interface skeleton describes geometric boundaries used to build a functional surface (i.e. named *f*). Use skeletons are introduced so as to be able to proactively define the product evolution in the use phase. These skeletons give information about both extreme boundaries of the move (i.e. *g*) and one intermediate use skeleton (i.e. *gi*), on which the product will be designed, navigating between boundaries. The intermediate skeleton can be instantaneously modified with defined parameters (i.e. last column of Table 2). Translation of a skeleton in the x, y and z axis, as well as rotation in the x, y and z axis are the two types of allowed parameters. The integration of those skeletons in CAD tools enables the designer to directly work in a dynamic context changing in regard to the chosen configuration. The idea was that the designer can choose one configuration and directly visualize the product in the chosen representation during design processing.

Table 2. Some skeletal descriptions of transformation primitives

Primitive name	Assembly skeleton	Interface skeleton	Use skeleton with parameter	
RevoluteTrf	k_1 line k_2 plane	f_1 surface	g_1, gi_2, g_3 points	α_x
CylindricalTrf	k_1 line	f_1 surface	g_1, gi_2, g_3 points g_4, gi_5, g_6 surface	x, α_x
PrismaticTrf	k_1 line	f_1 surface	g_1, gi_2, g_3 surface	x

4   Case Study

This section follows the three main steps: product architecture, mereotopological definition and skeletons description, for the dynamic design of transformable product. Here the objective is to formally define a "Transformer toy" having two distinct configurations, such as a mechanical digger and a fighting humanoid robot. The next step is to design this "Transformer toy" in a routine manner, as the geometry of both configurations is assumed to be known.

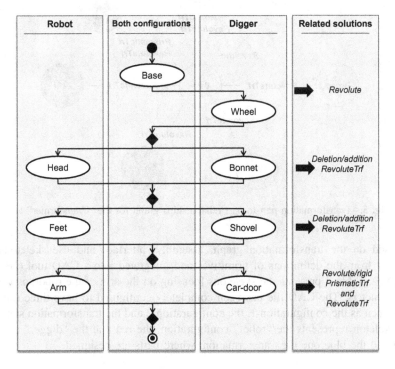

Fig. 4. Transformation diagram of the case study

Figure 4 presents the transformation diagram showing parts and their related solutions (i.e. mereotopological relationships or kinematic pairs). Here, the product architect has decided that the robot requires a head, feet and arms, as well as the digger needs a shovel, a bonnet and a car-door. Three of these six components (i.e. head, feet and arms) were necessary for the robot configuration and were useless for the digger configuration. In this case, the idea was to hide and show these components at the right time using a revolute pair. The shovel could also bring stability to the robot. Concerning the arm/car-door relationships, the idea was to use prismatic pair to move aside the arm from the body and a revolute pair to move the arm (cf. Table 4). Without the preliminary translation of the arm, the rotation would not be possible.

With this information, a transformation graph (cf. Fig. 5) containing all parts has been drawn. Some parts (e.g. bonnet and head) are linked, as one should appear in one configuration and be deleted in the other one. As such, the transformation graph integrates information from previous information with novel transformation primitives earlier defined. For instance, the product architect proposes a transformation part-to-part relationships graph. The kinematic pairs are defined for both configurations in the same graph. The transformation mereotopological description provides new information to the designer.

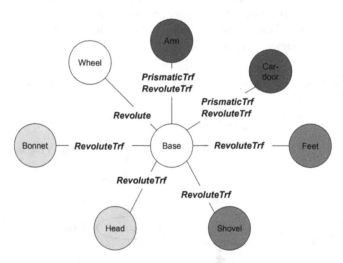

Fig. 5. Transformation part-to-part relationships graph for the "Transformer" toy

Based on the transformation graph, assembly, interface and use skeletons are extracted from the definitions of primitives and integrated into a CAD tool (i.e. here Catia V5). Table 3 presents the skeletons focusing on the arm of the robot, as well as the parameters. The CAD file has been completely configured to have three different states, such as the configuration 1, the configuration 2 and the transformation step. The pink skeleton represents the "robot" configuration, the red one the "digger" configuration and the blue one the transformation, where parts are designed.

Table 3. Skeletons representation and behaviour according to the selected configuration

Configuration	Skeletons representation and parameters
Configuration 1	DesignTable.1, configuration row: 2 — Line | Configuration_choice | PrismaticTrf\x | RevoluteTrf\angle_proj_x | RevoluteTrf\angle_proj_y : 1 Transformation 100mm 70,7mm 70,7mm; 2 Configuration1 0mm 100mm 0mm; <3> Configuration2 300mm 0mm 100mm
Transformation (g_1, g_{i5}, g_6, g_3, k_1, g_{i2}, f_1, g_4)	DesignTable.1, configuration row: 1 — Line | Configuration_choice | PrismaticTrf\x | RevoluteTrf\angle_proj_x | RevoluteTrf\angle_proj_y : 1 Transformation 100mm 70,7mm 70,7mm; 2 Configuration1 0mm 100mm 0mm; <3> Configuration2 300mm 0mm 100mm
Configuration 2	DesignTable.1, configuration row: 3 — Line | Configuration_choice | PrismaticTrf\x | RevoluteTrf\angle_proj_x | RevoluteTrf\angle_proj_y : 1 Transformation 100mm 70,7mm 70,7mm; 2 Configuration1 0mm 100mm 0mm; <3> Configuration2 300mm 0mm 100mm

With these novel skeletons, the designer can create both parts (i.e. the arm/car-door and the base part of the robot/digger) as in Table 4 by modeling volume and shape. The CAD tree is presented in Fig. 6 with *PrismaticTrf* and *RevoluteTrf*, as well as two CAD bodies (i.e. Arm and Body) directly related, thanks to publications, to skeletons and the choice of the configuration. This CAD tree has been structured to highlight the research work. As such, the designer is aware that:

- The prismatic pair to extract the arm from the body is limited by a surface (use skeletons of the *PrismaticTrf* from Table 2), whose distance has been previously chosen by the product architect thanks to the parameter x;

Table 4. Focus on the arm of the toy transformation skeletons

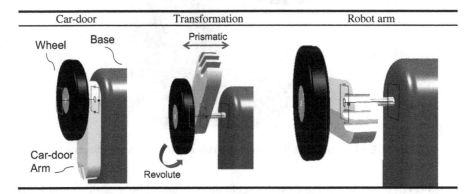

Car-door	Transformation	Robot arm

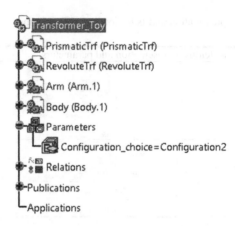

Fig. 6. CAD tree of the arm/car-door design

- The revolute pair is constrained between 0 and 90°;
- The robot can undergo the prismatic pair once the rotation (use skeletons of the **RevoluteTrf**) is one more time at the original point (limited with the α parameter chosen by the product architect).

Contrary to current static CAD tools, here several visions related to product configurations are presented. Consequently, the designer can choose, on which vision/configuration of the transformable product, he wants to work. This dynamically simulates the evolution of the product and enables checking the upholding of kinematic pairs thanks to novel use skeletons. For instance, the arm needed to be locked in mechanical digger configuration, so an added structure (i.e. highlighted parts in Fig. 7) was proposed by the designer.

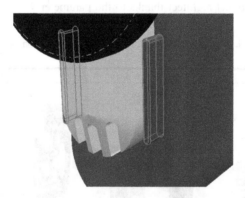

Fig. 7. Locking structure from product architect's transformation diagram

However, novel architectural product definition is limited because of current CAD tools. To go further, a new kind of interactive and dynamic CAD tools should be developed. Indeed, CAD tools are currently used for static design and not for the design of transformable or evolving products. This future CAD tool could have for instance a sliding cursor enabling visualizing both configurations and the intermediate steps of the transformation. Product design evolving in space and time is the key issue in the future.

5   Conclusions and Future Work

This paper has presented the first step of the research works motivated by literature review on transformation in the design phase. Compared to current works, here transformable products are designed from an architecture based on skeletons. The transformation primitives of the product have been formally defined using mereotopology and relying on skeletons. Indeed, assembly and interface skeletons have been reused from previous works and use skeletons have been created so as to make designers aware of boundaries of kinematic pairs move. Use skeletons are directly linked to parameters, which enable product architect to modify distances or angles at the preliminary stages of design. This product definition has also been integrated in CAD tools so as to design in a dynamic manner from a detailed architecture. It brings to the designer the opportunity to see the product evolution in the design phases.

In future work, this definition will be included in a design methodology so as to design transformable products. This novel methodology will ensure collaborative work through Product Lifecycle Management by linking the product definition to the transformation sequence, and will be integrated in CAD tools.

References

1. Ferguson, S., Tilstra, A.H., Seepersad, C.C., Wood, K.L.: Development of a changeable airfoil optimization model for use in the multidisciplinary design of unmanned aerial vehicles. In: ASME 2009 International Design Engineering Technical Conferences and Computers and Information in Engineering Conference, pp. 57–68 (2009)
2. Kiritsis, D.: Closed-loop PLM for intelligent products in the era of the Internet of things. Comput. Aided Des. **43**(5), 479–501 (2011)
3. Singh, V., Skiles, S.M., Krager, J.E., Wood, K.L., Jensen, D., Sierakowski, R.: Innovations in design through transformation: a fundamental study of transformation principles. J. Mech. Des. **131**(8), 081010 (2009)
4. Son, J.J., Shu, L.H.: Role of transformation principles in enabling environmentally significant behavior. In: Dornfeld, D., Linke, B. (eds.) Leveraging Technology for a Sustainable World, pp. 563–568. Springer, Heidelberg (2012). https://doi.org/10.1007/978-3-642-29069-5_95
5. Camburn, B.A., Guillemette, J., Crawford, R.H., Wood, K.L., Jensen, D.J., Wood, J.J.: When to transform? Development of indicators for design context evaluation. In: ASME 2010, International Design Engineering Technical Conferences and Computers and Information in Engineering Conference, pp. 249–266 (2010)

6. Kuhr, R., Wood, K., Jensen, D., Crawford, R.: Concept opportunity diagrams: a visual modeling method to find multifunctional design concepts. In: ASME 2010 International Design Engineering Technical Conferences and Computers and Information in Engineering Conference, pp. 193–205 (2010)
7. Huang, Y.-J., Chan, S.-Y., Lin, W.-C., Chuang, S.-Y.: Making and animating transformable 3D models. Comput. Graph. **54**, 127–134 (2016)
8. Wang, B.: The future of CAD 2019 as predicted by Solidworks (2009). http://www.nextbigfuture.com/2009/10/future-of-cad-2019-as-predicted-by.html
9. Kalyanasundaram, V., Lewis, K.: A function based approach for product integration. J. Mech. Des. **136**, 041002 (2014)
10. Literman, B., Cormier, P., Lewis, K.: Concept analysis for reconfigurable products. In: ASME 2012 International Design Engineering Technical Conferences (2012)
11. Gruhier, E., Demoly, F., Kim, K.-Y., Abboudi, S., Gomes, S.: A theoretical framework for product relationships description over space and time in integrated design. J. Eng. Des. **27**(4–6), 269–305 (2016)

Empty Space Modelling for Detecting Spatial Conflicts Across Multiple Design Domains

Arun Kumar Singh[1,2(✉)], B. Gurumoorthy[2], and Latha Christie[1]

[1] Microwave Tube Research and Development Centre (DRDO), Bangalore 560013, India
arunsingh_asks@yahoo.com
[2] Centre for Product Design and Manufacturing, Indian Institute of Science,
Bangalore 560012, India

Abstract. This paper discusses identification and decomposition of empty spaces in Computer Aided Design (CAD) model for detecting spatial conflicts across multiple design domains. An Algorithm has been developed to identify empty spaces in CAD model and decompose it to a level, where it can be correctly associated with the connected domains, states and requirements. Knowledge capture and representation have been demonstrated with System Modelling Language (SysML) diagrams using SysML tools. SysML blocks have been introduced to define intended empty spaces, product states and design domain in SysML structure diagrams. Association of these blocks with neighboring parts, has also been discussed. A case study of heat sink assembly has been taken for Empty space modelling.

Keywords: SysML · Empty space modelling · Spatial conflict

1 Introduction

Product designs are carried out with objectives to satisfy multifunctional domain requirements. In every product design, some spaces are intentionally left empty to satisfy specific requirements of different domains. For example space may have been provided for electrical insulation, thermal isolation, clearance for moving part, port accessibility, Electron beam or Radio frequency interaction, expansion of material, tool access, sensors, bolts accessibility, welding tools, or for removal/replacement of parts. There may be cases, where the same space is used for different purposes but in different product states. The space, which has been provided for moving parts clearance in operation state also serves the purpose for accessibility in maintenance state. That is the same space, which is used for two different purposes but in different states. Knowledge regarding these space usage for moving part clearance under operation state, may not have been documented or is not available to designer, who is searching for empty space to locate new module into the product. This may create spatial conflict with workspace of other designer in the same domain or with other domain designers. This also incurs time wastage; if these spatial conflicts are detected and resolved through conventional methods of multi-domain design stakeholder reviews. Electro-Mechanical systems

© IFIP International Federation for Information Processing 2017
Published by Springer International Publishing AG 2017. All Rights Reserved
J. Ríos et al. (Eds.): PLM 2017, IFIP AICT 517, pp. 223–230, 2017.
https://doi.org/10.1007/978-3-319-72905-3_20

exhibit more examples of these types of conflict. Designers from different domains have spatial conflicts, who claim over same empty space in coupled design iterations at different timelines.

CAD tools only hold the geometry information of the product, while beyond geometry information is not captured in CAD models. Product design information like requirements, product states, and actors involved at different product states, functional model and behaviour model, is not available in CAD model. Use of tools like System Modelling Language (SysML) by incorporation of system engineering domain, provides a way to capture and to represent product's non-geometry design knowledge. Problem at hand needs identification of intended empty spaces and its decomposition to correctly associate a portion of this empty space with the corresponding non-geometry information.

This problem for spatial conflict detection can be divided mainly into three levels: first level is identification of bulk of Empty space available in products, decomposition of this bulk empty space block into smaller empty space blocks and incorporation of non-geometry product knowledge by modelling it as system level domain information in SysML. Second level is building associativity among these empty spaces, product parts and SysML Information. The third level is spatial conflict detection using first two levels of information. In this paper, first level has been attempted.

2   System Modelling Language (SysML) Model and Diagrams

Before identification of empty spaces in product, methods are needed for capturing and representing non-geometry product knowledge. There are various product models available to capture non-geometry product information like NIST Core Product Model (CPM) [1, 2], its extension Open Assembly Model (OAM) [3] and Methodology and tools Oriented to Knowledge-based engineering Applications (MOKA) [4, 5]. These product models have classes to define product form, assembly structure, function, behavior and technology. These models are developed in Unified Modelling Language (UML). These product models do not have classes to define empty spaces and its associations with product knowledge. In recent times, more studies have been done to improve UML for incorporating system engineering domain information. SysML [6] is the extension of UML, which is developed to provide standard system modelling tools. SysML supports capturing requirements of system and capturing structural & behavioral models. SysML also supports equation based behavior through constraint blocks. Block Definition Diagrams (BDD) and Internal Block Diagrams (IBD) are used to define classes and instances. BDD and IBD are extended from UML structure diagram. SysML contains two new diagrams namely requirement diagram and Parametric Diagram, which were not present in UML2 diagrams.

Use of SysML tools, provides the way to capture, represent and associate the product's non-geometry information. There are no direct methods in SysML to resolve spatial conflicts of product design, as it is only a modelling language. Higher modelling efforts are needed to model information manually in SysML for any product. Hence automation of knowledge capture should be a criteria to generate information wherever possible by interfaces and standards. Bringing information in structured form inside SysML, can be a step towards interoperability as information is available in open standards and in structured form like XML. Having information in system engineering domain brings new challenges of maintaining consistency among developing models. Different designers use different design tools which do not communicate directly and have been proposed to be integrated by common framework of system engineering domain [7].

It is intended to detect spatial conflicts at different timelines of product lifecycle. In Building Information Management (BIM) tools, 4D modeling is used to detect such spatial conflicts [8]. It is like 3D modelling with an additional time variable. In product lifecycle, the time variable can be considered as product states. Product goes through manufacturing and assembly after design completion. Then it may go to transportation state before getting commissioned for operation. It may require periodic maintenance. A typical SysML product state diagram has been shown in Fig. 1. Product Design may involve designers from different domains, using different tools and working on product at different timelines. There can be domains involved in product design like structural, thermal, manufacturing, ergonomics, electrical, electro-magnetic etc.

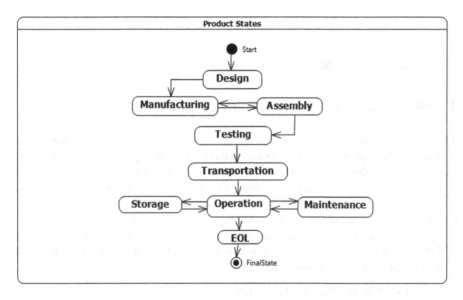

Fig. 1. Typical product states and transitions in a product lifecycle

CAD tools hold product geometry information so the same CAD tools should be holding the geometry of the empty spaces. Empty space block geometry data can also be saved in open standards like STEP, if multi-domain tools have to access this information. Other information for these blocks should be inside the SysML Product Model. SysML blocks have been introduced to define intended empty spaces. Blocks (Classes) for Empty space, product states and design domain, have been added in SysML Block Definition Diagram (BDD) shown in Fig. 2. An assembly is composed of parts and empty space blocks. An assembly can also aggregate other subassemblies. This has been shown in Fig. 2 by having a self-aggregation. Empty space blocks have direct associations with parts, product states and design domains with a multiplicity of (0 *) as shown in Fig. 2. These blocks can have inferred associations with requirements and functional diagram through Parts, states or domains.

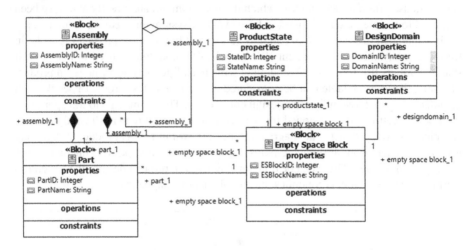

Fig. 2. SysML Block Definition Diagram (BDD) with empty space block

3   Identification and Decomposition of Empty Spaces

The first step in spatial conflict detection is identification of empty spaces available to be used at that design state. CAD tools are used for 3D modelling of product components and assemblies. There are different levels of sub-assemblies used to make the design modular in nature. Empty spaces available for modelling at part level are different when same parts are assembled together to from an assembly. Identification of these spaces then becomes an assembly level affair than to find it on part level.

Code has been generated to identify and decompose empty spaces for assemblies in SolidWorks with Visual Basic Application (VBA) API. These are the steps used in code for identification and decomposition of Empty Spaces

- Extract solid bodies from the Product Assembly into a new part.
- Calculate Bounding Box Dimensions surrounding these solid bodies.
- Create a Solid Block with the bounding box dimensions not merging it with the existing solid bodies.
- Subtract Product solid bodies from the bounding box main block.
- Extract planes/surfaces derived from selected faces from Product Assembly.
- Split this empty space block into a number of solid bodies using extracted planes.
- Save these blocks into a separate folder as separate entities. Convert these parts into assembly feature in SolidWorks to make every empty space block editable and to have mating features based on the part associations.

SysML Diagrams have been generated using open source code Papyrus on Eclipse IDE. Figure 3 shows the schematic of envisaged code interaction with CAD model and SysML model to fully automate the task of knowledge capture. SysML data is held in XML format, which makes it easy to expose and interface it with other applications and tools. A commercial CAD system SolidWorks is being used, only for accessing geometry. STEP has been chosen to store the product geometry data for the proposed implementation as that makes the solution vendor neutral.

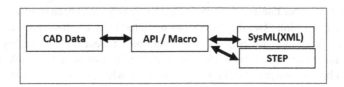

Fig. 3. Schematic showing code interaction with CAD and SysML

4   Case Study

A heat Sink assembly, which is used to cool electronic circuits has been taken as a case study for empty space identification and decomposition. SysML Requirement diagram has been shown for Heat Sink assembly in Fig. 4. Heat sink requirements are composed of electronic circuit requirements, thermal design requirements and manufacturing feasibility shown in diagram. Maximum allowable temperature limits are decided by the Electronic circuit component datasheets, which falls into the electronic domain. Thermal designer does fan selection and designs heat sink parameters like fin length,

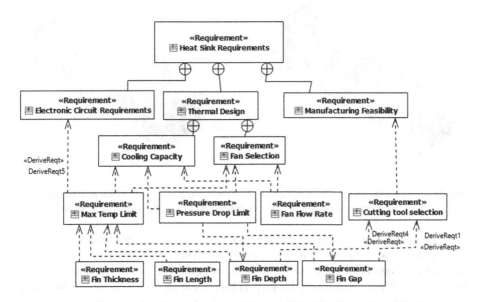

Fig. 4. SysML requirement diagram for Heat Sink Assembly

depth, gap and width. Fan flow rates and pressure drops are associated with fan selection. Final pressure drops depend upon heat sink fin parameters like fin depth and fin gap. The same parameters are driven by the manufacturing domain as these have to be fabricated and the cutting tool should be available to machine these fins gaps with that fin depth. Complexity of associativity and design dependency for a simple heat sink design, have been depicted using this SysML requirement diagram.

3D Model for Heat sink assembly has been generated in SolidWorks and is shown in Fig. 5a. Bounding box coordinates are calculated and a Bounding box solid body is created with these coordinates as shown in Fig. 5b. This box has been used as main block and remaining heat sink assembly has been subtracted from it. This results into the part shown in Fig. 5c, which are empty spaces available in Heat Sink Assembly. As seen there are counter bore holes made for screws needed to assemble heat sink. But other than these, a bulk of space is available as single part, which needs to be further decomposed.

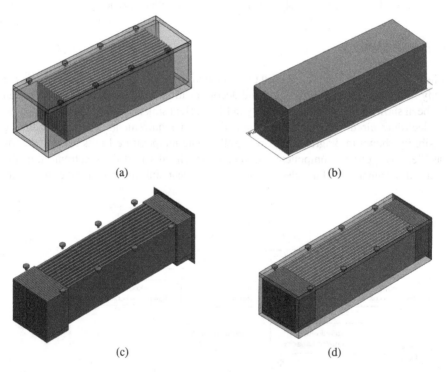

Fig. 5. (a) 3D model of Heat Sink Assembly. (b) Bounding Box, (c) Identified and decomposed Empty spaces. (d) Empty space solid bodies assembled back with the Heat sink assembly.

Face selections are made to split the bulk volumes into smaller blocks, which are used to decompose this block into smaller blocks. This empty space model has been inserted back into heat sink assembly and shown in Fig. 5d. Decomposition is needed to such a level that can correctly identify and represent air flow between two fins with a decomposed block. Any obstruction made in-between heat sink fins, restricts air flow under operation and in turn reduces heat sink cooling capacity of device. Any part located in airflow path should be a conflict with thermal domain.

All these empty space blocks can be captured in SysML IBD with block definitions, which are done in BDD as shown in Fig. 2. At present IBD has been created using SysML Tool Papyrus as shown in Fig. 6. Heat Sink, Enclosure and Decomposed Empty space blocks are modelled as instances inside heat sink assembly IBD. Connections have been shown to represent associations among them. Generation of IBD and connections have been envisaged to be done automatically in future.

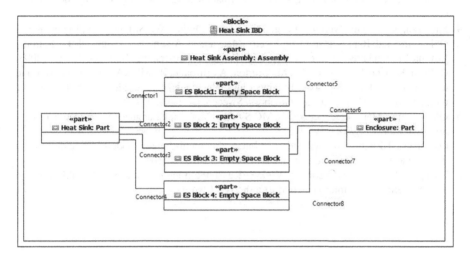

Fig. 6. Internal Block Diagram (IBD) for Heat Sink Assembly showing only selective empty space block instances and association with parts.

5 Conclusion

New blocks have been defined in SysML model for empty spaces, parts, assemblies, product states and domains. These blocks can be used to capture and represent knowledge inside CAD tools. Identification and decomposition of empty spaces inside CAD have been discussed and code has been generated for automation task. SysML diagram has been generated in SysML tools to model CAD assembly structure and generated empty space blocks.

Association of this knowledge with Empty space blocks inside CAD tools has not been done now and has been proposed for future work. Spatial Conflict detection, which needs first two level of information of Empty space blocks, SysML information and their associations, is proposed for future work.

Acknowledgement. The First author is thankful to Director, Microwave Tube Research & Development Centre (MTRDC) for providing the opportunity and encouragement in carrying out the work presented in the paper.

References

1. Fenves, S.J., Foufou, S., Bock, C., Sriram, R.D.: CPM2: a core model for product data. J. Comput. Inform. Sci. Eng. **8**(1), 014501 (2008). ASME
2. Foufou, S., Fenves, S.J., Bock, C., Rachuri, S., Sriram, R.: A core product model for PLM with an illustrative XML implementation. In: Proceedings of the PLM International Conference on Product Lifecycle Management, pp. 21–32. Inderscience Publishers, Lyon, July 2005
3. Rachuri, S., Han, Y.-H., Foufou, S., Feng, S.C., Roy, U., Wang, F., Sriram, R.D., Lyons, K.W.: A model for capturing product assembly information. J. Comput. Inf. Sci. Eng. **6**(1), 11–21 (2006)
4. Sudarsan, R., Young-Hyun, H., Feng, S.C., Roy, U., Fujun, W., Sriram, R.D., Lyons, K.W.: Object-oriented Representation of Electro-Mechanical Assemblies Using UML. National Institute of Standards and Technology, NISTIR 7057, Gaithersburg, MD 20899, USA (2003)
5. Oldham, K., Kneebone, S., Callot, M., Murton, A., Brimble, R.: MOKA – a methodology and tools oriented to knowledge-based engineering applications. In: Proceedings of the Conference on Integration in Manufacturing, Goteborg, Sweden, pp. 198–207 (1998)
6. OMG (Object Management Group). OMG Systems Modelling Language Specification (2015). http://www.omg.org/spec/SysML/1.4/
7. Qamar, A., Törngren, M., Wikander, J.: Integrating multi-domain models for the design and development of mechatronic systems. In: INCOSE 2010 (2010)
8. Zhang, Z.: Detecting and resolving Work-Space Congestions and Time-Space conflict through 4D - Modeling In the micro level, Master thesis (2016)

Design and Development of Orthopedic Implants Through PLM Strategies

Andrea Patricia Murillo Bohórquez, Clara Isabel López Gualdrón(✉),
and Javier Mauricio Martínez Gómez

Escuela de Diseño Industrial, Universidad Industrial de Santander, Bucaramanga, Colombia
Andre_murillo25@hotmail.com, {clalogu,javimar}@uis.edu.co

Abstract. The main research purpose in this work was to propose strategies to reduce uncertainty, setbacks and development times involved into orthopedic implants design process. For research proposal, it was used as reference a manufacturing framework design, based on simulation environments tools and PLM strategies. In addition, this research was carried out to define a model of practices which facilitated process interoperability in osteosynthesis implant development. The model proposed focused on product definition stages and manufacturing as a workflow which defined stages, processes, activities and roles in production of implants with collaborative work scheme in PLM. As part of model execution, a case study was developed in a technology-based company which produces osteosynthesis implants. Finally, the research compared traditional processes in this company with the new model proposed, in order to determine obtained improvements.

Finally, this comparison shows reduction in repetitive operations and uncertainty into the processes. Besides, quality of final design was improved like high precision and time reduction.

Keywords: Technologies integration · Design process · Manufacturing design Medical device development

1 Introduction

Medical devices are health care products, and these kind of goods has been becoming one of the most profitable areas in medicine [2], in part at increase in average life expectancy, degenerative diseases [3], musculoskeletal system pathological conditions, trauma caused by accidents (traffic, sports, and domestic) and risky life practices [4]. The expectations of market shared for new product development of orthopedic medical devices is growing up. For health care companies, is an imperative need to improve their capabilities to developing innovative products [1] through design activities integrated in new product development process.

Epidemiological studies show that more than seventy percent of any trauma cases have required surgery treatment, and usually a fracture also has required to be reduced by ostheosyntesis implant. Hence, an implant must be adapted anatomically to restore

J. Ríos et al. (Eds.): PLM 2017, IFIP AICT 517, pp. 231–240, 2017.
https://doi.org/10.1007/978-3-319-72905-3_21

as well as possible a broken bone [5]. However, development of orthopedic implants might be complex, because a piece of an anatomical structure must be replaced or reduced, partially or totally [2].

These orthopedic devices require to merging activities performed by CAx software during definition and development process [6]. However, innovation of medical devices in technology-based companies is an intricate process, and require multidisciplinary approaches to knowledge, such as medicine, engineering and design [6]; these sort of products could lack adequate process development, if controls, technology management [7], and regulations were not attended [8]. Likewise, depending on products complexity, difficulties can arise when iteration activities happen, or obtaining a physical product [9]. This landscape is a challenge for organizations that must generate patient-friendly products, and ensure patient safety. Finally, these products must comply with current health regulations and being profitable [2].

Specific design and performance requirements were defined to accelerate innovation and product launching [10]; this approach is known as life product life-cycle management (PLM) and is applied in New Product Development (NPD) process. PLM technologies purpose is to offer managerial tools to improving product development process. PLM is referenced as well as a strategy oriented to provide business solutions. Given these points, project resources and areas like product definition, process integration, people and systems, those were high interested areas for applying this kind of strategies. These strategies are well-timed to articulate goals, data and processes of product development from each department, in order to share information through collaborative approach; in other words, these strategies are aimed more particularly at better organization of product development processes from each department to share the information [11]. Strategies have the ability to address complex products with a large number of technical components, or components developed by different organizational teams [12]. Also, it is looking for reduce complexity of products, increase productivity in processes, reduce cost and shorten processing times by optimizing workflow [13].

CAx tools are a form to integrate some software in a workflow model to create new products. These software tools have been used in production of plastic parts [16], engineering parts [17], and robotics [18]. With these kind of software many companies have achieved outcomes successfully, focusing on product development, manufacturing cycle times and production costs reduction [19].

Through PLM, integration of CAx tools with the intention to improve the accuracy of medical devices is possible, obtaining a significative development time reduction [3, 14, 15], equally drop in uncertainty level that normally is evident in medical devices development process. In effect, practices to improve efficiency in design and manufacturing process were created by incorporating advances in information technology, systematization of product definition and development activities. CAx tools such as Computer Aided Design (CAD) to modeling parts, Computer Aided Manufacturing (CAM) oriented to make or produce components or products, and Computer Aided Engineering (CAE) to verify mechanical behavior of material and quality of the workpiece by simulation techniques; those have been integrated as PLM technologies.

In spite of the important contributions achieved through PLM in areas such as: aerospace [13], aeronautics [20], textiles [11] modular products [21], and productive processes, there are few contributions about PLM in medical sector and orthopedic implants development. Those are oriented on using PLM as a tool only for product management in their economic life [6], or improving biomedical systems, by merging clinical processes and PLM with the intention to increase patient attention quality [22].

In summary, according with the explanation about problems which have been solved through PLM strategies in other sectors, therefore, the authors of this research made a preliminary study using a diagnostic tool [9]. In this diagnosis, weaknesses were identified in areas like business, product and project management, collaboration and integrated workflow. Based on the diagnosis performed, the main purpose of this research was proposing a model of practices by PLM strategies in function to improve osteosynthesis implant design process. The paper is structured as follows: In Sect. 2 describes the methodology. In Sect. 3, explains the proposal and main results of case study. Finally in Sect. 4, the article concludes with a discussion of limitations.

2 Methodology

For present research, an exploratory study was chosen, so methodology was structured according to design thinking (DT) approach. DT is a process for problem-solving oriented to the practice, allowing approaches at product development into the company, and identifying weaknesses related with customized solutions.

In the first stage, researchers applied a diagnostic tool on product lifecycle management with the aim of identify capabilities and weaknesses into the company, specifically in product development. Information was obtained through interviews, which had done to the manager and technical staff. A line of questions were formulated about "which is the problem", "why is being generated and how it affects product development". Also, a field observation was hold in order to checking methodology followed by company.

In second stage, a case study was defined. Obtained data were analyzed about a product manufactured by the company. Times of processes, relationship of contact area between bone and plate, and finally resources required for model implementation.

Finally, in third stage, according to the analysis and previous evaluations, a new workflow was proposed based on PLM strategies, with the aim to develop a design process for osteosynthesis implants. For verification purposes, the new workflow was applied and analyzed by comparative evaluation with the model made by company. The evaluation scope was verifying design solutions physically, comparing times of each process. The accuracy of plate it was verified by measuring the contact area between bone and plate. Once workflow and software tools were defined, PLM strategies through project data management (PDM) were applied. With that in mind, activities for implant development in the case study were integrated.

3 Results

3.1 Diagnostic

The main results obtained from the case study, carried out in the osteosynthesis implant company, according to preliminary analysis, the company's mature capabilities. The four main levels such as: Business, product and project management and the last level collaboration integration are described below.

Business management: New product development has been performed by the company in organized way, based on market supply and competition offers alternatives. There were no collaborative information systems within the organization, so the main software tools (CAD, Office, etc.) were using on independently. The "Know How" of the company resides mainly in people, owing to workers experience, and no common source of knowledge was available inside organization.

Product management: The stages evaluated in the design of a product were focused on conceptual definition, design and detail engineering. Management of documentation which had been generated by each application took as a reference a shared folders system by organization, which had stored their documents manually. It is essential to have a software to allow plans visualization and to facilitate supervision in modifications that has made.

Project management: The project control tools were not found.

Collaboration in integration: Workflow in product design process was lineal and sequential, preventing different user's involvement in creation of technical files, in order to get better changes tracking. Product design and manufacturing departments acted separately, having their own information systems.

The analysis of weaknesses in the company workflow regarding definition process and osteosynthesis implants manufacturing was deployed in Fig. 1. Design process were highlight in blue, manufacturing process in green, production in orange, and finally, problems in red. These problems were presented in obtaining a reference model, for the design of the plate, the product design and the manufacturing processes, by example metal bender and fixture. Designing process involved on these devices has been complex, because it is responsible for generating specific curvatures in the plate and fixing those during the manufacturing processes. Difficulties during manufacturing processes might generate extensive development times, repetitions of activities and material losses.

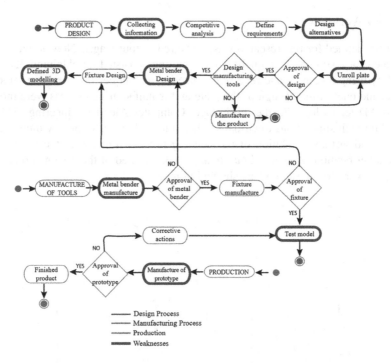

Fig. 1. Company workflow. (Color figure online)

3.2 Case Study

The case study was carried out in an SME Colombian dedicated to design and manufacture of orthopedic implants like plates, screws and nails. The selection of the case study was defined according company's needs to manufacture a product. Mainly this type of plates implies necessary the design of specialized devices for manufacturing it. Main problem identified was a poor accurate of plate for proximal tibia at bone, which led to duplicate process and prolong times for product development. Table 1 shows a reference SWOT matrix, identifying weaknesses, opportunities, and threats from the company.

Table 1. SWOT matrix

Strengths	Weaknesses
- Novelty or improvements to the products	- Absence of virtual models of bones
- Make efficient the design process	- Realization of unnecessary processes - They do not follow the methodology - Absence of CAD files - Information management
Opportunities	Threats
- Knowledge and management of the existing production environment	- Low costs of imported products - Knowledge management

3.3 New Workflow

Workflow defined for this research was structured in four stages. New activities were integrated for testing a piece quality. The first one consisted on obtaining 3D virtual model by using a scanner and reverse engineering techniques to get a bone reference. The second one, virtual design of the plate and manufacturing devices were modeled using CAD technology. In the third stage, Computer Aided Engineering CAE was applied through simulations to virtual verification of plate performed by finite element analysis and virtual simulation of the bending process. Finally, in the fourth stage, physical verification was carried out, making a 3D printed of the designed plate. New integrated workflow system where shown in Fig. 2.

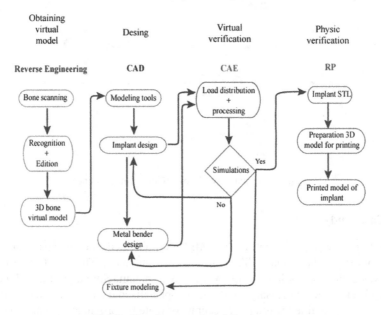

Fig. 2. New integrated workflow system

Differences between obtained data with the new design process defined by integrated workflow system and the company process was due in part, because new workflow was based on virtual and simulation environments, instead of manual processes. These new design processes also allowed biomechanical analyzes that reduced iterations and uncertainties during the plate development process. As new PLM technologies generated more advantages over older technologies. However, this change implies updating design area in the company with other processes, tools and skills.

To evaluate fulfillment of the objectives set out in this research, a comparative evaluation was made between traditional model developed in the company, and the workflow proposed according to PLM strategies. Additionally, this study evaluated times for each activity performed by company process and it was compared them with times and activities of workflow proposed in Table 2. This comparison has showed a decrease in development times, and also decrease in amount of resources demanded by workflow proposed, compared with processes and activities that company currently does.

Table 2. Comparison between the traditional company process and the workflow proposed

Activity	Company process	PLM workflow
	Time	Time
Obtaining virtual model	02:00	00:15
Implant design	128:30	11:30
Unroll plate	01:00	–
Biomechanical analysis of plate	–	00:50
Devices design (fixture and metal bender)	100:00	03:05
Biomechanical analysis of metal bender	–	01:20
Test model	03:00	01:15
Total (Hours: minutes)	**234:30**	**18:25**

Likewise, the quality of practices applied to get plate design was verified through measuring bone to plate contact. Hence, data from areas of contact were obtained to plate made by company process and plate made by PLM workflow and these data were compared.

Table 3 showed that with integration of PLM technologies process, having the geometry required and adjusted was more accurate. This was evident with an increase in the contact area, respect to the company process, which results were 16% in longitudinal section and 2,5% in the cross section.

Table 3. Comparison of areas of contact between bone and plate

Variable	Company process	Workflow proposed	Percent areas of contact incremented
Contact longitudinal section area	123,85 mm^2	143,85 mm^2	16%
Contact cross section area	23,67 mm^2	24,27 mm^2	2,5%

Finally, in Fig. 3, information about activities and roles of the product development integrated on PDM was presented. This PLM strategy improved interoperability between design and manufacturing departments, reducing development times and improved process management.

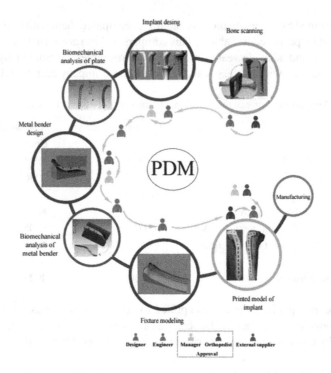

Fig. 3. PDM system.

4   Conclusions

The executed process had allowed a proposed workflow in design process of orthopedic implants. This process was developed with a methodological approach based on PLM strategies and scientific literature [8–13]. Outputs showed in time decrease were about approximately 92% in design process, according to company process showed in Table 2. In addition, new workflow evidenced that communication and information exchange between design and manufacturing departments was improved through PDM strategies applied in design and manufacturing process, obtaining collaboration and integration for those areas.

Workflow implementation not generated economic impacts, because the study case was conducted through a theoretical assessment. Given the scope of the study, it was not contemplated deploying workflow in the company, but at the same time, some proposed strategies were implemented. The new single workflow was taken into account for the development of orthopedic plates. Other products offering by company such as screws and nails have different development processes, which do not require integration of proposed technologies.

Proposed workflow will by PLM strategies help to prevent possible design mistakes by virtual and simulation environments, involving verification during all stages. These tools are used to make decisions before product manufacturing and market release.

According to software tools applied in the workflow, as reverse engineering and biomechanical analysis, those allow to get more accurately geometries, design parts, reducing development times, reiterative manual activities, and improving management resource. Finally, use of PLM strategies facilitated manufacturing processes into the company, integrating organizational structure, stages of development, work activities, roles and controls. The workflow proposed in this study proved to have better results in product definition stage, evidenced Fig. 2, as well as an enhancement in control process and effectiveness.

Acknowledgment. The authors would like to thank QE company and VIE through project Code 937 Fm-2016-1.

References

1. Global Market Insights: Orthopedic Devices Market Size, Trends (2017)
2. Khan, W., Jaffe, M., Domb, A.: Implantable medical devices. In: Advances in Delivery Science and Technology, pp. 33–59 (2014)
3. Cronskär, M.: On Customization of Orthopedic Implants- From Design and Additive Manufacturing to Implementation (2014)
4. Radu, C., Roşca, I.: Some contributions to the design of osteosynthesis implants. Est. J. Eng. **15**(2), 121 (2009)
5. Kucklick, T.R.: The Medical Device R & D Handbook (2006)
6. Díaz Lantada, A.: Handbook on Advanced Design and Manufacturing Technologies for Biomedical Devices. Springer, New York (2013). https://doi.org/ 10.1007/978-1-4614-6789-2
7. Songkajorn, Y., Thawesaengskulthai, N.: Medical device innovation development process. Int. J. Innov. Technol. Manag. **11**(4), 1450027 (2014)
8. Medina, L.A., Okudan, G.E., Wysk, R.A.: Supporting medical device development: a standard product design process model. J. Eng. Des. **24**(2), 83–119 (2013)
9. Fundación Prodintec: Herramienta de Autodiagnóstico de la Gestión del Ciclo de Vida del Producto (2010)
10. Gecevska, V., Chiabert, P., Anisic, Z., Lombard, F., Cus, F.: Product lifecycle management through innovative and competitive business environment. J. Ind. Eng. Manag. **3**(2), 323–336 (2010)
11. Segonds, F., Mantelet, F., Nelson, J., Gaillard, S.: Proposition of a PLM tool to support textile design: a case study applied to the definition of the early stages of design requirements. Comput. Ind. **66**, 21–30 (2015)
12. Bruun, H.P.L., Mortensen, N.H., Harlou, U., Wörösch, M., Proschowsky, M.: PLM system support for modular product development. Comput. Ind. **67**, 97–111 (2015)
13. Mas, F., Arista, R., Oliva, M., Hiebert, B., Gilkerson, I., Rios, J.: A review of PLM Impact on US and EU Aerospace industry. Procedia Eng. **132**, 1053–1060 (2015)
14. Pietzsch, J.B., Paté-cornell, M.L.: Stage-gate process for the development of medical devices. J. Med. Device **3**(2), 021004 (2009)
15. Chandrasegaran, S.K., Ramani, K., Sriram, R.D., Horváth, I., Bernard, A., Harik, R.F., Gao, W.: The evolution, challenges, and future of knowledge representation in product design systems. Comput. Des. **45**(2), 204–228 (2013)

16. Mercado-Colmenero, J.M., Paramio, M.A.R., Perez-Garcia, J.M., Martin-Doñate, C.: A new hybrid method for demoldability analysis of discrete geometries. Comput. Des. **80**, 43–60 (2016)

17. Xia, Z., Wang, Q., Wang, Y., Yu, C.: A CAD/CAE incorporate software framework using a unified representation architecture. Adv. Eng. Softw. **87**, 68–85 (2015)

18. Park, K., Kim, Y.S., Kim, C.S., Park, H.J.: Integrated application of CAD/CAM/CAE and RP for rapid development of a humanoid biped robot. J. Mater. Process. Technol. **187**, 609–613 (2007)

19. Lyu, G., Chu, X., Xue, D.: Product modeling from knowledge, distributed computing and lifecycle perspectives: a literature review. Comput. Ind. **84**, 1–13 (2017)

20. Mas, F., Oliva, M., Ríos, J., Gómez, A., Olmos, V., García, J.A.: PLM based approach to the industrialization of aeronautical assemblies. Procedia Eng. **132**, 1045–1052 (2015)

21. Bruun, H.P.L., Mortensen, N.H., Harlou, U., Wörösch, M., Proschowsky, M.: PLM system support for modular product development. Comput. Ind. **67**, 97–111 (2015)

22. López, A.S., Del Valle, C., Escalona, M.J., Lee, V., Goto, M.: Patient lifecycle management: an approach for clinical processes. In: Ortuño, F., Rojas, I. (eds.) IWBBIO 2015. LNCS, vol. 9044, pp. 694–700. Springer, Cham (2015). https://doi.org/10.1007/978-3-319-16480-9_67

Digitization and Preservation of Cultural Heritage Products

Abdelhak Belhi[1,2(✉)], Sebti Foufou[3,4], Abdelaziz Bouras[1], and Abdul H. Sadka[5]

[1] CSE, Qatar University, Doha, Qatar
{abdelhak.belhi,abdelaziz.bouras}@qu.edu.qa
[2] DISP Laboratory, University Lumière Lyon 2, Lyon, France
[3] Lab. Le2i, Université de Bourgogne, Dijon, France
sfoufou@u-bourgogne.fr
[4] New York University Abu Dhabi, Abu Dhabi, UAE
sfoufou@nyu.edu
[5] Brunel University, London, UK
abdul.sadka@brunel.ac.uk

Abstract. Cultural heritage encompasses various aspects of a nation's history. Cultural heritage artifacts are considered as priceless items that need special care. Since the wide adoption of new digital technologies, documenting and storing cultural heritage assets became more affordable and reliable. These records are then used in several applications. Researchers saw the opportunity to use digital heritage recordings for long-term preservation. They are considering cultural heritage artifacts as products, and the history behind them as a product lifecycle. In this paper, we present the research progress in cultural heritage digital processing and preservation, highlighting the most impactful advances. Additionally, we present the CEPROQHA project which is a new approach aiming at achieving cost-effective acquisition and digital preservation for cultural heritage artifacts in Qatar.

Keywords: Cultural heritage · PLM · 3D modeling · Semantic enrichment
Digital preservation · CEPROQHA project

1 Introduction

Cultural heritage (CH) digitization and preservation are two complex processes that involve several underlying techniques and algorithms to make CH mockups available for current and future generations. Digital content preservation is inspired from the manufacturing industry where companies use adapted archival platforms and PLM frameworks to store critical data and knowledge about important facts at each stage of product lifecycle. This data can be very important in the future for several reasons such as avoiding previous mistakes or for iterative purposes.

In this paper, we consider cultural heritage assets as products, their history as a lifecycle, and study their lifecycle preservation from a product viewpoint. In order to express the need behind the long term-preservation of cultural heritage several concepts

© IFIP International Federation for Information Processing 2017
Published by Springer International Publishing AG 2017. All Rights Reserved
J. Ríos et al. (Eds.): PLM 2017, IFIP AICT 517, pp. 241–253, 2017.
https://doi.org/10.1007/978-3-319-72905-3_22

need to be introduced. In the following, we present three major concepts: *Digital heritage* where we describe the impact of digital imaging technologies on CH, *Digital obsolescence* where we highlight the dangers of data extinction, and finally we introduce *Long-term digital preservation* which is the current solution for data extinction.

1.1 Digital Heritage

All nations around the world give a high value to their culture and traditions. The long-term preservation of the national moral identity is the concern of every nation. Cultural heritage assets are priceless items with a very high historical value. Maintaining and conserving these assets is a top priority for all communities.

Since the emergence of digital technologies, museums and CH reconstruction and conservation organizations are considering adapting these technologies for cultural heritage digitization. Museums are digitizing their collections not only for cultural heritage preservation, but also for making their collections accessible for a larger audience in an attractive way, like using Virtual Reality (VR), Augmented Reality (AR), 3D TV, etc. These technologies are integrated into web based platforms adapted to cultural content consumption (Fig. 1).

Fig. 1. Virtual museums tours

This new form of exhibition opened a new era for cultural heritage. Recent studies showed that only 10% of the global cultural heritage assets are exhibited in museums [1]. The other 90% are deposited in museums archives because of their non-importance compared to other more attractive artifacts, or simply because of their heavy physical degradation. Digital solutions like virtual museums can overcome these issues using tools like 3D model digital curation. In fact, the digital copy of a CH asset can be curated making its restoration cost-effective and more reliable. It can also be linked to a digital collection and valued with semantic enrichment by linking it to other attractive artifacts or simply highlighting its history.

1.2 Digital Obsolescence

Nowadays, with the wide adoption of information technology, every organization has to adapt its resources to be part of the digital era. However, with the high evolution pace of technology, the fear from digital obsolescence became more important than the fear from physical data loss. Digital obsolescence, or data extinction, is the state where the archived data becomes no more readable or usable. This obsolescence has two major reasons: the first one is the hardware obsolescence: the media storing the data is obsolete (for example the 5.25″ and 3.5″ floppy disks) or physically degraded. The second reason, which is the most important, is software obsolescence. This type of obsolescence can have several reasons, mainly the loss of the required knowledge to interpret the data, like what can happen for early CAD formats like GEM or IBM CAD [2]. To overcome these issues, several researchers are focusing on how to preserve the data for long-term archival [3–5]. This research ranges from data formats, best practices, to standards and frameworks.

1.3 Long-Term Digital Preservation

Digital preservation is a common process in the manufacturing industry [3, 6]. Recently, digital preservation became primordial in many sectors like: the medical field, historical and cultural fields, e-commerce, e-government, etc. From another side, the increasing performance of processing systems and the dropping costs of archival media are encouraging knowledge based organizations to consider digital preservation.

Digital preservation is not a generic process that can be applied directly in every context. In fact, the needs for the preservation of data for a car parts manufacturing company are different from those of a pharmaceutical company.

The majority of digital preservation approaches relies on the OAIS RM (Open Archival Information System Reference Model) [7]. OAIS is a conceptual reference model intended for the management, archival and long-term preservation of digital documents. It is considered as milestone achievement in long-term digital preservation.

OAIS describes the processes, the duties of each actor, and the overall architecture for a sustainable long-term digital archiving system. These characteristics guarantee and ensure the long-term availability of the archived data, and protect it from all kind of hazards (mainly digital obsolescence).

The rest of this document is organized as follows: In section two, we present a survey of cultural heritage digitization techniques, enrichment, content management and preservation. This is followed in section three by a brief description of some projects related to cultural heritage preservation. In section four, we present CEPROQHA which is a new research project aiming for cost-effective 3D acquisition and digital preservation for cultural heritage artifacts.

2 Related Work

Digital preservation for cultural heritage is widely studied. Several research projects are funded all over the world to establish, not only standards and good practices, but also some novel ideas in order to adapt existing approaches from other fields to the field of cultural heritage. Data about cultural heritage is stored in several file formats. Digital preservation is about the standards and best practices that guide the acquisition and the conservation steps. In this section, we discuss the impact of 3D technologies on cultural heritage, and present a survey of current innovations related to long-term digital heritage acquisition, enrichment, content management and digital preservation.

2.1 3D Digital Heritage Acquisition and Modeling

The massive advances in 3D imaging had a positive impact on digital heritage. Some researchers are comparing this impact to the one of photography in the 19th century [8]. 3D acquisition for cultural heritage assets is very critical, since assets are very fragile and their handling requires special care. The scanning of cultural heritage assets is very complicated compared to normal objects. In fact, CH assets often require restricted access and cannot be easily manipulated (touching, moving, rotating, etc.), which further complicates their scanning process [9]. Nowadays, with the advances in imaging capture and processing technologies, high quality captures can be performed using handheld devices. Software like: SELVA3D [10], Smoothie 3D [11] or AutoDesk 123D [12] can transform a 2D still image to a digital 3D model. These programs take as input different images, taken from several viewpoints, and generate a 3D model as shown in Fig. 2.

Fig. 2. Original item (Left) and its 3D model (Right)

For large objects, solutions involving a moving video camera, like SLAM technologies [13] or the Google Tango project [14], are often considered. These technologies can be used to capture large surface areas and monuments cost-effectively using computer tablets and smartphones.

In the cultural heritage sector, 3D modelling is still based on conventional techniques. For large size sites, commercial tools like AgiSoft Photoscan [15], AutoDesk 123D [12], Pix4D [16], Arc3D Web service [17] or even Potomodeler [18] are used. These tools are cost-effective as they can use images captured by average consumer devices like smartphones or tablets cameras. However, they suffer drawbacks such as time efficiency, and the lack of instantaneous feedback because of the separation between the acquisition and the modelling steps. In fact, the user doesn't get an instantaneous feedback. So, and in case the modelling fails, the user must take additional shots and the whole modelling process needs to be repeated. Recently, some high-end techniques were proposed. For instance, the CultLab3D [19] is a high-end 3D scanning system for cultural heritage assets digitization. However, this system is very expensive and cannot handle all types of assets (size limitation). Besides, this system is not portable as it consists of a large 3D scanner (see Fig. 3).

Fig. 3. CultLab3D professional scanner

Given the limitations of the aforementioned approach, in our work, we need a new 3D scanning framework, which must be able to scan all types of assets, with no size limitation. More importantly, it must be cost-effective, portable and give instantaneous 3D models.

Many academic research has been undertaken in the field of 3D modelling of CH assets. These researches were pioneered by the Digital Michelangelo Project [20]. Some of these researches were also undertaken by the Visual computing lab of ISTI-CNR [8]. Generally, researchers focus on the use of several techniques like: laser triangulation, Photogrammetry, Structured light, time of flight, Stereo vision, and others [21, 22]. For example, a new Photogrammetry and minimal image network adapted to the cultural heritage context is proposed in [23]. Other researchers are combining industrial techniques like Arc3D [17] and MeshLab [24]. Unfortunately, all these systems are very complex, lack cost-effectiveness and time efficiency. In addition, the majority of these systems are limited to specific use cases, as they are not designed with a user-centric approach.

3D Holoscopic imaging is an advanced true 3D imaging system. This technology enables full 3D immersion without special headgear [25–27], and offers the simplest form of recording and playing back a true 3D scene.

2.2 Data Enrichment

Data enrichment is the practice of enhancing, refining, valuing and linking the raw data. Semantic enrichment for cultural data has been an active and fruitful field of research in previous years. In 3D cultural heritage context, linking the collected data is a critical mission for many reasons. This process is tedious and requires a lot of analysis. 3D annotations are used to semantically enrich shapes, adding more knowledge to the 3D model. These annotations are associations between selected portions of the 3D shape and some data describing it.

The metadata schemes for cultural data are defined by several standards like the CIDOC-CRM or the CRMdig ontologies [28]. These standards aim at sharing cultural heritage information by a common and stretchable semantic scheme.

Several approaches tackled the semantic enrichment challenge of 3D models like AIM@SHAPE [29], 3D-COFORM [30], Focus K3D [31], CULTURA [32], V-MusT [33, 34]. Some are using interactive annotations, some others are studying how to include more information in 3D model files (like X3D, VRML or others) [35], while other approaches are focusing on machine learning techniques to automatically generate these annotations [36].

2.3 Content Management

Museums around the world use special software applications to manage their CH inventory e.g. Software like MuseumSoftware [37], Adlib [38] and Museumplus [34]. These tools are data management systems used for cataloguing purposes. They list some data about assets illustrated by 2D images.

Some novel approaches were introduced too. 3D-COFORM, for example, used a secured repository infrastructure to store and manage 3D cultural data. We can also cite other frameworks like [39] where the authors presented a centralized content management system (CMS) adapted to cultural heritage with advanced functionality like semantic queries and distributed storage.

However, since new digital technologies emergence and the progress in 3D imaging, the application of 3D visualisation technologies has become very reliable and cost-effective, especially in the content consuming market with technologies like 3D television, Virtual Reality (VR) and Augmented Reality (AR). Nowadays, virtual museum software products like *Versoteq* [40] or *3DStellwerk* [41] are used to create virtual museum tours adapted to variety of content consuming platforms (VR Headset, 3D TV, Smartphones and tablets, Etc.). 3D cultural heritage content is very attractive for consumers and considered as very lucrative. Several other software like *SketchFab* [42], which is a web-based 3D visualisation framework, focus on the 3D presentation of cultural heritage models.

The Fedora based 3D repository presented in [43] is a good example of a complete 3D digital heritage CMS. It has two core parts. The first part is a digital objects repository storing, aggregating, managing and extracting digital objects in a wide range of formats and data types. The second core component is a semantic resource index which establishes an indexing data structure for a complex information mapping for relations between an object and its components. This data structure is basically an ontology.

2.4 Digital Preservation

Due to the wide use of digital technologies to capture and store cultural heritage, the need to preserve this data for the future is becoming very important, especially because of the high value of the assets. Digital preservation is becoming more reliable than physical preservation, thanks to the increasing performance of processing systems and the dropping costs of archival media.

Digital Obsolescence is an alarming threat to every knowledge management organisation. These organisations fear the loss and the non-usability of their critical data in the future, especially that new technologies are being widely adopted [44].

Digital preservation is currently studied as a solution for digital obsolescence. The initial approach to digital preservation was the OAIS system (Open Archival Information System) in the mid 90's. This model established a platform and a definition of initial best practices and concepts of digital preservation [6, 7]. From this milestone, several research projects focused on digital preservation, like *ERPANET* which studied digital knowledge exchange, *LOTAR* which aimed at establishing long term preservation standards for digital data like 3D CAD models, and PDM (Product Data Management) [45]. For 3D content preservation, *MIT FAÇADE* [46], *DEDICATE* [47], and *DuraArk* [48] studied standards and techniques to archive and preserve 3D architectural data for long term use.

The 3D data topic is very challenging when it comes to digital preservation. A 3D model by itself is not very descriptive. It needs to be enriched with semantic annotations and metadata. The first problem with this metadata is about how to define it and where to store it. In fact, if the data is separated from the 3D model file, it can be easily lost [43]. Besides, if the archiving operator omits some important features of the digitized asset, this error can be fatal in the future.

The first requirement is very clear. The overall output must be usable for future processing (future-proof). The main problem with 3D models is the interoperability. For example, some proprietary (closed) file formats are becoming obsolete because of restrictions to their use (closed source and ad-hoc structure) [43]. The inability to use custom software to process this data is a major drawback. These issues led to the creation of new 3D file formats like X3D, VRML and COLLADA, which are widely used nowadays. From another side, several metadata standardisation approaches exist. The most impactful one is the CIDOC-CRM, which is an ontology describing the relationships and the concepts used in the context of cultural documentation [28, 43].

3 Progress and Efforts for Cultural Heritage Preservation

In this Section, we present the overall goals and the approaches used within several research projects related to cultural heritage digital preservation. These projects are mostly EU funded.

3D-COFORM Project (2008-12-01 to 2012-11-30). This project aim is to establish a tool for the digitisation of cultural heritage artefact to bring more realistic representations, better documentation and higher cost-effectiveness of digitisation.

The 3D-COFORM project addresses all aspects of 3D-capture, 3D-processing, semantics of shape, material properties, metadata and provenance, integration with other sources (textual and other media), search, research and dissemination to the public and professional alike.

3D-COFORM also studies the business aspect for the exploitation of 3D aspects and the socio-economic impact [30].

3D VIVANT Project (2010-03-01 to 2013-05-31). 3D VIVANT global aim is to develop a tool that captures video using a novel 3D video technology. This technology is based on 3D Holoscopic imaging. For playback, the project uses holography to provide immersive and ultra-high resolution presentation of 3D content. Various 3D Holoscopic video processing algorithms, such as 3D codecs and 3D object segmentation, as well as search and retrieval techniques are developed to optimize broadcasting and search [49].

VENTURI Project (2011-10-01 to 2014-09-30). VENTURI is an ambitious initiative which aims at developing and creating a pervasive Augmented Reality (AR) paradigm for mobile devices using advanced 3D technologies and adapted content management framework, where available information will be presented in a 'user' rather than a 'device' centric way. VENTURI goal is also to maintain and optimize current and future mobile platforms adapting its content type and performance settings to each platform to ensure continuity and enrich use cases [50].

V-Must Virtual Transnational museum network (1-02-2011 to 31-01-2015). V-MusT is an EU-FP7 funded project aiming to provide software tools and best practices to the heritage sector, to promote and develop virtual museums for preservation, education and entertainment purposes. The project investigates also the cohesion that exists in research and aims at reorienting the current research topics [33].

ArchéObjets 3D Project (2015-2016). The 'ArchéObjets 3D' Project is funded by Lyon University's PALSE IPEm. This project aims to develop a new 3D scanning technology for hand-held 3D devices like smartphones and tablets. The acquired data is then processed and used in the cultural heritage preservation context. The project main interest is to explore different aspects of 3D rendering and apply them to the various cultural heritage asset types [51].

PRESIOUS Project (2013-02-01 to 2016-01-31). PRESIOUS project [52] aim is to investigate and propose new solutions for the difficulty and inefficiency of the 3D digitisation process of cultural heritage assets, the quantification of stone (statues) monument degradation, and the reconstruction of objects from large numbers of constituent fragments. Using a common core of geometric processing, analysis and retrieval methods, PRESIOUS developed predictive geometric augmentation technologies targeted to the above problems [52].

DURAARK Project (2013-02-01 to 2016-01-31). DURAARK project aim is to develop a new digital preservation framework for architectural data (especially preserving 3D data). This new approach will enhance and redefine access mechanisms, which are generally based on metadata schemes. The new approach will not only focus on the retrieval, but also on fully exploiting the data by different semantic levels. DURAARK will also focus on the future-proof of the preserved data [48].

PREFORMA Project (2014-01-01 to 2017-12-31). PREFORMA [53] aim is to study and implement a better quality standardised file format for cultural information content preservation. It also focuses on formalizing a conformity process for the preservation input (tests and checks).

PREFORMA intended to adapt known archival processes like the OAIS model, specify the critical factors and establish the quality standards that the input data must comply with in order to achieve a sustainable long term preservation.

INCEPTION Project (2015-06-01 to 2019-05-31). The main objective of INCEP-TION [54] is to develop a new 3D modelling technique adapted to cultural heritage with an inclusive approach for time-dynamic reconstruction. INCEPTION focuses on how to preserve the time line of assets. This methodology will result in accessible 3D models for every user group. INCEPTION aims also at creating an open standard Web Semantics for Building Information models (BIM) adapted to cultural heritage.

LOng Term Archiving and Retrieval – LOTAR PROJECT. The main aim of the LOTAR Project [45] is to design, and maintain standards for long term archiving, preservation, and retrieval of data models, especially 3D CAD models and PDM data. The project is conducted by a consortium of aviation and aerospace OEMs and suppliers. LOTAR approach follows the OAIS models and adapts it to the requirement of the aerospace industry.

4 CEPROQHA Project

The State of Qatar is a good example of a fast-growing country with a great and long history. Preserving nation's culture is a key challenge in Qatar National vision 2030 and the Qatar National Development Strategy (2011–2016).

Qatar is also leading a new "Smart Nation" initiative whereby the goal is to create a smart, modern, and future proof country. One of the key tasks to achieve this goal is the digital preservation of Qatar's cultural assets.

CEPROQHA[1] is a cooperative research project between Qatar University and Brunel University (UK), funded by the Qatar National Research Fund (QNRF) under the National Priorities Research Program (NPRP). The project goal is to study how to digitally preserve Qatar's Cultural Heritage. CEPROQHA aims also at developing a bespoke 3D Holoscopic imaging framework that will bring a novel and cost-effective approach to the acquisition, reconstruction, curation, content management, and long-term preservation of cultural heritage assets.

CEPROQHA is aiming to make innovations in:

- Cost-effective acquisition and 3D modelling: The majority of 3D scanning approaches lacks efficiency (photogrammetry) or cost-effectiveness (Laser scanning). CEPROQHA will use innovative technologies like 3D Holoscopic imaging and advanced digital curation processes to achieve efficient and cost-effective 3D acquisition and modelling.
- Interoperability and representation of 3D cultural heritage assets: The resulting 3D models must be available in a format that can be rendered for any content consuming platform such as different display types or different representation formats like virtual walk-through. Future 3D visualisation techniques are required following the fast development in the media industry. Hence, interactive visualisation of static 3D objects as well as dynamic visual experience by virtual walk-through is required.

---

[1] Cost-Effective High-Quality Preservation and Restoration of Qatar Cultural Heritage through Advanced Holoscopic 3D Imaging.

- Enrichment, content management and long term preservation: All digitised assets must be linked, annotated and semantically enriched. The content management shall support user annotation, search and retrieval capabilities as well as tools for user-specific data processing and visualisation. Data management should preferably be performed using cloud-based services and storage capabilities. Digital preservation will be deeply studied. CEPROQHA will establish standards and best practices for digital preservation in cultural heritage environment. The overall architecture must comply with established standards to achieve sustainable long term digital preservation.

The CEPROQHA project will benefit from its partners experience in research and innovation in the 3D imaging field. In addition, the project aims at applying available technology to the context of cultural heritage with the perspective of making innovations in 3D acquisition and modelling, 3D content management and annotation and digital long-term preservation.

Overall, CEPROQHA aims are:

- Develop a new evolutionary 3D Holoscopic acquisition approach.
- Develop a new enrichment, processing and reformatting plug-ins for 3D models.
- Develop a bespoke content management system for 3D cultural heritage assets.
- Develop a new and innovative preservation process adapted to cultural heritage assets.

5   Conclusion

In this paper, we highlighted the advances and most important achievement in the cultural heritage digital preservation field. Cultural heritage artifacts can be treated as products. Their history is a lifecycle that has to be preserved. The high value of CH assets and their specificities require the development of a bespoke preservation framework. Our study covered these basic requirements, starting from 3D acquisition and enrichment, followed by CH content management, and finally, the long-term digital preservation. We also surveyed some projects related to CH acquisition, curation, management, and preservation.

At the end of this document, we presented the CEPROQHA project which our team is part of. CEPROQHA is an innovative approach toward CH digital management and preservation. The CEPROQHA team is really committed to make an innovative proof of concept for 3D digital preservation of the Qatari cultural heritage using cutting edge 3D imaging technologies.

Acknowledgement. This publication was made possible by NPRP grant 9-181-1-036 from the Qatar National Research Fund (a member of Qatar Foundation). The statements made herein are solely the responsibility of the authors.

References

1. Santos, P., Ritz, M.: CultLab3D – fast and economic, high quality 3D digitization of cultural heritage artifacts. In: Fritsch, D. (ed.) Photogrammetric Week 13, pp. 319–322 (2013)
2. Deljanin, S.: Digital obsolescence. INFOtheca-J. Inform. Librarianship **13**(1), 43–53 (2012)
3. Barbau, R.: A reference architecture for archival systems with application to product models (2013). https://tel.archives-ouvertes.fr/tel-00924492
4. Barbau, R., Krima, S., Rachuri, S., Narayanan, A., Fiorentini, X., Foufou, S., Sriram, R.D.: OntoSTEP: enriching product model data using ontologies. Comput.-Aided Des. **44**, 575–590 (2012). https://doi.org/10.1016/j.cad.2012.01.008
5. Barbau, R., Lubell, J., Rachuri, S., Foufou, S.: Toward a reference architecture for archival systems. In: Bernard, A., Rivest, L., Dutta, D. (eds.) PLM 2013. IFIPAICT, vol. 409, pp. 68–77. Springer, Heidelberg (2013). https://doi.org/10.1007/978-3-642-41501-2_8
6. Wilkes, W., Brunsmann, J., Heutelbeck, D., Hundsdörfer, A., Hemmje, M., Heidbrink, H.: Towards support for long-term digital preservation in product life cycle management. Int. J. Digital Curation **6**, 282–296 (2011). https://doi.org/10.2218/ijdc.v6i1.188
7. Lee, S.: Standardization of digital archiving and OAIS reference model. J. Inform. Manage. **33**, 45–68 (2002). https://doi.org/10.1633/JIM.2002.33.3.045
8. Scopigno, R., Callieri, M., Cignoni, P., Corsini, M., Dellepiane, M., Ponchio, F., Ranzuglia, G.: 3D models for cultural heritage: beyond plain visualization. Computer **44**, 48–55 (2011). https://doi.org/10.1109/MC.2011.196
9. Pavlidis, G., Koutsoudis, A., Arnaoutoglou, F., Tsioukas, V., Chamzas, C.: Methods for 3D digitization of cultural heritage. J. Cult. Heritage **8**, 93–98 (2007). https://doi.org/10.1016/j.culher.2006.10.007
10. Selva3D - Transform images into 3D models online. https://www.selva3d.com
11. Smoothie-3D. http://www.smoothie-3d.com
12. Autodesk 123D. http://www.123dapp.com
13. Brutto, M., Meli, P.: Computer vision tools for 3D modelling in archaeology. Int. J. Heritage Digital Era **1**, 1–6 (2012). https://doi.org/10.1260/2047-4970.1.0.1
14. Google Tango. https://get.google.com/tango
15. AgiSoft, LLC: Agisoft photoscan. Professional edn. (2014)
16. Pix4D. https://pix4d.com
17. ARC 3D Web Service. http://www.arc3d.be
18. PhotoModeler. http://www.photomodeler.com
19. Singh, G.: CultLab3D: digitizing cultural heritage. IEEE Comput. Graphics Appl. **34**, 4–5 (2014). https://doi.org/10.1109/MCG.2014.48
20. Levoy, M.: The digital Michelangelo project. Comput. Graphics Forum **18**, 13–16 (1999)
21. Sansoni, G., Trebeschi, M., Docchio, F.: State-of-the-Art and applications of 3D imaging sensors in industry, cultural heritage, medicine, and criminal investigation. Sensors **9**, 568–601 (2009). https://doi.org/10.3390/s90100568
22. Pieraccini, M., Guidi, G., Atzeni, C.: 3D digitizing of cultural heritage. J. Cult. Heritage **2**, 63–70 (2001). https://doi.org/10.1016/S1296-2074(01)01108-6
23. Alsadik, B., Gerke, M., Vosselman, G.: Automated camera network design for 3D modeling of cultural heritage objects. J. Cult. Heritage **14**, 515–526 (2013). https://doi.org/10.1016/j.culher.2012.11.007
24. MeshLab. http://www.meshlab.net

25. Swash, M., Aggoun, A., Abdulfatah, O., Li, B., Fernandez, J., Tsekleves, E.: Holoscopic 3D image rendering for autostereoscopic multiview 3D display. In: 2013 IEEE International Symposium on Broadband Multimedia Systems and Broadcasting (BMSB) (2013). https://doi.org/10.1109/BMSB.2013.6621683

26. Aggoun, A., Tsekleves, E., Swash, M., Zarpalas, D., Dimou, A., Daras, P., Nunes, P., Soares, L.: Immersive 3D holoscopic video system. IEEE Multimedia **20**, 28–37 (2013). https://doi.org/10.1109/MMUL.2012.42

27. Aggoun, A.: 3D holoscopic imaging technology for real-time volume processing and display. Signals Commun. Technol., 411–428 (2010). https://doi.org/10.1007/978-3-642-12802-8_18

28. CIDOC-CRM, CRMdig. http://doc.objectspace.org/cidoc

29. Falcidieno, B.: Special session AIM@SHAPE project presentation. In: Proceedings Shape Modeling Applications (2004). https://doi.org/10.1109/SMI.2004.1314520

30. Pitzalis, D., Kaminski, J., Niccolucci, F.: 3D-COFORM: Making 3D documentation an everyday choice for the cultural heritage sector. Virtual Archaeol. Rev. **2**, 145 (2011). https://doi.org/10.4995/var.2011.4571

31. Catalano, C.: FOCUS K3D Road map for future research. Technical report. http://www.focusk3d.eu

32. CULTURA (Cultivating Understanding and Research through Adaptivity). http://www.cultura-strep.eu

33. v-must | Virtual Museum Transnational Network. http://v-must.net

34. Collection Management Software for Museums. http://www.zetcom.com

35. Santos, P., Serna, S.P., Stork, A., Fellner, D.: The potential of 3D internet in the cultural heritage domain. In: Ioannides, M., Quak, E. (eds.) 3D Research Challenges in Cultural Heritage. LNCS, vol. 8355, pp. 1–17. Springer, Heidelberg (2014). https://doi.org/10.1007/978-3-662-44630-0_1

36. Llamas, J., Lerones, P.M., Zalama, E., Gómez-García-Bermejo, J.: Applying deep learning techniques to cultural heritage images within the INCEPTION project. In: Ioannides, M., Fink, E., Moropoulou, A., Hagedorn-Saupe, M., Fresa, A., Liestøl, G., Rajcic, V., Grussenmeyer, P. (eds.) EuroMed 2016. LNCS, vol. 10059, pp. 25–32. Springer, Cham (2016). https://doi.org/10.1007/978-3-319-48974-2_4

37. PastPerfect: The World's Leading Museum Collection Software. http://www.museumsoftware.com

38. Adlib - Flexible Software for Archives, Museums and Libraries. http://www.adlibsoft.com

39. Pan, X., Schiffer, T., Schröttner, M., Berndt, R., Hecher, M., Havemann, S., Fellner, D.W.: An enhanced distributed repository for working with 3D assets in cultural heritage. In: Ioannides, M., Fritsch, D., Leissner, J., Davies, R., Remondino, F., Caffo, R. (eds.) EuroMed 2012. LNCS, vol. 7616, pp. 349–358. Springer, Heidelberg (2012). https://doi.org/10.1007/978-3-642-34234-9_35

40. Versoteq. http://versoteq.com

41. 3D STELLWERK. http://3dstellwerk.com

42. Sketchfab. http://sketchfab.com

43. Felicetti, A., Lorenzini, M.: Metadata and tools for integration and preservation of cultural heritage 3D information. Geoinformatics FCE CTU **6**, 118–124 (2011). https://doi.org/10.14311/gi.6.16

44. Doyle, J., Viktor, H., Paquet, E.: Preservation metadata - a framework for 3D data based on the Semantic Web. In: 2008 Third International Conference on Digital Information Management (2008). https://doi.org/10.1109/ICDIM.2008.4746811

45. LOng Term Archiving and Retrieval. http://www.lotar-international.org

46. MacKenzie, S.: Future-proofing architectural computer-aided design: MIT's FACADE project. In: Peyceré, D., Wierre, F., Koch, C. (eds.) Architecture et archives numériques - L'architecture à l'ère numérique: un enjeu de mémoire, édition bilingue français-anglais, pp. 408–423. Editions InFolio (2008)
47. DEDICATE Project. http://gtr.rcuk.ac.uk/projects?ref=AH%2FJ008265%2F1
48. DuraArk project. http://duraark.eu
49. Steurer, J., Pesch, M., Hahne, C.: 3D holoscopic video imaging system. Hum. Vis. Electron. Imaging XVII (2012). https://doi.org/10.1117/12.915294
50. Venturi Project. https://venturi.fbk.eu
51. Arché3DObjet Project blog. http://archeorient.hypotheses.org/6692
52. PRESSIOUS Project Website. http://www.presious.eu
53. PREFORMA Project Website. http://www.preforma-project.eu
54. INCEPTION Project Website. http://www.inception-project.eu

Towards Modelling and Standardisation Techniques for Railway Infrastructure

Chen Zheng[1], Samir Assaf[2], and Benoît Eynard[1(✉)]

[1] Department of Mechanical Systems Engineering, Sorbonne Universités,
Université de Technologie de Compiègne, UMR CNRS 7337 Roberval,
CS 60319, 60203 Compiègne Cedex, France
{chen.zheng,benoit.eynard}@utc.fr
[2] Institut de Recherche Technologique Railenium Technopôle Transalley,
180 rue Joseph-Louis Lagrange, 59308 Valenciennes Cedex, France
samir.assaf@railenium.eu

Abstract. Modelling and standardisation for railway infrastructure has attracted the attention from both academia and industry for a long time. Building Information modelling (BIM) derived from the area of building construction and is currently on the rise in infrastructure projects. However, in the domain of railway infrastructure, BIM is not advanced enough for productive use due to the lack of the railway specific requirements. In order to propose an effective modelling and standardisation technique for railway infrastructure, International Union of Railway (UIC) leads the RailTopoModel project. The RailTopoModel intends to be used in all business processes dealing with the design, construction, operation and maintenance of the railway infrastructure. The paper presents the details of RailTopoModel with one case study based on a railway network. The new dimension for the further development of RailTopoModel in the context of Product Lifecycle Management (PLM) is then presented. Finally, the implementation of the RailTopoModel and its new dimension into the PLM numerical platform is discussed.

Keywords: Building Information Modelling · Railway infrastructure
RailTopoModel · railML · Product Lifecycle Management

1 Introduction

Building Information Modelling (BIM) originates from product models. Charles Eastman, who is considered as the "father of BIM", put forward the concept "Building Product Model" in 1999, which finally led to what is today known as BIM [1]. The definition of BIM which has been widely accepted is proposed by International Organisation for Standardisation (ISO). According to the ISO, BIM is defined as "shared digital representation of physical and functional characteristics of any built object which forms a reliable basis for decisions" [2]. In recent years, BIM attracts increasing attention of both academia and industry due to many benefits and resource savings during design, planning and construction of new building [3].

© IFIP International Federation for Information Processing 2017
Published by Springer International Publishing AG 2017. All Rights Reserved
J. Ríos et al. (Eds.): PLM 2017, IFIP AICT 517, pp. 254–263, 2017.
https://doi.org/10.1007/978-3-319-72905-3_23

BIM derived from the building domain; however, it is currently on the rise in other fields. The German Federal Ministry of Transport and Digital Infrastructure states that BIM will become an integral part of future governmental infrastructure projects [4]. This trend shows that the dimension of infrastructure project has been taken into consideration by BIM. Moreover, some elements closely related to the Product Lifecycle Management (PLM), such as change management, maturity assessment, business process, etc., have been integrated into BIM. The above introduction indicates that the scope of application of BIM becomes increasingly large; however, in the domain of railway infrastructure BIM is not advanced enough for effective use due to the lack of the railway specific requirements.

The RailTopoModel, initiated by the International Union of Railway (UIC), is one typical model and standard of railway infrastructure [5]. The RailTopoModel will be firstly presented in details in the paper. However, the RailTopoModel is a model and not a language, so it is not design for exchanging data. In order to fulfil the data exchange among different stakeholders of one infrastructure project, the railML is proposed to define a standard data exchange format based on the RailTopoModel [6]. One case study will be then provided to demonstrate the application of the RailTopoModel and the railML for describing the infrastructure of a railway network. Finally, the paper discusses the new dimension for the further development of RailTopoModel in the context of Product Lifecycle Management (PLM). The details of RailTopoModel will be presented in next section.

2 RailTopoModel

The RailTopoModel project, led by the UIC with contributions from several industrial and academic partners in railway infrastructure, aims to define a universal description of railways business objects, independent of usages, structured in layers (topology, referencing, infrastructure, signalling, project lifecycle...) and open to future developments [5]. The modelling principles of the RailTopoModel will be firstly introduced hereafter.

2.1 Modelling Principles

The generic description of the railway topology is considered as the basic part of the RailTopoModel. Based on such generic description, two modelling principles are applied in RailTopoModel: **topology of railway network** and **multilevel architecture**.

Topology of railway network principle indicates that the RailTopoModel only describes the logical parts of the railway network and therefore independent of any physical or technical items used to represent it. According to this principle, all resources of the railway network are represented by nodes, and only nodes; edges represent relations between nodes, and only relations.

Multilevel architecture principle adopted by the RailTopoModel indicates that the structure of one railway network can be described in different levels of details [7]. Three detail levels of the railway network are proposed by the RailTopoModel: micro level, meso level and macro level. Switch or buffer stops that are connected by tracks can be represented in micro level; meso level can be used to represent the operating points that are connected by one or more tracks; while operating points connected with each other via single connections can be found in macro level (Fig. 1).

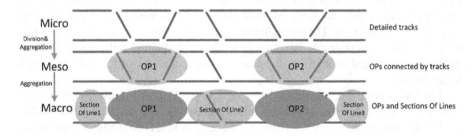

Fig. 1. Three detail levels of railway network represented by RailTopoModel (adapted from [5])

The RailTopoModel, describing the structure and the topology of the railway network with different levels of details, is represented by the Unified Modelling Language (UML). Based on the language UML, the RailTopoModel defines a universal description of railway business objects. The following section details the RailTopo-Model by explaining each package and class represented by the UML class diagram.

2.2 Global View of RailTopoModel

UML is a general-purpose, developmental, modelling language that is intended to provide a standard way to visualise the design of a system [8]. A package may contain classes, objects, use cases, components, nodes, node instances and even other package, thus providing a global view of model to stakeholders [9].

Figure 2 presents the global view of RailTopoModel represented by UML package diagram. The RailTopoModel intends to include all the domains related to the railway infrastructure. Different domains are studied and developed by different working groups of RailTopoModel project. Figure 2 shows the domains proposed by RailTopoModel of current version. These domains are represented by seven packages: **Base, PositioningSystem, Topology, Location, NetEntity, Infrastructure** and **Project**. Every package contains the classes and the relationships between them. The following section chose the **Topology** package as an example to introduce the classes and their relationships in package.

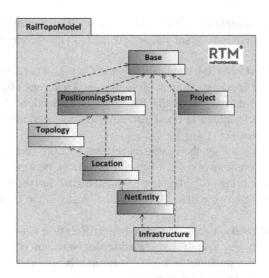

Fig. 2. Global view of RailTopoModel represented by UML diagram (Color figure online)

2.3 Topology Package of RailTopoModel

The RailTopoModel is proposed based on the generic description of the railway topology. Therefore the **Topology** package is considered as the basic part of the Rail-TopoModel and is chosen to introduce the details of the RailTopoModel.

Considering the **topology of railway network** principle presented in Sect. 2.1, nodes are conceptually embodied by **NetElement** class, and edges by **Relation** class in the Topology package. By applying the **multilevel architecture** principle, the **CompositionNetElement** class is derived from the **NetElement** class, which allows the assembly of nodes into bigger nodes, and zooming in and out from one level to another.

The **PositioningNetElement** class is derived from the **CompoistionNetElement** class, which indicates that a net element requires at least one positioning system.

The **AssociatedNetElement** class define topological structures and location information in relation between "**NetElement**" instances or between one "**NetElement**" instance and location information for "**NetEntity**" instances. The **AssociatedNetElement** has three attributes, **intrinsicCoordBegin**, **intrinsicCoordEnd and keepOrientation**. The **intrinsicCoordBegin** and **intrinsicCoordEnd** attributes are used to represent the start and end locations of the "**NetEntity**" instance in relation to the "**PositioningNetElement**" which is used for positioning within the network. The **keepOrientation** attribute is represent by a Boolean data type, which is used to present whether the child **LinearElement** keeps the same orientation as parent **LinearElement**.

The **LinearElement** class is derived from "**PositioningNetElement**". It can be used to represent two different situations. The first situation is the uninterrupted track between two adjacent switches, or between a switch and an adjacent buffer stop. "Uninterrupted" means that there are no other switches in that connection (i.e., micro level structure). The second situation is the line section between two adjacent Operational Points, would be an important class of nodes to be used at macro level.

The **NonLinearElement** class is also derived from "**PositioningNetElement**". It is used to present the operational point and net extremity in the railway network at macro level.

The **ElementPartCollection** class defines the collection of net elements to be aggregated into the higher level net element. Two classes, **OrderedCollection** and **UnorderedCollection** are derived from the **ElementPartCollection** class, dedicated to ordered net elements (required to build a route) and unordered net element (bulk list without need for routes).

The **Relation** class defines the connexity relation between two net elements in the connexity graph of the network. In a functional railway network, each instance of "**Relation**" typically brings together two "**NetElement**" instances. In other words, "**Relation**" can be seen as the base class to define edges in the **topology of railway network** principle.

The **PositionedRelation** class is derived from **Relation** class, which defines an oriented relation between exactly two "**PositioningNetElements**" instances. Three attributes, **navigability, positionOnA** and **PositionOnB**, using the enumeration type, are presented in the **PositionedRelation** class.

A compartment listing the attributes (AB, BA, Both and None) for the enumeration is placed to indicate the **Navigability** of the **PositionedRelation** class. If one connected "**NetElement**" instance is designated code "**A**", the other connected "**NetElement**" instance is designated code "**B**", the attribute "**AB**" (or "**BA**") indicates that it is possible to move a train from NetElement A (or B) to NetElement B (or A). The Attribute **Both** (or **None**) indicates that it is (not) possible to move a train from A to B as well as from B to A.

A compartment listing the attributes (0 and 1) for the enumeration is placed to indicate the usage of the **PositionedRelation** class. If the value of **positionOnA** is 0, the "Relation" is using the start of NetElement A, while if the value of **positionOnA** is 1, the "Relation" is using the end of NetElement A.

The Topology package is chosen to introduce the details of the RailTopoModel in this section. Above introduction on the Topology package indicates that the global objective of RailTopoModel is to provide a model, capable of supporting simulations for railway systems. However, RailTopoModel is a model and not a language, so it is not designed for exchanging data. Based on the RailTopoModel, the railML is proposed to define a standard data exchange format. In other words, the railML revolutionises the sharing of information structured by RailTopoModel in the railway industry. Next section will present the details of railML (Fig. 3).

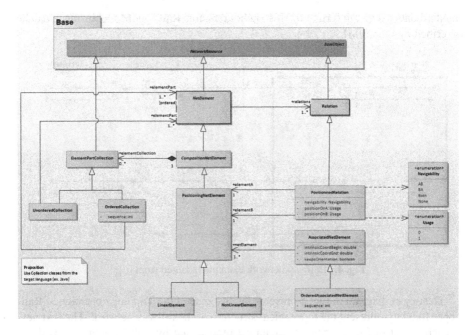

Fig. 3. Topology package

2.4 Data Exchange Format for RailTopoModel: railML

The railML is an XML-based exchange format dedicated to the rail domain and its multiple business. People use railML as the data exchange format. Since 2002, the railML.org initiative is dedicated to developing and enhancing a standardised open-source data exchange format [10]. Originally initiated from German and Swiss industry parties, it today consists of a diverse community from all over Europe. Currently railML 2.3 is the official version, and three different subschemas: Timetable, Rolling Stock and Infrastructure are presented in this version. The subschemas such as MetaData and Interlocking, are under construction and to be published with the railML 3.0 which will be released in September 2017 [11].

In order to show the application of RailTopoModel/railML for representing the railway infrastructure, a case study of one railway network will be presented in next section.

3 Case Study

The provided case study is the railway network adapted from [6], which is presented in Fig. 4. The topological structure can be represented by instantiating the Topology package of the RailTopoModel. For the sake of clarity, a part of the railway network is chosen (the part in the blue box in Fig. 2) to present the application of RailTopoModel in representing the railway network's topological structure. In order to provide a standard data exchange format to all stakeholders, this RailTopoModel instance can be described by the railML.

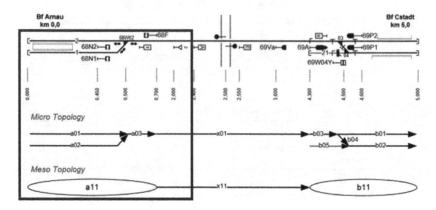

Fig. 4. Railway network example (adapted from [6])

The object diagram in Fig. 5 presents the instance of the Topology package of Rail-TopoModel to represent the topological structure of the railway network. The text next to each object in Fig. 5 shows the data set represented by railML, which provides a standard data exchange format of the RailTopoModel instance to all stakeholders.

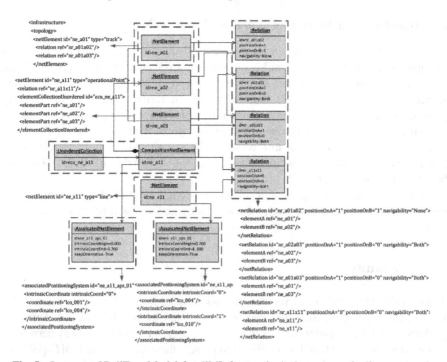

Fig. 5. Instance of RailTopoModel & railML for topological structure of railway network

In this section, the RailTopoModel is firstly presented in details in this section. The railML is then presented because it can provide a standard data exchange format for the RailTopoModel. One case study based on a railway network is chosen to demonstrate the application of the RailTopoModel and the railML for describing the infrastructure of a railway network.

As presented in Sect. 1, currently BIM not only requires the infrastructure information, it intends to integrate the data closely related to the PLM as well.

The RailTopoModel aims to define a universal description of railways infrastructure objects to facilitate the collaboration of different work group and eventually to reduce the collaborative project; however, compared with BIM, the elements related to the PLM has not been fully integrated into the RailTopoModel of current version.

Nowadays, the RailTopoModel is still under continuous development. Next section will discuss the new dimension of RailTopoModel for PLM.

4   New Dimension of RailTopoModel for PLM

PLM is a "systematic, controlled concept for managing and developing products and related information". It ensures "the management and the control of product process (product development, production and product marketing)" and provides "the order-delivery process, the control of product related information throughout the product life cycle, from the initial idea to the scrap yard" [12]. By considering the PLM dimension in the domain of railway network, the elements related to the PLM can be generally divided into two parts: PLM Infrastructure (Infra) and PLM Rolling Stock (RS). The two parts of the PLM dimension for the RailTopoModel will be discussed hereafter.

4.1   PLM Infrastructure

The RailTopoModel is considered as one typical model and standard of railway infrastructure, so the geometrical and locational information of basic parts existing in the railway network, such as switch point, crossing, train detection element, train protection element, derailer, signal and level crossing, can be described and integrated into the RailTopoModel's Infrastructure package. However, the data related to the PLM Infra mean more than that. The data describing the PLM Infra can be generally divided into four categories: (1) infrastructure layout data, (2) logical data, (3) manufactured equipment data and (4) project management data.

Infrastructure layout data ensure the physical integration between the equipment and buildings along the track, including the topographic information - these data have already been covered by the RailTopoModel of current version. Logical data describe the functional breakdown structure of the railway system and other system engineering data, such as the behaviour of the system. Manufactured equipment data describe thinly the geometry of the equipment for manufacturing, installing or maintenance purposes. Project management data correspond to an infrastructure project itself, which relies on the descriptive data.

The comparison result between the data represented by the RailTopoModel and the data required by the PLM Infra indicates that the data required by the PLM Infra have been partially represented by the RailTopoModel.

As to the logical data, functional structure and behaviour for all the net entities of the railway system have not been represented by the RailTopoModel. The functional structure and behaviour for the net entities should be further developed.

The third category of data required by the PLM Infra is the manufactured equipment data. On the one hand, the geometry of the net entities has been described by the net entities represented in Infrastructure package; on the other hand, the position of net elements is described in a very precise way by the Location package.

The last category of data is the project management data. The Projects package has been partially presented in the current version of RailTopoModel to represent the information related to the collaborative project. However, the relationship between the Projects package and the Infrastructure package has not been presented in current version, so the project corresponding to an infrastructure cannot be synergistically described.

4.2   PLM Rolling Stock

The term "rolling stock" in the considered context refers to building and operating a train. The PLM RS covers the following categories: (1) requirement specification data, (2) design & industrialisation data, (3) logistic data, (4) change management data and (5) maintenance data.

Requirement specification data supports the train constructors and the equipment providers in exchanging requirements through dedicated computer-aided means. Design & industrialisation data supports the model-based data exchange among different disciplines during the design and industrialisation process. Logistic data ensures the consistency of logistic data from the constructors to the customers (or vice versa). Change management data ensure the continuity between the constructor's information system and the change management tool of their suppliers or customers. Maintenance data refers to the data related to maintenance information of rolling stocks.

However, the data related to the rolling stock cannot be described by the current version of RailTopoModel. In order to describe the data related PLM RS, the RailTopoModel should be further developed. New packages which can represent the above categories of data should be integrated into the current version of RailTopoModel.

5   Conclusion

In the context of BIM for railway infrastructure, the paper firstly introduces the RailTopoModel, one typical model and standard of railway infrastructure. The standard data exchange format based on the RailTopoModel - railML, fulfilling the data exchange among different stakeholders of one infrastructure project, is then presented. One case study of a railway network is provided to demonstrate the application of the RailTopoModel and the railML for describing the infrastructure of a railway network. Finally, the paper discusses the new dimension for the further development of RailTopoModel in the context of Product Lifecycle Management (PLM).

The future work will focus on the PLM numerical platform in which the RailTopo-Model and its new PLM dimension can be implemented. Nowadays, various PLM platforms have been developed. Many of them prove to be successful in developing not only industrial tools but also exchange and collaboration standards around the digital processes throughout the whole lifecycle in different domains. The RailTopoModel is now under continuous development in aligning with the PLM numerical platform. It is believed that, by implementing the RailTopoModel into the PLM numerical platform, different stakeholders of one project can achieve a multidisciplinary collaboration during the whole lifecycle of the railway infrastructure and eventually reduce the development cost and leading-time.

References

1. Eastman, C., Teicholz, P., Sacks, R., Liston, K.: BIM Handbook: A Guide to Building Information Modeling for Owners, Managers, Designers, Engineers and Contractors. Wiley, Hoboken (2011)
2. ISO 29481-1: Building information modeling - information delivery manual - Part 1: methodology and format (2016)
3. Volk, R., Stengel, J., Schultmann, F.: Building information modeling (BIM) for existing buildings - literature review and future needs. Autom. Constr. **38**, 109–127 (2014)
4. Federal Ministry of Transport and Digital Infrastructure: Road map for digital design and construction-introduction of modern, IT-based process and technologies for the design, construction and operation of assets in the built environment (2015)
5. IRS-Internatial Railway Solution: RailTopoModel-Railway Infrastructure Topological Model. International Union of Railways, Paris (2016)
6. Augele, V.: Comparative analysis of building information modelling (BIM) and RailTopoModel/railML in view of their application to operationally relevant railway infrastructure (2016). https://www.railml.org/en/public-relations/scientific-p-pers.html?file=files/download/papers/230117_TUDresdenAugele_TermpaperComparisonRTMIFC.pdf
7. Kuckelberg, A.: Graph databases and railway operations research requirements. In: Proceedings of EDBT/ICDT Workshops, Brussels, Belgium (2015)
8. Eynard, B., Gallet, T., Roucoules, L., Ducellier, G.: PDM system implementation based on UML. Math. Comput. Simul. **70**, 330–342 (2006)
9. Booch, G., Rumbaugh, J., Jacobson, I.: The Unified Modeling Language User Guide. Addison-Wesley, Massachusetts (1998)
10. Nash, A., Huerlimann, D., Schütte, J., Krauss, V.P.: railML-a standard data interface for railroad applications. WIT Trans. Built Environ. **74**, 233–240 (2004)
11. Rahmig, C.: railML infrastructure v3 concept -ideas and concepts for a new infrastructure model. Braunschweig, Germany (2014). http://documents.railml.org/events/slides/2014-03-26_rahmig-railml3infrastructure.pdf
12. Saaksvuori, A., Immonen, A.: Product Lifecycle Management. Springer, Berlin (2002)

A Process Mining Based Approach
to Support Decision Making

Widad Es-Soufi[✉], Esma Yahia, and Lionel Roucoules

Arts et Métiers ParisTech, CNRS, LSIS, 2 cours des Arts et Métiers,
13617 Aix en Provence, France
{Widad.ES-SOUFI,Esma.YAHIA,Lionel.ROUCOULES}@ensam.eu

Abstract. Currently, organizations tend to reuse their past knowledge to make good decisions quickly and effectively and thus, to improve their business processes performance in terms of time, quality, efficiency, etc. Process mining techniques allow organizations to achieve this objective through process discovery. This paper develops a semi-automated approach that supports decision making by discovering decision rules from the past process executions. It identifies a ranking of the process patterns that satisfy the discovered decision rules and which are the most likely to be executed by a given user in a given context. The approach is applied on a supervision process of the gas network exploitation.

Keywords: Process mining · Decision mining · Process patterns
Decision-making · Business process

1 Introduction

Business process is defined as a set of activities that take one or more inputs and produce a valuable output that satisfies the customer [1]. In [2], authors define it as a set of activities that are performed in coordination in an organizational and technical environment and provide an output that responds to a business goal. Based on these definitions, the authors of this paper describe the business process, as a set of linked activities that have zero or more inputs, one or more resources and create a high added value output (i.e. product or service) that satisfies the industrial and customers constraints. These linked activities represent the business process flow and are controlled by different process gateways (And, Or, Xor) [3, Sect. 8.3.9] that give rise to several patterns (pattern 1 to 9 in Fig. 1) where each one is a linear end-to-end execution. The "And" gateway, also called parallel gateway, means that all the following activities are going to be executed in several possible orders. The "Or" gateway, also called inclusive gateway, means that one or all the following activities are going to be executed based on some attributes conditions. The "Xor" gateway, also called exclusive gateway, means that only one following activity among others, is going to be executed based on some attributes conditions.

© IFIP International Federation for Information Processing 2017
Published by Springer International Publishing AG 2017. All Rights Reserved
J. Ríos et al. (Eds.): PLM 2017, IFIP AICT 517, pp. 264–274, 2017.
https://doi.org/10.1007/978-3-319-72905-3_24

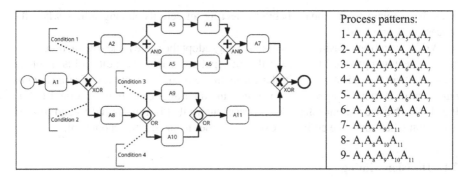

Fig. 1. Example of process patterns (expressed in BPMN http://www.bpmn.org/)

The presence of gateways in business processes results in making several decisions based on some criteria like experience, preference, or industrial constraints [4]. Making the right decisions in business processes is tightly related to business success. Indeed, a research that involved more than a thousand companies, shows an evident correlation between decision effectiveness and business performance [5].

In [6], authors explain that the process of decision-making can be broken down into two sub processes: The global and the local decision making. In this research, authors focus on the global decision making and aim at developing a generic approach that assists engineers in managing the business process associated with the life of their products or services. The approach automatically proposes a predicted ranking of the business process patterns, that are the most likely to be executed by a given user in a given context. This comes down to exploring these patterns and the decisions that control them in a complex business process, i.e. where all gateways are present (Fig. 1). Authors assume that this objective can be achieved using process mining techniques.

This paper is organized as follows. In Sect. 2, a literature review on decision and trace variants mining are discussed. The proposed approach is presented in Sect. 3 and then illustrated in a case study in Sect. 4. Finally, the discussion of future work concludes the paper.

2   Literature Review on Decision and Trace Variants Mining

Process mining is a research field that supports process understanding and improvement, it helps to automatically extract the hidden useful knowledge from the recorded event logs generated by information systems. Three types of applications in process mining are distinguished: *discovery*, *conformance*, and *enhancement* [7]. In this paper, authors focus on the *discovery* application, namely, the *decision mining* and the *trace variants mining*. A brief summary is provided of each.

Decision mining is a data-aware form of the process discovery application since it enriches process models with meaningful data. It aims at capturing the decision rules that control how the business processes flow (e.g. conditions 1,2,3,4 in Fig. 1). In [8], authors define it as the process in which data dependencies, that affect the routing of each activity in the business process, are detected. It analyses the data flow to find the rules that explain the rationale behind selecting an activity among others when the process flow splits [9].

While executing a business process, one may adopt the same logic several times (e.g. always executing pattern 1 in Fig. 1, rather than patterns 2 to 6, if condition 1 is enabled). This results in the existence of similar traces in the recorded event log. *Trace variants mining* aims at identifying the trace variants and their duplicates (e.g. patterns 1 to 9 in Fig. 1). Each trace variant refers to a process pattern that is a linear end-to-end process execution where only the activities execution order is taken into account [6].

2.1 Decision Mining

The starting point of the most common decision mining techniques is a recorded event log (i.e. past executions traces) and its corresponding petri net[1] model that describes the concurrency and synchronisation of the traces activities. To automatically generate a petri net model from an event log, different algorithms were proposed. The *alpha algorithm, alpha++ algorithm, ILP miner, genetic miner*, among others, are presented in [10], and the *inductive visual miner* that was recently proposed in [11].

Many research works contribute to decision mining development. In [8], authors propose an algorithm, called *Decision point analysis*, which allows one to detect decision points that depict choice splits within a process. Then for each decision point, an exclusive decision rule (Xor rule) in the form "*v op c*", where "*v*" is a variable, "*op*" is a comparison operator and "*c*" is a constant, allowing one activity among others to be executed is detected. The *decision point analysis* is implemented as a plug-in for the ProM[2] framework. In [12], authors propose a technique that improves the *decision point analysis* by allowing one to discover complex decision rules for the Xor gateway, based on invariants discovery, that takes into account more than one variable, i.e. in the form "v_1 *op c*" or "v_1 *op* v_2", where v_1 and v_2 are variables. This technique is implemented as a tool named *Branch Miner*[3]. In [13], authors propose a technique that embeds decision rules into process models by transforming the Xor gateway into a rule-based Xor gateway that automatically determines the optimal alternative in terms of performance (cost, time) during runtime. This technique is still not yet implemented. In [14], authors propose an approach to derive decision models from process models using enhanced decision mining. The decision rules are discovered using the *decision point analysis* algorithm [8], and then enhanced by taking into account the predictions of process performance measures (time, risk score) related to different decision outcomes. This approach is not yet implemented. In [15], authors propose a method that extends the *Decision point analysis* [8] which allows only single values to be analysed. The proposed method takes into account time series data (i.e. sequence of data points listed in time order) and allows one to generate complex decision rules with more than one variable. The method is implemented but not publicly shared. In [16], authors propose a process mining based technique that allows one to identify the most performant process path by

---

[1] https://en.wikipedia.org/wiki/Petri_net.

[2] http://www.promtools.org/.

[3] http://sep.cs.ut.ee/Main/BranchMiner.

mining decision rules based on the relationships between the context (i.e. situation in which the past decisions have taken place), path decisions and process performance (i.e. time, cost, quality). The approach is not yet implemented.

In [9], authors introduce a technique that takes the process petri net model, the process past executions log and the alignment result (indicating whether the model and the log conform to each other) as inputs, and produces a petri net model with the discovered inclusive/exclusive decision rules. It is implemented as a *data flow discovery* plug-in for the ProM framework. Another variant of this plug-in that needs only the event log and the related petri net as inputs is implemented as well. In [17], authors propose a technique that aims at discovering inclusive/exclusive decision rules even if they overlap due to incomplete process execution data. This technique is implemented in the *multi-perspective explorer* plug-in [18] of the ProM framework. In [19], authors propose an approach to explore inclusive decision rules using the *Decision point analysis* [8]. The approach consists in manually modifying the petri net model by transforming the "Or" gateway into an "And" gateway followed by a "Xor" gateway in each of its outgoing arcs.

2.2 Trace Variants Mining

Different researches were interested in trace variants mining. In [20], authors propose an approach based on trace clustering, that groups the similar traces into homogeneous subsets based on several perspectives. In [21], authors propose a *Pattern abstraction* plug-in, developed in ProM, that allows one to explore the common low-level patterns of execution, in an event log. These low-level patterns can be merged to generate the process most frequent patterns which can be exported in one single CSV file. The *Explore Event Log (Trace Variants/Searchable/Sortable)* visualizer[4], developed in ProM, sorts the different trace variants as well as the number and names of duplicate traces. These variants can be exported in separate CSV files, where each file contains the trace variant, i.e. process pattern, as well as the related duplicate traces.

2.3 Discussion

In this paper, authors attempt to discover the decision rules related to both exclusive (Xor) and inclusive (Or) gateways, as well as the different activities execution order. Regarding decision mining, the algorithm that generates the petri net model should be selected first. Authors reject the algorithms presented in [10] and select the *inductive visual miner* [11] as the petri net model generator. Indeed, experience has shown that only the *inductive visual miner* allows the inclusive gateways to be identified by the decision mining algorithm. This latter should afterward be selected.

The research works presented in [8], [12–16] attempt to discover exclusive decision rules considering only the exclusive (Xor) gateway. The work presented in [19] considers the inclusive and exclusive decision rules discovery, but the technique needs a manual modification of the petri net model which is not practical when dealing with complex processes. Therefore, authors assume that these works are not relevant for the

---

[4] https://fmannhardt.de/blog/process-mining-tools.

proposition and consider the works presented in [9, 17] which allow the discovery of both inclusive and exclusive decision rules. Moreover, authors assume that the *data flow discovery* plug-in [9] is more relevant since the experience has shown that the other one [17] could not correctly explore the decision rule related to the variables whose values do not frequently change in the event log.

Regarding *trace variants mining*, authors do not consider the approach presented in [20] as relevant for the proposition since the objective is to discover the patterns that are exactly similar, i.e. patterns with the same activities that are performed in the same order. The work presented in [21] and the *Explore Event Log* visualizer are considered as relevant for the proposition. Since none of the proposed techniques allow one to export a CSV file that contains only the trace variants and their frequency, authors assume that exploring trace variants using the *Explore Event Log* visualizer is more relevant because the discovered patterns can be exported in separate CSV files, which facilitates the postprocessing that needs to be made.

3   Decision and Trace Variants Mining Based Approach

The approach presented in Fig. 2 is the global workflow of the proposal and enables the achievement of the current research objective through seven steps.

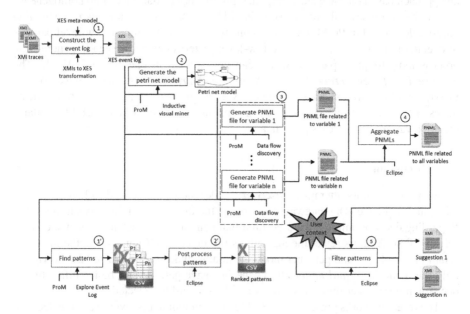

Fig. 2. Overview of the proposal (expressed in IDEF0 https://en.wikipedia.org/wiki/IDEF0)

The first step of the approach concerns the construction of the event log from the past process executions. These latter represent the process traces generated with respect to the trace metamodel depicted in [22, 23] and expressed in XMI (XML Metadata

Interchange) format. These traces should be automatically merged into a single XES[5] (eXtensible Event Stream) event log in order to be processed in ProM, the framework in which the selected decision mining technique is developed. This automatic merge is implemented using ATL[6] (Atlas Transformation Language).

The second step concerns the generation of the petri net model from the event log. To this end, the *inductive visual miner* is used. Having both the event log and its corresponding petri net model, the decision mining practically starts using the *data flow discovery* plug-in as discussed in Sect. 2.

The third step aims at deriving the decision rules related to all the variables in the event log and exporting them in a single PNML[7] (Petri Net Markup Language) file. PNML is a XML based standardized interchange format for Petri nets that allows the decision rules to be expressed as guards, this means that the transition from a place (i.e. activity) to another can fire only if the guard, and thus the rule, evaluates to true. For instance, condition 1 in Fig. 1 is the decision rule that enables the transition from A_1 to A_2. The experience has shown that when all the variables in the event log are considered in the decision mining, some decision rules related to some of these variables may not be derived as expected, the origin of this problem is not yet clear. Therefore, to avoid this situation and be sure to have a correct decision rule, authors propose to execute the *data flow discovery* plug-in for each variable, this results in as much decision rules as variables (step 3 in Fig. 2).

The PNML files, that are generated in step 3, should be automatically merged into one single PNML file that contains the complete decision rules, i.e. related to all the event log's variables (step 4 in Fig. 2). This automatic merge is implemented using the Java programming language.

In parallel with decision mining (finding the Or and XOR rules), the trace variants mining can be performed in order to find the end-to-end processes (e.g. patterns 1 to 9 in Fig. 1). The *Explore Event Log* visualizer, as discussed in Sect. 2, is used to explore patterns in an event log. The detected patterns are then exported in CSV files where each file contains one pattern and its duplicates (step 1' of Fig. 2). To fit our objective, the patterns files need to be automatically post processed. This consists in computing the occurrence frequency of each pattern and removing its duplicates and then creating a file that contains a ranking of the different, non-duplicate, patterns based on their occurrence frequency (step 2' in Fig. 2). This post processing is implemented using the Java programming language.

During a new process execution, the ranked patterns file is automatically filtered to fit both the discovered decision rules and the user's context (user's name, date, process type, etc.). In other words, the patterns that do not satisfy the decision rules and those that are, for example, performed by another user than the one that is currently performing the process are removed. As a result, a ranking of suggestions (i.e. patterns that are the most suitable for the current user's context) are proposed to the user (step 5 in Fig. 2). The selected pattern is, then, captured and stored in order to enrich the event log.

---

[5] http://www.xes-standard.org/.

[6] https://en.wikipedia.org/wiki/ATLAS_Transformation_Language.

[7] http://www.pnml.org/.

4 Case Study: Supervision of Gas Network Exploitation

Systems supervision is a decision-based activity carried out by a supervisor to survey the progress of an industrial process. It is a business process that produces an action, depending on both the supervision result and the set-point (i.e. target value for the supervised system), that resolves systems malfunction. The authors of this paper present a supervision case study where the supervisor of an industrial process should take, in the shortest time, the right decision in case an alarm is received. The challenge here is to provide this supervisor with a ranking of the process patterns that are the most likely to be executed in his context. The proposed approach is verified under a specific supervision process related to gas network exploitation.

The process starts by receiving the malfunction alarm. The Chief Operating Officer (COO) has, then, to choose the process that best resolves the problem in this context. This latter can be described by the field sensors values, season, supervisor's name, etc. The first step of the proposed approach is to transform the already captured sixty traces of this supervision process into a single XES event log (step 1 in Fig. 2) and then generate its corresponding petri net model (step 2 in Fig. 2). Then, from the event log and the petri net model, generate the decision rules for each variable and export them in PNML files (step 3 in Fig. 2). In this process, the decision variables are: Pressure, season, network status, flow rate, human resource (the decision rule related to the pressure variable is depicted in Fig. 3). These PNML files are then merged into one single PNML file that contains the complete decision rules related to all the decision variables (step 4 in Fig. 2).

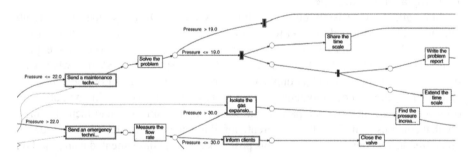

Fig. 3. Discovered decision rules for the pressure variable

In this process, based on both pressure value and season, the COO decides whether to send an emergency or a maintenance technician. If the emergency technician is sent (i.e. the decision rule: *((pressure > 22millibars) and (season ≠ fall))* evaluates to true), he has then to decide which action should be performed based on the measured flow rate. If the decision rule *((pressure ≤ 22millibars) and (season = fall))* evaluates to true, then the maintenance technician is sent. Moreover, if the rule *(pressure < 19millibars)* evaluates to true, then in addition to sending the maintenance technician, the supervisor should extend the time scale then share it and write the problem then share it. In this last case, the inclusive logic is transformed into a parallel logic, and thus the activities may be executed in different possible orders.

In parallel with the decision rules mining, the step 1' and 2' in Fig. 2 are performed; the patterns that are contained in the event log are discovered (Fig. 4a) then exported in CSV files and finally post processed by removing each pattern's duplicates and computing their occurrence frequency. If we consider all the possible process patterns and the different rules, it is possible to construct the BPMN process depicted in Fig. 5.

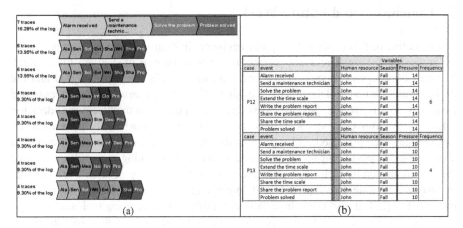

Fig. 4. (a) Discovered patterns, (b) proposed patterns

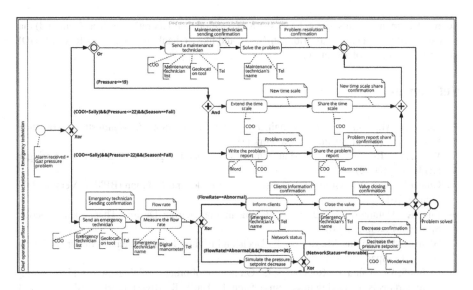

Fig. 5. Part of the resulting supervision process with the different rules (expressed in BPMN)

These patterns (Fig. 4a) are, then, filtered based on the current context and the decision rules that are generated (step 4 in Fig. 2). For instance, if the alarm is received in the fall by John, and the pressure of the supervised network equals to 18 millibars which is less than both 22 and 19 millibars (Fig. 5), the approach proposes two possible patterns to solve the problem (Fig. 4b), where the first one "P12" is the most frequently used in this context.

5   Conclusion and Future Work

The objective of this paper is to support engineers in their decision-making processes by proposing the most relevant process patterns to be executed given the context. Through the proposed approach, the past execution traces are first analysed and the decision rules that control the process are mined. Then, the patterns and their occurrence frequency are discovered, postprocessed and filtered based on the discovered decision rules and the user context parameters. A ranking of the most likely patterns to be executed are then proposed. This approach illustrates the feasibility of the assumption about using process mining techniques to support decision making in complex processes that are controlled by inclusive, exclusive and parallel gateways. Future work consists in fully automating the approach and integrating it in the process visualizer tool presented in [22]. It also consists in evaluating this approach, using real-world design and supervision processes, with respect to some performance indicators such as execution time, quality of the proposed decisions, changes propagation, etc.

Acknowledgments.   This research takes part of a national collaborative project (Gontrand) that aims at supervising a smart gas grid. Authors would like to thank the companies REGAZ, GDS and GRDF for their collaboration.

References

1. Hammer, M., Champy, J.: Reengineering the Corporation: A Manifesto for Business Revolution. Harper Business, New York (1993)
2. Weske, M.: Business Process Management: Concepts, Languages, Architectures. Springer, Heidelberg (2012)
3. Object Management Group, "Business Process Model and Notation (BPMN) Version 2.0," January 2011
4. Iino, K., Hatamura, Y.: Decision-Making in Engineering Design: Theory and Practice. Springer, London (2006)
5. Blenko, M., Mankins, M., Rogers, P.: Decision Insights: The Five Steps to Better Decisions. Bain & Company (2013)
6. Es-Soufi, W., Yahia, E., Roucoules, L.: On the use of process mining and machine learning to support decision making in systems design. In: Harik, R., Rivest, L., Bernard, A., Eynard, B., Bouras, A. (eds.) PLM 2016. IAICT, vol. 492, pp. 56–66. Springer, Cham (2016). https://doi.org/10.1007/978-3-319-54660-5_6

7. Van Der Aalst, W.: Process mining: overview and opportunities. ACM Trans. Manag. Inf. Syst. (TMIS) **3**(2), 7 (2012)
8. Rozinat, A., Aalst, W.M.P.: Decision mining in business processes. BPM Center Report BPM-06-10 (2006). BPMcenter.org
9. de Leoni, M., van der Aalst, W.M.P.: Data-aware process mining: discovering decisions in processes using alignments. In: Proceedings of the 28th Annual ACM Symposium on Applied Computing, Coimbra, Portugal, pp. 1454–1461 (2013)
10. van Dongen, B.F., Alves de Medeiros, A.K., Wen, L.: Process mining: overview and outlook of petri net discovery algorithms. In: Jensen, K., van der Aalst, W.M.P. (eds.) Transactions on Petri Nets and Other Models of Concurrency II. LNCS, vol. 5460, pp. 225–242. Springer, Heidelberg (2009). https://doi.org/10.1007/978-3-642-00899-3_13
11. Leemans, S.J.J., Fahland, D., van der Aalst, W.M.P.: Exploring processes and deviations. In: Fournier, F., Mendling, J. (eds.) BPM 2014. LNBIP, vol. 202, pp. 304–316. Springer, Cham (2015). https://doi.org/10.1007/978-3-319-15895-2_26
12. de Leoni, M., Dumas, M., García-Bañuelos, L.: Discovering branching conditions from business process execution logs. In: Cortellessa, V., Varró, D. (eds.) FASE 2013. LNCS, vol. 7793, pp. 114–129. Springer, Heidelberg (2013). https://doi.org/ 10.1007/978-3-642-37057-1_9
13. Catalkaya, S., Knuplesch, D., Chiao, C., Reichert, M.: Enriching business process models with decision rules. In: Lohmann, N., Song, M., Wohed, P. (eds.) BPM 2013. LNBIP, vol. 171, pp. 198–211. Springer, Cham (2014). https://doi.org/10.1007/978-3-319-06257-0_16
14. Bazhenova, E., Weske, M.: Deriving decision models from process models by enhanced decision mining. In: Reichert, M., Reijers, Hajo A. (eds.) BPM 2015. LNBIP, vol. 256, pp. 444–457. Springer, Cham (2016). https://doi.org/10.1007/978-3-319-42887-1_36
15. Dunkl, R., Rinderle-Ma, S., Grossmann, W., Anton Fröschl, K.: A method for analyzing time series data in process mining: application and extension of decision point analysis. In: Nurcan, S., Pimenidis, E. (eds.) CAiSE Forum 2014. LNBIP, vol. 204, pp. 68–84. Springer, Cham (2015). https://doi.org/10.1007/978-3-319-19270-3_5
16. Ghattas, J., Soffer, P., Peleg, M.: Improving business process decision making based on past experience. Decis. Support Syst. **59**, 93–107 (2014)
17. Mannhardt, F., de Leoni, M., Reijers, Hajo A., van der Aalst, Wil M.P.: Decision mining revisited - discovering overlapping rules. In: Nurcan, S., Soffer, P., Bajec, M., Eder, J. (eds.) CAiSE 2016. LNCS, vol. 9694, pp. 377–392. Springer, Cham (2016). https://doi.org/ 10.1007/978-3-319-39696-5_23
18. Mannhardt, F., de Leoni, M., Reijers, H.A.: The multi-perspective process explorer. In: BPM (Demos), pp. 130–134 (2015)
19. Sarno, R., Sari, P.L.I., Ginardi, H., Sunaryono, D., Mukhlash, I.: Decision mining for multi choice workflow patterns. In: 2013 International Conference on Computer, Control, Informatics and Its Applications (IC3INA), pp. 337–342 (2013)
20. Song, M., Günther, C.W., van der Aalst, W.M.P.: Trace clustering in process mining. In: Ardagna, D., Mecella, M., Yang, J. (eds.) BPM 2008. LNBIP, vol. 17, pp. 109–120. Springer, Heidelberg (2009). https://doi.org/10.1007/978-3-642-00328-8_11
21. Jagadeesh Chandra Bose, R.P., van der Aalst, W.M.P.: Abstractions in process mining: a taxonomy of patterns. In: Dayal, U., Eder, J., Koehler, J., Reijers, Hajo A. (eds.) BPM 2009. LNCS, vol. 5701, pp. 159–175. Springer, Heidelberg (2009). https://doi.org/ 10.1007/978-3-642-03848-8_12

22. Roucoules, L., Yahia, E., Es-Soufi, W., Tichkiewitch, S.: Engineering design memory for design rationale and change management toward innovation. CIRP Ann. Manufact. Technol. **65**(1), 193–196 (2016)

23. Es-Soufi, W., Yahia, E., Roucoules, L.: Collaborative design and supervision processes meta-model for rationale capitalization. In: Eynard, B., Nigrelli, V., Oliveri, S., Peris-Fajarnes, G., Rizzuti, S. (eds.) Advances on Mechanics, Design Engineering and Manufacturing. Lecture Notes in Mechanical Engineering, pp. 1123–1130. Springer, Cham (2017). https://doi.org/10.1007/978-3-319-45781-9_112

PLM and Education

PLM in Engineering Education: A Pilot Study for Insights on Actual and Future Trends

Joel Sauza Bedolla[1], Gianluca D'Antonio[1(✉)], Frédéric Segonds[2], and Paolo Chiabert[1]

[1] Politecnico di Torino, corso Duca degli Abruzzi 24, 10129 Turin, Italy
{joel.sauza,gianluca.dantonio,paolo.chiabert}@polito.it
[2] Ecole Nationale Supérieure d'Arts et Métiers, 151 bd. de l'Hôpital, 75013 Paris, France
frederic.segonds@ensam.eu

Abstract. Universities around the world are teaching PLM following different strategies, at different degree levels and presenting this approach from different perspectives. This paper aims to provide preliminary results for a comprehensive review concerning the state of the art in PLM education. This contribution presents the design and analysis of a questionnaire that has been submitted to academics in Italy and France, and companies involved in a specific Master program on PLM. The main goal of the survey is to collect objective and quantitative data, as well as opinions and ideas gained from education expertise. The collected results enable to depict the state of the art of PLM education in Italian universities and to gain some insights concerning the French approach; the structure of the survey is validated for further worldwide submission.

Keywords: Product lifecycle management · Education · Survey

1 Introduction

Product Lifecycle Management (PLM) is a key factor for innovation. The PLM approach to support complex goods manufacturing is now considered as one of the major technological and organizational challenges of this decade to cope with the shortening of product lifecycles [1]. Further, in a globalized world, products are often designed and manufactured in several locations worldwide, in "extreme" collaborative environments.

To deal with these challenges and maintain their competitiveness, companies and professional organizations need employees to own a basic understanding of engineering practices, and to be able to perform effectively, autonomously, in a team environment [2]. Traditional methodologies for design projects (i.e. with collocated teams and synchronous work) could be effective until a few decades ago, but they are insufficient nowadays.

Thus, engineering education has changed in order to provide students with some experience in collaborative product development during their studies. It is essential to train students to Computer Supported Collaborative Work (CSCW) [3], and PLM is a means for students to structure their design methodology. Indeed, before starting an efficient professional collaboration, future engineers must be mindful of how this

© IFIP International Federation for Information Processing 2017
Published by Springer International Publishing AG 2017. All Rights Reserved
J. Ríos et al. (Eds.): PLM 2017, IFIP AICT 517, pp. 277–284, 2017.
https://doi.org/10.1007/978-3-319-72905-3_25

approach works, and how tasks can be split between stakeholders. Thus, from an educational point of view, the PLM approach can be considered as a sophisticated analysis and visualization tool that enables students to improve their problem solving and design skills, as well as their understanding of engineering systems behaviour [2]. Moreover, PLM can also be a solution to face one of the main problems in our educational system: the fragmentation of the knowledge and its lack of depth [3].

The main research question from here is: "How can we, as engineering educators, respond to global demands to make our students more productive, effective learners? And how can PLM help us to achieve this goal?". At the state of the art, the information about PLM education is fragmented. Hence, the aim of this paper is to propose a survey structure to collect quantitative data about the existing university courses in PLM, identify the most common practices and possible improvements to closer adhere to the needs of manufacturers.

The remainder of the paper is organized as follows: in Sect. 2, an analysis of literature concerning recent changes in educational practices in engineering education is presented and the state of the art of PLM education is settled. Then, the survey structure is presented in Sect. 3. The results are presented in Sect. 4: data collected from Italian universities are presented, as well as the results of the test performed in France to validate the survey structure. Finally, in Sect. 5, some conclusive remarks and hints for future work are provided.

2   State of the Art

In literature, there is no evidence of a complete and full review of how PLM is taught in higher institutions around the world. Still, partial works can be found. Gandhi [4] presents the educational strategy employed by three US universities. Fielding et al. [5] show examples of PLM and collaborative practices implemented in higher education institutions from the United States and France. Sauza et al. [6] performed a two-step research. The first attempt consisted in a systematic research of keywords (i.e. PLM education, PLM certification, PLM course, PLM training) in the principal citation databases. Nevertheless, the analysis of scientific literature was limited to some specific programs of a limited quantity of countries. For this reason, the research was extended to direct research on universities' websites. The inclusion criteria for institutions was the attendance to one of the two main events in scientific and industrial use of PLM: (i) the IFIP working group 5.1 PLM International Conference, and (ii) Partners for the Advancement of Collaborative Engineering Education. The review process covered 191 universities from Europe, Asia, America and Oceania. It was found that there is a high variety in the topics that are presented to students, departments involved in the course management, the education strategy and the number of hours related to PLM.

The analysis presents useful insights. However, the research methodology based on website analysis was not sufficient and may present some lacks. In some cases, websites did not present a "search" option and this limited the accessibility to information. Moreover, during the research, some issues with languages were experienced: not all of the universities offered information in English, and for this reason, the universities were not considered. In some other cases, information was presented in the curricula that can be accessed only to institution members. The specific didactics nature of this study is precisely in that it brings researchers and professors from engineering education to work explain their vision of how PLM is taught. The objective is to get real participatory innovation based on integration of the PLM within a proven training curriculum in engineering education. One step further, we prone that by stimulating the desire to appropriate knowledge, innovative courses are also likely to convince a broad swath of students averse to traditional teaching methods and much more in phase with their definition as "digital natives" [7].

This paper is intended to be the first step of a broader effort to map the actual situation of PLM education around the world. This contribution presents the methodology employed to scientifically collect information from universities. Before going global, a first test has been made to evaluate the robustness of the tool in the authors' countries of origin, where the knowledge of the university system structure was clear.

3 Methodology

In order to get insights on the state of the art in PLM education, a survey structured in three parts has been prepared.

The first part is named "Presentation": the recipient is asked to state the name of his institution and to provide an email address for possible future feedbacks. Further, he is asked to state whether he is aware about the existence of courses in PLM in his institution or not, and if he is in charge of such courses. In case of positive reply, the recipient is invited to fill the subsequent part of the survey.

The second part of the survey aims to collect objective information to describe the PLM course. In particular, the following data are required:

– The level at which the course is taught (among B.Sc, M.Sc, Ph.D, Master);
– The curriculum in which the course is taught (free reply);
– At which year the course is taught, and the overall duration of the curriculum (values constrained between 1 and 5);
– The department in charge of the course (free reply);
– If PLM is taught in a devoted course (Yes/No) or as a topic in a broader course (Yes/No);
– The name of the course (free reply) and its duration;
– If software training is included (Yes/No) and which software is used.

Finally, in the third part of the survey, subjective data are collected to measure the interest of the recipient in teaching the PLM approach and the interest of the students in this topic (both in a likert 1–5 scale). Further, an opinion about the duration of the course is required (not enough/proper/excessive) and whether the presentation of applied case studies or the contribution of industrial experts are included in the course. A space for further free comments is also available.

The invitations to fill the survey have been organized in two steps. First, a full experiment has been made in Italy. The official database owned by the Italian Ministry of Education and University has been accessed to identify the academics to be involved. In Italy, academics are grouped according to the main topic of their research. Therefore, the contacts of all the professors and researchers working in the closest topics to PLM have been downloaded, namely: (i) Design and methods of industrial engineering; (ii) Technologies and production systems; (iii) Industrial plants; (iv) Economics and management Engineering; (v) Information elaboration systems; (vi) Computer science. This research led to a database consisting of 2208 people from 64 public universities. A first invitation and a single reminder have been sent; the survey, realized through a Google Form, has been made accessible online for 2 weeks in January 2017.

The second step consisted in inviting a small set of academics from French universities through focused e-mails: 11 replies have been collected. 11 replies have been collected. Further, a similar survey has been submitted to French companies employing people that has been attending a Master in PLM in the years 2015 and 2016.

4   Survey Data Analysis

4.1   Results from the Italian Sample

The overall number of replies from Italian academics is equal to 213, from 49 different institutions. Among this sample, 124 people do not have information about PLM courses in their universities; therefore, they were not asked further questions. The 89 respondents aware about a PLM course belong to 36 universities; among them, 40 professors are directly involved in teaching PLM. A synthetic overview of the results is provided in Fig. 1; the map of the Italian universities in which PLM is taught is shown in Fig. 2.

Degree level. In the sample of 36 universities, PLM is taught at different levels. The Master of Science is the most common: 53 courses have been identified. In 22 cases, PLM is also taught at the Bachelor level. Furthermore, there are 4 courses devoted to Ph.D. candidates and 2 Masters are organized. The latter two Master courses are organized in the Polytechnic universities of Torino and Milano; however, the first one has recently moved to University of Torino.

Curricula. There is a variety of curricula involved in teaching PLM. Course for Management Engineering and Mechanical Engineering are organized (23 occurrences each). The area of Computer Science is also involved (23 occurrences): topics concerning the architecture of PLM systems, or the so-called Software Lifecycle Management are taught. Moreover, PLM courses are also provided in Industrial Engineering (6 occurrences), Automotive Engineering (B.Sc. at Polytechnic University di Torino) and Building Engineering (Ph.D. course at Politecnico di Bari).

Type of course. The teachers involved in teaching PLM state that this topic is mostly dealt in broader courses, such as Drawing, Industrial Plants, Management. A devoted course is organized only in three cases: (i) "Product Lifecycle Management" at Polytechnic University of Milano (M.Sc. course for Management Engineers, 50 h); (ii) "Methods and tools for product lifecycle management" at University of Bergamo (M.Sc.

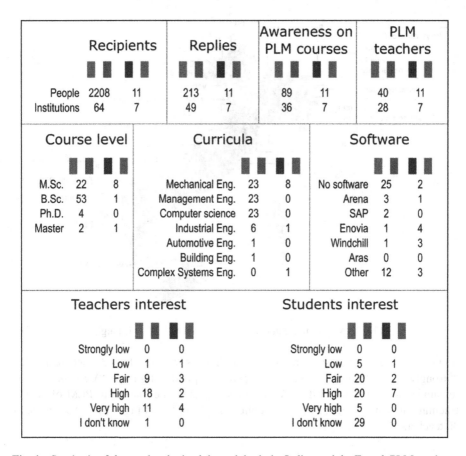

	Recipients		Replies		Awareness on PLM courses		PLM teachers	
	■■ ■■		■■ ■■		■■ ■■		■■ ■■	
People	2208	11	213	11	89	11	40	11
Institutions	64	7	49	7	36	7	28	7

Course level			Curricula			Software		
	■■ ■■			■■ ■■			■■ ■■	
M.Sc.	22	8	Mechanical Eng.	23	8	No software	25	2
B.Sc.	53	1	Management Eng.	23	0	Arena	3	1
Ph.D.	4	0	Computer science	23	0	SAP	2	0
Master	2	1	Industrial Eng.	6	1	Enovia	1	4
			Automotive Eng.	1	0	Windchill	1	3
			Building Eng.	1	0	Aras	0	0
			Complex Systems Eng.	0	1	Other	12	3

Teachers interest			Students interest		
	■■ ■■			■■ ■■	
Strongly low	0	0	Strongly low	0	0
Low	1	1	Low	5	1
Fair	9	3	Fair	20	2
High	18	2	High	20	7
Very high	11	4	Very high	5	0
I don't know	1	0	I don't know	29	0

Fig. 1. Synthesis of the results obtained through both the Italian and the French PLM teachers.

course for Management Engineering, 48 h); (iii) the aforementioned Master course held in Torino.

Practical activities. Among the 40 PLM teachers, 25 of them do not use software to support their educational activity. Some courses deploy Arena, Enovia, the PLM module embedded in SAP, Windchill. Other solutions, developed by smaller software houses are also used. Among the respondents, no one uses Aras Innovator, a PLM solution that has a license model inspired by open source products. However, in the majority of the teachers (27), industrial case studies are presented to show the role of PLM in managing product information and to provide students with a practical demonstration of the possible benefits coming from its implementation. Furthermore, interventions from industrial experts, aiming to show the practical implications of the theoretical notions taught in frontal lectures, are planned by 21 teachers.

Interest in PLM. The interest of students in PLM is variable: the replies are equally distributed among "Low" or "Fair" (25 occurrences) and "High" or "Very high" (25

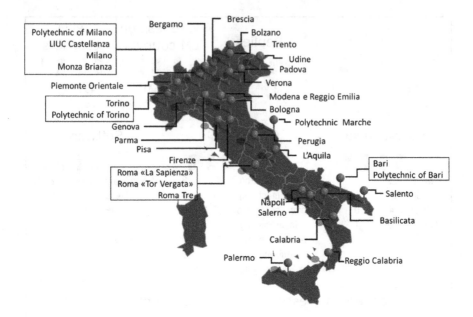

Fig. 2. Map of the Italian universities in which PLM is taught.

occurrences). The interest of replicants in PLM is variable too: 34 people replied "Strongly low", "Low" or "Fair"; 34 people replied "High" or "Very high"; the remainder sample states "I don't know". As expected, the interest in PLM of people teaching this topic is high: 29 people replied "High" or "Very high" (out of a sample of 40 teachers).

4.2   Results from the French Sample

On the French side, 11 replies were collected from 7 different Universities and School of Engineering. All the respondents teach PLM courses in their Universities. Similarly to the Italian sample, PLM is mostly taught in the M.Sc. level: beside a Master course, one B.Sc. and 8 M.Sc. courses were mapped. Most of the courses (8) are devoted to Mechanical Engineers. In 6 cases, a specific course is designed for PLM; further, in the Ecole supérieure d'électricité settled in Châtenay-Malabry the so-called 'PLM week' is organized. The duration of the PLM courses mainly ranges between 32 and 64 h, which is an appropriate duration, according to the teachers; conversely, in the broader courses, the time spent in teaching PLM is lower than 6 h. The only Master mapped through the survey is held in Ecole Nationale Supérieure d'Arts et Métiers (Paris): the duration is equal to 350 h, with high interest of the participants.

A reduced version of the survey was also sent to a small set of French companies to map internal courses in PLM.7 replies have been obtained.: 3 were from large companies in the field of aeronautics, textile and consulting, and 4 were small-medium companies from the PLM and BIM sector. 57% of these companies declare they have courses dedicated to PLM. The name of the courses are various. In particular, a textile enterprise has course structured in 11 modules as business process:

1. Line plan Management
2. Color Management
3. Material Management
4. Product/Colorway Merchandising Management,
5. Material. Color Development and Approval management
6. Product Specification management,
7. Market and Distribution Selection
8. Product Sample/Approval management,
9. Supplier Management and Vendor Collaboration
10. Reports and Dashboards
11. Quality Management

Another company has a specific training course on PLCS Training Over-view and PLCS Training Technical Walkthrough; focused on data management using standards. Time for these courses ranges from 2 to 40 h, depending on the complexity of the concept developed.

5   Conclusions

The present paper presented a methodology for a systematic overview about university education in PLM. A survey has been submitted to all the Italian academics performing research and teaching activities in fields related with PLM. The percentage of respondents in the Italian experiment was approximately 10%, which is in line with the expectations of the authors: these replies enabled to identify PLM courses in 36 different universities, mainly located in the north-central part of the country, which is characterized by a higher density of industries. However, to have a successful realization of the survey a complete database of university teachers is mandatory.

The proof-of-concept realized on the French sample led to good results: no criticalities have been found in the survey. Hence, the next steps of the work are the creation of the recipients database and the full-scale experiment. Then, the experiment can be replicated in other countries, to have a more exhaustive picture about PLM education. We plan to rely on Bloom taxonomy of educational objectives to sharpen the skills taught in PLM courses [8].

Our research question was: "How can we, as engineering educators, respond to global demands to make our students more productive, effective learners? And how can PLM help us to achieve this goal?". A first insight given to this research question is the proposal, as an ultimate goal, of the creation of a network made of PLM teachers, that will enable mutual exchange of expertise, teaching material, exercises and practices. To reach this goal and to wider our approach to IFIP WG 5.1 community, a first step could be the creation of shared storage space for documents that allow any user to teach PLM at any level.

Acknowledgments. The authors are grateful to the colleagues and industrials that replied to the survey.

References

1. Garetti, M., Terzi, S., Bertacci, N., Brianza, M.: Organisational change and knowledge management in PLM implementation. Int. J. Prod. Lifecycle Manag. **1**(1), 43–51 (2005)
2. Chen, Z., Siddique, Z.: Web-based mechanical engineering design education environment simulating design firms. In: Innovations in Engineering Education 2004: Mechanical Engineering Education, Mechanical Engineering Technology Department Heads, Anaheim, USA (2004)
3. Pezeshki, C., Frame, R., Humann, B.: Preparing undergraduate mechanical engineering students for the global marketplace - new demands and requirements. In: ASEE Annual Conference Proceedings, Salt Lake City, USA (2004)
4. Gandhi, P.: Product lifecycle management in education: key to innovation in engineering and technology. In: Fukuda, S., Bernard, A., Gurumoorthy, B., Bouras, A. (eds.) PLM 2014. IAICT, vol. 442, pp. 121–128. Springer, Heidelberg (2014). https://doi.org/10.1007/978-3-662-45937-9_13
5. Fielding, E.A., McCardle, J.R., Eynard, B., Hartman, N., Fraser, A.: Product lifecycle management in design and engineering education: international perspectives. Concur. Eng. Res. Appl. **22**(2), 123–134 (2014)
6. Sauza-Bedolla, J., Mora-Orozco, J., Guarin-Grisales, A., D'Antonio, G., Chiabert, P.: PLM in a didactic environment: the path to smart factory. Int. J. Prod. Lifecycle Manag. **9**(4), 333–352 (2016)
7. Prensky, M.: Digital natives, digital immigrants Part 1. On the Horiz. **9**(5), 1–6 (2001)
8. Bloom, B.S., Krathwohl, D.R., Masia, B.B.: Bloom Taxonomy of Educational Objectives. Allyn and Bacon, Boston (1984)

Preliminary Study on Workshop Facilitation for IoT Innovation as Industry-University Collaboration PLM Program for Small and Medium Sized Enterprises

Satoshi Goto[1,2(✉)], Osamu Yoshie[1], Shigeru Fujimura[1],
and Kin'ya Tamaki[3]

[1] Graduate School of Information, Production and Systems,
Waseda University, Tokyo, Japan
satoshi-goto@fuji.waseda.jp,
{yoshie,fujimura}@waseda.jp
[2] Business Transformation Management, PTC Japan Co. Ltd., Tokyo, Japan
[3] Human Innovation Research Center, Aoyama Gakuin University,
Tokyo, Japan
kinya.tamaki@gmail.com

Abstract. The global manufacturing business is in the new era of industrial revolution based on digital data across the whole business processes. Internet of Things (IoT) is one of extremely high expected technologies. They contribute product lifecycle management (PLM) process, such as remote monitoring of field service and predictive quality reliability engineering design. However, it assumes significant difficulties for small and medium sized enterprises (SME) to launch rapidly IoT solution for their business efficiency or strategic differentiation. Thus, this paper proposes a pragmatic IoT Innovation workshop approach for such SMEs' employees. This is as an industry-university collaboration PLM educational program utilizing both design thinking business methodology and commercial IoT application technology hands-on. It also introduces outcomes as a preliminary phase for empirical study on this workshop approach that deployed for a local city in the Far East area.

Keywords: Internet of Things · Workshop facilitation
Industry-university collaboration · Design thinking
Product lifecycle management · Educational and training approach

1 Introduction

The global and distributed industrial world has been producing various business trends and case studies in terms of product lifecycle management (PLM) process in the past decade [1]. In addition to such PLM approach, nowadays, a large business operating on a global scale would be aiming for the realization of smart connected product and smart factory where IoT technology is applied in industry while investing capital on a grand scale [2].

© IFIP International Federation for Information Processing 2017
Published by Springer International Publishing AG 2017. All Rights Reserved
J. Ríos et al. (Eds.): PLM 2017, IFIP AICT 517, pp. 285–296, 2017.
https://doi.org/10.1007/978-3-319-72905-3_26

On the other hand, what is the current situation of small to medium enterprises (SME)? They are limited due to having small scale and range of business. Securements of capital or human resources are also not always enough. However, in order for the industries in national country to continue developing, the contribution from SMEs making use of a widely spread regional network is essential. For example, the German SME comprises 99.6% of all enterprises in the country [3].

Based on such so-called fourth industrial revolution taking place, it is significantly meaningful for SME's whole product lifecycle to conduct investigative research into the strategic direction relating to information communication technology (ICT).

At present the authors are working on empirical research and business development via stakeholders' consensus building methods in the creation of vision and strategy [4]. This includes a study of IoT enabled commercial PLM application software for supporting IoT functionality which is installed on the main product of a manufacturing business [5]. We have been also working on research relating to the methods of agreement formation which can efficiently conceive a new business model in response to the product lifecycle process of discrete manufactures. This is to develop engineering and business management education program regarding PLM system as a part of industry-university collaboration [6].

With the background as described as above, this paper reports on a result from trial evaluation of "business initiative workshop on internet of things (IoT)" that we developed. Section 2 outlines the basic structure of the workshop developed in this research, expected types of participants as well as the technology which will be experienced. Section 3 reports the result of the preliminary trial implemented by the participating monitors in respect of the workshop methodology developed by our research team. Then in Sect. 4 the purpose and efficacy of the business modelling method called "design thinking [7]" applied in this workshop will be discussed. At the same time it discusses existing issues relating to industry-university collaboration.

In the final section, Sect. 5, it concludes relating to industry-university collaboration program for the promotion of new industries in a local area while concluding this research.

2 Basic Concept

2.1 Configuration of Workshop Agenda

This workshop is designed for employees and managers who are working at the local SME. It aims to be a short term and intensive human resources developmental lecture. This is a unique three discussion package, which are (1) business modeling, (2) technology hands-on and (3) field work out of the workshop seminar room. It configures for seven hours per a day and three consecutive days in total.

Day 1 – Value Identification. This workshop delivers as a group discussion format. It utilizes design thinking business methodology. With this, the participants are made aware of insights relating to IoT businesses. Finally, each group shall draw up a hypothesis of a new business model idea to tackle in the future.

Day 2 – Technology Experience. It experiences commercial ICT applications relating to the latest IoT and Augmented Reality (AR). This allows the participants to realize a practical work on computers. With this, it can validate out whether or not the imaginary new business model created on day 1 can be technologically supported with such ICT technologies.

Day 3 – Value Planning. This whole day is a field work exploring the local town where the participants work at. The participants visit that area in person. There are also opportunities for them to directly interview the local businesses people regarding their business strategy or stance so that the participants can understand the issues faced by the area. Participants can finally define a practical business model journey to improve the specific points of view considering with the contents of Day 1 and 2.

2.2 Assumed Profile of the Participants

The following is the expected profile of participants in this workshop. The premise is that the participants should be working at local SME. For example, middle class workers in local SME with the following experience or jobs was assumed to be a potential participant.

- A proprietor, successor or head of department
- A leading core human resource who is a future potential executive
- A specialist with interest in new business development and strategy setting
- A system engineer on business systems; e.g., CAD, PLM, ERP and CRM systems
- A middle manager interested in latest technology of the world such as IoT and AR

2.3 Opportunity to Experience of State-the-Arts Technologies

In addition to group discussions, it provides the opportunity to get real experience of state-of-the-arts technology solutions and application platforms such as IoT, AR, CAD and PLM application software that the manufacturing industries are working on. A hands-on session will be provided to the participants.

3 Case Study as a Preliminary Trial Workshop

In order to proof of the workshop concept, a preliminary trial workshop was implemented in city K. The city is an industrial area since the latter half of 19th century. It has been leading business region of manufactured metals, cars and energy industry as the place of origin of Japan's modern industry. However, looking back over the past 15 years, it's hard to say that there has been progress in economy of manufacturing activities. With the arrival of super aging society, many local industries would be remaining on a plateau. Local SME particularly fear serious business results downturn. In other words, it's thought that strengthening the imagination of new business planning and conception of new technological development while appreciating the full lifecycle of a product or a service is something that is needed urgently.

In such industry background, with area W in city K with a historical and industrial backdrop, the trial workshop was held. Inviting monitor participants, it deployed the verification and evaluation of the workshop concept. The implemented agenda and results were as follows. By the way, the author's university is located in area W.

3.1 Date and Time

- Date: 14, 15 and 16 September, 2016 (consecutive three days)
- Time: from 10:00 a.m. through 5:00 p.m. (net 6 h except for break time)

3.2 Venue and Place

- Workshop room 1: A classroom at university campus of our research team
- Workshop room 2: A meeting room at local community center in area W
- Field work area: Four locations (shopping street, historical business grade area, fish processing company and fruit and vegetable market)

3.3 Member

- 6 Workshop Participants - residing in city K (as monitor participants)
- 1 Workshop Facilitator - experienced in this industry for 30 years
- 1 Application Specialist - operating experience of IoT and AR technologies

3.4 Technology

The information communication technology (ICT) used in this trial workshop was the ThingWorx as an IoT development platform and Vuforia as augmented reality soft-ware. Both were produced by PTC Inc. which is one of the global leaders providing the market with commercial IoT and AR technology and solutions [8].

Note: As this was the first preliminary trial, both CAD and PLM applications were not prepared yet. We are planning to implement them as the next trial in late 2017.

3.5 Specific Session Streams

The following shows the actual agenda structure, timetable and content implemented over a total of three days. The intensive workshop over three days was formed of a total of 20 independent sessions. The following Tables 1, 2 and 3 are introduced the session streams:

Day 1: Hypotheses Definition on IoT Innovation;
Day 2: User Experience with State-of-the-Arts ICT Technologies;
Day 3: Conception of New Business Strategy through Field Observations.

Table 1. Day 1: Hypotheses Definition on IoT Innovation

Session #, Topic, (duration)	Session Activity in Day 1
1-A, Warming up (15 min)	As an ice breaker, each person introduced themselves and shared their thoughts on their impression of area W in city K, such as the lifestyle there and the current status of the region
1-B, Confirmation of business topics (45 min)	As the start of the workshop, a questionnaire was filled in by the participants in advance. From this, the participants attempted to hypothesize the direction of business strategy
1-C, Specifying problems to be solved (60 min)	The 26 types of IoT use case [4] used by our research team were categorized using the "2x2 matrix" method which is one of the methods for design thinking [12]. These use cases were shared between participants and whether new ideas and discoveries popped up was confirmed among the group members
1-D, Confirmation of business strategy (60 min)	From the above use cases categorized using the 2x2 method, one that a group member thought most important use case was specified as a start point, a discussion was conducted regarding what the original business "objectives" would be using IoT. By using the design thinking method called "value graph", a brainstorm took place giving consideration so that group members are not swayed by pre-conceptions, regarding what purpose of IoT technology would be used as a mean in businesses. There was a challenge to see whether a new idea for applying IoT technology may come to mind
1-E, IoT use case introduction (30 min)	The facilitator presented significant IoT business case studies which are already being developed in the world. These aim to be hints for the participants in conceiving new businesses in the future
1-F, Customer value chain analysis (60 min)	"CVCA: Customer Value Chain Analysis [9] " method was used and based on an imaginary business hypothesized in 1-B, the spread of value chain from a client's point of view was analyzed. From this, a discussion was further deepened to be about who the true final customer is, what the correlation status between related cooperating business and one's own company and whether value chains between in-company organizations are appropriate
1-G, IoT Proto-typing (45 min)	Participants made to specify three places out of the customer value chain diagram drawn up in 1-F in which business improvement or benefit of differentiation may be obtained by applying IoT application. IoT application's screen image to be drawn in those places was pseudo-designed on sketch book. In other words, this was a "paper prototyping" session
1-H, Group Presentation (45 min)	In order to explain the things which have been discussed in the day, a 5-min presentation was given by each group. The imaginary local business, its business issues, measures which should be tackled as well as the control of IoT application thought to be needed as well as their benefits were presented. Finally, the opinions of all the participants were shared in a Q&A session

Table 2. Day 2: User Experience with State-of-the-Arts ICT Technologies

Session #, Topic, (duration)	Session Activity in Day 2
2-A, Review of the first day (30 min)	All the steps from day 1 implemented the day before were reviewed by all participants and the details of work for day 2 were shared and everyone motivated themselves
2-B, Hypothesis creation of daily topics in business (60 min)	The imaginary business conceived in the previous day's discussions was considered in order to share among everyone the topics which may crop up on a day-to-day running of the business based on keywords (three per person) provided by the participants. With this, participants could be made aware constantly of how the IoT applications shown in this second day can become a solving procedure for some business issues
2-C, Experience controls in commercially available IoT/AR application development environment (210 min)	Starting with a lecture on the summary of ThingWorx functionality, practical controlling was experienced of commercially available IoT platforms such as the specific ThingWorx' screen operations, data import of pseudo sensor data and settings on the screen display as well as remote controls. In the latter half, each participant used their own smart phones as the AR device for Vuforia which is PTC's AR platform and the code for AR which had been prepared in advance as workshop materials was given out. With this the participants confirmed the new possibilities for IoT solution when AR technology is incorporated into IoT
2-D, Q&A session after operating experience (30 min)	Questions and answers were exchanged between the participants and facilitator relating to the technological functionality of ThingWorx or Vuforia for which real operation was experienced. In addition, a free debate was conducted between the participants regarding how this technology can play a part in the innovation for future regional improvement and in resolving issues in SME businesses
2-E, Explanation in advance on the progression of day 3 (30 min)	The participants went outside of the workshop room (indoor) on day 3. By realizing fieldwork in which a practical opportunity which is as specific as possible regarding area W in city K, a plan was established to continue the area search. For this a study to gain prior knowledge regarding the area W is essential. Specifically, the monitor participants took it home as homework. The outcomes were to be shared in the group discussion on the following day

Table 3. Day 3: Conception of New Business Strategy through Field Observations

Session #, Topic, (duration)	Session Activity in Day 3
3-A, Reflection of day 1 and 2 setting goal of Day 3 (30 min)	As the first step in day 3, repeated confirmation was given among the participants regarding the experience gained of the latest IoT/AR technology as well as the discussions implemented in the two days' agenda and the points for field observation on the third day were discussed. This clarified the aims and meaning of the site survey on day 3 for all participants. The discussion took place in a waiting room at the railway station closest to area W which is the starting points of the field survey
3-B, Field observation A: local shopping street (60 min)	Our real field research started from a railway station. We explored through a local shopping street in the central part of area W and identify the current state of shops. For example, this area was successful coal industry until 50 years ago. Hence we visited various places relating to that at the time and discussed in those locations regarding the changes in industry and economy since then as well as the ups and downs of the manufactured product lifecycle
3-C, Field observation B: historically preserved area (60 min)	In area W, there is a famous yard of bridge in Asia. There was a discussion on the business backdrop at the time of the bridge being constructed (in 1962) and a further discussion on the pros and cons on the local industry and such product lifecycle of the construction structure (a bridge). Around the seaside road in area W, there was a brainstorming of the current topics based on observation of how the old offices for each business were being preserved. From this, a group discussion was implemented in respect of the gap between the businesses that the participants had hypothesized on the first day and the actual situation seen/heard on site. In particular, for the foreign students residing in area W, how did this area's situation come across? Moreover, there were discussions using CVCA defined on the first day in respect of the strategy for supporting people to stay in area W as well as topics involved in the human resources flow over to the big cities such as Shanghai, Singapore and Tokyo

(continued)

Table 3. (*continued*)

Session #, Topic, (duration)	Session Activity in Day 3
3-D, Field observation C: Fish processing company (60 min)	We moved over to area T on the opposite coast of the port on a ferry boat and visited a historical fish processing company established 100 years ago. We had a lecture by a manager on a specific agenda of the business revolution of the company over the past 100 years. It was a great change through the product lifecycle and a history of global competition. We also identified key issues arising in the business during economic downturn and business transfers as well as how they dealt with
3-E, Field observation D: Fruit and vegetable market (60 min)	A research explorer was taken around a local fruit and vegetable market where most of the shops have now closed down. The participants had a discussion regarding the reasons why such a market has disappeared. "Five whys" method was also used to test the specificity of the hypothesis of the underlying cause among participants. Moreover, a vegetable shop that has managed to maintain the business were observed and a discussion conducted among the participants as to why the shop has managed to continue business and also what is required in order to push their business further
3-F, Hypothetical examination of next generation business strategy and a summary of feel observation (75 min)	As a summary of the three days' activities, a discussion was conducted with all the participants reflecting the field observation gained throughout the final day on issues, strategies and directions for bringing a new future industrial in-novation in area W; the possibility of new products and services and the topics involved in realizing them. The discussion took place in a local public community building at area W in city K
3-G, Final summary (15 min)	All the activities over the three days were reflected upon by all the participants and mutual evaluations were defined as well as proposals about how each would contribute going forward

4 Discussion

4.1 Key Outcomes of Workshop Content

This workshop was a short-term intensive session over three days. This trial was characterised by the fact that the following real experiences from three viewpoints were provided to the participants.

Outcome 1. The basic method of "design thinking" was used to provide a place for group work in order to conceive efficiently an innovative hypothesis.

Outcome 2. The innovative hypothesis conceived the actual operating experience for the participants the latest commercial ICT solutions such as IoT and AR. This provided a great opportunity for the participants to experience immediately both value of technology and business strategies at the same timing.

Outcome 3. While getting the participants to keep hold of the business theory and experienced technological theory, a field observation was provided. With this, it provided the ability for participants to conceive more practical products and services for the local community area.

With the above three outcomes incorporated, the short-term intensive business work-shop over three days contributed to enable more sense of achievement to be obtained by the participants and also for the host. There was a possibility that it can efficiently collect voice of local region within a shorter period of time compared to other similar workshops.

In reality, the implemented trial workshop evaluated to be effective in creating a more realistic approach compared to conventional simple questionnaire survey with the stereotypical analysis results. Furthermore, compared to individual interview style which can only cover a few businesses situation, this workshop was an academic survey method which has a cost-effectiveness and efficient as a value of group discussion.

4.2 Efficacy of Design Thinking Method Adoption

In order to efficiently collect opinions and to smoothly obtain the future business concept hypotheses from the participants, this workshop attempted to use a lot of the methods provided in "Innovation dialogue guidebook 2013 [10]". It developed by MECSST (Japan Ministry of Education, Culture, Sports, Science and Technology). The guidebook is developed referring to the design thinking methodology of Stanford d.school. For example organizing topics and measures by dividing into four phenomena based on the "2 × 2 matrix [12]" method became a means for participants to start using intellectual imagination. Team work within groups was used in order to tackle issues such as what are the goals for the future and whether new methods and ideas can be synchronized using "value graph". With "CVCA", it was possible to carefully analyse what the final client or company organization providing the existing value without using the information/data of the relevant stakeholders in the region based on a fixed concept. Those of design thinking methods were used a lot on the first day in this workshop and a lot of idea insights could be provided by the participants.

4.3   Mutual Benefit as an Industry-University Collaboration

Currently in various regional cities around Japan, the industrial and academic world is collaborating on various topics as part of the industry-university collaboration programs. Hence social and industrial problems specific to regions are being tackled. However for both parties, it's not necessarily true that they get the same benefit out of the industry-university collaboration program. From the business activity point of view, it goes without saying that practical results contributing to the benefit of businesses are highly in demand. From the point of view of academic researchers, it's probably true that as much as possible of empirical data should be collected for use in research.

Generally, if sufficient merit in participating in this workshop cannot be obtained for the participants from firms cooperating, the workshop format information collecting method does not always work. Therefore, we very much focused on providing the participants practical key two benefits at one time. One is a method for conceiving next generation business strategy in a short period of time; another one is a practical experience of state-of-the-arts commercial ICT technology such as IoT and VR.

4.4   Voice of Monitor Members – Pros and Cons

The representative feedback from the monitor members of this workshop are shown below. Their feedback will be valuable insights for our next steps to work on this workshop methodology development and improvement.

> *"Firstly I thought that strategy building was to see and feel myself and start being aware for the first time. Hence I understood the importance of questioning everything. To understand something very well is to keep asking questions regarding its cause. Through the workshop today I understood things that I would not have been able to understand just from studying on the desk."* Ms. A (workshop participant)

> *"It did not only end with the discussions of IoT technology. I could learn about how to distinguish objectives from means in terms of business point of view. Moreover, there haven't been many opportunities to get to know the town that I live in so I am grateful that I have been given this precious opportunity."* Mr. B (workshop participant)

> *"I experienced things I'd never thought about previously at this workshop. I specialize in computer science so I was thinking, if one does a technical job, and then there is no need to worry about the business. However after three days design thinking, I have lost most of the thoughts I had previously. I felt that being aware of being customer focused is good work and being a good worker. The most important point is that the local town is different in each place visited. In other words, the businesses to which they are suited to are all different."* Mr. C (workshop participant)

> *"As my 30 years experiences as a facilitator, I saw that this was a unique value as an intensive workshop combining with business modelling and technology hands-on. However, whether people actually working in businesses can participate in this workshop, taking such "three days off" consecutively away from their work needs further consideration regarding the purpose of participation and aims of the activities of the participants."* Mr. D (workshop facilitator)

5   Conclusion and Future Works

It conducted a preliminary verification with the aim of evaluating the workshop concept. This workshop could be concluded to be a method with a higher satisfaction of participants with usefulness, efficiency in information collection and superiority in cost-effectiveness that cannot be seen in other similar workshops as mentioned the above. However, it is also true that participants of this preliminary trial were still graduate school students or researchers of the research facility that the authors are a part of. Even so, the evaluation from the participants of the practical workshop that we trialled on this occasion was relatively good. Methods and agenda used in this workshop can be concluded to be valuable for future implementation as one of the methods of efficient information collection in considering a regional revival.

Forward looking, it's thought that there is a need to build some sort of industry-academy collaborative facility to instruct the planning/operation of the workshops developed here. In particular, it's thought that developing core people with strong expertise such as facilitators or coordinators in running workshops is quite urgent. By the way, the author's university has been accepting many of international students since 2003 [11]. This allows the local participants to be aware of brand new global idea in the future; our research team is currently planning to work on next research and consideration working with the city K's promotion team regarding the challenging topics of local industry-university collaboration PLM program.

Acknowledgements. This work was supported by The Japan Society for the Promotion of Science (JSPS) Grant-in-Aid for Scientific Research (C) No. 15K00495 and (B) No. 26282088.

References

1. Bhatt, S., Tseng, F.H., Maranzana, N., Segonds, F.: Scientometric study of product lifecycle management international conferences: a decade overview. In: Bouras, A., Eynard, B., Foufou, S., Thoben, K.-D. (eds.) PLM 2015. IFIP AICT, vol. 467, pp. 672–683. Springer, Cham (2016). https://doi.org/10.1007/978-3-319-33111-9_61
2. Porter, M.E., Heppelmann, J.E.: How smart, connected products are transforming companies. Harv. Bus. Rev. **93**(10), 96–114 (2015)
3. IfM   Bonn.   http://www.ifm-bonn.org/statistiken/mittelstand-im-ueberblick/#accordion= 0&tab=1. Accessed 12 Feb 2017
4. Goto, S., Trolio, E., Yoshie, O., Tamaki, K.: Multi-party interactive visioneering workshop for smart connected products in global manufacturing industry considering PLM. In: Harik, R., Rivest, L., Bernard, A., Eynard, B., Bouras, A. (eds.) PLM 2016. IAICT, vol. 492, pp. 501–511. Springer, Cham (2016). https://doi.org/10.1007/978-3-319-54660-5_45
5. Goto, S., Yoshie, O., Fujimura, F.: Internet of Things value for mechanical engineers and evolving commercial product lifecycle management system. In: The IEEE International Conference on Industrial Engineering and Engineering Management (2016)
6. Tamaki, K., Park, Y.W., Goto, S.: A professional training programme design for global manufacturing strategy: investigations and action project group activities through industry-university cooperation. Int. J. Bus. Inf. Syst. **18**(4), 451–468 (2015)
7. Stanford University Institute of Design. http://dschool.stanford.edu. Accessed 12 Feb 2017

8. PTC Inc. http://www.ptc.com/internet-of-things. Accessed 12 Feb 2017
9. Donaldson, K.M., Ishii, K., Sheppard, S.D.: Customer value chain analysis. Res. Eng. Des. **16**(4), 174–183 (2006)
10. Ministry of Education, Culture, Sports, Science and Technology (MECSST). http://www. mext.go.jp/a_menu/shinkou/sangaku/1347910.htm. Accessed 12 Feb 2017
11. Yoshie, O., Wang, L.: Building hub for global human resource development and lessons learned from it, Waseda Institute of Political Economy Working Paper Series No. E1520 (2016)
12. 2X2   Matrix.   https://dschool-old.stanford.edu/groups/k12/wiki/29e5a/2X2_Matrix.html. Accessed 31 Mar 2017

PLM in Education – The Escape from Boredom

Bernhard Fradl[✉], Anita Sohrweide[✉], and Felix Nyffenegger[✉]

HSR, Rapperswil, Switzerland
{bernhard.fradl,anita.sohrweide,felix.nyffenegger}@hsr.ch

Abstract. PLM and particularly the thoughts behind Closed-Loop PLM are a complex matter and almost every aspect of an industrial enterprise is affected by it. The real-world complexity and the role of PLM in a company are hard to explain to students, particularly in an abstract university environment. In fact, only few students manage to build a link between the abstract theory and the daily challenges of companies. Linking the reality with commonly accepted theory and new aspects from research requires a model that can showcase how theory works in real world, but is simple enough to be explained in a reasonable amount of time.

To achieve this goal in education, a scenario around a product in its eco-system has been created. Physically, it is built on very common and easy to use technologies (Lego, Arduino, 3D printed parts). Yet, all relevant organizational aspects, processes, and IT tools are present as in a modern, up-to-date company (ERP, PLM, Configurator, CAD, etc.). This allows to understand the different aspects of PLM based on a hands-on example. For instance, it is possible to explain and experience the impact of an assemble-to-order strategy on engineering, the sales department, service, and the assembly line, by actually doing it.

This paper discusses a novel approach in the education of PLM that addresses students, but also people from industry. Eventually, the educational model also serves as a platform to discuss real world problems with industry and discuss and test new approaches (digitization, industry 4.0) and their impact along the life-cycle of their product.

Keywords: PLM · Education · Closed-Loop PLM · Lego · Arduino · Integration
Digital twin · Eco-system · Elaboration model

1 Introduction and Challenge

PLM has become a widely-used concept and strategic component in today's industrial companies. Moreover, it is part of an engineer's daily business. Understanding the concepts of PLM will help developers to build sustainable products and contribute to commercial success of their company. Therefore, HSR (university of applied science of Rapperswil) and probably many other institutions consider PLM as a fundamental part of engineering education.

© IFIP International Federation for Information Processing 2017
Published by Springer International Publishing AG 2017. All Rights Reserved
J. Ríos et al. (Eds.): PLM 2017, IFIP AICT 517, pp. 297–307, 2017.
https://doi.org/10.1007/978-3-319-72905-3_27

Yet, understanding why an industrial company needs PLM and how PLM affects an enterprise is challenging. It needs broad knowledge reinforced by good examples. Engineers need to understand the details (e.g. how their decisions affect other connecting parts, electronics or software), but also understand the big picture (e.g. understanding impact on services and the business model, be aware of subsequent processes, etc.). With increasing complexity of products and organizations, more disciplines are involved in product development and communication becomes essential. Increasing pressure on delivery time and production costs or concepts for digitization also force engineers to think outside their specialized domain.

In the educational environment at HSR we want to prepare our students to master these challenges. In the core disciplines we aim to advance them to level 5 or 6 according to Bloom's taxonomy [1]. Thus, they should be able to draw their own conceptual decision (e.g. on a concept of product architecture) and be able to justify and stand this decision.

However, we discovered that these real-world situations can only be solved in a reasonable amount of time for limited problems. The bigger the complexity of the situation, the bigger the gap between theory and reality (see Fig. 1). Consequently, it takes more time to understand the problem and its constraints. Unfortunately, time in an educational environment is limited. Therefore, we were looking for a concept, where students need less time to understand the situation around the problem, but still are exposed to a reality-like situation that allows problem-based learning and reflection as suggested by Mazur [2, 3].

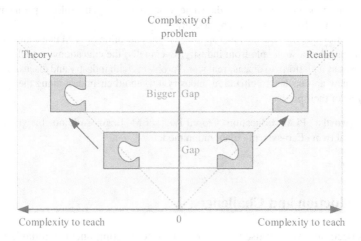

Fig. 1. Growing complexity creates a bigger gap to be closed with a transfer example.

The obvious solution to close this gap in the context of PLM would be to create a company with its products, organization, processes, and tools. A company where students can gain practical experience, investigate concepts, and get immediate feedback from trial and error. An example that builds up from basic to complex and allows the students to get familiar with, maybe even over several semesters. It should allow to connect the topics and issues from various courses.

Neither a product nor an industrial company and customers for such an attempt existed. But continuing to teach such a dry, abstract, and complex topic without the possibility to gain experience was no option. A different approach was followed: A platform where one would be able to experience all this complexity and deal with it. An environment where learning PLM is fun.

2 Didactic Approach

An essential concept of education is the transfer from fundamental principles to the problems of the real world [4–6]. Good examples and practical exercise can help closing the gap between those two [7] as shown in Fig. 1. Often such examples cover only a single problem taken out of context. Building examples for single topics and taking them out of context may help. Multiple such examples may complete the "bridge", but with increasing complexity the chances to create a complete picture drop, as illustrated in Fig. 2. In addition, the more complex topics or problems get, the more complex education of the corresponding theory will be.

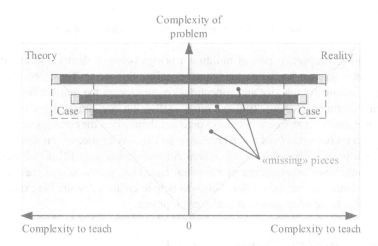

Fig. 2. Missing pieces to connect different transfer examples.

Hence, instead of taking complexity out or isolating it, a large example that can cover many topics was considered. Inside that example, the different topics and aspects were sorted by difficulty to explain them and their constraints and their connection to other topics. It should help to develop the full picture over time with increasing complexity. It should allow reflecting new theory on a known environment anytime.

"Full stack" Example. To solve the problem of these missing pieces a different method was found. Instead of explaining topics with new examples for every new topic one example for many topics was created, that aims at covering both the simple but fundamental, as well as the complex problems (Fig. 3). Students should be able to connect the conceptual dots of the topic themselves or with help of interactive reflection.

Depending on the nature of the problem, reflection can be among peers, or accompanied by the teacher.

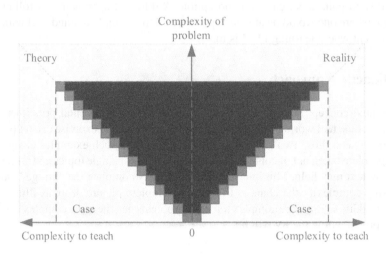

Fig. 3. One "full stack" example covering the majority of topics.

Goals. Another important part of building a bridge between theory and reality is to create a first-hand experience on what impact certain actions have. Therefore, apart from fulfilling a certain complexity and educational requirements the real challenge was to create an environment where "trial and error", reflection, and practicing is possible. A setup where students can figure out and experience themselves the consequences of their actions with no risks involved and a chance to go back. We endeavor creating an environment for problem-based learning, where curiosity takes over [2]. Eventually, this leads to continuous development of the setup based on questions and theories from students and other interested parties. This will help to create a sustainable example that still is flexible to be adopted to the latest development.

3   The Setup of the Transfer Example

Our setup to build a bridge between complex PLM theory and the challenges in a realistic company can be divided in three major parts: a physical product, a business environment, and the relevant IT landscape. While the physical product is based on prototyping tools (Lego, 3D prints, and Arduino), the business plan, organization, and processes of the exemplary companies are based on real figures. Also, the IT landscape is mostly built with known enterprise solutions.

3.1 Product

The product needed to suffice these major requirements:

i. First and foremost, the product needed to be a mechatronic product with enough structural complexity to explain the aspects of classical PLM and interdisciplinary engineering. Mechanical engineering students at HSR are confronted with all kinds of modules from electronics, mechatronics, and robotics. The approach of letting students use their knowledge and build something increases their motivation and even more important, their perspective on the whole product in terms of systems engineering and not just as single actors or sensors.

ii. Second, to be able to explain theories around modularization and the complexity of configurations the product needed to be modular. In a second step the whole system was formed to become an assemble-to-order product. This then also allows to dig deeper into complex structure matters and brings some more focus to the selling process and the customer with his specific needs.

iii. Third, to cover the business side and current hot topics of the industry the product also needed to be servitized. A decision was made to create a "Machine as a Service" business model around the product.

A pick-and-place robot was chosen as the product. The robot collects and sorts LEGO "packages" based on their RFID tag. To be able to quickly try out new concepts, new versions, or to just compare old to new without having to spend too much money, LEGO Technic was the optimal tool for this. Since our students learn programming on the Arduino platform, the control of the machine was implemented on Arduino with a "hacked" interface to LEGO (electronic bridges and 3D printed parts for mechanical

Fig. 4. The pick-and-place robot.

interfaces to LEGO). A very similar product with a similar mechanical concept exists in real world which helps to create the final link to the real world (Fig. 4).

3.2 Companies in an Ecosystem

To emphasize the importance of the organization, processes, and business models in relation to a product and to give students a wider perspective, two virtual companies were created. A company called "Sortic" that produces the pick-and-place machine, as well as a company called "Dropkick" representing the customer.

Sortic. In order to show and discuss the impact and dependencies between product and business model the company Sortic offers two ways of bringing machines to their customers. One is the "conventional" way of simply configuring and selling a complete pick-and-place system based on specifications of the customer. The other way is to offer the complete system as a service and just sell the work the machine does. This way, the machine remains the property of Sortic and it is in their interest to increase the lifetime of their products.

Dropkick. A company founded by a couple of IT guys who found a clever algorithm that finds the fastest route through a city. Using that algorithm, they started a small delivery service that offers pick-up and delivery to any place within a city. The cost of that service depends on how fast a package must be delivered. If it is not time sensitive, the package will be brought to a central hub, where packages will be sorted depending on the algorithm's shortest and most efficient route through the city. This is where Sortics machine comes into play. As a start-up, Dropkick does not have enough money to buy a machine and as IT guys they do not want to handle machines nor recruit somebody that can. So, the service that Sortic offers is optimal for Dropkick.

3.3 Processes Coverage

The example aims at education of future engineers in the world of digitization. Therefore, from the very beginning, PLM was considered as a closed loop process that covers all the essential processes and disciplines around the life of a product as described by Kiritsis et al. [8] or Cerri et al. [9]. In our scenario, this holistic approach can be vividly transferred to the two companies of the eco-system.

Design and Development. The core competence of Sortic is the development of automation solutions. Due to the nature of the product, Sortic follows a systems engineering process and develops towards a mechatronic product structure. Also, a modular architecture is essential to their success, since Sortic follows an ATO (Assemble-to-Order) strategy. Students learn how to translate market requirements into a modular product structure. The "machine-as-a-service" business model also pictures what development of a service product means and how it is linked to the technology or equipment. All data in the collaboration between development and operations is present in corresponding

PLM and ERP systems. This allows also to explore typical change management tasks and taking decisions on actual data.

Sales. The sales process of Sortic needs configuration. In this setup, the specific needs of Dropkick are applied on the platform product and finally result in an order BOM (Bill of Material). In this process, the view of the customer and technical constraints of the platform must be matched. In addition, students can be challenged by requirements from Dropkick, which are not foreseen in the ATO concept of Sortic. This allows debating if the new requirement should be sold either as an ETO (Engineering-to-Order) component or become part of the platform or if it should be denied.

Production. Sortic has a need for production management. For students of industrial engineering, the engineering BOM is given, and they must create a production concept which covers issues like:

- Which assemblies can be produced in Kanban?
- How will the final assembly look like?
- What is the cost for different lot sizes?

Mechanical engineers will meet a given production concept and get feedback, on how well their product structure approach fits the thinking of operations – again material for intense debates.

Sourcing. Some parts of the LEGO/Arduino model (e.g. the motor or the base plate for the robot module) can easily be upscaled to industrial products. With this information, different sourcing strategies can be investigated and "tested in the wild". Because Sortic does have a business plan and a realistic sales plan, all necessary figures are available. In some cases, students even propose design optimizations for cheaper sourcing.

Service. As mentioned above, in our scenario Dropkick did not buy the machine. They only buy machine hours, or more precisely they buy "sorting capacity". To achieve the promised percentage of uptime, the Sortic machines were designed towards condition based monitoring. Typical maintenance scenarios can be tested and the importance of installed base data and the product history become obvious. In more advanced courses, this scenario also allows to experiment with IoT and machine-to-cloud communication, and predictive maintenance.

Innovation. The generalization side of the closed loop model has not yet been integrated into the transfer model. Future work will be done on the feedback loop from data generated by real instances of the model leading into new design decisions. We envision many of these models, maybe even adopted by other universities or institutions, to create actual big data.

3.4 IT Tools (in the Landscape)

Around the product and the companies, a complete IT landscape was set up and configured to show how tool support, but also constraint typical business processes. Our IT architecture reflects a typical setup of a company with a higher degree of PLM maturity.

During product design and the different engineering processes the central hub and the single source of truth is the PLM system, in our case "Aras Innovator". For the development process "Siemens NX" is used as an M-CAD, Fritzing as E-CAD, and versioning tool "Git" to store and manage the Arduino code base. Additionally, the software "Simio" is used to create different kinds of simulations for internal use as well as for customers. These tools all store their data in Aras.

To create customer specific products and orders in the sales process, a plant configurator is used ("PX5" by Perspectix). It is directly connected to the ERP system. For the operations processes, a cloud-based ERP solution called "myfactory" was fully configured and established. One major advantage of this cloud-based approach is the possibility to create copies of a complete setup in a couple of minutes. This allows to give each student his own ERP environment.

To interface the different solutions (particularly for release and change management), a web-services based architecture was deployed and linked with "NodeRed", a visual programming tool that allows fast prototyping and easy connection of a large variety of communication protocols.

To create digital twins and link the machines with all their data to the cloud, a variety of tools on Microsoft's "Azure Cloud" was introduced. This allows to follow novel concepts such as machine learning with neural network and other analytics tools. This, however, is currently part of our research and covered by student thesis, not in lectures.

4   Implementation in the Educational Environment

At HSR the setup explained above has been implemented. It runs under the name "Lifecycle Lab". This Lab is a place where you can experience all the processes by actually doing them and figuring out what impact certain actions can have. It is also a place to make everyone aware of how important it is to take care of your data and how you can generate value and advantages if your applications and tools are properly configured and work as intended.

Learning units typically consist of theory, transfer, application, and reflection. The Lifecycle Lab offers building blocks to create tutorials for transfer, execute exercises in the lab environment, and allow reflection in the full context of Sortic and Dropkick. Based on the situation, it is up to the teacher if he chooses and inductive approach and starts with theory or to start with a tutorial in the lab environment and builds up theory in a deductive way. In either case, examples from real world will complete the picture. These can now be isolated, since the transfer example allows to create the links.

4.1 Application in Courses

The fictive companies Sortic and Dropkick as an example for the real world quickly found a partial introduction into many courses starting from the first semester and reaching into a specialization course for PLM implementation practice. Figure 5 gives an overview of the courses that interact with the Lifecycle Lab. Particularly the interaction between industrial engineers and mechanical engineers around product architecture and production management is worth mentioning. Initial frustration of mismatching approaches from both side hast the potential to turn into common understanding for each other's needs.

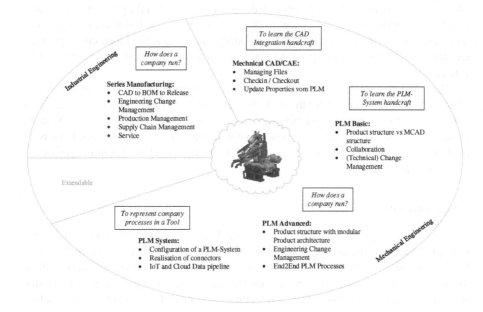

Fig. 5. Education Courses

Apart from the regular education courses, a post educational course for PLM responsibles in the industry is held every summer. In some cases, there is also a special training program for a specific company. In this context, the Lifecycle Lab proofed to be helpful in the opposite way. It allows to easily step out of the constraints and maybe frustration of the customer's situation. Thus, concepts can be discussed with less emotions and therefore in a more objective way. After all, it's just a toy.

5 Conclusion and Outlook

The chosen setup with a product and all the tools around it and consistent data flows has proven to be a good base to explore different topics along the lifecycle of that product. The "Lifecycle Lab" can make you aware of details, of major communication issues or the pitfalls of digitization. Even experienced PLM consultants are eager to try out new ideas on our model and gets fast results. Building up the lab was also fertile journey for the team doing it. It created debates about concepts, which were as real as in any PLM project, especially between the mechanical perspective and manufacturing.

5.1 Sandbox for New Theories

There are several points where the setup of the transfer example has proven to be extremely helpful. One of which is the possibility to quickly create new products, modules, or variants thanks to LEGO and 3D-printing.

The lab allows to understand how processes and data around the lifecycle of products are linked. For example, it can be observed, how new variant in the product architecture affects production, sales and service on the level of processes, but also on the level of data. It acts as a simulator to test different concepts and understand their consequences. Eventually, it also serves as a platform for research to validate new and uncertain PLM concepts.

The setup also proved optimal for continuous development by advanced students along with bachelor and master thesis. Different aspects of PLM, product, and business development can be refined and missing connections of the dots in our example can be closed. Especially in the field of "predictive maintenance" different topics have been explored and implemented into the lab which can be used to show different approaches of connected products.

5.2 Footprint

The transfer example of the LEGO robot started as an attempt to find a better, bigger example to explain the complex theory of PLM. Nowadays it's much more than that. Professors and assistants from different areas and disciplines want to join and contribute to the project. From different perspectives, they see the lab as a good place to sensitize students as well as customers how interconnected different topics are. Often creating value out of PLM requires an interdisciplinary effort.

A positive effect was also achieved in terms of a common vocabulary. All stakeholders in this collaboration started to use common language and built up an understanding for each other's perspectives - the fundament of sustainable collaboration.

5.3 Next Steps

After the first feasibility experiments where the robot sent sensor data to the cloud and first discussions around "digital twins", it became clear that one possible next step would be that similar setups could be started on different places all around the globe. They would clearly profit from each other. Each setup would produce data that could be used for many existing and new theories. The data from one machine could improve the setup of another one, physically or software wise. As an open-source project, everybody who wants to contribute has the opportunity – the possibilities seem endless.

Ultimately, the knowledge gained from "playing with toys" in a large scale would be solid enough to be applicable not just in education, but also in industrial challenges.

Current and new topics (digitization, industry 4.0) can be tested in our lab and the actual application inside a company becomes cheaper and less risky.

Eventually, without realizing it, students that contribute to this project would find themselves in a real global collaborative and interdisciplinary development scenario. However, there is still a long way to go.

Acknowledgements. These persons strongly contributed to the success of our educational approach by supporting financially or with regards to content: Bernd Leonhard, Prof. Dr. Roman Hänggi, Prof. Dr. Katarina Luban, Prof. Dr. Daniel Politze, Prof. Dr. Daniel Keller, Prof. Dr. Margit Mönnecke, Prof. Dr. Hanspeter Gysin, André Kälin and his crew, David Lauchenauer and his crew, Kevin Hausammann, Georgios Kiouplidis, Severin Scherrer, Samuel Wetter, Rene Mettler, Simon Hersche, Alain Ritschard, Florian Schletzak, Urs Meier, and Florian Fischli.

References

1. Bloom, B.S.: Taxonomie von Lernzielen im kognitiven Bereich. Taxonomy of educational objectives & lt, Beltz-Studienbuch, vol. 35 (1972)
2. Mazur, E.: Education: farewell, lecture? Science (80-.) **323**(5910), 50–51 (2009)
3. Mazur, E.: Peer instruction: a user's manual. Am. J. Phys. **67**(4), 359 (1999)
4. Perkins, D.N., Salomon, G.: Teaching for transfer. Educ. Leadersh. **46**(1), 22–32 (1988)
5. De Rijdt, C., Stes, A., van der Vleuten, C., Dochy, F.: Influencing variables and moderators of transfer of learning to the workplace within the area of staff development in higher education: research review. Educ. Res. Rev. **8**, 48–74 (2013)
6. Merriam, S., Leahy, B.: Learning transfer: a review of the research in adult education and training. PAACE J. Lifelong Learn. **14**, 1–24 (2005)
7. Stangl, W.: Lerntransfer. http://arbeitsblaetter.stangl-taller.at/LERNEN/Lerntransfer.shtml
8. Kiritsis, D., Bufardi, A., Xirouchakis, P.: Research issues on product lifecycle management and information tracking using smart embedded systems. Adv. Eng. Inform. **17**(3–4), 189–202 (2003)
9. Cerri, D., et al.: Proposal of a closed loop framework for the improvement of industrial systems' life cycle performances: experiences from the linkeddesign project. Procedia CIRP **29**, 126–131 (2015)

BIM

BIM-FM and Information Requirements Management: Missing Links in the AEC and FM Interface

Julie Jupp[1(✉)] and Ramsey Awad[2]

[1] University of Technology Sydney, Ultimo, Australia
julie.jupp@uts.edu.au
[2] University of Newcastle, Callaghan, Australia
ramsey.awad@newcastle.edu.au

Abstract. A steady shift in the value added from building information modelling (BIM) to architectural, engineering and construction (AEC) activities to those of facilities management (FM) is seeing increasing emphasis on whole-of-life thinking and associated information requirements management practices. Little is known about the process of identifying, documenting, generating and harmonizing BIM data inputs with FM data outputs in the Australian construction industry. Grounded on empirical evidence from a case study that transverses client and project team perspectives, this exploratory paper identifies missing links in the AEC and FM interface. The study describes the issues surrounding the collection and harmonization of BIM data inputs (as-built deliverables at handover) and the identification of (and connection to) FM data outputs. With the limitation of an exploratory and interpretive case study, the intention is to provide a contribution to academics and practitioners with grounded, stakeholder-related insights.

Keywords: Building information modelling · Facilities management
Information requirements management · Case study

1 Introduction

Much has been written about the technologies, processes and policies underpinning the implementation of BIM in the AEC/FM industry. With regard to case studies on the implementation of BIM-FM fewer investigations exist. The technologies, processes, policies and people required to support the collection, harmonization and connection of BIM data inputs to FM data outputs are yet to be mapped relative to the boundary conditions of a client's operations and the new building project being procured. Existing research describes BIM-FM projects as an often ad-hoc discovery and learning process with a lack of a clear implementation 'methodology' defined at the outset of the project to support the specification and management of information requirements. Further, case studies on this topic, have in part, reflected large pilot projects undertaken by Tier 1 contractors in the delivery of public works projects. This perspective on 'best'

© IFIP International Federation for Information Processing 2017
Published by Springer International Publishing AG 2017. All Rights Reserved
J. Ríos et al. (Eds.): PLM 2017, IFIP AICT 517, pp. 311–323, 2017.
https://doi.org/10.1007/978-3-319-72905-3_28

practice can diminish industry to those leading enterprises that have achieved high levels of internal integration in their approach to digital engineering. A look behind the scenes reveals a not less powerful and absorbing ecosystem amongst smaller Tier 2/3 firms with more modest levels of maturity in internal integration and a distinct lack of BIM-FM know-how. A glimpse at the daily business of such project initiatives unveils a raft of interdependent issues confronting BIM for FM implementation.

High levels of uncertainty compound the challenges surrounding the start of a BIM-FM initiative. AEC teams and owners inexperienced in the application of BIM technologies, processes and protocols for use in the operational phases increases the technical risks, which surround the scope and difficulty of the BIM-FM implementation problem not being well understood (or defined) at the outset. Owners should first undergo digital FM transformations internally so as to align with the newly available data and capabilities of BIM-enabled FM. Thus, in parallel to managing internal organizational change, owners requiring the delivery of 'FM-ready' BIM datasets by project teams prior to the completion of their own FM integration initiatives – and therefore without careful specification of the information requirements are managing complex problems with high levels of uncertainty. The owner's changing organizational context and any connected project environment will therefore be characterized by rapid technological change and high levels of learning. AEC/FM stakeholders may therefore be required to extend beyond their traditional roles, responsibilities and scope of works.

Recent works have studied BIM-FM implementation challenges (e.g., see [1–7]). Difficulties faced by Australian AEC/FM stakeholders in this context remain largely undocumented. A lack of understanding in the Australian AEC/FM industry therefore exists relative to AEC and FM information requirements specification and management process and as a consequence, AEC and owner/operator decision making are being based on 'acts-of-faith'. This research study is therefore an attempt unpack the complexity surrounding information requirements management and elucidate the nature and structure of undertaking a BIM for FM initiative. Grounded on empirical evidence from a case study on a university building project with an inexperienced client and a Tier 2 contractor, we explore the BIM-FM implementation problem using the following two-part research question:

[RQ1:] How are BIM-FM information requirements specified and managed across project phases – relative to the identification, documentation, collection and harmonization of data inputs; and connection with FM data outputs? And

[RQ2] What links are missing in the AEC and FM stakeholders interface when specifying and managing BIM for FM information requirements?

The remainder of the paper is divided into four sections. Section 2 provides a brief review of related literature. Section 3 presents the research methodology, data collection and analysis methods. Section 4 presents the findings and discusses the issues identified. Section 5 concludes the paper, synthesizing the observations in a discussion before identifying the limitations and implications of the research.

2 Background

ISO15686-1 defines maintenance as the "Combination of all technical and associated administrative actions during service life to retain a building or its parts in a state in which it can perform its required functions." [8, p2]. In the standardization initiatives surrounding the application of BIM to the maintenance phase of a facility, a central issue has been how to specify, document, generate, collect, structure and exchange digital information to enable its connection across different disciplines participating throughout the building life cycle. Recent studies focusing on the value of as-built datasets (virtual building models) to operations and facilities maintenance (O&FM), highlight difficulties surrounding their creation [9, 10], demonstrating that there is often no clear strategy for data harmonization or keeping the BIM model "alive" after handover. Whilst proponents of BIM assert its effectiveness in enabling process integration and information management (avoiding information losses incurred when transitioning from one team to another), a critical assumption remains that each group has the ability to "add to and reference back to all information they acquire during their period of contribution to the BIM model" [11]. Such aspirations for fully coordinated datasets and seamless information management appear to be far from reality.

The building life cycle is both complex and fragmented [12], and across each phase, information requirements differ and serve different purposes [13]. Whilst, information generated upstream should be available in downstream phases in a continuous data flow [14], research shows that current industry practices result in disconnected islands of data at each phase [1–5]; when data is communicated, the transfer most often occurs as a one-off event to the subsequent phase [13]. Consequently, the harmonization and connection of information to O&FM remains limited. As O&FM activities are multidisciplinary, there are extensive information requirements. The flow of information is restricted largely due to ineffective and inefficient exchange of information among AEC/FM stakeholders and each discipline's unique information systems. Building design and production call for information to be exchanged between AEC stakeholders across project phases to coordinate and integrate the various building systems within the project. Building O&FM remains largely disconnected from project phases with handover and commissioning activities being poorly defined, coordinated and managed due to schedule and budget constraints [15]. The O&FM data 'island' therefore suffers from ineffective and inefficient use as it requires the delivery of accurate and high quality data at building handover, which largely depends on having construction, supplier and O&FM expertise involved earlier in the design phases.

To maximize the use of buildings and minimize operational costs, the requirements of O&FM must be considered from project inception and verified throughout each phase [16]. Various initiatives have tried to support this aim. For example, the buildingSMART Data Dictionary (bSDD) [17], known as the International Framework for Dictionaries (IFD) and defined in ISO 12006-3 [18], was developed as a terminology standard for BIM libraries and ontologies. The IFD library is most useful when used in combination with the Industry Foundation Class (IFC) schema and the Information Delivery Manual (IDM) approach. Together, this approach is capable of describing what kind of information is exchanged by providing a mechanism that allows the creation of unique IFD IDs, connecting information from existing databases to IFC (Industry Foundation Classes) data models [19]. IFC4 is the latest version of the ISO 16739 standard [20] and has brought significantly improvements in energy and performance analysis, environmental impact values, integration of ifcXML and mvdXML into specification and improved documentation [21].

A further initiative to span the AEC-FM divide is the COBie (Construction Operations Building information exchange) specification [22], which denotes how information may be captured during design and construction and provided to facility operators. This method provides a spreadsheet of the same exact information available in the IFC file in a way that is easier to human to understand. The main objective of COBie is to provide for: (i) an IFC reference standard so as to directly support software information exchange, and (ii) a spreadsheet that can be used to capture building and operations data. Supporting the use of COBie is the Facility Management Handover Model View Definition [22]. The model view definition (MVD) identifies all the objects in IFC file necessary to support COBie and the relationship between these objects. MVD defines the process for determining the appropriate exchange requirements from the IFC schema for any particular use, representing them in an Information Delivery Manual (IDM) [23]. However, there are few studies documenting the implementation of this integrated approach to the capture of processes and exchange requirements.

The application of OmniClass has also progressed the pursuit of BIM-FM. OmniClass is a standard that combines multiple existing classification systems for many subjects into a single unifying system, which is based on ISO 12006-2, Organization of Information about Constructions Works – Part 2: Framework for Classification of Information [24]. However, whilst this standard establishes common concepts used in building information exchange, it is a guidance document and has no explicit rules for implementation [25]. As a result, Omniclass can be implemented in different ways and, used on its own, is seen by some as having the potential to create inconsistencies [13] and should be used in conjunction with e.g., IFD, so as to enable the access and viewing of data via an unambiguous classification system.

In the United Kingdom (UK), the HM Government's BIM Programme has mandated 'Level 2 BIM' (file-based collaboration and library management) on all centrally-procured Government projects, which was enforced mid-2016. Within this policy, the need for the provision of structured data for asset information models is recognised in the UK PAS1192-3:2014, 'Specification for information management for the operational phase of assets using building information modelling' [26]. PAS1192-3:2014 specifies an information management methodology for the operational phase of assets based on open BIM standards and data specifications – COBie [26]. PAS 1192-3:2014 utilizes a hierarchical structure encompassing four information requirements specification processes, namely the: organization information requirements (OIR), employer information requirements (EIR), asset information requirements (AIR) and project information model (PIM). The support of asset and facility managers in specifying their information needs takes the form of an Asset Information Model

(AIM) and is thus aimed at enabling the production of a data model that can be linked to the as-built BIM model, which contains all digital information required for operation [26]. It is intended that the AIM then be communicated to lead designers and contractors. However to meet the information needs of owner/operators, accurate data must be generated, collected and exchanged throughout project delivery phases, and not left as a 'clean-up' activity that occurs just prior to- or after- building handover. From this perspective, the process of defining EIR by the owner – and upon which the AIM depends – is fraught with difficulty [13]. Missing links in the AEC-FM interface arise from a lack of quality control mechanisms, since whilst the minimum set of information requirements for an EIR is specified in the PAS 1192-2 [27], an EIR's definition necessitates requirements for all disciplines involved in project delivery and operations.

Further, EIR specifications do not currently account for a method to define, collect and document data input requirements from AEC and FM stakeholders. This deficiency reflects other critiques of BIM for FM initiatives to date, which demonstrate implementation deficiencies relative to the early involvement of O&FM expertise, i.e., the 'closed-loop' engineering problem, [28, 29]. This is complicated by a lack of detailed quality control systems in construction that facilitate digital deliverables during project phases, and whilst the definition of data drops with specifications for information content and granularity, (e.g., COBie data drops in the UK [16]), can help capture and verify client requirements are being met, the specification of progressive model content schemas which rely of definitions of the 'Level of Development' (LOD), are problematic. Bolpagni [31] highlights the difficulties arising from a lack of a "univocal approach to the definition and management of the content of a virtual building model". Several definitions of LOD exist, (e.g., 'Level of Detail' and Level of Information), resulting in subjectivity, interpretation and inconsistency.

Implementing BIM-FM not only requires the delivery of accurate 'as-built' datasets at project completion that fulfill a client's (often undefined) request for an 'FM-ready' BIM model, but also requires that operations and maintenance (O&M) documentation, asset hierarchies, and building classification systems correspond with the metadata contained in the model. These responsibilities often fall on (inexperienced) main contractors to audit, verify and harmonize data inputs with the owner's O&FM data outputs. In doing so, it is necessary to consider the owner's existing and future information systems, processes and protocols, whilst at the same time working with design consultants and subcontractors to ensure accurate, high quality data inputs. Where a lack of integration across an owner's existing O&FM systems and inconsistencies in operational workflows exist, the task of data harmonization can become an intractable one. An integrated and consistent approach to digital FM is therefore primary in obtaining the benefits of BIM.

Within this context, regulatory frameworks and in particular contract procurement methods will have a major impact on the successful delivery of as-built datasets and of the timely harmonization of data inputs with O&FM data outputs. The nature of most contractual frameworks applied to govern the design, construction and commissioning phases of projects predate the use of BIM [32] – particularly the delivery of digital assets for the purpose of building life-cycle management. Contractual frameworks can therefore obstruct than rather support the use of BIM in O&FM. Compounding these challenges are the constraints of low levels of client-side knowledge and modest BIM and digital FM implementation budgets. Studies that describe BIM for FM typically focus on the project delivery phases and overlook client-side challenges surrounding the continuous improvement and ongoing investment requirements that BIM-FM approaches necessitate in operations. In a study on the Sydney Opera House (SOH), the nature and substantial size of ongoing investment in a BIM-FM strategy is highlighted [33]. A substantial investment in initial modelling costs, continuing costs of maintaining and managing models, developing flexible and scalable database integration platforms combined with the development costs of a visual engine (or BIM-FM interface) present a variety of known unknowns as well as unknown unknowns that must be risk managed from the outset.

3   Research Methodology

The objective of this research is to investigate challenges surrounding the specification and management of information requirements that support the use of BIM in FM, with focus on the AEC and FM interface. We selected an exploratory research strategy, based on a single-case study approach, which used an interpretive epistemological perspective [34]. From November 2016 to March 2017 an intensive study into a Tier 2 construction firm ('ContractorT2') and a university client and O&FM team ('Uni-Client') was undertaken. The study concentrated on the interfaces between stakeholders during the design and construction of a new building project. As case study research strongly relies on the case context [34], characteristics of ContractorT2, UniClient and project background are outlined below.

ContractorT2 is an Australian owned private company that derives the majority of its revenue from the provision of construction services. From a financial viewpoint, ContractorT2 features revenues of approximately AUD $520 million and comprises approximately 400 employees. As a Tier 2 contractor, the company aims to differentiate its construction services via innovation and quality from competitors. For this purpose, ContractorT2 approaches projects based on an integrated and accredited project management system with services are aimed at providing value and risk management to their clients using BIM to ensure a best value for money with a smooth delivery.

UniClient is an Australian public university with approximately 40,000 students. The building project that forms the setting of this case study is a 16 story building and is the latest and most significant development in the university's campus master plan. Running concurrently with the design and construction of the building project, Uni-Client is defining a new "concept of building operation" to determine seven key aspects of asset management: (a) high level operating approach, (b) required roles and resources, (c) scope of assets to be defined in asset management, (d) required functions and processes across campus, (e) interfaces to financial management and other university systems, (f) mapping of workflows, and (g) reporting and auditing systems. The approach of UniClient's digital FM transformation strategy is to ensure it can be used not just for the new building, but existing buildings as the transformation process will be a multi-year, multi-project program of projects. Further, key change management activities are underway to support UniClients digital transformation – moving from a "reactive repair and replace" culture to a "proactive and predictive" one.

UniClient's technology brief informed ContractorT2 (and other project stakeholders) via its translation into the project's BIM Execution Plan (BEP). The client's aspirations centered on BIM's potential to deliver a fully documented building at handover with supporting O&M documentation that can be used and updated throughout the operations phase. To deliver data inputs to UniClient's O&FM systems, a range of FM functions and systems were accounted for. The main requirements were:

- BIM-based input data to ensure a record of initial asset information, and as a means of documenting change to the campus' built environment.
- BIM-based input data to automatically link and download to existing computer-aided facility management (CAFM) asset register and management module. Data relating to the asset should be posited in the CAFM and linked back into the BIM model.
- Use of Construction Operations Building information exchange (COBie) protocol to enable asset data synchronisation between model and CAFM asset mgmt. module.
- Interface between CAFM, building management system (BMS) and Security Systems to allow for live data feed, changing from a reactive to pro-active fault tolerant culture.
- Integration with Geographic Information System (GIS) data to map in ground services and make information available to CAFM.
- Interface with space management system using web-based interface for space planning, operations and reporting activities.

Semi-structured interviews built the main foundations of the study, with other sources of evidence informing the findings, including archival records (e.g., strategic documents and management plans) and digital artifacts (e.g., software applications and models). Overall, 12 interviews across the two organizations were undertaken on a face-to-face and remote basis. In line with the scope of the BIM-FM implementation problem, we included stakeholders from across the design consultant and sub-contracting teams. Following the exploratory nature of the research, we adapted grounded theory techniques [35] for data analysis. Open, axial, and selective coding procedures were then utilized. During the coding procedures, NVIVO 10 was utilized to assure consistent and efficient data analysis.

4 Findings

In the case study, missing links in the AEC-FM interface of BIM-FM implementation were identified. Table 1 presents the gaps and obstacles perceived by interviewees in order of the greatest coding frequency, with each of the ten issues discussed below.

#1 – Lack of Application & Awareness of Intl. Standards & Guidelines: AEC stakeholders had limited detailed knowledge about the application of international standards and guides (e.g., those established in the UK and US) to support information

Table 1. Gaps and obstackles to the specification and management of information requirements

No.	Challenge
#1	Lack of Application & Awareness of Intl. Standards & Guidelines
#2	Deficiencies in Contractual Frameworks and BIM Execution Plans
#3	Missing Stakeholders during Design Phases
#4	Lack of IFC and COBie Support for Asset Data
#5	Multiple Breaks in Information Flow
#6	Heterogeneous Data Inputs and Outputs
#7	Deficiencies in & Varying Commitment to Modelling
#8	Lack of Whole-of-life Thinking
#9	Lack of BIM-FM competency assessment
#10	Deficiencies in BIM-FM Benefits and Business Cases

requirements specification and quality control management processes. The AEC project team lacked information about the assets and actual operations, and did not have a guide to support the collection of requirements. The information requirements specification and quality management methods utilized lacked in appropriate policy coverage across project delivery. It was perceived that the focus of existing approaches to BIM lies on the design and production phases, with processes and protocols to support handover, commissioning and operations requirements largely being neglected. Further, feedback loops after practical completion had not been planned.

#2 – Deficiencies in Contractual Frameworks and BIM Execution Plans (BEP): The BEP was perceived as a multi-layered and extensive document addressing design consultants, contractor and suppliers. However, being a construct-only contract, ContractorT2 was not able to control of the entire collaborative effort (as in a DnC or Managing Contractor delivery), and therefore the BEP was not able to consider information requirements across the entire project in a thorough and timely manner. Modelling requirements and workflows were therefore ill-defined in light of the model uses that were required, particularly for the ultimate purpose of supporting O&FM.

#3 – Missing Stakeholders during Early Design Phases: During the pre-construction phase, the contractor's information management task was complicated by their limited ability to affect the requirements management process, and in particular data drops. This was largely seen to be due to the absence of suppliers. Without appropriate contractual agreements and protocols in place, collaboration was an obstacle to key data-drops and milestones during design. Despite client-side BIM-FM objectives, AEC and FM stakeholders remained disconnected. Further, whilst information exchange was given a high priority, due to challenges rooted in different information systems, this issue was left largely unresolved. The software itself was not seen as the bottleneck, but rather the lack of early stakeholder engagement and information sharing.

#4 – Lack of IFC and COBie Support for Asset Data: The use of IFC4 and COBie were initially tested by the contractor so as to map asset register requirements in IFC4 and COBie 2.4. Testing on the project (and previous projects) by the contractor had shown

that some of the main requirements were not directly supported. Whilst some of the non-supported fields were part of data drops, gaps were identified in O&FM information (e.g., costs breakdown, asset value, accumulated depreciation, and sources of spare parts). Whilst the possibility of including additional information in IFC and COBie files using custom property sets was raised, consensus within ContractorT2 was that this process would be too time consuming and relied on the design team and subcontractor's cooperation as it was necessary to first identify which components were not correctly exported to IFC, before then defining correct IFC types and entities.

#5 - Multiple Breaks in Information Flow: As a result of the above issue coupled with the discipline-specific information system landscapes, the contractor was confronted with multiple occurrences of breaks in information flow across project phases. A seamless transition from requirements specification to design and engineering, simulation and analysis, to construction planning, manufacturing, and onsite construction did not exist. Building model data exported from ArchiCAD and imported into Revit interrupted information flows and reduced AEC stakeholder confidence in model consistency, reinforcing information 'silos'.

#6 - Heterogeneous Data Inputs and Outputs: From a tool perspective, AEC and FM stakeholders were challenged by boundary conditions such as information protocols and software standards. On the one hand, in working with multiple consultants and subcontractors it was difficult for the main contractor to impose different data input requirements, yet in some cases failure to do so resulted in redundant design consultant models. On the other hand, the owner had difficulty in specifying data output requirements and mapping functions from the various asset and FM software used. Further, the CAD tools used across project stakeholders reflected their own tool portfolio. Heterogeneous and contrarious information requirements resulted and management of data inputs by contractor was significantly challenged.

#7 - Deficiencies in & Varying Commitment to Modelling: Deficient use of modeling standards and varying levels of modelling commitment across both AEC and FM teams was a common theme. Whilst for many interviewees, BIM-FM was typically equated with a central repository for building data, the significance of human factors was emphasized relative to inconsistencies across information standards, software and modelling practices inherent within that repository. Understanding the relevance of quality control systems and information requirements management as a holistic strategy entrenched into the project culture was not an established thinking.

#8 – Lack of Whole-of-life Thinking: A lack of a 'lifecycle' approach in the development and use of BIM-FM protocols presented a significant challenge. Without whole-of-life thinking being driven from the client, the O&FM needs could not be addressed adequately by the contractor. Although the client had a vested interest in the long-terms benefits of BIM, the BEP and contractual framework did not include key methods to attain these goals, (e.g., PAS 1192-3:2014 and EIR for Facilities and Asset Management).

#9 – Lack of BIM-FM competency assessment: There was a consensus that key members of the project stakeholders did not yet have the required level of BIM-FM knowledge or experience required. This meant that the competencies required to deliver successful outcomes were either being learnt on-the-fly or resulting in poor data delivery. The lack of BIM-FM competency assessment and the willingness of the client to blindly trust the project teams presents a substantial risk to the realization of BIM-FM's return on investment. However whilst competency assessment was seen as important it was not perceived as being an essential part of tender processes. It was however seen as critical to distinguish between those BIM-FM competencies that are essential prerequisites and those that could be learned on the job.

#10 – Deficiencies in BIM-FM Benefits and Business Case: Whilst benefits for adopting BIM in the AEC sector are well known, the client organization was in the early stages of developing and implementing a business case for BIM-FM campus wide. The common perception was that most of the documented, quantifiable benefits of BIM are related to the design and production phases, with a lack of evidence and metrics on the benefits BIM to FM. The case to support the required (and ongoing) investment in BIM-FM was seen by the client to rely on its value to not only supporting FM functionalities - such as space and asset management - but also in managing operational risks; e.g., code compliance, asset certification, environmental performance monitoring, emergency response, and predictive operational safety and scenario planning. Whilst the existence of an effective benefits delivery and management process was lacking within the client organization it *was* perceived as necessary to supporting mutual co-operation of project and operational management functions.

5 Discussion

Some of the identified challenges are similar to related BIM-FM studies, e.g., [1–7], whereas others identify issues specific to this study and its context. For example, challenges #2 ("*Deficiencies in Contractual Frameworks and BEP*") and #4 ("*Lack of IFC and COBie Support for Asset Register Data*") are counted among these. Wider influences are identified relative to how Australian AEC and FM stakeholders are impacted by and can influence each issue. To illustrate this, Table 2 provides a stakeholder analysis of 'impacted by' and 'power to influence' the ten challenges identified relative to the project context, shown as *high* (*h*), *medium* (*m*), or *low* (*l*).

From the analysis, it can be observed that not only the owner and contractor are impacted by the issues identified but also the FM team, design consultants, suppliers. Few challenges therefore exist that individual stakeholders can address alone. Referring back to the underlying research questions, the findings reinforce that the specification and management of information requirements are constrained by conditions that span project phases and discipline responsibilities but cannot be influenced by all equally.

These ten issues identified contribute to the research discussion in a number of ways. First, these challenges relate to the specification and management of information requirements across project phases and discipline responsibilities, which highlights an underlying deficiency surrounding the lack of quality control mechanisms in

Table 2. Stakeholder analysis of information requirements management issues

#	Challenges	Impacted by					Power to Influence				
		Owner	FM team	Contractor	Design consultants	Suppliers	Owner	FM team	Contractor	Design consultants	Suppliers
1	Lack of Application & Awareness of Intl. Standards & Guidelines	h	h	h	m	m	h	m	h	m	m
2	Deficiencies in Contractual Frameworks & BIM Execution Plans	h	l	h	h	l	h	l	m	m	l
3	Missing Stakeholders during Procurement & Design Phase	h	h	h	m	h	h	l	l	m	l
4	Lack of IFC & COBie Support for Asset Data	h	h	h	m	h	l	l	l	l	l
5	Multiple Breaks in AEC/FM Data and Information Flow	h	h	h	m	h	h	l	m	m	l
6	Heterogeneous Data Input and Output Requirements	m	h	h	m	m	m	h	h	m	m
7	Deficiencies in & Varying Commitment to Modelling	h	h	h	h	h	h	l	h	h	h
8	Lack of 'Whole-of-life' Thinking	h	h	m	l	l	h	h	m	l	l
9	Lack of BIM-FM competency assessment	h	h	h	m	m	h	l	m	l	l
10	Deficiencies in BIM-FM Benefits and Business Cases	h	h	h	m	l	h	m	l	l	l

information requirements management processes in construction. Quality management systems (QMS) established in conformity with ISO 9000 standards have a twenty-year tradition in the automotive and aerospace industries. The most recent issue of the ISO 9001 standard (2015) focuses on technology risk management, the innovation implementation process, and information management. Secondly, with respect to the loosely coupled stakeholders in the BIM-FM landscape, although the development of a QMS for information management will require the joint optimization of related processes and workflows, development will be difficult. As many technological, processual, and policy steps have to be climbed on the path to successful BIM-FM implementation, transformation of existing approaches to quality control in construction will be gradual. Finally, whilst this is a starting point, integrated procurement, organizational change management and detailed commissioning processes represent other essential activities. The relevance of the social component of information requirements management in the BIM-FM implementation process is highlighted by the study's findings; as a dynamic socio-technical system, developing QMS for BIM-FM requires further research in this regard.

The advantages of a single-case study go hand-in-hand with its limitations. Although a typical construction company and client was investigated, research findings are not representative or generalizable across the construction industry. Data analysis is also interpretive and the exploratory nature of the study does not ensure exhaustiveness. However the study raises potential directions for further research. Validating the challenges identified using a mixed method or quantitative research design would provide further insight. To capture a broader perspective, multiple case studies may be useful to investigate other project contexts and provide a valuable corpus to begin a comparison. From this perspective, it may then be possible to map identified challenges with potential solutions. For these activities this study acts as a point of origin.

References

1. Whyte, J., Lindkvist, C., Ibrahim, N.H.: From Projects into Operations: Lessons for Data Handover. University of Reading, DIRC, Working Paper (2011). www.reading.ac.uk/
2. Arayici, Y., Onyenobi, T., Egbu, C.: Building information modelling (BIM) for facilities management (FM): the mediacity case study approach. Int. J. 3-D Inf. Model. (IJ3DIM) 1(1), 55–73 (2012)
3. Kelly, G., Serginson, M., Lockley, S., Dawood, N., Kassem, M.: BIM for facility management: a review and a case study investigating the value and challenges. In: Proceedings of the 13th International Conference on Construction Applications of Virtual Reality, pp. 30–31 (2013)
4. Codinhoto, R., Kiviniemi, A.: BIM for FM: a case support for business life cycle. In: Fukuda, S., Bernard, A., Gurumoorthy, B., Bouras, A. (eds.) PLM 2014. IAICT, vol. 442, pp. 63–74. Springer, Heidelberg (2014). https://doi.org/10.1007/978-3-662-45937-9_7
5. Kassem, M., Kelly, G., Dawood, N., Serginson, M., Lockley, S.: BIM in facilities management applications: a case study of a large university complex. Built Environ. Proj. Asset Manag. 5(3), 261–277 (2015)
6. Ibrahim, K.F., Abanda, F.H., Vidalakis, C., Woods, G.: BIM-FM: input versus output data. In: Proceedings of the 33rd CIB W78 Conference, 31st October – 2nd November, Brisbane, Australia (2016)
7. Ashworth, S., Tucker, M., Druhmann, C., Kassem, M.: Integration of FM expertise and end user needs in the BIM process using the employer's information requirements (EIR). In: Proceedings of CIB World Building Congress, vol. 5 (2016)
8. ISO: ISO 15686-1, Buildings and constructed assets: Service life planning – Part 1: General principles and framework, International Organization for Standardization, Geneva, Switzerland (2011)
9. Ashworth, S., Tucker, M., Druhmann, C.: The Role of FM in Preparing a BIM Strategy and employer's information requirements (EIR) to Align with Client Asset Management Strategy, p. 218 (2016)
10. Xuesong, L., Eybpoosh, M., Akinci, B.: Developing as-built building information model using construction process history captured by a laser scanner and a camera. In: Construction Research Congress (2012)
11. Bew, M., Underwood, J.: Delivering BIM to the UK market. In: Underwood, J., Umit, I. (eds.) Handbook of Research on Building Information Modeling and Construction Informatics: Concepts and Technologies, pp. 30–64. IGI Global (2010)
12. Hitchcock, R.J.: Improving building life-cycle information management through documentation and communication of project objectives. In: Proceedings of Modeling of Buildings through their Life-Cycle, vol. 150, p. 358 (1995)
13. Pinheiro, S.V., Corry, E., O'Donnell, J.T.: Requirements for a BIM-based life-cycle performance evaluation framework to enable optimum building operation. In: 32nd International CIB W78 Conference, Eindhoven, The Netherlands, 27–29 October 2015, pp. 639–648. EUT (2015)

14. Man, Q., Wang, Y., Li, H., Chang, Y., Martin, S.: Life-cycle information flow management system. Intl. J. Digit. Content Technol. Appl. **7**(8), 857 (2013)
15. Carmichael, D.G.: Project Planning, and Control. Routledge, Abingdon (2006)
16. BSRIA: The Soft Landings Framework, BSRIA (2009)
17. ISO Standard: ISO 12006-3:2007 Building construction: Organization of information about construction works, Part 3: Framework for object-oriented information (2007)
18. buildingSMART: IFD Library for buildingSMART 2012 (2012)
19. Laakso, M., Kiviniemi, A.: The IFC standard - a review of history, development, and standardization. J. Inf. Technol. Constr. (ITcon) **17**, 134–161 (2012)
20. ISO Standard: ISO 16739:2013 Industry Foundation Classes (IFC) for data sharing in the construction and facility management industries (2013)
21. Liebich, T.: IFC4 - The New buildingSMART Standard: What's new in IFC4? (2013)
22. East, W.E.: Construction Operation Building Information Exchange, USACE ERDC (2007)
23. Belsky, M., Sacks, R.A., Brilakis, I.: Semantic enrichment engine for building information modelling. Comput. Aided Civ. Infrastruct. Eng. 261–274 (2016)
24. ISO 12006-2: Building construction – Organization of information about construction works - Part 2: Framework for classification, ISO (2015)
25. Cemesova, A.: Enhancing BIM-based data transfer to support the design of low energy buildings, Doctoral dissertation, Cardiff University (2013)
26. BSi: PAS 1192-3:2014 Specification for information management for the operational phase of assets using BIM, BSi Limited, London (2014)
27. BSi: PAS 1192-2:2013 - Specification for information management of the capital delivery phase of construction projects using building information modelling, British Standards Institution, BSI, London (2013)
28. Anderson, A., Marsters, A., Dossick, C.S., Neff, G.: Construction to operations exchange: challenges of implementation COBie and BIM in a large owner organization. In: Construction Research Congress, Purdue University, IN, May, p. 15 (2012)
29. Reefman, R., van Nederveen, S.: A controlled integral product model (IPM®) in building and construction. In: Proceedings of CIB W78-W102 2011: International Conference, France (2012)
30. Jupp, J.R.: Incomplete BIM implementation: exploring challenges and the role of product lifecycle management functions. In: Bernard, A., Rivest, L., Dutta, D. (eds.) PLM 2013. IAICT, vol. 409, pp. 630–640. Springer, Heidelberg (2013). https://doi.org/10.1007/978-3-642-41501-2_62
31. Bolpagni, M., Ciribini, A.L.C., Bolpagni, M., Ciribini, A.L.C.: The information modeling and the progression of data-driven projects. In: Proceedings of WBC 2016, Finland (2016)
32. London, K., Singh, V., Taylor, C., Gu, N., Brankovic, L.: Building information modelling project decision support framework. In: Dainty, A. (ed.) Proceedings of 24th Annual ARCOM Conference, Cardiff, UK, Association of Researchers in Construction Management, vol. 2, pp. 655–664 (2008)
33. Ebbesen, P., Karlshøj, J., Bonke, S., Jensen, P.A.: Information system strategies in facilities management–based on five process studies. In: Proceedings of CFM's 2nd Nordic conference: FM Research and Practice: Does FM Contribute To Happiness in the Nordic Countries (2016)
34. Yin, R.K.: Case Study Research: Design and Methods, 4th edn. SAGE Pub., CA (2009)
35. Strauss, A.L., Corbin, J.M.: Grounded Theory in Practice. Sage, Thousand Oaks (1997)

Automating Conventional Compliance Audit Processes

Johannes Dimyadi[✉] and Robert Amor

Department of Computer Science, University of Auckland, Auckland, New Zealand
{jdim006,trebor}@cs.auckland.ac.nz

Abstract. Any product, especially those with safety features or concerns, is normally subject to compliance audit with various standards and legal requirements at different stages throughout its lifecycle. These requirements are typically conveyed in voluminous written natural language texts requiring much expert interpretation. The compliance audit process has conventionally been a manual undertaking, which is known to be laborious, costly, and error-prone. In an era of increased legislation and electronic representations of products, it is prudent that some of these manual processes should be automated. This paper describes the capabilities of an automated compliance audit framework that can be incorporated into the compliance management of a product lifecycle. Apart from the product data model that is subject to audit, essential components of the framework include machine-readable legal knowledge and executable audit process models, support for supplementary human input and interface with simulation tools.

Keywords: Automated compliance audit processes ·
Computable legal knowledge · Building information modelling

1 Introduction

The lifecycle of a product from inception, through design and manufacture, to service and end-of-life stages, is subject to compliance audit processes one way or another, be it legislative, regulatory, or contractual. For example, major purchasers often impose on their suppliers to be ISO 9001 certified to demonstrate that their operation is in accordance with specified quality management system (QMS) requirements. This means there are clearly defined quality control processes in place that can be used to audit the production and the products for compliance with applicable standards.

In the domain of AEC/FM (Architecture, Engineering, Construction & Facilities Management), any component of a building structure is a product that must be designed to comply with legal requirements governing safety and quality standards before it can be consented for installation or construction. The compliance audit process has conventionally been a manual undertaking, which is inefficient, resource intensive and error-prone. A study in New Zealand has shown that 10% efficiency gain in the domain would bring about a 1% boost in the annual gross domestic product [1], which is currently worth in excess of USD75 million per annum.

There have been numerous research attempts over the last half of the century to automate compliance audit processes in the domain [2, 3], but there are only a handful

© IFIP International Federation for Information Processing 2017
Published by Springer International Publishing AG 2017. All Rights Reserved
J. Ríos et al. (Eds.): PLM 2017, IFIP AICT 517, pp. 324–334, 2017.
https://doi.org/10.1007/978-3-319-72905-3_29

of successful implementations reported to date [4, 5] and most of them only have limited applications. The main challenge remains with accessing and processing the right information efficiently and effectively. Legal knowledge, in particular, is conveyed in voluminous paper-based documents in natural language text written for human interpretation. Recent advances in the fields of artificial intelligence has made, for example, natural language processing techniques available for machines to extract and interpret legal text [6]. However, this approach is not yet matured sufficiently to be fully exploited in real-world applications. More importantly, however, not all legal text can be processed by machines alone. There are implicit types of legal knowledge that only human experts can understand and interpret in a certain context, especially under extraordinary circumstances. Human experts are equipped with intuition and tacit knowledge, and have the ability to draw on their years of experience to make judgments and conclusions reasonably quickly. Moreover, many types of legal knowledge cannot be predefined easily due to their dependency on dynamic factors, which must be evaluated by dedicated computational or simulation processes.

The conventional compliance audit process is procedural in nature, which lend itself to automation. However, there are still roles in the process that are best played by human experts such as specifying what information to retrieve from which sources and how to process them. Machines excel in executing instructions efficiently and accurately and so should be given such a role to play in the process.

Ultimately, there needs to be a practical compliance audit framework where human experts can specify the audit procedure each time, and the product model and legal knowledge are both treated as independent input components to the process engine.

1.1 Human-guided Automation Process

An essential ingredient of the aforementioned practical framework is maintaining direct human involvement in the audit process by allowing human experts to specify the correct type of information to retrieve and sources where they can be retrieved from, and also how they can be processed. The tasks involved are already part of the conventional manual design procedure, so it should be relatively straightforward to transfer the knowledge across for machine processing. One method is to formally document the procedure in a standard process model that can be used as an input component to the framework, which can then be executed in the computing environment, thereby automating the conventional process.

1.2 Product Data Model (PDM) and Building Information Modelling (BIM)

A PDM (Product Data Model) defines the structure of a product model, which is a source and repository of information on the development of a product [7] and a subset of PLM (Process Lifecycle Model) that is primarily concerned with information exchanged during the design phase of the product's lifecycle. PDM is the subject to be audited for compliance. In the context of this paper, this is taken to be equivalent to the compliant building design data captured in a building model developed using the open standard BIM (building information modelling) approach.

The open standard method of exchanging general product data is ISO 10303 STEP (Standard for the Exchange of Product model data. In the context of the AEC/FM domain, the open standard specifically for exchanging generic building data is ISO 16739 IFC (Industry Foundation Classes) [8]. For a specific application such as the compliance audit in a sub-domain, a subset of the IFC schema known as the model view definition (MVD) can be used to exchange selected and targeted information [9]. As in the conventional practice, separate MVDs can be used to represent different design packages (or product models) related to different design disciplines such as architectural, structural, fire safety, and so on.

1.3   Human and Machine-Readable Legal Knowledge Representation

A legal knowledge representation is what PDM/BIM must be audited against. As an ingredient of the framework, there needs to be a standard digital version of all legal documents that are human and machine-readable. For interoperability, it is pertinent that an open standard model is used to represent these documents.

Two emerging open standards, i.e. LegalDocML [10] and LegalRuleML [11], being developed by OASIS (Organisation for the Advancement of Structured Information Standards), have the potential of being used for this purpose. An important feature of these standards is that they allow the literal and logical content of any paper-based document to be represented and maintained coherently. Furthermore, they support data exchange in open standard XML (Extensible Markup Language), which further promotes interoperability.

2   Automated Compliance Audit Framework

The automated compliance audit framework (Fig. 1) described in this paper is capable of executing instructions embedded in a process model, referred to as CDP (compliant design process), and processing information retrieved from the PDM/BIM (product/building model or MVD), LKM (legal knowledge model), and other supplementary sources (manual human inputs and external simulation processes).

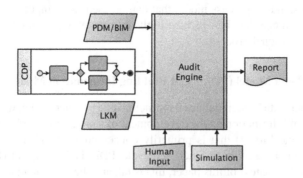

Fig. 1. Automated compliance audit framework (adapted from [13])

The core of the framework is an audit engine that incorporates a dedicated BPMN-compliant process engine. LKM and PDM/BIM are queried by the process engine like any standard information models for compliance assessment in accordance with the specification and instructions in the CDP.

Two optional input components of the framework are manual human inputs and any specified outputs returned by external computation or simulation processes [12]. These supplementary inputs are often necessary to supply information that may be missing from the PDM/BIM or LKM, or to help determine parameters that cannot be predefined or are dependent on dynamic environmental conditions such as air temperatures.

The output of the framework is a set of reports for each CDP highlighting any violation or compliance items that cannot be automatically determined and that may require further attention or processing.

3   Executable Compliant Design Processes (CDP)

A building design is subject to multiple compliant design processes relating to different building components or aspects such as architectural, structural, fire safety, electrical and mechanical services, or others. In conventional practice, designers typically follow industry standard procedures, which may or may not be documented, to develop various design solutions that are compliant with applicable standards and regulatory requirements. The procedural design task is amenable to automation as each step of the procedure can be mapped into respective activities in an executable process model.

3.1   CDP as a Component of Legal Knowledge

Legal documents contain provisions that may not all be applicable to every situation. There are multiple compliance paths present in each legal document. Choosing a set of scenarios leads to a particular path of compliance. Selecting a different set may result in an entirely different path. Each compliance path represents a compliant design procedure that can formally be documented as a CDP for computer execution. Each CDP is, therefore, a component of the legal knowledge conveyed by the document.

It is the designer's role to evaluate and decide which compliance path to follow (or which CDP to use) and whether or not the resulting compliant design is deemed satisfactory. Such a decision making process typically requires an intimate knowledge of different compliant design options, considerations of cost-benefits, the acceptable level of risks and safety margins. These are human attributes that are difficult to transfer to machines. On the other hand, machines are far superior than humans in terms of executing repetitive instructions efficiently and accurately. Therefore, it is considered appropriate and natural for human experts to resume an active role of providing direct guidance to the automation process by means of instructions specifying sources of information and what information to retrieve, and how the information is to be processed. Machines are simply given the role of doing what they do best, which is to execute specified instructions.

3.2 BPMN-Compliant CDP

The sequence of steps in a typical compliant design procedure can be represented as a series of activities, events, and sequence flows in a process model such as the open standard Business Process Model and Notation (BPMN) [14], as shown in Fig. 2. The current BPMN standard (BPMN 2.0) promotes extensibility and interoperability by supporting data exchange in XML natively. One important type of activity in a BPMN-compliant process model is the script task, which allows embedding of computer scripts that convey user-specified instructions such as where to retrieve which information from and how to use the collected information to perform specific calculations.

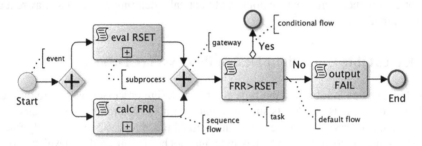

Fig. 2. Exemplar BPMN-compliant CDP

Enterprise BPMN 2.0-compliant process engines generally support standard computer scripting languages such as Javascript, Groovy, and Python, for use with the script task. For specific applications such as the compliance audit in a particular domain, however, it may be necessary to develop a domain-specific BPMN-compliant process engine that incorporates a purpose-built domain specific language. This may be necessary for handling certain concepts and types of information that are specific to the domain. Exemplar domain-specific languages that have been used in conjunction with BPMN-compliant CDP include the high-level query language RKQL (Regulatory Knowledge Query Language) [13] and BIMRL (BIM Rule Language) [15].

4 Legal Knowledge Model (LKM)

There are two aspects to the legal knowledge conveyed by legal documents, namely the document structure and text (or the literal content) and the semantics (or the logical content). It is considered essential for any computerized legal document to provide separate representations of the literal and logical content of the document that allows them to be maintained coherently. The literal content representation maintains user familiarity with the look and feel of the original text, which would promote its adoption in practice. The logical content representation is primarily intended for machines to process, but also allows human experts to manage and maintain. A Legal Knowledge Model (LKM) pertains to both representations operating together as one entity.

4.1 LegalDocML

LegalDocML [10] is a standardization of Akoma Ntoso (Architecture for Knowledge-Oriented Management of African Normative Texts using Open Standards and Ontology) [16], which can be used to represent the literal content of a legal document. The current version of the schema is Akoma Ntoso 3.0, which has gained popularity in the legal domain for representing legislative and judicial documents. LegalDocML is compatible with an existing European standard CEN MetaLex [17], which has been used to represent the entire set of Dutch regulations.

Among other features that have been developed using open standards, LegalDocML supports document workflow tracking with the ability to capture the entire lifecycle of a document, and provides an automatic version control and tight coupling with its LegalRuleML counterpart.

As it is exchanged in XML, any LegalDocML representation of a legal document can be rendered in user-friendly readable formats such as HTML or plain text while maintaining the structure and literal content of the source document. This allows the user to navigate a digital version of a legal document in the same way as they would do with the original paper-based document.

4.2 LegalRuleML

LegalRuleML [11] is inherited from RuleML [18] with extended features specific to the formalization of norms, guidelines, and legal reasoning. This emerging open standard can be used to represent the logical content of any legal document.

As the name implies, LegalRuleML enables normative provisions to be represented as rules. The encoding of norms into rules is currently a manual process. It is expected that the development of LegalRuleML representations of legal documents is to be undertaken by the same government agencies responsible for authoring the legal documents in the first place. However, NLP and other AI techniques may soon be able to assist in automating some of the encoding process.

Each rule represented in LegalRuleML has a unique key that is associated with its source provision in LegalDocML Any changes in the source text in LegalDocML would trigger the need to update its rule representation in LegalRuleML.

5   Worked Example

As a worked example, a common workflow that is used repeatedly throughout various stages of a building's life-cycle has been selected. This workflow checks if the opening direction of a door from any space is compliant with provisions in the fire regulations. For this example, the provisions of the New Zealand Building Code has been selected. The is taken from Paragraph 3.2.6 "Direction of Opening" of the C/VM2 document [19], which stipulates that *"Doors...shall be hung to open in the direction of escape...These requirements need not apply where the number of occupants...using the door is no greater than 50"*.

In another word, this regulatory provision prescribes that any door used for exit by potentially more than 50 people from a space must swing open in the outward direction.

5.1 Space Activity and Occupant Load

The potential occupant load of a space can often be determined by the type of primary activity designated for the space. This is particularly relevant for spaces with the potential capacity of accommodating a large number of people. For example, the expected occupant load in a space where the crowd is normally standing as part of the activity would be higher than if the same space is furnished for a different activity with some seating arrangements such as couches or sofas.

The activity of a space may change multiple times throughout the lifecycle of the building. Consequently, the expected occupant load of the space also changes accordingly. Therefore, it is necessary for building designers and operators to audit building components in the space (such as the door and its opening direction) for compliance as changes occur in the designated use or activity type of the space.

In a conventional procedure, knowing the activity type of a space, one can look up the prescribed occupant load density (defined as the number of persons per unit floor area) from the building code or building regulations. Given the floor area of the space and the occupant load density, the potential occupant load can then be calculated.

5.2 Exemplar CDP

An exemplar CDP that represents a compliance path implied by the selected regulatory provision given in this worked example is shown in Fig. 3. This workflow describes the procedure of checking the opening direction of a door from a space based on the occupant load of the space for compliance with the specified requirement.

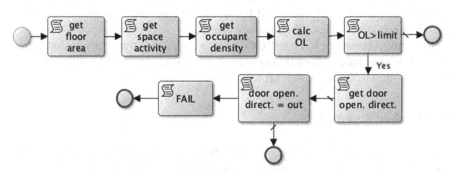

Fig. 3. CDP to check compliant door opening direction

In this CDP, it is assumed that the occupant load of the space is not available from the building model (PDM/BIM), but the type of activity designated for the space is known. Otherwise, the information may be provided via supplementary manual input.

The CDP starts by retrieving the floor area of a space from PDM/BIM. This is followed by a sequence of tasks to retrieve the space activity type, look up the prescribed occupant load density based on the activity, and then calculate the occupant load. The next task is to look up the required upper limit that shall not be exceeded from LKM (i.e. 50 in this case) and check if the calculated occupant load is within this threshold. If the occupant load is less than 50, then no further check is required and the audit process is deemed completed. Otherwise, the next task is to the check the opening direction of the door of the space and decide if it passes or fails the audit.

An exemplar instruction (in RKQL script) embedded into the task of calculating the occupant load (OL) is shown below as the BPMN-compliant XML representation of the script task (i.e. an excerpt of the CDP given in Fig. 3):

```
<scriptTask id="PO_p1037">
  <incoming>PO_p1036</incoming>
  <outgoing>PO_p1043</outgoing>
  <script>SET OL =(floorArea/occupantDensity)</script>
</scriptTask>
```

5.3 Information from PDM/BIM

Provided that the building model contains a space (*IfcSpace* object), it is very likely that it also contains the floor area information, which is one of its defined quantity. The other piece of information expected from the PDM/BIM for this worked example is the space activity designation, which may or may not be present in the model, but it can be made available through supplementary input either directly into the PDM/BIM or supplied separately through the CDP as part of the process.

In the IFC4 specification (also in IFC2x3 version), the space activity designation is conveyed by *OccupancyType* of the *Pset_SpaceOccupancyRequirements* property set related to the *IfcSpace* object. This property set also includes *OccupancyNumber* and *AreaPerOccupant*, which can both be used to convey the information needed for the compliance audit process, if required. The floor area of a space is specified in IFC4 schema by *NetFloorArea* of the *Qto_SpaceBaseQuantities* quantity set related to the *IfcSpace* object.

5.4 Information from LKM

In accordance with the instruction in the CDP, the process engine would extract the occupant load density associated with the activity type from the LKM, if it was not specified in the PDM/BIM. This exemplar regulatory provision is obligatory in nature and can be represented in LegalRuleML as shown in the excerpt below:

```
<lrml:PrescriptiveStatement key="3.2.6_R1.K01">
  <ruleml:Rule>
    <ruleml:if>
      <ruleml:Atom>
        <ruleml:Rel>greater than</ruleml:Rel>
        <ruleml:Var>occupantLoad</ruleml:Var>
        <ruleml:Data>50</ruleml:Data>
      </ruleml:Atom>
    </ruleml:if>
    <ruleml:then>
      <lrml:Obligation>
        <ruleml:Atom>
          <ruleml:Rel>doorOpenDirection</ruleml:Rel>
          <ruleml:Con>out</ruleml:Con>
        </ruleml:Atom>
      </lrml:Obligation>
    </ruleml:then>
  </ruleml:Rule>
</lrml:PrescriptiveStatement>
```

The rule representation contains one condition, i.e. the occupant load of the space under audit is greater than 50. Otherwise, the rule is not applicable. If the condition is true, then the consequent of the rule is that the opening mode of the door must be in the outwards direction to pass the audit process. Otherwise, it would fail the audit process.

In the LegalRuleML excerpt above, the rule has a unique key of "3.2.6_R1.K01", which is associated with the same key in the source LegalDocML representing the original text of Paragraph 3.2.6 in the C/VM2 document. This object relationship feature enables version control and tracking of any amendment in the source text, which would prompt an update of the rule representation, as necessary.

6   Conclusion

This paper has described a practical approach of automating compliance audit processes with a simple example to demonstrate how an open standard process model can be used to specify how to access and process the required information. Conventional audit processes are laborious and error-prone because humans are tasked with accessing and processing information repetitively, which is an activity that can be performed much more efficiently and accurately by machines.

Automation is possible when computer representations of the product and legal knowledge are available. However, human experts should retain their roles in designing the compliance audit process (CDP) and give instructions as necessary, thereby providing a guidance to the automation process. As each CDP is a formal documentation of a design procedure, it can be audited and validated for correctness. This would minimise any human error in the process, especially when the CDP is intended to be used multiple times across different projects.

References

1. Nana, G.: Assessment of the Economic Impact of Efficiency Improvements in Building and Construction. Business and Economic Research Limited, Wellington, New Zealand (2003)
2. Dimyadi, J., Amor, R.: Automated building code compliance checking - where is it at? In: 2013 19th International CIB World Building Congress, pp. 172–185. Queensland Institute of Technology, Brisbane (2013)
3. Eastman, C., Lee, J., Jeong, Y., Lee, J.: Automatic rule-based checking of building designs. J. Autom. Constr. **18**, 1011–1033 (2009)
4. Ding, L., Drogemuller, R., Rosenman, M.A., Marchant, D., Gero, J.: Automating code checking for building designs - designcheck. In: Proceedings of the CRC for Construction Innovation International Conference, Gold Coast, Australia, pp. 1–16 (2006)
5. Khemlani, L.: CORENET e-PlanCheck: Singapore's automated code checking system. http://aecbytes.com/buildingthefuture/2005/CORENETePlanCheck.html
6. Dragoni, M., Villata, S., Rizzi, W., Governatori, G.: Combining NLP approaches for rule extraction from legal documents. In: Proceedings of the workshop on "Mining and Reasoning with Legal Texts" collocated at the 29th International Conference on Legal Knowledge and Information Systems, pp. 1–13 (2016)
7. Zhou, Z.D., Ai, Q.S., Liu, Q., Yang, W.Z., Xie, S.Q.: A STEP-compliant product data model for injection moulding products. Int. J. Prod. Res. **47**, 4497–4520 (2009)
8. ISO 16739: ISO 16739:2013 Industry Foundation Classes (IFC) for data sharing in the construction and facility management industries. International Organization for Standardization, Geneva, Switzerland (2013)
9. Hietanen, J., Lehtinen, S.: MVD and SimpleBIM (whitepaper) (2014)
10. OASIS: OASIS LegalDocumentML (LegalDocML) TC. https://www.oasis-open.org/committees/tc_home.php?wg_abbrev=legaldocml
11. Palmirani, M., Governatori, G., Rotolo, A., Tabet, S., Boley, H., Paschke, A.: LegalRuleML: XML-based rules and norms. In: Olken, F., Palmirani, M., Sottara, D. (eds.) RuleML 2011. LNCS, vol. 7018, pp. 298–312. Springer, Heidelberg (2011). https://doi.org/10.1007/978-3-642-24908-2_30
12. Dimyadi, J., Amor, R., Spearpoint, M.: Using BIM to support simulation of compliant building evacuation. In: Proceedings of the 11th ECPPM, Limassol, Cyprus, pp. 511–518 (2016)
13. Dimyadi, J., Clifton, C., Spearpoint, M., Amor, R.: Computerizing regulatory knowledge for building engineering design. J. Comput. Civ. Eng. **C4016001**, 1–13 (2016)
14. ISO/IEC 19510: ISO/IEC 19510:2013 Information Technology - Object Management Group Business Process Model and Notation., Geneva, Switzerland (2013)
15. Dimyadi, J., Solihin, W., Eastman, C., Amor, R.: Integrating the BIM rule language into compliant design audit processes. In: Proceedings of the 33th CIB W78 International Conference 2016, Brisbane, Australia pp. 1–10 (2016)
16. Palmirani, M., Vitali, F.: Akoma-Ntoso for legal documents. In: Sartor, G., Palmirani, M., Francesconi, E., Biasiotti, M. (eds.) Legislative XML for the Semantic Web. LGTS, vol. 4. Springer, Dordrecht (2011). https://doi.org/10.1007/978-94-007-1887-6_6

17. Boer, A., Winkels, R., Vitali, F.: MetaLex XML and the legal knowledge interchange format. In: Casanovas, P., Sartor, G., Casellas, N., Rubino, R. (eds.) Computable Models of the Law. LNCS (LNAI), vol. 4884, pp. 21–41. Springer, Heidelberg (2008). https://doi.org/10.1007/978-3-540-85569-9_2

18. Boley, H., Paschke, A., Shafiq, O.: RuleML 1.0: the overarching specification of web rules. In: Dean, M., Hall, J., Rotolo, A., Tabet, S. (eds.) RuleML 2010. LNCS, vol. 6403, pp. 162–178. Springer, Heidelberg (2010). https://doi.org/10.1007/978-3-642-16289-3_15

19. MBIE: C/VM2 Verification Method: Framework for Fire Safety Design For New Zealand Building Code Clauses C1-C6 Protection from Fire. The Ministry of Business, Innovation and Employment, Wellington, New Zealand (2014)

From Traditional Construction Industry Process Management to Building Lifecycle Management

Ada Malagnino[✉], Giovanna Mangialardi, Giorgio Zavarise, and Angelo Corallo

Department of Engineering for Innovation, University of Salento, Lecce, Italy
{ada.malagnino,giovanna.mangialardi,giorgio.zavarise,
angelo.corallo}@unisalento.it

Abstract. Building Information Modeling (BIM) is an innovative approach based on a virtual model, which allows to manage all the information about the building. This approach is applicable to all the phases of the building process, but many surveys show the lack of BIM implementation in the use e maintenance phases. The BIM use in the management phase represents a unexpressed potentiality, a differentiating factor compared to Product Lifecycle Management (PLM), a holistic approach able to oversee the whole life cycle of a product and the information connected with it, widespread and consolidated in the manufacturing sector. Starting from this assumptions, in an empirical study, the paper presents a qualitative investigation into the current situation of the processes management of the constructed heritage in a French real estate company. The case study proposes the integration of the PLM and BIM approaches, that could be defined as Building Lifecycle Management (BLM), in order to close the gap of the traditional method.

Keywords: BIM · PLM · BLM · Management · AEC industry

1   Introduction

The increased attention given to sustainability and use of new technologies in the construction industry requires new approaches that take into account the entire life cycle of the building. The building sector, in fact, accounts for about 40% of final energy consumption in EU [1] and it is the largest consumer of raw materials in the world, with less than a third of recycled waste materials [2]. To this end, several applications and researches are based on the need to innovate traditional building processes from both methodological and technological point of view. In the Architecture, Engineering and Construction (AEC) Industry this trend is reflected in the Building Information Modeling (BIM), where "M" has also the meaning of Model and Management [3], widespread in many contexts such as USA and UK or in the countries from Asia-Pacific [4] and it is taking off in others nations, like in Italy [5]. Application of BIM to building processes responds to a strong need to bring innovation to construction industry, that is generally slow to change and currently suffers the economic crisis effects. The main resistances lie in the inability to regulate the production of an asset that cannot be

© IFIP International Federation for Information Processing 2017
Published by Springer International Publishing AG 2017. All Rights Reserved
J. Ríos et al. (Eds.): PLM 2017, IFIP AICT 517, pp. 335–344, 2017.
https://doi.org/10.1007/978-3-319-72905-3_30

standardized and in the complexity of ensuring interoperability among the various actors involved in the process. Strong parallelism, also reported in many interdisciplinary studies in literature [6–8], was found between BIM, or rather BLM, and PLM, an innovative and holistic approach used by manufacturing industry to manage the product life cycle. PLM, by integrating data, processes, business systems, and people [9], can represent an opportunity to extend its methodological and technological maturity to the buildings whole life cycle management. In this frame, the opportunity to study both PLM and BIM approaches, by highlighting the strengths, weaknesses and possible contact points, results to be an interesting challenge for the built heritage of a major French real estate company (I3F Group), which manages the entire life cycle of its buildings. The case study is justified by the processes complexity, the multiplicity of the actors involved, the large number of used software applications, that cause high risk of errors and loss of time and costs. The main interest of the company is to improve the built heritage management and this study gives a contribution to achieve this result by a qualitative research that lead to a critical analysis of the traditional management processes. This research, by analysing the "As Is" of the French company activities management, aims to integrate BLM approach to optimize processes, by proposing a new conceptual model that would benefit from BIM, thanks to the specificities linked to the building process, but also from PLM, in relation to its consolidated experience in the whole process management in the industrial sector. The paper is divided into 6 Sections. Section 2 presents a brief review of the literature, of the technologies on the market and of their application for the management and maintenance of other similar cases. Section 3 introduces the research settings and method. Section 4 presents the empirical case study and Sect. 5 presents findings which are structured according to the proposed conceptual model (To Be), concluding the paper with a discussion on the challenges identified and on future developments.

2 Background

The Product Lifecycle Management is a strategic business approach for the effective creation, management and use of corporate intellectual capital, from a product's initial conception to its retirement [10]. PLM systems support the product management during its life cycle, facilitating coordination and collaboration among different stakeholders. Hence, PLM is not only a software, but it is a methodology that unifies management dimensions (processes), economic dimensions (costs and revenue), technical dimensions (activities and staff) and technological ones (IT systems) [11]. "Currently, PLM is being used in a wide range of industries. It is used in discrete manufacturing, process manufacturing, distribution and service industries, as well as in research, education, military and other governmental organizations" [9]. The Building Information Modeling seems very similar to the Product Lifecycle Management [12]. BIM is "the process of creating and using digital models for design, construction and/or operations of projects", according to Succar [13]. It is centred around an Information Model, which is "the virtual representation of the physical characteristics of a facility from inception onwards. It serves as a shared information repository for collaboration throughout the facility's lifecycle" [14]. Therefore, BIM can be viewed as a virtual process that allows all design team members (owners, architects, engineers, contractors, and suppliers) to collaborate more accurately and efficiently than using traditional processes [15]. Integration between BIM and PLM is a subject of much discussion as several important international studies show [12, 16–18]. Both BIM and PLM approaches are based on the idea of managing the whole product life cycle, so that phases and actors of the process become linked. Each approach is focused on a 3D virtual model that contains all the necessary information about the product, which can be a building or an infrastructure for BIM and an industrial product for PLM. Actually, the most widespread BIM technologies are fully concentrated on visualisation and internal consistency checking to detect errors during the design and construction process [19]. Compared to PLM, which is applied to all the phases of product life cycle, this represents only a section of the entire cycle [8, 12]. Recently, consistent efforts have been made to enrich the traditional 3D BIM with the 4D, 5D, or even 6D and 7D dimensions, by trying to cover all phases of the building life [20]. This solution has been named Building Lifecycle Management or Unified Project Management (UPM) [21, 22]. BLM is an emerging concept which aims to consolidate design, engineering, construction, financial aspect, energy usage and facilities data in a central database for a holistic picture of a building process [23]. Through a Building Lifecycle Platform (BLP), BLM seeks to improve the level of information sharing among stakeholders at different phases of the project life cycle and to reduce the building information exchange barriers [24]. BLM could be seen as a way of developing a project strategy on its full life cycle and providing a mechanism of an information flow integrated management in the framework of an integrated IT environment. It aims to transform separate contractors into teams and separate tasks into processes in order to obtain a more effective and less costly implementation of such operations in the whole construction project life cycle [20]. To achieve this result, benefits and best practices issued from PLM are used to enhance BIM towards BLM [25, 26]. As regards management process, BIM should gain from PLM a more detailed definition of procedures, responsibilities and data structure, given that there is a lack of document management, version and status control and traceability of information. Integration of PLM methodologies in BIM system could facilitate capturing and coordination of the current and past projects information, as well as it could optimize the resources and strategic goals of an enterprise. This can enhance the decision-making efficiency, promote better use of resources and support agile problem-solving. Such a comprehensive information consolidation along with business intelligence tools facilitates uncovering, use and reuse of best practices in design, requirements management and project workflows. Change management features of PLM solutions enable tracking design, fabrication and construction changes in projects and ensure consistency of working information by different project entities [27]. The relation between BIM and PLM can therefore be considered inclusive and BLM represents the model that ensures this inclusion [26]. Building owners and operators are driving the AEC industry to achieve higher levels of BLM adoption by demanding process improvements and technological innovations. As the use of BLM grows, so does the amount of digital project information. As a consequence, companies need a more integrated approach for capturing, managing, and sharing data among increasingly different project teams, in order to maximize the business benefits of BLM processes. For this purpose, several PLM platforms are adapted to be used for AEC Industry projects, demonstrating the importance of integration between a consolidated approach and Building Information Modeling. For instance, Lascom (a software publisher in the field of PLM data management) met CSTB (*Centre Scientifique et Technique du Bâtiment*) in 2011 with the *Centre de Recherche Finlandais* VTT as a partner, to create Lascom AEC BIM Edition web platform. The aim of the project was to adapt the proven PLM process for managing documents online with business workflows. Another example is Dassault Systèmes 3DEXPERIENCE platform, which offers PLM applications that leverage BIM data for the AEC Industry. Also Siemens dedicates a section to BIM, through Siemens PLM for AEC and Infrastructure solution, that supports building process from design phase to maintenance phase. The result of the BLM innovation process is that big companies like Hickory Group in Australia and Skanska Group in Finland [7] are becoming aware of the benefits that integration between PLM best practises and BIM could bring not only in the initial phases of the process (design and construction), but also during use and maintenance phase [28, 29] and apply PLM solution to manage data.

3 Research Settings and Method

On the base of the state of the art, BIM approach is not considered sufficient to optimize the management of a real estate company's construction heritage, and PLM is not adapted to the construction industry peculiarities. Starting from this evaluations, this research aims to integrate BIM and PLM approaches to give a BLM setting to Immobilière 3F activities, that represents the case study of the present research. The complexity and variety of its activities in all the construction industry process management make it a good empirical example for the analysis of the application of BLM. A qualitative research on the company management processes was carried out, pinpointing all the activities and their related actors, divided into internal and external actors. Furthermore, for each activity a detailed study on software utilized by each actor was carried out. Data collection, which began in September 2014 and finished in December 2014 during a period of internship in 3F offices in Paris, involved analysis of project documents (project plans, contract documents, reports), qualitative observation of the activities as a participant actor and semi-structured interviews with company staff. In this way, the researcher had a firsthand experience with participants and had the possibility to record a lot of information. Face-to-face interviews involved unstructured and open ended questions, by covering a range of topics related to the research problem, such as information exchange method, documents management, interactions with external actors, technologies. Twelve employees with different roles were interviewed and each interview, which took place at the end of the period of internship, lasted approximately thirty minutes (see Table 1). From the data collected, workflow processes and information management were mapped, and the set of information was systemized, crossing the various phases of the process (conception and design, construction management, use and maintenance, demolition or refurbishment) with actors and software.

Table 1. Interviewees

Sector	Title	#Interviewed
Urban development	Architecture and urban planning manager	1
Real estate management	Delegated project manager	1
Construction operations management	Project manager	3
	Project manager assistant	3
Urban renovation	Project manager	2
	Project manager assistant	2

The analysis of the management processes enabled the individuation of the bottlenecks that were worked out in order to achieve a better organization and, as a consequence, time and costs savings. The PLM system provides a guidance on system requirements, above all as regards phases automation, through standard procedures definition. A solution for each bottleneck was detected among the system features and a management process conceptual model was proposed to improve company activities quality.

4 Case Study

The case study is represented by a French real estate company, Immobilière 3F, that manages 245.000 social housing units, commercial premises and residential homes in France. In detail, I3F deals with buildings construction, real estate management, buildings maintenance, urban renewal, territorial development, apartment rental and selling. The company plays different roles according to the different activities. It is, in fact, owner, developer, contracting entity, supervisory body, management body, etc. and it uses its internal organisational set-up for managing all the processes, from the beginning to the end. In the generic process some external actors are involved, such as territorial authorities, architects and engineers, construction company and other professionals. I3F previously expressed its interest in BIM and carried out a feasibility study to implement the BIM approach to its activities. This empirical study aims to give a further contribute by including PLM best practices through a customized BLM method. To this purpose, a detailed analysis was carried out specifically on new construction process, rather than renovation or urban renewal process, because it involves a greater number of actors and phases and it is more comprehensive. Data collected during the qualitative research have been processed firstly to understand the As Is, by finding and mapping the relationships among activities, actors involved an software used (Fig. 1), secondly to identify the issues that caused waste of time and delays, increasing of costs and risks of errors, communication difficulties and lack of documentation traceability. Based on these results, a study of PLM requirements is carried out in order to acquire some best practices that could benefit the company management processes. PLM requirements that have been identified as possible solutions for the company As Is issues, have been adapted to the construction industry and customized to the case study specificity.

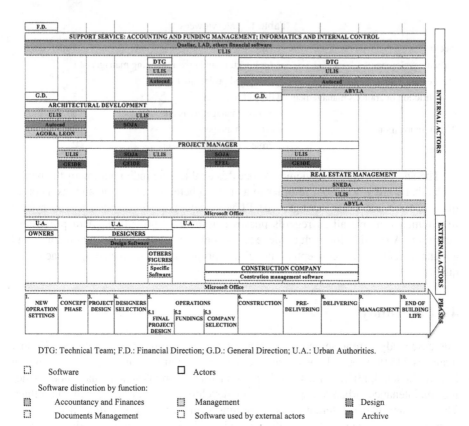

DTG: Technical Team; F.D.: Financial Direction; G.D.: General Direction; U.A.: Urban Authorities.

☐ Software   ☐ Actors

Software distinction by function:

▦ Accountancy and Finances   ☐ Management   ▦ Design
☐ Documents Management   ☐ Software used by external actors   ▦ Archive

Fig. 1. "As Is" of the French company activities management

As shown in Fig. 1, where process phases, actors and software are systemized in order to underline interactions and to have a better comprehension of the case study complexity, the company uses many software applications not interoperable and each one for a specific activity. For instance, GEIDE is an online archive available by the staff; LEON is a tool for budget evaluation; SOJA is used to manage purchases; etc. ULIS is the only management tool that is used in different activities, thanks to specific modules for each thematic area, i.e. construction activities, real estate management, financial and accountancy management, technical management. Data analysis points out that technological systems are not linked and management processes are not automated. In addition, each project manager uses Excel spreadsheets, data are entered manually and documents exchange is done on paper form or through .pdf files. Another bottleneck is represented by the lack of automatic check on files versions uploaded and standard format. As regards the second result of data analysis, the authors propose a new process conceptual model based on an integrated BIM and PLM environment, named BLM environment, by identifying the main solutions at the above-mentioned bottlenecks, following described (To Be):

- all the procedures should be well defined, highlighting the interactions among actors and clarifying the communication rules;
- Information exchange should take place on a BLM platform that contains the IFC model;
- All the actors, even the secondary ones, should use BLM tools to optimize exchange information time;
- The supervisory body, represented by the BLM manager, should have access to information during the whole construction process to verify that all the procedures are effectively respected;
- In the detailed design phase designers (architects, structural engineer, service engineer, safety engineer) should validate the project after clash detection;
- Each actor should have the access to the BLM model in a defined phase and should have the possibility to do defined operations;
- For each project a digital dossier should be automatically created, where maintenance data organization is standardised. Information about use phase can optimize energy consumption and expenditure and provide feedback.

5   Findings

The new process conceptual model (Fig. 2) scope is to give a solution to the issues related to the lack of interoperability among software and internal and external actors by using a common environment, where exchange of information is in real time and each actor uses standard formats. The interoperability concept that this work aims to is the level 3 of the technical roadmap adopted by BuildingSmart, an international organisation which aims to improve the exchange of information between software applications used in the construction industry[1]. The new system allows the transition from a traditional approach to an industrial one and from a consequential phases process to a circular phases process, where a global vision of the project during its life cycle is given by PLM principles. In this work, BLM is considered as a method which can close the gap between BIM and PLM maturity. In detail, instead of the different software applications used by the staff, a BLM platform, that enables communication among design, management and maintenance software, will be used. Furthermore, precise procedures and roles definition are established in order to guarantee traceability and a valid supervision method. Thanks to the new conceptual model, internal and external actors have a defined role in each phase of the process and are allowed to add information and manage the virtual model in according to standard procedures. For example, when construction works begin, designers have no longer access to virtual model information, but data will be available to next phases actors and to the BLM manager. During the construction phase the model is enriched by information added by building company and, at the end of this phase, only 3F staff can manage data on BLM platform. Data have to be structured in according to standard schemes and all the actors must use a unique language to avoid waste of time. System provides deadlines alerts and automatic checks of operations, as well as the opportunity to reduce the number of software applications used by the company,

---

[1] http://buildingsmart.org/standards/technical-vision/technical-roadmaps/.

thanks to the possibility to manage different types of information on the same platform. The BLM manager is the supervisor of the entire process, who unifies all the phases and gives a common direction to company activities. All these considerations are made with a view to improve facility management phase, where an informative model of the building is the key to manage efficiently the building.

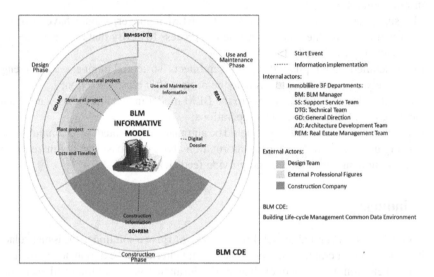

Fig. 2. "To Be"- conceptual model of the company management process

6   Conclusions and Future Developments

The construction industry is taking a new and evolutionary phase, reshaping strategic visions, processes and products, thus supporting the implementation strategies of the BLM approach. An important role in this phase is played by information technologies that allow cooperation among all the process actors, interoperability, construction phase management and building maintenance management for the reduction of design errors and rework in construction and to optimize the real estate management. These benefits are due to an enriched platform, that correlate BIM and PLM features. The BLM environment gives life to new processes, resulting from the integration of different operative levels, and is able to activate and radically improve the productivity of the construction sector. PLM best practices, as results from literature study and as this empirical study confirms, are the key to bring innovation into a sector that is still linked to traditional approaches, far from industry 4.0 and circular economy concepts. BLM turns out to be the method that will innovate the management of building heritage as regards spaces, energy consumptions, maintenance. The present work results could be extended and adapted to other 3F processes, like renovation process or urban renewal. This research is limited by the lack of a pilot case analysis to verify the effectiveness of the new conceptual model proposal. In addition to that, this work is referred to a process of data collection that took place in 2014, and because of this, it couldn't be possible to obtain information in subsequent stages of the qualitative analysis that could improve the accuracy of the study. To overcome the limitations of this research, it could be useful to evaluate a real case where a BLM approach is applied to 3F activities. Another future development will be the application of this BIM/PLM integrated approach to the Regional Agency for house and living (ARCA) Social Housing management in Italy, considering the national context and customizing software and platform to the regional authority activities.

Acknowledgement. The elaboration of this paper has been possible thanks to I3F, that permitted the study of its activities and gives useful information. We would like to thank Mariangela Lazoi, researcher at University of Salento, for her advice as regards PLM.

References

1. ENEA: Italy's Energy Efficiency Annual Report – Executive Report (2016)
2. World Economic Forum: Shaping the Future of Construction: A Breakthrough in Mindset and Technology (2016). https://www.weforum.org/reports/shaping-the-future-of-construction-a-breakthrough-in-mindset-and-technology
3. Eastman, C.M., et al.: BIM handbook: a guide to building information modeling for owners, managers, designers, engineers and contractors. Wiley, Hoboken (2011)
4. Panuwatwanich, K., et al.: Factors affecting the current diffusion of BIM: a qualitative study of online professional network. In: Creative Construction Conference, Budapest (2013)
5. Working Group UNI: CT033-GL05 Coding of products and processes in the building industry. Approved parts 1, 4 and 5 of the first standard Italian technique on BIM (2017)
6. Jupp, J.R., Nepal, M.: BIM and PLM: comparing and learning from changes to professional practice across sectors. In: Fukuda, S., Bernard, A., Gurumoorthy, B., Bouras, A. (eds.) PLM 2014. IAICT, vol. 442, pp. 41–50. Springer, Heidelberg (2014). https://doi.org/10.1007/978-3-662-45937-9_5
7. Holzer, D.: Fostering the link from PLM to ERP via BIM. In: Fukuda, S., Bernard, A., Gurumoorthy, B., Bouras, A. (eds.) PLM 2014. IAICT, vol. 442, pp. 75–82. Springer, Heidelberg (2014). https://doi.org/10.1007/978-3-662-45937-9_8
8. Jupp, J.R., Singh, V.: Similar concepts, distinct solutions, common problems: learning from PLM and BIM deployment. In: Fukuda, S., Bernard, A., Gurumoorthy, B., Bouras, A. (eds.) PLM 2014. IAICT, vol. 442, pp. 31–40. Springer, Heidelberg (2014). https://doi.org/10.1007/978-3-662-45937-9_4
9. Stark, J.: Product Lifecycle Management, 2nd edn. Springer, London (2011)
10. Amann, K.: Product Lifecycle Management: Empowering the Future Of Business. CIM Data, Inc. (2002)
11. Terzi, S., Bongiardina, C., Macchi, M.: Product Lifecycle Management: Definizione, caratteristiche e trend evolutivi (2011)
12. den Otter, A., Pels, H.J., Iliescu, I.: BIM versus PLM: risks and benefits, Francia, Sophia Antipolis, 26–28 October 2011
13. Succar, B.: Handbook of research on building information modelling and construction informatics: concepts and technologies. In: Underwood, J., Isikdag, U. (eds.) Building Information Modelling maturity matrix. In: Information Science Reference, pp. 65–103. IGI Publishing (2009)
14. Suermann, P., Issa, R.: Evaluating industry perceptions of building information modeling (BIM) impact on construction. ITcon, J. Inf. Constr. **14**, 574–594 (2009)

15. Carmona, J., Irwin, K.: BIM: who, what, how and why (2007). facilitiesnet.com, http://www.facilitiesnet.com/software/article/BIM-Who-What-How-and-Why-7546

16. Reefman, R.J.B., Van Nederveen, S.: A controlled integral product model (IPM®) in building and construction. Francia, Sophia Antipolis, 26–28 Oct 2011

17. Jupp, J.R., Singh, V.: A PLM perspective of BIM research initiatives. Int. J. Prod. Lifecycle Manage. **9**, 180–197 (2016)

18. Jupp, J.R.: Cross industry learning: a comparative study of product lifecycle management and building information modelling. Int. J. Prod. Lifecycle Manage. **9**(3), 258–284 (2016)

19. Kim, H., et al.: Generating construction schedules through automatic data extraction using open BIM (building information modeling) technology. Autom. Constr. **35**, 285–295 (2013)

20. Ustinovičiusa, L., et al.: Innovative research projects in the field of building lifecycle management. Procedia Eng. **122**, 161–171 (2015)

21. Froese, T.: Future directions for IFC-based interoperability. In: ITcon, vol. 8, Special Issue IFC - Product models for the AEC arena, pp. 231–246 (2003). http://www.itcon.org/2003/17

22. Migilinskasa, D., et al.: The benefits, obstacles and problems of practical BIM implementation. Procedia Eng. **57**, 767–774 (2013). Elsevier

23. Hu, W.: Information lifecycle modeling framework for construction project lifecycle management. In: International Seminar on Future Information Technology and Management Engineering (2008)

24. Liu, Q., Gao, T., Wang-Jian, P.: Study on building lifecycle information management platform based on BIM. Res. J. Appl. Sci. Eng. Technol. **7**, 1–8 (2014)

25. Bricogne, M., et al.: Building lifecycle management: overview of technology challenges and stakeholders (2011)

26. Bouguessa, A., Forgues, D., Doré, S.: La complémentarité entre le Building Information Modeling (BIM) et le Product LifeCycle Management (PLM) en passant par le Lean Construction (LC), Vols. CSCE 2013 General Conference-Congrès général 2013 de la SCGC (2013)

27. Aram, S., Eastman, C.: Integration of PLM solutions and BIM systems for the AEC industry. In: Proceedings of the 30th ISARC, Canada, Montréal, pp. 1046–1055 (2013). [compl.]

28. Kassem, M., et al.: Built environment project and asset management. In: BIM in Facilities Management Applications: A Case Study of a Large University Complex, vol. 5, pp. 261–277. Emerarld (2015)

29. Saaksvuori, A., Immonen, A.: Product Lifecycle Management. Springer, Heidelberg (2004)

BIM and PLM Associations
in Current Literature

Giovanna Mangialardi[✉], Carla Di Biccari, Claudio Pascarelli,
Mariangela Lazoi, and Angelo Corallo

Department of Engineering for Innovation, University of Salento, Lecce, Italy
{giovanna.mangialardi,carla.dibiccari,
claudio.pascarelli,mariangela.lazoi,
angelo.corallo}@unisalento.it

Abstract. Building Information Modeling (BIM) and Product Lifecycle Management (PLM) have been associated many times in recent literature and the possibilities for their integration or to be mutually used as a source of lesson learned has been envisaged. The paper proposes to analyze, through a systematic literature review approach, the existing state of art of previous studies that has already examined relations between BIM and PLM. The main objective of the paper is to understand the real nature of BIM-PLM association for better directing future research developments.

Keywords: BIM · PLM · BLM · Review

1 Introduction

Assuring efficient and effective management, collaboration and sharing processes is fundamental to ensure the right actions sequences necessary to achieve a good project or a good product, avoiding errors, losses of time and compartmentalized situations where professionals assumed separate and strictly defined roles with discipline-based responsibilities. This is valid both for a complex product in the Manufacturing Industry and for a complex building in the Architecture, Engineering and Construction (AEC) one. In the automotive and aerospace industries the development process management, and the storage and control of product related data, occurred since the late '80s, first with the PDM (Product Data Management) [1] that was later included in the PLM paradigm, emerged in 2001 [2]. The PLM for Corallo et al. [3] "is a strategic business approach that supports all the phases of product lifecycle, from concept to disposal, providing a unique and timed product data source. Integrating people, processes, and technologies and assuring information consistency, traceability, and long term archiving, PLM enables organizations to collaborate within and across the extended enterprise". Therefore, the PLM, supported by Information Technologies, sets up highly complex production and management tasks. In the construction sector, this systematization of processes, people and resources, is known in literature as Building Information Modeling. This term became popular only in 2002 [4], thanks to J. Laiserin, even if C. Eastman starts talking about it in the late '70s [5]. Today it is diffusely recognized "as set of interacting policies, processes and technologies

© IFIP International Federation for Information Processing 2017
Published by Springer International Publishing AG 2017. All Rights Reserved
J. Ríos et al. (Eds.): PLM 2017, IFIP AICT 517, pp. 345–357, 2017.
https://doi.org/10.1007/978-3-319-72905-3_31

generating a methodology to manage the essential building design and project data in digital format throughout the building's life cycle" [6, 7]. Theoretically, BIM should cover all the phases of a construction life cycle but at the moment, it is mainly focus on the design phase. Furthermore, its current state of development shows that many others researches can and must be done in view of the benefits deriving from its adoption [8].

Many publications cited the terms BIM and PLM contextually for different reasons, sometimes assuming they are two sides of the same coin, sometimes that they share similarities and sometimes that one is part of the other. Therefore, as a preliminary study of a broader project focused on the realization of a BLMS (Building Lifecycle Management System), this paper aims to analyze studies discussing about BIM and PLM in the same context in order to fix the current authors' points of view and addressing future research. The research wants to clarify scientific literature position about the nature of the association between BIM and PLM concepts through a systematic literature review approach of papers that have already examined this relation (i.e. as definition, as industries where they are adopted, as types and reasons of the association).

The next section of the paper describes the research method and, in particular, the papers selection and assessment. In Sects. 3, 4, 5 and 6, definitions, industries, type of associations and benefits, based on the literature review are respectively, explained. A final section of conclusion and further developments ends the paper.

2 Research Method

This study uses a literature review process to compare and fully understand the current state of association between Building Information Modeling and Product Lifecycle Management, in order to reach a shared interpretation and better direct future research developments.

Between the systematic and narrative literature review approaches [9], the choice has been in favour of the systematic literature review that allows to reach the following objectives: establish the nature of the relationship between BIM and PLM, comparing their definitions and meanings, their respective industries, the degree of association and the potential benefits deriving from their adoption, to identify fields to focus future research. The key characteristics of the systematic review method adopted in the present research are: planning the review on the basis of keywords and search terms with a replicable and defined search strategy. The literature review cannot be considered exhaustive but represent a significant vision of a current research interest at international level.

2.1 Selection and Assessment Process

The papers search was carried out through three important indexed electronic scientific databases: Web of Science (www.webofknowledge.com), Scopus (www.scopus.com) and Scholar (scholar.google.it). The research took place until May 2017. The criteria for searching was four combination of words: "PLM" and "BIM"; "PLM" and "Building Information Modeling"; "Product Lifecycle Management" and "BIM";

"Product Lifecycle Management" and "Building Information Modeling". The search in Web on Science, conducted into "Title" and "Topic", returned 10 articles, instead, the search in Scopus, conducted into "Title", "Keywords" and "Abstract", found 23 articles (10 of them were the same of Web of Science), two of which were not available for download. The search in Scholar, conducted into "Advanced Research" on "Article Title", from 2007 to 2017, returned 13 articles, (the same reported by the other databases), five of which were not taken in consideration due to the language (Chinese, Russian). As a result, a total of 23 scientific papers were identified.

The first step of the reviewing process is the preparation of a matrix to record authors notes about each article, providing a standard structure. In detail, the 23 papers were evaluated in ascending chronological order using a structured form with 12 columns including: title, publication year, source, authors with affiliations, abstract, keywords, document type, study focus, definitions of BIM/PLM, industrial issues, degree of association, benefits of association.

The second step of the research method, is the realization of a summary, in a critical way, about the significant data identified for each paper. Contents are compared and discussed. The following points are analyzed: the definition of BIM/PLM, a list of industrial features in the adoption of BIM or PLM, the type of association between BIM and PLM, and, finally, the benefits highlighting in the treatment of BIM and PLM in the same context. The results of this comparative review are reported in the following paragraphs.

3 Definitions

Before the development of his research, almost each author of the analyzed papers, states which definition of BIM and PLM refers to. These definitions can be considered as a first hint of the nature of the association observed later. Some nouns (i.e. approach, IT system, process) and attributes (i.e. object-oriented, model-driven, inclusive synonyms) were found to be very common across definitions. Table 1 classifies the selected papers both according to nouns used in the definition of BIM and/or PLM(i.e. approach, IT system, process, and their synonyms) and the attributes (i.e. object-oriented, model-driven and their synonyms).

Table 1. Summary of BIM and PLM definition classification

	Nouns			Attributes	
	Approach	IT system	Process	Object-oriented	Model driven, model
BIM	[10–16, 37–39]	[11, 12, 16–25, 38]	[11, 26]	[10, 12, 15–17, 19, 22–24, 26, 27]	[11, 13, 15, 16, 21, 22, 28, 29, 39]
PLM	[10–12, 22, 26, 37, 38]	[10, 11, 13, 17, 18, 20–22, 25–29]	[11, 26]		[11]

BIM and PLM have been described by means of one or more definitions, depending on the aim of the research. Some papers used all the three nouns at once. This can be a hint of a multifaceted nature of both concept. The most numerous group seems to be that of authors who considered BIM and/or PLM as an IT system. On the other hand, PLM has never been described through the attribute 'object-oriented'. When they are seen as IT systems, papers listed even the main functionalities of PLM systems ([13, 18, 21, 22, 26]) and of BIM systems; [26] also produces a scheme to easily visualize overlapping functionalities of the two systems.

4 Industries in the Reviewed Papers

All the papers refer to AEC Industry in general as typical sector for BIM application. [27] focuses specifically on civil structures and [25] focuses on modular building construction as an industrialized sector. The papers dealing with PLM, refer to Complex Manufacturing Sectors and, in detail, to the Automotive and Aerospace Industry. [19, 24] refer to the Shipbuilding Industry as a sector with an incomplete adoption of PLM that would benefit from BIM. [10, 17, 18] expose cases of AEC companies that have already adopted PLM in their organizational management.

Almost every paper included in this review highlights that processes, projects and products are "complex" in both sectors, but for [11, 12, 18] AEC and manufacturing industries have specific structural, background and traditional characteristics, different technology applications, methods, scope of business and tools.

The AEC industry, whose supply chain management is more project-based, is characterized by small or medium sized companies with innovation deficit and small economic resources to invest in expensive and integrated technologies. Indeed, the level of technology adoption ranges from low to medium with consequent lack of process commonality, standardization and integration between IT processes and software. The industries are highly fragmented and remain rooted in local context. The projects are different every time.

Conversely, Manufacturing companies, whose supply chain management is product-based, are larger, more globalized and consolidated. These aspects facilitate greater investments in innovative digital applications and guarantee long standing and collaborative relationships with customers. Generally, the Manufacturing industry is characterized by higher levels of IT integration and adoption of PLM system. Not all manufacturing companies have a holistic view of the whole product lifecycle but their structure, IT equipment and more mature mentalities help this transition. Accordingly, six different characteristics of the AEC industry for BIM application and of the Manufacturing one for PLM application were identified and synthesized in Table 2.

Despite of several different current characteristics identified, almost each paper includes potential future similarities for companies adopting BIM and/or PLM. In detail, for both industries, data governance, information management, storage and distribution, are important for the whole building/product lifecycle, together with the new competencies and digital skills required [10–12, 21]. For example, for [21] the "Advanced use and management of digital product data that shortens time-to-market, gives tools for product information distribution and changes management, better and

Table 2. Industry characteristics

Sector type	Characteristic					
	Firms dimension	Data management and tool	IT adoption	Industry organization	Product type	Supply chain management and industry structure
BIM						
AEC Industry (all papers) Shipbuilding Industry [19, 24]	Small and Medium [10, 17, 18, 37]	Largely separate application modules. 3D CAD, CAM, CAE, 4D – 5D BIM. [10, 21]	Low and medium [10, 11, 18, 37, 39]	Highly fragmented [10, 11, 23, 37], Localized [10, 11] Multidisciplinary and heterogeneous team [19, 22, 24, 37] Slowness to changes [23] Low integration [39]	Complex project, components and process [10, 13, 14, 16, 19–27] Individual nature of the project [19, 23, 24]	Project Based [10, 17, 18, 23], High variation in project structures and delivery methods [18] Short Term and more isolated relationships with client [10, 37] Lack of process commonality, standardization and integration [10, 11, 23, 37, 38]
PLM						
Complex Manufacturing Sectors and in detail Automotive and Aerospace Industry (all papers) Shipbuilding Industry [19, 24] AEC Industry [10, 17, 18]	Big, globalized and consolidated [10, 11, 37]	Higher Levels of integration. PLM [39] application modules, PDM, 3D CAD, CAM, CAE. Information modeling architectures, development toolkits, business app [10, 21]	Long experienced of PLM and ERP use, but with different levels of adoption [10, 12, 17, 18, 21, 23]	Partially integrated "islands of information" [11] Globalized and consolidated [10]	Complex product [10, 13, 18, 20, 21, 23–26]	Product based [10, 11] Long Standing and collaborative relationships with client [10, 37] Lack of a holistic view of users of information [11] Engineering methods. Support decision-making from whole life cycle perspective [10, 37]

reliable tools for customer requirements", and for [10] "collaborative ways of working, procurement methods, and process planning" are advantages desired in both construction and mechanical engineering industries, although there are structural barriers like the lack of vertical and horizontal integration.

5 Types of Association

Since in the sample of analyzed papers, BIM and PLM are often put in reference, in this section, the aim is to describe the nature of this association. The analysis identified four types of BIM-PLM association to which the papers can be led back: sharing similarities, being different entities, being complementary entities, being comparable (Table 3).

When BIM-PLM share similarities, whether defined as systems, approaches or models, they have something in common, for example as in [11] "relative to their approach to data sharing, project management, organization of teams around deliverables and timelines and object based visualization activities." [39] affirms that they share similarities but "differ for technical and organizational integration".

Papers that treat BIM and PLM as different entities, are those like [17] that keeps them as two worlds apart, considering BIM as an enabler to link PLM to ERP, or papers that conceive them for different functions as in [18, 29] where PLM is a unifying platform for data produced by BIM-based authoring tools, or in [14] where BIM integrated with 3D capturing processes can move towards "a special kind of Product Life cycle Management (PLM), Building Life cycle Management (BLM)". Similarly in [21] BIM's function is producing digital product data and information (authoring tools like CAD, CAM, CAT) and PLMs' is handling digital product information. In this group there is also [15] that sees BIM as an approach for design and analysis that offers a static view of the building, PLM, instead can simulate the management and is associated with the dynamic view of the building in time.

PLM and BIM were "complementary" when together they were said capable of creating a whole complete new entity. In [22] BIM and PLM together create something different, i.e. BLM. In [26], instead, they are complementary systems to fully implement Lean methodology in Construction.

On the other hand, four papers state they are fully comparable; for example [27] says that they are "comparable virtual models" and [20] considers them as two "collaborative applications". In [23] the type of association is not clearly stated, even if PLM is among paper keywords, it appears only in a figure caption "Commissioning/as-built BIM must keep PLM in mind" with no further explanation.

Table 3. Types of BIM/PLM association

Share Similarities	Different	Complementary	Comparable
[10–13, 19, 37–39]	[14–18, 21, 29]	[22, 26, 39]	[20] … collaborative applications [25] … information management frameworks [27] … comparable virtual models [28] … BIM is an immature PLM

Looking at the association purpose, the reviewed papers have been gathered according to the four most common reasons: learning lessons already known in other industries where the other system has been previously applied and more knowledge has been matured, suggesting the integration of PLM functionalities to BIM, loosely integrating PLM systems and BIM, adopt some BIM aspects into PLM (Table 4).

Table 4. BIM/PLM scope of association

Lesson learned in other industries	BIM Inherits functionalities from PLM	PLM learns from BIM	PLM system loosely integrated with BIM
[10–12, 17–19, 22, 24, 27, 28, 37, 39]	[13–16, 22, 25, 26, 29, 37, 38]	[19]	[18, 21]

In general, BIM and PLM have been associated in order to transfer functionalities and characteristics from PLM to BIM, or from the manufacturing world where PLM was born to the construction, as also noticed in [10]: "the motivations of previous PLM-BIM comparisons have typically surrounded the transfer of PLM functions and industry characteristics from the complex manufacturing industries to the construction industry." In many papers, BIM is considered as incomplete, it especially seems to lack collaboration and facility management functionalities [16, 21, 27]. Furthermore, [16] also points out that tools alone are not sufficient for BIM implementation but "drastic changes in term of work practices, staff skills, relations with client and participants of project implementation team as well as contractual arrangements are required". Only [20] suggests that collaboration should be enabled in both systems. In [14, 16, 22, 26, 39] the integration of BIM with PLM functionalities can lead to Building Lifecycle Management (BLM) considering BLM as the PLM version for the construction industry. Similarly, [29] introduces Construction Product Lifecycle Management (CPLM), a term for a PLM that is specific for the construction industry. In an early article [15] this concept is even called 4D PLM. Moreover [14, 15, 19–21, 24, 27] focus more on the authoring or 3D modeling aspects of both BIM and PLM in order to clarify the type of Association of BIM/PLM, by defining the similarities, differences, complementarity and the comparison. Interestingly [25] compares BIM to what Product Information Modeling (PIM) is in manufacturing: a structure that represents the data model for a specific product in manufacturing that can enable the interoperability of PLM [30].

6   Benefits from BIM/PLM Integration

According to the analyzed papers, a classification based on the benefits derived from BIM and PLM integration is provided. In general, it emerges that the construction industry stands to benefit more in learning from PLM application and from the professional practice in the industrial sector ([10, 11, 18, 25, 37, 39]). These researches show that the main aspects missing in AEC industry could benefit by the great experience of PLM application in manufacturing industry in sharing of information at various stages of the life cycle. In particular, the AEC facility management needs horizontal integration of several disparate systems, management of business workflow, using a shared database for all the phases.

For [10] "the construction industry is still in the early phases of BIM adoption and therefore stands to benefit most in learning from the experiences of manufacturing industries". Other researches (e.g. [10, 14, 15, 17, 21, 22, 26, 27, 29]), try to integrate the two systems, because they are viewed as complementary. In detail, while [17] integrates BIM to link PLM with ERP and [37] cites BOM and Product structure as the missing links to fully exploit BIM; the others researches focus their attention on Project management systems and suggest to apply their functionalities for a better management of digital product data in all the phases of the construction process, including facility management. All take the benefits of the management process from PLM to BIM methodology.

Benefits are generally always similar, as it can be seen in Table 5, and they are focused on the Construction Industry where BIM is actually, in a phase of development and can benefits from PLM that is a more mature topic. The major advantages are: the increase of productivity, more cost efficient and sustainable manufacturing and production, optimization of design, minimize production waste, manage supply chain, standardize components of products and manage product changes and adoptions.

Table 5. Advantages of the comparison

	Advantages		
	Kind of integration	Capabilities and functionalities involved	Kind of benefit
[10, 11, 18, 25, 37, 39]	Construction Industry learns from case studies of PLM and professional practice Lesson Learned from PLM Construction Industry uses PLM system Insight in closed loop PLM research and practices	New activities, roles/responsibilities, knowledge competencies, and supply chain relationships Horizontal integration of several disparate systems Business workflow Integration of existing PLM platforms with BIM servers Comprehensive information consolidation with business intelligence tools Change management features of PLM solutions Using a shared database. Create a hybrid system BIM-IoT-PLM	Addressing shortcomings in collaborative design in the AEC industry and enhance project performance Facilitating the capturing and consolidating information of the current and past projects as well as resources and strategic goals of an enterprise Enhancing efficient decision-making Promoting better use of resources and support agile problem-solving Facilitating the uncovering, use and reuse of best practices in design, requirements management and project workflows Tracking design, fabrication and construction changes in projects and ensuring consistency of working information by different project entities Reduction of the ownership cost Increase productivity, optimize design, minimize waste, manage supply chain, standardize components of products and manage product changes Closed loop BLM

(*continued*)

Table 5. (*continued*)

	Advantages		
	Kind of integration	Capabilities and functionalities involved	Kind of benefit
[17, 37]	Integrating BIM with PLM and ERP	Software environment, Integration of the information system, BOM, product structure	Be more transaction-oriented, standardization, increased connectivity
[10, 13–15, 21, 22, 26–29]	BIM and PLM combined	Merge functionalities Facility/project management. PDM. Lean features BIM should become a mature PLM or an integrated part of it	More cost efficient and sustainable manufacturing and production Capacity of PLM system to unify and control various tasks and steps of the construction industry PLM simulates project management, calculating the precise resource demand on a 3D model, to determine Gantt and to assess effectively alternatives

7 Findings

Comparing, learning from one another, looking for similarities and differences are not new concepts when it comes to BIM and PLM. Authors believe these are interesting current fields of research and of the twenty-three papers reviewed, many have been published in 2016, demonstrating the relevance of this topic.

Starting from definitions (Table 1), even if it is not uncommon that an author refers to both BIM and PLM as "approaches", IT system is the most spread noun to define them. This could mean that even if a strategy or a methodology lies behind BIM and PLM, without information technology the implementation would be difficult, if not impossible. Most papers use more than one of the nouns at the same time to define BIM and PLM, proving their multi-faceted nature. On the other side, "Object-Oriented" is an exclusive attribute of BIM. The parallel with Object Oriented Programming is intuitive and also found in [31, 32].

The analysis of the respective industries highlights the current transition phase and the several challenges that characterize the Construction Industry from a cultural, economic, technological and sociological point of view, as found in [11, 17, 22, 28]. Even if there are still many differences between the manufacturing and construction sectors, both are calling for new skills, performance standards, interoperability, training and an IT system that covers the whole lifecycle of complex products or buildings. Furthermore, the use of innovative technologies and methodologies in AEC industry is now steadily expanding, since it has reached a high level of awareness. As highlighted in [37] a mere integration of BIM and current PLM solutions based on discrete manufacturing, won't be able to satisfy the actual needs of the construction industry. BIM should inherit customized functionalities and features from PLM (mainly to enable collaboration and Facility Management) to become complete and effective in its scope or to evolve towards BLM [39]. Still, there is no agreement on the relationship between PLM and BLM. For some authors they are the same approach for lifecycle management, the first for manufacturing products, the second for construction products. Others refer to BLM as the sum or integration of BIM and PLM.

In Sect. 6 the advantages deriving from the integration point out that: "Sharing knowledge and experiences in the implementation and use of PLM and BIM should be understood as an essential source of continuing improvement and innovation for both paradigms" as asserts [11], even if the reviewed articles underline much more the advantages of PLM application in AEC industry, at different degree of association. Another important benefit for AEC derives from PLM lessons learned. It emerges that it is necessary to extend, like current PLM applications for complex products, the BIM technologies across the entire lifecycle, especially along the facility management phase, gaining benefit from a "unifying platform that captures, integrates and shares the object-based information generated by BIM-based authoring, analysis, and simulation applications" [18]. In general, what seems to emerge is the unsatisfied need of managing the full lifecycle of a construction in a collaborative way and that BIM currently is not able to do it. Functionalities, features and best practices already mature PLMs in the complex product manufacturing, should be customized to the specific context of construction industry to effectively manipulate BIM models.

8   Conclusions and Further Developments

This study explores the relationship between BIM and PLM using a structured approach for the literature review through a qualitative analysis of the contents coming from selected papers. The scope is to provide a better understanding of the context, principles, technologies and practices underpinning a future technological implementation. The study is motivated by recent research on BIM and PLM and their relationship to lead in the extension of BIM through BLM.

The first important conclusion is, logically, that PLM seems to be considered more mature than BIM, whether as an approach, an IT system or a process. Most researches focused on the benefits of BIM inheriting PLM lesson learned, functionalities or even the full system.

Secondly, with respect to BIM many aspects of PLM have been analyzed so far, from collaboration to user management, knowledge and data management, configuration and change management. Gaps are discovered in the possibilities of learning from PLM configuration views, which is a key concept in the dedicated literature [33]. This concept is, in fact, already linked to BIM in [34] by citing Gielingh's stages [35]: "as required, as designed, as planned, as built as used as maintained, as demolished," as a way to model product lifecycle following a traditional linear lifecycle. Since it is still missing a concrete comparison about configuration management in BIM against PLM, it will be a focus on future research on this topic.

Thirdly, the authors this paper believe that there is a general confusion about the meaning of BIM and in plain language it has assumed lately broader implications or dimensions or "perspectives" (design, estimation, construction process, building lifecycle, performance and technology [40]).

As methods and IT solutions are born to satisfy specific needs, the reviewed papers converge to the construction industry's need of managing the full lifecycle of a building in a collaborative way on a centralized object oriented model. In order to fully satisfy this need, the AEC industry should reach the digitization level of Complex manufacturing industry. The evolution of concepts that led to the modern meaning of BIM as reported by [40], reminds us that BIM originated from Building Product Structure. The recent studies of [25, 37], respectively pointing out that BIM is what PIM is to PLM and that product structure could be the "missing link in the BIM approach", bring us to consider the product structure as one of the most important features of BIM together with its being "object-oriented". Calling BLM the solution to the construction industry's need of managing the full lifecycle of a building in a collaborative way on a centralized object oriented model would better focus the aims of academic and software research. The same could happen if the common language would associate BIM more to its important feature of PIM.

Finally, from the study emerges that the relationship between BIM and PLM data model (or PIM) has not been investigated enough in the light of contemporary IT and many uncertainties are still observable in the use of BIM, PLM and BLM so the need for a standard terminology is highlighted. Therefore further research are needed on these topics.

References

1. Saaksvuori, A., Immonen, A.: Product Lifecycle Management. Springer, Heidelberg (2002). https://doi.org/10.1007/978-3-540-24799-9
2. Stark, J.: Product Lifecyle Management. Springer, London (2015). https://doi.org/10.1007/978-0-85729-546-0
3. Corallo, A., Latino, M.E., Lazoi, M., Lettera, S., Marra, M., Verardi, S.: Defining product lifecycle management: a journey across features, definitions, and concepts (2013)
4. Laiserin, J.: Comparing Pommes and Naranjas (2002), http://www.laiserin.com/features/issue15/feature01.php. Cited 14 Jan 2017
5. Eastman, C.M.: An Outline of the Building Description System. Institute of Physical Planning, Carnegie-Mellon University, Pittsburgh (1974)
6. Penttilä, H.: Describing the changes in architectural information technology to understand design complexity and free-form architectural expression (2006)
7. Succar, B.: Building information modelling framework: a research and delivery foundation for industry stakeholders (2009)
8. Azhar, S.: Building information modeling [BIM]: Trends, benefits, risks, and challenges for the AEC industry (2011)
9. Bryman, A., Bell, E.: Business Research Methods. Oxford University Press, New York (2007)
10. Jupp, J.R.: Cross industry learning: a comparative study of product lifecycle management and building information modelling. Int. J. Prod. Lifecycle Manage. 9(3), 258–284 (2016)
11. Jupp, J.R., Nepal, M.: BIM and PLM: comparing and learning from changes to professional practice across sectors. In: Fukuda, S., Bernard, A., Gurumoorthy, B., Bouras, A. (eds.) PLM 2014. IAICT, vol. 442, pp. 41–50. Springer, Heidelberg (2014). https://doi.org/10.1007/978-3-662-45937-9_5

12. Jupp, J.R., Singh, V.: Similar concepts, distinct solutions, common problems: learning from PLM and BIM deployment. In: Fukuda, S., Bernard, A., Gurumoorthy, B., Bouras, A. (eds.) PLM 2014. IAICT, vol. 442, pp. 31–40. Springer, Heidelberg (2014). https://doi.org/10.1007/978-3-662-45937-9_4

13. Jupp, J.R.: Incomplete BIM implementation: exploring challenges and the role of product lifecycle management functions. In: Bernard, A., Rivest, L., Dutta, D. (eds.) PLM 2013. IAICT, vol. 409, pp. 630–640. Springer, Heidelberg (2013). https://doi.org/10.1007/978-3-642-41501-2_62

14. Fadli, F., Barki, H., Shaat, A., Mahdjoubi, L., Boguslawski, P., Zverovich, V.: 3D capture techniques for BIM enabled LCM. In: Bouras, A., Eynard, B., Foufou, S., Thoben, K.-D. (eds.) PLM 2015. IAICT, vol. 467, pp. 183–192. Springer, Cham (2016). https://doi.org/10.1007/978-3-319-33111-9_17

15. Popov, V., Mikalauskas, S., Migilinskas, D., Vainiūnas, P.: Complex usage of 4D information modelling concept for building design, estimation, scheduling and determination of effective variant. In: Ukio Technologinis ir Ekonominis, pp. 91–98 (2006)

16. Migilinskasa, D., Popov, V., Juocevicius, V., Ustinovichius, L.: The benefits, obstacles and problems of practical bim implementation. In: 11th International Conference on Modern Building Materials, Structures and Techniques, MBMST 2013. Procedia Engineering (2013)

17. Holzer, D.: Fostering the link from PLM to ERP via BIM. In: Fukuda, S., Bernard, A., Gurumoorthy, B., Bouras, A. (eds.) PLM 2014. IAICT, vol. 442, pp. 75–82. Springer, Heidelberg (2014). https://doi.org/10.1007/978-3-662-45937-9_8

18. Aram, S., Eastman, C.: Integration of PLM solutions and BIM systems for the AEC industry. In: Proceedings of the 30th ISARC, Montreal, Canada, pp. 1046–1055 (2013)

19. Luming, R., Singh, V.: Comparing BIM in construction with 3D modeling in shipbuilding industries: is the grass greener on the other side? In: Bouras, A., Eynard, B., Foufou, S., Thoben, K.-D. (eds.) PLM 2015. IAICT, vol. 467, pp. 193–202. Springer, Cham (2016). https://doi.org/10.1007/978-3-319-33111-9_18

20. Desprat, C., Luga, H., Jessel, J.P.: Hybrid client-server and P2P network for web-based collaborative 3D design. In: WSCG 2015 Conference on Computer Graphics, Visualization and Computer Vision, Plzen, Czech Republic (2015)

21. Heikkilä, R., Hovila, J., Ahola, M., Nevala, K., Schäfer, T.: Digital product process for construction product industry. In: Proceedings of the 28th ISARC, Seoul, Korea, pp. 734–739 (2011)

22. Bricogne, M., Eynard, B., Troussier, N., Antaluca, E., Ducellier, G.: Building lifecycle management: overview of technology challenges and stakeholders. In: IET International Conference on Smart and Sustainable City, ICSSC 2011, pp. 1–5. IET, Shanghai (2011)

23. Oberoi, S., Holzer, D.: Mechanical contractors: the key for supply chain integration in lifecycle BIM. Int. J. Prod. Lifecycle Manage. 9(3) (2016)

24. Ran, L., Singh, V.: Building information modelling-enabled best practices in AEC and takeaways for Finnish shipbuilding industry. Int. J. Prod. Lifecycle Manage. 9(3) (2016)

25. Ramaji, I.J., Memari, A.M.: Product architecture model for multistory modular buildings. J. Constr. Eng. Manage. 142(10) (2016)

26. Bouguessa, A., Forgues, D., Doré, S.: La complémentarité entre le Building Information Modeling [BIM] et le Product LifeCycle Management [PLM] en passant par le Lean Construction [LC]. In: GSCE 2013 General Conference, Montreal, Canada (2013)

27. Nöldgen, M., Harder, J., Wassmann, W.: Closing the GAP in BIM – an engineering approach. In: IABSE Symposium Report, IABSE Conference Geneva 2015: Structural Engineering: Providing Solutions to Global Challenges. International Association for Bridge and Structural Engineering, Geneva (2015)

28. Reefman, R.J.B., Van Nederveen, G.A.: Knowledge management in an integrated design and engineering environment. In: eWork and eBusiness in Architecture, Engineering and Construction: ECPPM 2012. CRC Press, Reykjavik (2012)

29. Shin, H.M., Lee, H.M., Oh, S.J., Chen, J.H.: Analysis and design of reinforced concrete bridge column based on BIM. In: The Twelfth East Asia-Pacific Conference on Structural Engineering and Construction. Elsevier Ltd., Hong Kong (2011)

30. Foufou, S., Fenves, S.J., Bock, C., Rachuri, S., Sriram, R.D.: A core product model for PLM with an illustrative XLM implementation. In: International Conference on Product Lifecycle Management (2005)

31. Ahn, S., Park, M., Lee, H., Yang, Y.: Object oriented modelling of construction operations for schedule-cost integrated planning, based on BIM. In: Proceedings of the International Conference on Computing in Civil and Building Engineering, Nottingham (2010)

32. Ibrahim, M., Krawczyk, R.: The level of knowledge of CAD objects within the building information model. In: Association for Computer-Aided Design in Architecture 2003 Conference, pp. 172–177 (2003)

33. Eigner, M., Fehrenz, A.: Managing the product configuration throughout the lifecycle. In: PLM11-8th International Conference on Product Lifecycle Management (2011)

34. Eastman, C.M.: Building Product Models: Computer Environments, Supporting Design and Construction. CRC Press, Boca Raton (1999)

35. Gielingh, W.: General AEC reference model [GARM]. ISO TC184/SC4 (1988)

36. Vartiainen, P.: On the principles of comparative evaluation 8(3), 359–371 (2002)

37. Boton, C., Rivest, L., Forgues, D., Jupp, J.: Comparing PLM and BIM from the product structure standpoint. In: Harik, R., Rivest, L., Bernard, A., Eynard, B., Bouras, A. (eds.) PLM 2016. IAICT, vol. 492, pp. 443–453. Springer, Cham (2016). https://doi.org/10.1007/978-3-319-54660-5_40

38. Den Otter, A., Pels, H.J., Iliescu, I.: BIM versus PLM: Risks and benefits (2011)

39. Kubler, S., Buda, A., Robert, J., Främling, K., Le Traon, Y.: Building lifecycle management system for enhanced closed loop collaboration. In: Harik, R., Rivest, L., Bernard, A., Eynard, B., Bouras, A. (eds.) PLM 2016. IAICT, vol. 492, pp. 423–432. Springer, Cham (2016). https://doi.org/10.1007/978-3-319-54660-5_38

40. Latiffi, A.A., Brahim, J., Fathi, M.S.: The development of building information modeling (BIM) definition. Appl. Mech. Mater. 567, 625–630 (2014)

What Do Students and Professionals Think of BIM Competence?

Manish Yakami, Vishal Singh[(⊠)], and Sunil Suwal

Rakentajanaukio 4A, Otaniemi, 02150 Espoo, Finland
Vishal.Singh@aalto.fi

Abstract. Building Information Modeling (BIM) can have significant positive influence on the productivity and efficiency of construction projects. Hence, BIM competence is increasingly important in Architecture Engineering and Construction education. This paper aims to build a better understanding of BIM skills requirement to help the planning and implementation of BIM curriculum. A literature review was conducted initially to identify a set of BIM skills reported through previous studies. Thereafter, a questionnaire-based survey was conducted with students, researchers, and industry professionals to validate the identified set of skills, and assess respondents' perception of BIM competence and requisite skills. This paper presents the results from the survey.

1 Introduction

Building Information Modeling (BIM) is perceived differently by different trades within the construction sector. BIM today refers to a product (B-I-Model), an activity (B-I-Modeling), as well as a system (B-I-Management). The use of BIM in projects can have significant impact on quality, resource efficiency, and reduction in construction time and cost (Eastman et al. 2008). Research studies such as Gillian and Kunz (2007) have shown tangible benefits of BIM in projects. BIM can be used for various purposes throughout the project lifecycle, and increase the overall productivity. Since BIM relates to products, processes as well as people, the BIM way of working requires active collaboration and communication between the project participants. Team members from different disciplines need to work with BIM data, supported by the BIM professionals. BIM tools provide various possibilities for collaboration and exchange of data. A dedicated BIM manager for the projects is often seen as a requirement today. Thus, active cooperation between stakeholders is critical to successful BIM implementation.

Consequently, BIM education has become one of the key requirements in Architecture Engineering and Construction (AEC) education (Yalcinkaya and Singh 2015). BIM can empower the current and future AEC professionals to accomplish increase in productivity, waste reduction, and creation of a sustainable future through a combination of technical, methodological, procedural and organizational skills and competences. Thus, BIM education should also include individual as well as team skills and competences.

Nonetheless, because BIM is a relatively new topic in AEC education, and because the best practices in BIM education are yet to emerge, BIM courses are often taught as

© IFIP International Federation for Information Processing 2017
Published by Springer International Publishing AG 2017. All Rights Reserved
J. Ríos et al. (Eds.): PLM 2017, IFIP AICT 517, pp. 358–368, 2017.
https://doi.org/10.1007/978-3-319-72905-3_32

technology training without any theory or collaborative learning. In contrast, industry values both technical as well collaborative skills, as the base for better integration and growth of the future employees (Ahn et al. 2012). Hence, the open questions are:

What is the right balance of technical and non-technical skills that BIM education should deliver? How do the combination of skills differ based on the desired role, for example, BIM manager, BIM modeler, etc.? But, before we can answer these questions, we need to look at the following research questions:

1. What does the construction industry think about BIM competence?
2. Is BIM competence required for all AEC graduates?
3. What type of BIM competencies should the AEC graduates have?
4. What BIM competencies are needed for individuals, teams and organizations?

2 Research Method

Initially a literature review was conducted, which was followed by empirical studies using an online questionnaire survey. The literature review provided necessary information on BIM, BIM skills, and BIM education. The survey questionnaire, based on the review, was used to collect primary data to understand the current perception of BIM competence among industry practitioners, students and researchers.

2.1 Literature Review

According to Succar et al. (2013) *"Individual BIM competencies are the personal traits, professional knowledge and technical abilities required by an individual to perform a BIM activity or deliver a BIM-related outcome. These abilities, activities or outcomes must be measurable against performance standards and can be acquired or improved through education, training, and/or development."*

Several authors highlight the need for BIM skills in the AEC industry. For example, Fan et al. (2014) emphasize the need for a relationship between the BIM skills of a person and their understanding of intricacies of the field for which BIM is used. Mohd and Ahmad Latiffi (2013) mention that skilled BIM workforce helps in cost reduction and improved time management through clash detection. Wu and Issa (2014) anticipate BIM education as a solution to brisk up the BIM learning curve, though they recognize that the competencies of fresh graduates is not enough to satisfy the work-related demand. Instead, they suggest that BIM education prepares graduates to be ready to the extent that the organizations can shape BIM competencies of these graduates as per their own need (Fig. 1).

Yarmohammadi and Ashuri (2015) emphasize BIM competence regarding the coordination of building services, and how, a team leader with high BIM competence can have major impact on the progress and coordination of the project. Taiebat and Ku (2010) report that the construction industry prefers to have future employees with deep conceptual knowledge of BIM rather than those with BIM application skills only.

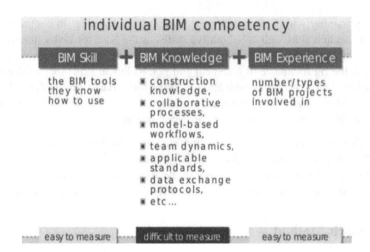

Fig. 1. Individual BIM Competence - (performance measurement & improvement, Succar et al. (2013))

A growing trend of new positions such as BIM professor and BIM manager shows the increasing need for BIM competent workforce. Project managers are likely to have a role as BIM managers. However, Rahman et al. (2016) state that skill sets needed for project managers and the BIM managers are different. The authors also highlight that skills like teamwork and communication are required in the curricula.

Dossick et al. (2014) emphasize that BIM curriculum should also include the understanding of computer application concepts and BIM processes. Davies et al. (2015) also focus on the soft skills like collaboration and communication, negotiation, teamwork, leadership and conflict management. Similarly, Barison et al. (2011) look into individual competencies such as aptitude, qualifications, skills/abilities, knowledge and attitude, noting professional need for the position in both foundational and functional ways.

Table 1 summarizes the essential skills required for graduates, based on the review.

Table 1. Summary of key BIM skills based on literature review

Authors: BIM Competencies and skills
Rahman et al. (2016): Teamwork, communication, understand BIM standards & workflow
Succar et al. (2012): Leadership, estimation, documentation & detailing, model management
Eadie et al. (2014): Collaboration
Wei et al. (2014): 3D coordination, modeling, design review, site utilization planning
Murphy (2014): Technical knowledge, planning & administration, strategy & policy, programme management
Sturts et al. (2014): Coordination and collaboration
Davies et al. (2015): Conflict management, communication, negotiation, teamwork, leadership
Barison et al. (2011): Teamwork, leadership, analytical thinking, BIM applications, creativity
Succar and Sher (2014): Leadership, collaboration, facilitation, organizational management

2.2 Design of the Questionnaire Survey

Based on the literature review, a survey questionnaire was designed with two sections: (1) BIM section and (2) BIM skills and competencies section. All the questions were mandatory to answer. Marginal questions such as gender and age were avoided. After asking about their role, respondents were prompted to select their professional background, and their work experience in BIM. Question 4 asked about the definition of BIM, where the respondents could choose one or more answers from a list of pre-stated definitions. Question 5 asked about the need for BIM competent employees in the industry. Questions 6 and 7 asked about the requirement for national level BIM competence certification, and who could be responsible for the certification. In the open-ended question 8, respondents could write their opinion about BIM skills and competences, fluency in BIM applications, knowledge of the development of BIM, and BIM experience. Using a 3-point scale, the respondents had to mark their answers as most or least important. Question 9 asked respondents about skills and competencies.

The second section of the survey continued with BIM skills and competencies. Multiple choices on BIM skills for BIM managers, BIM coordinator, BIM designer, and BIM team, based on the literature, were listed by the author for the respondents to rate on a scale of 10, with 1 being the most important skill for the position and 10 as least important. Finally, in Question 14 the respondents were given a list of skills to choose from, and self-assess and rate their own competence levels in those skills.

2.3 Data Collection and Survey Results

Around 105 emails were initially sent to BIM professionals and students. A link to the survey was also posted in BIM related groups in Linkedin.com. Respondents were assured that all the data collected from the survey will remain anonymized.

From the pool of 120 potential responses, the survey received 46 responses altogether. Thus, the final response rate at the time of closing the survey was 38.33%.

Section 1: BIM questionnaire

Figure 2 shows the breakdown of respondents. Others (e.g. BIM managers, project managers, consultants) and researchers were the most represented groups. Civil/Structural Engineers and Construction/design/business managers were most common disciplinary backgrounds. In addition, Responses to Question 3 suggest that 82% of the respondents had reasonable (self-assessed) experience with BIM, showing that BIM has become popular in the AEC industry.

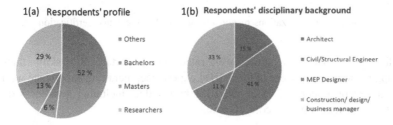

Fig. 2. Respondents profile based on questions 1 and 2 in the survey

In Question 4, four pre-defined options were given to choose from, Fig. 3. Most respondents selected option D, indicating that the wider view of BIM is more prevalent.

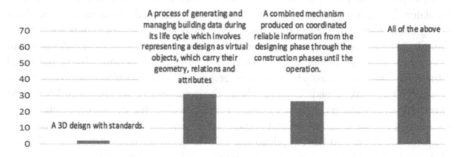

Fig. 3. Description of BIM

As seen in Fig. 4, 80% respondents see the need for BIM competent engineers. More than 50% see the need for certifications systems, while 16% feel it is not required. The respondents suggest that educational bodies and professional associations should provide BIM competence certification. Others suggest EU level certifications. Around 20% think that the BIM application vendors should provide competence certifications.

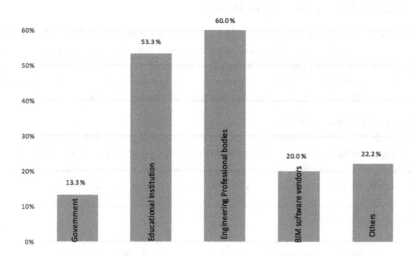

Fig. 4. Organizations responsible for BIM competence certification

All aspects of BIM competence were rated to be important. BIM skills (fluency in BIM applications) got a score of 90%, BIM experience, including experience with BIM applications got a score of 78%, and BIM knowledge, including awareness of BIM related developments got a score of 70%.

In the open-ended question 9, respondents were asked to list 10 most important skills that are required for BIM professionals. Different skills were listed by the respondents, of which, the most common skills are listed in Table 2.

Table 2. Most important BIM skills as listed by the respondents

Communication	Problem solving capabilities
Leadership	Enthusiasm for learning
Collaboration and coordination	Interoperability
Process understanding	Time management
LOD concept	Negotiation skills
Application skills	Project management
Knowledge about BIM standards and National BIM guidelines	
Experience in use of VDC/Big room method	
Understanding about working environment of another discipline	

Section 2: BIM skills and competence

Section two of the survey mainly focused on BIM skills. The respondents' were given a pre-defined list of skills to rate as per their perceived importance. Although these questions were close-ended, the answers were not very different from the open-ended list created by the respondents in the previous section. In Question 10, respondents were able to choose the essential skills needed for BIM managers, Fig. 5. The most valuable skills for BIM managers, as rated by the respondents, are collaboration, knowledge about BIM development, fluency in BIM applications, and technical skills.

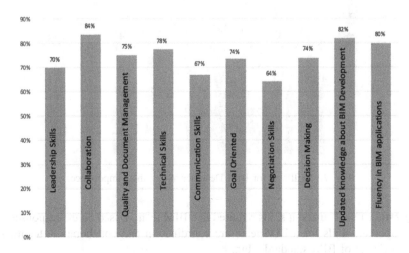

Fig. 5. Skill sets as per their importance for BIM Manager

For BIM coordinators the most important skills, based on the responses, Fig. 6, are knowledge about BIM standards, and updated knowledge about BIM developments. The other important skills are leadership and application skills. Surprisingly, communication skills and creativity got relatively low ratings.

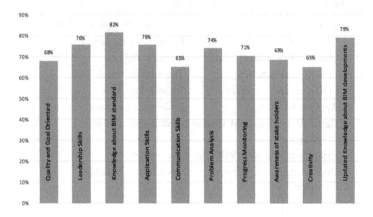

Fig. 6. Skill sets as per importance for BIM Coordinator

For BIM designer, the highest rated skills include updated knowledge of BIM development, application skills, and knowledge of BIM standards. The results show that BIM designers require BIM skills and BIM knowledge, Fig. 7.

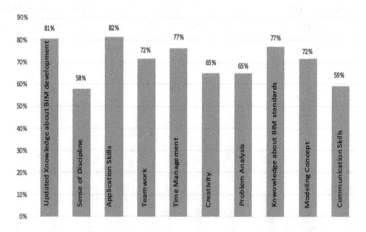

Fig. 7. Skill sets for BIM Designer as per their importance

Question 13 asked about skills required in a BIM team. Based on the responses, the most important skills for a BIM team are coordination and collaboration, teamwork, and knowledge of BIM standards, Fig. 8.

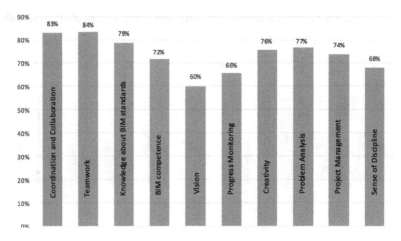

Fig. 8. Important skills for BIM Team.

The last question asked the respondents to self-assess and report their own skills relevant to a BIM profession, Fig. 9. The most commonly reported skills are coordination and collaboration, teamwork, application skills, knowledge about BIM standards, and modeling concepts, followed by problem analysis, time management, goal orientation, and leadership. The weakest self-assessed skill is related to creativity.

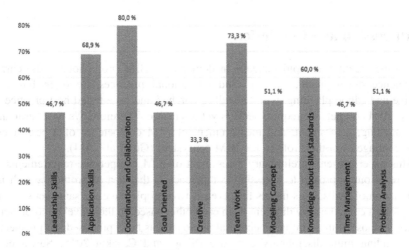

Fig. 9. BIM skills possessed by the respondents

Figure 10 shows average, self-assessed skills and competences of the respondents.

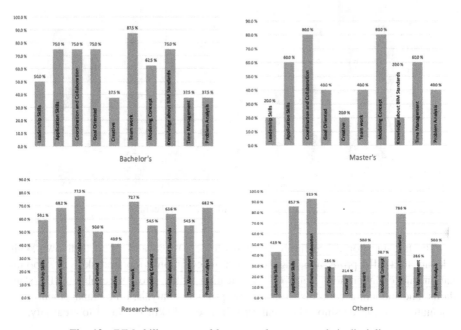

Fig. 10. BIM skills possessed by respondents as per their discipline

3 Discussion and Conclusion

Due to the recent and rapid increase in demand for BIM professionals, the current competence development, training, and educational practices are often based on reactive and adhoc planning, while a well-researched and time-tested best practice for diverse BIM competence requirements is yet to emerge. Therefore, we need structured understanding, assessment, and measurement of BIM competence of a person or a team, contingent on their role in the BIM ecosystem (Gu et al. 2014).

This paper presents preliminary assessment of BIM competence requirements. At the core of our approach to assessing competence is the idea of profiles, which is a combination of skills. This means that even if two people have the same set of skills, their profiles could be very different from each other based on their level of competence in each of those skills. Similar conceptual approach has been proposed with respect to understanding multi-disciplinary expertise (Singh and Casakin 2015; Suwal et al. 2016). This representation allows individuals and teams to self-assess their own unique profile, and assess how well they fair or compare with the typical profile expected for a particular job. For example, in Fig. 10 we see how the profile of a typical bachelor student is different to the typical master student. An individual student can use this average to compare how they are similar or different to their peers. Such a comparison can, not only allow an individual to identify gaps in their own skill-sets, but it can also be used to strategically build their own unique profile that stands out from others.

In terms of the findings from the survey, there were a few surprises. For example, for BIM professionals such as BIM Managers, who lead a unit from the organization, the authors had expected that skills like leadership, communication, negotiation, and decision-making would be rated higher than what we found in the responses. Similarly, the survey results for BIM coordinator were opposite to what the authors had expected. Nonetheless, as expected collaboration and coordination are seen among the most important competencies required for BIM personnel as well as the BIM team.

Most participants in their feedback appreciated initiating a survey on this research topic. While the findings are only a preliminary study, further studies are planned to revise the questionnaire and the competencies listed in the current set.

References

Ahn, Y.H., Annie, R.P., Kwon, H.: Key competencies for US construction graduates: industry perspective. J. Prof. Issues Eng. Edu. Pract. **138**(2), 123–130 (2012)

Barison, M.B., Santos, E.T.: The competencies of BIM specialists: a comparative analysis of the literature review and job ad descriptions. In: Proceedings of the International Workshop on Computing in Civil Engineering, ASCE, Reston, VA (2011)

Davies, K., McMeel, D., Wilkinson, S.: Soft skill requirements in a BIM project team. In: Proceedings of 32nd CIB W78 Conference, 27th–29th October 2015, Eindhoven, The Netherlands (2015)

Dossick, C.S., Lee, N., Foleyk, S.: Building information modeling in graduate construction engineering and management education. In: ICCCBE 2014 (2014)

Eadie, R., Comiskey, D. McKane, M.: Teaching BIM in a multidisciplinary department. In: Proceeding of Education, Science and Innovations (2014)

Eastman, C., Teicholz, P., Sacks, R., Liston, K.: BIM Handbook: A Guide to Building Information Modeling for Owners, Managers, Designers, Engineers, and Contractors. Wiley, Hoboken (2008)

Fan, S.L., Skibniewski, M.J., Hung, T.W.: Effects of building information modeling during construction. J. Appl. Sci. Eng. **17**(2), 157–166 (2014)

Gillian, B., Kunz, J.: VDC use in 2007: significant value, dramatic growth, and apparent business opportunity. CIFE Technical report #TR171, December 2007 (2007)

Gu, N., Singh, V., London, K.: BIM ecosystem: the co-evolution of products, processes and people. In: Kensek, K.M., Noble, D. (eds.) Building Information Modeling: Building Information Modeling in Current and Future Practice, pp. 197–209. Wiley, Hoboken (2014)

Mohd, S., Ahmad Latiffi, A.: Building Information Modeling (BIM) application in construction planning. In: 7th International Conference on Construction in the 21st Century (CITC-VII), Bangkok (2013)

Rahman, R.A., Alsafouri, S., Tang, P., Ayer, S.K.: Comparing building information modeling skills of project managers and BIM managers based on social media analysis. Procedia Eng. **145**, 812–819 (2016)

Singh, V., Casakin, H.: Developing a computational framework to study the effects of use of analogy in design on team cohesion and team collaboration. In: Weber, C., et al. (eds.) 20th International Conference on Engineering Design (ICED 2015), Milan, July 27–29, pp. 101–110 (2015)

Succar, B., Sher, W., Williams, A.: An integrated approach to BIM competency assessment, acquisition, and application. Autom. Constr. **35**, 174–189 (2013)

Succar, B., Sher, W.: A competency knowledge-base for BIM learning. Australas. J. Constr. Eco. Build.-Conf. Ser. **2**(2), 1–10 (2014)

Succar, B., Sher, W., Williams, A.: Measuring BIM performance: five metrics. Archit. Eng. Des. Manage. **8**(2), 120–142 (2012)

Suwal, S., Singh, V., Shaw, C.: Towards a framework to understand multidisciplinarity in BIM context - education to teamwork. In: CIB World Building Congress, pp. 658–672 (2016)

Taiebat, M., Ku, K.: Industry's expectations of construction school graduates' BIM skills. In: 2010 Proceedings of ASC Conference, Boston (2010)

Wei, W.U., Raja, R.A.: Key issues in workforce planning and adaptation strategies for BIM implementation in construction industry. In: 2014 Construction Research Congress (2014)

Wu, W., Issa, R.: BIM education and recruiting: survey-based comparative analysis of issues, perceptions, and collaboration opportunities. J. Prof. IssuesEng. Edu. Pract. **140**, 04013014 (2014)

Yarmohammadi, S., Ashuri, B.: Exploring the approaches in the implementation of BIM-based MEP coordination in the USA. J. Inf. Technol. Constr. **20**, 347–363 (2015)

Yalcinkaya, M., Singh, V.: Patterns and trends in Building Information Modeling (BIM) research: a latent semantic analysis. Autom. Constr. **59**, 68–80 (2015)

Cyber-Physical Systems

Lean Thinking in the Digital Era

Laura Cattaneo[1(✉)], Monica Rossi[1], Elisa Negri[1], Daryl Powell[2,3], and Sergio Terzi[1]

[1] Department of Management, Economics and Industrial Engineering, Politecnico di Milano,
Piazza Leonardo da Vinci, 20133 Milan, Italy
{laura1.cattaneo,monica.rossi,elisa.negri,
sergio.terzi}@polimi.it
[2] Kongsberg Maritime AS, Horten, Norway
[3] Department of Economics and Technology Management,
Norwegian University of Science and Technology, Trondheim, Norway
daryl.j.powell@ntnu.no

Abstract. The Industry 4.0 concept represents a paradigm shift where physical objects are seamlessly integrated into information networks. This promises to enable a more effective infrastructure in which the design, development, manufacturing and support activities that represent the key parts of a product's life cycle are closely integrated through the presence of real-time information and big data, arising from sensors, Cyber Physical Systems, Internet of Things and social networks. The challenge is to understand how to use this extensive information in order to enhance product value and to improve industrial productivity. Since information must be displayable, reusable and available in real-time, the fourth industrial revolution is already well-aligned with lean thinking, which promotes information visualization, including the just-in-time delivery of materials and information, as well as the *zero defects* ideal to quality management. Moreover, Lean thinking forces the development of human resource capabilities, through the adoption of scientific problem solving and continuous improvement approaches. These approaches must continue to underpin the leadership and employee development activities required in light of Industry 4.0. Through a systematic literature review, this paper describes the current state of the art in order to understand how lean thinking should be implemented in the context of the smart factory, and provides an initial contribution to the emerging debate around the roles of "Lean Thinking in the Digital Era".

Keywords: Lean thinking · Digital era · Industry 4.0 · Smart manufacturing
Productivity · Lean 4.0

1 Introduction

Today, consciously or not, industries have to compete in a data-driven world, where the volume of available data is continuously increasing thanks to the development of technologies such as digital platforms, sensors, mobile phones, etc. [1]. In this context, the range of applications and opportunities has grown exponentially, provided that industries are able to capture data intrinsic value. Data come from different sources, have

© IFIP International Federation for Information Processing 2017
Published by Springer International Publishing AG 2017. All Rights Reserved
J. Ríos et al. (Eds.): PLM 2017, IFIP AICT 517, pp. 371–381, 2017.
https://doi.org/10.1007/978-3-319-72905-3_33

different formats, affect different parts of the value chain and are essential to learning and knowledge-creation. The big challenge is ensuring that users get the most from the data, i.e. using it to increase the probability of making the right decisions, in the right context and for the right reasons. Indeed most companies are capturing only a fraction of the potential value of data and analytics and the biggest barriers companies face in extracting value from data are organizational, since companies struggle daily to incorporate data-driven insights into day-to-day business processes [1]. This problem statement presents a series of questions that need to be answered by carrying out research in this field: *Who is in charge to manage data and data sources within companies? What kind of analysis and models should be implemented to learn from the information contained in Big Data? Which manufacturing system may ideally include data-driven insights into day-to-day business processes? How does the concept of productivity change in the digital context?*

Lean thinking is still the most powerful philosophy to optimize operations throughout the entire manufacturing enterprise, focusing on continuous process improvements driven by customer demand, on rooting out production inefficiencies and engaging all the employees in the application of lean principles and actions like value creation, waste elimination, respect for people and continuous improvement [2, 3]. Specific attention should be paid to product and process development where lean thinking promotes the creation, use and reuse of knowledge for learning purposes [4]. Developing products and manufacturing processes is much more effective when based on formal and properly managed knowledge that prevents the company from taking wrong decisions and leads towards a better definition of customer value [5]. For the sake of knowledge formalization and learning, the access, interpretation and use of data will become increasingly more paramount for competitive advantage during the fourth industrial revolution. And the lean principles of *doing what is needed, how it is needed, when it is needed* [6] seem to translate here into enabling a system to *provide the information that is needed, when it is needed, where it is needed, and in the right format (how it is needed).* This is certainly not an easy task in such a chaotic "big data ocean". Hence, it would seem natural to find a way to understand how lean thinking can serve as enabler of Industry 4.0 and the digital era.

The paper is organized as follows: in Sect. 2 the research statement is outlined, explaining the rationale of the research and introducing the framework of Industry 4.0 and smart manufacturing, by exploring what kinds of information are available thanks to sensors, Internet of Things (IoT), social networks, IT platforms and so on. In Sect. 3 we present the state of the art regarding lean thinking in the digital era. Finally, a critical analysis on the findings is discussed in Sect. 4, with the objective of creating a common understating on existing studies, delineating open issues and research directions in the field of "Lean in the Digital Era".

2 Research Design

Lean thinking in the digital era drives the rational of this research, which starts with this initial framing paper and will continue with more in depth reasoning and fact-based findings in due course. The overall objective of the study will be to understand how data and analytics tools could underpin lean thinking (and vice versa) in order to ultimately deliver customer value centric products, by fulfilling customer requirements and increasing industry productivity. As a first contribution to such a debate, this paper starts the illustration of the current research status on lean thinking and Industry 4.0, through a systematic literature review, in order to provide an overview, synthesis and a critical assessment of previous research, challenge existing knowledge and identify and define novel research problems and research questions [7]. The paper presents the illustration of the existing literature by querying the main academic databases, around the keywords "Industry 4.0", "Smart Manufacturing" and "Lean", [8], as will be illustrate in the Sect. 3.

2.1 Industry 4.0 in the Data-Driven World

In the recent years, the volume of available data and information has grown exponentially, coming from digital platforms, wireless sensors, social networks and mobile phones. In the meanwhile data storage capacity has increased and its cost is drastically lowered. Computer power opened the way to the development of new and sophisticated algorithms [1]. We are entering a new industrial era, called Industry 4.0. This term has been coined at the 2011 Hannover Fair by Siegfried Dais (Robert Bosch GmbH) and Henning Kagermann (Acatech) [9] and it represents a politically established target for the production industry, intending to apply the principles of Cyber-Physical Systems (CPS), internet and future-oriented technologies and smart systems, with enhanced human-machine interaction paradigms [10–12]. It is currently being operationalized in different national initiatives, some examples are "Industry 4.0" in Germany, "Industry 2025" in Switzerland, "Smart Manufacturing" in USA, "Industria 4.0" in Italy, "Norge 6.0" in Norway, "Usine du Futur" in France and "High Value Manufacturing" in UK. Thus, its name has not yet been consolidated at an International level. Each of these national initiatives has led to the creation of various entities and programs, to leverage on technologies that allow easy integration of interconnected intelligent "things" inside the shopfloor with the objective to build smart, adaptive and resource efficient factories which can integrate the business processes and values in the whole supply chain [9]. The technological basis for the Industry 4.0 is the Internet of Things (IoT), first proposed in 1999 by the MIT [13]. In IoT, physical objects (i.e. the "things") are remotely sensed and controlled for a tighter integration between the physical and digital worlds, creating networks of "things" able to autonomously collect and flow data to other objects through the internet thanks to an embedded connectivity at electronic and software level [14]. Thanks to such radical technological developments, IoT is now mature and can be exploited cost-effectively at an industrial level within the so-called Industry 4.0. This consists of the use of intelligent manufacturing technologies linked to be able to communicate and deliver copious amounts of sensed data in real-time to allow having better predictability and optimization capabilities with respect to the production plant and higher customization levels in the products [15, 16]. Therefore, Industry 4.0 is anticipated to be one of the keys to facing the turbulent and unpredictable market contexts currently faced by many manufacturing companies, characterized by shorter product lifecycles, frequent introduction of new and customized products, and shorter delivery lead times [17–19]. Industries and companies in front of this new challenging context feel that they may take advantages from data and analytics, but some questions arise and some points should be clarified.

3   Lean Thinking in the Digital Era: Literature Review

3.1   Review Method

The paper focuses on the discussion based on the findings retrieved from a systematic literature review of the state of the art of lean thinking in the digital era [8, 20]. We perform the literature review of scientific articles by filtering articles according to the keywords "Industry 4.0", "Smart Manufacturing" and "Lean", which are the basic concepts of our research framework. Since the concept of "Industry 4.0" is connected to national initiatives with no recognized consolidation at an international level (as mentioned in the previous paragraph), we choose to extend our search to include other related terms, in order to capture documents that do not explicitly belong to the "Industry 4.0" domain but are factually related to parallel initiatives. We know that concepts are not only expressed using specific terms, they are also described and paraphrased. This is of particular importance when looking at emerging phenomena or new research areas, as these are generally still establishing a specific terminology to talk about the research domain in its various aspects [7]. It is worth pointing out that this paper aims at giving an exhaustive systematic literature review around the above mentioned keywords, though the paper is part of an on-going broader literature review, that will include additional keywords, as discussed in the conclusion in Sect. 4.

Scientific documents are selected through the most popular scientific works search engine (*Scopus, Google Scholar, Web of Science, Science Direct, Wiley Online Library, World Wide Science, Base, Emerald*) and we stop the research when repetition of materials reaches a significant value [8].

We perform two different searches, combining "Industry 4.0" AND "Lean", and "Smart Manufacturing" AND "Lean". The terms are searched for in the titles, abstracts and keywords. Among the results, we perform a first selection of scientific documents filtering the language and the subject. In terms of language only English documents are taken into account in this research. Regarding the subject, we select papers belonging to these subject areas: *business, management* and *accounting, computer science, economics, econometrics and finance, engineering, chemical engineering, mathematics, energy and environmental science, earth and planetary science, decision science, neuroscience and social science*. By applying these filters, we deal with a total of 458 documents (including articles, proceeding papers and master theses). In this number, some articles appear more times as they appear in different search engines. After the first selection of documents, we perform three stages of filtering, following [20]: screen titles, read abstracts and screen full texts. After filtering, irrelevant papers are rejected, and we deal with a total of 42 documents. Table 1 illustrates the number of documents found in each search engine, for both the keywords combination.

Table 1. Documents' sample

	Industry 4.0 AND lean	Smart manufacturing AND lean
Scopus	19	54
Google Scholar	18	19
Web of Science	31	38
Science Direct	52	7
Wiley Online Library	17	7
World Wide Science	26	35
Base	18	74
Emerald	34	9
Total (458 documents)	215	243

3.2 Descriptive Analysis

The search and filtering selection process results in 42 scientific documents. We find 24 proceeding papers, 14 Journal articles, 2 book chapters and 2 Master theses. Among all the documents, 21 documents appear as result of different databases. The most repeatedly found document is [21], that appears as result in five different databases (Scopus, Web of Science, Science Direct, World Wide Science, Base).

In Fig. 1 we illustrate the distribution of the 42 papers over time. Since we do not use the publication year as a filter, the oldest document we find has been published in 2010, [22]. We can observe that after 2012 there is a significant increase in publications: this is aligned with the introduction of the Industry 4.0 concept [9].

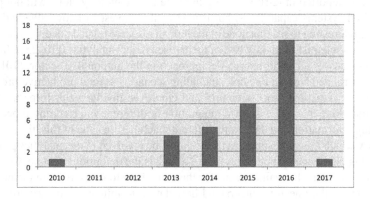

Fig. 1. Distribution of papers over time.

3.3 Information Extraction

Analysing the documents identified with the research methodology described in the previous paragraph, we perform an initial analysis to delineate the state of the art of the defined research framework, to highlight if and how lean thinking and Industry 4.0/smart manufacturing are connected, to identify which arguments are mainly investigated and to point out which gaps exist.

To investigate which topics are discussed by the selected documents, we fix *a priori* a list of keywords in order to divide documents by arguments. These keywords are relative to specific lean topics (e.g. *human resources, value stream, learning, requirements, productivity*) and to particular Industry 4.0 aspects (e.g. *Cyber Physical Systems, Internet of Things, big data*). We search also for other keywords that, basing on our experiences, could be relevant for this research, such as *Information and Communication Technology (ICT), Product Lifecycle Management (PLM), business models, data analytics* and *data scientists* [1]. Results are reported in Table 2. Developing our literature analysis, we found that similar keywords have been obtained as results also in [23], where the authors, doing an opposite process, generate representative Industry 4.0 and lean thinking keywords through a text analysis.

Observing the results summarized in Table 2, we see that one third of the selected documents writes about ICT, comprising computerized technologies, such as CAD and CAE systems, that preceded the introduction of the Industry 4.0 and are already seemingly integrated into lean manufacturing environments. This is confirmed by the fact that most of the articles speaking about ICT result from the "Lean" AND "Smart Manufacturing" search.

After ICT keywords, the most recurrent keywords are related to lean thinking: *human resources* (13 documents), *value* (12 documents), *requirements* (11 documents) and *productivity* (10 documents). Among these topics, biggest attention is given to human resource. As reported in [24], investing in the latest technology alone will not provide the required systems capabilities, but it is crucial to invest in knowledge and people skills. It is interesting to see that none of the human resource related documents explicitly mention data scientists and only two of them discuss data analytics ([10, 25]). In particular [25] discusses a hybrid lean-agile approach in the automotive sector. [10] speaks about "Control and Human Factors", including scenarios as total productive/preventive maintenance, statistical process control and employee involvement. In particular, the authors underline that IoT assists in integration of different value adding processes by combining information and data from different machines. In spite of this, the authors do not clarify which human resource activities must be involved in the analytics processes. Another big challenge that emerges from Table 2 is the definition of value. Companies have to understand what value means for them and how to measure it. In the new data-driven context, they need to understand how data can influence industry productivity and performance and how to quantify this. These concepts are so far scarcely studied, as we see from Table 2 there are few connections between "Value", "Productivity" and the data world, i.e. "Cyber Physical Systems", "Internet of Things" and "Data Management". Among the common results, [10] indirectly writes of productivity, saying that financial benefits could be measured as a reduction or elimination of redundant wastes.

[11] underlines that lean manufacturing system's performance can be integrated into CPS control algorithms, suggesting that Just-In-Time was the highest performing system. But the authors conclude their work by pointing out that further studies are needed to analyse the influence on performance variables and to investigate the necessary capital investment to actually implement Industry 4.0 on the shop floor.

Table 2. Lean and digital topics recurrence in publications. Documents that are not directly cited in the text are reported with first author and year.

Topic	Articles	Conference proceedings	Other	Tot
ICT	[22] [V.G. Smelov, 2014] [I. Veza, 2016] [M.S. Amalnik, 2015] [R. Mason-Jones, 2006]	[27] [S. Ulonska, 2013] [M. Lanz, 2014] [N. Gjeldum, 2016] [E. Rauch, 2016] [S.W. Doh, 2016] [P. Dallasega, 2016] [B. Mrugalska, 2016]	[D. Ivanov, 2017]	14
Human resources	[10, 25] [P. Edwards, 2016] [S.V. Sibatrova, 2016]	[24, 27] [Hanna Theuer, 2013] [I. Giuliano, 2014] [M. Boscoianu, 2015] [D. Kolberg, 2015] [S.W. Doh, 2016] [R.J. Eleftheriadis, 2016]	[M.T.M. Ramadan, 2016]	13
Value	[25] [V.G. Smelov, 2014] [S.E. Chick, 2014] [I. Veza, 2016]] [S.V. Sibatrova, 2016]	[I. Giuliano, 2014] [G. Ringen, 2014] [U. Hurt, 2015] [E. Rauch, 2016] [S.W. Doh, 2016] [B. Wang, 2016]	[M.T.M. Ramadan, 2016]	12
Requirements	[11, 25, 26] [T. Chen, 2017]	[24] [S. Ulonska, 2013] [A. Ojamaa, 2013] [R.J. Eleftheriadis, 2016] [J. Um, 2015] [E. Rauch, 2016]	[Hanna Theuer, 2013]	11
Productivity	[10, 25] [I. Veza, 2016] [T. Chen, 2017]	[23] [M. Lanz, 2014] [H. Huang, 2015] [S.V Sibatrova, 2016]	[M.T.M. Ramadan, 2016] [O. Gunaydi, 2016] [D. Ivanov, 2017]	10
Cyber-physical systems	[10, 11, 26] [S.V Sibatrova, 2016]	[27] [D. Kolberg, 2015] [S.W. Doh, 2016] [R.J. Eleftheriadis, 2016] [Z. Stojkic, 2016]		9
Internet of things	[10, 11, 25] [S.V Sibatrova, 2016]	[23] [M. Lanz, 2014]		6
PLM	[V. G. Smelov, 2014] [M.S. Amalnik, 2015]	[27] [S. Ulonska, 2013] [N. Gjeldum, 2016] [E. Rauch, 2016]		6
Data management	[R. Mason-Jones, 2006] [S.E. Chick, 2014]	[S. Ulonska, 2013] [A. Ojamaa, 2013]	[M.T.M. Ramadan, 2016]	5
Learning		[21, 24] [N. Gjeldum, 2016] [S.J. Blochl, 2016]		4
Data analytics	[10, 25] [J. Um, 2015]		[O. Gunaydi, 2016]	3
Big data	[10] [S.V Sibatrova, 2016]	[J. Cao, 2016]		3
Business model	[V.G. Smelov, 2014]			1
3D printing	[T. Chen, 2017]			1
Data scientist				0

Few papers, among those selected, explicitly talk about "Cyber Physical Systems" (9 documents), "Internet of Things" (6 documents) and "Big data" (3 documents). For example, [24] focus on automated manufacturing, discussing organizational capabilities and tools required to enable transformation into Industry 4.0. However, the authors write that the dominant technologies within Industry 4.0 are expected to be I(C)T, electronics and robotics, never talking about data, CPS or IoT. They write that it is important to execute value-creating activities with the correct information input and suggest that the use of prototypes enable rapid learning minimizing mistakes. These prototypes can be produced combining Computer-aided solutions and Virtual Reality. [26] describes work on a common, unified communication interface in order to digitise lean production methods and how CPSs have been used to encapsulate and retrofit workstations. Nonetheless in [26] the technological bases of Industry 4.0 (such as Big Data and IoT) are never mentioned. Among the papers talking about data technologies, [10] is particularly interesting, since the authors explicitly state when CPS, IoT and Big Data can be used as solutions for lean principles implementation. Nonetheless, they observe that some researches in Industry 4.0 are purely theory-oriented and not readily adaptable to a real-life application. Also [11] tries to explain the potential advantages that lean could achieve in combination with CPS and IoT, supporting the fact that Industry 4.0 must be integrated into the comprehensive lean theory framework. However, they also state that the Industry 4.0 initiative has a high probability to fail if it is not put into the right context by considering fundamental manufacturing principles. [26] says that there is a need for research to understand how CPSs can be integrated into existing production environments and to realize what processes they can support.

We observe also that there are few links between lean practices, Product Lifecycle Management (PLM) and the digital world, since only 6 documents discuss PLM. It is interesting to notice that, among these articles, no one is directly connecting with IoT and Big Data and only [27] writes about CPS. Furthermore, none of them are concerned with data management and data analytics.

We can conclude that although there is an extant body of literature dealing with lean thinking and the digital era, the fundamental Industry 4.0 technologies, big data and PLM principles are seldom mentioned, suggesting that the research stream is still in its infancy.

4   Conclusion and Future Research

This paper is intended to start a broader discussion on how lean thinking can and should be integrated in the digital era. Since the 1990s, the widespread adoption of lean thinking within and across industries has contributed to a truly *lean world* [28]. More recently, the digital era allows us to deal with lots of information, arising from sensors, CPS, IoT and social networks. The challenge is to understand how to use these technologies in order to build on the fundamentals of lean thinking and create even more value and to improve industrial productivity. In particular, information must be displayable, reusable and must be provided to the right person, in the right format, at the right moment. Lean thinking has vast potential in the digital era since it promotes information visualization, the just-in-time delivery and achieving more with less, for example using no more information than is required. Moreover, lean thinking has an impact on human resources (customer involvement, employee involvement, leadership development) and on problem-solving techniques, to manage information in a proper way, knowing what, how, when and why information must be available. Therefore, the integration of digital technologies with lean manufacturing seems reasonable and beneficial. Nonetheless, a number of fundamental issues remain unaddressed. Further research must be carried out to address the following areas:

- To investigate the machine-human interaction and to understand how to integrate new professional functions such as data scientists in the current manufacturing environment [1]. Although software can run algorithms to explore data, there is still a need for human resources to be able to manage different challenges: to understand the context from which the data arises, to interpret the data and sometimes to translate data languages and to choose suitable analyses methods. In "data driven" problems (unsupervised learning), data scientists must be able to extract hidden information from data and use them to better explain or solve situational problems. In "problem driven" situations (supervised learning), data scientists must be able to find a way to extract data from suitable sources and to use them to test hypotheses. In both cases, data scientists must be able to provide the right knowledge, to the right person, in the right moment and with the right language and should be able to speak with other specific industrial resources (business partners, designers, employees, etc.). Automatically this means implementing lean thinking, which aims to provide the right amount of information, to the right person, in the right moment and in a displayable and reusable format.
- To understand how to define the industrial productivity in the context of *digitalized lean*, and to understand how to measure it.
- To understand when data are useful or even necessary during the product life cycle. In particular IT tools connected with PLM should contribute to collect, manage, share and make available all information of the products (and in principle also services) along the whole life cycle. It should be natural that existing software solutions must be integrated with suitable statistical tools and algorithms able to perform analyses to extract value and re-usable information from different data sources such as sensors, CPS, IoT and social networks.

This literature review is a starting point for a more exhaustive systematic review, where we want to study in depth the connection between lean thinking and digital technologies. We will perform a more comprehensive analysis, completing the keywords research adding other main keywords such as "data", "digital", "big data" and "human". Qualitative analysis should be replaced by a quantitative analysis, following for example what was carried out in [23], with more emphasis on specific aspects such as human skills integration and technology-human interactions, interconnectivity of data and product life cycle management, and the definition of the industrial productivity in a *digitalized lean world*.

Further and deeper studies will be conducted to complete the literature review adding some specific industrial cases, in order to observe how industries are changing and enhancing their productivity applying *lean digital thinking*.

Acknowledgments. This work was partly funded by the European Commission through *Manutelligence* (GA_636951) Project and by the Research Council of Norway through the *SmartChain* Research Project.

References

1. Henke, N., Bughin, J., Chui, M., Manyika, J., Saleh, T., Wiseman, B., Sethupathy, G.: The Age of Analytics: Competing in a Data-Driven World. McKinsey Global Institute, New York (2016)
2. Scheel, O., Eitelwein, O., Monaha, S., Koelbli, M.: Digital Lean: The Next Operations Frontier. A.T. Kearney, Chicago (2015)
3. Womack, J.P., Jones, D.T., Roos, D.: The Machine That Changed the World. Rawson Associates, Free Press, New York (1990)
4. Rossi, M., Morgan, J., Shook, J.: Lean product and process development. In: Netland, T.H., Powell, D.J. (eds.) The Routledge Companion to Lean Management, Routledge (2017)
5. Rossi, M., Cattaneo, L., Le Duigou, J., Fugier-Garrel, S., Terzi, S., Eynard, B.: Lean product development and the role of PLM. In: Harik, R., Rivest, L., Bernard, A., Eynard, B., Bouras, A. (eds.) PLM 2016. IAICT, vol. 492, pp. 183–192. Springer, Cham (2016). https://doi.org/10.1007/978-3-319-54660-5_17
6. Womack, J.P., Jones, D.T.: Lean Thinking: Banish Waste and Create Wealth in Your Corporation. Simon & Schuster, New York (1996)
7. Boell, S.K., Cecez-Kecmanovic, D.: On being 'Systematic' in literature reviews in IS. J. Inf. Technol. **30**, 161–173 (2015)
8. Page, D.: Systematic literature searching and the bibliographic database haystack. Electron. J. Bus. Res. Methods **6**(2), 171–180 (2008)
9. Jazdi, N.: Cyber physical systems in the context of Industry 4.0. In: 2014 IEEE International Conference on Automation, Quality and Testing, Robotics, pp. 1–4 (2014)
10. Sanders, A., Elangeswaran, C., Wulfsberg, J.: Industry 4.0 implies lean manufacturing: Research activities in industry 4.0 function as enablers for lean manufacturing. J. Ind. Eng. Manag. **9**(3), 811–833 (2016)
11. Rüttimann, B.G., Stöckli, M.T.: Lean and Industry 4.0—twins, partners, or contenders? A due clarification regarding the supposed clash of two production systems. J. Serv. Sci. Manag. **9**(6), 485–500 (2016)
12. Garetti, M., Fumagalli, L., Negri, E.: Role of ontologies for CPS implementation in manufacturing. MPER Manag. Prod. Eng. Rev. **6**(4), 26–32 (2015)
13. Ashton, K.: That 'Internet of Things' thing. RFiD J. **22**(7), 97–114 (2009)
14. Sarma, S., Brock, D.L., Ashton, K.: The networked physical world. Auto-ID Center White Pap. MIT-AUTOID-WH-001, pp. 1–16 (2000)
15. Davis, J., Edgar, T., Porter, J., Bernaden, J., Sarli, M.: Smart manufacturing, manufacturing intelligence and demand-dynamic performance. Comput. Chem. Eng. **47**, 145–156 (2012)
16. Negri, E., Fumagalli, L., Garetti, M., Tanca, L.: Requirements and languages for the semantic representation of manufacturing systems. Comput. Ind. **81**, 55–66 (2016)
17. Meredith, J., Akinc, U.: Characterizing and structuring a new make-to-forecast production strategy. J. Oper. Manag. **25**, 623–642 (2007)
18. Salvador, F., Forza, C.: Configuring products to address the customization-responsiveness squeeze: a survey of management issues and opportunities. Int. J. Prod. Econ. **91**, 273–291 (2004)

19. Hu, S.J.: Evolving paradigms of manufacturing: from mass production to mass customization and personalization. In: Forty Sixth CIRP Conference on Manufacturing Systems, vol. 7, pp. 3–8 (2013)
20. Ming, T.M., Jabar, M.A., Sidi, F., Wei, K.T.: A systematic literature review of computer ethics issue. J. Theor. Appl. Inf. Technol. 78(3), 360–372 (2015)
21. Diez, J.V., Ordieres-Mere, J., Nuber, G.: The hoshin kanri tree. Cross-plant lean shopfloor management. In: 5th Conference on Learning Factories, vol. 32, pp. 150–155 (2015)
22. Lavrin, A., Zelko, M.: Moving toward the digital factory in raw material resources area. Acta Montan. Slovaca 15(3), 225–231 (2010)
23. Martinez, F., Jirsak, P., Lorenc, M.: Industry 4.0. The End Lean Management? In: The 10th International Days of Statistics and Economics, pp. 1189–1197 (2016)
24. Synnes, E.L., Welo, T.: Enhancing integrative capabilities through lean product and process development. In: 6th CIRP Conference on Learning Factories Enhancing, vol. 54, pp. 221–226 (2016)
25. Elmoselhy, S.A.M.: Hybrid lean-agile manufacturing system technical facet, in automotive sector. J. Manuf. Syst. 32, 598–619 (2013)
26. Kolberg, D., Knobloch, J., Zühlke, D.: Towards a lean automation interface for workstations. Int. J. Prod. Res. 55, 1–12 (2016)
27. Eleftheriadis, R.J., Myklebust, O.: A quality pathway to digitalization in manufacturing thru zero defect manufacturing practices. In: Proceedings of 6th International Workshop of Advanced Manufacturing and Automation, January 2016
28. Netland, T.H., Powell, D.J.: A lean world. In: Netland, T.H., Powell, D.J. (eds.) The Routledge Companion to Lean Management, Routledge (2017)

The Evolution of the V-Model: From VDI 2206 to a System Engineering Based Approach for Developing Cybertronic Systems

Martin Eigner[✉], Thomas Dickopf[✉], and Hristo Apostolov[✉]

Institute of Virtual Product Engineering, University of Kaiserslautern,
Gottlieb-Daimler-Straße, Building 44, 67663 Kaiserslautern, Germany
{Eigner,Thomas.Dickopf,Apostolov}@mv.uni-kl.de

Abstract. By talking about complex systems, systems engineering is always named as the only way out for the enhancement of system understanding and the reduction of system complexity in the design process. After an identification of the essential aspects and concepts for pursuing systems engineering, this paper shows how well these key factors are integrated in today's methodologies for developing mechatronic and cybertronic systems. The content of this paper is based especially on current and previous research activities on the field of model-based development at the Institute of Virtual Product Engineering.

Keywords: Systems engineering · Cybertronic systems · System design Design methodologies · System Lifecycle Management · Complex systems

1 Introduction and Motivation

Contemporary and future technological products are multi-disciplinary systems developed by multiple engineering disciplines with a significant level of complexity [1]. By talking about complex systems, we talk about systems with a large number of diverse and highly interconnected elements. These systems are characterized by dynamic system boundaries and cross-linkages between their elements [23]. Systems like these, which have the capabilities to communicate with each other, collect and distribute information or are able to autonomously adapt their behavior based on information available across different systems, are termed as Cyber Physical Systems (CPS) [2, 3] or Cybertronic Systems (CTS) [4, 5]. In order to handle the rising complexity of today's innovative and multi-disciplinary products, it is necessary to rethink and refine current design methodologies, processes, IT solutions as well as the entire enterprise organization. This paper shows an approach how essential aspects and concepts of systems engineering can be integrated in the development process of mechatronic systems in a model-based way to support the reduction of system complexity in the design process of mechatronic and cybertronic systems. In order to analyze todays design processes regarding to the incorporation of systems engineering aspects, chapter two gives a brief overview of design methodologies and extensions in the field of mechatronic and cybertronic systems. While chapter three identifies essential aspects and basic ideas each systems engineering process should include,

J. Ríos et al. (Eds.): PLM 2017, IFIP AICT 517, pp. 382–393, 2017.
https://doi.org/10.1007/978-3-319-72905-3_34

chapter four compares how well the different approaches from chapter two implements them. This paper ends with chapter five, which summarizes the results after demonstrating how the introduced approaches complement each other.

2 Development of Mechatronic and Cybertronic Systems

2.1 VDI 2206 – Design Methodology for Mechatronic Systems

During the last decades, dozens of methodical approaches for the development of new products or the further development of existing products have emerged in the field of mechatronic systems development [6]. The best known representative of these methodologies is the guideline VDI 2206 [7]. As a supplement to the guidelines VDI 2221 (systematic approach to the development and design of technical systems and products) and VDI 2422 (systematical development of devices controlled by microelectronics), VDI 2206 is intended to describe the methods of developing mechatronic systems. The objective of this guideline is to provide methodological support for a cross-domain development especially in the early phase of development, concentrating on system design. As a whole, the guideline consists of three essential elements: a general problem-solving cycle as a micro-cycle, the V-model as a macro-cycle, and predefined process modules for recurrent working steps. In the description of the micro-cycle, the guideline VDI 2206 refers to the problem-solving cycle used in systems engineering (see [8]). In general, the micro-cycle supports the work on predictable and consequently plannable subtasks as well as the solution process of suddenly occurring and unforeseeable problems. The macro-cycle guides along the logical sequence of important sub-steps in the development of mechatronic systems. Based on ideas from software development, the generic procedure is implemented along the V-model (see [9, 10]). Some of these sub-steps, which keep recurring when designing mechatronic systems, are described in the guideline in a more concrete way. The process module system design is essential for the interdisciplinary development. Its aim is to establish a cross-domain system architecture. This architecture describes the main operating characteristics of the future product. Therefore, the overall function of a system is broken down into main sub functions, which are assigned to suitable operating principles or solution elements [8].

2.2 The MVPE Model for Multidisciplinary Product Development

The MVPE Model is an extension of the VDI guideline 2206, more precisely an extension of the macro-cycle of the guideline, which has been developed at the Institute of Virtual Product Engineering (University of Kaiserslautern, Germany) in the last years [6, 11–13]. The extensions focus on two essential points: the support of the left "wing" of the V-model by methods from model-based systems engineering and on the seamless integration and management of data from the entire product lifecycle by a System Lifecycle Backbone. With regard to the left "wing" of the V-model, *Eigner et al.* identifies three levels of modeling: modeling and system specification, modeling and first simulation, and discipline specific modeling (see Fig. 1) [11]. On the specification level, the system is described by qualitative models, which include the system requirements as well as the functional und logical system structure. These models are descriptive and cannot be simulated. For an early system description, [11] recommend the use of modeling languages like SysML. The second level, modeling and first simulation, focuses on the integration of quantitative aspects by the creation and use of multidisciplinary simulation models (in e.g. Matlab or Modelica). On the last level, the system is modeled more precisely in a discipline-specific way. These models include discipline-specific aspects like e.g. concrete geometry representations and built by specific CAx tools. Parallel to these overlapping levels, the information artifacts or model elements are differentiated in requirements (R), functions (F), logical architecture elements (L) and physical parts (P), which are modeled in languages using authoring tools along the three levels of modeling [13].

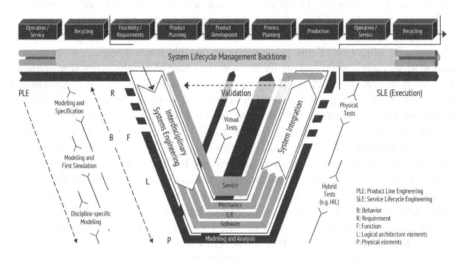

Fig. 1. The MVPE-model (after [13])

Gilz developed a SysML-based interdisciplinary approach for the creation of a model-based system architecture based on a functional and logical breakdown in the early phase [12]. This approach, the SE-VPE method, guarantees both "horizontal" and "vertical" traceability along the different model elements (R-F-L-P) and is as well construed for a transfer of this elements into a System Lifecycle Management (SysLM) solution. Similar to Product Lifecycle Management (PLM), SysLM [14–16] is a general information management solution extending PLM to the early development phase and all disciplines along the lifecycle including services [13].

2.3 The mecPro² Architectural Framework

With the fourth industrial revolution in engineering, mechatronic systems enhanced to cybertronic systems. To handle the complexity of such innovative, interdisciplinary, and interconnected products and their production systems, a rethinking of current design methodologies, processes, IT solutions, and the entire enterprise organization is needed [17]. The German research project mecPro^2 (Model-based Engineering of Products and Production Systems) seized on this requirements and created a concept to increase the efficiency of development projects in the field of Cybertronic Systems by using Model-Based Systems Engineering [18]. One result of the project is the mecPro^2 Architectural Framework. Integrated in the mecPro^2 Process Framework (another result of the research project [5]) the Architectural Framework is an interdisciplinary, model-based approach to describe a system during the phase of system design supported by the modeling language SysML. The mecPro^2 Model Framework, as an essential part of the architectural framework, forms the foundation for the description of the technical system in the early phase (see Fig. 2). It implements basic ideas of various development methodologies in the fields of mechatronic, mechanic, electric/electronic, software and systems engineering [17, 18], especially the RFLP approach from the MVPE model [6, 11], the viewpoints of the SPES Modeling Framework [19], the consideration of principle solutions [20, 21], and the subdivision in requirement and solution space including the three axes of detailing, variability and concretisation derived from the so-called Munich Model of Product Concretisation [21].

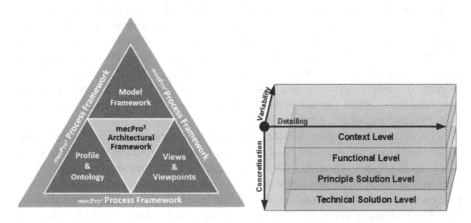

Fig. 2. The mecPro^2 architectural framework and its model framework [18]

As shown in Fig. 2, the description of the system consists of four levels with increasing solution concretization. On the context level the system is described as a black box with its interfaces. The focus of this level is the translation of natural language requirements into a system model. This includes the distinction of the system of interest in regard to its context-based environment as well as a detailed description of the expected system behavior. On the functional level, non-redundant and solution neutral system functions are identified based on the defined system behavior. The result of this level is a hierarchical and structural depiction of the system functionality including all material, energy and signal flows. On the principle solution level, the technical aspects, which realize the desired function, are considered. Therefore, principle solution alternatives should be systematically identified, analyzed and evaluated to make an optimal selection with respect to the requirements. The evaluation and selection should be made in two stages: first with respect of the degree of fulfilment of a function and second with respect of the degree of fulfilment of possible principle solution structures, which are based on the functional structure of the level before. On the technical solution level, the maximum concretization of a solution, for which an organizational unit is responsible for, is reached. The concept to identify the final system structure is similar to the one of the principle solution level. Thereby, solution components will be identified, which realize the system functions by applying the chosen principle solution [17, 18].

3 Systems Engineering

All methodologies and approaches of chapter two include or are based on concepts or aspects from the field of systems engineering. In general, especially if technical products become more and more complex, systems engineering e.g. model-based systems engineering looks like a common concept to solve the problem [8, 22, 23]. *INCOSE* describes System Engineering as an interdisciplinary approach for the realization of successful systems by considering the whole problem [24]. In the context of problem solving, *Haberfellner et al.* describes systems engineering as the methodical factor that helps to synchronize other problem solving factors to find the best solution [23]. Therefore, the system design in system engineering is based on two fundamental concepts. Systems thinking as a mindset, that enables a better understanding and redesign of complex systems, and a procedure model based on basic principles and components to support the development and realization of a solution by subdividing them into understandable sub-steps [8, 23].

Systems thinking supports holistic thinking within interdependencies as well as the differentiation and the structuring of the system. Thereby, it contains the essential terms as well as exemplary approaches for the description and illustration of complex object, without unallowed prohibited simplifications. *Crawley et al.* defined four tasks, which base on the essential features of a system to aid people in practicing systems thinking [22]. The first task is to identify the system, its form, and its function. Each system has form and function, whereby the form is the instrument of function. In the most cases, the primary function of a system is clear. The second task is to identify the entities of a system, their form and functions as well as the system boundary and context of use. System entities are, in general, also systems, which have a form and a function. The system of interest itself could be an entity of a larger system. Important to know is, what is part of the system under development and what is interacting with the system in its context? Based on this, task three helps to identify what are relationships among the entities of the system and at the boundary. Each link between the system entities as well as links to entities outside the system have a formal and functional character. The fourth task is to identify the emergent properties of the system based on the functions of the entities and on their functional interactions. It is the synergy that gives the system its power, because through the interaction between the entities a new function or characteristic arise, that is greater than the sum of the functionalities of its parts [22]. *Haberfellner et al.* clarify in their approach, that system thinking can be characterized by different perspectives of the system [23]. Therefore, it is essential to describe the system by models, which specify a specific problem of the reality in an abstract and simplified way. The identified perspectives are environmental, impact, structure, and hierarchical oriented. The environmental orientated perspective serves to identify factors, which influence the system or get influenced by it. The impact oriented perspective considers the system - like the first perspective - as a black box. But here, the focus is on the determination of the input and output values. The structure orientated perspective helps to identify, understand and determine the internal structure of the system. This includes dynamic aspects like object, energy or information flows, processes or mechanisms of action. The hierarchical perspective considers the system from two sub-perspectives. The first one is a bottom-up perspective, which considers the system as part of another system. Through this, new comprehensive system delimitation that supports a holistic thinking becomes visible. The second perspective is a top-down one, which shows the system breakdown into its subsystems on different levels. In this scope a system of systems evolves, if systems are getting joined into one system, if a system gets integrated into another one, or if the system of interest was developed independent from the other parts and can realize its functions independently from a specific system context [23].

Like in fields of mechanical, mechatronic, electrical/electronical or software engineering, in systems engineering a lot of procedure models and methodologies have been developed over the last years as well [24]. *Haberfellner et al.* identified four essential basic ideas each procedure model should include [23]. These principles are:

(1) starting from the rough and going to the details
(2) consideration of alternative solutions
(3) divide the process into chronological steps (phases)
(4) use a formal guideline (problem-solving cycle)
    to find for each problem a solution

The first principle is related to several points already mentioned in the context of systems thinking. Thereby, the engineer should start with a large field of consideration for the system that will be restrict step by step. This includes the region of interest (the system and its environment) as well as the design of solutions. Starting with a system as a black box, the levels of detail and concretization will increase stepwise until all system entities and their connections are known (white box). With each level of solution concretization variability occurs. This means that there could be more than one solution to solve the problem. To obtain the best result, it is important to analyze, compare and evaluate these alternatives. In general, this could be alternatives on a very early level of the solution finding process, where each alternative based on different basic idea, or alternatives that are based on the same principle solution but disagree in the pre or final design. The third idea describes a macro strategy that extends the first two ideas. It divides the solution finding process into chronological steps and defines decision and corrections nodes with the aim to reduce complexity as well as the risk of wrong decisions. This allows to jump back to a preceding phase and/or to focus on a different solution alternative. The problem-solving cycle describes a reusable micro-strategy, which can be used in each step of the development process. In general, it is based on the identification of a problem, the search of alternative solutions strategies as well as their analysis, evaluation, and final selection [23].

Systems engineering, in general, includes more than systems thinking and a procedure module which helps to turn a problem into a solution. Especially business needs, which are considered in the project management are as much as important as the technical needs. This paper, however, deals only with the aspects mentioned in this chapter.

4 Comparison Based on Essential Systems Engineering Aspects

While the second chapter with the VDI 2206 guideline, the MVPE model and the mecPro^2 Architectural Framework gives a specific overview about design methodologies in the field of mechatronic and cybertronic systems, chapter three introduces essential aspects and principle ideas a system development process based on concepts of systems engineering should include. Table 1 gives an overview, whether and to what extent these fundamental aspect of Systems Engineering are included in the presented methodologies and approaches of chapter two.

As seen as in Table 1, each approach includes one or more of the identified essential aspects and concepts of systems engineering. While the VDI 2206 is very abstract on the identified points, individual views of the mecPro^2 Architectural Framework can be assigned to the criteria. This is because the VDI 2206, on the one hand, looks at the entire development process from the requirements up to the finished product and, on the other hand, the VDI 2206 is a general guideline, which should guide the engineer during the development process. Whereas the mecPro^2 Architectural Framework is a specific methodological and model-based approach developed specifically for the system design phase of cybertronic systems. Although the MVPE model is an extension of the V-model from VDI 2206. It extends the scope of the view by the increase of the System Lifecycle Management Backbone to the entire life cycle and contains - with the SE-VPE method - a model-based procedure for the system design phase. While in the sense of cybertronic, mecPro^2 focuses primarily on a context-related description of the system, the focus of the SE-VPE method is mainly on the integration and administration of the essential system elements into a Product Lifecycle Management environment. This is especially evident in the rows 'environmental orientated perspective' and 'impact orientated perspective' of Table 1. In general the SE-VPE method served as an important basis for the development of the mecPro^2 Architectural Framework.

Table 1. Comparison of design approaches based on essential systems engineering aspects

	VDI guideline 2206	MVPE model	mecPro^2 architectural/model framework
Focus of the approach	Product Development Process	Product Development Process and Product Lifecycle Management	System Design
System Thinking			
Environmental oriented perspective			
- Identification of the systems context of use	Not explicitly described	Implicit by the technical system requirements analysis (SE-VPE method)	Context Level (ContextDefinitionView)
- Identification of the system			Context Level (ContextDefinitionView)
- Identification of the system boundary and its environment			Context Level (ConlextDefinitionView, ContextUseCaseView)
Impact oriented perspective			
- Identification of die main system function	System design (setting up the function structure)	Functional flow definition (SE-VPE method)	Context Level (ContextUseCaseView)
- Identification of die interactions between the system and its environment (function)	System design (setting up the functional structure)		Context Level (ContexFlowView)
- Identification of die interfaces between the system and its environment (form)	Not explicitly described		Context Level (ContextlnterfaceDefinitionView)
Hierarchical oriented perspective			
- Identification of the system entities	System design (search for operating	Logical system modeling -	Principle Solution Level Technical Solution Level

(*continued*)

Table 1. (*continued*)

	VDI guideline 2206	MVPE model	mecPro² architectural/model framework
	principles and solution elements)	black box view (SE-VPE method)	
- Identification of die system entities' functions	System design (setting up the function structure)	Functional breakdown definition (SE-VPE method)	Functional Level (FunctionalB lockDefinitionView)
Structure oriented perspective			
- Identification of the interactions between system entities (function)	System design (search for operating principles and solution elements)	Logical system modeling — white box view (SE-VPE method)	Functional Level (FunctionalStructureView)
- Identification of die interfaces between system entities (form)	Not explicitly described		Functional Level (Funct i onalS true mre View)
- Creation of a system architecture (mapping of functional system structure to element based system structure)	Implicit during the search of operating principles and solution elements at the system design	F-L Allocation Modeling (SE-VPE method)	Functional Level Technical Solution Level
Basic Ideas of a Procedure Model			
- Starting from the rough and going to the details	Not explicitly described	From black box to white box views along RFLP	Along the axes of concretization and detail
- Consideration of alternative solutions	Included in the problem- solving cycle	Not included	Principle Solution Level Technical Solution Level
- Divide the process into	A guide for the basic procedure	V-model and hi system	Through the levels of the model framework and the process framework

(*continued*)

Table 1. (*continued*)

	VDI guideline 2206	MVPE model	mecPro² architectural/model framework
chronological steps	is offered by the V-rnodel	design along RFLP	
- Use a formal guideline (problem-solving cycle) to find a solution for each problem	Reference to the SE problem-solving cycle of [8]	Not explicitly explained by the SE-VPE method	Principle Solution Level Technical Solution Level

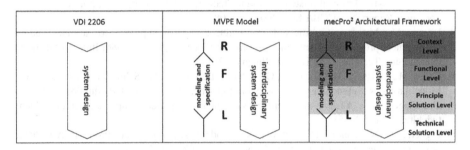

Fig. 3. Integration of the mecPro² architectural framework into the system design phase

5 Conclusion and Outlook

Based on the statement that systems engineering helps to reduce the complexity of today's products [23, 24], this paper identified essential aspects and concepts a system engineering-based approach should include. Therefore, chapter four analyzed whether and to what extent these aspect are included in the selected methodologies for mechatronic and cybertronic development. Due to the fact that the introduced approaches build upon each other and represent enhancements, the level of fulfillment increases with each approach. Nevertheless, each approach has its own right of consent. While the VDI 2206 describes a general guideline for the development of mechatronic systems, the MVPE model - especially with its SE-VPE method and the mecPro² Architecture Framework - represent methodical and model-based procedures for the design process. Since the mecPro² approach focusses exclusively on the design phase, there is no problem to integrate it into the interdisciplinary system design phase of the MVPE model (see Fig. 3). However, the SE-VPE method is not to be replaced by the mecPro² Architectural Framework, but it is an important alternative, especially for the specification of very complex systems.

Acknowledgments. The authors would like to acknowledge the German Federal Ministry of Education and Research (BMBF) and the Project Management Agency Karlsruhe (PTKA) for founding the research project mecPro^2 (funding code 02PJ2573).

References

1. Eigner, M., Stelzer, R.: Product Lifecycle Management – Ein Leitfaden für Product Development und Life Cycle Management, 2nd edn. Springer, Heidelberg (2009). https://doi.org/10.1007/b93672
2. Broy, M.: Cyber-physical systems: Wissenschaftliche Herausforderungen bei der Entwicklung. In: Broy, M. (ed.) Cyber-Physical Systems: Innovation durch softwareintensive eingebettete Systeme, pp. 17–31. Springer, Heidelberg (2010). https://doi.org/10.1007/978-3-642-14901-6_2
3. Lee, E.A.: Cyber Physical Systems: Design Challenges. University of California, Berkeley, Technical Report No. UCB/EECS-2008-8 (2008)
4. Eigner, M., Muggeo, C., Dickopf, T., Faißt, K.G.: An approach for a model based development process of cybertronic systems. In: Proceedings of the 58th Ilmenau Scientific Colloquium. Technische Universität Ilmenau (2014)
5. Cadet, M., Meissner, H., Hornberg, O., Schulte, T., Stephan, N., Schindler, C., Aurich, J.C.: Modellbasierter Entwicklungsprozess cybertronischer Produkte und Produktionssysteme - Grundlagen, erste Ansätze und weiteres Vorgehen. Stuttgarter Symposium für Produktentwicklung 2015 (2015)
6. Eigner, M., Roubanov, D., Zafirov, R.: Modellbasierte virtuelle Produktentwicklung. Springer, Heidelberg (2014). https://doi.org/10.1007/978-3-662-43816-9
7. VDI 2206: Entwicklungsmethodik für mechatronische Systeme – Design methodology for mechatronic systems. Beuth, Berlin (2004)
8. Daenzer, W.F., Huber, F.: Systems Engineering – Methoden und Praxis. Verlag Industrielle Organisation, Zürich (1992)
9. Bröhl, A.P.: Das V-Modell – Der Standard für die Softwareentwicklung. Oldenbourg, München (1995)
10. Flath, M., Kespohl, H., Möhringer, S., Oberschelp, O.: Entwicklung mechatronischer Systeme. In: Entwicklungsumgebungen Mechatronik – Methoden und Werkzeuge zur Entwicklung mechatronischer Systeme, Bd. 80. HNI-Verlagsschriftenreihe, Paderborn (2000)
11. Eigner, M., Gilz, T., Zafirov, R.: Proposal for functional product description as part of PLM solution in interdisciplinary product development. In: 12th International Design Conference – Proceedings of the Design 2012, pp. 1667–1676. University of Zagreb, Zagreb (2012)
12. Gilz, T.: PLM-Integrated Interdisciplinary System Models in the Conceptual Design Phase Based on Model-Based System Engineering. Band 13 Schriftenreihe VPE. Technische Universität Kaiserslautern, Kaiserslautern (2014)
13. Eigner, M., Dickopf, T., Apostolov, H., Schaefer, P., Faißt, K.-G., Keßler, A.: System lifecycle management: initial approach for a sustainable product development process based on methods of model based systems engineering. In: Fukuda, S., Bernard, A., Gurumoorthy, B., Bouras, A. (eds.) PLM 2014. IAICT, vol. 442, pp. 287–300. Springer, Heidelberg (2014). https://doi.org/10.1007/978-3-662-45937-9_29

14. Sendler, U.: Industrie 4.0 – Beherrschung der industriellen Komplexität mit SysLM (Systems Lifecycle Management). In: Sendler, U. (ed.) Industrie 4.0 – Beherrschung der industriellen Komplexität mit SysLM, pp. 1–20. Springer, Heidelberg (2013). https://doi.org/10.1007/978-3-642-36917-9_1
15. Eigner, M.: Modellbasierte Virtuelle Produktentwicklung auf einer Plattform für System Lifecycle Management. In: Sendler, U. (ed.) Industrie 4.0 – Beherrschung der industriellen Komplexität mit SysLM, pp. 91–110. Springer, Heidelberg (2013). https://doi.org/10.1007/978-3-642-36917-9_6
16. Eigner, M.: Das industrial internet. In: Sendler, U. (ed.) Industrie 4.0 grenzenlos. X, pp. 137–168. Springer, Heidelberg (2016). https://doi.org/10.1007/978-3-662-48278-0_9
17. Eigner, M.; Dickopf, T.; Huwig, C.: An interdisciplinary model-based design approach for developing cybertronic systems. In: 14th International Design Conference – Proceedings of the Design 2016, pp. 1647–1656. University of Zagreb, Zagreb (2016)
18. Eigner, M.; Dickopf, T.; Schulte, T.; Schneider, M.: mecPro^2 - Entwurf einer Beschreibungssystematik zur Entwicklung cybertronischer Systeme mit SysML. In: Tag des Systems Engineering 2015, pp. 163–172. Hanser, München (2015)
19. Pohl, K., Hönninger, H., Achatz, R., Broy, M.: Model-Based Engineering of Embedded Systems – The SPES 2020 Methodology. Springer, Heidelberg (2012). https://doi.org/10.1007/978-3-642-34614-9
20. VDI 2221: Methodik zum Entwickeln und Konstruieren technischer System und Produkte – systematic approach to the development and design of technical systems and products. Beuth, Berlin (1993)
21. Ponn, J., Lindemann, U.: Konzeptentwicklung und Gestaltung technischer Produkte – Systematisch von Anforderungen zu Konzepten und Gestaltlösungen. Springer, Heidelberg (2011). https://doi.org/10.1007/978-3-642-20580-4
22. Crawley, E., Cameron, B., Selva, D.: System Architecture – Strategy and Product Development for Complex Systems. Pearson Higher Education, Hoboken (2016)
23. Haberfellner, R., de Weck, O., Fricke, E., Vössner, S.: Systems Engineering – Grundlagen und Anwendung. Orell Füssli, Zürich (2012)
24. INCOSE: Systems Engineering Handbook – A Guide for System Life Cycle Processes and Activities. Wiley, Hoboken (2015)

Replacement of Parts by Part Agents to Promote Reuse of Mechanical Parts

Hiroyuki Hiraoka[✉], Atsushi Nagasawa, Yuki Fukumashi, and Yoshinori Fukunaga

Chuo University, Tokyo, Japan
hiraoka@mech.chuo-u.ac.jp

Abstract. Replacement of parts is a crucial task for the reuse of parts. In this paper, functions of part agent we are developing that support the reuse are described. A part agent manages life cycle of a part using a network agent and an RFID tag attached on the part and generates advices for the user on the maintenance of the part in order to promote the reuse. Part agent we are developing to support the replacement has the following functions. First function is to detect deterioration of the part from its sensory data. As an example, simple 3d of manipulator is developed with modularized link structure. Part agent is assigned for each module and generates advice on its replacement. Second function is to calculate the possibility of failures of part based on causal relation among user operations and detected events. Third function is to support users to disassemble used parts. Part agent generates disassembly procedure of the part and shows it to the user using augmented reality technique. In this paper, the planned scheme for part agent to support reuse of part with these functions is described and preliminary result of the development is shown.

Keywords: Part reuse · Replace · Part agent · Life cycle

1 Introduction

The effective reuse of mechanical parts is important for the development of a sustainable society [1]. To realize effective part reuse, it is essential to manage individual parts over their entire life cycle because each individual part has a different reuse history. However, it is difficult for manufacturers to predict such information due to the uncontrollable and unpredictable diversity of user behavior. For factories and plants, there are various effective methods such as in the domain of reliability engineering have been developed to maintain multiple machines and equipments in shop floors. However, users in home have difficulty to apply such methods to their appliances and vehicles and to decide when their part should be replaced with which used part in the market. This is because, firstly, users have various single products to which methods to maintain multiple similar machines in a floor are difficult to apply. Secondly, most users do not have access to appropriate maintenance information on his parts and products. Based on these considerations, we propose a scheme whereby a part "manages" itself and supports user maintenance activities.

© IFIP International Federation for Information Processing 2017
Published by Springer International Publishing AG 2017. All Rights Reserved
J. Ríos et al. (Eds.): PLM 2017, IFIP AICT 517, pp. 394–403, 2017.
https://doi.org/10.1007/978-3-319-72905-3_35

In this paper, we focus on replacement of parts and propose functions of part agent to support users to replace parts, as we consider replacement of parts is a core task in reuse of parts. It consists of two subtasks that are decision of parts to be replaced and support of user to disassemble the part. Proposed concepts and architecture of part agent's functions to support replacement of parts is described.

The concept of part agent is described in Sect. 2. In Sect. 3, after the issues on part replacement are described, framework of part agent to replace a part is described. Functionalities of part agent we are developing for this purpose are described in Sect. 4. Section 5 summarizes the paper including remaining issues.

2 Part Agent

A part agent manages all information about its corresponding part throughout its life cycle. The proposal assumes the spread of networks and high-precision RFID technology [2]. A part agent is generated at the manufacturing phase of core parts, when an RFID tag is attached to its corresponding part. The part agent identifies the ID of the RFID tag during the part's life cycle, tracking the part through the network. We chose an RFID tag for identification because RFIDs have a higher resistance to smudge or discoloration than printed bar codes during the long period of a part's life cycle.

Figure 1 shows the conceptual scheme of the part agent. The part agent communicates with various functions within the network and collects the information needed to manage its corresponding part such as product design information, predicted deterioration of parts, logistic information, or market information. It also communicates with local functions on-site, such as sensory functions that detect the state of the part, storage functions for individual part data, and management and control functions of the product. Communication is established using information agents that are subordinate network agents generated by the part agents.

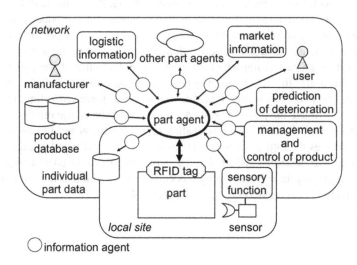

Fig. 1. Conceptual schema of part agent

In this paper we describe a part agent system we are developing based on this fundamental scheme to support user on replacement of part.

3   Framework of Part Agent for Replacement of Parts

3.1   Replacement of Parts

Challenges in promoting reuse of parts include selection of parts to be replaced and disassembly of those parts. The decision whether a certain part should be replaced or not is made based on monitored state of the part and its diagnostics. Methodologies on condition-based maintenance and predictive maintenance of product have been developed such as [3, 4]. In addition to detection and diagnostics of current situation of parts and products using these methods, it is better to take in consideration their expected future state by forecasting the future stages of the life cycle. Users need help on decisions on whether a part should be replaced or not and, in case of replacement, when and with which part it should be replaced.

Disassembly of a part from its assembly is necessary in order to execute the replacement of parts. Most disassembly procedures are provided in design stage of the product. However, it may not be applicable to disassemble used parts because of the degradation and deformation of fastening components over a long time. Assistance is required for disassembly operators to find alternative disassemble procedures.

To resolve these issues, we are developing functions of part agents that help users replace parts.

3.2   Agent Framework for Replacement of Parts

Based on the consideration described above, we are developing a framework of part agent that supports user to replace a part as shown in Fig. 2. It consists of four components; detection of deterioration based on assembly model of the product, prediction of failures based on causal relations of probable events, prediction of part behavior based on life cycle of the part, and advice generation of replacement of the part.

Deterioration of part is important information to determine if the part should be replaced. Detection of the deterioration by part agent is described in Sect. 4.3. Possibility of failure of the part is also important for the purpose. Bayesian estimation we are developing to estimate the possibility of part failure based on causal relations of events is described in Sect. 4.2. With the information on deterioration and failure possibility, part agent foresees the future states of part based on its life cycle and evaluates current possible options as described in Sect. 4.1. Part replacement is advised if the replacement is evaluated as appropriate. Disassembly procedure of the part that is required to execute the replacement is generated as described in Sect. 4.4.

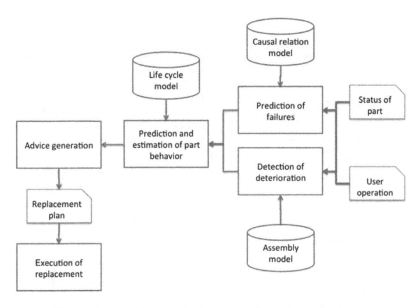

Fig. 2. Proposed framework of part agent for replacement of parts

4   Planned Functions of Part Agent for Replacement of Parts

4.1   Generation of Advice by Part Agent Based on Life Cycle Model

Figure 3 shows a basic framework for a part agent to advise its user based on the life cycle model of a part. A life cycle model consists of life cycle stages and life cycle paths that represent transfer between them. At each time step, the part agent predicts possible states of the part in the near future, and evaluates the options of actions in order to give advice to the user [5].

A part agent expands the life cycle to evaluate every options of expanded life cycle path for several time steps in the future. Figure 4(a) shows a simple example of the life cycle model. Circles represent life cycle stages that include produce, sell, use, repair, and dispose. Arrows depict life cycle paths. The part agent expands this life cycle of the part to represent possible changes in its life cycle over time. Figure 4(b) shows an expanded life cycle of the part starting from the "use" stage.

The evaluation of actions in the life cycle is based on two kinds of information. One is the possibility of failures, explained in the next section and the other is the simulated state of the part, including its environmental load, benefit, and cost. These values are estimated for every life cycle stage in the near future using the current status of the part and information about its deterioration. Possibility of failures is also taken into consideration in the estimation of life cycle stage. The evaluation is performed as described below.

The expanded life cycle represents possible changes in the life cycle of the part over time. An expanded life cycle path represents a transfer from an expanded life cycle stage to another stage in one time step. Each expanded stage has values required or generated

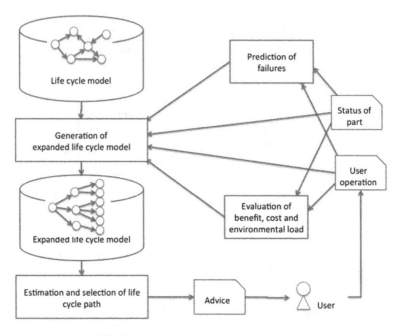

Fig. 3. Generation of advice by part agent

there for the step, such as cost, environmental load, and benefit. Probability is assigned to each expanded life cycle path. It represents a probability that the part agent takes that path and is estimated considering the probability of failures of the part.

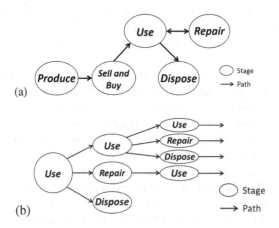

Fig. 4. Expansion of life cycle model

Figure 5 describes how a part agent selects the next stage using the expanded life cycle of the part. The figure shows an example situation in which the current life cycle stage shown in the left is a "Use" stage and the possible candidate stages in the next time step are Stage1, Stage1', and Stage1". A circle denotes an expanded life cycle stage with its property value such as V1, V2 and V3. An arrow denotes an expanded life cycle path with its probability such as p12, p13 and p14. To evaluate each possible candidate stage, its expected value of a property is calculated, taking into consideration the series of paths in the future. A series of stages connected with the paths is defined as a "route." The property values for the next stages and their probabilities are collected for all possible routes that could occur in the future. The expectation is then calculated for each route by multiplying the sum of the property values and the product of probabilities, as shown in Eq. (1).

$$EV = \sum_{route} \left(\sum_{stage\_in\_route} V * \prod_{path\_in\_route} P \right) \tag{1}$$

where, EV is the expected value of a candidate in the next stage with considering the future stages,. V is the sum of the property values for the stages in a route, and P is the accumulated probability of the paths in the route.

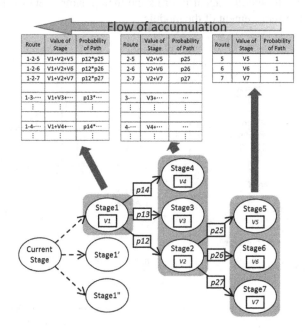

Fig. 5. Process of accumulating the values of the life cycle

We apply this schema to generate advice on replacement of the part.

4.2 Qualitative Prediction of Failures

Predicting the occurrence of failure is one of the most important and the most difficult tasks. Considering its probabilistic nature, we applied a Bayesian network to the failure model that represents causal relations between the failure of the part with the operations of its user and the current status of the part [6]. The system estimates possibility of failures based on observed events such as detected status of the part, user inputs and other detected events. We have still issues to apply this scheme to practical application. One of those issues is creation of the failure model and, as a first step, we are considering a method to improve the failure model based on a library of causal relations [7].

4.3 Detection of Deterioration of Modules

Deterioration of a part affects its performance, operational cost and environmental load. Many methods and systems have been reported to detect deterioration of products. In this paper, we are developing a system, as shown in Fig. 6, to control the manipulator and to detect deterioration of part using part agent [8]. A simple robotic manipulator shown in Fig. 7 is built for a target product. A part agent is devised for each module that consists of a link and a joint. We are developing a part agent that detects deterioration of module while controlling it. When a module agent detects the level of deterioration exceeds the limit, the module agent informs the manipulator agent of the fact and it generates a plan of replacement of the module.

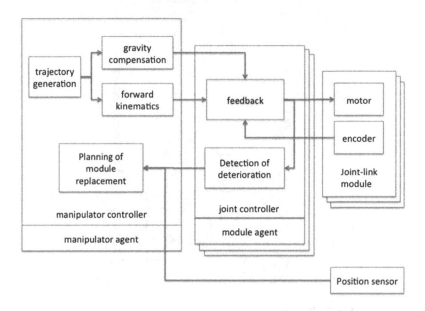

Fig. 6. Detection of deterioration for module of robot manipulator

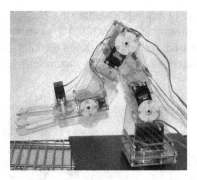

Fig. 7. A simple robotic manipulator for the experiment

4.4   Adaptive Disassembly Plan for Replacement of Part

In order to replace a part, the part must be disassembled from its assembly. A disassembly procedure is provided that is generated at the design phase of the product. However, the predefined procedure may not be applicable for used parts that are used for a long period because of the altered materials such as rust and deformation of the part. We are developing adaptive disassembly planning system that generates multiple alternative disassembly procedures as shown in Fig. 8. Instructions for the disassembly procedure are displayed overlaid on the captured image of assembly.

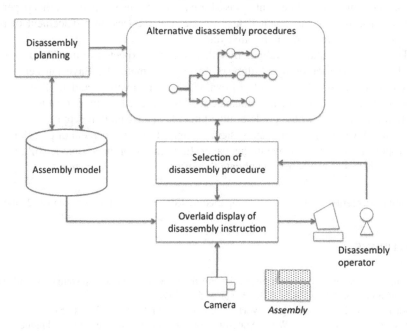

Fig. 8. Adaptive disassembly plan for replacement of part

Figure 9 shows an image of a simple assembly that is displayed with the disassembly instruction overlaid by a prototype system [9]. The system identifies the parts in the assembly using marker-based recognition technique and displays the disassembly instruction with arrow based on disassembly operations generated using assembly model.

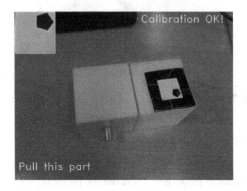

Fig. 9. Overlaid display of disassembly instruction for a simple assembly

5   Conclusion

Replacement of parts is an essential task for executing reuse of parts. In this paper, we propose functions of part agent that gives the user advices on replacement of parts considering the future state in the life cycle.

The function creates the advice by calculating the expected future TPI of the part based on its deterioration and failure probability estimated by Bayesian network. A simulation of the system is made to evaluate its effectiveness and its first result is reported. We expect flexible maintenance will be achieved using part agents with this function for the cases where predetermined maintenance cannot be applied.

We are developing a part agent system to support the replacement of parts based on the proposed scheme described in this paper. Elaboration of the system is still required and experiments is necessary to validate the effectiveness of the system.

Acknowledgements.   This work was supported by JSPS KAKENHI Grant Number 24560165.

References

1. Hauschild, M., Jeswiet, J., Alting, L.: From life cycle assessment to sustainable production: status and perspectives. Ann. CIRP **54**(2), 535–555 (2005)
2. Borriello, G.: RFID: tagging the world. Commun. ACM **44**(9), 34–37 (2005)
3. Hashemian, H.M., Bean, W.C.: State-of-the-art predictive maintenance techniques. IEEE Trans. Instrum. Measur. **60**(10), 3480–3492 (2011)

4. Jin, C., Ompusunggu, A.P., Liu, Z., Ardakani, H.D., Petre, F., Lee, J.: A vibration-based approach for stator winding fault diagnosis of induction motors: application of envelope analysis. In: Annual Conference of the Prognostics and Health Management Society 2014 (2014)
5. Nanjo, K., Yamamori, Y., Yokoki, Y., Sakamoto, Y., Hiraoka, H.: Maintenance decisions of part agent based on failure probability of a part using Bayesian estimation. In: The 22nd CIRP Conference on Life Cycle Engineering, Sydney (2015)
6. Hiraoka, H., Ueno, T., Kato, K., Ookawa, H., Arita, K., Nanjo, K., Kawaharada, H.: Part agent advice for promoting reuse of the part based on life cycle information. In: Nee, A., Song, B., Ong, S.K. (eds.) 20th CIRP International Conference on Life Cycle Engineering, pp. 337–342. Springer, Singapore (2013). https://doi.org/10.1007/978-981-4451-48-2_55
7. Fukunaga, Y., Yokoki, Y., Hiraoka, H.: Bayesian network for the reuse of mechanical parts using part agents. In: 2016 JSPE Autumn Meeting, Ibaraki, G63 (2016) (in Japanese)
8. Fukumashi, Y., Hiraoka, H.,: Parts exchange using part agents - development of the experimental system-. In: EcoDesign Products & Service (EcoDePS) Symposium 2016, 3–4 2016 (2016) (in Japanese)
9. Nagasawa, A., Hiraoka, H.: Part agent's support for disassembly of mechanical product. In: 16th International Conference on Precision Engineering, Hamamatsu, Japan (2016)

Role of VR Throughout the Life of Low Volume Products Towards Digital Extended Enterprises

Simo-Pekka Leino[1(✉)], Antti Pulkkinen[2], and Juha-Pekka Anttila[1]

[1] VTT Technical Research Centre of Finland Ltd., Tampere, Finland
Simo-Pekka.Leino@vtt.fi
[2] Tampere University of Technology, Tampere, Finland

Abstract. This paper discusses the role of virtual reality from the perspective of PLM, based on several industrial case studies. As a result of the research a virtual reality in PLM utilization model is proposed. The proposed model regards virtual reality value creation and prerequisites from PLM perspective. Utility of the model is discussed from business management point of view.

Keywords: Virtual reality · Virtual prototyping · Framework
Extended enterprise

1 Introduction

Virtual Reality (VR) technology is living its renaissance, thanks to entertainment business. However VR has a great potential in industry as well, but the demands and benefits are somewhat different. Additionally real value and preconditions of VR are still often unclear in industry [1]. Simultaneously, PLM concept itself is evolving and expanding from engineering data management towards genuine innovation and business platform. Naturally, this affects the PLM architecture as well. In this context, VR should be connected to PLM model and business value.

This paper discusses the role of VR from the perspective of product lifecycle management (PLM) based on several industrial case studies. In the context of this research, VR applications and virtual environments (VE) are user friendly interfaces to product models such as virtual prototypes (VP). In other words: virtual prototyping is a methodology and process perspective, a virtual prototype is a model of the design object, VEs are the way of experiencing and interacting with the model, and VR represents the technology utilized in virtual prototyping [1]. The extended [1] concept Intermediary Virtual Prototyping (IVP) underscores the many layers and dimensions of VP from technical advantages (immersion, interaction) of VR to the expanded mediating object of product related activity system connecting VR and VP also to PLM framework. VR based VP is widely seen as an enabling technology for intensifying product processes [2]. VP techniques also facilitate better concurrent engineering [3], Kansei engineering [4] and communication among cross-functional teams. The VEs enable engineers to consider product lifecycle downstream issues earlier in the product design phase, and

© IFIP International Federation for Information Processing 2017
Published by Springer International Publishing AG 2017. All Rights Reserved
J. Ríos et al. (Eds.): PLM 2017, IFIP AICT 517, pp. 404–415, 2017.
https://doi.org/10.1007/978-3-319-72905-3_36

make design changes even in the conceptual design stage [5, 6]. Nevertheless, VP could be utilized more efficiently and systematically, but according to our experiences companies are today lacking an understanding and knowledge of the real value and significance of VP (see e.g. [7]. There is a "paradox" of common statements of the high utility of VP and simultaneously a relatively low level of real adoption in industry [1].

The scientometric study of [8] concerning PLM International Conferences between 2005 and 2014 listed ten most frequent keywords of research papers. It is no surprise that not VR or VP are included in that list. In PLM2015 one or two of papers were related to the subject, and 2016 conference coverage was not remarkably bigger. Word "virtual" gives five articles, and "VR" none in a keyword search of International Journal of

Table 1. Characterization of the industrial case studies

	P M	P G	E D	P Z	M	P	M a	P U	S	E P	C E
PM product management, PG project management, ED engineering design, PZ productization, M manufacturing, P production, Ma maintenance, PU product upgrade, S suppliers, EP engineering partners, CE customers/end users											
Design for maintenance and manufacture	x	x	x			x				x	
Improve ergonomics and safety, reliability and maintenance. Support product lifecycle management and documentation											
Maintenance training	x	x	x				x				
Using VR for training and assessment of new maintenance tasks of new generation mining machines											
Cabin of future	x	x	x								x
Real-time VR, simulators and virtual prototyping in the assessment of human-machine interaction systems with end users during new product development projects											
Productization (NPD, prototyping)	x	x	x	x	x	x			x		
Introduce the new engine module for productization and production, assembly and maintainability assessment											
Productization (NPD, prototyping)	x	x	x	x	x	x			x		
Improve combined mass-customization and manual maintainability and easy assembly during new product development											
Productization (NPD, ramp-up)	x	x	x	x	x	x	x	x			
Using VR and virtual prototyping in order to optimize combination of time-to-market, time-to-standard production, time-to-profit											
Product updates	x		x	x		x					
VR based virtual prototyping for improved integration of engineering design and production in product development of forest machines											
Product upgrades	x	x	x	x	x		x	x	x	x	x
VR and AR aided upgrading of old mining machines in order to meet new legislation, environmental and safety regulations											
Sourcing (extended enterprise)	x		x						x	x	x
Using VR based virtual prototyping as an improved collaboration and communication means within internal and external stakeholders of a mining machine manufacture value chain											

Product Lifecycle Management. Therefore we reasoned that VR and VP should be integrated to the body of knowledge of PLM, where this paper aims to contribute. Relative to PLM, this research aims to answer following questions: How VR applications can be categorized? Where are the main benefits of VR? What are the essential enablers of VR utilization? The rest of this paper is structured as follows: Research approach is shortly described. After that the "VR utilization framework in PLM" is introduced and discussed. Finally main conclusions are summarized.

Research method was based on industrial case studies (Table 1) including interviews, workshops, process and information modelling, and comparison of past and ongoing development projects. Nature of the case study is action research, meaning that the aim is on analyzing the present challenges and changing the situation in the company. The research approach is constructive and as a result of the research a VR in PLM utilization model is proposed. From the business perspective, companies are studied with a resource based view (see [9]).

1.1 Background

In a 2016 finished Accelerate research project goal was to improve integration of engineering design and production in product development of a forest machine manufacturer. VR based VP and 3D-CAD were proposed and piloted as one means for reaching the goal. In the project ten people (see Table 1) were interviewed, and detailed result can be found in [10].

In a 2016 finished similar type of research project called Promagnet (report available[1]), fifteen mid- and senior managers from nine internal business functions (see table) of a mining machine manufacturing company were interviewed. Topic of the interviews was a past very challenging new product development project. Results and conclusions are treated in [1].

Current Dexter (Digital Extended Enterprise) research project expanded stakeholders to include three manufacturing suppliers of welded sheet structures, machined parts, sub-assemblies, and modules of mobile mining machines. Aim of the project is to improve productivity by means of digital technology. The suppliers deliver parts and sub-assemblies for both standard production and prototypes. Based on interviews and workshops, improved use of 3D-models and virtual prototypes has been recognized as one of the main target areas.

In a 2016 finished EU funded FP7 research project called Use-it-Wisely aim was to establish business models and platforms that enable life-long adaptation of high investment product-services. The Finnish cluster case focused on upgrading old mining machines in order to meet new legislation, environmental and safety regulations [11]. VR and AR were selected and piloted as means for improving communications and collaboration between upgrade project stakeholders. In the tool trial phase, ten people from the mining equipment manufacturing and service company were interviewed concerning the utility of VR in upgrading projects [12].

---

[1] http://hightech.dimecc.com/system/attachments/files/000/000/053/original/
DIMECC_MANU_Final_report_ebook.pdf?147947392.

LEFA (New Generation Human-centred Design Simulators for Life-cycle-efficient Mobile Machines) project developed user-centred design methods for mobile working machines based on VR and virtual prototypes [13]. Two participating companies represented manufacturers of mining and construction machines and container handling equipment.

2 VR Utilization Framework in PLM

The utilization model includes five main layers (Fig. 1): Digital Extended Enterprise, Processes, Tools, PLM content, and Data management. Extended enterprise is the dynamic organizational structure where VR-based product processes are executed. The product processes can be principally categorized in two dimensions as virtual (models, information flows) and physical (material flow), and product-based and service-based. The fundamental idea of using VR and VP is to create projections of the physical product processes and material flows as well as physical product based services to the virtual side.

Engineering design is traditionally transforming [14] demands of customers, users and society into requirements specifications, product concepts, embodiments designs and finally detailed design specifications in the virtual product quarter (1). In the physical product quarter, design specifications are released to sourcing, part manufacturing, and production/assembly (2). A finished product individual is shipped to a customer where it is operated, maintained and finally disposed. However, the lower section of the process layer, namely virtual (3) and physical services (4) often are vaguer and less precisely defined.

In extended enterprises product related processes such as part manufacturing, assembly, prototyping, maintenance, and product upgrades are provided as services. Because in extended enterprise collaboration, parallelism and information flows are essential capabilities, these services and related product properties should be designed concurrently. Therefore the virtual service section becomes very interesting from the VR in PLM perspective. The stakeholders and actors of extended enterprises participate to the virtual product-service processes with different perspectives bringing their diverse knowledge. Furthermore, based on our industrial case studies, the process layer includes four different VR utilization types: (A) New product development (NPD), (B) standard production support, (C) standard service support and product individual upgrade support (D).

2.1 VR Value Creation

Using VR and IVP, the properties and functions of physical products as well as related services and processes can be discussed and evaluated earlier, before physical manufacture and assembly. Additionally, for instance product-based services, such as maintenance work tasks can be designed before building the physical products and systems. VR enables better understanding of product models and information for unexperienced people, thus improved communication and knowledge sharing between stakeholders, decreased uncertainty, and better quality fast decision making [1, 9, 15–17]. The stakeholders can virtually test and train the use of the products, which may lead to improved

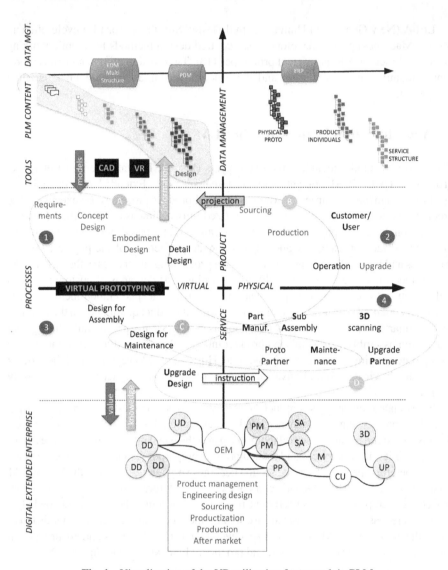

Fig. 1. Visualization of the VR utilization framework in PLM

usability and ergonomics [18]. The potential business impact of VR may also be derived from a more holistic view of the product-service system [3]. Generally, early prototyping should be seen as a management tool and means for learning [19]. More detailed value creation dimensions and mechanisms are discussed in [1]. There main value creation dimensions include processes, people (organization and individuals), and business management. This paper extends the value creation context to wider product lifecycle and on the other hand to extended enterprises.

In PLM, life phases of products can roughly be divided [20] into the Beginning of Life (BoL) - design and manufacture; the Middle of Life (MoL) – operation and support;

and the End of Life (EoL) – retire or upgrade. This view is different from marketing, where a product life is divided into five phases: introduction, growth, maturity, saturation and degeneration [21]. The following Table 2 summarizes the value creation mechanisms during the three main product life phases.

Table 2. Examples of value creation mechanisms during the three main product life phases and PLM dimensions

	Process	People	Business
New product development (BoL)	Requirements validation, concept design and validation, design reviews, prototyping, marketing, production ramp-up	Communication and understanding, organizational learning, knowledge creation and sharing, shared mental models, revealing contradictions	time-to-market, time-to-serial production, decreased physical prototyping cost, decision making decreased uncertainty, productivity (information), value-chain design
Standard production support (BoL)	Engineering change, design for assembly, part manufacturing, sub-assembly services, knowledge feedback	Transferring skills and information from NPD to standard production, ability to improve one's work	time-to-profit, productivity (material), balanced performance and core competence, value-chain optimization
Standard services (MoL)	Design for maintenance, product-service co-design, sales and marketing	Involvement of new stakeholders, service training	Prototyping partner, service innovations
Upgrade support (EoL)	Upgrade design, fitting an upgrade solution to an old product individual, design reviews, sales, illustration of upgrade offering, 3D-scanning	Involvement of new stakeholders, knowledge capture, commitment	New upgrade business models, improved productivity (information and material), upgrade partner relationships

Generally engineering change requests and modifications are made too late in NPD projects, leading to costly rework with physical prototypes. VR and design reviews allow finding design flaws early, thus engineering changes can be made before manufactured physical prototypes [1, 22]. This leads to decreased time-to-market and time-to-profit.

When a new product is ramped-up to production, it is important to effectively transfer information and knowledge from product development to standard production, and equally important to transfer knowledge back to design engineers. This can be supported by VR and digital manufacturing approach [23]. In the middle of life, the product is operated and maintained. With the use of VR and IVP, these actions can also be designed. Product upgrades in the end of life are special types of services. Profitability of product upgrade service projects may often be questionable because the actual status of the upgrade target is not known, and communication between customers, service people, suppliers and design engineers is difficult. VR is a means to visualize scan-based and 3D-CAD models so that customer and other stakeholder requirements as well as proposed design solutions can be validated before building the physical system. Productivity is increased because unproductive rework and information search can be decreased [11].

2.2 Preconditions for Value Creation

As stated before, the benefits of virtual prototyping cannot be attained for free. Certain preconditions and pre-requisites are needed before VR and VP really create value for internal and external customers. As [24] stated, the success of VR aided design requires both technical and organizational prerequisites. Also [3, 25] argued that "virtual engineering" cannot lead to a significant improvements when put to existing processes. [26] argued that virtual prototyping also requires "virtual confidence". In [1] these preconditions are discussed in details. The next paragraphs give a short summary of them divided to dimensions of processes, organization and technology since they are often seen as the main dimensions of PLM.

Processes Implications: In the big picture, effective utilization of VR and IVP requires actually a paradigm change in engineering design and product development which are the essential processes that produce and utilize virtual product models. IVP should be understood as a pivotal process within PLM. The product process should be frontloaded so that e.g. assembly and maintainability can be analysed and improved using the virtual prototypes. Naturally, the frontloading affects how the design maturity, i.e. the 3D product model and structure should evolve in order to support all stakeholders.

Organizational Implications: It is important to recognize and respect the internal customers both inside the company and in the extended enterprise. Thus, a culture that encourages openness, knowledge sharing and sharing unfinished models as well as constructive feedback is required. IVP should be organized in dynamic multi-disciplinary teams that are not based on the formal line organizations or company boundaries, but rather on the required knowledge of all stakeholders. On the other hand, utilization of VR in IVP creates new roles such as VR developers and design review organizers. From the financial perspective, it should be understood that VR and IVP do not belong just to a single organizational unit (e.g. engineering design), but to whole business and product lifecycle.

Technological Implications: As VR and IVP are discussed here from a PLM perspective, implications to product model and data management are interesting. The above described changed and frontloaded product processes require capabilities for managing parallel product model structures. The virtual prototype structure often is different from the design structure (EBOM) and from e.g. manufacturing structure (MBOM) since it is typically a simplified and restricted model made for a certain purpose [1]. Effective utilization of IVP also requires efficient bi-directional data flow between VR and CAD/ EDM including data conversion and simplification as well as meta-data transfer. PLM should provide capabilities for giving feedback directly on the virtual prototype model and that information should be available for design engineers in their working environment i.e. CAD/EDM. A "baseline" or "as-built" model structure is proposed as a frame for information and knowledge flow as well [1, 23]. The upgrade solution of old product individual requires capability to transform and manage point clouds or other scanned 3D data in order to be utilized in VR, see more e.g. in [11].

3   Discussion

Utilization of VR and IVP can be considered as manifestations of industry digitalization. Digitalization increases transparency both internally and between companies [27], which is goal of Extended Enterprises. Term"Extended Enterprise" probably originates [28] in Chrysler Corporation where it was used for improving information exchange and decreasing cost in value chains. According [29] Extended Enterprise (EE) consists of collaborating upstream and downstream companies from raw material production even to end customers creating value to market. The EE approach requires a new organizational strategy aiming to overall optimization, deep collaboration, flexibility and change from linear and sequential process toward parallelism [30]. Practically, EE collaboration requires mechanisms that enable collaboration and communication between heterogenous organizations and systems [31]: Conceptual models, data-models, organizational structures and processes, and technical solutions like software tools. According to [28] this kind of development requires more than ad-hoc reactions to changing situations. It requires commonly accepted practices aiming to systemic and holistic knowledge management and business benefits [29]. Digitalization of EEs require recognition and analysis of relevant concepts and technologies [27].

This paper discusses how VR, IVP and PLM could possibly provide for the demanded collaboration mechanisms and systematic development of EEs. From the perspectives of problem solving and improved productivity, development of relationships between stakeholders is one of the most essential success factors [28]. Lowering the barriers between organizations and internal departments has been the goal for a long time, but in reality development has rather been towards more siloed organizations in order to simplify management in the world of ever more complicated products and complex business models [32].

The Germany based concept Industry4.0 is an example of value network digitalization including disruptive and social innovations. Concerning digitalization and Industry4.0, a key question is what kind of impacts supply chains will face in future [27]. VR has been seen as a means for effective collaboration [33]. Extended enterprise and IVP [1] as business and social concepts and VR as a piece of technology boost new innovations, because [32] they enable better communication and collaboration of people from different organizations with different backgrounds.

PLM as a Platform: Management of product lifecycle objects, collaboration between stakeholders, analysis of challenges, and making decisions are tasks of PLM [34]. Therefor VR as a technology and IVP as a methodology should be seen as part of companies' PLM models and architectures. [35] for instance has concluded that in automotive industry there is a growing demand for visual simulations which drives towards rethinking product processes and PLM.

As was reasoned before, service design is one of the major value creating processes where VR can be utilized. [36] proposed a value creation framework that could be expanded with VR. Servicization requires better integration of products and services, thus effective collaboration and digital continuity [37]. Compared to physical products, services are generally under-designed and ineffectively developed, because manufacturing companies still have a traditional engineering approach to the tangible part of engineering leaving the intangible service element to intuitive processes and methods [21, 38]. On the other hand, PLM increasingly focuses on the whole product lifecycle, both the product types and individuals, promising to manage all related data and information [21]. VR and IVP should be seen as enablers of effective product-service design when the data and processes really support them. Also [38] have discussed using VR for interaction between service providers and clients, and visualizing new service concepts.

The concept of "Closed-loop PLM" of [34] takes even greater upon the holistic product lifecycle closing the information gaps between different phases and processes of the product life both backwards and forwards [21]. This requires knowing all product lifecycle activities, how information is created, used, modified, accumulated and even utilized in the next generation products [34]. As described before, VR and IVP could help here too when integrated in PLM.

4 Conclusion

The proposed framework for utilization of VR includes the dimensions of product life-cycle stages, extended enterprise stakeholders and disciplines, value creation, managerial and technical implications. The framework was reflected with the industrial case studies and business benefits. From the extended enterprise perspective, VR and IVP enable improved knowledge sharing and transparency between the stakeholders. The proposed framework supports decision making and planning of VR investments in the context of PLM architecture development. This paper also contributes to research by discussing the closed-loop PLM concept, involving virtualization of product-service system development.

Acknowledgements. This research was funded and supported by Tekes, EU, Dimecc and participating organizations.

References

1. Leino, S.-P.: Reframing the value of virtual prototyping intermediary virtual prototyping – the evolving approach of virtual environments based virtual prototyping in the context of new product development and low volume production. Tampere University of Technology (2015). http://www.vtt.fi/inf/pdf/science/2015/S89.pdf
2. Leino, S.-P., Riitahuhta, A.: State of the art of virtual engineering based human-machine system lifecycle knowledge transfer and management. In: Proceedings of TMCE 2012, 7–11 May 2012, Karlsruhe, Germany, pp. 573–586 (2012)
3. Ovtcharova, J.G.: Virtual engineering: principles, methods and applications. In: International Design Conference - DESIGN 2010, pp. 1267–1274 (2010)
4. Arrighi, P.-A., Maurya, S., Mougenot, C.: Towards co-designing with users: a mixed reality tool for kansei engineering. In: Bouras, A., Eynard, B., Foufou, S., Thoben, K.-D. (eds.) PLM 2015. IAICT, vol. 467, pp. 751–760. Springer, Cham (2016). https://doi.org/10.1007/978-3-319-33111-9_68
5. Cecil, J., Kanchanapiboon, A.: Virtual engineering approaches in product and process design. Int. J. Adv. Manuf. Technol. **31**, 9–10 (2007)
6. Seth, A., Vance, J.M., Oliver, J.H.: Virtual reality for assembly methods prototyping: a review. Virtual Reality **15**(1), 5–20 (2011)
7. Aromaa, S., Leino, S., Viitaniemi, J., Jokinen, L., Kiviranta, S.: Benefits of the use of virtual environments in product design review meeting, pp. 355–364 (2012)
8. Bhatt, S., Tseng, F.H., Maranzana, N., Segonds, F.: Scientometric study of product lifecycle management international conferences: a decade overview. In: Bouras, A., Eynard, B., Foufou, S., Thoben, K.-D. (eds.) PLM 2015. IAICT, vol. 467, pp. 672–683. Springer, Cham (2016). https://doi.org/10.1007/978-3-319-33111-9_61
9. Leino, S.-P., Koivisto, T., Riitahuhta, A.: Value of virtual prototyping – a strategic resource based view. In: Proceedings of the 19th International Conference on Engineering Design (ICED 2013), pp. 249–261 (2013)
10. Videnoja, J.: Implementation of Virtual Prototyping in the Context of Product Update Projects and Low Volume Production. Tampere University of Technology (2016)
11. Leino, S.-P., Aromaa, S., Helin, K.: Rock crusher upgrade business from a PLM perspective. In: Grösser, S., Reyes-Lecuona, A., Granholm, G. (eds.) Dynamics of Long-Life Assets. Springer, Cham (2017). https://doi.org/10.1007/978-3-319-45438-2_12
12. Aromaa, S., Väänänen, K.: Suitability of virtual prototypes to support human factors/ ergonomics evaluation during the design. Appl. Ergon. **56**, 11–18 (2016)
13. Aromaa, S., Leino, S.-P., Viitaniemi, J.: Are companies ready for the revolution in design – modelling maturity for virtual prototyping. In: International Conference on Engineering Design (ICED 2013) (2013)
14. Hubka, V., Eder, E.: Theory of Technical Systems: A Total Concept Theory for Engineering Design. Springer, Heidelberg (1988). https://doi.org/10.1007/978-3-642-52121-8
15. Gomes de Sá, A., Zachmann, G.: Virtual reality as a tool for verification of assembly and maintenance processes. Comput. Graph. **23**, 389–403 (1999)
16. Lindskog, E., Berglund, J., Vallhagen, J., Johansson, B.: Visualization support for virtual redesign of manufacturing systems. Procedia CIRP **7**, 419–424 (2013)
17. Leino, S.-P., Pulkkinen, A.: Design for human – virtual engineering is a media for knowledge transfer. In: Proceedings of DESIGN 2012, The 12th International Design Conference, pp. 1507–1514 (2012)
18. Ottosson, S.: Virtual reality in the product development process. J. Eng. Des. **13**, 159–172 (2002). 823

19. Golovatchev, J., Schepurek, S.: Early prototyping in the digital industry: a management framework. In: Bouras, A., Eynard, B., Foufou, S., Thoben, K.-D. (eds.) PLM 2015. IAICT, vol. 467, pp. 335–343. Springer, Cham (2016). https://doi.org/10.1007/978-3-319-33111-9_31

20. Wiesner, S., Freitag, M., Westphal, I., Thoben, K.: Interactions between service and product lifecycle management. Procedia CIRP **30**, 36–41 (2015)

21. Wuest, T., Wellsandt, S., Thoben, K.-D.: Information quality in PLM: a production process perspective. In: Bouras, A., Eynard, B., Foufou, S., Thoben, K.-D. (eds.) PLM 2015. IAICT, vol. 467, pp. 826–834. Springer, Cham (2016). https://doi.org/10.1007/978-3-319-33111-9_75

22. Di Gironimo, G., Lanzotti, A., Tarallo, A.: A virtual reality framework for the design review of complex industrial assemblies: case study on the interiors of superjet 100 aircraft. In: Horváth, I., Rusak, Z. (eds.) Proceedings of TMCE 2014, 19–23 May 2014, Budapest, Hungary, pp. 1553–1560 (2014)

23. Leino, S.-P., Jokinen, L., Anttila, J.-P., Pulkkinen, A.: Case study on engineering change management and digital manufacturing. In: Bouras, A., Eynard, B., Foufou, S., Thoben, K.-D. (eds.) PLM 2015. IAICT, vol. 467, pp. 591–600. Springer, Cham (2016). https://doi.org/10.1007/978-3-319-33111-9_53

24. Zimmermann, P.: Virtual reality aided design: a survey of the use of VR in automotive industry. In: Talaba, D., Amditis, A. (eds.) Product Engineering - Tools and Methods based on Virtual Reality, pp. 277–296. Springer, Heidelberg (2008). https://doi.org/10.1007/978-1-4020-8200-9_13

25. Damgrave, R.G.J., Lutters, E., Drukker, J.W.: Rationalizing virtual reality based on manufacturing paradigms. Procedia CIRP **21**, 264–269 (2014)

26. Oscarsson, J., Jeusfeld, M.A., Jenefeldt, A.: Towards virtual confidence - extended product lifecycle management. In: Bouras, A., Eynard, B., Foufou, S., Thoben, K.-D. (eds.) PLM 2015. IAICT, vol. 467, pp. 708–717. Springer, Cham (2016). https://doi.org/10.1007/978-3-319-33111-9_64

27. Pfohl, H., Yahsi, B., Kurnaz, T.: The impact of industry 4.0 on the supply chain. In: Hamburg International Conference of Logistics (HICL) (2015)

28. Post, J.E., Preston, L.E., Parker, M.: Managing the extended enterprise: the new stakeholder view. Calif. Manage. Rev. **45**(I), 6–28 (2002)

29. Spekman, R.E., Davis, E.W.: Risky business: expanding the discussion on risk and the extended enterprise. Int. J. Phys. Distrib. Logist. Manage. **34**(5), 414–433 (2004)

30. Belkadi, F., Bernard, A.: Trust-based patterns for the management of inter-enterprises collaborations in context of extended enterprise. In: IFAC-PapersOnLine, pp. 1186–1191 (2015)

31. Chen, D., Vernadat, F.: Standards on enterprise integration and engineering — state of the art. Int. J. Comput. Integr. Manuf. **17**(3), 235–253 (2004)

32. Kane, G.C., Palmer, D., Phillips, A.N., Kiron, D., Buckley, N.: Strategy, not Technology, Drives Digital Transformation. Becoming a digitally mature enterprise. MIT Sloan Management Review (2015)

33. Brettel, M., Friederichsen, N., Keller, M., Rosenberg, M.: How virtualization, decentralization and network building change the manufacturing landscape: an industry 4.0 perspective. Int. J. Mech. Aerosp. Ind. Mechatron. Eng. **8**(1), 37–44 (2014)

34. Jun, H., Kiritsis, D., Xirouchakis, P.: Research issues on closed-loop PLM. Comput. Ind. **58**, 855–868 (2007)

35. Rehfeld, I.: Virtual reality as an integral part of product lifecycle management (PLM). In: Joint Virtual Reality Conference of EGVE-ICAT – EuroVR (2010)

36. Wang, P.P., Ming, X.G., Zheng, M.K.: A framework of value creation for industrial product-service. In: Bouras, A., Eynard, B., Foufou, S., Thoben, K.-D. (eds.) PLM 2015. IAICT, vol. 467, pp. 311–320. Springer, Cham (2016). https://doi.org/10.1007/978-3-319-33111-9_29
37. Mahut, F., Bricogne, M., Daaboul, J., Eynard, B.: Servicization of product lifecycle management: towards service lifecycle management. In: Bouras, A., Eynard, B., Foufou, S., Thoben, K.-D. (eds.) PLM 2015. IAICT, vol. 467, pp. 321–331. Springer, Cham (2016). https://doi.org/10.1007/978-3-319-33111-9_30
38. Cavalieri, S., Pezzotta, G.: Product – service systems engineering : state of the art and research challenges. Comput. Ind. **63**(4), 278–288 (2012)

Storytelling Platform for Virtual Museum Development: Lifecycle Management of an Exhibition

Chaowanan Khundam[✉] and Frédéric Noël

Univ. Grenoble Alpes, CNRS, G-SCOP, 38000 Grenoble, France
{chaowanan.khundam, frederic.noel}@g-scop.inpg.fr

Abstract. Digital heritage applications have been widely developed through Virtual Reality (VR) technologies as known as Virtual Museum (VM). Devices and digital contents are significantly increasing and may support interaction system to immerse users into VM. Due to rapid changes of technologies, a platform to develop an exhibition should support to change devices and also to optimize interaction system used in VM. However, usually, both devices organization and contents structure on a platform is still lacking efficient management to support alternative interaction in general. The development and maintenance process of a VM exhibition must be undertaken in an integrated mode. We propose a storytelling platform for developing virtual exhibition with high-level abstractions providing adaptive interaction system. An exhibition's lifecycle management will be useful for maintenance and service in VM when technologies evolved over time. Our framework has 2 sub-processes: development of storytelling platform and development of interaction system. A storytelling template provides a flexible service to manage an exhibition and adapt it to various devices and interaction techniques. Interaction system evaluation will be deployed to maintain an exhibition and support user learning in VM.

Keywords: Virtual reality · Virtual museum · Digital storytelling
Interaction system

1 Introduction

In digital content era, thousands physical bricks of information are converted to become a digital content. There are many devices and technologies which allow users to access data and to visualize and to interact with virtual world [1]. Virtual reality (VR) technologies have been used for various purposes. Virtual museum is one branch that applies VR for demonstrating actual objects or architecture with mock-up as three-dimensional models [2]. Virtual exhibition applies VR concepts with multimedia information and computer graphic technology. The design and development of virtual museum's exhibition also considers interactivity in the system to allow users to learn about collection of history with content that they are interested in [2]. Virtual museum becomes a large multimedia center where users easily access information and can convey the contents through interaction between users [3]. It allows users to gain knowledge from the

© IFIP International Federation for Information Processing 2017
Published by Springer International Publishing AG 2017. All Rights Reserved
J. Ríos et al. (Eds.): PLM 2017, IFIP AICT 517, pp. 416–426, 2017.
https://doi.org/10.1007/978-3-319-72905-3_37

museum more easily but the keystone remains a good storytelling. We need a storytelling to drive virtual environment behavior while the interaction is the modality to follow this story. There is a kind of disconnection between the initial specification of the exhibition and its implementation and delivery. A good product development expects to fill this gap.

Storytelling becomes a major part to create interactive content for a virtual museum and use stories as instruments for suspenseful knowledge transferring [4]. In order to create a virtual museum exhibition, storytelling platforms will be the tool to help developer defining elements in a scene and makes stories. Non-linear storytelling is a kind of interactivity content [5], users get involved into the story to interact with a content. To design and develop an exhibition as non-linear storytelling, the contents will be considered in term of user interaction where interaction system is concerned. Here, devices and interaction techniques are also considered for designing interactive contents. Most of virtual museum's exhibitions have been designed limited to selected devices. Maintenance and service of interaction system will be restricted to the contents of all development process that will be complicated for exhibition management due to the fact that there is no lifecycle management for an exhibition to support technologies change over time.

Therefore, storytelling platform acts as the major specification of any exhibition. We propose high-level abstraction to define all event and action in a scene that must be translated into low-level technical user interactions. Thus, end user (visitor) interactions will respect high-level abstraction whatever devices are finally used. The platform aims to be part of the lifecycle management of an exhibition.

2 Related Works

Authoring tools are majority to support an application development. We focus on manual narrative authoring [6] and interaction system is also concerned. Hence, the platform will provide not only story generation but also VR interaction system. Storytelling platform for virtual museum exhibition is related to VR platform which mainly provides functions to develop virtual environments and device plugin support. Educational game-authoring tool is another platform concerned to storytelling with an enjoyment goal. Advantages and disadvantages of each platform will be considered respect to application in the field of virtual museum exhibition.

2.1 VR Platforms

There are several platforms for creating a VE by a developer who handle several kinds of devices. VR Juggler [7] is a virtual platform providing a virtual reality environment independent of operating system. This platform supports many graphics engines and network distribution through the NetJuggler module but no high-level support for application distribution. AVANGO/NG [8] is a distributed scene graph framework. It applies a generic field container programming interface based on OpenSceneGraph and develops an entire application with Python scripting support. Vizard [9] is VR toolkit for interactive 3D content, scripting with Python undertaking many commercial devices and also achieving extraordinary rendering including multi-user, clustering, and multi-channel abilities. InVRs [10] implements Collaborative Virtual Environments (CVEs) approach in the form of a highly extensible, flexible, and modular framework with pre-defined navigation and interaction techniques. Configurable via XML, it has a network distributed virtual world using OpenSG as a scene graph engine. pSIVE [11] platform allows easy setting up of VEs with interactive content and also has a generic model to be applied in different contexts by non-expert users. pSIVE is a good platform to study device switching with pre-defined interaction techniques that selection and navigation techniques will be used to compare potential of each device. 3DVIA Studio [12] is an interactive 3D application platform by LUA scripting language. There are many GUI tools to work on models and animations in scenes. Providing integration with VR/AR systems and also realistic interactive 3D by advance rendering, physics and animation engine support to create immersive virtual reality project. Unity3D [13] is high perform-ance 3D rendering and physics engine for game developer which can be applied for creating VR application. With various device plugin supports, Unity3D is able to export an application towards many operating systems, useful for interaction techniques studying. However, the application development remains based on pre-selected device. To switch device we have to edit programming part for a correct application control due to devices restriction.

Most VR platforms are proposed to be a tool for VEs development and support developer to handle devices configuration. However, storytelling to support and to organize story structure is still lacking. There is some platform providing high-level abstraction to define object behaviors in general for interaction which could be improved as educational game or storytelling platform.

2.2 Educational Game-Authoring Tools

WEEV [4] is an educational game creation framework. The system is built upon <e-Adventure> [14], a game authoring platform. WEEV implemented three tools to edit main element which are Actor editor, World editor and Story editor using visual programming language to represent a story based on interaction between user and game. Thinking Worlds [15] is an authoring platform for VEs focused on creating structured learning experiences. It is a commercial tool that facilitates development of serious 3D games. This platform attempts to create more complex scenes which required more 3D rendering engine and also camera and character control through the scene. Adventure Author [16] is a platform based on visual programming language as WEEV is. The development of this platform focuses on linear stories without real interactivity. Thus, it is easy to create educational stories rather than games. StoryTec [17] is another visual programming language like Adventure Author for serious game creation. However, it supports to create non-linear stories to encourage creativity rather than educational game. StoryTec has powerful expressiveness for story creation via a Story editor enabling non-linear stories. Storytelling Alice [18] is proposed to teach programming concept for students but also provides many features to create animated stories. Story-telling Alice includes high-level animation that enables users to program interaction between elements which provides 3D character and scenery with custom animations. Adventure Game Studio [19] and Adventure Maker [20] are platforms for game developer with 2D animation support. In contrast, these platforms do not provide tools for storytelling or educational features which are not targeted to educator. These platforms have GUI editor to support content editing on the scene based on point and click gaming. If we considered both, Table 1. shows educational game-authoring tools have abilities for developing structured learning and VR platform lacks. By the way, educational game-authoring tools tried to advance their engine to be high performance in 3D while most VR platforms support these features. The creation of an exhibition in virtual museum needs to have a storytelling platform which supports of educational features for user learning but also advanced 3D engine and device switching. Therefore, it would be great to combine good features of each platform together. Furthermore, development process is still lacking of lifecycle management which should be considered into storytelling platform. The process should carry out according to product lifecycle phase as well as conceive, design, realize and service. The design of a storytelling platform for virtual museum exhibition will have methodologies based on exhibition lifecycle management which improves exhibition development process as described in next section.

Table 1. Existing environment capacities

Platform	Main approach	High-level	Storytelling support	Animation support	Multi-users	Device support	Interaction technique	Complexity
VR Juggler	XML Scripting	No	No	Yes	Yes	Many	Scripting	High
AVANGO/NG	Scripting	Yes	No	No	Yes	Many	NA	High
Vizard	Scripting + GUI Editor	Yes	NA	Yes	Yes	Many	Scripting	High
InVRs	XML Scripting	NA	NA	Yes	Yes	Many	Pre-defined	High
3DVIA Studio	LUA Scripting	Yes	No	Yes	No	Desktop	Point and Click	High
pSIVE	GUI Editor	No	No	NA	Yes	Many	Pre-defined	Low
WEEV	Visual Language	Yes	Yes	Yes, 2D	No	Desktop	Point and Click	Low/ High
Thinking Worlds	Hybrid	Yes	Yes	Yes	No	Desktop	Point and Click	Low
Adventure Author	GUI Editor	NA	Yes	NA	No	Desktop	Point and Click	High
StoryTec	Visual Language	Yes	Yes	NA	No	Desktop	Point and Click	NA
Storytelling Alice	Visual Language	Yes	Yes	Yes	No	Desktop	Point and Click	Low
Adventure Game Studio	GUI Editor	No	NA	Yes, 2D	No	Desktop	Point and Click	High
Adventure Maker	GUI Editor	No	NA	No	No	Desktop	Point and Click	High
Unity3D	GUI Editor	NA	NA	Yes	Yes	Many	Scripting	Very High

3 Storytelling Platform

As a top–down design of engineering workflow, storytelling platform is focused on high-level functional requirements. High-level abstraction is decomposed into lower level structures and specifications until the physical implementation layer is reached. The specification phase is the definition of exhibition requirement. This starts with the design of scene components, defining basic entities and some event controlling and then high-level behaviors will be defined as action logics. From this specification, storytelling platform will be developed. Then the design phase is where the details design and development starts. An exhibition will be developed on the platform as a storytelling project. Next it comes the realization phase; physical implementation is handling here. The complete project will be launched into the low-level functions where interaction system is used. Finally, the service phase serves for interaction system providing system maintenance as well as reuse of project. Collaborative Virtual Environments (CVEs) may support this phase to transfer exhibition project to a specific interaction system. When technology is changed former exhibition project is transferred again for new technology.

3.1 Development of Storytelling Platform

The design of scene components will be applied to develop storytelling platform. The Viewer is a tool to display virtual environment in 3D. All entities are handled in the Asset manager while event and action part will be specified in the Event editor. Here, high-level abstract model will be defined into a scene with events and actions corresponding to storytelling needs. When all entities in a scene have been determined, an execution part will be addressed by a runtime engine to perform interactive stories in real time and interact at low-level connection. The translation between the high-level abstract model and low-level connections should be automated so far as we can do it. Figure 1. Shows the process and architecture of platform which has the following basic components:

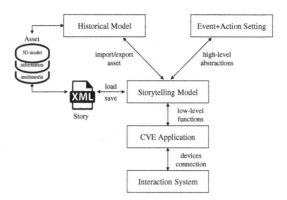

Fig. 1. Exhibition development architecture

A Viewer: A viewer is a display window to present entities as virtual environments and cooperate with Asset manager for entities editing. Viewer provides graphic engine to handle rendering and lighting in the scene. There are 2 modes that use the same window which are storytelling mode for editing and runtime mode to present the result of storytelling mode.

Asset manager: Asset manager is a tool panel to carry out all entities imported into the scene. When each model has been imported, entities will be loaded into a manager panel. Entities can be a representation of a building, artifact, actor, information or avatar. These will keep entities as scene graph data structure.

Event editor: Event and action have been designed already then implemented to the visual setting in the Storytelling platform. Event editor provides GUI panel to connect each event component together: Entity, Event and Action. Entity will be selected directly in the 3D scene while events and actions are selected in a GUI template. Condition is added into an event for flexibility of logic assignment to be a rule for Action. Event editor is the tool for defining high-level abstractions for every scene, events and actions for all entities provide a common template for every storytelling.

Runtime engine: Provides runtime mode in the Viewer to test the result from storytelling mode when event and action have been assigned. Event and action are interpreted to execute and perform entities in the scene in real-time interaction. We see how the story is going on and if interaction works well or not. Low-level functions can be implemented and tested on this stage. Before to execute the runtime engine, the connection with low-level interaction system is exported.

Low-level connection is a part of a top-down design workflow. High-level abstraction is decomposed into a lower level for physical implementation. This is compatible with vertical transformation as propose in Model Driven approaches [21, 22]. High-level abstraction related to the entity as defined while event and action allow developer to connect the device which is independent of event setting anyway. Here, storytelling platform enables device changing through event and action by Event editor and low-level functions are applied by interaction follows device's characteristic as shown in Fig. 2.

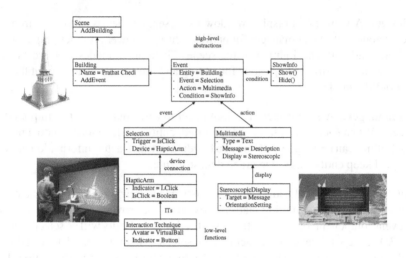

Fig. 2. Vertical transformation as model driven approach

3.2 Development of Interaction System

Interaction system on our Storytelling platform uses Collaborative Virtual Environments (CVEs) to be the tool for running an application (This tool is internally developed at the laboratory). In order to connect devices to an application, CVE is expected to manage device connection in the system through a CVE's server. Moreover, interaction techniques (ITs) are methods to let user perform a task within VEs via user interface. ITs are influenced by input devices, but the same device may be used for many ITs for the same task [23]. On the other hand, it may be possible to implement a given IT using several different input devices. ITs studying is essential for system development to use of various devices and to improve system when new technologies arise. Therefore, development of interaction system through CVE will support exhibition lifecycle management especially during maintenance and service phase.

ITs design: Interaction tasks are the method to interact with VEs while ITs are the way to perform interaction tasks. To design ITs, the first step will begin with ITs classification. Universal interaction tasks are partitioned into separable subtasks, each of which represents technique component calls taxonomy. Taxonomy is not only a characterization of interaction tasks, but also as a design space. Taxonomy is the intermediate-level of ITs implementation to the lower level. In our Storytelling platform, interaction tasks are separated to be 3 genres of ITs which are Selection, Manipulation and Navigation [21].

Device setting on platform: In Event editor, only connected device can be chosen and then ITs will be selected for managing scene behavior. A same input device can select different IT already designed and the same ITs can be used with different input device also. Storytelling platform provides ITs management. Some ITs are probably reuse with other devices by keeping all ITs into a database from where each device can be retrieved.

Device management: Usually, CVE is used for collaboration and interaction of multiple users to work together on VR application [24]. However, CVE does not provide only multiple users in the system, but also enable using multiple devices together in the same application. Thus, CVE is the tool which facilitates flexibility when using devices and supports device management of Storytelling platform. Interaction system of our platform will address low-level implementation of device which supports devices service while high-level abstractions maintain the content events and actions in the exhibition.

4   Case Study

We expect to build an exhibition about history of Prathat temple, the crucial temple model of South East Asia. There have been various legends of Prathat temple. One legend mentioned that the Buddha relics (the teeth of the Lord Buddha) have been kept inside. The relics were moved from Tontha Buri by Prince Thanakuman and Princess Hem-chala. It has been assumed that the original form of Prathat was Mondop, a structure with four arches and a pyramidal roof topped with five tiers as Srivijaya style. Then, in 1700BE, Theravade doctrine of Lanka has been prosperous and spread to Nakhon Si Thammarat, as a result Chedi of Theravade was constructed to cover the original one. This becomes a typical model of Theravade in the south of Thailand and influentially spreads to adjacent areas.

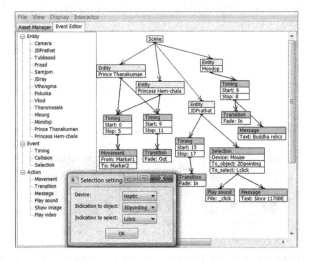

Fig. 3. An example of Event editor on drag and drop canvas and selection setting for device and IT management.

The storyteller expects to make an exhibition to tell this story with Storytelling platform by transforming history in term of text to be an interactive learning exhibition. First, all entities models are loaded into the database as historical model which are able to edit transformation value within the scene. The story is modelled at a high-level abstraction by Event editor which has 3 main components: Entity, Event and Action. Each component is drag and drop node on a canvas. We make relations by linking nodes from Entity to Action through Event which is editable on setting menu. The example scene in Fig. 3 has 4 Entities which are two Actors Prince Thanakuman and Princess Hem-chala and two buildings named Mondop and JDPrathat. At beginning of the scene, we set two actors moving from Marker1 to Marker2 with 5 s duration to present the relics were moved from Tontha Buri by them. When approach to Marker2, Mondop will appear to show the original form of Prathat which kept the relics inside and these actors will fade away at the seconds 11. Then the building JDPrathat will be faded-in and we set more input event by adding Selection with respect to device. When this model is selected, the scene will play clicking sound and show message as defined.

Selection event will depend on selected device which can be setting up the interaction technique to select the Building. Here, indication to object is a method to point to any object while indication to select is a selection method. These parameters of IT have been defined respect to device which can choose directly from setting menu. When the device is switched to other one and completely defines new IT. All actions that related to the event still work even device has been changed by flexibility of high-level design. In this example, Selection defined a mouse to be a default device. This platform allows story-teller to change device to other one e.g., a Haptic arm and assign indication to object and to select which calls IT. Although storyteller would like to use the old device, the platform provides capabilities to manage IT directly and still using the same logic. Finally, specification of ITs will be translated into executable interaction system follows selected devices. Figure 4. Shows high-level abstraction can be transformed the story to various devices.

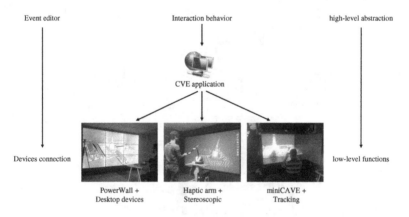

Fig. 4. Transformation of storytelling model to low-level functions with various devices.

5   Conclusion

We propose new methodologies for exhibition development in VM to support its management. We believe that it will also support the whole exhibition lifecycle. Devices organization and contents structure are addressed by the Storytelling platform which has efficient management to support alternative interaction in general. Engineering work-flow as a top–down design provides a high- level interaction abstraction model where storytelling models specific interaction behavior to drive interaction in a scene. Devices and ITs are handled through a CVE.

According to product lifecycle phase, concept design is supported by our Storytelling platform which specifies the exhibition interaction. Service phase is processed after an evaluation method to keep an exhibition maintained and operational. We claim that Storytelling platform provides an adaptive interaction system which will supports user learning when applied to VM. This implementation is useful to deploy not only for the development of VM exhibition, but also for industrial engineering where interactive content and interaction system are required.

At this step the overall architecture of our exhibition development system is ready. A first demonstrator provides a storytelling modeler and we have a first converter of a story into a runtime environment. We continue developing this platform and we will analyze devices and ITs for each story to classify their specific potential to support user learning in VM.

Acknowledgments. This research was supported by Franco-Thai scholarship (French Government) and Walailak University, Thailand.

References

1. Styliani, S., Fotis, L., Kostas, K., Petros, P.: Virtual museums, a survey and some issues for consideration. J. Cult. Herit. **10**(4), 520–528 (2009)
2. Pujol. L.: Archaeology, museums and virtual reality. Revista digital de humanidades, UOC (2004). (http://www.uoc.edu/humfil/articles/eng/pujol0304/pujol0304.pdf)
3. Walczak, K., Cellary, W., White, M.: Virtual museum exhibitions. IEEE Computer **39**(3), 93–95 (2006)
4. Marchiori, E.J., Torrente, J., Del Blanco, Á., Moreno, G.P., Sancho, P., Fernández, M.B.: A narrative metaphor to facilitate educational game authoring. Comput. Educ. **58**(1), 590–599 (2012)
5. Spaniol, M., Klamma, R., Sharda, N., Jarke, M.: Web-based learning with non-linear multimedia stories. In: Liu, W., Li, Q., Lau, R.W.H. (eds.) ICWL 2006. LNCS, vol. 4181, pp. 249–263. Springer, Heidelberg (2006). https://doi.org/10.1007/11925293_23
6. Kybartas, B., Bidarra, R.: A survey on story generation techniques for authoring computational narratives. IEEE Trans. Comput. Intell. AI Games **9**, 239–253 (2016)
7. Bierbaum, A., Just, A., Hartling, P., Meinert, K., Baker, A., Cruz, N.C.: VR Juggler: a virtual platform for virtual reality application development. In: Proceedings of IEEE Virtual Reality, pp. 89–96 (2001)
8. Kuck, R., Wind, R., Riege, J., Bogen, K.M., Birlinghoven, S.: Improving the avango vr/ar framework: lessons learned. In: Workshop Virtuelle und Erweiterte Realität, pp. 209–220 (2008)
9. WorldViz: Vizard VR Software Toolkit. http://www.worldviz.com/products/vizard
10. Anthes, C., Volkert, J.: inVRs – a framework for building interactive networked virtual reality systems. In: Gerndt, M., Kranzlmüller, D. (eds.) HPCC 2006. LNCS, vol. 4208, pp. 894–904. Springer, Heidelberg (2006). https://doi.org/10.1007/11847366_92

11. Souza, D., Dias, P., Santos, D., Santos, B.S.: Platform for setting up interactive virtual environments. In: IS&T/SPIE Electronic Imaging, International Society for Optics and Photonics (2014)
12. 3DVIA Studio, Dassualt Systemes. http://www.3dvia.com/studio
13. Unity3D game engine. https://unity3d.com
14. Torrente, J., Del Blanco, Á., Marchiori, E.J., Moreno, G.P., Fernández, M.B.: <e-Adventure>: introducing educational games in the learning process. In: 2010 IEEE Education Engineering (EDUCON), pp. 1121–1126 (2010)
15. Thinking Worlds. http://www.thinkingworlds.com
16. Robertson, J., Nicholson, K.: Adventure author: a learning environment to support creative design. In: Proceedings of the 6th International Conference on Interaction Design and Children, pp. 37–44. ACM (2007)
17. Göbel, S., Salvatore, L., Konrad, R.: StoryTec: a digital storytelling platform for the authoring and experiencing of interactive and non-linear stories. In: Automated Solutions for Cross Media Content and Multi-channel Distribution, AXMEDIS 2008, pp. 103–110. IEEE (2008)
18. Kelleher, C., Pausch, R., Kiesler, S.: Storytelling alice motivates middle school girls to learn computer programming. In: Proceedings of the SIGCHI Conference on Human Factors in Computing Systems, pp. 1455–1464. ACM (2007)
19. Adventure Game Studio. https://www.adventuregamestudio.co.uk
20. Adventure Maker. http://www.adventuremaker.com
21. Calvary, G., Coutaz, J., Thevenin, D., Limbourg, Q., Bouillon, L., Vanderdonckt, J.: A unifying reference framework for multi-target user interfaces. Interact. Comput. **15**(3), 289–308 (2003)
22. Coutaz, J., Calvary, G.: HCI and software engineering for user interface plasticity. In: Handbook: Fundamentals, Evolving Technologies, and Emerging Applications, Human-Computer Interaction, 3 edn., pp. 1195–1220 (2012)
23. Bowman, D.A.: Interaction techniques for common tasks in immersive virtual environments. Doctoral dissertation, Georgia Institute of Technology (1999)
24. Wright, T., Madey, G.: A survey of collaborative virtual environment technologies. University of Notre Dame-USA, Technical report, pp. 1–16 (2008)

Modular Design and Products

Automatic Configuration of Modularized Products

Joel Sauza-Bedolla[1], Stefano Amato[2], Alfredo Fantetti[2], Andrea Radaelli[2], Alex Saja[2],
Gianluca D'Antonio[1(✉)], and Paolo Chiabert[1]

[1] Politecnico di Torino, corso Duca degli Abruzzi 24, 10129 Turin, Italy
{joel.sauza,gianluca.dantonio,paolo.chiabert}@polito.it
[2] Alta Scuola Politecnica, corso Duca degli Abruzzi 24, 10129 Turin, Italy
{stefano.amato,alfredo.fantetti,andrea.radaelli,
alex.saja}@asp-poli.it

Abstract. In business to business manufacturing, a major competitive advantage comes from the personalization of the product for the customer. In order to customize a product, companies go through a long process of customer interviews and specialized product development processes: this results in a time-consuming design phase and in a highly variable production process. In this paper, a method to improve the efficiency of product development and manufacturing, keeping a high degree of customization, is presented. A standardization effort is performed to identify a set of interchangeable components and to define a set of functional constraints. The consequences of such standardization are a dramatic reduction of the time expected to design and produce an item, as well as in lowered degree of variability of both the manufacturing process and the warehouses content. The presented methodology has been applied to a manufacturer of ink dispensing systems.

Keywords: Mass customization · Modularization · Product configurator
Standardization

1 Introduction

Manufacturing companies are facing the well-known antithesis between high product variety and fast delivery time. Highly-customized products must be designed and produced into an increasingly competitive environment, and must satisfy the multifaceted needs of their customers; this leads to an intense effort for continuous and fast re-designs [1]. In the last years, different authors [2, 3] pointed out that a product configurator is an effective tool to support the response to this contrast. Customer requirements are quickly individuated, while his choices are guided through an automatic process that ends with a finite number of standardized products. Hence, the re-design effort for the company is severely reduced, whereas, from the customer perspective, service perception and satisfaction are improved [4]. An automatic product configuration also supports some central phases of Product Life cycle Management (PLM), in terms of possibility to automatically generate Bill of Materials (BOM), and to integrate internal functions of the company [5]. However, although these tools can be extremely effective on both

© IFIP International Federation for Information Processing 2017
Published by Springer International Publishing AG 2017. All Rights Reserved
J. Ríos et al. (Eds.): PLM 2017, IFIP AICT 517, pp. 429–439, 2017.
https://doi.org/10.1007/978-3-319-72905-3_38

the internal and external performances, their implementation usually needs non-trivial efforts and money investment, and thus become prohibitive for small-sized companies. The present paper aims to develop a scalable methodology for the implementation of a product configurator, mainly devoted to Small-Medium Enterprises (SMEs) designing industrial machinery and scalable products whose structure can be decomposed in para-metrical modules. The methodology is validated through a case-study: a product config-urator has been implemented into a small company that assemblies machines for mixing inks.

The rest of the paper is organized as follows: the state of the art analysis is discussed in Sect. 2. The methodology for the implementation of a product configurator developed in this work is presented in Sect. 3. The case-study and the validation of the model are presented in Sect. 4. Conclusive remarks and hints for future developments are presented in Sect. 5.

2 State of the Art

Product configuration has been an area of active research in the last years. Several ways to implement a product configurator have been proposed; depending on the chosen approach, different cost, development time and effort, configurator quality can be achieved. Felferning et al. [6] showed a method based on modeling the product using the Unified Modeling Language (UML) that can then be interpreted automatically by a configuration engine. Haugh et al. [7] compared seven different strategies to develop product configurators, each with its advantages and drawbacks for handling projects according to complexity, duration, and risks. Yang et al. [8] presented an approach for encoding configuration models into the Dynamic Constraint Satisfaction Problems (DCSP). Gembarski and Lachmayer [9] introduced a process model for defining multi-variant products. Wang et al. [10] described a method for modularizing existing products improving design efficiency. Although these works deploy different approaches, the following basic steps can be identified:

Step 1. *Preliminary analysis.* This step consists in interviewing product experts and consulting company documentation to retrieve information about the knowl-edge and reasoning process underlying product development as well as on the projects formerly dealt.

Step 2. *Knowledge representation.* This step consists in structuring the acquired infor-mation in a form that a computer system can utilize to solve a task. According to the chosen representation the literature classifies product configurators in the following categories [11, 12]:

- Rule-based: product knowledge is expressed as a set of rules or implications. The system can draw conclusions using the logical process of deduction.
- Model-based: the product is represented through decomposable entities and interactions between their elements.
- Case-based: the knowledge necessary for reasoning is a set of records of configurations sold to former customers. The system attempts to solve the

current configuration problem by finding a similar, previously solved problem and adapting it to the new requirements.

Step 3.   *Configurator implementation*. The last step consists in implementing a software able to take in input the customer requirements, analyze them, and provide all the product information and specification necessary to validate the design and start the manufacturing phase.

Nevertheless, many investigations about the implementation of product configurators were focused on specific case-studies, and lacked generality. In particular, such researches mainly focused on the development of company-customized product configurators [13], sometimes with obsolete techniques [14]. Custom-built software can offer a direct and more effective improvement of firms' performance, but this implementation technique certainly requires an expensive Information Technology (IT) consultancy support [2]. This investment often discourages SMEs that aim to implement a product configurator.

Thus, an analysis on the support that new technologies and tools can provide in developing novel, cheaper solutions can be valuable. In particular, the present work aims to extend the state of the art by presenting a standard methodology applicable, even through low cost tools, to SMEs that aim to implement a product configurator to improve their performances by preserving a high product variety, and ensuring compliance with delivery time schedules.

3   Methodology

The three steps summarized in the previous section play a crucial role in integrating a product configurator within a company. However, the methodologies proposed in literature do not take into account the standardization tasks: this step plays a key role, especially in SMEs offering products with high customization or flexibility levels. Therefore, a four-steps methodology (shown in Fig. 1) is proposed here: the standardization tasks are placed between the Preliminary analysis and the Knowledge representation. The description of each step and the corresponding sub-steps is provided in the following.

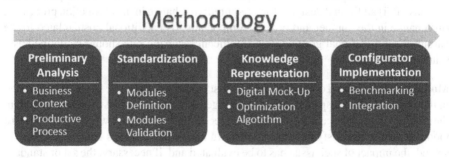

Fig. 1. Schematic of the methodology to achieve a product configurator presented in this work.

3.1 Preliminary Analysis

The analysis of the company's requirements for the configurator is performed with a two-sided approach: an analysis of the external factors (business analysis) and internal aspects (productive processes).

Business Context Analysis. The preliminary analysis begins with a deep analysis the core business of the company. A significant timespan must be identified to study company processes: internal tasks must be decomposed, in order to understand the reasons of possible issues, time wastes, and delivery delay. Further, the communication channels between the company and its customers are studied: an overview of customers' requirements and constraints provides a basic idea about the general architecture of the configurator and its interface with the users.

Productive Process Analysis. A deep analysis of the products delivered in the observation timespan is necessary to define the features most frequently requested by the customers and the solutions most frequently provided by the company. This statistical analysis provides valuable information and suggestions for the subsequent standardization step. Moreover, this approach allows to directly evaluate the design efforts performed in the development of each product variant, outlining the amount of resources that could be saved by implementing a standard product configurator.

3.2 Standardization

The statistical analysis previously performed provides data useful to define a number of frequently adopted elements. In fact, one of the main goals of the product configurator is to reduce product variety to a limited set of variants. Therefore, the recurring elements must be standardized in order to avoid the proliferation of such variants: they are decomposed into elementary functional blocks and sets of standard modules are defined. Two phases are necessary:

Modules definition. The results of the preliminary analysis highlight the most frequently used components and the impact that each variant to the standard product has in terms of: (i) additional design efforts required; (ii) change in the production processes; (iii) change in the number and type of components; (iv) additional costs related to the variant. Each functional group with a significant recurring rate should be defined as a standard module.

Modules validation. To validate the set of standard modules, the projects performed in the observation timespan (or even in a longer time interval) must be checked again: the requirements of the customers have to be reconsidered, to check whether the standard modules enable to satisfy such necessities. In case some requests cannot be properly solved, the impact of such issue has to be evaluated and, if necessary, the set of standard modules must be enlarged.

3.3 Knowledge Representation

The objective of this stage is to create a library of reusable parts to virtually represent the product and to display a mockup of the product to the client. Moreover, in order to allow the easy evaluation of product variants, an optimization algorithm must be employed.

Digital Mock-Up. The standard modules have to be implemented into a library of parts and components designed with a modeling software, possibly in 3D. Nowadays, many CAD software allow connecting detailed parametric technical drawings of each part into a variable assembly. These platforms can store all the components, modules and assemblies, permitting to modify with basic instructions their main geometrical and appearance features. This possibility can be used to apply optional changes to a standard product, to obtain fast 3D product representations.

Optimization algorithm. One of the main issues in the final product definition is to find the best combination of modules according to the defined requirements. Hence, the definition of an optimization algorithm is necessary. A constrained optimization problem must be solved, where the modules are decision variables and the user's requirements represent the problem constraints. A quantity f to be optimized must be chosen. Possible choices for the objective quantity may include space occupation or economical costs. Therefore, for a given set of input requirements, the algorithm should find the best combination of modules which optimizes the objective quantity.

3.4 Configurator Implementation

The last step of the methodology consists of: the definition of the requirements of the system, the choice of the configurator software, and the implementation of the formalized knowledge. Selecting a configurator software already available on the market allows to exploit the advantages of software reuse [15]: lower production and maintenance costs, shorter implementation time, and increased software quality. Instead, creating a completely new configurator software would require an unaffordable financial effort for small and medium enterprises.

Benchmarking. In order to choose the software that best fits the needs of the company, all the existing configurator platforms must be considered. A feature matrix to compare the available alternatives must be deployed: each row is one of the requirements provided by the Preliminary analysis, which can be weighted according to a priority scale. Then the alternative which satisfies the most "Must have" requirements is selected, if the price is considered acceptable by the company; in case of ties, the alternative having the most "Nice to have" requirements is chosen. An example of such feature matrix is presented in the case study discussion.

Integration. In order to provide effective results, the configuration system must be well integrated into the company business processes as well as with the other IT systems deployed. First, the configurator must support the automated generation of sales quotes and other specification documents, such as blueprints, BOM, and detailed product specifications. Further, the configurator can be required to communicate with other information systems, such as: the ERP, for order fulfillment, or PDM systems, for archiving custom product variants.

4 Case Study

The methodology presented in Sect. 3 has been applied to a small manufacturing company in the area of Turin (Italy) that produces integrated dispensing systems for ink, paint and chemical dispensing and mixing. Due to an increasing product demand, the company decided to improve the design and production efficiency for a family of products. Thus, the implementation of a product configurator has been considered as a main objective by the company board and the presented methodology devoted to SMEs has been applied. In the following, data concerning machines specification will be anonymized to preserve industrial secret.

4.1 Preliminary Analysis

Business Context Analysis. The complete business analysis of the company is described in [16]. In the following, key aspects are presented. The company customers are both large and small businesses, which require automated dispensing systems for a huge array of applications. In particular, a subset of the company products has been considered, with prices ranging between 30-45 k€ and need long times for delivery (approximately 10 weeks), since the majority of them are actually tailor made in an engineering-to-order (ETO) approach.

Productive Process Analysis. When a customer requests a quotation, a company engineer is chosen as project chief and is in charge of designing a machine fulfilling the requested requirements. Since the company employs several engineers with different expertise, the lack of a standard design methodology leads to a huge product variability: the same set of requirements provided to different engineers can result in final products with different configurations. This approach leads to design and manufacturing inefficiencies. The years 2014-15 have been selected as observation timespan: in this period, 18 machines of the selected family have been designed and produced.

The requirements for each order and the solutions provided by the company have been carefully analyzed. An example of typical structure for a machine is shown in Fig. 2. Product analysis led to the following results. First, the dispensing head – which releases the final ink mixture into a small bucket – was found to be usually placed at one extremity of the machine. Second, two kinds of raw material containers, with different volume, are mostly used: they will be labeled Large Container (LC) and Small Container (SC). Third, one pump per each container is placed to carry the raw material towards the dispensing head; two types of pumps (A and B) are generally used for the two types of containers respectively.

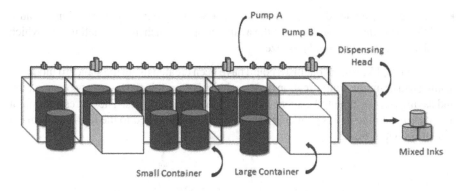

Fig. 2. Representation of a machine based on the non-modular design approach.

The main design constraint was the maximum encumbrance of the machine imposed by the customer. Each designer dealt with this issue by proposing steel structures of different sizes. Furthermore, project chiefs stated that three kinds of requirements need particular attention: (i) Topology: space occupation and containers accessibility; (ii) Layout: position occupied by the different containers (LC should be close to the dispensing head) and pumps capacity; (iii) Maximum allowable structure length: profile section resistance, maximum loads.

4.2 Standardization

Modules definition. 15 modules were defined. Among the different constraints, topology was the most limiting in the design process, as the machine size is often in contrast with the space management of the facilities where it is to be installed. Each module consists in a structural part, a set of pumps, hydraulic and electrical connections and room for the containers. The modules differ for:

- type of containers: the modules can host (i) only LC; (ii) only SC; (ii) both the two types of containers;
- number of containers: three different standard lengths, based on the size of the steel profiles have been used (labeled L1, L2, L3);
- accessibility: modules can host containers (i) on both the sides or (ii) on a single side, for example to support installations close to wall.

Modules validation. The 18 analyzed projects have been redesigned through the set of standard modules, with the following results:

- 7 projects were totally accomplished, with a space occupation close to the original project, with a max difference of 1% (~ 10 cm).
- 7 projects were accomplished with an overlength smaller than 10%; the maximum surplus was equal to 70 cm on a 8.2 m machine;
- 1 project was accomplished with overlength greater than 10%;

- 3 projects were considered to be not solvable with standard modularization, because of the particular conformation of the available space, such as too small rooms, which did not comply with modules size.

Therefore, 15 projects out of 18 could have been created using the standard modules, leading to a dramatic simplification in the technical office job, the inventory organization and saving a lot of time to be spent in more challenging designs. The representation of a standardized machine is shown in Fig. 3; it can be compared to the non-standardized design shown in Fig. 2.

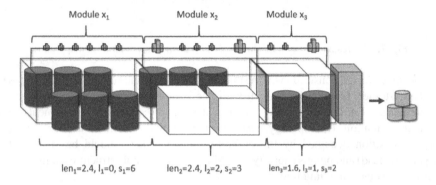

Fig. 3. Representation of a machine based on the modular design approach.

4.3 Knowledge Representation

Digital Mock-Up. The standard modules defined in the previous step have been modelled with a 3D CAD software already available in the company; a parametric design approach was adopted. The parametric models have been used, at a higher level, to propagate data between different layers of the assembly (interpart links) and to create associative copies of geometry between parts (constraints links).

Optimization algorithm. The Preliminary analysis showed that the variable to be optimized was the surface occupied by the machine. Hence, the chosen objective function f to be minimized has been the total length of the configuration. The following attributes were defined for each module: (i) length, denoted by len_i; (ii) width, denoted by wid_i; (iii) number of large containers, denoted by l_i; (iv) number of small containers, denoted by s_i. The subscript $i = 1, \ldots n$ denotes the identification for each module; in the present case study, $n = 15$.

Variables for the customer requirements were also defined: LCC and SCC denote, respectively, the number of the requested large and small containers. The size of the room – supposed to be rectangular – is stored in the variable $R = (R_1, R_2)$. The variable c is used to model the length of the dispensing head; δ is used to determine the orientation of the machine in the space. The following optimization problem has been obtained:

$$\min \sum_{i=1}^{n} len_i x_i \quad \text{subject to} \begin{cases} \sum_{j=1}^{n} l_i x_i \geq LCC \\ \sum_{i=1}^{h} s_i x_i \geq SCC \\ WID = \max_{j \text{ s.t. } x_j>0} wid_j \\ len_i x_i + c \leq (1 - \delta)R_1 + \delta R_2 \\ WID \leq \delta R_1 + (1 - \delta)R_2 \\ x_i \in N \quad \forall i \in \{1,..,n\} \\ \delta \in \{0, 1\}, \quad WID \geq 0 \end{cases}$$

As this represents an LP problem, exact solution methods can be used, such as the Branch & Bound. The optimizer has been developed using the C# programming language to accommodate the needs of the company; to handle the LP problem, the open source library COIN-OR was used. Finally, an executable program, automatically run by the configurator, reads the inputs from the graphical user interface, loads the specific attributes of the modules, solves the optimization problem and yields as output a list of modules (optimal configuration) back to the configurator.

4.4 Benchmarking and Development

The research of existing software led to an initial set of approximately 20 configurator systems. A first analysis enabled to reduce this selection to four alternatives: A = Autodesk Configurator 360, B = Tacton CPQ, C = KBMax, D = MyCustomizer.

Table 1. Requirements matrix of the developed case-study.

		Alternatives			
Requirements	Priority	A	B	C	D
Bill of material generation	Must have	✓	✓	✓	✓
Web access	Must have	✓	✓	✗	✓
Multilingual support	Nice to have	✓	✓	✓	✓
3D visualizations	Nice to have	✓	✓	✓	✗
Engineering drawings generation	Must have	✓	✓	✓	✗
Integration with the company CAD	Must have	✓	✓	✓	✗
Extensible trough API	Must have	✓	✓	✓	✓
Mobile platforms support	Nice to have	✓	✓	✗	✓
Free trial	Nice to have	✓	✗	✗	✗

The full features matrix is shown in Table 1. The Alternative A best fits with such requirements. Data collected from the user through the web application are sent to the optimizer, which computes the best machine configuration. In turn, the optimizer provides the Alternative A with the machine configuration to generate the 3D visualizations, the specifications documents and the blueprints, which are embedded and shown to the user. Furthermore, the cost of the software licenses amounts to about 4500€ per year and they are considered acceptable by the company board. At the moment of writing this paper, the integration between the configurator and the company ERP system was not yet developed.

5 Conclusions

Product configurators are an effective tool to balance the needs of product customization and manufacturing process standardization. However, a high effort is often needed to implement a configurator within a company, resulting in a low spread of such tool in SMEs. In this paper, a methodology to effectively realize, through low cost means, such tool is presented and validated through a case-study.

However, beside the mere implementation issues, further aspects must be considered. For example, internal issues may arise: employees could perceive this tool as a competitor in the workforce, a serious threat to their job. To tackle such issues, a multi-faceted approach is necessary: the management must point out that the configurator does not represent a substitute of human workforce, but represents a support to deal with repetitive tasks.

Furthermore, the definition and modelling of the standard modules is a time consuming activity which has to be considered by the company board. Resources also need to be allocated for the creation of an efficient optimization algorithm, either by hiring an external consultant or creating the algorithm with the company internal resources.

The presented approach results particularly effective with Engineering-To-Order (ETO) companies, whose core business consists in modular products, or whenever a parametrical modular decomposition is effectively possible. In fact, the results of this method are strictly bounded to the simplicity of the product, as an excessive product variety could introduce considerable difficulties in the implementation of an automatic configurator.

Research in this field could drive to the creation of an effective, affordable product configurator that generates these benefits for a larger number of companies, and could be a further step towards the popular concept of the Industry 4.0, pursuing the objective of a completely automated interaction between customer requirements and manufacturing sector.

Acknowledgments. This work has been supported by Alta Scuola Politecnica (ASP), an educational programme funded by Politecnico di Torino and Politecnico di Milano (Italy) devoted to promising students in Engineering and Architecture, based on ad-hoc courses and the development of multidisciplinary projects. http://www.asp-poli.it. The authors also thank Inkmaker srl, the industrial partner that supported this project.

References

1. ElMaraghy, H., Schuh, G., ElMaraghy, W., Piller, F., Schonsleben, P., Tseng, M., Bernard, A.: Product variety management. CIRP Ann. Manuf. Technol. **62**(2), 629–652 (2012)
2. Zhang, L.L., Helo, P.T., Kumar, A., You, X.: Implications of product configurator applications: an empirical study. In: International Conference on Industrial Engineering and Engineering Management (2015)
3. Salvador, F., Chandrasekaran, A., Sohail, T.: Product configuration, ambidexterity and firm performance in the context of industrial equipment manufacturing. J. Oper. Manag. **32**, 138–153 (2014)
4. Trentin, A., Perin, E., Forza, C.: Increasing the consumer-perceived benefits of a mass-customization experience through sales-configurator capabilities. Comput. Ind. **65**, 693–705 (2014)
5. Terzi, S., Bouras, A., Dutta, D., Garetti, M., Kiritsis, D.: Product lifecycle management - from its history to its new role. Int. J. Prod. Lifecycle Manag. **4**(4), 360–389 (2010)
6. Felfernig, A., Friedrich, G., Jannach, D.: Conceptual modeling for configuration of mass-customizable products. Artif. Intell. Eng. **15**(2), 165–176 (2001)
7. Haug, A., Hvam, L., Mortensen, N.H.: Definition and evaluation of product configurator development strategies. Comput. Ind. **63**(5), 471–481 (2012)
8. Yang, D., Ming, D., Chang, X.-K.: A dynamic constraint satisfaction approach for configuring structural products under mass customization. Eng. Appl. Artif. Intell. **25**(8), 1723–1737 (2012)
9. Gembarski, P.C., Lachmayer, R.: Forward variance planning and modeling of multi-variant products. Procedia CIRP **21**, 81–86 (2014)
10. Wang, P., Liu, Y., Nee, A.: Modular design of machine tools to facilitate design for disassembly and remanufacturing. Procedia CIRP **15**, 443–448 (2014)
11. Blecker, T., Abdelkafi, N., Kreutler, G., Friedrich, G.: Product configuration systems: state of the art, conceptualization and extensions. In: Eight Maghrebian Conference on Software Engineering and Artificial Intelligence, Sousse, Tunisia (2004)
12. Sabin, D., Weigel, R.: Product configuration frameworks - a survey. IEEE Intell. Syst. Appl. **13**(4), 42–49 (1998)
13. Kristanto, Y., Lelo, P., Jiao, R.J.: A system level product configurator for engineer-to-order supply chains. Comput. Ind. **72**, 82–91 (2015)
14. Forza, C.: Product configuration and inter-firm coordination: an innovative solution from a small manufacturing enterprise. Comput. Ind. **49**(1), 37–46 (2002)
15. Sommerville, I.: Software Engineering, 9th edn. Pearson, London (2011)
16. D'Antonio, G., Mottola, S., Prencipe, G., Rosa-Brussin, A., Sauza-Bedolla, J., Chiabert, P.: Deployment of product configurators: analysis of impacts within and outside the user company. In: IFIP 14th International Conference on Product Lifecycle Management, Seville (2017)

Deployment of Product Configurators: Analysis of Impacts Within and Outside the User Company

Gianluca D'Antonio[1(✉)], Sara Mottola[2], Giovanni Prencipe[2], Arianna Rosa Brusin[2], Joel Sauza Bedolla[1], and Paolo Chiabert[1]

[1] Politecnico di Torino, corso Duca degli Abruzzi 24, 10129 Turin, Italy
{gianluca.dantonio,joel.sauza,paolo.chiabert}@polito.it
[2] Alta Scuola Politecnica, corso Duca degli Abruzzi 24, 10129 Turin, Italy
{sara.mottola,giovanni.prencipe,arianna.rosa}@asp-poli.it

Abstract. Today many companies throughout the world recognize the need to provide outstanding service to customers: for both mass market products and products devoted to professionals, an increasing level of customization is required. This, in turn, leads to high variability in design and manufacturing processes. Hence, a structured approach to manage such variability is necessary. For an effective mass-customization program, two organizational design principles could be introduced: (i) the definition of a set of standard modules and functional criteria; (ii) the development of a tool enabling customers designing his own product. The present paper aims to analyze the impacts of a product configurator, both inside and outside of a manufacturing company. Within the internal analysis, the studied aspects include business model transformation, organization change, economic benefits. The external impacts mainly involve supply chain effects, consequences on brand perception, and impacts on society. The presented analysis is applied to a manufacturer of machines for mixing inks.

Keywords: Mass customization · Modularization · Product configurator
SCM-NPD alignment · Impacts

1 Introduction

In the last years, customers demand has been characterized by increasingly specific and complex requirements, leading to a broadened product variety. The direct effect of this phenomenon is the necessity, for companies, to produce high volumes of customized goods. However, beside customers satisfaction, companies must also keep manufacturing profitability and remain competitive. Therefore, the increase of product variety must cope with strategies for cycle time reduction, adaptation to changing (or new) markets and transformation of product development processes [1].

A strategy to overcome some of the above-mentioned issues is Mass Customization (MC): it is the ability to supply customized products or services through flexibility in processes, integration and agility [2] in the supply chain.

© IFIP International Federation for Information Processing 2017
Published by Springer International Publishing AG 2017. All Rights Reserved
J. Ríos et al. (Eds.): PLM 2017, IFIP AICT 517, pp. 440–449, 2017.
https://doi.org/10.1007/978-3-319-72905-3_39

In literature, strategies for managing MC have already been developed. For example, Mikkola and Skjøett-Larsen [3] showed how MC can be achieved through the integration of the customer in the supply process, with co-design and, in some cases, co-production. Another way to deal with MC is the implementation of a product configurator, a software-based expert system that supports the user in the creation of product specifications by restricting the way to combine predefined entities and their properties [4]. Unfortunately, often Small and Medium Enterprises (SMEs) cannot afford the adoption of such tool; a methodology devoted to this kind of companies to tackle this issue is presented in [5]. However, the adoption of a product configurator may lead to significant changes in the organization of a company, with an impact relatively higher than in big companies. Hence, the present paper aims to present a comprehensive methodology for the overall analysis and evaluation of the changes related to the introduction of a product configurator. Furthermore, the implication of this tool as an important step for the shift from an Engineering-to-order (ETO) to an Assembly-to-order (ATO) strategy will be analysed in detail.

The remainder of the paper is organized as follows: in Sect. 2 the state of the art is reviewed. The methodology for evaluating the impact of product configurator is described in Sect. 3. The case-study to validate the methodology is presented in Sect. 4: it is based on a manufacturer of machines for mixing inks. Conclusive remarks and hints for future works are provided in Sect. 5.

2   Literature Review

The development in Information Technology (IT) made available also for SMEs a class of software tools called 'product configurator': they are "a software-based expert system that supports the user in the creation of product specifications" through the combination of different standard modules [4], and enable to reduce the trade-off between product variety and delivery time [6]. A standard module is a consistent product unit that can be identified and replaced in the product architecture several times to boost product variety and adaptability [7]. A product configurator is an important tool for the alignment of the supply chain to a new product development, assuring the coordination between the development of new products and the business processes [8]. Moreover, configuration design has been recognized as an effective means to implement mass customization [9].

Empirical studies were performed in order to identify all the consequences that a product configurator generates for a company and its surrounding environment. The findings from the literature can be classified in the following two classes.

Impacts on the internal business activities. Zhang et al. [10] developed an analysis on the implications of product configurators on companies' business activities. Changes result in sales order processing, generation of BOMs and manufacturing documentation. Such changes can be supported by the integration between the product configurator and the Enterprise Resource Planning (ERP) of the company [8]. The automation of traditionally manual activities leads to a substantial reduction in the time necessary for processing orders and for design [8, 10] and, in turn, to an overall lead time reduction which is particularly significant for engineering oriented companies [4]. In highly-complex products, the adoption of a product configurator also drives to improved quality, preservation of knowledge, lowered time for employees training and improved certainty of delivery [4]. The latter point is achieved from the standardization of the selling process, which reduces the possibility of changes by the customer in the product design after the order has been approved.

Other impacts on the internal business activities, in terms of performance improvements, are identified by Zhang [10]: increased correct sales order, increased customers' orders and increased IT capacity. Beside the business tasks, possible changes concerning the company internal organization must be taken into account. The automation of design activities may lead employees to reject the novel tool, considering it as a threat for their position [10].

Impacts on the supply chain. The effective adoption of a product configurator requires tight collaboration and integration with the two terminal nodes of the supply chain system, namely customers and suppliers. A product configurator promotes co-design processes in which the customers are actively involved in the design of their product, and, in some cases, in the production [3]. Hence, considering both sides of the supply chain, suppliers and customers become key partners. To this purpose, Belkaldi [7] underlines the importance of linking a modular product strategy with the suppliers' selection, particularly for original equipment manufacturers (OEM).

3 Methodology

In order to evaluate the effects due to the adoption of a product configurator on both the company and its supply chain, a four steps methodology has been developed. It is partially based on the frameworks proposed in [11, 12]. In the two-dimensional matrix, shown in Fig. 1, different managerial approaches are proposed based on the level of complexity and customization of products. In the second framework, different variables have been considered for the purpose of supply chain alignment, from a point a view of

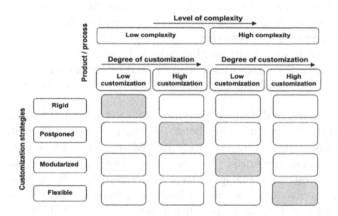

Fig. 1. Interpretative framework for mass customization. Picture taken from [11].

NPD and supply chain design, planning and management. The original contribution of this work is the adaptation of these models to small ETO companies, which is currently missing in literature.

3.1 Analysis of the as-is Business Model

A preliminary analysis is necessary to point out the initial background. In particular, a deep awareness about the company business model, the stakeholders, their role and interaction with the supply chain is necessary. The business model canvas [13] is an effective tool to support this task.

In particular, the *value proposition* of the products to be managed through the configurator must be analyzed. The target *customers* for such products are identified, as well as the valuable features they are willing to pay for. This step is crucial, since the configurator adoption also impacts on the *relationship* and the *communication* between the company and its customers. *Key activities* and *resources* are analyzed to identify the outsourced activities, the suppliers and their role. The key *partners* represent the upstream side of the supply chain and could be integrated into the manufacturing process, on the basis of the specific strategy implemented. Finally, *revenues streams* and *costs* are strictly linked to the other elements of the business model: they support, in the following steps, the analysis of the economic impacts.

3.2 Analysis of the Internal Organization

In this phase, the causality relationships tied to configurator adoption are analysed: on the one side, the reasons leading to this decision must be stated; on the other side, the expectations on future performances must be evaluated, as well as the actions and the technical decisions necessary to develop and implement the solution. Finally, the activities required to integrate the configurator into the supply chain and bring it to a fully working regime must be described.

The effective adoption of a product configurator requires that an appropriate manufacturing strategy is set and implemented. In particular, product and process standardization, decoupling point positioning and material flow setting represent the main strategic levers. To this purpose, a framework for decision support has been proposed by Brun and Zorzini [11]; it considers two factors – product complexity and customization level – to identify the most suitable manufacturing strategy. The two above-mentioned factors could be interpreted as "Internal/technological product variety" and "External/required product variety". Since the volume is linked to the product variety, through a strong trade-off - the higher the variety granted to lower the volume realizable [14] – this model seems to be particularly comprehensive. This framework has been validated for medium and big companies; however, since SMEs are often required to directly face the trade-off among the variety, volume and customization (e.g. mass customization), hybrid strategies can also be considered.

Finally, some considerations are done with respect to the product life cycle length and the innovation rate within the market. In fact, the introduction of a product configurator cannot make the system rigid at all with respect to the product innovation over time, but should support it.

3.3 Analysis of the Supply Chain

Beside the manufacturing strategy redefinition, the alignment between the product development and the supply chain must also be considered: the modularization of the finite product also involves the suppliers.

Here, the framework developed in [12] is adopted to analyze the impacts of modularization on the products variety and on the supply chain integration and collaboration. The application of this framework requires the introduction of the product configurator to be considered as an independent variable. Then the effects of this novel element on the supply chain are analysed, as well as the link between product modularity and innovation. A schematic representation of the framework is shown in Fig. 2.

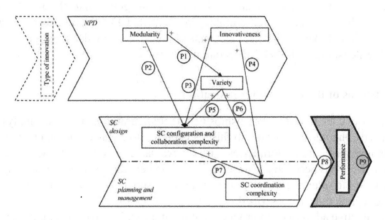

Fig. 2. Framework for supply chain alignment. Picture taken from [12].

3.4 Definition of the to-be State

The last step of the methodology is represented by the definition of the target condition: a description of the company and the supply chain, after having introduced the product configurator and set the manufacturing strategy, is made.

All these factors are synthesized within a comprehensive framework, which has to join the business model canvas and the supply chain representation. An overview of the methodology is shown in Fig. 3.

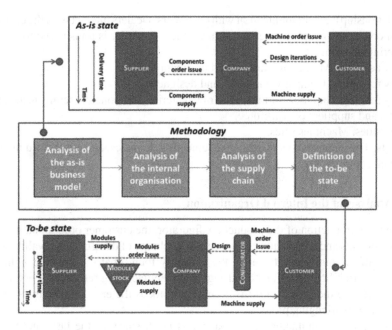

Fig. 3. Framework for the followed methodology.

4   Case Study

In this section the methodology presented in the previous section is applied to a real case study. The introduction of a product configurator within an Italian SME that assemblies dispensing systems for inks and paintings is considered. The analysis presented in this work involves the most customizable family of products.

The introduction of a product configurator is strongly supported by the company; in particular, the design lead time is expected to be dramatically shortened and the accuracy of the design is supposed to be increased, due to a more inclusive approach in customers involvement. However, most of the existing product configurators are designed for business-to-customer companies; here, the challenge is to shift the approach to a business-to-business company.

4.1   Analysis of the as-is Business Model

The business model canvas has been used to perform the analysis of the current state of the company.

- Value proposition. Dispensing systems for mixing inks and paintings are sold; the portfolio is composed by highly customizable products.
- Customers. Producers and retailers of inks and paintings; they are spread all over the world.

- Relationship and communication with customers. Dealers interact with the customers and collect the orders for new machines. Then, the order is transmitted to the engineering department.
- Key activities.Marketing, design, and upstream logistics.
- Key resources. Company engineers and designers.
- Key partners. Suppliers of materials (raw material, components, semi-finished products) and suppliers of workforce.
- Revenues. Machines sales.
- Costs. The main sources of cost are engineering, logistics, and outsourced manufacturing activities.

4.2 Analysis of the Internal Organization

Before the introduction of the product configurator, the customer order contained a set of requirements and a company employee was in charge of designing and validating the structure of the machine. However, the company found that the products exhibit an excessive variability, affecting both design and manufacturing resources. Therefore, an action to reduce the design effort is necessary to focus the existing resources in more added value, challenging projects.

A postponed manufacturing approach was used, since all the tasks necessary to provide a customer with his product were performed after the order is signed. Further, in agreement with the Wortmann classification, the company could be classified as an ETO manufacturing system.

In the company vision, the adoption of product configurator was accompanied by a standardization effort, with the aims of reducing the effort necessary for designing highly customized machines and maintaining a high level of perceived flexibility. The company portfolio exhibit a low innovation rate; this long life cycle does not require frequent changes in product definition, hence modules do not need frequent updates.

The methodology to develop standard modules is presented in [5]. This approach leads to a potential increase of product variety: several variants can be obtained by combining the modules in different ways, on the basis of customers' requirements. Therefore, the complexity of the product is increased, although standardization can ease product management.

Hence, after the implementation of the product configurator a hybrid approach mixing postponement and modularization is to be pursued. The most common and required parts of the machines can be modularized and assembled during idle times. Conversely, the realization of non-standard parts is dealt in a postponed approach.

The definition of standard modules can lead to the desired reduction of design times; however, the overall lead time is shortened since an order decoupling point is introduced between the modules preparation and the final assembly phase, as shown in the next step.

4.3 Analysis of the Supply Chain

The deployment of the hybrid manufacturing approach, made of postponement and products modularization, also requires tight collaboration and integration with the suppliers. The company at stake requires partners to supply both components and materials, as well as workforce to assembly the finite product.

Suppliers of physical entities may be required to provide entire modules rather than simple components. Since such modules can be assembled before an order is issued, the suppliers can organize their work in an autonomous manner. The company just needs a limited amount of modules and components in the warehouse, to face customization requests or priority orders. On the other side, such modules and the operators for the final assembly must be provided to the company as soon as an order is issued: hence, a security stock level of modules must be kept and the production plans must be aligned with the needs of the company.

4.4 Definition of the to-be State

After the introduction of the product configurator, the major changes in the business model involve the relationship and the communication with the customers. The new system enables to involve the customer into the process, through a product co-design; this, in turn, leads to change one of the tasks included in the key activities. Furthermore, important changes must be highlighted in terms of key resources: the configurator could be strong resource for building and keeping a competitive advantage on the market. In fact, the novelty factor of using a product configurator also into a B2B market and, in particular, within this specific industry, could create a differentiation with respect to the other competitors during the first period. As pointed out in the previous section, the relationship with the key partners is also transformed because a higher level of integration and collaboration with the suppliers is necessary. Revenues are expected to increase because of an expected increase of orders [10] moreover a possible premium price could be applied in order to have very fast deliveries. Finally, costs are expected to be decreased: the shortened lead time, the effort reduction in design and the optimized material management lead to higher efficiency. Furthermore, the increased accuracy in the order technical features will result in a reduction of reworking activities.

All these changes lead to shift the initial ETO configuration towards an Assembly-to-Order (ATO) system. This paradigm change is marked by the introduction of an order decoupling point between the production of different modules and the assembly phase of the finite product. As a consequence, the final assembly can start as soon as the order arrives from the product configurator. A strategic inventory level is kept in order to satisfy the average demand. This approach, in turn, leads to a balance between the material availability and the inventory costs: modules are always available at stock, but over-stock costs are avoided.

The impacts on the internal organization must be carefully handled. As stated, the product configurator affects design, which is a key activities. The deployment of an automation tool for this task can be misunderstood by the employees; the company must clarify that the configurator is used to replace repetitive, boring tasks and to focus the resources on more challenging projects with a higher added value.

The decreasing of delivery lead time and the increased accuracy are impacts affecting both the company and the entire supply chain. In fact, the reduced lead time allows the company and the suppliers to better organize their manufacturing systems and directly link them to the demand, and to reach significant internal economies; with respect to the customer, the reduction of lead time leads to a differential factor, a competitive advantage, if comparing the company with its competitors.

The increased accuracy avoids the occurrence of reworking costs or the application of penalties for the company; while the customer can surely base itself on a reliable manufacturing system.

5   Conclusions

The present paper has provided insights regarding the deployment of a product configurator within an ETO company. The product configurator represents an effective way to deal with mass customization. In order to make it work effectively, it requires deep changes in terms of both production processes and supply chain structure. These changes result into the transformation of the ETO system in an ATO, allowing the repositioning of the order decoupling point.

A four-step methodology has been presented in order to describe all the phases necessary to start-up the configurator and achieve a steady-state condition, and to assess the impact of such tool in a multi-faced way: the business model, the internal structure and the relationships with the suppliers of a company. The methodology is devoted to support SMEs, overcoming the limit of the literature, which is mainly focused on big companies. The methodology has been validated through the case study of a company that assembles machines for mixing inks and paintings. At the moment of writing this paper, the company is validating the configurator and is starting its deployment. The main challenge for system implementation has been the lack of structured knowledge. The size of the company and the ETO approach led to a proliferation of practices and solutions which – in some cases – were not the best ones. Thus, a fundamental step for this approach is to structure company expertise according to standard criteria; to guarantee the success of this task, the cooperation of company executives and employees is mandatory.

Acknowledgments. This work has been supported by Alta Scuola Politecnica (ASP), an educational Programme funded by Politecnico di Torino and Politecnico di Milano (Italy) devoted to promising students in Engineering and Architecture, based on ad-hoc courses and the development of multidisciplinary projects. http://www.asp-poli.it.

References

1. Eigner, M., Fehrenz, A.: Managing the product configuration throughout the lifecycle. In: 8th International Conference on Product Lifecycle Management, Eindhoven, Netherlands, pp. 396–405 (2011)
2. Davis, S.M.: Future perfect. Addison-Wesley, Boston (1987)
3. Mikkola, J.H., Skjott-Larsen, T.: Supply-chain integration: implications for mass customization, modularization and postponement strategies. Prod. Plann. Control 15(4), 352–361 (2004). https://doi.org/10.1080/0953728042000238845
4. Haug, A., Hvam, L., Mortensen, N.: Definition and evaluation of product configurator development strategies. Comput. Ind. 63(5), 471–481 (2012). https://doi.org/10.1016/j.compind.2012.02.001
5. Sauza Bedolla, J., Amato, S., Fantetti, A., Radaelli, A., Saja, A., D'Antonio, G., Chiabert, P.: Product configuration: a standardization methodology to support mass customization. In: 14th International Conference on Product Lifecycle Management, Seville, Spain (2017)
6. Forza, C., Salvador, F.: Product configuration and inter-firm coordination: an innovative solution from a small manufacturing enterprise. In: The Fourth SMESME International Conference Technology Transfer in SMEs, Aalborg, Denmark (2002)
7. Belkadi, F., Gupta, R.K., Vlachou, E., Bernard, A., Mourtis, D.: Linking modular product structure to suppliers' selection through PLM approach: a frugal innovation perspective. In: Harik, R., Rivest, L., Bernard, A., Eynard, B., Bouras, A. (eds.) PLM 2016. IAICT, vol. 492, pp. 227–237. Springer, Cham (2016). https://doi.org/10.1007/978-3-319-54660-5_21
8. Hvam, L., Bonev, M., Denkena, B., Schürmeyer, J., Dengler, B.: Optimizing the order processing of customized products using product configuration. Prod. Eng. 5(6), 595–604 (2011). https://doi.org/10.1007/s11740-011-0334-x
9. Zhou, C., Lin, Z., Liu, C.: Customer-driven product configuration optimization for assemble-to-order manufacturing enterprises. Int. J. Adv. Manufact. Technol. 38, 185–194 (2008). https://doi.org/10.1007/s00170-007-1089-6
10. Zhang, L.L., Helo, P.T., Kumar, A., You, X.: An empirical study on product configurators' application: implications, challenges and opportunities. In: The 17th International Configuration Workshop, Vienna, Austria, pp. 5–10 (2015)
11. Brun, A., Zorzini, M.: Evaluation of product customization strategies through modularization and postponement. Int. J. Prod. Econom. 120(1), 205–220 (2009). https://doi.org/10.1016/j.ijpe.2008.07.020
12. Pero, M., Abdelkafi, N., Sianesi, A., Blecker, T.: A framework for the alignment of new product development and supply chains. Supply Chain Manag. Int. J. 15(2), 115–128 (2010). https://doi.org/10.1108/13598541011028723
13. Osterwalder, A., Pigneur, Y.: Business Model Generation. A Handbook for Visionaries Game Changers and Challengers. John Wiley & Sons, Hoboken (2010)
14. Slack, N., Brandon, J., Johnson, R., Betts, A.: Operations and Process Management. Principles and Practice for Strategic Impact. Pearson, London (2012)

Secure Modular Design of Configurable Products

Henk Jan Pels[(✉)]

Phi Knowledge Process Enabling b.v., Nuenen, Netherlands
h.j.pels@phi-kpe.nl

Abstract. Design of complex configurable products is a hard task. Testing of all variants is often impossible because the number of variants is orders of magnitude larger than the total life cycle production volume. Modular design is advocated as solution but cannot guarantee that if one variant works OK another will not cause errors. This paper proposes, based on a similar method for modular database system design, a theory for modular design of mechanical systems that poses the concept of module independence, to enable design and test of module families as a separate unit while offering formal conditions to assure that no variant of the module family will cause failures when integrated in the end-product. This allows system verification and testing to be done per module family with no need to test individual end product variants. The method is illustrated with a simple example of a mechanical design, but not yet applied in practice.

Keywords: Modular design · Product configuration · Module independence

1 Introduction

A configurable product is defined by a number of parameters. By assigning proper values to the parameters a specific product can be configured to fit the requirements of a customer. When one or more parameters control the selection out of a set of interchangeable components, the design is called modular and the interchangeable components are called modules. Product configuration is applied massively in modern industry in order to increase product variety. Especially automotive industry depends heavily on product configuration, such that numbers of product variants within one model range up to 10**20 and larger.

The design of a configurable product is a complex task. Where designing a single product first time right is still a challenge, the design of a consistent product family, with all necessary rules to make sure that every allowed variant will be manufacturable and will work properly, is a huge task, especially because 100% testing is impossible when the number of variants is orders of magnitude larger than the total life cycle production volume.

Controlling the change process in a configurable product environment is as complex as the original design. Every product family will have numerous changes during its life time. Every change in a module may cause conflicts with other modules. Maintaining

J. Ríos et al. (Eds.): PLM 2017, IFIP AICT 517, pp. 450–461, 2017.
https://doi.org/10.1007/978-3-319-72905-3_40

the consistency of a configurable product is a huge task. This research proposes a secure method for design and maintenance of configurable products.

2   Modularity Overview

The generic meaning of module is "exchangeable component". The term modularity is used to describe the use of common units to create product variants. It aims at the identification of independent, standardized, or interchangeable units to satisfy a variety of functions [1, 2]. For decomposing a system into modules often Design Structure Matrix [3, 4] is used where components with relatively more interactions are combined into one module. Components that are not assigned to any module are called independent. Three types of modularity are distinguished: component swapping, component sharing and bus. Four types of interaction are mentioned by [5]: spatial, energy, information and material. Modularity is viewed by [6] as depending on two characteristics of a design: (1) similarity between the physical and functional architecture of the design, and (2) minimization of incidental interactions between physical components. [7] Discusses modularity in the context of integrated process and product design in order to obtain flexibility in terms of increased number of product variants. An approach from the operations management point of view is found in [8]. Their qualitative research results in correlations between type of modularity and complexity of production and supply chain. The modular design of production management systems is discussed in [9–12].

All methods for design of modular products aim at reduction of design cost, but non offers a possibility to prove that two modules are exchangeable in the sense that if one functions without failure in a larger system, the other will as well. Changes in a modular system can be implemented by changing one or more modules and replacing the old versions by the new ones. A method to prove that that if the new module version is consistent in itself, it will also be consistent in the whole system, could reduce considerably the maintenance cost for complex configurable products. This paper discusses such a method for secure modular design.

3   Research Question and Approach

When the number of variants is much larger than the total lifecycle production volume, it is unrealistic to test all possible combinations, so it is desirable to have a method to test individual modules independent from the total product, with certainty that all module variants will operate properly in the total system, regardless the choices made for other modules. Also it is desirable to be able to design and verify modules independently, in order to avoid endless design iterations. The problem is that there are many relationships between the components, which may cause failure under non frequently occurring conditions. When there are complex relationships between the components of a product, a change in one component may cause failure in other components. This means that the effort for a change increases with the complexity of the product. If we assume that the frequency of changes also increases with the complexity of the product, we may conclude that maintenance cost will increase with the square of the complexity. This paper describes a method to define module independence as a provable property that enables to design, verify and test a module as a separate entity and yet ensure that the module will not cause failures in other modules during manufacturing or operation. Note that the term module independence as defined in this paper is very different from the term as cited [3, 4] in the previous section.

The research builds upon a modular design methodology developed for large database information systems [13, 14]. The concept of module independence is translated from database systems to mechanical systems and illustrated with an example. This paper explains how the theory can be applied in mechanical design, but does not describe validation in practice.

4 Configurable Products and Product Families

4.1 Some Terminology

The traditional approach in manufacturing is to design a product once and produce identical copies many times. The need for increased variety led to introduction of the concept of product families [15, 16]. Understanding product families requires quite some abstract thinking, so precise definition of terms is helpful:

- A **product instance** is a specific, single, manufactured product, as can be touched, sold to and used by a customer,
- A **product type** is defined by a product model, such that each two product instances, manufactured according to this model, are equivalent to the user,
- A **product family** is a class of **product variants**, defined by a number of parameters with specified value ranges. Each choice of parameter values defines a product variant. A product variant may be either a product family itself, or a product type.

Product is used as generic term: it can be an end-product, a sub-assembly or a mono part, and for each of them instance, type or family. A component is a product that is intended to be used as part of an assembly. The implementation of a change in the design of a modular product can be viewed as creating a changed version of a module and exchanging the old module version with the new one.

4.2 Definition of Module

As stated above a module is an exchangeable component. That means that in a specific assembly it can be exchanged with another variant of the same product family. When it is not feasible to test the behavior in the end-product of each variant individually, we need formal rules to predict the consistent exchangeability of the whole family. Since a module, in order to be a functional part of a larger system, must have relationships (share space, energy, information or material) with other parts of the system, it is impossible to check consistency of a module without knowledge of some specifications of those other parts. Therefore a module must have interfaces, showing the necessary specifications of related parts in the system. Consequently, in this paper, we define a module as:

A module is a product family or product type including the specification of its interfaces.

This means that a module specification consists of two parts:

1. The **own domain** which holds the specification of the component itself,
2. The **foreign domain** which holds specifications of related components.

The own domain can be split into two parts:

1. The **public domain** with the own specifications that may occur in the public domain of other modules,
2. The **private domain** with the specifications that are hidden for other modules.

Note that in this definition a module interface differs from the usual interpretation of interface as a physical port to exchange or share space, energy, information or material. A module interface is a set of specifications. The foreign domain is the module's model of its environment, the public domain is the model the module shows of itself to its environment. So in this paper a module interface is defined from the design point of view rather than form an operational point of view.

The essential property of a module is that it can be changed and verified without any other knowledge of the total system than its foreign domain, such that, after verification, it can be integrated in its intended position in the total system, without causing any failures during assembly or operation. This property is called **module independence**.

Supposing that a module type is always a variant of a family of mutually exchangeable components, we call a module independent when:

It can be verified and tested to operate properly in the intended product, without knowledge of the intended product other than specified in the module's foreign domain.

It may be clear that the designer of a module may only change specifications in the own domain of the module. When changing a specification in the public domain, he must check which other modules are using this specification and negotiate with the designers of those modules whether the intended change is acceptable. A desirable, but not self evident property is that the designer can change any specification in the private domain without causing conflicts with other modules. The designer is not allowed to change any specification in the foreign domain of his module, since those are the responsibility of another designer.

4.3 Module Independence in Databased Systems

The concept of module independence has originally been developed for data based information systems, which consist of a set of applications that operate on a common database. Maintenance of complex databased information systems appears to be expensive because a change in one application or its database subschema, may cause failures in other applications. These errors cannot always be detected in tests, because it happens that state changes propagate slowly along different elements of the database until a fault occurs in an application that does not even have any data element in common with the changed application. Since any data element may be related, directly or via applications, to any other data element in the total database, every change must be verified against the whole database.

A database is defined by a database schema that specifies object classes, their attributes and constraints that limit the allowed combinations of attribute values. Constraints can refer to single attributes (like "the value must be a positive integer") or to multiple elements (like "this value must be unique within the object class population"). In this way the database schema defines the state space of the database. Applications perform operations on the database, which can be [1] reading data and performing computational operations on them or [2] writing data in order to add or change data. A fault occurs when an application tries to execute a not allowed state change (like writing a negative integer) or when a value read from the database causes failure of a computational operation (like division by zero). Since the database state space is defined by its schema, it is theoretically possible to check each operation against every possible set of values.

A database module is a subset of object classes and constraints together with a set of applications that operate on only those classes. The subset of element specifications and constraints forms the **module-subschema**. The module state space is obtained by projecting the database state space on the module schema. It is evident that constraints make only sense for a module when all elements referenced in the constraint are in the module subschema. Modules interact through interfaces in the form of shared object classes. Each class is owned by a single module and only applications of the owner module are allowed to write on this object class. This means that the applications of a module may read all elements in its subschema, including foreign elements, but update only own elements. On basis of the usage rights the subschema of a module can be divided in own, private, public and foreign domains, consistent with the definitions above.

Verification of the design of the subschema and applications of a module must make sure that each computational operation is defined for all possible values of the attributes that are referred to and that each change operation results in an element of the state space (meaning it does not conflict with any constraint). It is clear that a change in the design of the foreign domain may cause an own operation to fail on an unanticipated value, while a change in the public domain may cause failure of an operation of another module. The desirable property of module independence must guarantee that each module can be designed, operated and maintained with only knowledge of the module and its interfaces. This property is defined as:

> *A module is independent in a total schema if and only if every state change that is allowed according to its subschema, is also allowed according to the total schema, and every element of the module state space is a valid state for all its operations.*

Independence means that a module can be designed, used and changed without risk of failures in the total database, with only knowledge of its subschema. This means that new or changed applications as well as changes in the own domain of the subschema, need to be checked only against the subschema of the module without knowledge of the database structure nor applications outside that subschema.

It has been proven [13] that:

a database module is independent in a database schema, if every constraint in the database schema that refers to an element of the own domain of the module, does not refer to any element outside the subschema of the module.

In practice this means that modules must be designed without using any knowledge that is not specified in the subschema of the module. Note that independence of a module is defined in the context of the total database schema of which it is a subschema. Independence is not a property of a module on its own, but of the module in a specific environment.

4.4 Module Independence in Mechanical Systems

The property of independence as defined above for a database module is exactly the property we wish to have for modules in mechanical systems. If we can extend the concept of module independence from databased information systems to complex mechatronic products, we would have a tool to design modular systems that can be proven correct by proving that each single module is correct. In this paper we extend this concept to the design of mechanical products. However, we expect that the conclusions will stay valid when electronic and other technologies are added.

A mechanical product is an assembly of ultimately mono parts. Some parts can have variable positions because of elastic properties or degrees of freedom in assemblies. A mono part is specified in terms of features like cube or cylinder. Each feature compares to an object class in a database. Each variable of the feature compares to an attribute of the object class and each actual value for a variable to an attribute value. Some variables specify possible movements of the construction during operation (e.g. axle rotation). We call them dynamic variables. When in the part model all static (non-dynamic) variables have singular values, the model specifies a product type. When one or more static variables have a value range assigned, the model specifies a product family. An assembly is defined by a Bill of Materials, where each BoM-line specifies a part with its relative position in the assembly. If the what-used variable of a BoM-line specifies a set of possible parts, it defines a product family based on exchangeable parts.

Constraints in a database schema correspond to constraints in a mechanical design, that limit the range of allowed values of variables. Examples are mutual fit for connected components, design volumes and limits on force, mass, speed, temperature etc. The own domain of the module is the product model itself. The public domain of a module is the list of own elements and constraints that may be referred to (known by) other modules. The foreign domain is the list of elements and constraints of other modules that may be referred to (relied upon) in this module. Private, public and foreign domains together form the **module model**.

Based on this analogy between database systems and mechanical systems, we can define the condition for module independence as:

a module of a mechanical system is independent in the system model, if every constraint in the system model that refers to an element of the own domain of the module, does not refer to any element that is not specified in the module model.

In the following section we will apply this interpretation of a modular mechanical product model on a simple example.

4.5 Example

Let's take the simple example of a metal block (further referenced as Block) with a cylindrical hole and a metal cylinder (Cylinder) that can rotate in the hole (see Fig. 1). Block has attributes l, w, and h for its outer dimensions. Further is has axis and d for axis and diameter of the hole. The origin of Block is where the axis meets its left side in its point of gravity; the x-axis equal to axis and parallel to the length of Block. Width is parallel to y-axis and height parallel to z-axis. Cylinder has attributes l and d. The origin is the center of the left end. The x-axis is the axis of Cylinder.

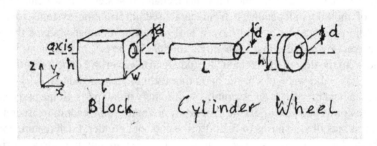

Fig. 1. Mechanical design with three modules

Suppose Cylinder is intended to rotate in the hole of Block. Then the following constraints could apply:

C1. The axes of the hole and the cylinder coincide,
C2. The difference between hole- and cylinder diameter must be between 1% and 2% of hole diameter,
C3. No end of the cylinder is inside the hole.

Because independence is not a property of a module on its own, but of a module in an assembly, the structure of the assembly must be known in order to be able to check independence. Therefore we define assembly Assy with bill of material:

$$\{Part1: Block(0, 0, 0, 0, 0, 0),$$
$$Part2: Cylinder(0, 0, 0, rotation, 0, 0)\}.$$

This BOM specifies that the x y and z-axes of Block and Cylinder coincide and that Cylinder can rotate around the x-axis.

In order to be an independent module, the designer of Block needs to know all Cylinder specifications that are referenced in the constraints:

$$Cylinder.axis, Cylinder.d, Cylinder.l, Part2.$$

These form the foreign domain of Block and the public domain of Cylinder. Similarly, the foreign domain of Cylinder must specify all hole variables that are mentioned in constraints:

$$Block.axis, Block.d, Part1.$$

These become the public domain of Block. Note that Assy, Block and Cylinder are product families, since several variables have value ranges. This makes Assy a configurable product. Constraint C1 is satisfied in the positions of the parts. Constraint 2 an 3 remain as configuration constraints. Rotation is a dynamic variable. Note that in this example the private domain of Cylinder is empty.

Now suppose the system is extended with a wheel, to be mounted on Cylinder, with right planes of Wheel and Cylinder equal. The bill of material line is:

$$Part3: Wheel(Cylinder.l-Wheel.l, 0, 0, 0, 0, 0).$$

The following constraints control the correct mounting of Wheel:

C4. $Wheel.d = Cylinder.d$,

C5. $Cylinder.lLength-Block.l-Wheel.l > Wheel.h/10$,

C6. $Cylinder.l > 10.Wheel.l$.

Because of these constraints the designer specifies the foreign domain of Wheel as:

$$Cylinder.d, Cylinder.l, Block.l, Part2, Part3.$$

This makes all relevant constraints 'visible' for module Wheel, so Wheel is independent in Assy. However, the Wheel design introduced a constraint that refers to a specification of Block, and thus destroys the independence of Block. This may cause trouble, when configuring a product. Suppose that parameter values for Wheel and Cylinder have been set and a value for Block.l has to be chosen. Since the Block module does not know Wheel, it cannot check constraint C5 and may cause a clash between Block and Wheel. To restore independence of Block, Wheel.l must be added to the foreign domain of Block.

The example shows how the features and bills of material in the model of a mechanical product correspond to object classes in databases. Feature and BoM variables correspond to attributes of objects. Constraints in a mechanical model limit value ranges of variables like constraints in a database schema limit attribute values. The distinction between static and dynamic variables adds a nuance to mechanical models: static attributes define variants of product families while dynamic variables define the behavior of the product during operation.

5 Discussion

Although the example is extremely simple, it shows how module independence depends on constraints and how ignored constraints cause failures (like when adding Wheel in the example). Constraints are essential for system consistency and thus for managing changes. Therefore it is paramount that all constraints are explicitly specified in the module models and that for every constraint it is clear to which elements it refers. In our experience this is not common in current design practice. Also CAD and PLM systems do not support the maintenance of lists of design constraints, other than, to some extent in the requirements management function. An important task of reviewers is to check for implicit constraints, that are not specified in the design but nevertheless relied upon for any design decisions.

A difference between databased and mechanical systems is that the first have only dynamic variables (attributes), that are used and modified by applications, while a mechanical system has 3 types of variable use:

1. design variables: get their value by design,
2. configuration variables: get their value when configuring a variant,
3. dynamic variables: get their value by operation.

The rules for module independence apply to all of them. When designing a module type, module independence ensures that, although the module has been designed with only foreign domain knowledge of the system, the module will not cause failures when mounted or operated in that system. Simulation should check that dynamic variables do not violate constraints during operation. When designing configurable components, the value ranges of the configuration attributes (also called parameters or options) can be checked against the constraints in only the module schema to ensure that all variants will function consistently in the system. Simulation can be done per module, for a limited range of configuration variable value combinations, which makes a much smaller number of runs than simulating all system variants.

By controlling module independence, a configurable product can be designed module by module. In its design a module must specify its foreign and public domain and all constraints referring to them. An important design decision is how much knowledge the module needs to use about its environment, and what knowledge the module wants to keep private in order to maintain freedom of change and flexibility of the product. Very important is that each module specifies all constraints its design relies upon for proper fit and function. Each constraint must specify explicitly the set of elements to which it refers, as well as the owner module of each element. This specification is the basis for independence checks. Although in the example the public domains are mirrored from the foreign domains of other modules, this is not required. In order to increase flexibility of the design, a module should aim for weak constraints on its foreign domain (allowing a broad range of values) in order to be less sensitive for changes in its environment. At the same time it should aim at constraints on its public domain to be stronger than necessary for its current design, in order to prevent avoidable limitations on future changes. In other words: keep your public state space smaller than your environment currently requires and keep your foreign state space larger. A general rule for modular design is: keep interfaces as simple as possible.

When adding a module to an assembly, it must be checked that:

1. All its foreign elements are specified as public element in the owner module of the element,

2. All its constraints referring to foreign elements, correspond to equal or stronger constraints specified in other modules,
3. All own elements that occur in foreign domain of other modules, are in the public domain,
4. All constraints in other modules that refer to own elements, are visible in the module model, in the sense that all elements they refer to, are specified in its public or foreign domain and are equal or stronger than the corresponding own constraints.

This means that in a modular design every constraint that hits an interface is specified separately in all related modules and need not be identical. Designers may choose to specify constraints for their foreign domain weaker than specified in the other modules and thus verifying for more possible states, in order to be prepared for a broader range of variants in future and to be less sensitive for constraint changes in other modules. Also they may choose to have own constraints on their public elements that are stronger than the constraints they actually show in their public domain, in order to be less sensitive to future changes in the environment.

Changes in a modular design can be:

1. Adding, changing or removing features in a mono component,
2. Adding, changing or removing BoM-lines,
3. Changing values for design variables,
4. Changing value ranges of static variables to change the set of possible variants of a product family.

Like in database systems, enlarging the value range of a variable, may cause, after some time of operation, or even after several design changes in other modules, values for variables in other modules, that never occurred before and cause failures that could difficultly be foreseen. Module independence prohibits such failures.

Module independence is a property of a module in a system. So a module that is independent in one system, can be dependent in another system. The bad news is that every change in a system can in principle destroy independence of any module in the system. The good news is that a simple check of the reference domains of constraints is sufficient to ensure that independence is conserved. If a conflict with the independence rule is detected, the designer who's change causes the conflict, has to inform the responsible designer of the other module so that this designer can negotiate what adaptation in which module is best to restore independence.

When the wheel was added as a third module, it appeared that wheel and cylinder were independent, but wheel and block were not, even though there is not a direct connection between them. The designer of the wheel is responsible for this error: he used a constraint that referenced Block, but did not take proper action. This shows how responsibility for system failures can be assigned to module owners, on basis of independence rules: it can be that not the current change is the real cause, but an earlier change in anther module.

6 Conclusion

The research goal was to find a method for secure interchangeability of modules. The method for modular decomposition of large database system [9, 13] has been translated to mechanical design in such a way that the database rule for database module independence could be applied to mechanical module independence. This means that we may consider the proposed method to be proven.

The method enables to design, test and change modules independent from the total system and then check independence in the system using the system list of reference domains of constraints. This check is relatively easy and can even be automated. We believe that this method can substantially reduce design cost for complex configurable products. However, for practical application of this method CAD-systems need to extended with the possibility to specify interfaces and PLM systems with the function to maintain constraint lists.

A goal for future research is to validate this theory in practice. One of the issues to be researched is how to achieve a really complete system list of constraints since many mechanical designers are not used to document them accurately. Database technology hardly puts a limit on variable values, so constraints only exist if they are specified by design. In mechanical system material properties pose many constraints on value ranges of many variables, not only geometrical, but also in terms of force, speed, temperature, electro magnetic radiation etc. Sometimes such constraints are only discovered in heavy test conditions. This means that mechanical module independence cannot prevent failures because of previously unknown physical phenomena.

References

1. Huang, C.C., Kusiak, A.: Modularity in design of products. IEEE Trans. Syst. Man Cybern. A **28**(1), 6677 (1998)
2. Gershenson, J.K., Prasad, G.J., Zhang, Y.: Product modularity: definitions and benefits. J. Eng. Des. **30**(3), 295–313 (2010)
3. AlGeddawy, T., ElMaragry, H.: Reactive design methodology for product family platforms, modularity and parts integration. CIRP J. Manuf. Sci. Technol. **6**, 34–43 (2013)
4. Bonvoisin, J., Halstenberg, F., Buchert, T., Stark, R.: A systematic literature review on modular product design. J. Eng. Des. **27**(7), 488–514 (2016)
5. Pimmler, T.U., Eppinger, S.D.: Integration analysis of product decompositions. In: ASME Design Theory and Methodology Conference Minneapolis, MN, September 1994, pp. 343–351 (1994)
6. Ulrich, K., Tung, K.: Fundamentals of product modularity. In: Sharon, A. (ed.) Issues in Design/Manufacture Integration 1991, pp. 73–79. ASME, New York (1991)
7. Kusiak, A.: Integrated product and process design: a modularity perspective. J. Eng. Des. **13**(3), 223–231 (2002)
8. Salvador, F., Forza, C., Rungutasanatham, F.: Modularity, product variety, production volume, and component sourcing: theorizing beyond generic prescriptions. J. Oper. Manage. **20**, 549–575 (2002)
9. Pels, H.J., Wortmann, J.C.: Decomposition of information systems for production management. Comput. Ind. **6**(6), 435–448 (1985)

10. Pels, H.J., Wegter, G.J.: Conceptual integration of databases for computer integrated manufacturing. In: Bo, K., Warman, E.A., Estensen, L. (eds.) Proceedings of 2nd International Conference on Computer Aided Production and Engineering (CAPE 1986), Copenhagen, 20–30 May, 1986, North-Holland, pp. 455–472 (1987)
11. Pels, H.J.: Conceptual integration of distributed production management databases. In: Proceedings of IFIP WG5.7 Working Conference on Design, Implementation and Operation of Databases for Production Management, Barcelona, May 1989, North-Holland (1989)
12. Pels, H.J., Erens, F.J.: Dynamic integration: an approach for the design of integrated manufacturing systems. In: Hirsch, B.E., Thoben, K.-D. (eds.) 'One-of-a-Kind' Production: New Approaches, IFIP Transaction B: Applications in Technology, North-Holland, pp 101–110 (1992)
13. Pels, H.J.: Geïntegreerde Informatiebanken, Modulair ontwerp van het conceptuele schema, Dissertation Eindhoven University of Technology, Stenfert-Kroese, Leiden (1988) (in Dutch)
14. Pels, H.J.: Modularity in product design. In: Tichem, M., et al. (eds.) Proceedings of the 3rd WDK Workshop on Product Structuring, Jun 26027, Delft University of Technology (1998). ISBN 90-370-0169-6
15. Erens, F.J.: The synthesis of variety: developing product families. Dissertation Eindhoven University of Technology (1996)
16. Erens, F.J., Verhulst, K.: Architectures for product families. Comput. Ind. **33**(2–3), 165–178 (1997)

Modular Architectures Management with PLM for the Adaptation of Frugal Products to Regional Markets

Farouk Belkadi[1(✉)], Ravi Kumar Gupta[1], Stéphane Natalizio[2], and Alain Bernard[1]

[1] Ecole Centrale de Nantes – LS2N, UMR CNRS 6597, Nantes, France
{farouk.belkadi,Ravi-Kumar.Gupta,alain.bernard}@ls2n.fr
[2] AUDROS Technology, Lyon, France
snatalizio@audros.fr

Abstract. Nowadays companies are challenged with high competitiveness and saturation of markets leading to a permanent need of innovative products that ensure the leadership of these companies in existing markets and help them to reach new potential markets (i.e. emerging and mature market). Requirements of emerging markets are different in terms of geographic, economic, cultural, governance policies and standards. Thus, adopting existing European product to develop new products tailored to emerging markets is one possible strategy that can help companies to cope with such challenge. To do so, a large variety of products and options have to be created, managed and classified according to the requirements and constraints from a target regional market. This paper discusses the potential of PLM approach to implement the proposed modular product design approach for the adaptation of European product and production facilities to emerging markets. Using modular approach, the product design evolves iteratively coupling the configuration of various alternatives of product architectures and the connection of functional structures to their contexts of use. This enables the customization of adapted product to specific customer's needs.

Keywords: PLM · Modular architecture · Product features · Co-evolution

1 Introduction

Customer's requirements fluctuate across geographical regions, standards, and context of use of the product of interest, whereas global production facilities to address such requirements are constrained by local governing policies, standards, and local resources availability. In order to address emerging market's needs and adapt existing product development facilities, it is important to analyze and evaluate different possibilities of product solutions against specific requirements of one regional market.

An emerging market is generally characterized as a market under development with less presence of standards and policies comparing to mature markets in the developed countries [1]. To respond to the competition from these emerging countries, frugal innovation is considered as a solution to produce customized products in a shorter time for improving the attractiveness of western companies [2]. Frugal innovation or frugal engineering is the process of reducing the complexity and cost of goods, and their production. A frugal product is defined in most industries in terms of the following attributes: Functional, Robust, User-friendly, Growing, Affordable and Local. The details of these attributes are given in [3, 4].

As per the study [5], these frugal attributes are not always sufficient for adapting existing product development facilities in European countries to emerging markets. Several additional factors can influence consumer behavior as well such as cultural, social, personal, psychological and so on. To answer this demand, companies have to provide tangible goods and intangible services that result from several processes involving human and material resources to provide an added value to the customer.

However, looking to the large variety of markets, customer categories, needs and characteristics, companies have to create and manage a huge variety of products and services, under more complex constraints of delivery time reduction and cost saving. To do so, optimization strategy should concern all steps of the development process, including design, production, packaging and transportation [6].

Generally, three categories of product are distinguished depending on the level of customization and the consideration of customer preferences, namely: (i) standard products that don't propose any customization facility; (ii) mass customized product offering customization on some parts of the product, and (iii) unique product developed to answer specific customer demand. Despite this variety, every product is defined through a bundle of elements and attributes capable of exchange and use. It is often proven that modular architectures offer high advantages to support creation and management of various product architectures from the same family. Taking advantage from this concept, this paper proposes the use of a modular approach to address the emerging market requirements through the adaptation of original products. The key issue is the use of PLM (Product Lifecycle Management) framework as a kernel tool to support both the management of product architectures and the connection of these architectures with production strategies. The specific use case of product configuration of mass customized product is considered as application context.

The next section discusses the main foundation of modular approach and its use for the configuration of product architectures. Section 3 discusses the implementation of the proposed approach in Audros software. Audros is a French PLM providing a set of flexible tools adaptable to a lot of functional domains through an intelligent merge of the business process model, the data model generator and the user interface design. Finally, Sect. 4 gives the conclusion and future works.

2   Product Configuration Strategies Within Modular Approach

2.1   Product Modular Architectures

Product architecture is the way by which the functional elements (or functions) of a product are arranged into physical units (components) and the way in which these units interact [7]. The choice of product architecture has broad implications for product

performance, product change, product variety, and manufacturability [8]. Product architecture is thought of in terms of its modules. It is also strongly coupled to the firm's
development capability, manufacturing specialties, and production strategy [9].

A product module is a physical or conceptual grouping of product components to
form a consistent unit that can be easily identified and replaced in the product architecture. Alternative modules are a group of modules of the same type and satisfy several
reasoning criteria/features for a product function. Modularity is the concept of decomposing a system into independent parts or modules that can be treated as logical units
[9, 10]. Modular product architecture, sets of modules that are shared among a product
family, can bring cost savings and enable the introduction of multiple product variants
quicker than without architecture. Several companies have adopted modular thinking or
modularity in various industries such as Boeing, Chrysler, Ford, Motorola, Swatch,
Microsoft, Conti Tires, etc. [11]. Hubka and Eder [12] define a modular design as
"connecting the constructional elements into suitable groups from which many variants
of technical systems can be assembled". Salhieh and Kamrani [13] define a module as
"building block that can be grouped with other building blocks to form a variety of
products". They also add that modules perform discrete functions, and modular design
emphasizes minimization of interactions between components.

Generic Product Architecture (GPA) is a graph where nodes represent product
modules and links represent connections among product modules according to specific
interfaces (functional, physical, information and material flow) to represent a product
or a set of similar products forming a product family. A GPA represents the structure of
the functional elements and their mapping into different modules and specifies their
interfaces. It embodies the configuration mechanism to define the rules of product variant
derivation [14]. A clear definition of the potential offers of the company and the feasibility of product characteristics could be established for a set of requirements [15].
Figure 1 shows an example of modular product architecture for the case of bobcat
machine, including the internal composition of modules and the interaction between

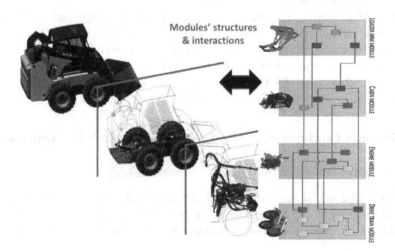

Fig. 1. Example of generic product architecture of Bobcat machine (adapted from [16]).

them [16]. The similar concepts mentioned in the literature are 'building product architecture', 'design dependencies and interfaces' and 'architecture of product families', which can be used for the development of GPA. The GPA can be constructed by using different methods presented in the literature [17, 18].

2.2 Construction of Modular Architectures

The use of the modular approach should propose the facility to work in different configurations. The concept of GPA can give interesting advantages for these issues. Indeed, by using existing GPA to extract reusable modules, a first assessment of interfaces compatibilities and performance of the selected modules can be performed regarding various product structures. Thus, module features are defined to support these assessments and used to link process specifications, production capabilities, and all other important criteria involved in the product development process. As the developed GPA is a materialization of the existing products, the adaptation of these products to the new market requirements will be obtained through some swapping, replacing, combining and/or modification actions on the original product architectures.

In fact, the application of customer-driven product-service design can follow one of two ways processes; either collectively through generic product architecture by mapping all the requested functions, or by mapping functions individually through features and then configuring product modules (cf. Fig. 2). In this last case, more flexibility is allowed for the selection of products modules and consequently more innovative possibilities for the final product alternatives. However, more attention is required for the global consistency of the whole structure. The concept of "feature" is considered as a generic term that includes technical characteristics used for engineering perspective as well as inputs for decision-making criteria, useful for the deployment of customer-driven design process in the context of adaptation of existing European product and development facilities to an emerging market.

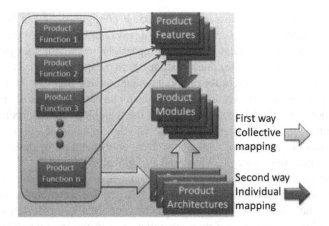

Fig. 2. Two ways product configuration strategies for identification of modules for a product

In the first case, starting from existing solutions implies a high level of knowledge about the whole development process and will reduce considerably the cost of adaptation to a new market. Using individual mapping of modules, the second way will give more possibilities to imagine new solutions (even the design process doesn't start from scratch) by reusing modules that are not originally created for the identic function. The implementation scenarios detailing these two ways are the following:

- **Configuration 1: Mapping of Requested Functions to GPA.** The starting point in this configuration is the existing product families, really produced to meet certain functions and sold to customers in other markets. The goal is then to adapt the definition of modules regarding the new requirements according to their level of correspondence with existing functions, the importance of each customer option, and possible compatibilities between local production capabilities and those used for the realization of the original product. The modular approach is used to satisfy set of functions collectively through GPA by mapping all the functions required.
- **Configuration 2: Mapping set of functions to modules through features.** In the second configuration, the modular approach is used to satisfy functions individually through features. More attention is given to product modules separately regardless of the final products structures involving these modules. This is also the case when the previous product structures contain partial correspondence with new requirements. This configuration offers more innovation freedom for the design of new product but include a strong analysis of interface compatibilities across modules. In this configuration, we go from the interpretation of the functions to identify all modules' features and then, search if there are some adequate modules and then configure these modules to possible products architectures.

3   Implementing Modular Approach in PLM for the Configuration of Customized Product

By using modular architectures, different product configurations can be built as an adaptation of existing products or the creation of new ones through the combination and connection of existing modules developed separately in previous projects. Product Configuration is already used for mass customization perspective [19]. This can be also used to increase product variety for regional adaptation and improve the possibility to the customer to choose between different options for an easily customized product with low production cost. This is possible through the matching among product modules, process modules and production capabilities. The development of a product for a new market can then be obtained through a concurrent adjustment of the designed architecture and the production strategy, considered as a global solution.

Following this approach, the involving of the customer into the product development process is made through an easier clarification of his needs as a combination of functions and options. These functions/options have to be connected in the design stage to pre-defined modules. Customers are then engaging only in the modules which they are interested in and presenting a high potential of adaptation. In the production side, alternatives of process are defined for each alternative of product configuration so that all the proposed options presented in the product configurator are already validated in terms of compatibility with the whole product architecture and production feasibility. This ensures more flexibility in the production planning.

Figure 3 shows a global scenario connecting a product configurator with the PLM. Following this scenario, the customer can visualize different options for one product type and submit his preferences. These options are already connected to a list of predefined models which are designed previously and stored in the PLM. The selection of a set of options will activate various product architectures in the PLM. Based on the selected set of options, the designer extracts the related product architectures. For every option as displayed to the customer in the configurator, a set of modules alternatives are available in the PLM and can be managed by the Designer to create the final product architecture as a combination of existing architectures.

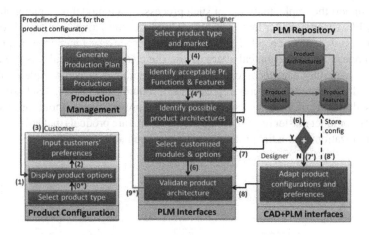

Fig. 3. Scenario of product configuration with PLM

In addition, when selecting the product family and the target market, the PLM interfaces provide a first filtering of modules respecting the target market requirements.

The creation of the predefined models in the PLM is part of a design process which is fulfilled in the design department based on the configuration strategies presented in Sect. 2.2. For each target market or potential category of customers, every type of product is presented with its main architecture connected to a set of alternative architectures. Each alternative implements one or more product options that are tailored to specific regional markets by means of related alternatives of production process.

The main question to be resolved in this design stage concerns the characteristics which the concept of modules should adopt in order to cope with the co-evolution strategy of product architecture and production process, respecting customization constraints. In this case, specific features are defined with the module concept as decision-making criteria to support the product configuration process within a co-evolution perspective as given below:

- Criticality: The importance of a module in the final product architecture regarding the importance of the related option/function to the customer. This will help the designer to choose between solutions in presence of some parameters conflicts.
- Interfacing: The flexibility of one module to be connected with other modules in the same architecture. This increases its utilization in various configurations.
- Interchangeability: The capacity of one module to be replaced by one or more other modules from the same category to provide the same function. Based on this feature and the previous one, the customer can select only compatible options.
- Process Connection: It gives information about the first time the related module is used in the production process and the dependency with other assembly operations. This is particularly important if the company aims to propose more flexibility to the customer for selecting some options although the production process is started.

To support the implementation of such process, a data model is implemented in the Audros PLM to manage a large variety of product alternatives connected to several alternatives of production (cf. Fig. 4). In this model, every function is implemented through one or several technical alternatives. The concept of "module" is used to integrate one (and only one) technical solution in one product structure. Every product is composed of several structures representing product alternatives. Each structure is composed of a set of modules and connectors that present one or more interfaces. The concept of product master represents the models of mature products that will be available for customization within the product configurator and able.

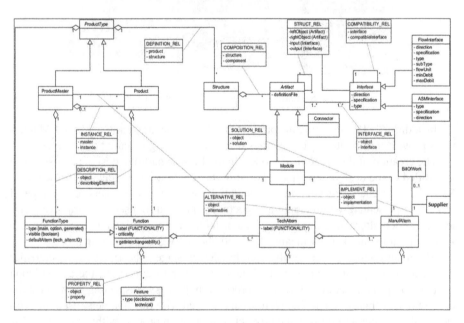

Fig. 4. PLM data model implementing modular approach

Based on this data model, several scenarios are defined as an implementation of the construction and use processes of modular architectures (see Fig. 2). These scenarios concern, for instance, the creation of original products from scratch or from the adaptation of existing ones, the connection between PLM and product configurator for the ordering of new customized product and the connection PLM-MPM (manufacturing process management) for the realization of the selected alternatives, etc.

A recognition scenario of the ordering and customization of a frugal product based on the adaptation of an existing one, using PLM is described as follow. The customer or the marketing department choose an existing product as a base and define customization to be applied to adapt the product by the design office.

- Actors: Customer/Marketing department of the company + Design department
- Goal: select the product to be customized and ordered
- Pre-condition:
    - If request comes from the Marketing department, a new product family will be developed with options.
    - If the request comes from the customer, a new customer order with customization will be considered.
- Post condition: Instance of the product master is created, request is sent to design
- Events and interactions flow:
    - The user chooses product type and target market
    - The system returns the list of suitable options
    - The user creates an order for the desired products
    - The system creates a new product, instance of chosen product master
    - The user selects the options
    - The system analyzes the order and identifies suitable modules for each option
    - The system filters the alternatives of modules for each function regarding the interfacing and compatibility criteria
    - The system generates potential alternatives of product architecture
    - The system sends a notification of design request to design office.

The Graphical User Interface (GUI) of the PLM tool has been designed to provide flexible and user-friendly manipulation of any type of product structure as well as its different modules and features. The global template of the GUI is the same for all screens, but the content adapts itself depending on the data to be managed and the context of use (Scenario and Use). With this GUI, the user will have a unified interface that will help the designer for the design of a frugal product and its co-evolution with the production process as follow:

- Create and analyze various product architectures at any level, from different point of view (functional, technical solutions, compatibility, manufacturing, etc.)
- Promote re-use and adaptations of existing solutions in the design of product architectures. This is based on the searching facilities for object (function, modules, alternatives ...) in a very simple and quick way.
- Manipulate product and production data (create/modify/adapt solutions)
- Access easily to all related documents like market survey, customer feedback, etc.

The following figure (cf. Fig. 5) presents the main GUIs of the proposed PLM platform as used in the proposed frugal design process. The flexibility of this platform takes advantage from the use of the "effectivity parameter" describing the link between two PLM objects. The effectivity parameters, displayed in the GUI, are used for data filtering as well as representation and manipulation of objects during the configuration process. There is no limit for the definition of effectivity parameters. Examples of effectivity parameters used in the case of frugal product configuration are: Criticality; Customization; Manufacturing plant; Sales country; Product option/variation; and Begin/end date of validity.

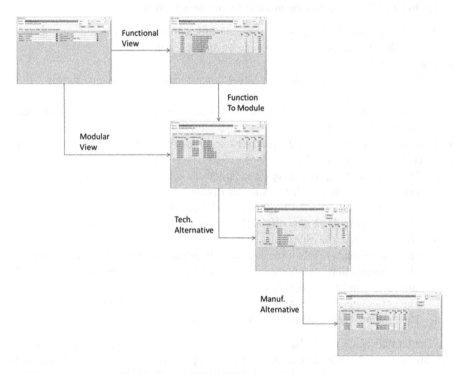

Fig. 5. Several PLM GUIs as a whole process

4   Conclusion

PLM tool configuration for the representation and the management of Product modular architectures has been introduced so as to respond to the requirements of adapting product-service design and production in a customer-driven context. The focus is the tailoring of mature product solutions to customer's needs in emerging market. Module features have been defined to help translate the regional customer requirements into product functions and product structure design. It is also used to connect the product design to production planning as well as other downstream activities.

The modular design approach for the adaptation of European product to emerging markets has been proposed for this objective. The proposed modular product design approach is actually under implementation for supporting the configuration and customization of aircrafts in aeronautic domain and the co-design of production systems tailored to regional markets. Another application, in domestic appliance industry concerns the integration of the customer in the definition of product variety through a smart organization of feedback survey following modular structures, highlighting the preferences of potential customers in a target regional market. Software interoperability and information exchanges between involved tools in these industrial scenarios is ensured using PLM framework, considered as a hub.

Acknowledgement. The presented results were conducted within the project "ProRegio" entitled "customer-driven design of product-services and production networks to adapt to regional market requirements", funding by the European Union's Horizon 2020 research and innovation program, grant agreement n° 636966.

References

1. MSCI Market Classification Framework (2014). https://www.msci.com/
2. Khanna, T., Palepu, K.G.: Emerging giants: building world-class companies in developing countries. Harvard Bus. Rev. **84**(10), 60–72 (2006)
3. Bhatti, Y.A., Khilji, S.E., Basu, R.: Frugal Innovation: Globalization, Change and Learning in South Asia. Chandos Publishing, Oxford (2013). ISBN 978-0857094643
4. Berger, R.: Frugal products, Study results (2013)
5. Gupta, R.K., Belkadi, F., Bernard, A.: Adaptation of European product to emerging markets: modular product development. In: 15ème Colloque National AIP-PRIMECA, 12–14 April 2017, La Plagne, France (2017)
6. Ferrell, O.C., Dibb, S., Simkin, L., Pride, W.M.: Marketing: Concepts and Strategies, 5th edn. Houghton Mifflin, Abingdon (2005). ISBN 9780618532032
7. Ulrich, K.T., Eppinger, S.D.: Product Design and Development, 3rd edn. McGraw-Hill, New York (2004). ISBN 0-07-247146-8
8. Ulrich, K.: The role of product architecture in the manufacturing firm. Res. Policy **24**, 419–440 (1995)
9. Pimmler, T.U., Eppinger, S.D.: Integration analysis of product decompositions. In: Proceedings of ASME Design Theory and Methodology Conference, DE, vol. 68, pp. 343–351 (1994)
10. Jiao, J., Tseng, M.M.: Fundamentals of product family architecture. Integr. Manuf. Syst. **11**(07), 469–483 (2000)
11. O'Grady, P.J.: The Age of Modularity: Using the New World of Modular Products to Revolutionize Your Corporation. Adams & Steele, Iowa City (1999)
12. Hubka, V., Eder, E.W.: Theory of Technical Systems. Springer, Heidelberg (1998)
13. Salhieh, S.M., Kamrani, A.K.: Macro level product development using design for modularity. Robot. Comput. Integr. Manuf. **15**, 319–329 (1999)
14. ElMaraghy, H., Schuh, G., ElMaraghy, E., Piller, F., Schonsleben, P., Tseng, M., Bernard, A.: Product variety management. CIRP Ann. Manuf. Technol. **62**(2), 629–652 (2013)
15. Forza, C., Salvador, F.: Application support to product variety management. Int. J. Prod. Res. **46**(3), 817–836 (2008)

16. Bruun, H.P.L., Mortensen, N.H., Harlou, U.: Interface diagram: design tool for supporting the development of modularity in complex product systems. Concurrent Eng. **22**(1), 62–76 (2014)
17. Jiao, J.R., Simpson, T.W., Siddique, Z.: Product family design and platform-based product development: a state-of-the-art review. J. Intell. Manuf. **18**, 5–29 (2007)
18. Bruun, H.P.L.: PLM support to architecture based development contribution to computer-supported architecture modelling. Ph.D. Thesis, DTU Mechanical Engineering, Technical University of Denmark (2015)
19. Daaboul, J., Da Cunha, C., Bernard, A., Laroche, F.: Design for mass customization: product variety vs process variety. CIRP Ann. Manuf. Technol. **60**(1), 169–174 (2011)

A Multi-leveled ANP-LCA Model
for the Selection of Sustainable Design Options

Manel Sansa[1(✉)], Ahmed Badreddine[2], and Taieb Ben Romdhane[1]

[1] LISI, Institut National des sciences Appliquées et de Technologies,
Université de Carthage, Centre Urbain Nord BP 676, 1080 Tunis, Tunisia
manel.sansa@outlook.com, benromdhane.t@topnet.tn
[2] LARODEC, Institut Supérieur de Gestion de Tunis,
41 Avenue de la liberté, 2000 Le Bardo, Tunisia
ahmed.badreddine@gmail.com

Abstract. The aim of this paper is to propose a new model for the selection of sustainable design options. This model is based on the environmental, the economic, and the social life cycle assessments. It deals with the uncertainties and the imprecisions due to the technological choices and their potential impacts since early design phase of the product. The proposed model is based on four principles, namely: Early integration, life cycle thinking, functionality thinking, and the multi-criteria concept. A case study is presented to validate the applicability of the proposed model on the design of batteries.

Keywords: Sustainable design · Eco-design · ELCA · EcLCA · SLCA
Fuzzy ANP

1 Introduction

The sustainable development has become widely embraced by industries. It links the concept of sustainability to the social, economic and environmental challenges faced by humanity [1]. To this end, designers have to improve the reliability of the product since its design phase. Despite the acknowledgment of the sustainability approaches, its application has been limited to single aspects which the best known is the eco-designs approaches [2]. The implementation of the design strategies is not an easy task due to the lack of necessary roadmaps [3]. In this context, many tools are available, the most suitable ones are the Environmental Life Cycle Assessment (ELCA) [4], the Economic Life Cycle Assessment (EcLCA) [5], and the Social Life Cycle Assessment (SLCA) [6]. However, these methods are more complex at an early stage of the design phase since they require significant data through all the life cycle phases which leads to uncertain and imprecise results. To this end, we propose a new model which combines the eco-design strategies with the concept of sustainable development. This model aims to select the optimal sustainable design option for a product at an early stage using simplified ELCA, EcLCA and SLCA and the fuzzy ANP [7–9]. The remainder of this paper is laid out as follows: Sect. 2 presents the problem statement and the motivation. Section 3 describes and details the different steps of the proposed model. Section 4 presents the implementation of the model on a case study. Finally, Sect. 5 concludes the research.

© IFIP International Federation for Information Processing 2017
Published by Springer International Publishing AG 2017. All Rights Reserved
J. Ríos et al. (Eds.): PLM 2017, IFIP AICT 517, pp. 473–486, 2017.
https://doi.org/10.1007/978-3-319-72905-3_42

2 Problem Statement and Motivation

In the literature, several researches have been conducted on the sustainable design. Table 1 summarizes the most recent ones.

Table 1. The related works on sustainable design

Existing works	Sustainable design			Early integration	Life cycle thinking	Functionality thinking	Multi-criteria concept	Uncertainties issues
	E	Ec	S					
Romli et al. [10]	X	N.A	N.A	Design process	The use of LCA	Quality function deployment, functional unit	The use of LCA	N.A
Wang et al. [11]	X	N.A	N.A	Design process	The use of LCA	Functional unit	Criteria defined for each life cycle phase	Fuzzy logic
Ng and Chuah [12]	X	N.A	N.A	Design process	The use of rough-cut LCA	Functional unit	AHP	Fuzzy logic, Evidential Reasoning
Fragnoli et al. [13]	X	Ergonomic issues	Safety issues	Redesign process	N.A	Function analysis	Environmental, quality and costs indices	N.A
Bereketli and Genevois [14]	X	X	X	Design process	N.A	QFDE	AHP	Fuzzy AHP
Younesi and Roghanian [15]	X	X	Product quality	Design process	N.A	QFDE	ANP	Fuzzy logic, DEMATEL

According to the related works and the international standards [2, 4, 16], the following principles are recommended for designers in order to achieve a sustainable design: (i) **Early integration**: The improvement of the environmental performance of the product must be considered at early stages of the design process because such improvement will be more difficult if the product is already developed. (ii) **Life cycle thinking**: The consideration of all the stages of the life cycle is necessary to better locate where and how the product can affect the environment, the economy and the society. (iii) **Functionality thinking**: The purpose and performance requirements of the products must be taken into account through the life cycle analysis. (iiii) **Multi-criteria concept**: The combination between criteria such as environment, economy and society must be considered through the design process.

In addition, most of the related works (See Table 1) have ignored the economic and social aspects. Their proposed frameworks treated only the environmental issues. Moreover, these researchers pointed out the complexity of the complexity of the LCA method at the design phase which leads to uncertain results and unsuitable design decisions.

To overcome these weaknesses, our proposed model is based on simplified ELCA, EcLCA, and SLCA methods. The simplified life cycle assessment was proposed by Ng [17] as a rough-cut LCA in order to address the complexity of the full LCA and to obtain the environmental performance of the desired product with the available data. Then, our idea is to connect these results to a multi-leveled fuzzy Analytic Network Process [7–9] for decision support.

3   A New Model for the Selection of Sustainable Design Options

The proposed model is outlined in Fig. 1. The model selects the optimal sustainable design option for a specific product during its design phase taking into account its life cycle phases LCP_j where $j = [1..5]$, LCP_1 is the extraction of raw materials, LCP_2 is the manufacturing, LCP_3 is the distribution, LCP_4 is the use and maintenance and LCP_5 is the end of life. This model is based on an environmental, economic, and social life cycle assessments conducted on each option on the basis of a unique functional unit which is a quantified description of the main function of the product. The functional unit is considered as a mutual reference between the three life cycle assessments. The model is detailed as follows:

Let PDO_i be the set of the product's design options where $i = [1..n]$ and n is the number of design options.

Let PDOs be the selected optimal sustainable design option.

- For each PDO_i, the environmental, economic, and social impacts are assessed on the basis of multi-criteria and life cycle approaches in order to evaluate the impacts through all the life cycle phases. The results of these assessments are a set of environmental indicators EI_x, economic indicators ECI_y and social indicators SL_z

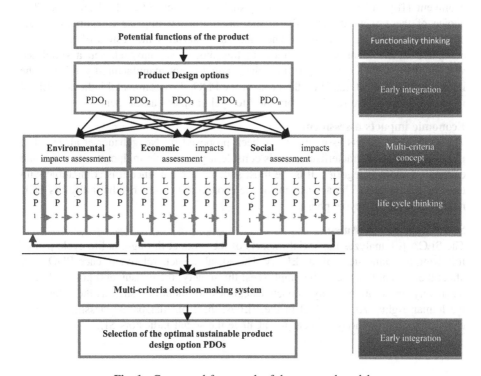

Fig. 1. Conceptual framework of the proposed model

where x, y and Z are the numbers of the set of environmental, economic and social indicators.

- For each life cycle phase LCP_j, the priority weights relative to each PDO_i are computed through a multi-criteria decision-making system using the environment, the economy and the society as criteria, and the aforementioned indicators as the relative sub-criteria.
- For each PDO_i, the global score is computed on the basis of the calculated priority weights per life cycle phase, the PDOi with the highest score is the selected option PDO_S.

3.1 Impacts Assessement

Environmental impacts assessment
The potential environmental impacts of the product are assessed using the ELCA method taking into account all the phases of the life cycle [4]. It allows the definition of the environmental profile of the product for each PDO_i. this method consists of four main iterative steps: The first defines the goal and the scope of the study. The second determines the inventory of the elementary and intermediate flows related to the environment. The third is dedicated to the assessment of the environmental impacts related to the identified flows. In fact, these latter are classified and characterized by impacts and damage categories. At this stage, environmental databases such as the ecoinvent [18] and aggregation methods such as Impact 2002+ [19] are used. The choice of these methods depends on the environmental impacts categories and the consideration of time and space. The final step interprets the results of the studies compared to the identified objectives. In this model, we have chosen a simplified version of the full ELCA [17]. In fact, the product is not manufactured yet. Thus, the inventory data are estimated on the basis of the PDO_i. Environmental indicators EI_x of impacts categories are resulted from the life cycle impacts assessment.

Economic impacts assessment
The economic impacts assessment has been proposed by Neugebauer et al. [5]. The EcLCA proposes characterization tools considering economic midpoint categories and endpoint damage categories. It is the most suitable version since it is compatible with the ELCA structure. The assessment of the economic impacts results indicators ECI_y relative to each life cycle phase.

Social impacts assessment
The SLCA [6] analyzes the social impacts of the product through its life cycle phases following the same steps of the ELCA. The social impacts relative to each PDO_i may affect the stakeholders (e.g. the employees, the society, the consumers) positively and negatively. In addition, many impacts categories are identified such as the safety and the human rights. As described in the ELCA, there are databases, classification and characterization methods in order to calculate the social indicators SI_z.

3.2   Selection of the Optimal Sustainable Design Option

At this stage, on the basis of the indicators computed above, the optimal sustainable product design option PDO$_S$ is selected using the fuzzy ANP [9]. The choice of this method is due to the dependency among the three aspects and the uncertainty and imprecision of the ELCA, EcLCA, and SLCA results and the judgments of the decision-makers. The fuzzy ANP considers triangular fuzzy numbers denoted l, m, and u where l is the smallest possible value, m is the most promising value and u is the largest possible value. These parameters describe a fuzzy event and their relative membership function is defined below [20]:

$$\mu(x) = \begin{cases} \frac{x-l}{m-l} & if \quad l \le x \le m \\ \frac{u-x}{u-m} & if \quad m \le x \le u \\ 0 & Otherwise \end{cases} \tag{1}$$

Therefore, the fuzzy pair-wise comparison matrix $\breve{M}$ is presented below:

$$\breve{M} = \begin{pmatrix} (1,1,1) & (E_{12}^l, E_{12}^m, E_{12}^u) & \cdots & (E_{1n}^l, E_{1n}^m, E_{1n}^u) \\ (\frac{1}{E_{12}^u}, \frac{1}{E_{12}^m}, \frac{1}{E_{12}^l}) & (1,1,1) & \cdots & (E_{2n}^l, E_{2n}^m, E_{2n}^u) \\ \vdots & \vdots & \ddots & \vdots \\ (\frac{1}{E_{1n}^u}, \frac{1}{E_{1n}^m}, \frac{1}{E_{1n}^l}) & (\frac{1}{E_{2n}^u}, \frac{1}{E_{2n}^m}, \frac{1}{E_{2n}^l}) & \cdots & (1,1,1) \end{pmatrix} \tag{2}$$

Where $E_{ij}^{l,m,u} = \left(E_{ij}^l, E_{ij}^m, E_{ij}^u\right)$ and $E_{ji}^{l,m,u} = (\frac{1}{E_{ij}^u}, \frac{1}{E_{ij}^m}, \frac{1}{E_{ij}^l})$ are the fuzzy preference which compare the ith with the jth element where i (resp.j) = [1..n] is the number of rows (resp. columns) of the matrix $\breve{M}$. The weights relative to each element k of the matrix $\breve{M}$ where k = [1..n] and n is the number of the elements, are computed as follows: Let $W_k^{l,m,u} = \left(W_k^l, W_k^m, W_k^u\right)$ be the triangular fuzzy weight relative to the kth element of the matrix $\breve{M}$. $W_k^{l,m,u}$ is computed using the logarithmic least squares method given in Eq. (3) [20].

$$W_k^{l,m,u} = \frac{\left(\prod_{j=1}^n E_{kj}^{l,m,u}\right)^{1/n}}{\sum_{i=1}^n \left(\prod_{j=1}^n E_{ij}^{l,m,u}\right)^{1/n}} \tag{3}$$

Since the ANP method is applied for each life cycle phase, we suggest the multi-leveled fuzzy ANP. The criteria relative to our model are: The environment (E), the economy (Ec), and the society (S). The sub-criteria are: EI$_x$, ECI$_y$, SI$_z$. The alternatives are: The product design options PDO$_i$. We note that all the fuzzy pair-wise comparison matrices are determined using (2) and all the fuzzy weights are computed using (3). The steps to conduct the fuzzy ANP relative to the proposed model are outlined below:

Let $W_{IC}^{l,m,u}$ (resp. $W_{DC}^{l,m,u}$, $W_{SC}^{l,m,u}$, $W_A^{l,m,u}$) be the set of weights relative to independent (resp. dependent criteria, sub-criteria, alternatives).

Let $W_C^{l,m,u}$ (resp. $W_{OP}^{l,m,u}, W_{GP}^{l,m,u}$) be the set of overall priority weights relative to criteria (resp. sub-criteria, alternatives).

Let GS_i be the global score of each PDO$_i$.

1. Determine the comparison matrix between each criterion by supposing that they are independent and compute $W_{IC}^{l,m,u}$.
2. Determine the comparison matrix between each criterion by considering the dependency among them and compute $W_{DC}^{l,m,u}$.
3. Compute $W_C^{l,m,u}$ by multiplying $W_{IC}^{l,m,u}$ and $W_{DC}^{l,m,u}$.
4. Determine the comparison matrix between the sub-criteria with respect to the criteria and compute $W_{SC}^{l,m,u}$.
5. Compute $W_{OP}^{l,m,u}$ by multiplying $W_C^{l,m,u}$ and $W_{SC}^{l,m,u}$ for each sub-criterion.
6. For each LCP$_j$, determine the comparison matrix between the alternatives with respect to each sub-criterion.
7. Compute $W_A^{l,m,u}$ and then $W_{GP}^{l,m,u}$ for each alternative by multiplying $W_A^{l,m,u}$ and $W_{OP}^{l,m,u}$.

Once $W_{GP}^{l,m,u}$ are computed for all the life cycle phases, the last step is to compute the GS_i for each PDO$_i$ by summing the W_{GP} of each life cycle phase.

4   Case Study

In order to illustrate the proposed model, we present its application within a company that designs and manufactures electronic products for a specific usage. Designers have chosen to apply the proposed model for the selection of the optimal battery technology with the aim to design a sustainable product.

4.1   Identifying the PDO$_i$

To simplify the application of the proposed model, only four batteries technologies noted as design options PDO$_1$, PDO$_2$, PDO$_3$, and PDO$_4$ are defined in Table 2 in order to select the most sustainable one.

Table 2. The types and properties relative to each PDO$_i$

PDO$_i$	Type of chemistry cell	Technical data		
		Nominal voltage (V)	Cycle durability (cycles)	Specific energy (Wh/kg)
PDO$_1$	Lithium iron phosphate	2	1000–2000	90–120
PDO$_2$	Lithium nickel cobalt aluminum oxide	3	1000–1500	200–260
PDO$_3$	Lithium manganese oxide	2.5	300–700	100–150
PDO$_4$	Lithium cobalt oxide	205	500–1000	150–200

- PDO$_1$: **Lithium iron phosphate (LiFePO$_4$)**. This option consists of a graphite carbon anode and an iron phosphate cathode. It is characterized by a lower specific energy, a longer life span and a better specific power than the other lithium ions batteries. PDO$_1$ offers good safety characteristics regarding the users and manufacturers consider it as a potential replacement for the common lead acid batteries. The materials have low costs and do not harm the environment compared to the other options [21].
- PDO$_2$: **Lithium nickel cobalt aluminum oxide (LiNiCoAlO$_2$)**. This battery consists of a graphite carbon anode and a nickel cobalt aluminum oxide. The aluminum offers specific energy and power and a long-life span. However, the costs relative to this option are high and the percentage of its safety is very low [22].
- PDO$_3$: **Lithium manganese oxide (LiMn$_2$O$_4$)**. This option consists of a graphite carbon anode and a manganese oxide cathode. It is considered safer than lithium cobalt in terms of overheating risks and also less expensive. PDO3 is known for its high power but less capacity and a short life span. In addition, it is composed of non-toxic material which does not treat the environment and the human being [23].
- PDO$_4$: **Lithium cobalt oxide (LiCoO$_2$)**. This battery is composed of a graphite carbon anode and a cobalt oxide cathode. It is characterized by its high specific energy which has increased its market share. However, the cobalt material is known for its high costs. Besides, PDO$_4$ has a short life span and a low thermal stability compared to the remaining options. Regarding the environment and the society, this battery contains material with very low percentage of toxicity but these materials may harm the environment and the human-being in case of improper disposal at the end of life [21].

4.2 Conducting a Life Cycle Assessment

For each PDO$_i$, simplified EcLCA, and SLCA methods have been conducted using the Quantis software and the Ecoinvent 2.2 database [18]. The three assessments are based on a unique functional unit which is the use of the battery for five years. All the collected data are normalized to the functional unit and then treated in order to evaluate the potential impacts. At this stage, the IMPACT 2002 + method [19] has been chosen. For simplicity reasons, the endpoint indicators are computed and taken into account in the case study.

Environmental assessment

As shown in Fig. 2, four impacts indicators, namely; EI$_1$: human health, EI$_2$: ecosystem quality, EI$_3$: climate change, and EI$_4$: resources are computed for each PDO$_i$ through all the life cycle phases. We can remark that all PDO$_i$ have approximately the same impacts on the human health in LCP$_1$ ($\approx$22%). In fact, all options are lithium based and this element is extracted through lithium mining. This process is considered harmful for the environment. Besides, the exposure of workers to the lithium dust for a long period causes respiratory problems and air pollution. In addition, PDO$_1$ and PDO$_3$ have the same impacts in LCP$_4$ ($\approx$28%) regarding the climate change due to the carbon emissions when charging the batteries. Moreover, PDO$_1$ has greater impact on the climate change in LCP$_2$ ($\approx$28%) and LCP5 ($\approx$24%) because it generates more carbon

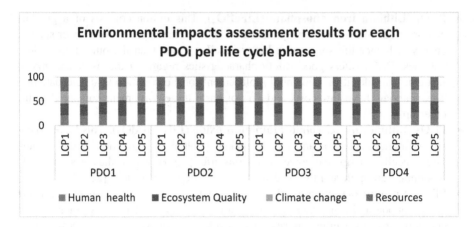

Fig. 2. Results of the ELCA impacts assessment

dioxide during these phases compared to the other PDO_i. Also, we can remark that PDO_2 has a significant impact on the ecosystem quality ($\approx 25\%$) and the human health ($\approx 24\%$) especially in LCP_2 and LCP_5 because the aluminum is considered as a toxic metal and it has significant effects on the aquatic and terrestrial ecosystems due to the emission of this metal during the manufacturing phase and its disposal at the end of life phase. PDO_1 and PDO_3 have lower impacts on the human health ($\approx 23\%$) in LCP_5 than PDO_2 and PDO_4 ($\approx 25\%$). In fact, manganese and iron have lower toxicity percentage whereas nickel and cobalt belong to the hazardous material category. Finally, we can remark that all PDO_i have approximately the same impacts on LCP_3 due to the assumptions that the distribution phase is similar for all options regarding the distance and the fuel consumption and emissions (i.e. $EI_1 \approx 24\%$, $EI_2 \approx 25\%$, $EI_3 \approx 25\%$, $EI_4 \approx 26\%$).

Economic assessment
Two indicators are computed from the impacts assessment of the EcLCA as illustrated in Fig. 3: ECI_1: economic prosperity and ECI_2: economic resilience. ECI_1 is estimated through the profitability, productivity of the organization and the consumer satisfaction deduced from the market share of the product. ECI_2 expresses the ability to prevent changes without drawbacks for the economic stability [5]. We can note from Fig. 3 that PDO_2 and PDO_4 have the highest impact on the economic prosperity due to the high costs of the raw materials ($\approx 50\%$), manufacturing ($\approx 40\%$), and the end of life treatments, and the end of life treatments ($\approx 28\%$). In addition, PDO_1 and PDO_3 have the highest impact on the economic resilience especially during LCP_4 ($\approx 65\%$) since the level of competitiveness on the market has increased due to investments on improving the nickel metal hybrid and the absorbed glass mat batteries that are characterized by their low costs, safer for the environment, and affordable by the consumer.

Social assessment
The impacts assessment relative to the SLCA results an indicator that estimates the well-being of stakeholders SI_1 (See Fig. 4). In this context, the stakeholders are all

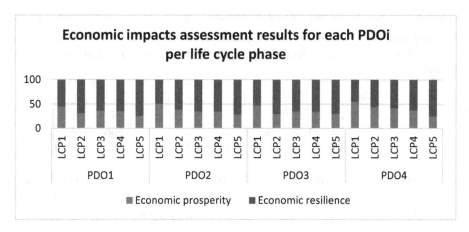

Fig. 3. Results of the EcLCA impacts assessment

human-being that are involved within the product (i.e. employees, consumers, managers, governors).

As shown in Fig. 4. we can remark that PDO_2 and PDO_4 have significant impacts on the human well-being particularly during LCP_2 ($\approx 26\%$) and LCP_4 ($\approx 28\%$). In fact, the workers are exposed to hazard materials as well as the consumers. PDO_1 and PDO_3 have the lowest impacts on all phases since they offer good safety characteristics and consist of non-toxic materials.

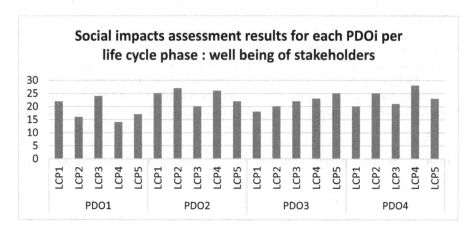

Fig. 4. Results of the SLCA impacts assessment

4.3   Selecting the Optimal Sustainable Design Option

Following the steps of the fuzzy ANP, the first step is to set the main comparison matrix $\tilde{M}$ for the criteria E, Ec, and S using (2) with respect to the goal which is the selection of PDO$_S$. Supposing that the criteria are independent, the comparison is based on a judgment scale predefined using (1) [9]. $\breve{M}$ is defined on the basis of the judgments of the designers taking into account the properties of the different PDO$_i$ and obtained as follows:

$$
\tilde{M} = \begin{pmatrix}
 & & E & & & & Ec & & & S & \\
E & 1 & 1 & 1 & 3 & 3.5 & 4 & 5 & 5.5 & 6 \\
Ec & 0.25 & 0.285 & 0.333 & 1 & 1 & 1 & 1 & 0.666 & 0.666 \\
S & 0.166 & 0.181 & 0.2 & 1.5 & 1.5 & 1 & 1 & 1 & 1
\end{pmatrix}
$$

For example, the Environment (E) is moderately to strongly preferred than the Economy (Ec) with respect to the goal. Then, considering the dependencies between the criteria, we set the matrix $\breve{M}_{inter-dependencies}$ by comparing the criteria with respect to each other's. For instance, we compare Ec and S with respect to E. $\breve{M}_{inter-dependencies}$ is obtained as follows:

$$
\tilde{M}_{inter-dependencies} = \begin{pmatrix}
 & & E & & & Ec & & & S & \\
E & 1 & 1 & 1 & 0.449 & 0.4 & 0.449 & 0.5 & 0.5 & 0.5 \\
Ec & 0.224 & 0.222 & 0.224 & 1 & 1 & 1 & 0.5 & 0.5 & 0.5 \\
S & 0.775 & 0.777 & 0.775 & 0.55 & 1.6 & 0.55 & 1 & 1 & 1
\end{pmatrix}
$$

Then, we obtain two comparison matrices for the sub-criteria EI$_x$, ECI$_y$ with respect to E and Ec respectively. Since we have one social sub-criteria, the relative weight is equal to 1. We present in Table 3 all the weights relative to E, Ec, S, EI$_x$, EI$_y$, SI$_z$ computed using (3).

At this stage, for each LCP$_j$, seven comparison matrices for PDO$_i$ with respect to EI$_x$, EI$_y$, and SI$_z$ are identified from the judgments of designers on the basis of the impacts assessments results shown in Figs. 2, 3 and 4. since the same step is performed for each LCP$_j$, we present the results of the application of the fuzzy ANP for LCP$_1$. The seven comparison matrices for the PDO$_i$ with respect to EI$_x$, EI$_y$ and SI$_z$ are detailed in Table 4. The following step is to determine the priority weights relative to each PDO$_i$

Table 3. The overall priority weights relative to the criteria and the sub-criteria per LCP$_1$

Criteria	W$_C$			Sub criteria	W$_{SC}$			W$_{OP}$		
	l	m	u		l	m	u	l	m	u
E	0.3277	0.3281	0.328	EI$_1$	0.3096	0.3241	0.3489	0.1014	0.1063	0.1144
				EI$_2$	0.2603	0.2623	0.2467	0.0853	0.0861	0.0809
				EI$_3$	0.1503	0.1316	0.1576	0.0492	0.0431	0.0517
				EI$_4$	0.2797	0.2818	0.2467	0.0917	0.0924	0.0809
Ec	0.2614	0.2614	0.2614	ECI$_1$	0.25	0.2222	0.2	0.0653	0.0581	0.0522
				ECI$_2$	0.75	0.7777	0.8	0.1961	0.2033	0.2091
S	0.4107	0.4104	0.4104	SI$_1$	1	1	1	0.4107	0.4104	0.4104

Table 4. The comparison matrices relative to PDO$_i$ with respect to EI$_x$, EI$_y$ and SI$_z$ for LCP$_1$.

	PDO$_1$			PDO$_2$			PDO$_3$			PDO$_4$		
	l	m	u	l	m	u	l	m	u	l	m	u
EI$_1$												
PDO$_1$	1	1	1	1	1.5	1.5	1	0.5	0.5	1	1.5	1.5
PDO$_2$	0.666	0.666	1	1	1	1	0.333	0.285	0.25	1	0.666	0.666
PDO$_3$	2	2	1	4	3.5	3	1	1	1	1	2	2
PDO$_4$	0.666	0.666	1	1.5	1.5	1	0.5	0.5	1	1	1	1
EI$_2$												
PDO$_1$	1	1	1	1	2	2	3	4	4.5	1	2	2
PDO$_2$	0.5	0.5	1	1	1	1	0.333	0.285	0.25	1	0.666	0.666
PDO$_3$	0.222	0.25	0.333	0.2	0.222	0.333	1	1	1	0.2	0.181	0.166
PDO$_4$	0.5	0.5	1	0.666	0.666	1	6	5.5	5	1	1	1
EI$_3$												
PDO$_1$	1	1	1	1	2	2	0.333	0.285	0.25	1	1.5	1.5
PDO$_2$	0.5	0.5	1	1	1	1	0.333	0.25	0.222	1	0.5	0.5
PDO$_3$	4	3.5	3	4.5	4	3	1	1	1	3	3.5	4
PDO$_4$	0.666	0.666	1	2	2	1	0.25	0.285	0.333	1	1	1
EI$_4$												
PDO$_1$	1	1	1	1	0.5	0.5	0.333	0.222	0.2	1	0.5	0.5
PDO$_2$	2	2	1	1	1	1	0.2	0.181	0.166	1	1.5	1.5
PDO$_3$	5	4.5	3	6	5.5	5	1	1	1	5	5.5	6
PDO$_4$	2	2	1	0.666	0.666	1	0.166	0.181	0.2	1	1	1
ECI$_1$												
PDO$_1$	1	1	1	5	5.5	6	3	4	4.5	5	7	9
PDO$_2$	0.166	0.181	0.2	1	1	1	0.333	0.222	0.2	3	4.5	5
PDO$_3$	0.222	0.25	0.333	5	4.5	3	1	1	1	5	6	7
PDO$_4$	0.111	0.142	0.2	0.2	0.222	0.333	0.142	0.166	0.2	1	1	1
ECI$_2$												
PDO$_1$	1	1	1	0.2	0.181	0.166	0.333	0.25	0.22	0.2	0.142	0.111
PDO$_2$	6	5.5	5	1	1	1	3	4.5	5	0.333	0.222	0.2
PDO$_3$	4.5	4	3	0.2	0.222	0.333	1	1	1	0.2	0.166	0.142
PDO$_4$	9	7	5	5	4.5	3	7	6	5	1	1	1
SI$_1$												
PDO$_1$	1	1	1	3	4.5	5	0.2	0.181	0.166	0.333	0.285	0.25
PDO$_2$	0.2	0.222	0.333	1	1	1	0.2	0.166	0.142	0.333	0.222	0.2
PDO$_3$	6	5.5	5	7	6	5	1	1	1	0.333	0.285	0.25
PDO$_4$	4	3.5	3	5	4.5	3	4	3.5	3	1	1	1

for LCP$_1$ as presented in Table 5. Then, W$_{GP}$ is obtained by multiplying $W_A^{l,m,u}$ and $W_{OP}^{l,m,u}$.

Finally, the global score GS of each PDOi is computed by summing the W$_{GP}$ of the PDO$_i$ per life cycle phase. W$_{GP}$ and GS are presented in Table 6.

Table 5. The priority weights relative to PDO_i with respect to EI_x, ECI_y, SI_z, for LCP_1

PDO_i	W_A						
	EI_1	EI_2	EI_3	EI_4	ECI_1	ECI_2	SI_1
W_A^l							
PDO_1	0.2375	0.3358	0.156	0.1323	0.5496	0.0502	0.1127
PDO_2	0.1631	0.2823	0.1312	0.1385	0.1193	0.2312	0.0572
PDO_3	0.3995	0.0783	0.5567	0.6095	0.2867	0.0962	0.326
PDO_4	0.1997	0.3034	0.156	0.1196	0.0443	0.6223	0.504
W_A^m							
PDO_1	0.2339	0.4135	0.1966	0.0888	0.5815	0.0462	0.127
PDO_2	0.1356	0.2802	0.1021	0.1573	0.1078	0.2492	0.055
PDO_3	0.4394	0.0655	0.5406	0.6253	0.2661	0.1009	0.3201
PDO_4	0.191	0.2406	0.1605	0.1284	0.0445	0.6035	0.4978
W_A^u							
PDO_1	0.2432	0.3692	0.1972	0.0959	0.5997	0.04773	0.1393
PDO_2	0.1509	0.2966	0.1223	0.1434	0.1015	0.2818	0.0644
PDO_3	0.3696	0.0661	0.5192	0.6249	0.2471	0.1158	0.3261
PDO_4	0.2361	0.268	0.1611	0.1356	0.0516	0.5546	0.4701

Table 6. The overall priority weights and global score relative to PDO_i

PDO_i	W_{GP}					GS
	LCP_1	LCP_2	LCP_3	LCP_4	LCP_5	
PDO_1	0.1704	0.379	0.1509	0.4294	0.3859	1.5158
PDO_2	0.1411	0.1566	0.2837	0.1645	0.2454	0.9912
PDO_3	0.2997	0.2155	0.2222	0.2331	0.1917	1.1622
PDO_4	0.3886	0.2489	0.3432	0.173	0.177	1.3307

According to Table 6, PDO_1 has the highest score. This option is considered the most suitable for the design of the product since it generates the minimum environmental, economic, and social impacts through all the life cycle phases.

5 Conclusion

In this paper, we proposed a new model for the selection of the optimal sustainable design option. Our contribution is mainly observed through the integration of the environmental, economic, and the social aspects by using simplified assessment methods and by adding a multi-criteria decision making for the selection of a sustainable design option. In addition, we highlighted through the case study the extension of the eco-design concept towards a sustainable design. In fact, we used the inventory data collected from similar previous designs of the batteries. These data are then classified and their relative impacts are evaluated by categories of indicators. The results showed that PDO_1 is the optimal sustainable design option. This option generates the least impacts through the life cycle phases comparing to the remaining options. It consists of non-toxic materials and has low costs. PDO_1 is considered safe for the consumer. Moreover, the experts confirmed the coherence of the obtained results with studies on similar batteries. However, it is important to note that these results depend on the time and space aspects due to the choice of the IMPACT 2002+ method.

References

1. Bruntland, G.: World commission on environment and development (WCED), Our common future (1987)
2. ISO 14062, Environmental Management-Integrating Environmental Aspects into Product Design and Development (2002)
3. Pigosso, D.C., Rozenfeld, H., McAloone, T.C.: Ecodesign maturity model: a management framework to support ecodesign implementation into manufacturing companies. J. Clean. Prod. **59**, 160–173 (2013)
4. ISO 14044, Environmental Management–Life Cycle Assessment, Requirements and Guidelines (2006)
5. Neugebauer, S., Forin, S., Finkbeiner, M.: From life cycle costing to economic life cycle assessment—introducing an economic impact pathway. Sustainability **8**, 428 (2016)
6. Dreyers, L., Hauschild, M., Schierbeck, J.: A framework for social life cycle impact assessment. Int. J. Life Cycle Assess. **11**, 88–97 (2006)
7. Saaty, T.L.: Decision Making with Dependence and Feedback: The Analytic Network Process. RWS Publications, Pittsburgh (1996)
8. Zadeh, L.: Fuzzy sets. Inf. Control **8**, 338–353 (1965)
9. Mikhailov, L., Madan, G.: Fuzzy analytic network process and its application to the development of decision support system. IEEE Trans. Syst. Man Cybern. Part C Appl. Rev. **33**, 33–41 (2003)
10. Romli, A., Prickett, P., Setchi, R., Soe, S.: Integrated eco-design decision-making for sustainable product development. Int. J. Prod. Res. **53**, 549–571 (2015)
11. Wang, X., Chan, H., White, L.: A comprehensive decision support model for the evaluation of eco-designs. J. Oper. Res. Soc. **65**, 917–934 (2014)
12. Ng, C., Chuah, K.: A hybrid approach for environmental impact evaluation of design options. Int. J. Sustain. Eng. **9**, 1–11 (2016)
13. Fargnoli, M., De Minicis, M., Tronci, M.: Design management for sustainability: an integrated approach for the development of sustainable products. J. Eng. Technol. Manag. **34**, 29–45 (2014)
14. Bereketli, I., Genevois, M.: An integrated QFDE approach for identifying improvement strategies in sustainable product development. J. Clean. Prod. **54**, 188–198 (2013)
15. Younesi, M., Roghanian, E.: A framework for sustainable product design: a hybrid fuzzy approach based on Quality Function Deployment for Environment. J. Clean. Prod. **108**, 385–394 (2015)
16. Marques, B., Tadeu, A., De Brito, J., Almeida, J.: A perspective on the development of sustainable construction products: an eco-design approach. Int. J. Sustain. Dev. Plan. **12**, 304–314 (2017)
17. Ng, C., Chuah, K.: Evaluation of design alternatives' environmental performance using AHP and ER approaches. IEEE Syst. J. **8**, 1185–1192 (2014)

18. Wernet, G., Bauer, C., Steubing, B., Reinhard, J., Moreno-Ruiz, E., Weidema, B.: The ecoinvent database version 3 (part I): overview and methodology. Int. J. Life Cycle Assess. **21**, 1–13 (2016)
19. Jolliet, O., Margni, M., Charles, R., Humbert, S., Payet, J., Rebitzer, G., Rosenbaum, R.: IMPACT 2002+: a new life cycle impact assessment methodology. Int. J. Life Cycle Assess. **8**, 324–330 (2003)
20. Onut, S., Kara, S., Isik, E.: Long term supplier selection using a combined fuzzy MCDM approach: a case study for a telecommunication company. Expert Syst. Appl. **36**, 3887–3895 (2009)
21. Scrosati, B., Garche, J.: Lithium batteries: Status, prospects and future. J. Power Sources **195**, 2419–2430 (2010)
22. Chen, C.H., Liu, J., Stoll, M.E., Henriksen, G., Vissers, D.R., Amine, K.: Aluminum-doped lithium nickel cobalt oxide electrodes for high-power lithium-ion batteries. J. Power Sources **128**, 278–285 (2004)
23. Thackeray, M.M., Johnson, C.S., Vaughey, J.T., Li, N., Hackney, S.A.: Advances in manganese-oxide 'composite' electrodes for lithium-ion batteries. J. Mater. Chem. **15**, 2257–2267 (2005)

New Product Development

Towards Smart Product Lifecycle Management with an Integrated Reconfiguration Management

Michael Abramovici, Jens Christian Göbel, Philipp Savarino$^{(\boxtimes)}$,
and Philip Gebus

Chair of Information Technology in Mechanical Engineering (ITM),
Ruhr-University Bochum, Bochum, Germany
philipp.savarino@itm.rub.de

Abstract. Recent ICT innovations determine dramatically changes of traditional products towards intelligent, connected Smart Products. These product-related changes also imply the need for a fundamental adaption and enhancement of traditional Product Lifecycle Management approaches. Analyzing the main characteristics of Smart Products reveals that lifecycle management approaches for Smart Products especially have to extend their focus on the product use phase. A core challenge in this context is to provide suitable methods and IT tools for the reconfiguration of Smart Products across different engineering domains. This contribution introduces a conceptual approach for the reconfiguration of Smart Products, which considers the dynamical changes of virtual and physical product instances based on the virtual product twin. This approach was implemented and validated prototypically in a model-environment considering smart vehicles, that where temporarily reconfigured during their use phase.

Keywords: Reconfiguration · Smart Products
Product Lifecycle Management · Virtual twin

1 Configuration of Traditional and Reconfiguration of Smart Products

Recent innovation in Information and Communication Technology (ICT) have begun to dramatically change traditional products towards intelligent, connected Smart Products (SP). Characteristic features of Smart Products are their capability to communicate and interact with their environment and other Smart Products by using Internet-based services [1]. They have a high degree of personalization and autonomy, a large number of multidisciplinary components, the ability to react in real-time and their dynamic reconfiguration potential during their whole lifetime [2]. Especially the high amount of software components enables a tremendous potential for IT-based reconfiguration, e.g. like a (temporary) parking assistant for a smart vehicle. However such a reconfiguration requires suitable methods and IT tools e.g. for the management of virtual and physical product instances that exceed common Product Lifecycle Management approaches [3].

© IFIP International Federation for Information Processing 2017
Published by Springer International Publishing AG 2017. All Rights Reserved
J. Ríos et al. (Eds.): PLM 2017, IFIP AICT 517, pp. 489–498, 2017.
https://doi.org/10.1007/978-3-319-72905-3_43

A reconfiguration can be generally described as a modification of a product instance to meet new requirements [4]. Considering Smart Products, reconfiguration processes during the use phase primarily aim at:

- The general technical improvement of product classes (e.g. the implementation of new software releases for a new generation of smart vehicles).
- The individual improvement of product instances by enhancing the functional amount (e.g. IT-based parking assistance systems for smart vehicles) or IT-services (e.g. a cloud-based, individually improved energy management for smart vehicles).

As a conceptual basis for the methodological reconfiguration of Smart Products, existing product configuration approaches providing initial customer specific virtual product models can be used. The normative standard ISO 10007 defines configuration units, which are entities within a configuration that provide a specific end use function. These configuration units are part of a configuration management model that also addresses the change management of these units during a reconfiguration [5]. However, this requires knowledge of all product instance configuration units along the entire product lifecycle. The management of configuration units can also be done by using product configurators aiming at the mass customization of products. They base on system of rule describing dependencies and requirements between configuration units. These rules have to be maintained and updated along a product's lifecycle, too [6]. The IEC 61499 standard defines function blocks to manage control unit configurations with a focus on (agile) manufacturing systems [7]. This methodological approach has been enhanced in several research works by addressing reconfiguration issues with a focus on electronic or software components [8, 9].

Smart vehicles can be regarded as a representative example for a Smart Product due to its complexity and commercialization, which is also part of cross sectoral smart systems (e.g. smart energy systems). The analyses of reconfiguration processes of smart vehicles have shown that in contrast to the previously mentioned approaches for an initial, customer specific configuration of virtual product model variants a Smart Product configuration additionally requires:

- A continuous development and enhancement of virtual product models considering the compatibility to existing virtual product models that are part of product instances in the use phase.
- An individual management of all product instances across all engineering domains.
- A synchronization of the initial virtual product configuration models and the multiple reconfiguration variants of all product instances.
- A continuous development and enhancement of the configuration knowledge for all physically existing product instances.
- An integration of external service providers that can be integrated into the reconfiguration process of Smart Products during their use phase.

In our previous contribution at the PLM16 conference we presented a conceptual approach considering virtual product twins as integrated components of Smart Products [10]. As a result of our follow-up research activities this paper focusses on the ability of virtual twins to serve as an enabler for Smart Product reconfiguration.

2 Virtual Twins as Enabler for the Reconfiguration of Smart Products

While the traditional product development concept can be sufficient for the management of the initial virtual product configuration models, the management of virtual product instance models for the reconfiguration of Smart Products along the entire lifecycle is characterized by an enormously high complexity. The consistent, situational consideration of virtual product models including the integration of product use data exceeds traditional Product Lifecycle Management methods. In this section, we will show how virtual product twins can serve as an approach for the integrated consideration of virtual product lifecycle models and product use data.

2.1 Virtual Product Twin Concept

As mentioned in Sect. 1, product configurations of Smart Products dynamically change along the entire product lifecycle. This leads to a new spectrum and history of virtual product models based on previous product instance versions. Specific characteristics of Smart Products like autonomy and IT-based reconfiguration services however require also the consideration of product use data as an extended lifecycle management approach. Therefore, the concept of the virtual product twin is introduced for the management of all the virtual product models as well as the product use data (Fig. 1). In this context, different terms addressing similar research questions, like for example product avatars as a product-instance centric management concept, arose in the past decade [11]. In the scope of Smart Products, the virtual twin can be considered as the notion, where the data of each stage of the product lifecycle is transformed into information and is made seamlessly available to subsequent stages [12]. The transformation into information can be e.g. the intention to analyze the data within its semantic context or the use of the data to predict the product's behavior.

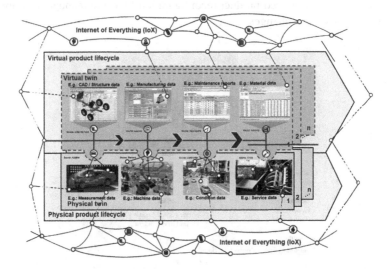

Fig. 1. Conceptual model of a virtual product twin for the lifecycle of a Smart Product.

As every virtual twin has a physical twin, the separation between a virtual and a physical lifecycle is necessary. As Smart Products combine highly interdisciplinary components from different engineering domains like mechanics, electronics and informatics, the virtual twin needs to synchronize context-specific multi-disciplinary models with the respective physical twin. This integration enables e.g. a reconfiguration like a temporary IT-service for a customer based on product structure data, CAD-models and software component versions [10]. Exemplary specific product instance models and data generated along both virtual and physical product lifecycles are shown in Fig. 1. In the early phases of the virtual product lifecycle, e.g. the product structure is defined, while in the following phases the management of maintenance reports is focussed. Analogously, the pictured physical lifecycle describes data that is primarily generated in different lifecycle stages by the physical product twin. This can refer to service data in a product's late lifecycle stage for example, which can be used for conclusions about a product's component condition and the possibility of further usage. However, data from the physical product lifecycle cannot be ignored when aiming at the composition of a product's comprehensive digital copy. E.g., product condition data is of essential importance in order to describe the current behavior or status of product. Therefore, they must be part of the virtual twin.

Considering that the data from every lifecycle phase is transformed into information and is made seamlessly available to subsequent phases, the amount of information available through the virtual twin increases together with the product's lifecycle stages. Consequently, this refers to a higher spectrum of context-specific deployment possibilities of the virtual twin of a Smart Product in the late phases of the product's lifecycle.

2.2 Reconfiguration Lifecycle of Smart Products During Their Use Phase

The changes in engineering affected by the transformation from traditional to Smart Products demand a rethinking regarding the relations between the generic variant development in the traditional product development phase and the affiliated product configuration. The introduced product reconfiguration lifecycle management approach (Fig. 2) addresses these changes.

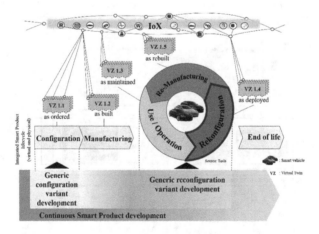

Fig. 2. Reconfiguration lifecycle in the product use phase.

The given approach includes a continuous Smart Product development phase that can be regarded as a lifecycle-attending instead of an early-lifecycle only element, which is addressed by traditional Product Lifecycle Management methods. Consequently, the provider of a Smart Product is highly involved in all lifecycle phases. The initial early phases of Smart Products lead to generic, modular, virtual product models and structures, which are the basis for the configuration of individual, customer-specific product variants. Common technical solutions for the customer-specific configuration are for example online product configurators that are highly popular in the automotive sector (e.g. BMW). The resulting configuration however describes the product only to a specific point in time or in a defined status for the distribution that can be subject to various reasons of change. Hence, the initial configuration by the customer is only one state (as ordered) that can be part of traditional PLM-approaches. However, this state varies dynamically along the entire lifecycle e.g. due to stochastic influences or necessary adjustments. Likewise, the product condition can be defined as an as built configuration after the manufacturing and distribution process, before entering a cyclic process in the use phase consisting from use/operation (as maintained), reconfiguration (as deployed) and re-manufacturing (as rebuilt). The different shapes of the physical product twin along the entire product lifecycle require simultaneously the adjustment of the virtual product twin (compare the different versions of the virtual product twins in Fig. 2). The generic reconfiguration options during the use phase are part of the continuous product development. Therefore, the customer can individualize his product further while choosing from variants that did not necessarily had to be existent during the very first configuration. Regarding a smart vehicle, this can refer to either mechanic, electronic or software components or more likely, to a combination of those that can be reconfigured depending on their compatibility. For example an IT-service such as a parking assistant can be offered as a (temporary) reconfiguration providing a given sensor technology, although this service has not been part of the company's product portfolio at the time of the initial configuration. A core challenge is the synchronization of the initial virtual product configuration models with the multiple, reconfigured variants of the product instances. The necessary models regarding the configuration knowledge for the introduced reconfiguration cycle in Fig. 2 are product structure models (e.g. BOM or structure trees) including the attached product models (e.g. metadata of the product components or CAD-models). Source for this data can be Product Lifecycle Management (PLM) systems, however due to the complexity of Smart Products the necessary knowledge can be scattered over different PLM systems in an engineering collaboration partner network [13]. In order to offer reconfiguration options during the use phase as a result of the continuous product development, this knowledge needs to be centralized as it is part of the virtual product twin (compare Sect. 2.1).

Hence, the virtual twin can be considered as a fundamental element when enabling a reconfiguration such as the previously introduced example of a parking assistant. As a first step, the product instance configuration has to be identified which can be done by analyzing the given product structure. After that, the necessary structural components for the parking assistant have to be compared to those identified regarding the compatibility of the reconfiguration option. This step does not necessarily include only configuration knowledge that has been created in-house, but has to consider engineering-knowledge from the whole partner network as mentioned above. After the rule-based compatibility checks have been conducted successfully, the implementation of the component-related reconfiguration can be initialized. Considering the implementation of the reconfiguration as a transformation of the product instance, this must be consequently regarded as a transformation of the virtual product twin as well.

3 Model Environment for the Reconfiguration of Smart Products

This section introduces a realization of the previously presented approach of the reconfiguration of Smart Products based on virtual products twins by transferring it to a model environment. The setup of this model environment consists of a conceptual and experimental part that were deduced from the use case in Sect. 3.1.

3.1 Considered Use Case

The use case in this section shall emphasize the benefit of the reconfiguration cycle while underlining the need for virtual twins in order to profit from a continuous product development. It describes the reconfiguration process of a smart vehicle, which will be the basis for the conceptual design of a reconfiguration platform followed by the implementation by means of a developed software-prototype. The basic idea of this use case is that a customer is owner of a smart vehicle whose functions can be temporarily or constantly altered. At first, the physical product instance is identified and connected to the respective virtual twin. A compatibility check considering the product instance configuration and all possible reconfiguration options follows. This includes all options that are currently available according the continuous product development process. The compatible, offered reconfiguration option in this use case is a parking lot detection assistant. Upon activation of the IT-service by the customer, the virtual twin changes analogously as part of the reconfiguration process. After the implementation, the IT-service enables the retrieval of free parking lot positions detected by sensors from other smart vehicles as soon as they pass an empty parking box. Finally, the customer can navigate to the free parking lot.

3.2 Components of a Cloud-Based Reconfiguration Platform

In order to realize the reconfiguration approach for Smart Products in their use phase based on virtual product twins, the cloud-based reconfiguration platform architecture has been developed. It allows the integration of the necessary product instance data as well as the management of the reconfiguration options and rules (Fig. 3).

The reconfiguration platform consists of two main sections: Functional modules that combine all operational units for the reconfiguration process and data sources that provide the necessary data for the reconfiguration process.

The central unit of the data providing section is the **virtual product twin database**. It assures the assignment of virtual product models from the entire lifecycle to the physical product instances via wireless connection e.g. as part of a service of an Internet of Things (IoT) platform. The virtual product models for the virtual product

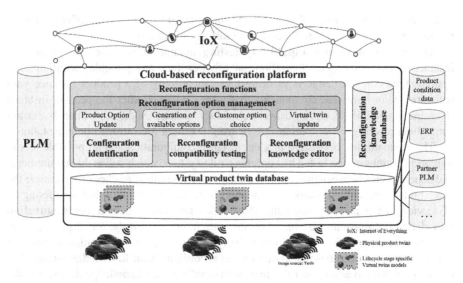

Fig. 3. Extension of the traditional PLM-concept by a cloud-based reconfiguration platform for Smart Products.

twin database are supplied by Product Lifecycle Management (PLM), e.g. by considering product structure data, and enterprise resource planning (ERP) systems of the entire partner network, as the complexity of Smart Products requires a highly flexible engineering-collaboration. Additionally, product condition data from the physical lifecycle has to be considered as part of the virtual product twin database as well. They can be used to trigger reconfiguration events, e.g. when passing a threshold.

Core of the function modules is the **reconfiguration option management**. The product option update is responsible for the consideration of the continuous product development notion. The basic idea is to keep the possible (re)configuration variants up to date in the sense of including newly developed variants while excluding those who are not part of the company's portfolio anymore. The second module is needed in order to generate only available reconfiguration options for each product instance. This assures that only those reconfiguration options are available for a product instance whose compatibility has been positively checked before. The customer choice option module is giving the customer the possibility to choose from the available reconfigurations, which can be realized by a graphical user interface. The fourth module is responsible for the continuous updating process of the virtual product twin. After the customer has chosen a reconfiguration option, the product instance changes as well as the virtual product twin.

Regarding the **configuration identification,** two different kinds of identification layers need to be considered: A general configuration is linking the physical product instance to all the related virtual product models as well as to the related physical lifecycle data. This refers e.g. to the assignment of the related CAD-models, current product structure or the localization of the present product position. The second layer addresses the product-internal selection of configuration units that are affected by the reconfiguration process (specific configuration identification).

The **reconfiguration compatibility testing** module checks the current product instance against missing configuration units that exclude any possible reconfiguration options. One core challenge is assuring the compatibility of a product instance with software and/or hardware components that were developed after the product instance (forward compatibility), e.g. by using neutral data formats. On the other hand, backward compatible reconfiguration options are offering potential for various implementations.

The compatibility between a product instance configuration and all possible reconfiguration options can be tested by applying a rule-system, which define the requirements and dependencies between the configuration units. These rules can check for example the availability of necessary sensors in a product instance configuration before offering an IT-service like a parking assistant. These rules are managed in a **reconfiguration knowledge database** and are based on the rules at the time of the initial product configuration but have to be updated respectively enhanced due to the continuous product development. This database is source for the **reconfiguration knowledge editor**. The editor is required to adjust the rules from the reconfiguration knowledge database to the existing product instance configuration with all the requirements and dependencies of the implemented configuration units.

3.3 Technical Implementation and Validation of the Platform

The cloud-based reconfiguration platform described in Sect. 3.2 was implemented and validated in a model environment. To model the characteristic properties of a Smart Product, the technical features of two Lego Mindstorm robots were augmented by using a Raspberry Pi to enable Internet-connectivity of sensor data like speed, position or distance to objects. Core of the reconfiguration platform is the cloud-platform "ThingWorx" commercially available by the provider "PTC". The service oriented architecture offers a broad range of interfaces, e.g. to the PLM-software "Windchill" (also PTC). Hence, ThingWorx offers the possibility to link physical lifecycle data (in our case retrieved by the sensors from the Lego Mindstorm robots like position data and ultrasonic data) with virtual lifecycle data (in our case product structure data from Windchill). Technically, the robots were described in ThingWorx as "things" and the product structure data as well as the sensor data were described as the things' "properties". According to previously defined query intervals, the BOM-data and data values from the ultrasonic-sensors as well as the robots' positions are updated constantly in order to monitor the product instance configuration and condition continuously. After an algorithm had checked the compatibility between the reconfiguration option "parking lot detection assistant" and the given product structure the software update was implemented. Following a necessary reboot, the robot was able to cyclical query the position of the other robot. Regarding the semantic context of the given use case the position of the Lego Mindstorm robot was always then transferred if the ultrasonic sensor at the side of the robot was exceeding a previously defined value. This position was indicating a free parking lot (see Fig. 4).

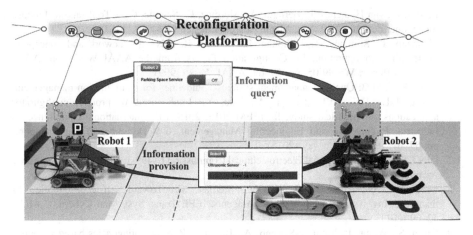

Fig. 4. Reconfiguration example based on virtual product twins.

4 Conclusion

Smart Products offer a tremendous potential for reconfiguration during their use phase due to their multidisciplinary properties. Especially the broad range of IT-services can enable an augmentation of functions by means of Internet technology in combination with hardware. This contribution showed the necessity of a continuous product development that is supported by a Product Lifecycle Management in order to access the full potential of reconfiguration offers for Smart Products. However, the dynamical reconfiguration of Smart Products is neither conceptual nor technological sufficiently addressed to the present day. Hence, a conceptual reconfiguration platform based on virtual product twins was introduced in order to take one step towards a higher reconfigurability of Smart Products during their use phase. Fundamental core of the virtual product twin concept was an integrated Product Lifecycle Management. The approach is especially characterized by its openness regarding the integration of more functional modules and data sources in order to transfer it to different Smart Product-Service Systems (Smart PSS). Challenges like latency and availability of needed Internet infrastructure, data security and access management questions as well as the scalability for a high number of product instances are still remaining. Current research activities focus semantic data management models and the integration of product behavior models into the reconfiguration cycle.

References

1. Abramovici, M.: Smart products. In: Lapierriére, L., Reinhart, G. (eds.) CIRP Encyplopedia of Production Engineering. Springer, Heidelberg (2014). https://doi.org/10.1007/978-3-642-35950-7_16785-1
2. Abramovici, M., Dang, H.B., Göbel, J.C., Savarino, P.: Systematization of IPS2 diversification potentials using product lifecycle data. Procedia CIRP **47**, 288–293 (2016)

3. Lutters, E., van Houten, F.J., Bernard, A., Mermoz, E., Schutte, C.S.: Tools and techniques for product design. CIRP Ann. Manuf. Technol. **63**(2), 607–630 (2014)
4. Männisto, T., Soininen, T., Tiihonen, J., Sulonen, R. (eds.): Framework and conceptual model for reconfiguration. In: Configuration Papers from the AAAI Workshop, AAAI Technical Report WS-99-05, pp. 59–64. AAAI Press (1999)
5. ISO 10007:2003: Quality management systems- Guidelines for configuration management
6. Zhang, L.L., Helo, P.T., Kumar, A., You, X.: Implications of product configurator applications: an empirical study. In: IEEM 2015: 2015 IEEE International Conference on Industrial Engineering and Engineering Management, 6–9 December 2015, Singapore, pp. 57–61. IEEE, Piscataway (2015)
7. DIN EN 61499: International Electrotechnical Commission 61499-1: Function Block - Part 1 Architecture (2013)
8. Lepuschitz, W., Zoitl, A., Vallée, M., Merdan, M.: Toward self-reconfiguration of manufacturing systems using automation agents. IEEE Trans. Syst. Man Cybern. C **41**(1), 52–69 (2011)
9. Olsen, S., Wang, J., Ramirez-Serrano, A., Brennan, R.W.: Contingencies-based reconfiguration of distributed factory automation. Robot. Comput.-Integr. Manuf. **21**(4–5), 379–390 (2005)
10. Abramovici, M., Göbel, J.C., Savarino, P.: Virtual twins as integrative components of smart products. In: Harik, R., Rivest, L., Bernard, A., Eynard, B., Bouras, A. (eds.) PLM 2016. IAICT, vol. 492, pp. 217–226. Springer, Cham (2016). https://doi.org/10.1007/978-3-319-54660-5_20
11. Hribernik, K.A., Rabe, L., Thoben, K.D., Schumacher, J.: The product avatar as a product-instance-centric information management concept. IJPLM **1**(4), 367 (2006)
12. Rosen, R., von Wichert, G., Lo, G., Bettenhausen, K.D.: About the importance of autonomy and digital twins for the future of manufacturing. IFAC-PapersOnLine **48**(3), 567–572 (2015)
13. Penciuc, D., Durupt, A., Belkadi, F., Eynard, B., Rowson, H.: Towards a PLM interoperability for a collaborative design support system. Procedia CIRP **25**, 369–376 (2014)

CAD Assembly Retrieval and Browsing

Matteo Rucco[1], Katia Lupinetti[1,2(✉)], Franca Giannini[1], Marina Monti[1],
and Jean-Philippe Pernot[2]

[1] IMATI- CNR, Genova, Italy
ruccomatteo@gmail.com,
{katia.lupinetti,giannini,monti}@ge.imati.cnr.it
[2] LSIS - Arts et Métiers ParisTech, Aix-en-Provence, France
jean-philippe.pernot@ensam.eu

Abstract. This paper presents a method for the retrieval and inspection of similar CAD assemblies in a database according to a user query. The method exploits the information on components' shape and relationships (e.g. contacts and regular patterns) automatically extracted from the STEP descriptions of CAD assemblies and stored in the so-called Enriched Assembly Model. It evaluates the similarity among assemblies in terms of the components' shapes and joints. A graphical interface highlighting the elements in the assembly similar to the query has been developed to facilitate the inspection of the obtained results.

Keywords: Assembly retrieval · Shape matching · Information visualization

1 Introduction

The large use of CAD (Computer Aided Design) and CAM (Computer Aided Manufacturing) systems in industries has generated a number of 3D databases making available a large amount of 3D digital models. The reuse of these models, either single parts or assemblies, and the exploitation of the knowledge associated with them are becoming an important way to facilitate new designs. To track and organize data related to a product and its lifecycle, modern CAD systems are integrated into PDM (Product Data Management) and PLM (Product Lifecycle Management) systems. Among others, the associated data usually involve the technical specifications of the product, provisions for its manufacturing and assembling, types of materials used for its production, costs and versioning. These systems efficiently manage a search based on textual metadata, which cannot be sufficient to effectively retrieving the searched data. Actually, standard parts, text-based annotation and naming convention are company- or operator- specific, thus difficult to generalize as search keys. To overcome these limitations, content-based algorithms for 3D model retrieval are being developed based on shape characteristics. A wide literature is available and some commercial systems provide shape-based model retrieval. [1–3] provide an overview of the 3D shape descriptors most used in the CAD domain. However, these descriptors focus solely on the shape of a single component, which is not adapted for more complex products obtained as assemblies. An effective

© IFIP International Federation for Information Processing 2017
Published by Springer International Publishing AG 2017. All Rights Reserved
J. Ríos et al. (Eds.): PLM 2017, IFIP AICT 517, pp. 499–508, 2017.
https://doi.org/10.1007/978-3-319-72905-3_44

assembly search cannot be limited to simple shape comparison among components, but requires also information that is not always explicitly encoded in the CAD models, e.g. the relationships and the joint constraints between assembly components.

In this paper, we present methods for the retrieval of globally and/or partially similar assembly models according to different user-specified search criteria [9] and for the inspection of the provided results. The proposed approach creates and exploits an assembly descriptor, called Enriched Assembly Model (EAM), organized in several layers that enable multi-level queries and described in Sect. 4.1. The rest of the paper is organized as follows. Section 2 provides an overview of related works. Issues related to assembly retrieval are described in Sect. 3, while Sect. 4 presents the assembly descriptor and the comparison procedure. Section 5 reports some of the obtained results, focusing on the developed inspection capabilities. Section 6 concludes the paper discussing on current limits and future work.

2   Related Works

Shape retrieval has been investigated far and wide in the recent years [1–4]. However, most of the work present in literature deal with the shape of a single component and do not consider other relevant information of the assembly such as the relationships between the parts. One of the pioneer works dealing with assembly retrieval was presented by Deshmukh et al. [5]. They investigate the possible usage scenarios for assembly retrieval and proposed a flexible retrieval system exploiting the explicit assembly data stored in a commercial CAD system. Hu et al. [6] propose a tool to retrieve assemblies represented as vectors of watertight polygon meshes. Identical parts are merged and a weight based on the number of occurrences is attached to each part in the vector. Relative positions of parts and constraints are ignored, thus the method is weak in local matching. Miura and Kanai [7] extend their assembly model by including structural information and other useful data, e.g. contact and interference stages and geometric constraints. However, it does not consider high-level information, such as kinematic pairs and some information must be made explicit by the user. A more complete system is proposed by Chen et al. [8]. It relays on the product structure and the relationships between the different parts of the assembly. The adopted assembly descriptor considers different information levels including the topological structure, the relationships between the components of the assembly, as well as the geometric information. Thus, the provided search is very flexible accepting rough and incomplete queries. Anyhow, most of the work require user support for the insertion of the required information and weakly support the analysis and browsing of the obtained results, which for large assemblies can be very critical. To overcome these limitations, in this paper, we present an assembly descriptor (i.e. the Enriched Assembly Model), which can support user requests based on different search criteria not restrained to the identification of assembly models with the same structure in terms of sub-assemblies, and tools for facilitating the inspection and browsing of the results of the retrieval process.

3   Assembly Retrieval Issues

Retrieving similar CAD assembly models can support various activities ranging from the re-use of the associated knowledge, such as production or assembly costs and operations, to part standardization and maintenance planning. For instance, knowing that a specific subassembly, which includes parts having a high consumption rate due to their part surrounding and usage, is present in various larger products may help in defining more appropriate maintenance actions and better planning of the warehouse stocks. Similarly, knowing that different products having problems share similar configurations can help in detecting critical configurations. Considering these scenarios, it is clear that simply looking for products (i.e. assemblies) that are completely similar to a given one is important but limited. It is therefore necessary to have the possibility to detect if an assembly is contained into another as well as local similarities among assemblies, i.e. assemblies that contain similar sub-assemblies. These relations can be described using the set theory. Being $\cong$ the symbol indicating the similarity according to given criteria, given two assemblies A and B, we say that:

A is ***globally similar*** to B iff for each component $a_i \in A$, $\exists\ b_h \in B$ s.t. $a_i \cong b_h$, for each relation $(a_i, a_j) \in A$, $\exists\ (b_h, b_k) \in B$ s.t. $(a_i, a_j) \cong (b_h, b_k)$ where $a_i \cong b_h$ and $a_j \cong b_k$

A is ***partially similar*** to B iff it exists $A' \subseteq A$ s.t. for each component $a_i \in A'$, $\exists\ b_h \in B$ s.t. $a_i \cong b_h$, for each relation $(a_i, a_j) \in A$, $\exists\ (b_h, b_k) \in B$ s.t. $(a_i, a_j) \cong (b_h, b_k)$ where $a_i \cong b_h$ and $a_j \cong b_k$

A is ***locally similar*** to B iff it exists $A' \subset A$ and $B' \subset B$ s.t. for each component $a_i \in A'$, $\exists\ b_h \in B'$ s.t. $a_i \cong b_h$, for each relation $(a_i, a_j) \in A$, $\exists\ (b_h, b_k) \in B$ s.t. $(a_i, a_j) \cong (b_h, b_k)$ where $a_i \cong b_h$ and $a_j \cong b_k$

The different types of similarities are depicted in Fig. 1. According to the given definitions, the models in Fig. 1(a) and (b) are globally similar, while both of them are partially similar comparing with the models in Fig. 1(c) and (d). In the end, model in Fig. 1(c) and (d) are locally similar, since they share a similar component.

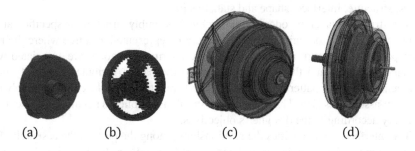

(a)   (b)   (c)   (d)

Fig. 1. Example of different type of similarities

Depending on the retrieval purpose, not only the criteria change but also the interest on the similarity among the parts or on their connections can have different priority. It is therefore important to provide flexible retrieval tools that can be adapted to the specific need and thus able to consider the various elements characterizing the assembly despite on how the assembly was described by the user (e.g. structural organization) or on the information available on the CAD model itself (e.g. explicit mating conditions).

In addition, it might be difficult to assess the effective similarity when various elements contribute to it. It is crucial to provide tools for gathering results according to the various criteria and for their inspection. This is very important in the case of large assemblies, where detecting the parts considered similar to a given assembly might be particularly difficult.

4   The Proposed Approach

Based on the above considerations, we propose a method for the comparison of assembly models exploiting various levels of information of the assembly. Differently from most of the work presented in literature, our method can evaluate all the three types of similarity described above. It uses a multilayer information model, the so-called Enriched Assembly Model (see Sect. 4.1), which stores the data describing the assembly according to three different layers, in turns specified at different level of details thus allowing a refinement of the similarity investigation. Depending on the type of requested similarity, an association graph is build putting in relation the elements of the EAM of two CAD models to be compared. The similar subset of these two models are then corresponding to the maximal clique of the association graph (see Sect. 4.2). To analyze the retrieved results, a visualization tool has been developed; it highlights the correspondences of the parts and provides statistics on the matched elements (see Sect. 5).

4.1   Enriched Assembly Model (EAM)

The EAM is an attributed graph, where nodes are the components and/or composing sub-assemblies while arcs represent their adjacency relations. It uses four information layers: structure, interface, shape and statistics [9].

The structural layer encodes the hierarchical assembly structure as specified at the design stage. In this organization, the structure is represented as a tree where the root corresponds to the entire assembly model, the intermediate nodes are associated with the sub-assemblies and the leaves characterize the parts. Attributes to specify parts arrangement (regular patterns of repeated parts) are attached to the entire assembly and to its sub-assemblies [10]. The organization in sub-assemblies is not always present and may vary according to the designer's objectives.

The interface layer specifies the relationships among the parts in the assembly. It is organized in two levels: contacts and joints. The first contains the faces involved in the contact between two parts and the degree of freedom between them. The joint level describes the potentially multiple motions resulting from several contacts between two parts [11].

The shape layer describes the shape of the part assembly by several dedicated descriptors. Using several shape descriptors helps answering different assembly retrieval scenarios, which can consider different shape characteristics and at different level of details. They include information like shape volume, bounding surface area, bounding box and spherical harmonics [12].

The statistics layer contains values that roughly characterize and discern assembly models. Statistics are associated as attributes to the various elements of the EAM. For the entire assembly and for each sub-assembly, they include: the numbers of sub-assemblies, of principal parts, of fasteners, of patterns of a specific type, of a specific joint type. To each node corresponding to a component, the statistics considered are: percentage of a specific type of surface (i.e. planar, cylindrical, conical spherical, toroidal, free form), number of maximal faces of a specific type of surface. Finally, for each arc corresponding to a joint between parts, the stored statistics include the number of elements in contact for a specific contact type.

The E.A.M. is created using ad hoc developed modules [9–11], which analyze the content of the STEP (ISO 10303-203 and ISO 10303-214) representation of the assembly and extract the required information.

4.2 EAM Comparison

Adopting this representation, if two models are similar, then their attribute graphs must have a common sub-graph. The similarity assessment between two EAMs can then be performed by matching their attribute graphs and finding their maximum common subgraph (MCS). The identification of the MCS is a well-known NP-hard problem and among the various techniques proposed for its solution [13] we chose the detection of the maximal clique of the association graph, since it allows identifying also locally similarities.

The association graph is a support graph that reflects the adopted high-level similarity criteria. Each node in the association graph corresponds to a pair of compatible nodes in the two attributed graphs according to the specified criteria. Associated arcs connect nodes if they have equivalent relations expressed as arcs connecting the corresponding nodes in the attribute graphs.

A clique is a sub-graph in which for each couple of nodes a connecting arc exists. For the clique detection we applied the Eppstein-Strash algorithm [14]. This algorithm represents an improved version of the algorithm by Tomita [15], which is in turn based on the Bron-Kerbosch algorithm for the detection of all maximal cliques in graphs [16]. As far as we know, Eppstein-Strash algorithm is up to now the best algorithm for listing all maximal cliques in undirected graphs, even in dense graphs. The performances of the algorithm are in general guaranteed by the degeneracy ordering.

The algorithm of Eppstein-Strash improves Tomita's algorithm by using the concept of degeneracy. The degeneracy of a graph G is the smallest number d such that every subgraph of $G(V, E)$ contains a node of degree at most d. Moreover, every graph with degeneracy d has a degeneracy ordering: a linear ordering of the vertices such that each node has at most d neighbors after it in the ordering. Eppstein-Strash algorithm first computes the degeneracy ordering; then for each node v in the order, starting from the first, the algorithm of Tomita is used to compute all cliques containing v and v's later neighbors. Other improvements depend on the use of adjacency lists for data representation. For more details we refer to [14].

Among all the maximal cliques present in the associated graph, we consider as interesting candidates of the similar sub-graphs only those having: (1) the majority of arcs corresponding to real joints between the corresponding components, (2) a number of nodes bigger than a specified value. In this way, priority is given to sub-graphs which contain a significant number of joined similar components, thus possibly corresponding to sub-assemblies. Then, for each selected clique, a measure vector is computed. The first element of the vector indicates the degree of the clique, while the others report the similarity of the various assembly characteristics taken into consideration for the similarity assessment. Depending on the search objectives the set of characteristics to consider may change. The default characteristics are the shape of the components and the type of joint between them. The examples and results discussed in the next section consider the default characteristic selection.

5   Result Visualisation

The proposed retrieval system has been implemented in a multi-module prototype system. The creation of the EAM description is developed by using Microsoft Visual C# 2013 and exploiting the Application Programming Interface (API) of the commercial CAD system SolidWorks. The matching and the similarity assessment module is developed by using Java and is invoked during the retrieval as a jar file. In the end, to analyze the obtained results, a browser view has been implemented. It is obtained by multiple dynamic web pages that are based on HTML5, jQuery, Ajax and PHP. Moreover, Mysql is used as database system, while X3D library is used for the STEP model visualization.

The system has been tested on assembly models obtained from on-line repositories [17–19] and from university students' tests.

Figure 2 shows an example of the developed user interface, where the design can choose an assembly model as query and set the required criteria of similarity. In this example, it is required to retrieve models similar for shape and joint. Some results of this query are shown in Fig. 3. The first model in the picture (top-left) coincides with the query model. The retrieved models are gathered together in the other views of Fig. 3. Each retrieved and displayed assemblies has a clique that has been detected in the association graph and satisfies the required conditions. The assemblies are visualized in X3D view that allows rotating, zooming and selecting the various 3D components of the retrieved assembly. Components are visualized in the transparency mode to make possible to see also the internal ones. Under each model, three bars are shown to quickly get an idea of how similar to the query the retrieved assemblies are. The first two indicate the percentage of coverage (i.e. percentage of matched elements) with respect to both the query and target model. Thank to these bars, the user can see the type of similarity (i.e. global, partial or local). If the green is not complete, it means that just a subset of the query model is matched, thus the similarity is locally. The global similarity is shown by the purple bar, if this bar is not complete, then the similarity is partial. The last bar shows the average shape similarity among the components associated with the displayed clique. Simply looking at the reported model and checking the purple bar, the user can notice that (except the first model which represents the query model) no models are globally similar to the query one according to the criteria he/she has specified. The first model in the second row is partially similar with the query one, since the query is completely included in it (see the green bar). Other models are locally similar with the query model, thus just a subset of the query model is included in them.

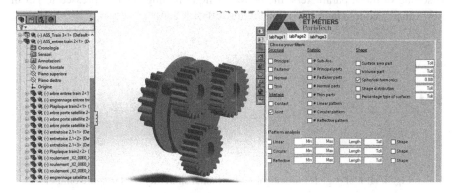

Fig. 2. An assembly model and the similarity criteria used for the matching

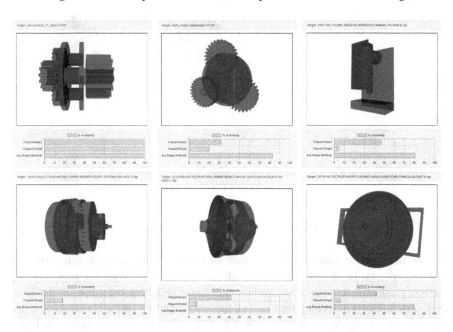

Fig. 3. A sample of the retrieved models for the proposed speed reducer query (top left) (Color figure online)

If the user wants to further analyze the levels of similarity of the chosen characteristics or to visualize all the subsets of matched parts, he/she can select one of the retrieved assemblies and a new browser page is prompted. Once selected, a new page as in

Fig. 4 is available, where the user can get the list of all the interesting clique, using the sliders at the top of window. With these sliders, the user can choose some thresholds that the proposed results have to satisfy. In particular, they refer to the dimension of the matched portion, the shape similarity measure and the joint similarity measure. After the setting of those parameters, the button "Clique finding" can be pressed to get the results displayed in a table as visible on the left of Fig. 5.

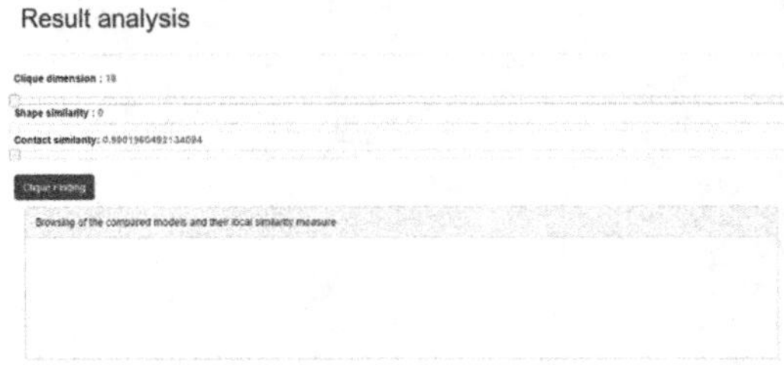

Result analysis

Clique dimension : 18

Shape similarity : 0

Contact similarity: 0.900198049214094

Clique Finding

Browsing of the compared models and their local similarity measure

Fig. 4. Initial page for investigating the model similarity (Color figure online)

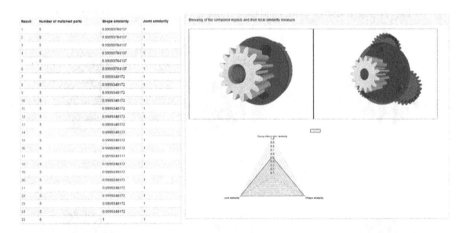

Fig. 5. Example of matching browsing

The rows of the table gather together all the matching portions that satisfy the required criteria. In this example, four information are accessible for each matching portion: an identification number, the number of matched parts, the shape similarity and the joint similarity. Selecting one of them, the corresponding clique is visualized within the assembly. It highlights the component correspondence with the query model using same colors for corresponding components in the two objects, as shown on the right part of Fig. 4. To easy the comparison according to several available criteria (here reported just the default ones), a radar chart is used. It illustrates the shape and joint similarities among the overall assembly in relation to the clique degree. This type of visualization is very useful to compare multiple data and to have a global evaluation in just a look. Moreover, the radar charts are convenient to compare two or more models on various features expressed through numerical values. The larger is the covered area, the more the two assemblies are similar. In the reported case, the user can observe immediately that the two models are not completely matched, even if they look very similar. This is because the gears in the two models have a significant different shape, which avoids including those parts among the matched one, thus decreasing the global level of similarity. On the other side, the retrieved portion completely satisfies the requests, thus reporting an assemment of 1.

6 Conclusions

In this paper, methods for the identification and evaluation of similarities between CAD assemblies are presented. While almost all of the products are made of assembled parts, most of the works present in literature are addressing the problem of similarity among single parts. For assemblies, the shape of the components is not the only characteristic to be considered. Increasing the number of elements to consider, augments from the one hand the possibility of adapting the search to specific user needs, and on the other hand the difficulty to evaluate the results. The method here described can consider all or a subset of the various aspects of the assembly, namely the shape of the components, their arrangements (i.e. patterns), their mating contacts and joints. The evaluation of the retrieved results is supported by exploiting colour variations in the 3D visualisation of the components in correspondence between the compared assemblies. Measures and statistics quantifying the similarity of the overall assemblies and of the matched subparts are reported according to the various considered characteristics.

In future work, we plan to introduce graph databases, such as Neo4j, for speeding-up the search of local similarity among big assembly models. We also intend to improve the clique-finding algorithm by allowing it to select automatically the dimension of the biggest clique. Moreover, we intend to involve the definition of a single measure for the overall ranking of the retrieved assemblies similar to a query one. This information will be displayed in an ad-hoc infographics, which will be developed for improving the user-experience.

References

1. Biasotti, S., Cerri, A., Aono, M., Hamza, A.B., Garro, V., Giachetti, A., Giorgi, D., Godil, A., Li, C. Sanada, C., Spagnuolo, M., Tatsuma, A., Velasco-Forero. S.: Retrieval and classification methods for textured 3D models: a comparative study. Visual Comput. Springer, Heidelberg (2015). http://doi.org/10.1007/s00371-015-1146-3. ISSN 0178-2789
2. Cardone, A., Gupta, S.K., Karnik, M.: A survey of shape similarity assessment algorithms for product design and manufacturing applications. J. Comput. Inf. Sci. Eng. 3(2), 109–118 (2003)
3. Iyer, N., Jayanti, S., Lou, K., Kalyanaraman, Y., Ramani, K.: Three-dimensional shape searching: state-of-the-art review and future trends. Comput.-Aided Des. 37(5), 509–530 (2005)
4. Tangelder, J.W., Veltkamp, R.C.: A survey of content based 3D shape retrieval methods. Multimedia Tools Appl. 39(3), 441–471 (2008)

5. Deshmukh, A.S., Banerjee, A.G., Gupta, S.K., Sriram, R.D.: Content-based assembly search: a step towards assembly reuse. Comput.-Aided Des. **40**(2), 244–261 (2008)
6. Hu, K.-M., Wang, B., Yong, J.-H., Paul, J.-C.: Relaxed lightweight assembly retrieval using vector space model. Comput.-Aided Des. **45**(3), 739–750 (2013)
7. Miura, T., Kanai, S.: 3D Shape retrieval considering assembly structure In: Proceedings of Asian Symposium for Precision Engineering and Nanotechnology 2009 (ASPEN 2009) (2009)
8. Chen, X., Gao, S., Guo, S., Bai, J.: A flexible assembly retrieval approach for model reuse. Comput.-Aided Des. **44**(6), 554–574 (2012)
9. Lupinetti, K., Giannini, F., Monti, M., Pernot, J.-P.: CAD assembly descriptors for knowledge capitalization and model retrieval. In: Proceedings of the Eleventh Symposium on Tools and Methods of Competitive Engineering - TMCE 2016, 09–13 May 2016, Aix-en-Provence, France (2016)
10. Lupinetti, K., Chiang, L., Giannini, F., Monti, M., Pernot, J.-P.: Use of regular patterns of repeated elements in CAD assembly models retrieval. In: Computer-Aided Design and Applications, vol. 14, no. 4 (2017)
11. Lupinetti, K., Giannini, F., Monti, M., Pernot, J.-P.: Automatic extraction of assembly component relationships for assembly model retrieval. In: Procedia CIRP, vol. 50, pp. 472–477 (2016). ISSN 2212-8271
12. Kazhdan, M., Funkhouser, T., Rusinkiewicz, S.: Rotation invariant spherical harmonic representation of 3d shape descriptors. In: Symposium on Geometry Processing, vol. 6 (2003)
13. Bunke, H., Foggia, P., Guidobaldi, C., Sansone, C., Vento, M.: A comparison of algorithms for maximum common subgraph on randomly connected graphs. In: Caelli, T., et al. (eds.) SSPR&SPR 2002. LNCS, vol. 2396, pp. 123–132. Springer, Heidelberg (2002). https://doi.org/10.1007/3-540-70659-3_12
14. Eppstein, D., Strash, D.: Listing all maximal cliques in large sparse real-world graphs. In: Pardalos, Panos M., Rebennack, S. (eds.) SEA 2011. LNCS, vol. 6630, pp. 364–375. Springer, Heidelberg (2011). https://doi.org/10.1007/978-3-642-20662-7_31
15. Tomita, E., Tanaka, A., Takahashi, H.: The worst-case time complexity for generating all maximal cliques and computational experiments. Theor. Comput. Sci. **363**(1), 28–42 (2006)
16. Bron, C., Kerbosch, J.: Algorithm 457: finding all cliques of an undirected graph. Commun. ACM **16**(9), 575–577 (1973)
17. Solidworks industrial designer. http://help.solidworks.com. Accessed 20 Feb 2017
18. GrabCAD Workbench. http://www.grabcad.com/. Accessed 22 Feb 2017
19. Product content everywhere. http://www.tracepartsonline.net/. Accessed 22 Feb 2017

Analysing Product Development Process and PLM Features in the Food and Fashion Industries

Elisa d'Avolio[1(✉)], Claudia Pinna[2], Romeo Bandinelli[1], Sergio Terzi[2],
and Rinaldo Rinaldi[1]

[1] Department of Industrial Engineering, University of Florence, Florence, Italy
{elisa.davolio,romeo.bandinelli,rinaldo.rinaldi}@unifi.it
[2] Department of Management, Economics and Industrial Engineering,
Politecnico di Milano, Milan, Italy
{claudia.pinna,sergio.terzi}@polimi.it

Abstract. The food and fashion industries are well-known as areas of excellence representing Italy globally. Their products include innovative features, have short lifecycles and a high level of customisation. Both the pipelines have to respond quickly to unpredictable demand in order to minimize stock-outs, forced mark-downs, obsolete inventory and they focus their Supply Chain (SC) strategies on quality and time-to-market. Although they are characterized by many different aspects, both leverage on the same point of strength: their internal Product Development (PD) process. The opposite occurs in the automotive industry, with its standard and functional products and its efficient pipeline centred on cost reduction. Starting from previous works presented during the last PLM conference (PLM16), the research aims at investigating similarities and differences between these sectors, focusing on their PD process and their main critical success factors. Moreover, the authors analyse how Food and Fashion companies are managing the entire set of information throughout PD and the strategic role of Product Lifecycle Management (PLM). In order to reach these goals, a multiple case study analysis has been performed, involving companies belonging to the Food and Fashion industries. The results will be relevant both for academics and practitioners. Indeed, there is a literature gap about this topic, because of the lack of researches concerning Food and Fashion PD. From the practitioners point of view, the results of this work will help Food and Fashion companies to support their business analysing the PD process and to better understand how the use of the PLM system could improve it.

Keywords: Product Development (PD) · Product Lifecycle Management (PLM)
Food industry · Fashion industry · PLM for food and fashion · Food and fashion

1 Introduction

Product Development (PD) represents the core process for many industries focusing on product quality and innovation. Food and Fashion companies are trying to streamline this process in order to reduce time-to-market and to be competitive in the international

© IFIP International Federation for Information Processing 2017
Published by Springer International Publishing AG 2017. All Rights Reserved
J. Ríos et al. (Eds.): PLM 2017, IFIP AICT 517, pp. 509–521, 2017.
https://doi.org/10.1007/978-3-319-72905-3_45

scenario. The two sectors are particularly linked in Italy, where they embody parts of the three F (food, fashion and furniture) driving "Made in Italy" to its success, due to the innate history and culture, creativity, design and lifestyle [1]. In this concern, the Food and Fashion are the two sectors where Italians trust more concerning the "Made in Italy" brand [2].

At first glance, Food and Fashion appear to be different and distant environments, especially because of product features from the final customer viewpoint. The fashion industry stresses the not-essential customer needs, i.e. the ones related to the irrational sphere of our mind. On the other hand, the food industry produces, more than other sectors, vital items that every customer chooses day-by-day; yet it also delivers more "fashionable" products that clients could do without (in particular processed foods, as chocolate, sweets, jams and so on). Hence, fashion could be recognisable in all those products that satisfy emotional and temporary needs, including food products. Moreover, analysing both the supply chains from the companies' perspective, they prove to be configured as "market responsive" instead of "physically efficient" [3]: their primary purpose is to respond quickly to unpredictable demand. Other similarities are related to product design and management. According to Fisher [3], Food and Fashion deliver innovative products instead of functional ones, characterised by short lifecycles, high contribution margin and high variety. Furthermore, they are also special products instead of standard ones, as suggested by Christopher et al. [4]: they are not stable in demand and include a high level of customisation.

An interesting leitmotiv between Food and Fashion supply chains is that PD represents the core process; in fact, it is always conducted in-house to retain the control over the involved tasks and resources. In this context, the use of the PLM system in support of PD process for both industries could be considered as a key driver of innovation that allow them to be successful in the market. Starting from previous works presented during the last PLM conference (PLM16), this research aims at investigating similarities and differences between the Food and Fashion sectors, focusing on their PD process and on their main critical success factors. Moreover, the authors analyse how Food and Fashion companies are managing the entire set of information throughout PD and the strategic role of PLM. The second section of the paper explores the literature related to Food and Fashion supply chains and PLM functionalities in order to pave the way for the further case study analysis. Then, Sect. 3 describes the methodology used to conduct the research and to obtain the main results, using both questionnaires and interviews. In the Sect. 4, the findings coming from the analysis of the interviews are shown. Finally, the paper concludes by presenting some thoughts and future research directions.

2   Literature Review

The first step within this study has been to gather as much information as possible about Food and Fashion supply chain chains, in order to distinguish the PD tasks and how they are linked with the other supply chain processes.

The fashion supply chain has been classified as agile [5] because it is market sensitive (closely connected to end-user trends), virtual (relying on shared information across all supply chain partners), network-based and process aligned (high degree of process interconnectivity between the network members). Food supply chain is not framed in a specific classification (e.g. lean or agile), but much interest is payed to its networked structure where producers, distributors and buyers/retailers [6, 7] contribute to generate value. Food and Fashion supply chains are above all described through case studies [8–14] and their processes appears to be very business-specific, so that a diagram of a generic fashion or food supply chain is still missing.

The second step through the literature review has been devoted to the PLM functionalities supporting PD in the Food and Fashion industries.

For the fashion industry, in particular, PLM means clear visibility into PD, sourcing, and pre-production processes and a more collaborative approach, through every phase of the lifecycle. Even if PLM is spreading since a decade within the fashion industry, very little is known in literature about PLM features and functionalities, while most of the papers are related to automotive cases [15]. Just few authors [16, 17], have discussed PLM implementation and adoption in fashion companies, highlighting the need for tailor-made functionalities.

PLM is becoming a very important solution also for the food industry. The use of this system allows food companies to provide different benefits, including: higher efficiency and productivity, increased product quality, reduced errors, greater profitability in PD and ensured regulatory compliance [18]. In this concern, several contributions dealing with themes related to the different phases of the product life cycle, (Beginning of Life BOL, Middle of Life MOL and End of Life EOL [19]) have been found in the scientific literature. It is also true that the term "product lifecycle management" [20] is a very broad topic [21, 22]. Indeed, considering the entire life cycle of the product, PLM is not often used as a unique term but it is more common to find other terms that indicate one of its specific phase, a specific method or the software names used in the different stages. In conclusion, it could be said that the level of knowledge of the PLM systems is still low also in the food sector from the literature point of view. As a result, the major part of the publications concerning PLM in the Food and Fashion industries is actually based on analyses conducted by consulting societies and specialized magazines. The lack of papers about PD process and PLM functionalities in Food and Fashion industries has triggered a deeper investigation into several companies, through a case study analysis, in order to reach the objective of this study.

3   Research Methodology

Case Study methodology has been adopted as research strategy. This works well with exploratory research because it can give those initial insights that are needed to find for the explorative cases [23]. In this work, multiple embedded case studies [24] have been applied to Food and Fashion companies. The aim of this study is to analyse the main Critical Success Factors (CSF) [25] in the two sectors, the PD activities [26] and how information are managed through PLM. In a first moment, the analysis has been held separately. In fact, two questionnaires with common topics and sections have been developed (customised for each specific sector) and then submitted to the selected companies to be investigated. Indeed, before to start the analysis, a common structure of the two questionnaires has been defined in order to obtain results that could be compared once the interview process was completed. The first step has been the identification of CSF, which are a limited number of key variables or conditions that have an impact on how successfully and effectively an organization meets its mission or the strategic goals of a program or project. Then, the PD process has been analysed and linked to the PLM functionalities, in order to investigate both process and information management.

The questionnaire has been divided into three sections. After that, the questionnaire structure has been defined and adapted for each sector. The next step was to identify the reference sample, so that the two analyses could be compared. In order to achieve homogeneity in the sample, companies selected have to respect all the following requirements: constituting a brand managing finished products, being owned brands, having at least a BU in Italy and an international profile and being medium-large firms established in their business for several years. After this first screening, it was decided to select those companies that are: (i) conducting PD activities in-house; (ii) showing different market positioning based on price (from low-end to high-end companies); (iii) including, for food companies, "fashionable" factors in the product (as a packaging with a certain appealing, the choice of a specific ingredient just for a specific period trend, and whatever is not primary food).

At this point, two groups of companies operating in the food and in the fashion businesses have been selected.

The five fashion companies interviewed manage leather goods, shoes and ready to wear products. According to [27] the cases range from the luxury market segment (cases 1, 2 and 3) to the lower-end brands (cases 4 and 5): this market segmentation is based on price levels. Case 1 and 3 conduct all the supply chain processes internally, while in the other cases production is outsourced to suppliers located in Italy and in Europe. Three cases have already implemented a PLM solution, while the remaining are using Product Data Management (PDM) and are evaluating to adopt PLM. Two main clusters have been identified: high-end/luxury companies, selling leather goods, prefer to focus on CSFs as quality and innovation and to retain in-house the majority of supply chain processes. They need to achieve innovation also in data management and have implemented an industry-specific PLM solution. The second cluster includes low-end companies, selling outerwear and childrenswear, that are competing on time to market (TTM) and decide to outsource production to suppliers. They are still not able to manage product information through PLM.

The seven food companies interviewed manage milk and yogurt, pasta and sauces and confectionery products. All the companies interviewed decided to outsource the distribution and sales phases. This is due to the fact that all the companies consider as core phases the R&D, purchase and production: this is the reason why they decide to leave them internally, being the phases that add more value to the final product.

Furthermore, food sector could be classified through different market segments basing on product categories: fresh products (case 1 and 5), pasta and canned food (case 2, 4 and 6) and confectionery products (case 3 and 7).

Moreover, just two companies are using the PLM system, while the remaining are adopting PDM and ERP. Some of the companies intend to adopt the PLM solution, while others do not even know the meaning of this system and the related benefits.

The selected companies have been contacted and asked for their willingness to be investigated through a case study; the companies analysed have been finally selected among those which indicated their availability for a field investigation. Case studies typically involve multiple sources of information [23]. In this research, they are: two questionnaires, which have been used as a guideline for many semi-structured interviews with the company's managers (IT and R&D managers); semi-structured and open interviews (the latest coming from consulting activities). Both questionnaires have been earlier validated and tested. Then they have been sent to the company's IT and R&D managers and discussed through an interview. The collected results have been elaborated and submitted to the company's managers for approval. In conclusion, the results obtained from the case studies have been validated by the company's top management. Once the responses of the two different questionnaires have been analysed, a comparison between Food and Fashion results has been performed and similarities and differences have been found.

4   Findings

This section describes the results coming from the case study analysis, deepening first of all the CSFs and challenges of the companies interviewed. Then, PD process, the related activities, data management and the role of PLM are analysed for both Food and Fashion industries.

4.1   Critical Success Factors

A background to acknowledge the strategic choices of the cases analysed is required to introduce the topics of PD and PLM in the Food and Fashion industries.

Fashion companies are orienting their efforts to improve products quality and to streamline their pipelines reducing TTM. Innovation is another important CSF, given the continuous progress entailed by new technologies and the attention paid by customers to digitalization. The luxury companies (cases 1,2,3) also leverage lots of their strategic decisions on the craftsmanship behind the manufacturing process, and on the brand reputation. While, companies belonging to the low-end market segment (cases 4 and 5) try also to reduce costs, transferring the manufacturing process to countries with cheap labour. These strategic goals are accompanied with several challenges, as (i) the need to develop premium quality products, (ii) the importance of style and design, (iii) the "Made in Italy" origin and (iv) the increasingly shorter product lifecycle.

Concerning the food industry CSFs, companies are focusing more on: quality, costs, customer satisfaction and TTM. As in the Fashion industry, also for the food companies, innovation is considered a key factor to improve and to develop a new product, ensuring its success in the market. Companies operating in pasta and confectionery sectors (cases 2, 3, 4, 6, 7) are more focused on the innovation of the product, in terms of meaning (changing the aesthetic of the product and assigning a certain meaning to a certain product) [28]. The reason why they decide to bet to the innovation of the meaning is usually related to two main factors: the product is not a primary food (in fact they produce sweets and pasta) and/or the recipe complexity is low (few and standard ingredients). On the other hand, company producing fresh products (cases 1,5) are more focused on quality, customer satisfaction and nutritional factors. These companies produce products subject to high perishability and are addressing to very important and delicate markets (such as food for children or elderly). The food industry faces different challenges, such as: (i) retail consolidation, (ii) ineffective innovation, (iii) increasing regulatory requirements and unclear regulations, (iv) empowered consumers, (v) increasingly complex global supply chains, (vi) sustainability, (vii) TTM.

4.2 PD Activities, Data Management and PLM Functionalities

Interviews and direct contacts with R&D and IT managers have allowed to analyse business processes, with a particular focus on PD and on how information are managed throughout product lifecycle. Figures 1 and 2 represent outlines of processes, tasks, PLM functionalities and other software solutions that Food and Fashion companies have validated and approved in a general meaning. PD and production are the main processes that constitute the beginning of life for Food and Fashion products and that have a relationship to PLM. Sub-processes are also aligned in Food and Fashion cases: planning, recipe/collection development, prototyping and test, engineering and production are representative of all the companies interviewed.

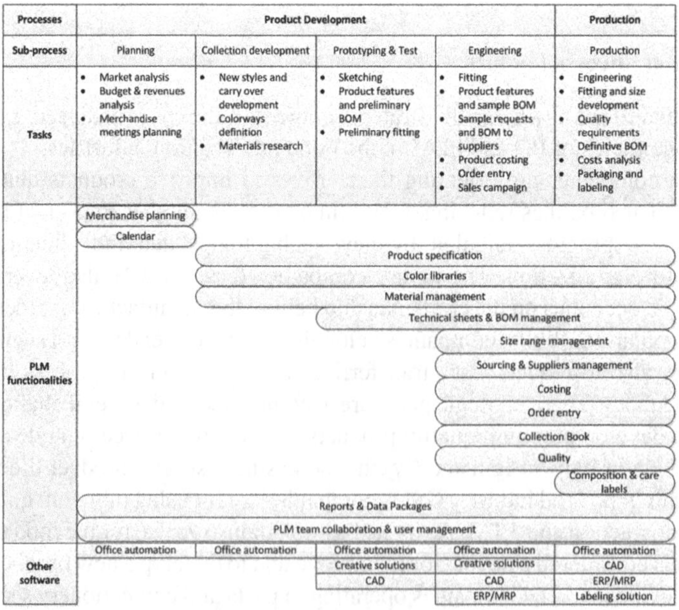

Fig. 1. Processes, tasks, PLM functionalities and other software in fashion companies

Information related to PLM functionalities, are based on the cases that are using it: they have implemented the same industry-specific solution, adding several customizations to the out-of-the box configuration.

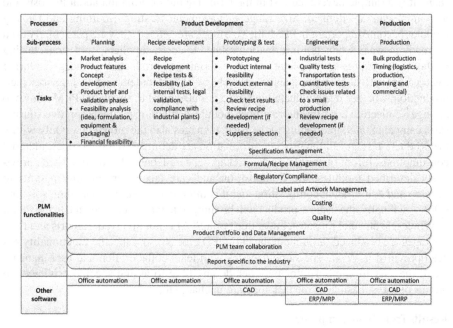

Processes	Product Development				Production
Sub-process	Planning	Recipe development	Prototyping & test	Engineering	Production
Tasks	• Market analysis • Product features • Concept development • Product brief and validation phases • Feasibility analysis (idea, formulation, equipment & packaging) • Financial feasibility	• Recipe development • Recipe tests & feasibility (Lab internal tests, legal validation, compliance with industrial plants)	• Prototyping • Product internal feasibility • Product external feasibility • Check test results • Review recipe development (if needed) • Suppliers selection	• Industrial tests • Quality tests • Transportation tests • Quantitative tests • Check issues related to a small production • Review recipe development (if needed)	• Bulk production • Timing (logistics, production, planning and commercial)
PLM functionalities	Specification Management				
	Formula/Recipe Management				
	Regulatory Compliance				
	Label and Artwork Management				
	Costing				
	Quality				
	Product Portfolio and Data Management				
	PLM team collaboration				
	Report specific to the industry				
Other software	Office automation	Office automation	Office automation CAD	Office automation CAD ERP/MRP	Office automation CAD ERP/MRP

Fig. 2. Processes, tasks, PLM functionalities and other software in food companies

Results from fashion companies

Concerning the fashion cases, PD begins with collection planning, when the Top management and Style managers take decisions about new collections, basing on budget, revenues, margins and analyses of market needs. Industry-specific PLM solutions include two main functionalities supporting collection planning, which are Merchandise Planning and Calendar: The Merchandise Planning module supports collection, product, and colourway planning by season to meet business objective. The Calendar module allows scheduling activities and milestones, both for products and materials. Office automation often completes data management with additional reports and aggregated information. Then, collection is developed: new products and carry over are identified, together with colourways and main materials. In PLM, the Product Specification module allows to define product details and build collections and the Material Management module is adopted to define materials, compositions labelling and material samples. At this stage, colour libraries are created, thanks to a specific PLM functionality, storing and grouping them by different criteria (e.g. season, collection, brand…). During the prototyping & test stage, the fashion product is still in a preliminary status, based on a sketch and few details. A preliminary fitting, that test the prototypes on models, is performed for shoes and ready-to-wear products. In addition to the modules described for collection planning, the Technical sheets and BOM management functionality is adopted to create bill of materials and to link products and materials. Creative solutions and CAD (Computer Aided Design) constitute additional software to manage prototypes and are usually interfaced with PLM. When the product progresses to the engineering stage, it is a sample developed just in the base size but information about its costs and its components are defined. Size range management, Costing, Sourcing and Quality modules become important in PLM: the size maps are defined (they are particularly used for ready-to-wear products); information related to costs, suppliers, quotations, testing methods, procedures and expectations on materials and products are managed. During sales campaign, fashion companies are able to collect orders and to organize their production, whether it is conducted in house or outsourced to suppliers. PLM allows to arrange a collection book through a proper module, containing products approved during sales campaign, and, interfacing to the ERP, manages also the order entry. Only within the production stage, all the product information are definitive (colours, sizes, material consumptions, bill of materials, costs, packaging, care labels). In addition to the previously described modules, the Composition and care labels functionality permits to develop and edit product composition and it is often interfaced with labelling software solutions. Finally, the fashion product will be shipped to the warehouses and to the Retail or Wholesale channel for sales, but at this point PLM is not involved. Reports and Data packages are produced throughout the entire PD process, so a specific functionality has been provided in PLM. The same happens with team collaboration and user management: the system administrator may decide any time to assign specific privileges to groups of users, basing on the task they are in charge to.

Results from food companies

Concerning food companies, the PD process starts with the phase of planning. The process usually begins with a market analysis, in order to understand the customer needs, the competitor positioning, with the different comparisons with industry standards (benchmark) and so on. Once the external factors have been fully defined, the next step is to identify if there are already similar products in the company portfolio. A brainstorming on technical and economics features is conducted in order to identify the product characteristics. Then, a first feasibility phase has to be developed, in order to evaluate the idea, formulation, equipment, packaging and financial feasibility. When this phase is concluded, a product brief is defined. The PLM functionalities supporting this preliminary phase are: Product portfolio and data management (supporting the continuous cultivation of product sets by prioritizing and managing PD and retirements), PLM team collaboration (supporting the collaborations between different teams and company functions) and Report specific to the industry (enabling the facilitation, automation, and control of the entire development process). The second macro-phase that characterize the food PD process is the recipe development phase. The first activity characterizing this phase is the recipe development. Once the recipe has been developed, this undergoes various evaluation stadiums (usually internal), starting from a laboratory validation, then a pilot plant validation, the industrial plant and finally a legal validation. The PLM modules supporting this phase are: Specification management, Formula/recipe management and Regulatory compliance. Formula and recipe management solution sustains the recipe development and its management. Specification management allows to capture the descriptions and quantities of ingredients, materials and other content, including process information needed to produce, package and ship a product. Regulatory compliance enables to identify what regulations, policies and obligations are applicable to the developing product. These functionalities support all the next phases of the process. If the recipe passes all ratings, then it is possible to move to Prototyping &Test phase. In this phase the production of the first prototypes is done observing if the realized products follow all the input specifications. A small batch of product is produced in order to be tasted both internally and externally. After that, the results of the tests will be analysed in order to understand whether changes to the recipe must be done. Therefore, a very important process characterizing this phase is the suppliers' selection. This phase is supported by the following PLM functionalities: Label and artwork management, Costing and Quality. Once the product is fully defined, it is possible to develop labels and artwork for different markets conforming to their preferences and regulations. Furthermore, product quality and costs are measured. These functionalities support the next PD phases, in order to constantly monitor costs and quality factors. The next macro-phase of the food PD process concerns the Engineering stage. The process owner verifies if the production line can handle the new product manufacturing. Different tests are performed, as industrial, quality, transportation and quantity tests. After that, quality tests must be done in order to check the quality of the industrialized products. It is usually produced a small number of products to check issues related to a small production. Finally, one or more transportation tests have to be done in order to understand how the product reacts to the various conditions during the different transports. Completed the Engineering phase, the actual production (bulk production) and the product launch are carried out.

4.3 Discussion: Similarities and Differences Between Food and Fashion Industries

The parallel interviews to Food and Fashion companies are compared in this section and several similarities and differences, influencing process and information management, are outlined. The main similarities and differences are listed below (Table 1):

Table 1. Food and fashion similarities and differences

Similarities & Differences	Description
Similarities	
Importance of the PD process	The case study has confirmed the relevance of PD in both the industries. PD is characterized by the same number of phases, assuming also the same meaning for both sectors
Customer-centric product design	Both the industries recognise the customer central role in the PD process
Importance of product innovation	Fashion companies have demonstrated how innovation is appealing for new consumers. Also, the food sector is focusing heavily on product innovation, which is gradually becoming one of the key factors that characterize successful food companies
High number of items	Food and Fashion companies manage lots of product variations, due to the high number of colourways for the fashion industry, and to different packaging and market-related customizations for the food industry
Importance of industry-specific PLM solutions	The cases have demonstrated that a general-purpose PLM system is not able to fit the needs of Food and Fashion companies. This is the typical situation in which "one size does not fit all". Both the industries require several functionalities that ask for an appropriate data model, provided by a custom solution or an industry-specific PLM, developed by a vendor with a particular focus on the sector
Differences	
Issues related to product obsolescence	Food product lifecycle is highly influenced from obsolescence and expiration dates while for fashion products, their lifecycle length is just a matter of seasonality and new trends
Issues related to regulatory compliance	PD in food companies cannot overlook regulatory compliance and market constraints. This is not an issue in the fashion industry
Differences in the sale channels	Fashion companies need to control the sales channels: the large part is also managing the Retail channel, as brand owners. Food companies sell their product to MRC (mass retail channels), losing any control over the sales channel
Differences in data model	The typical fashion item is an SKU (stock keeping unit), composed of a model, a colour and a size. The same structure is not replicated in the food products, which are characterised by a recipe and the value-added information come from the balancing quantities, more than from the single components
Different customer perception of product design	Even if design is fundamental for both the industries customers directly perceive product design in fashion items while, for the food sector, the appealing design is associated to the packaging more than to the product itself

5   Conclusions and Future Research Directions

This study has investigated the core process within Food and Fashion supply chains, i.e. PD. The first analysis has been a literature review about the PD process, its main tasks and the role of PLM, as a software and as a strategic business approach. Academic research is poor in terms of contribution related to PD in the Food and Fashion industries.

Hence, with the aim to analyse the main critical success factors in the two sectors, the PD activities and information management through PLM, a case study research has been performed. Two samples, one including fashion companies and the other one including food firms, have been identified and two different questionnaires (with the same structure) have been administered. The respondents from the fashion industry were high-end and low-end fashion companies: in three cases a PLM solution has been already implemented. The interviewed food companies managed different product categories (fresh products, pasta and canned food and confectionery products) and two cases have adopted a PLM solution. According to the case study analysis, the CSFs common to both the industries are product quality, TTM and innovation, while the challenges that these companies are facing appear to be more industry-specific.

The interviews have also allowed to deepen how PD process and information are managed in Food and Fashion companies: activities, PLM functionalities and the interfaces with other software solutions have been detailed in Figs. 1 and 2. Finally, a comparison between the two sectors has been performed, aiming at finding commonalities and differences. The main similarities that the authors have found are: importance of the PD process, customer-centric product design, importance of product innovation, high number of items managed and importance of industry-specific PLM solutions. Although, the following differences have been noticed: issues related to regulatory compliance, issues related to product obsolescence, differences in the sale channels, differences in data model and different customer perception of product design.

The results might be relevant for academics, because of the lack of researches concerning Food and Fashion PD. From the practitioners' point of view, the results of this work will help Food and Fashion companies to support their business, analysing the PD process and to better understand how the use of the PLM system could improve it.

A cross fertilization may be an interesting development of this research, allowing fashion companies to learn best practices related to PD and PLM from food firms and vice versa: for example, fashion products might be refined in their packaging and food industry might learn from the fashion product capability to be often renewed. Moreover, if we consider a particular merchandise category within the fashion industry, i.e. cosmetics, more commonalities will be found with the food companies, as the importance of regulatory issues. Cosmetics and food are also similar in terms of data model, because products are recipe-based, so that several PLM vendors have developed solutions fitting both the industries. A case study analysis might be performed in cosmetics companies, for their "fashion" nature and their affinity with food products. Other topics will be examined with a cross-industry approach: PD and PLM KPIs, PLM data model and the concept of "lean value chain". Finally, in order to close the examination of the three F driving "Made in Italy" to its success, several cases related to the Furniture industry might be included and analysed.

References

1. Aiello, G., Donvito, R., Grazzini, L., Halliburton, C., Wagner, B., Wilson, J., Godey, B., Pederzoli, D., Shokola, I.: An international comparison of 'Made in Italy' in the fashion, furniture and food sectors: an observational research study in France, Russia and The United Kingdom. J. Glob. Fash. Mark. **6**(2), 136–149 (2015)
2. Coldiretti. I valori dell'agroalimentare italiano nell'indagine Coldiretti-Swg, 16 Oct 2009 (2009). http://www.coldiretti.it/News/Pagine/770—16-10-2009.aspx
3. Fisher, M.: What is the right supply chain for your product.pdf. Harvard Bus. Rev. **2**, 105–116 (1997)
4. Christopher, M., Peck, H., Towill, D.R.: A taxonomy for selecting global supply chain strategies. Int. J. Logistics Manag. **17**(2), 277–287 (2006)
5. Christopher, M., Lowson, R., Peck, H.: Creating agile supply chains in the fashion industry. Int. J. Retail Distrib. Manag. **32**(8), 367–376 (2004)
6. Bloom, J.D., Hinrichs, C.C.: Moving local food through conventional food system infrastructure: Value chain framework comparisons and insights. Renew. Agric. Food Syst. **26**(1), 13–23 (2011)
7. van der Vorst, J.G.: Performance measurement in agri-food supply chain networks, an overview. In: Quantifying Agri-Food Supply Chain, pp. 13–24 (2006). Chap. 2
8. Gereffi, G., Lee, J.: A Global Value Chain Approach to Food Safety and Quality Standards, America (NY), vol. Global Heath, p. 52 (2009)
9. Taylor, D.H.: Value chain analysis: an approach to supply chain improvement in agri-food chains. Int. J. Phys. Distrib. Logist. Manag. **25**(10), 744–761 (2005)
10. van der Vorst, J.G.A.J., Beulens, A.J.M., de Wit, W., van Beek, P.: Supply chain management in food chains: improving performance by reducing uncertainty. Int. Trans. Oper. Res. **5**(6), 487–499 (1998)
11. Zokaei, A.K., Simons, D.W.: Value chain analysis in consumer focus improvement: a case study of the UK red meat industry. Int. J. Logist. Manag. **17**, 141–162 (2006)
12. Christopher, M.: The agile supply chain. Ind. Mark. Manag. **29**(1), 37–44 (2000)
13. Şen, A.: The US fashion industry: a supply chain review. Int. J. Prod. Econ. **114**(2), 571–593 (2008)
14. Barnes, L., Lea-Greenwood, G.: Fast Fashioning the supply chain: shaping the research agenda. J. Fash. Mark. Manag. **10**(3), 259–271 (2006)
15. d'Avolio, E., Bandinelli, R., Rinaldi, R.: Improving new product development in the fashion industry through product lifecycle management: a descriptive analysis. Int. J. Fash. Des. Technol. Educ. **8**(2), 108–121 (2015)
16. Segonds, F., Mantelet, F., Nelson, J., Gaillard, S.: Proposition of a PLM tool to support textile design: a case study applied to the definition of the early stages of design requirements. Comput. Ind. **66**, 21–30 (2015)
17. Jacob, M., Jonnro, E.: The drivers and factors influencing PLM adoption and selection, September 2015
18. Young, G.H.: PLM and the Food & Beverage Industry Conquering the Food Proving Value at Heinz. Agile Software Corporation (2004)
19. Kiritsis, D., Bufardi, A., Xirouchakis, P.: Research issues on product lifecycle management and information tracking using smart embedded systems. Adv. Eng. Inform. **17**(3–4), 189–202 (2003)
20. Terzi, S., Bouras, A.A., Dutta, D., Garetti, M., Kiritsis, D., Garetti, M.: Product lifecycle management–from its history to its new role. Int. J. Prod. Lifecycle Manag. **4**(4), 360–389 (2010)

21. Schuh, G., Rozenfeld, H., Assmus, D., Zancul, E.: Process oriented framework to support PLM implementation. Comput. Ind. **59**(2–3), 210–218 (2008)
22. Ameri, F., Dutta, D.: Product lifecycle management: Closing the knowledge loops. Comput. Aided. Des. Appl. **2**(5), 577–590 (2005)
23. Yin, R.K.: Case Study Research Design and Methods, 4th ed. vol. 5 (2009)
24. Yin, R.K.: Case Study Research: Design and Methods, vol. 26(1), pp. 93–96. SAGE Publications, Thousand Oaks (2003)
25. Cooper, R., Kleinschmidt, E.: Benchmarking the firm's critical success factors in new product development. J. Prod. Innov. Manag. **12**, 71–85 (1995)
26. Cooper, R.G.B., Kleinschmidt, E.J.: Winning businesses in product development: The critical success factors. Res. Technol. Manag. **50**(3), 52–66 (2007)
27. Saviolo, S., Testa, S.: Le imprese del sistema moda: Il management al servizio della creatività. Etas, Milan (2005)
28. Verganti, R.: Design, meanings and radical innovation: a research agenda. J. Prod. Innov. Manag. **25**(5), 436–456 (2008)

Applying Closed-Loop Product Lifecycle Management to Enable Fact Based Design of Boats

Moritz von Stietencron[1(✉)], Karl A. Hribernik[1], Carl Christian Røstad[2], Bjørnar Henriksen[2], and Klaus-Dieter Thoben[1,3]

[1] BIBA - Bremer Institut für Produktion und Logistik GmbH at the University of Bremen, Bremen, Germany
sti@biba.uni-bremen.de
[2] SINTEF Technology and Society, Trondheim, Norway
[3] Faculty of Production Engineering, University of Bremen, Bremen, Germany

Abstract. In the design of both leisure as well as professional boats, the experience of the boat designers and builders traditionally play a central role. To reach the desired customer satisfaction especially with high powered vessels, which often are used for decades, the tendency of overengineering is imminent. This is mainly based on the lack of reliable testing data and the high costs of towing tank tests and complex hydro dynamic simulations. The paradigm of Closed-Loop Product Lifecycle Management (PLM) can be employed as the enabling technology to overcome this lack of objectiveness by supplying the necessary product usage information to improve these processes. This paper presents an explorative approach towards a fact-based design and development process utilising distributed sensor data acquisition and high performance computing to enhance and validate the hydrodynamic simulations during the development process with the objective to reduce costs and uncertainties while increasing development speed and customer satisfaction. Beyond the related work and detailed description of the solution approach, this paper explores a concrete application experiment and gives conclusions on the applicability of Closed-Loop PLM as well as the other employed technologies.

Keywords: High performance computing · Closed-Loop PLM · IoT
Product development · Product usage information · Hydro dynamic simulations

1 Introduction

The trade of boat builders is a very traditional and cautious one, in which the personal knowledge of the craftsmen plays a central role. This imposes the industry with a number of limitations to both the productivity as well as the level of innovation that can be safely achieved from product generation to product generation.

While some categories of boat producers can adopt the processes from other mass production industries, this is not applicable for the manufacturers of specialised vessels, which need to find new and innovative approaches to combine expert knowledge with intelligent decision support. The paradigm of closed-loop Product Lifecycle Management

J. Ríos et al. (Eds.): PLM 2017, IFIP AICT 517, pp. 522–531, 2017.
https://doi.org/10.1007/978-3-319-72905-3_46

(PLM) postulates the shift from the traditional management of CAD-files towards a management of product information from all lifecycle phases.

This paper presents an approach to help specialised boat manufacturers to evolve their design and production processes based on real life product usage information.

2 Background and Motivation

Many producers of standardised, mass-produced boats have long abandoned the "craftsman"-approach to boat building and have heavily invested in a design driven process, which yields vessels, that fulfil the demands of a vast majority of common customers. However, the producers of small series vessels, and those with especially high demands to functional capabilities, are struggling to evolve their design and production processes as uncertainty and high investments currently do not calculate a promising business model. While the feedback from captains and boat-owners is usually anecdotal, without real data as the foundation for engineering decisions, many boats do have sensors, but, usually, the resulting data are neither collected nor transmitted to the boat manufacturer.

With the vision to improve the traditional process of designing small series of specialised boats and especially their hulls in a way, that eradicates the need for repetitive and costly rounds of prototype development, production and testing, we explored the possibilities to enhance the development process of boats for professional use by introducing real life product usage information and high performance computing (HPC) fuelled hydrodynamic simulations into the product design process.

In other domains different approaches towards product design and development processes which are not based merely on personal experience but also on actual product usage information – like fact-based design – have emerged over the recent years [1]. In fact-based design, in-situ information about product usage (usage information) is collected and consequently integrated into decision-making processes [2].

For the experiment a 6-step process for the usage of product usage information in vessel design was adapted, comprising the following steps:

1. Usage Data Collecting
2. Data Analysis
3. Design of Simulation Scenarios
4. Coupling of Data and Simulation
5. Running the Simulation
6. Creating a Better Boat

This paper will detail the related work and approach taken to address this idea and discuss the experiments results.

3   Related Work

This section presents an overview of three main topics – Fact-based design for boats, Product Lifecycle Management, and Internet of Things – which form the basis of the research presented in the subsequent chapters.

3.1   Fact-Based Design for Boats

In vessel design, the lack of data the customers' actual product usage patterns, results in a largely retrospective product-design based on experience, subjective judgments with external input only from certain customers or key persons. This often results in too high or wrong quality-standards and consequently over-processing. [1] However, a systematic product development approach needs to combine the knowledge from people that know the customers' demands and service requirements with that of the craftsmen producing the vessel. Product development research has explored several approaches, like concurrent engineering as a means to capture product usage information and mobilize them to enable reuse of the gained knowledge in the product development process [3]. Besides the trend towards a formalization of the product development process the capturing and utilization of product usage information is more and more seen as a competitive advantage in the domain. [4]

3.2   Product Lifecycle Management

Product Lifecycle Management (PLM) can be interpreted from the marketing as well as from the production engineering perspective. [5] The production engineering perspective on PLM has evolved from Product Data Management (PDM, also known as technical data management/TDM or engineering data management/EDM) [6]. It often divides the product's lifecycle into three main phases: beginning-of-life (BOL), middle-of-life (MOL) and end-of-life (EOL). [7] The BOL comprises steps such as product development, production and distribution and as primary focus of traditional PDM still is the "heart" of the conventional PLM.

With the emergence of paradigms like extended products, product service systems, functional products and the like, the need for a more extensive management of the product's lifecycle has been fostered. Thus, the latter phases of the product's lifecycle have gained more recognition in PLM. The MOL represents the use phase and the EOL the reverse logistics. [8] Figure 1 shows the three phases of a "closed-loop" product lifecycle with main processes.

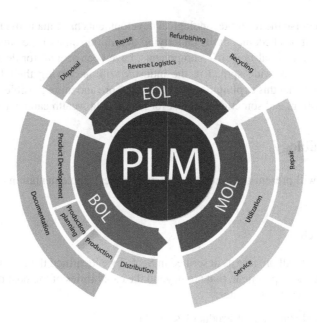

Fig. 1. PLM Phases and Processes; adapted from [9, 10]

The paradigm of closed-loop PLM describes an ecosystem in which stakeholders of a product can control product information originating from any phase in the product's lifecycle and utilize them throughout all lifecycle phases. [11] In this view it is crucial to combine information flows of as many product phases as possible – or ideally all. [12]

While BOL and EOL regularly are of little direct interest to the customer or end user, the MOL features direct interaction with the user. [10] While direct user interaction enables the straightforward creation of new business models, it also imposes a barrier between product and producer in the MOL phase, hindering direct access to product information from this phase. This is even increased in control and security sensitive industries like the maritime sector.

Therefore, the integration of the MOL phase as the regularly longest phase, requires, that technologies which enable product – producer interaction without customer involvement, like the Internet of Things (IoT) need to be employed.

3.3   Internet of Things

The product services of the 21st century are broadly supported by and reliant on the internet [13]. This trend is further increased by the possibilities of the Internet of Things (IoT). The Internet of Things can be seen as an evolution of the "old" human driven internet towards an internet which is driven by inanimate objects – things [14]. Originating in the wake of radio frequency identification (RFID) technology the IoT encompasses every object that participates in data exchange with other systems. It does not make any difference whether this exchange is multilateral or not, neither what sort of system is observed. [15]

While of course the recent technological developments have made the IoT the international trend it has become, by its underlying definition some of the simpler systems (like RFID), which qualify as IoT components, have been around for decades and are already respectively wide spread in the industry without having their full potential exploited. Now, that this exploitation is becoming more and more feasible for many use cases this existing, and sometimes almost forgotten, data wealth can be accessed.

4 Methodology

This section will present the approach and prototypical implementation chosen in the experiment.

4.1 Approach

Based on the overall process as described in Sect. 2 we identified the following tasks to be handled by the experiment, that are beyond the capabilities of the boat manufacturer and their engineering associates:

1. Capture and Handling of Product Usage Data
2. Management and Visualization of Data
3. Coupling of Data to Simulations

The design of the simulation and coupling of data to the simulation were executed by the simulation experts of the boat manufacturer and external subcontractors which are already involved in the boat design process.

4.2 Use Case

Hydrolift is a renowned Norwegian boat manufacturer that recently developed a new rescue vessel – the Hydrolift P42 – designed for high speed operations based on a modular design with focus on a high level of safety, functionality and cost of ownership.

In addition of being an innovative, efficient and a fast running vessel this new class also has great towing capacity and the possibility of carrying a watercraft. State of the art navigation equipment VHF, double chart plotters, radar and thermal imaging camera is also included. Our experiment has been carried out in parallel to the prototype testing and finalisation process.

4.3 Experiment

To achieve the first two objectives of the experiment, we implemented an IoT system for the collection, management and visualization of sensor data from the prototype vessels as a flexible system which was designed for ease of use and maximum flexibility on utilization. It is comprised of a data acquisition unit installed on the prototype boat (named the Universal Marine Gateway) and a cloud based data management and visualization application (named the HighSea Designer).

Capture and Handling of Product Usage Data. The data acquisition unit "Universal Marine Gateway" (UMG) is a modular data acquisition unit for product centric sensor data, which has been especially adapted to the marine domain. It was employed to collect sensor data from the boat's on-board systems which are connected via a NMEA2000 bus as well as dedicated sensors that have been strategically placed on the vessel.

The UMG has been implemented within the experiment in multiple versions depending on the vessel prototype status. Figure 2 shows the UMG as implemented on the final vessel prototype.

Fig. 2. The Universal Marine Gateway as implemented on final Hydrolift P-42 prototype

From the NMEA2000 bus the existing on-board systems can be accessed, which delivers access to an already vast number of vessel related data sources like fluid levels, engine and drivetrain status as well as weather, position, speed and more.

Beyond the pre-existing, yet not readily available, data set of the on-board systems, the simulation and product development experts have identified the need for advanced acceleration and orientation data from the vessel. To cater to this need two Bosch BNO055[1] system in package inertial measurement units have been installed, one at the hull's center of gravity (see Fig. 3, left) and one attached to the heavily dampened captain's chair (see Fig. 3, right).

---

[1] https://www.bosch-sensortec.com/bst/products/all_products/bno055.

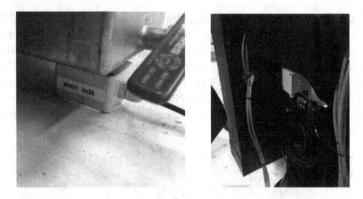

Fig. 3. Bosch BNO055 IMU sensor installations on Hydrolift P-42

Management and Visualization of Data. The cloud based HighSea Designer is a IoT platform which receives the sensor data from the UMG and manages them. Beyond the data management, it offers online data analysis and showcasing of different test runs for preselection before handing them over to the use in the further design processes.

Figure 4 gives examples of the graphical user interface which presents the data from a specific prototype test run.

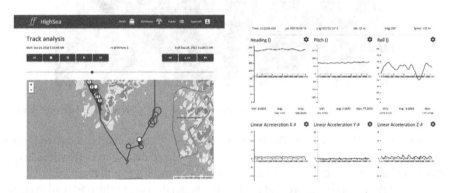

Fig. 4. Screenshot of Hydrolift P-42 test run analysis in the HighSea Designer

Coupling of Data to Simulations. While the first two objectives could be addressed from a technical direction the coupling of the sensor data from the test runs to the improved simulations was more a methodic task. It was decided in the experiment to pursue a two-fold approach:

1. Using preprocessed sensor data as input to the simulation scenario,
2. Comparing real-life sensor data to simulated data points observing the same object.

For both approaches the accelerations measured on the hull and the captain's chair were used as reference data and coupled with an adapted simulation model of the P-42. The simulations were run on the CINECA High Performance Computing Centre.

5 Results

The evaluation period of the experiment has enabled us to collect sensor data from over 100 test runs of the Hydrolift P-42 prototype.

Since the boat prototype has passed through different stages, with different technical system on-board, the data acquisition tool chain has encountered minor issues with short-term changes in configurations.

Based on the amount of sensor data it became apparent that in wide spread applications automated selection of relevant test runs would be advisable to enable easy selection of valid sensor data. The prototypical cloud application developed proved useful to conduct selection and validation of a smaller batch of test runs based on both the geo-profile of the test run as well as the sensor readings.

The data coupled simulations were dubbed in the experiment as "virtual sea trials". During the experimentation, it proved more achievable to utilize the real-life sensor data to verify the validity of the simulation results. And initiate an iterative process of simulation improvement, thus enabling the simulations to reach the necessary credibility.

From the concept of the virtual sea trials, validating the simulations based on real-life prototype run data, it is anticipated that the vessel design process can be significantly streamlined.

Figure 5 shows the impact of replacing repetitive prototype development, production and testing with a virtual sea trial. It is estimated that employing this approach can lead to savings of up to 15% on the prototype analysis and simulation efforts across the whole value chain.

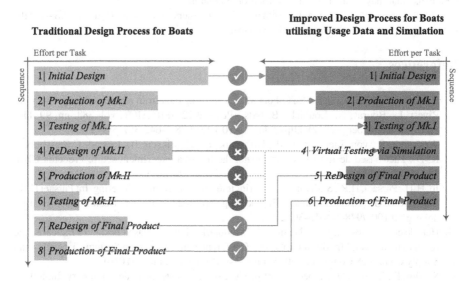

Fig. 5. Traditional (left) and Improved (right) design processes for boats

6 Conclusions

The research presented in this paper has explored a possibility of introducing fact-based design processes into the development of boats. A combination of real-life usage data captured from on-board systems as well as dedicated sensors and hydrodynamic simulations run in high performance computing centres has been chosen. The system implemented has successfully shown the potential of capturing sensor data from real-life test runs and transferring them back to the design process for use in or validation of simulations thus reducing uncertainties and development costs significantly.

Based on the successful experimentation in this experiment follow up developments have been initiated by the partners. Most notably the consortium has jointly engaged in the EC-funded project LINCOLN – Lean Innovative Connected Vessels[2] to expand both the development of the Internet of Things approach to vessel data capturing and usage as well as the employment of high performance computing and simulations for vessel design. However, the demonstrated approach not only holds potential for the boat developers' design and development processes; it also paves the way for new value adding business models which can be based on the now available usage data.

Acknowledgements. The research leading to these results has received funding from the European Community's seventh framework programme (FP7) under grant agreement No *609029* as well as the European Union's Horizon 2020 research and innovation programme under grant agreement No *727982*.

The contents of this paper reflect only the authors' view and the Commission is not responsible for any use that may be made of the information it contains.

The authors would like to thank the other projects partners – especially Hydrolift AS – for the support and openness in the creation of this paper.

References

1. Røstad, C.C., Henriksen, B.: ECO-boat MOL capturing data from real use of the product. In: Rivest, L., Bouras, A., Louhichi, B. (eds.) PLM 2012. IFIP AICT, vol. 388, pp. 99–110. Springer, Heidelberg (2012). https://doi.org/10.1007/978-3-642-35758-9_9
2. Wellsandt, S., von Stietencron, M., Hribernik, K., Henriksen, B., Røstad, C.C., Thoben, K.-D.: Fact-based design for leisure boats: the highsea-experiment setup. Procedia CIRP **38**, 74–77 (2015)
3. Jo, H.H., Parsaei, H.R., Sullivan, W.G.: Principles of concurrent engineering. In: Parsaei H.R., Sullivan W.G. (eds.) Concurrent Engineering, pp. 3–23. Springer, Boston (1993). http://doi.org/10.1007/978-1-4615-3062-6_1
4. Henriksen, B., Røstad, C.C., Naume, C.: Modularization fact-based design to increase "the room to maneuver." In: 6th International Conference on Information Systems, Logistics and Supply Chain ILS Conference 2016, June 1–4, Bordeaux, France (2016)
5. Sundin, E.: Life-cycle perspectives of product/service-systems: in design theory. In: Sakao, T., Lindahl, M. (eds.) Introduction to product/service-system design, pp 31–49. Springer, London (2009). http://doi.org/10.1007/978-1-84882-909-1_2

---

[2] http://www.lincolnproject.eu.

6. Terzi, S., Bouras, A., Dutta, D., Garetti, M., Kiritsis, D.: Product lifecycle management–from its history to its new role. Int. J. Prod. Lifecycle Manag. **4**, 360–389 (2010)
7. Kiritsis, D., Bufardi, A., Xirouchakis, P.: Research issues on product lifecycle management and information tracking using smart embedded systems. Adv. Eng. Inform. **17**, 189–202 (2003)
8. von Stietencron, M., Hribernik, K.A., Røstad, C.C., Henriksen, B., Thoben, K.-D.: An IoT fueled DSS for MOL Marine Auxiliaries management. In: Harik, R., Rivest, L., Bernard, A., Eynard, B., Bouras, A. (eds.) PLM 2016. IAICT, vol. 492, pp. 621–630. Springer, Cham (2016). https://doi.org/10.1007/978-3-319-54660-5_55
9. Hans, C., Hribernik, K.A., Thoben, K.D.: Improving reverse logistics processes using item-level product life cycle management. Int. J. Prod. Lifecycle Manag. **4**, 338–359 (2010)
10. Hribernik, K.A., von Stietencron, M., Hans, C., Thoben, K.-D.: Intelligent products to support closed-loop reverse logistics.In: Hesselbach, J., Herrmann, C. (eds.) Glocalized Solutions for Sustainability in Manufacturing, pp. 486–491 (2011). http://doi.org/10.1007/978-3-642-19692-8_84
11. Kiritsis, D.: Closed-loop PLM for intelligent products in the era of the Internet of things. Comput. Aided Des. **43**, 479–501 (2011)
12. Jun, H.B., Kiritsis, D., Xirouchakis, P.: Research issues on closed-loop PLM. Comput. Ind. **58**, 855–868 (2007)
13. Thoben, K.-D., Wortmann, J.C.(Hans): The role of IT for Extended Products' Evolution into Product Service Ecosystems. In: Emmanouilidis, C., Taisch, M., Kiritsis, D. (eds.) APMS 2012. IAICT, vol. 398, pp. 399–406. Springer, Heidelberg (2013). https://doi.org/10.1007/978-3-642-40361-3_51
14. Ashton, K.: That "Internet of things" thing. RFiD J. **22**, 97–114 (2009)
15. Atzori, L., Iera, A., Morabito, G.: The internet of things: a survey. Comput. Netw. **54**, 2787–2805 (2010)

Impact of PLM System in the New Food Development Process Performances: An Empirical Research

Claudia Pinna[1(✉)], Laureline Plo[2,3], Monica Rossi[1], Vincent Robin[3], and Sergio Terzi[1]

[1] Department of Management, Economics and Industrial Engineering, Politecnico di Milano, Piazza Leonardo da Vinci, 20133 Milan, Italy
{claudia.pinna,monica.rossi,sergio.terzi}@polimi.it
[2] Groupe POULT – Site de Montauban, Montauban, France
l.plo@groupe-poult.fr
[3] IMS Laboratory, University of Bordeaux, Talence, France
vincent.robin@u-bordeaux.fr

Abstract. Over the last few years, the food industry has become increasingly more relevant since it represents excellence not only at the European level, but also for the worldwide economy. Starting with this consideration, the main objective of this paper is to provide some elements that could support food companies to be successful in the market. In 2016, during the last PLM conference, the first results of a wider research were presented with the aim to understand how the PLM solution has been adopted into the food industry, and its limits and challenges of the deployment in this sector. This paper presents how the study has evolved through this year. Starting from this point, the impacts and effects from the use of the PLM solution on the New Food Development (NFD) process performances have been described. To identify these effects, a questionnaire was developed and used as a framework to support the data gathering process; each section of the questionnaire is described in the paper. Furthermore, the results of a preliminary empirical research based on a case study are shown. The results of this work will help both food companies and PLM vendors. Indeed, it will support PLM vendors to understand the food industry vision about their NFD process and performances. On the other hand, food companies will be able to better understand their NFD process, their NFD process performances and how they can use the PLM solution to affect their performances.

Keywords: New product development (NPD)
Product Lifecycle Mmanagement (PLM) · Food industry
New Food Development (NFD) · PLM for the food industry
NFD process performances

1 Introduction

Although food is considered a very important sector, companies operating in this area have to face several challenges to maintain and increase their competitive advantage [1, 2]. This paper starts from the results obtained in a previous study [3]. The aim of the

© IFIP International Federation for Information Processing 2017
Published by Springer International Publishing AG 2017. All Rights Reserved
J. Ríos et al. (Eds.): PLM 2017, IFIP AICT 517, pp. 532–543, 2017.
https://doi.org/10.1007/978-3-319-72905-3_47

previous study was to understand if the PLM solution is adopted in the New Food Development (NFD) process. In order to achieve this objective, we focused on: (i) the level of knowledge of the PLM solution in this sector, (ii) the main phases and activities characterizing the NFD process and (iii) the PLM functionalities supporting the NFD process. This paper presents how the study evolved throughout 2016. The first step of the current research is concerned with the analysis and adoption of the PLM solution in the NFD process. While the second step regards the analysis of the impacts and effects from the use of the PLM functionalities on the NFD performances. To identify these effects a questionnaire was developed, putting in evidence the NFD activities performances and how the PLM functionalities support the NFD process. Before it could be sent to the companies, the questionnaire had to be tested and validated, to verify the alignment with the defined expectations. In this paper, the results from the first pilot case has been presented. Thanks to this pilot case, the questionnaire has been revised and updated, in order to be submitted to the food companies sample. The paper starts, in Sect. 2, with a literature review about the level of knowledge from the PLM solution in the food sector. The following section, Sect. 3, describes a preliminary empirical research, which defines the research methodology, as well as the meaning and scope of the difference from each part of the questionnaire. In Sect. 4, the results of a Pilot Case have been presented and developed with the aim to test our questionnaire. Section 5 is dedicated to the discussion of the pilot case's results. Finally, Sect. 6 concludes the paper, presenting some thoughts about future research.

2 State of the Art on the Knowledge of the PLM Solution in the Food Sector

This first section of the paper adopts a qualitative methodology based on a literature review. The aim of the review is to understand the level of knowledge of the PLM solution in the food sector from a scientific point of view. The analysis was performed by following three main steps: (i) identify the keywords to be used, (ii) choose the database sources and (iii) analyse the results that were found by combining different keywords.

Starting from step one, three clusters of keywords were chosen and applied to retrieve the articles of interest. The first keyword group consisted of: "Product Life-cycle Management" and "PLM", while the second was composed of the following: "Food industry", "Food sector" and "Food". Keywords from each group were then combined, in order to expand the research results as much as possible. The searches were done separately for each keyword and applied to the journals' abstracts, title and keywords. Besides, authors did not set any restrictions related to time, but only for type, including articles and books sections. Furthermore, *Scopus* was chosen as the abstract and citation database of peer-reviewed literature. Sixty-two articles were collected, which became fifty-two after removing duplicates. The abstracts form each remaining article and book were then carefully read to assess criteria of relevance; articles that used the keywords in another semantic way were excluded. After evaluating of the abstracts, ten studies remained in the final selection of articles. These articles were extracted and read thoroughly, in full length. At the end, only three articles were considered in line with our field of interest.

The 3 interesting articles give a generic overview of how food companies could benefit from the use of the PLM solution. In fact, a complete discussion about how the PLM functionalities are used in the food industry has not yet been treated in literature.

Both Overbosch and Blanchard [5] and Granros [6] work's deal with the PLM solution on Quality and Food Safety Management topics. Pinna et al. [3] proposed a list of PLM functionalities supporting the product development process activities for the food industry. This study gives a brief overview about the usefulness of the IT solutions by the food companies to support the NFD process.

The fact that no articles dealing with the use of the PLM solution within the food industry have yet to be found, clearly shows the presence of a literature gap in this field. This is the reason why this study strives to address this topic.

3   Preliminary Empirical Research

3.1   Theoretical Framework and Research Questions

The main objective of the whole study is to understand how the use of the PLM functionalities impact the NFD process performances. To achieve this aim, we proposed a methodology based on four different activities:

- *A1:* to identify the main Critical Success Factors (CSFs) driving the company strategy supporting the NFD process
- *A2:* to identify which are the main performances evaluating the NFD activities
- *A3:* to understand how PLM functionalities support the NFD activities
- *A4:* to identify how PLM functionalities impact the identified performances

To provide an answer for each of these actions, a questionnaire was developed, with a section dedicated to each of them.

Figure 1 shows the theoretical framework and the logic sequence (steps 1 to 5) used to develop the 4 different sections of the questionnaire.

The first step identifies the CSFs that lead the strategy of the company. Step 2 allows us to analyse the PD process and its coherence with the strategy. Step 3 is focused on the links between activities of PD process and the PLM functionalities. Finally, in step 4, NFD performances are identified, trying also to understand the possible influence that PLM functionalities could have on them.

Table 1 shows the main research question and the research sub-questions. The latter corresponds to each section of the questionnaire.

3.2   Methodology – Research Strategy

In this work, Case Study is utilized as a research strategy. A multiple embedded case study will be developed. Specifically, the companies sample must respect the following characteristics:

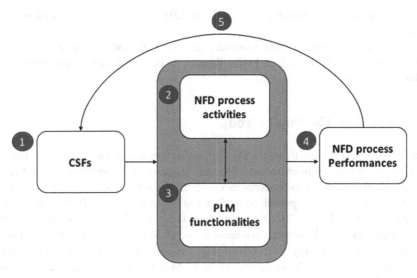

Fig. 1. Research theoretical framework

Table 1. Main research question and research sub-questions

RQ: How do PLM functionalities impact on the NFD process performances?	
sRQ1	Which are the main Critical Success Factors (CSF) driving the company strategy?
sRQ2	Which are the main performances evaluating NFD activities?
sRQ3	How do PLM functionalities support NFD activities?
sRQ4	How do PLM functionalities impact the identified performances?

- They must be classified as "*big companies*", due to the fact, large companies have a more formalized and structured NPD process. In addition, being the PLM solution costly for companies, it is largely used by large companies rather than small companies
- They must *use a PLM solution to manage their NFD process activities*

Questionnaires were used as a research tool. It was developed between September and November 2016. In December 2016, it was tested and validated through a Pilot Case. Moreover, in January 2017, the sample of food companies was fully defined. The selected sample was made up of about 20 companies. In order to have a complete view of how the PLM solution is used to support the NFD process, actors who mostly interface with this solution were chosen (R&D and IT managers). When initially trying to contact firms to conduct interviews, difficulty arose with finding a qualified employee, as well as working with their availability. During this phase, the collaboration with a PLM vendor leader in the food industry was very important.

The questionnaire was then submitted in the form of an interview. A standard protocol was followed and identified to be valid for each case study. The interview process took place from January 2017 until June 2017, and was then followed up with a results analysis.

As mentioned before, in order to validate and test the questionnaire, a first pilot case was developed, with the aid of Poult. Results of our pilot case is presented in the following section.

4   Pilot Case: The Poult Group

A pilot case study helps to refine the data collection plans with respect to both the content and the procedures to be followed. It assists to develop relevant lines of questions and provides some conceptual clarification for the research design as well [7]. For these reasons, it is important to explain the "Selection of the Pilot Case" and the "Scope of the Pilot Inquiry". Concerning the first question, Poult [4] has been chosen as the pilot case because it showed an interest to use PLM to manage its NFD process and also because it has already collaborated with the academia. In fact, some researchers were collaborating with the company on the PLM topic. This provides easy access to the case. The company was also selected because a study on their NFD process, information management and the actors involved in the NFD process had already been carried out. About the scope of the Pilot Inquiry, this pilot case has been chosen to improve its conceptualization of different types of PLM functionalities for different NFD performances and their related organizational effects.

4.1   Critical Success Factors (CSF)

The first step of our proposition is the identification of CSFs. Usually, CSFs are used to define key areas of activity and to identify the strategic indicators of the company [8]. These strategic indicators allow us to evaluate the "strategical interest" of the of PLM solution deployment. Since Poult wants to reduce the customer answer time and to ensure better continuity between the "product" innovations and their putting into production, the company CSFs are:

- the *sharing of information* by setting up a unique product repository enabling the company to maintain centralized, reliable and up-to-date information
- the *optimization of its processes* by sharing and capitalizing on knowledge
- the deploying a *structured methodology*, to develop new product
- the *analysis and the anticipation of the risks* linked to the product/process data.

4.2   NFD Phases and Activities

The phases and activities described in the previous study [3] describe a generic and standard NFD process. Nevertheless, some differences can be noticed when comparing companies. Since the different sections of our questionnaire are linked with the phases and activities of the NFD process, a check concerning the coherence of the terminologies and the related meanings is needed. In Table 2 the process phases and activities of Poult are presented.

Table 2. NFD process phases and activities of Poult and actors involved

NFD macro-phase	NFD activities	Actors
Customer's or internal (Poult's project) request for proposal	Send external NFD request Send internal NFD request Receive customer or internal request and carry out a preliminary study	Customers General (innovation challenge) Marketing "Product family" (R&D, marketing, trade, production)
Project launch	Plan the project Develop the recipe	R&D (Project Manager) General (innovation challenge)
Product test & feasibility	Test recipe (Lab and Industrial Testing) Study internal feasibility Study external feasibility	R&D (Project Manager + R&D technician) Production Customer Laboratory
Production, Launch and Commercialization	Manufacture, Launch and Commercialize	General (quality, production, trade, R&D....)

Table 3 shows the comparison between the standard process identified in the previous study [3] and the NFD process of Poult.

Overall, the description of generic NFD process seems to be similar to Poult's. Moreover, differences have been observed concerning two phases:

- *Plan the project*: Poult Company mainly sells its products under private label, which is to say that the retailers are the ones that impose their idea and define their need. Company in-house teams reflect on the product to be created, so that it adapts to our customers' strategy (mainly the retailer). Thus, the macro phase planning is mainly generated when they enter a process of development for a new product, following a need expressed internally (either by the marketing department after market study or after the innovation challenge conducted internally). In the case of an internal need, the company is a source of proposal and once the product is created, it is presented to the identified customers (retailers)

- *Define Recipe*: A first estimation of the technical and financial feasibility is carried out during phase zero, and then another during the definition of the recipe. In addition, the industrialization phase is carried out in parallel with the production phase and feasibility tests. In general, the production manager checks whether the manufacturing line can manage the production of the new product with all its technical and financial characteristics or not. Once the project team agrees, a small quantity of the products (industrial tests or laboratories) is produced to check if everything is okay before sending the samples to the customer and/or panel. If the customer seems satisfied with the products sent, then the product is ready to be launched on the market.

Table 3. Comparison between our standard process and Poult NFD process (Y: correspondence, N: difference)

NFD macro-phase	NFD activities	Y/N
Planning	Plan the project	No, unless developing a new product is a result of an internal need (exceptional case: the need usually arises from a customer)
	Define the recipe	No, unless developing a new product is a result of an internal need (exceptional case: the need usually arises from a customer)
Recipe definition	Study idea internal feasibility	No
	Develop the recipe	Yes
	Study recipe internal feasibility	Yes
Product test & feasibility	Make a prototype	Yes
	Study product internal feasibility	Yes
	Study product external feasibility	Yes
Industrialization	Industrialize	No
Production, launch and Commercialization	Manufacture, launch and commercialize	Yes

Once the various phases characterizing the Poult NFD process and the gap from the general process have been identified, it will be possible to go on with the identification of performances.

4.3 Main Performances Characterizing the NFD Activities

The main objective of this section is to understand how the food companies evaluate their NFD activities and how they define their performances. The results of this phase will help food companies to better understand their NFD activities, their NFD process performances and to support them in monitoring NFD activities over time. Mapping the KPIs characterizing each activity and assigning a grade of importance to each of them will allow to identify the most relevant NFD activities. Keeping the focus on the relevant activities, will provide greater value to the whole process.

In the specific case of Poult, the performance measurement remains an open question where there are multiple and shared opinions. The most widely used indicators within the Poult Group is related to the production (*overall rate of return*) and supply chain (*customer satisfaction*). Concerning the R&D, the main objective is to reduce the time and cost of the product development project. For this purpose, R&D focuses on projects general indicators, for example: the number of products that have emerged, the percentage of projects carried out in relation to the number of projects undertaken. The

Table 4. Poult NFD process activities and related performances

NFD activities	NFD process performances	Relevance
Study product internal feasibility	Indicator tracking panels referenced products Indicators panels new referencing *Customer satisfaction rate* = Total satisfactory panels/Total panels received	4
Study product external feasibility	The percentage of projects carried out in relation to the number of projects undertaken	3
Manufacture, launch and commercialize	***Production***: TRG is the product of 3 rates TRG = availability rate (TD) × efficiency rate (TE) × quality rate (TQ) ***Supply chain***: Litigation: number of lines in dispute/total number of order lines Delivered during the same period...	3

The column "Relevance" defines the degree of importance of the indicator (KPI), according to this scale: 1 = Not important; 2 = Low importance; 3 = Important; 4 = Very important

most important indicator for R&D remains the rate of satisfaction of the tasting panels. Table 4 shows the NFD process performances for each phase interested and the related relevance.

4.4 How Do PLM Functionalities Support NFD Activities?

According to the results obtained in 2016 [3], nine main PLM functionalities, supporting the NFD process, are taken into consideration. In this context, these functionalities are considered as a metrics of classification. Starting from these assumptions, we present the results related to the section of the questionnaire focusing on PLM functionalities (Table 5). The main objective of this section is to understand how PLM functionalities support the different NFD activities. The results obtained will help food companies to better understand the potentiality of the PLM categories and the impact on the NFD process activities. In fact, to use properly PLM functionalities, food companies must first understand the meaning and the capabilities of each and then to understand which activities of NFD process are supported. The knowledge about the main process activities and how the PLM functionalities support the analysed activities will allow food companies to maximize the benefits from the adopted solution.

4.5 Relation Between PLM Functionalities and NFD Process Performances

Finally, once both Value Added (VA) activities and PLM functionalities have been identified, it is possible to define the influence that each functionality has on each performance. In particular, the most interesting part for companies will be to focus on the value-added activities previously identified. In this way, companies can understand which are the performances that mostly represent their process and which must be kept

Table 5. PLM functionalities and NFD main activities, the Poult Pilot Case

PLM functionalities	NFD main activities supported	Actors involved (BU)
CAD design management	Not used	–
CAD for packaging design	Not used	–
Formula and recipe management	Develop recipe	R&D (Project Manager)
Label management	Study product internal feasibility	R&D (Project Manager) Quality
PLM team collaboration	Not used	–
Product portfolio and program management	Not used	–
Report specific to the industry	Study product internal feasibility Study product external feasibility	R&D (Project Manager) Quality
Regulatory compliance	Develop recipe Study product internal feasibility	R&D (Project Manager) Quality
Specifications management	Not used	–

under control. After that, thanks to the relation between PLM functionalities and NFD activities it is possible to identify the link between them. In this way, companies can select the PLM functionalities which mainly influence their value-added activities, and thanks to the monitoring of the related performances, they can identify the relative impact. This final step allows food companies to better understand how they can use these functionalities to improve their NFD activities, and consequently trying to achieve the main goals defined by the previous CSFs. Moreover, in order to achieve the best results, it is necessary that those who use the software functionalities have full knowledge of the tools they are using, including the relative capacities and capabilities. Below, in Table 6, the results related to the Poult Pilot Case are presented. The relation between PLM functionalities and performances could be positive, negative or neither: positive relation means that the use of the PLM functionalities has improved the performances, negative relation that the use of the PLM functionalities has decreased the performances and no relation means that the use of the PLM functionalities has no influence on the performances.

For this specific case, the analysis had to be restrict to the information that Poult highlights as important. In fact, only two of the NFD activities are both supported by PLM functionalities and measured by performance indicators. These phases are: "study product internal feasibility" and "study product external feasibility". Unfortunately, it is not possible to assign a relation between the use of PLM functionalities and NFD performances, due to these PLM functionalities having been deployed in the Poult group recently. Thus, the company is not in position to establish a precise analysis on the relations between the introduction of a PLM solution and the NFD process. Nevertheless, they assume that the implementation of a PLM within the Poult Group will

Table 6. Evaluation of the impact of PLM software categories on NFD process performances, the Poult's results

NFD activities	PLM functionalities	NFD process performances
Develop recipe	*Formula and recipe management* *Regulatory compliance*	No performance measured
Make a prototype	No PLM functionality supports this activity	No performance measured
Study product internal feasibility	*Label management* *Report specific to the industry* *Regulatory compliance*	The percentage of projects carried out in relation to the number of projects undertaken
Study product external feasibility	*Report specific to the industry*	Indicator Tracking panels referenced products Indicators panels new referencing *Customer satisfaction rate* = Total satisfactory panels/Total panels received
Manufacture, launch and commercialize	No PLM functionality supports these activities	***Production***: TRG is the product of 3 rates TRG = availability rate (TD) × efficiency rate (TE) × quality rate (TQ) ***Supply chain***: Litigation: number of lines in dispute/total number of order lines Delivered during the same period

influence the processes, and particularly the activities carried out within the R&D and quality services. Indeed, the construction of a single raw materials database will make it easier to research and use the data during the formulation phases. Improved data quality on raw materials results in less error in formulation. Within the quality department, the implementation of a PLM tool will allow automatic documentation in relation to the product/process from the data entered in the repository.

5 Research Results Discussion

The Poult Pilot Case helped us test, validate and refine the first version of the questionnaire. In this concern, changes have been done to the preliminary form proposed:

- *CSFs section has been moved*. In the first version of the questionnaire this section was positioned at the end. Interviewees proposed to move this section to the beginning in order to have a more complete view of the company, as well as to define the strategical objectives and to link the next sections, while keeping this information in mind
- *NFD process comparison*. A question about the comparison between the general NFD process proposed and the current one of the company was introduced. This

was done in order to better contextualize and customize the questionnaire based on the interviewed company

- *Link between CFSs and NFD performances.* This section has been deleted because it didn't add relevant information to the main research question defined

The other sections of the questionnaire were aligned with the Poult point of view. It was decided in some cases to improve the quality of the questions, in terms of presentation, but the meanings have not been changed. Concerning the Poult Case Study, what it could be said is that the main phases that have to be taken under consideration are the internal and external studies of product feasibility. These phases are managed with the support of some PLM functionalities, as Label management, Report specific to the industry and Regulatory compliance. In order to measure the performances of these activities three performances have been identified: the percentage of projects carried out in relation to the number of projects undertaken, the indicator tracking panels referenced products and indicators panels new referencing. Being a pilot case, the fact that it was not possible to identify a relation between PLM functionalities and NFD performances is not so relevant, because of the main scope of the inquiry. As said before, the scope of the pilot case is not data collection oriented (to answer the research question), but is used to refine, test and validate the case study tool (questionnaire).

6   Conclusions and Further Research

This study is part of a wider research project, whose main objective is to understand the influence of the PLM functionalities on NFD performances. The methodology used to achieve the research goal is case study. In order to obtain a methodologically efficient work, it is important to design a good research tool, which in this case is a semi-structured questionnaire. This paper shows the results relating to the final phase of the questionnaire design: The Pilot Case. The pilot case has been developed with the aid of a French company. Various corporate figures (R&D, Marketing and Production) have participated in this process, in order to obtain different points of view and a more complete improvement of the instrument. The results of the pilot case helped mostly to better refine it in terms of questions and structure. In fact, the results influenced the move of some sections within the questionnaire (because it seems to give a better logic sequence) and to eliminate other parts (because they don't add so much value). Nevertheless, some results have been obtained from the Poult interview, in particular: the most important NFD process phases for Poult are "Study Product Internal Feasibility", "Study Product External Feasibility" and "Manufacture, Launch and Commercialize". Nonetheless, only the phase of "Study Product Internal and External Feasibility" is supported by different PLM functionalities. The Manufacture, Launch and Commercialize activity is measured by different performances but no PLM functionalities are used to support it. It would be interesting to better investigate why they made this choice.

In conclusion, it is possible to say that the proper use of this research tool will allow food companies to: (i) better understand the NFD processes and activities, (ii) define, discover and monitor the NFD performances by giving them a relevance,

(iii) understand how the use of PLM tool can support the NFD process and (iv) understand how the PLM functionalities can affect the various activities of the process and as a result the performance associated with them. As the next research step, the questionnaire will be submitted to different food companies that are currently using the PLM functionalities, and then their answers will be analysed and evaluated in order to obtain a final answer to this research. From a scientific point of view, this work will help to fill a gap in literature about the use of the PLM in the food sector (in particular in support of NFD process). Moreover, also the results related to the NFD process performances, NFD process phases and activities and PLM functionalities supporting the NFD process will allow to enrich the contents about these topics, lacking in the scientific literature. Furthermore, from the practitioner point of view, this study will help PLM vendors to understand the food industry vision about their NFD process and performances. In addition, food companies will be able to better understand their NFD process, their NFD process performances and how they can use the PLM system to affect their internal performances. Fundamental element to achieve good results from the use of PLM functionalities is the knowledge of the tools. Food companies that want to manage their processes through these capabilities must therefore make sure they know the related potential in such a way that they can make the most of these functionalities.

References

1. Bachev, H.: Risk management in the agri-food sector. Contemp. Econ. **7**(1), 45–62 (2013)
2. Bloom, J.D., Hinrichs, C.C.: Moving local food through conventional food system infrastructure: value chain framework comparisons and insights. Renew. Agric. Food Syst. **26**(1), 13–23 (2011)
3. Pinna, C., Taisch, M., Terzi, S.: PLM in the food industry: an explorative empirical research in the Italian market. In: Harik, R., Rivest, L., Bernard, A., Eynard, B., Bouras, A. (eds.) PLM 2016. IFIPAICT, vol. 492, pp. 238–247. Springer, Cham (2016). https://doi.org/10.1007/978-3-319-54660-5_22
4. Groupe-poult: GROUPE-Poult (2017). http://www.groupe-poult.com/fr/
5. Overbosch, P., Blanchard, S.: Principles and systems for quality and food safety management. In: Motarjemi, Y., Lelieveld, H. (eds.) Food Safety Management: A Practical Guide for the Food Industry, pp. 537–558. Elsevier, Amsterdam (2013)
6. Granros, R.: Regulatory compliance for food safety. Control Eng. **56**(10), 50 (2009)
7. Yin, R.K.: Case Study Research: Design and Methods, vol. 26, No. 1. pp. 93–96. SAGE Publications, Thousand Oaks (2003)
8. Cooper, R.G.B., Kleinschmidt, E.J.: Winning businesses in product development: the critical success factors. Res. Technol. Manag. **50**(3), 52–66 (2007)

Implementing Total Lifecycle Product Sustainability Through True Lean Thinking

M. A. Maginnis[1](✉), B. M. Hapuwatte[2], and I. S. Jawahir[2]

[1] Department of Mechanical Engineering, Institute of Research for Technology Development (IR4TD), Lean System Program, University of Kentucky, Lexington, KY, USA
amaginnis@uky.edu
[2] Department of Mechanical Engineering, Institute for Sustainable Manufacturing (ISM), University of Kentucky, Lexington, KY, USA

Abstract. Recent expansion of the manufacturing industry's customer requirements include product lifecycle considerations covering environmental, economic and societal concerns. Awareness for the need to implement sustainable manufacturing (SM) practice continues to grow but the implementation rate appears to be relatively slow. In cases where successful SM implementation depends on the ability to compete in the marketplace in terms of quality and cost, lean manufacturing concepts have been applied to help manage the product lifecycle. Unfortunately, most lean manufacturing applications in SM focus on the use of basic lean tools such as 5S, visual management and kanbans, etc., implemented as a series of management-directed projects or Kaizen activities without full engagement of the people doing the work. Consequently, improvements made under these conditions are often short-lived and relatively limited. True Lean benchmarks the Toyota Production System (TPS) and includes often overlooked critical operational elements aimed at developing and sustaining team member engagement for continuous improvement (CI). This paper discusses important concepts of sustainable PLM and True Lean and introduces an integrated model called the 'Benevolent Production System' as a guide to continuously improve total lifecycle product sustainability.

Keywords: Benevolent Production System · Benevolent system
Lean manufacturing · True Lean · Lean thinking · Toyota Production System
Sustainable manufacturing · 6R concept · Product lifecycle management
Life-cycle

1 Introduction

Industries worldwide are facing more stringent and numerous regulation on processes and systems required to produce products through all stages of their lifecycle. While some organizations may see these regulations as obstacles, they can be also viewed as an expansion of customer requirements and therefore part of the value proposition for the customer. To be successful, sustainable manufacturing must meet the triple bottom-line (TBL) requirements designed to positively impact the economy, environment and society throughout a products' lifecycle. In many instances, meeting these

© IFIP International Federation for Information Processing 2017
Published by Springer International Publishing AG 2017. All Rights Reserved
J. Ríos et al. (Eds.): PLM 2017, IFIP AICT 517, pp. 544–553, 2017.
https://doi.org/10.1007/978-3-319-72905-3_48

demands will require the use of new manufacturing processes and materials to meet TBL requirements through the use of 6R (reduce, reuse, recycle, recover, redesign and remanufacture) [1] thinking. This can add significant complexity to product lifecycle management (PLM) and would require a (new) learning environment within participating organizations to master and continuously improve methods needed to take full advantage of the new processes and materials and economically meet market demands.

Lean manufacturing or 'lean' is a term coined to describe the Toyota Production System (TPS) and is a proven method to fulfill customer expectations in terms of quality and cost, by eliminating waste throughout the system [2, 3]. Unfortunately, most organizations focus on the application of lean tools (specific IE related concepts) and as a result, the failure rate for lean implementations has been estimated at between 70% to 98% [4]. However, done correctly, the application of TPS principles and practices or *True Lean*, which focuses on TPS and the thinking behind it [5], can create a learning environment resulting in sustained CI over long periods as demonstrated by Toyota [6, 7].

The authors of this paper believe that the successful application of True Lean thinking within organizations engaged in the application of any of the 6Rs of sustainable manufacturing could provide a significant strategic advantage in developing and meeting new market requirements. As in the more general application of lean mentioned above, the literature shows the application of lean manufacturing as a way to improve lifecycle sustainability has primarily focused on the use of lean-related tools, centered around a single aspect (mainly environmental) of manufacturing sustainability. Thus, in this paper, while discussing the integration of lean principles within sustainable manufacturing, a new concept called the *"Benevolent Production System"* (BPS) is introduced to support a more effective implementation model for sustainable manufacturing practices in industry through the integration of True Lean thinking.

2 Literature Review

2.1 Sustainable Manufacturing

According to Jawahir et al. [8], sustainable manufacturing (SM) practices occurring at the product, process and systems levels must reduce their negative impact on TBL aspects, while maintaining or improving both quality and overall lifecycle cost benefits which are generally not addressed by traditional or Green Manufacturing. Shuaib et al. [9] introduced the Product Sustainability Index (*ProdSI*) framework, to comprehensively and quantitatively evaluate all the important sustainability-related aspects of products, and provide an index to compare their sustainability content. In recent work, Hapuwatte et al. [10] identified the importance of *ProdSI*, especially when alternate manufacturing methods such as additive manufacturing are available, adding to the complexity of choosing the optimum sustainable designs and processes.

Jawahir et al. [11] also identified the importance of *'total lifecycle sustainable manufacturing'* to ensure all four major stages of a product's lifecycle (*Pre-manufacturing, Manufacturing, Use and Post-use*) are considered when evaluating SM. The literature further suggests the need for applying the 6R concept [1, 12] to successfully implement SM. This work also shows how each R can be incorporated into different stages of the lifecycle to enable a '*closed-loop material flow*', which is essential to maximize the product lifecycle sustainability [11]. While there is a considerable number of recent studies related to SM, the focus on implementing total lifecycle sustainable manufacturing is somehow limited.

In a related issue, Grieves [13] developed models describing the potential application of lean tools to address PLM issues. These models illustrate the effective use of information to reduce potential inefficiencies in product design, manufacture, support and disposal. Our work conceptually extends the application of lean principles/concepts to all aspects of total lifecycle sustainability, including the 6Rs, and systemically integrates the critical component of respect for the people doing the work (team members or TMs), emphasizing human development and engagement.

2.2   Conventional Lean Manufacturing and True Lean Thinking (TPS)

As mentioned above, lean manufacturing [2] was originally based on the Toyota Production System (TPS) [14] which was conceived as a method to fulfill customer expectations for high quality products while eliminating waste and reducing cost within the entire manufacturing system by fully utilizing the workers' capabilities. The literature [15, 16] focuses on a number of individual tools available within lean, such as 5S, Just-in-Time (JIT), problem solving, value and waste identification, cellular manufacturing, kanban systems, Single Minute Exchange of Dies (SMED), Total Productive Maintenance (TPM), Value Stream Mapping (VSM), etc. Literature sources [15, 17] also identify instances of implementing multiple lean concepts, emphasizing the importance of viewing lean as a philosophy rather than simply a set of individual tools [18]. However, some prior publications [15, 19] also identify the concept of respect for people, a core principle of TPS [20], as a primary missing component in most 'conventional' lean implementations. New [21] has compared the difference between the TPS idea of respect and dignity for people based on their ability to improve their work as opposed to the Western model of 'dignity at work' which emphasizes variety and autonomy in core activities without consideration of CI. In addition TPS also encompasses the concept of developing people by providing them with an environment to more fully utilize their capabilities as a reflection of Toyota's core principle of respect for TMs at every level [20, 21].

CI is the other core principle embodied in TPS, focusing on reducing cost while improving the product quality through waste elimination. It is a learning process focused on an ever-increasing understanding of individual processes performed using standard methods (standardized work), based on the idea of '*good method = good results*'. Unlike conventional thinking, according to TPS or True Lean (used interchangeably in this paper), the people doing the work have the greatest understanding of how to improve it. Basic misunderstandings of the thinking behind TPS has led to a huge variation in the definition of lean resulting in the need for the University of Kentucky (UK) Lean Systems Program (initiated by and still managed by Toyota Executives) to specifically define the term '*True Lean*' to describe their program [5]. According to the UK program, True Lean is defined as: '*the group by themselves, using systematic problem solving, to improve the work they do, towards the achievement of the company's targets and goals, when and only when the company culture is the reason the improvement occurs'.* According to this definition, the continuous application of systematic problem solving, based on the PDCA (Plan, Do, Check, Act) learning cycle [5, 6, 22] depends on the ability of the group to rapidly identify and eliminate abnormalities where the work is performed at every level of the organization. Incorporating successful problem solutions (countermeasures) into standardized work is the way to keep the problem from coming back, establishing a new baseline for CI and a strategic advantage for any organization [6].

2.3 Lean and Sustainable Manufacturing

Literature discussing the application of lean manufacturing or thinking in sustainable manufacturing is sparse and largely focuses only on the environmental aspect (discussion of 'Lean and Green' manufacturing). Yet, sustainability as discussed above must include all three aspects of TBL.

One case study [23] explores the implementation of the lean concept of waste elimination in SM, and states that lean transcends Green. Chiarini [24] illustrates how certain lean concepts such as VSM, 5S, cellular manufacturing, SMED and TPM can be used to improve the environmental impact of the manufacturing plants.

In some applications of Lean to Green manufacturing cited, lean is seen as a means to reduce (i.e., make the products, processes and systems 'leaner') the environmental impact of manufacturing through improved efficiency and waste reduction [25, 26]. In other studies [25, 27] its effectiveness is disputed based on insufficient evidence by citing the importance of conducting comprehensive lifecycle assessments to truly understand the total impact. However, at least some of the available literature [25, 28] agrees on the synergistic impact of implementing Lean and Green together. Rothenberg et al. [26] go so far as to conclude attention to human development factors such as training and jobs skills could enable even better identification of waste reduction opportunities.

As mentioned, creating a learning environment through the implementation of True Lean, represents an essential strategic advantage for practicing SM, not only to reduce waste and cost, but to deal with increasing complexities effecting every aspect of SM. However, the relationship between lean and SM has not been adequately studied. The concept of the Benevolent Production System introduced below is our attempt to integrate the two concepts in order to guide the development of CI capabilities in current and future sustainability activities.

3   Discussion

Figure 1 is based on Zhang et al. [29], and illustrates the product lifecycle stages of: Pre-manufacturing (PM), Manufacturing (M), Use (U) and Post-use (PU) shaded in purple, and their relationship to the 6Rs along with the gateways to each R. The figure has been adapted to distinguish between the material and information flows in order to reveal potential feedback loops essential for continuous learning.

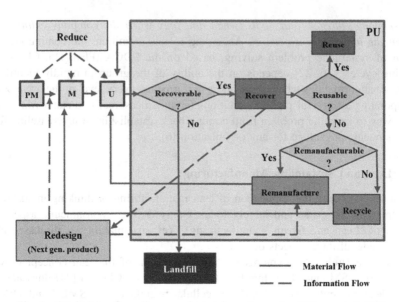

Fig. 1. 6R decision flow diagram adapted from the work of Zhang et al. [29]

The model presented in Fig. 2 illustrates the primary information feedback loop for total lifecycle product development (TLPD). This framework was developed by extending Shetty's conventional product development concept [30], which appears to neglect critical and formalized two-way communication between each stage of development. This is especially important between the "End-of-Life" and "Customer Requirements" stages because EOL concerns must be included in customer requirements to achieve total lifecycle sustainability. The occurrence of information flow between each stage of product development illustrated in Fig. 2 represents opportunities to apply true lean thinking as a way to develop continuous learning capabilities throughout a sustainable system. In sustainability, success is typically defined by the ability to meet the requirements of the TBL and are usually centered on the needs of the customer and the company. True Lean extends the definition of success to encompass the needs of the people engaged in creating the product (TMs), which, based on the success of TPS, can be expected to increase the ability of the system to meet the TBL requirements. It is the successful integration of the technical and human elements of the production system which results in what we call a *'benevolent production system'*.

Fig. 2. Primary feedback loop for total lifecycle product development (TLPD)

3.1 Definition of Benevolent Production System

As mentioned above, regulatory and other forces have resulted in the expansion of customer requirements to include improved sustainability content in manufactured products. As the section on lean manufacturing suggests (Sect. 2.2), a True Lean manufacturing system represents one of the most effective ways to manage product lifecycle issues for achieving safety, quality, cost, productivity and human resource development objectives to meet the increasingly complex customer demands upon sustainably manufactured products.

The *"Benevolent Production System"* (BPS) model illustrated in Fig. 3 is defined as the successful integration of the operational elements of TPS or a True Lean system with the primary elements of TLPD to create a CI operation based on 6R thinking. This system, like TPS, is centered on the core principles of CI and Respect for People [20]. The BPS model was developed using gap analysis based on the UK True Lean Operating Environment model [5] and general observations of sustainable manufacturing activities (6Rs & TLPD). Its purpose is to help provide a more focused pathway for developing CI capabilities within SM organizations.

Fig. 3. Benevolent Production System model representing the integration between True Lean and Sustainable Manufacturing

The system is referred to as '*Benevolent*' because it incorporates three basic criteria including: (1) the primary precepts of sustainability throughout the lifecycle, which strive to fully utilize existing resources with minimal impact on TBL; (2) it supports the highest customer satisfaction by promoting the production of quality products at lowest cost and on-time delivery; while (3) respecting society and the people who do the work. A benevolent production system therefore provides a win-win-win for the environment, economy and society (TBL).

3.2 Major TPS (True Lean) Operational Elements of BPS

The Benevolent Production System Model in Fig. 3 includes the core True Lean operational elements required to sustain CI [5]. We believe these elements are particularly compatible and important for the efficient implementation of sustainable manufacturing through the lifecycle of a product. Each of these element's importance and an example of how they relate in the SM environment is described below:

Customer/Product Focused: This is the focal point of the organization since only by providing products or services which meet customer needs in terms of cost, quality and deliverability will companies survive, especially in a global market. Here the knowledge management capabilities of PLM meet the operational elements of the BPS model to help ensure appropriate sustainable process pathways (6Rs) and products are identified and developed.

Systematic Problem-Solving (P/S): An effective systematic problem solving methodology must be in place throughout the organization (One System, One Voice) to protect the customer from receiving defective products or late deliveries. Each step of product lifecycle management requires effective problem solving that enables TMs to accurately identify a problem, find the root cause, develop effective countermeasures, implement and validate them, and finally (and most importantly) incorporated effective countermeasures into the TMs standard work to keep the problem from returning. This is an especially important activity during the product design stage where most of the decisions which impact the overall lifecycle sustainability are made.

Abnormality Management: To achieve effective systematic P/S you must be able to identify problems *when they occur*. This is done using the concept of 'built-in-quality' to create a system capable of identifying and eliminating defects as they occur. This helps distinguish between quick fixes, chronic problems and opportunities for improvement. SM strives for maximum resource utilization, therefore both problem conditions and improvement opportunities must be readily identifiable to continuously improve towards this goal.

Standard Processes: Identifying defects and waste (problems) means workers must clearly see the difference between normal and abnormal conditions which can only occur with standard processes in place. The more quickly a problem is identified the more likely the root cause can be determined and the problem eliminated. The current standard defines the baseline for improvement and supports the ability of TMs to perform normal, value added work and identify abnormalities and waste (problems) quickly. Maintaining and developing standard work also ensures problems are eliminated without reoccurrence. In implementing SM, standardization is essential to understand how design decisions impact the sustainability content of the product.

Engaged Staff: To perform standard processes and improve upon them, TMs must identify challenges to meeting expectations and opportunities for improvement. Without their engagement, which depends on trust, developing standards and identifying abnormal conditions becomes very difficult, increasing the likelihood of passing defects to the customer and increasing costs.

Clear Roles: Basic roles exist within the organization and at the level of production which identify who performs the normal, value added work (what the customer is willing to pay for) and who handles abnormalities, so that value added activities are not interrupted. With expanding involvement of people, SM requires efficient management of people.

Management Support Culture: Operationally, management requires visibility of the systems' status with respect to meeting customer needs. This is done through the use of Key Performance Indicator (KPI) boards to guide P/S activities at all levels of the organization. Management must also create an environment of trust between all employees so TMs feel safe and are encouraged to identify problems without fear of recrimination. The management culture supports P/S at all levels and encourages a process- focused mentality (good process = good results) by aligning HR policies to reward both method and results instead of results only or bottom line thinking. With the multi-lifecycle thinking of SM, besides the absolute necessity of having clear KPIs at all levels, and TMs involvement to meet them, there needs to be a thorough understanding of the methods used (rather than just a focus on the results) as the results must be reproducible and improved iteratively.

4 Conclusions

Both lean and sustainable manufacturing have been identified as two distinct concepts capable of enhancing important aspects of productivity and resource utilization. In particular, we contend the application of True Lean thinking to sustainability activities is expected to provide similar benefits as those experienced by Toyota and other 'lean' organizations. While the current literature contains studies which indicate some understanding of the application of 'lean' in sustainability, most, if not all studies appear to be limited to applying certain lean concepts or tools rather than taking a more integrated and systemic approach. Thus, one of the major objectives of this work was to explore opportunities to integrate TPS practices and principles with total sustainable product development and to understand the compatibilities and complementariness of both. Underlying philosophies of TPS, such as systematic problem solving, respect for people, CI, etc., were identified to be directly compatible with SM and 6R - a core part of implementation of total lifecycle product sustainability. As the literature review suggested, the people side of TPS is the most underrated, and even neglected, aspect in conventional lean implementations. Yet, it forms the basis for the engaged learning environment of (True) Lean, which enables the most effective use of human and other resources. The principle of Respect for Team Members in both TPS and the Benevolent Production System requires management to develop everyone in the organization and provide effective methods, training and resources so workers can be successful.

This respect ultimately leads to trust, which is the cornerstone of CI. Workers must feel safe to identify problems without recrimination and to contribute their knowledge towards finding effective solutions and prevent their reoccurrence.

The approach in this initial study provides a basis for the development of a broader framework incorporating True Lean and SM. Further work will attempt to expand and verify the concept of a Benevolent Production System in sustainable manufacturing applications.

References

1. Joshi, K., Venkatachalam, A., Jaafar, I., Jawahir, I.: A new methodology for transforming 3R concept into 6R for improved sustainability: analysis and case studies in product design and manufacturing. In: Proceedings of IV Global Conference on Sustainable Product Development and Life Cycle Engineering (2006)
2. Womack, J.P., Jones, D.T., Roos, D.: Machine that Changed the World. Simon and Schuster, New York (1990)
3. Liker, J.K.: The Toyota Way. Esensi (2004)
4. Graban, M.R.F.: Preventing Lean Failures (2005). http://leanfailures.blogspot.com/. 28 Feb 2017
5. Kreafle, K.: Models to support type 3 lean implementations. In: University of Kentucky, Lean Systems Certification Program Material (2007)
6. Maginnis, M.A.: The impact of standardization and systematic problem solving on team member learning and its implications for developing sustainable continuous improvement capabilities. J. Enterp. Transform. 3, 187–210 (2013)
7. Liker, J.K., Hoseus, M.: Toyota Culture. McGrawHill, New York (2008)
8. Jawahir, I.S., Badurdeen, F., Rouch, K.E.: Innovation in sustainable manufacturing education. In: 11th Global Conference on Sustainable Manufacturing, Berlin, Germany, pp. 9–16 (2013)
9. Shuaib, M., Seevers, D., Zhang, X., Badurdeen, F., Rouch, K.E., Jawahir, I.S.: Product Sustainability Index (ProdSI): a metrics-based framework to evaluate the total life cycle sustainability of manufactured products. J. Ind. Ecol. 18, 491–507 (2014)
10. Hapuwatte, B., Seevers, K.D., Badurdeen, F., Jawahir, I.S.: Total life cycle sustainability analysis of additively manufactured products. Procedia CIRP 48, 376–381 (2016)
11. Jawahir, I., Dillon, O., Rouch, K., Joshi, K.J., Venkatachalam, A., Jaafar, I.H.: Total life-cycle considerations in product design for sustainability: a framework for comprehensive evaluation. In: Proceedings of the 10th International Research/Expert Conference, Barcelona, Spain, pp. 1–10 (2006)
12. Jaafar, I., Venkatachalam, A., Joshi, K., Ungureanu, A., De Silva, N., Dillon Jr., O., et al.: Product design for sustainability: a new assessment methodology and case studies. In: Kutz, M. (ed.) Environmentally Conscious Mechanical Design, vol. 5, pp. 25–65. Wiley, Hoboken (2007)
13. Grieves, M.: Product Lifecycle Management: Driving the Next Generation of Lean Thinking. McGraw Hill Professional, New York (2005)
14. Sugimori, Y., Kusunoki, K., Cho, F., Uchikawa, S.: Toyota production system and kanban system materialization of just-in-time and respect-for-human system. Int. J. Prod. Res. 15, 553–564 (1977)
15. Bhasin, S., Burcher, P.: Lean viewed as a philosophy. J. Manuf. Technol. Manag. 17, 56–72 (2006)

16. Shah, R., Ward, P.T.: Lean manufacturing: context, practice bundles, and performance. J. Oper. Manag. **21**, 129–149 (2003)
17. Womack, J.P., Jones, D.T.: Lean thinking: Banish waste and create wealth in your organisation, vol. 397. Simon and Shuster, New York (1996)
18. Lander, E., Liker, J.K.: The Toyota Production System and art: making highly customized and creative products the Toyota way. Int. J. Prod. Res. **45**, 3681–3698 (2007)
19. Spear, S., Bowen, H.K.: Decoding the DNA of the Toyota production system. Harvard Bus. Rev. **77**, 96–108 (1999)
20. Toyota Business Practice (Internal training document) (2005)
21. New, S.: Celebrating the enigma: the continuing puzzle of the Toyota Production System. Int. J. Prod. Res. **45**, 3545–3554 (2007)
22. Deming, W.E.: The New Economics: For Industry, Government. Education. MIT Press, Cambridge (1994)
23. Miller, G., Pawloski, J., Standridge, C.R.: A case study of lean, sustainable manufacturing. J. Ind. Eng. Manag. **3**, 11–32 (2010)
24. Chiarini, A.: Sustainable manufacturing-greening processes using specific Lean Production tools: an empirical observation from European motorcycle component manufacturers. J. Clean. Prod. **85**, 226–233 (2014)
25. Dües, C.M., Tan, K.H., Lim, M.: Green as the new Lean: how to use Lean practices as a catalyst to greening your supply chain. J. Clean. Prod. **40**, 93–100 (2013)
26. Rothenberg, S., Pil, F.K., Maxwell, J.: Lean, Green, and the quest for superior environmental performance. Prod. Oper. Manag. **10**, 228–243 (2001)
27. Mollenkopf, D., Stolze, H., Tate, W.L., Ueltschy, M.: Green, Lean, and global supply chains. Int. J. Phys. Distrib. Logistics Manag. **40**, 14–41 (2010)
28. Bergmiller, G.G., McCright, P.R.: Are Lean and Green programs synergistic? Presented at the Industrial Engineering Research Conference (2009)
29. Zhang, X., Badurdeen, F., Rouch, K., Jawahir, I.: On improving the product sustainability of metallic automotive components by using the total life-cycle approach and the 6R methodology. In: 11th Global Conference on Sustainable Manufacturing, Berlin, Germany (2013)
30. Shetty, D.: Building blocks of new product design. In: Shetty, D. (ed.) Product Design for Engineers, pp. 8–12. Cengage Learning, Boston (2015)

Ontologies, Knowledge and Data Models

A Methodological Framework for Ontology-Driven Instantiation of Petri Net Manufacturing Process Models

Damiano Arena[(✉)] and Dimitris Kiritsis

École Politechnique Fédérale de Lausanne,
SCI-STI-DK ME, Station 9, 1015 Lausanne, Switzerland
{damiano.arena,dimitris.kiritsis}@epfl.ch

Abstract. In the last decade, the interest and effort towards the use of ontology-based solutions for knowledge management has significantly increased. Ontologies have been used in manufacturing to provide a formal representation of the domain knowledge in a way that is machine-understandable. However, despite the ability to formally represent the elements of a domain and their relations, ontologies themselves do not provide any kind of simulation and systems behaviour analysis capabilities.

Manufacturing system knowledge may be translated into specific executable models by exploiting experience and human logical deduction. This can be also achieved using ontologies and semantic reasoning.

The framework presented in this work, therefore, aims to explore a W3C standard for inference rules, such as Semantic Web Rule Language (SWRL), and OWL ontology models to transform elements of a Knowledge-Base (KB) into Petri Net (PN) primitives. The combination of semantics and mathematical modelling techniques applied to the analysis of a simple automated assembly station highlights the existence of modelling patterns and the effectiveness of inference rules to automatically instantiate PN-based manufacturing system models.

As results, the inference rules-driven instantiation of a semantically enriched PN model has two positive consequences: (i) the axioms upon which the manufacturing system ontology is built are easy-to-reuse; (ii) the semantics-based bridging of the analysed domains shows the possibility of further enriching the KB with both qualitative and quantitative assessment capabilities.

Keywords: Ontology · Semantic interoperability · Petri Net

1 Introduction

In the last decades, the manufacturing domain gained several benefits from the application of ontologies, such as the possibility to communicate in an unambiguous manner, the common terminology and semantic alignment, and an information infrastructure in which data are provided in a computational way [1]. The main applications of manufacturing domain ontologies were summarized by [2]. Among them, [3] introduces an interesting ontology-based framework to support integration of data in the Product Life

© IFIP International Federation for Information Processing 2017
Published by Springer International Publishing AG 2017. All Rights Reserved
J. Ríos et al. (Eds.): PLM 2017, IFIP AICT 517, pp. 557–567, 2017.
https://doi.org/10.1007/978-3-319-72905-3_49

Cycle (PLC). Beginning Of Life (BOL), Middle Of Life (MOL) and End Of Life (EOL) knowledge aiming to support the different phases of the PLC, from its conceiving and design to the disposal. As far as the design and production phases of a product are concerned, these use BOL knowledge (e.g. technical documentation, process/product requirements, etc.) to define the requirements specification in terms of activities and resources. However, process designing may need the employment of – quantitative or qualitative – analytics techniques that ensure the feasibility and reliability of the production process. Despite the ability to formally represent the elements of a domain (i.e. manufacturing process) and their inter-relations, ontologies themselves do not provide any kind of system behaviour analysis or simulation capabilities. In this regard, Petri Net is a general purpose graphical and mathematical modelling language that is used to describe a large variety of different systems [4]. PN formalism has clear semantics which unambiguously defines the structure and behaviour of each model, hence, forming the foundation for its formal analysis. It is based on very few primitives that allow the explicit description of both states and actions of the modelled system, which is moreover built upon true concurrency, instead of interleaving [5].

Generally, the development of a manufacturing model leverages modelling experience and logical deduction of the domain-specific elements from the real case to be represented. Such logical deduction can be also achieved through semantic reasoning, which is one of the pillar on which ontologies are based on [6]. Recently, ontology-based model transformation became a well-established approach adopted to generate and validate models according to a specific domain of analysis [7]. However, the transformation and mapping from domain abstract models (technology-independent) to technology-dependent models, such as PNs, is nowadays a crucial issues [8].

The paper is structured as follows: Sect. 2 presents the proposed 3-step approach of this research work. Section 3 introduces the ontologies design and their semantic alignment towards the achievement of a robust theoretical framework that allows ontology-driven instantiation of PN primitives. Semantics-based simulation and analysis of the inferred PN model is therefore described in Sect. 4.

2   Proposed Approach

The overall approach includes three main steps: (i) Semantic modelling and manufacturing data enrichment; (ii) Ontology-driven instantiation of PN models; (iii) PN-based simulation and analysis. Figure 1 shows the stepwise evolution of the information flow: from manufacturing data silos to PN-based model simulation and analysis reports by leveraging semantics. In particular, the application presented in this study deals with the use of data and information regarding an automated assembly station, with specific emphasis on the reliability of its components. The development of ontologies enables the enrichment of this data in a way that it is shareable and ubiquitously interpretable by machines. Thus, we propose a semantic framework built upon two ontological models, i.e. the so-called Automated Assembly Station Ontology (AASO) and the Petri

Net Ontology for Reliability modelling (PNO4R). This will therefore drive the instantiation of OWL[1]-like PN elements that resemble the design and production data semantically-enriched and stored in a KB.

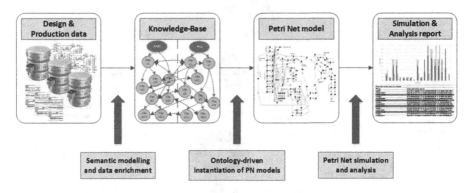

Fig. 1. Proposed approach

Once the model is instantiated, state-of-the-art tools[2,3,4] can be used to simulate the dynamic behaviour of the PN model and analyse the results, in a way that will yield maximum insight and help with decision-making.

3   Ontology Modelling

In this section, the structures of the above-mentioned AASO and PNO4R are described in terms of common OWL ontology modelling components, such as classes, object and data properties, along with an insight on inference rules.

3.1   Automated Assembly System Ontology

The Automated Assembly System Ontology (AASO) is a domain-specific ontology developed to gather and semantically-enrich the information regarding the presented case study, i.e. an assembly station. The overall ontological structure presented in Fig. 2 stems from an analysis of the available data regarding assembly operations, component failures and repair modes. The following classes have been, therefore, defined: *Station, Component, Activity, FailureMode, RepairMode, SystemState. Activity* refers to the operations that are performed by the *Station* while *Component* refers to all the parts that form the latter. Each *Activity* has a *SystemState* that may describe the system either before or after the occurrence of the *Activity*. *FailureMode* is the set of all the possible breakdowns that could take place, while *RepairMode* refers to the way such

---

[1]   Web Ontology Language https://www.w3.org/OWL/.

[2]   **GreatSPN Tool** http://www.di.unito.it/~greatspn/index.html.

[3]   **CPN Tools** http://cpntools.org/.

[4]   **ORIS Tool** http://www.oris-tool.org/.

failures may be fixed. Eventually, *CausesOfFailure* includes the reasons that have generated a specific failure.

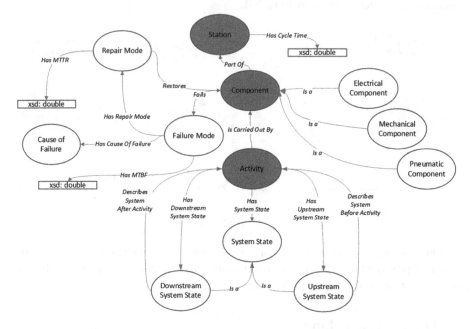

Fig. 2. Automated assembly system ontology

3.2 Petri Net Ontology

As far as the Petri Net Ontology (PNO) is concerned, among the various solutions proposed in literature, Gasevic and Devedzic [9] developed a UML Petri net ontology, called *Core Petri net ontology* considering both elements in common for all Petri net models and concepts that do not really exist in Petri net models to obtain more suitable synthetic concepts. Later on, the solution presented by Szymanski and colleagues [10] shows a PNO together with its upper ontology. Here, authors employed the Semantic Web Rules Language (SWRL) to express rules among primitives for instance to identify an active place (i.e. a place that contains a token) and an active transition (i.e. a transition that can fire).

This paper aims to use a hybrid approach, partly combining the research works mentioned above, in fact, here the structure of the so-called *Core Petri net Ontology* is extended with PN elements for Discrete Event Systems (DES) reliability modelling (Fig. 3), i.e. the PNO4R. SWRL-based rules are, then, exploited to automate the interpretation of PNO4R instances from the AASO ones.

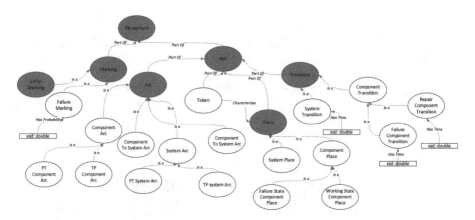

Fig. 3. Class hierarchy of Petri Net Ontology extended with DES reliability modelling elements (PNO4R)

Let us start from the introduction of the main elements: *Place, Transition* and *Arc, Initial Marking,* upon which each PN model is built. These have been defined as subclasses of the element *Net* despite [9] defines *Net* as a superclass of the *PN element.* Thus, according to the case study requirements, which will be introduced in the next section and stem from the use of Petri nets for reliability modelling and analysis, two subclasses of *Place* were identified: *ComponentPlace* and *SystemPlace. Component-Place* is a place at component level which can be either a *FailureStateComponentPlace* (if it represents the component in a failure state) or *WorkingStateComponentState* (if it represents the component when it is in available state). Conversely, *SystemPlace* includes places at system level, representing the various phases of the process.

Similarly, it is possible to further discern the *Transition* class into *ComponentTransition* and *SystemTransition. ComponentTransition* can be *FailureComponentTransition* or *RepairComponentTransition*, which characterizes respectively the breakdown event and the repairing activity. *SystemTransition*, instead, gathers transitions at system level describing the various activities of the system. The distinction of *Component* and *System* (Fig. 4) levels is due to the fact that the assembly process was discretized, then, different process phases were identified and modelled at higher level (system level). A set of components may, therefore, fail at each one of those phases and are modelled at a lower level (component level). For these reasons, the class called *Arc* is further specialised in four subclasses according to the elements that it connects. The first one is *ComponentToSystemArc* (i.e. the arc that connects the repair transition with the system place) and the second is *SystemToComponentArc* (i.e. the arc that connects the system place and the failure transition).

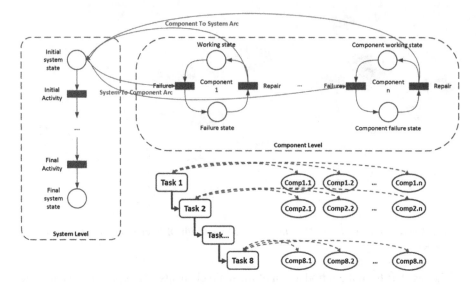

Fig. 4. Distinction between system and component levels

The third subclass is *ComponentArc*, which is further divided in *PTComponentArc* (i.e. arc linking a place representing the available component to a failure transition and arc linking place representing not available components to a repairing transition) and *TPComponentArc* (i.e. arc linking failure transitions to places representing not available components and arc linking repairing transition to places representing available components).

Then, *SystemArc* is similarly divided into *PTSystemArc* and *TPSystemArc* according to the connection at system level either from place to transition or from transition to place. Eventually, *Token* is the class meant to contain the tokens that the places could contain. However, the *Marking* class has been defined outside the *Net* class, and represents the set of all possible markings of the net. In particular, its subclass *FailureMarking* identifies the failing states of the systems.

3.3 Semantic Alignment

Generally speaking, an alignment between two ontologies "specifies a set of correspondences, and each correspondence models a bridge between a set of ontologies entities" [11]. Applying this definition to the present study means enabling the transformation of the elements of the AASO to the respective elements of the PNO4R. To this aim, the first step has been the introduction of a hybrid concept called *Module* (Fig. 5), which does not belong to neither the AASO nor the PNO4R. However, this modelling patter plays a crucial role in the alignment, since it is able to mediate between the AASO and PNO4R. In particular, the *Module* represents the behaviour of a component that may fail or be repaired in different ways and with a specific probability distribution.

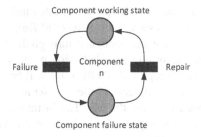

Fig. 5. Module: PN representation of a component behaviour

The instantiation process of PNO4R individuals and their properties is driven by SWRL-based rules. Starting from instances of AASO it is possible to create a congruent number of instances belonging to the PNO4R. The following relations have to be, hence, added to the semantic models in order to univocally link the elements of the two domains and avoid misinterpretations. Here, *System Level*, refers to all the discrete assembly phases and the states of the modelled system before and after each phase, while *Component Level* refers to modules resembling components that may fail at a specific state of the system (Table 1).

Table 1.   (left) System Level - (right) Components level owl class inter-links

System Level	
S1	Activity → SystemTransition
S2	SystemState → SystemPlace
S3	SystemState → SystemTransition
S4	SystemPlace → SystemTransition
S5	SystemPlace → SystemArc

Component Level	
C1	Module → FailureComponentTransition
C2	Module → RepairComponentTransition
C3	Module → FailureStateComponentPlace
C4	Module → WorkingStateComponentPlace
C5	Module → ComponentArc
C6	Module → ComponentToSystemArc
C7	Module → SystemToComponentArc

Due to a limited pages number, the class inter-links mentioned above cannot further described. Nonetheless, their indispensable statement will be better understood with two examples presented in the next section (S1 and C1).

4   Ontology-Driven Manufacturing Model Instantiation and Analysis: Case Study

The purpose of this section is to describe an application case, whose modelling requirements and data have been extracted from to [12]. In the latter work the authors proposed computational experiments to explore the validity of two different techniques to decompose a system. In order to reach their goal, they tested their methodology by means of a Petri net model, which resembles a part of an automated assembly shop.

At this point in time it is noteworthy to mention that the construct http://swrl.stanford.edu/ontologies/built-ins/3.3/swrlx.owl: *makeOWLThing*[5] plays a non-trivial role. This is indeed required to execute inference rules through the rule engine called *Drools*[6] that create a new element according to a deduction process based on existing OWL elements. Firstly, OWL knowledge and SWRL rules will be transferred to the SWRL engine. The latter uses a reasoner library in order to infer new axioms that will be eventually translated and loaded to actual the KB. The Instantiation of owl individuals of SystemTransition class resembling owl individuals of Activity (S1) is achieved by including the following rule in the ontology

Activity(?a)   ∧   ActivityHasDuration(?a, ?d)   ∧   swrlx:makeOWLThing(?st, ? a) → SystemTransition(?st) ∧ SystemTransitionHasDuration(?st, ?d) ∧ ActivityIsCharacterizedBy(?a, ?st)

This should be perceived as the backbone of the inferred PN model since most of the other modelling elements will be connected to those ones. Each OWL individual inferred through this rule is, therefore, related to *SystemTransitionHasDuration*, whose data property is inherited from the *ActivityHasDuration*, and then related to the *Activity* as well. Furthermore, here there is *ActivityIsCharacterizedBy* that has been defined as the inverse functional of *SystemTransitionCharacterizes*. This way, it is possible to connect instances belonging to the two different domain ontologies in a univocal manner.

The instantiation of individuals of the owl FailureComponentTransition inferred from the individuals of the owl class Module (C1) is achieved as follows. Each Module comprises of one FailureComponentTransition and one RepairComponentTransition. The former has a data property describing the λ, which is the inverse of the Mean Time Between Failures (MTBF). The SWRL rule, hence, aims to create the owl instance and make it inherit that property:

Module(?m)   ∧   Failure(?f)   ∧   ModuleCharacterizesFailure(?m, ?f)   ∧   FailureHasMTBF(?f, ?mtbf)   ∧   swrlx:makeOWLThing(?fct, ?m)   ∧   swrlb:divide(?l,   1, ? mtbf)   →   FailureComponentTransition(?fct)   ∧   FailureComponentTransitionHasLambda(?fct, ?l) ∧ ModuleIsComposedByFCT(?m, ?fct) ∧ FailureComponentTransitionCharacterizes(?fct, ?f)

4.1 Simulation of the Inferred PN Model

Hereafter the data used for the simulation of the PN model. This consists of 8 System Transitions (ST), 13 System Places (SP), 16 Component Transitions (CT), 36 Component Places (CP). There is only one module linked to each SP, which means that only one component may fail in a specific phase of the process. The available values are, therefore, the processing time of each activity, the failure rate (λ), and the repair rate (μ) as it is shown in Table 2. Then, the initial marking of the PN has been set as all the components are available and the process is ready to start.

Table 2. Reliability values and processing times

Activity	Time [h]	Component	λ [1/h]	μ [1/h]
A1	0.0192	BF	0.174	3.412
A2	0.0192	BR	0.295	3.386
A3	0.0185	MI	0.073	3.439
A4	0.0185	BI	0.004	5.042
A5	0.0204	FF	0.114	3.433
A6	0.0204	FW	0.074	3.461
A7	0.0204	FC	0.074	3.378
A8	0.0204	RF	0.194	3.409
Tback	0.0196	UC	0.367	3.385

Generally speaking, there are two kind of simulations: continuous and discrete [13, 14]. Here we propose the evaluation of the average number of tokens in a place and the transition throughputs by simulating the inferred PN through GreatSPN simulator, which exploits the Monte Carlo Simulation technique. Given the fact that the net has been built in a way that each place can contain at most one token, this measure reflects the probability of having a token in that place. The simulation results have been obtained through a so-called Basic GSPN (no colours) simulation with the Solver GreatSPN Confidence Interval 95% - Approximation 20% - Set batch length max: 31000.

4.2 Semantics-Based Analysis of the Results

Two key assessments have been carried out on the simulation results: the probability that a failure state component place has a token and the throughputs of the system (given by the simulation tool). Beside their semantical enrichment and storage in the KB, this can be queried in order to obtain: (i) the probability that a failure occurs on a specific component (Fig. 6); and (ii) the overall system availability (Fig. 7).

component	ComponentHasProbabilityToFail
MI	"0.0031379900268981"^^<http://www.w3.org/2001/XMLSchema#double>
FC	"0.0036769317614786"^^<http://www.w3.org/2001/XMLSchema#double>
FW	"0.003603079152595"^^<http://www.w3.org/2001/XMLSchema#double>
RF	"0.0093411466662446"^^<http://www.w3.org/2001/XMLSchema#double>
BF	"0.0078714671473149"^^<http://www.w3.org/2001/XMLSchema#double>
BR	"1.033900632191E-4"^^<http://www.w3.org/2001/XMLSchema#double>
FF	"0.0057082925242496"^^<http://www.w3.org/2001/XMLSchema#double>
BI	"8.82587424049E-5"^^<http://www.w3.org/2001/XMLSchema#double>
UC	"0.0174963998355185"^^<http://www.w3.org/2001/XMLSchema#double>

Fig. 6. Protégé SPARQL Query Tab: probability that a failure occurs on a specific component

SystemAvailability
"0.9489730440800767"^^<http://www.w3.org/2001/XMLSchema#double>

Fig. 7. Protégé SPARQL Query Tab: System availability

5 Conclusions

The conceptualization of a modelling framework based on ontologies and Petri nets has been thoroughly described. Efforts were made to clarify the interpretation of manufacturing concepts in the PN domain and vice versa, thus, paving the way towards a methodological framework to be used for ontology-based model transformation, PN-based simulation, and reliability analysis of a manufacturing system. The core part of this research concerns the development of two different models: the Automatic Assembly System Ontology (AASO) and the Petri Net Ontology for Reliability modelling (PNO4R). The latter represents an attempt of extension of an existing Petri Net ontological model with elements of reliability modelling for discrete event systems. This enabled the PN-based representation of the automated assembly station knowledge for reliability assessment. The structure of the model and the operating principles were eventually outlined. Finally, the achievement of semantic interoperability between the AASO and PNO4R enabled the SWRL rules-based instantiation of all the PN elements resembling a simple assembly process along with its simulation and analysis, showing the potentialities of the proposed approach, beside its soundness.

References

1. Schlenoff, C., Ivester, R., Libes, D., Denno, P., Szykman, S.: An Analysis of Existing Ontological Systems for Applications in Manufacturing and Healthcare. NIST (1999)
2. Negri, E., Fumagalli, L., Garetti, M.: Approach for the use of ontologies for KPI calculation in the manufacturing domain. In: Proceedings of the XX Summerschool of Industrial Mechanical Plants Francesco Turco, Napoli, Italy, 16–18 September 2015, pp. 30–36 (2015)
3. Kiritsis, D.: Closed-loop PLM for intelligent products in the era of the Internet of things. Comput. Des. **43**, 479–501 (2011)
4. Desel, J., Reisig, W.: The concepts of Petri Nets. Softw. Syst. Model. **14**(2), 669 (2015)
5. Jensen, K.: Coloured Petri Nets: Basic Concepts, Analysis Methods and Practical Use, vol. 1, Springer, Heidelberg (2013)
6. Motik, B., Rosati, R.: Reconciling description logics and rules. J. ACM (JACM) **57**(5), 30 (2010)
7. Roser, S., Bauer, B.: Ontology-based model transformation. In: Bruel, J.-M. (ed.) MODELS 2005. LNCS, vol. 3844, pp. 355–356. Springer, Heidelberg (2006). https://doi.org/10.1007/11663430_42
8. Silega, N., Noguera, M., Macias, D.: Ontology-based Transformation from CIM to PIM. IEEE Lat. Am. Trans. **14**(9), 4156–4165 (2016)
9. Gasevic, D., Devedzic, V.: Interoperable Petri Net models via ontology. Int. J. Web Eng. Technol. **3**(4), 374–396 (2007)
10. Szymański, K., Dobrowolski, G., Koźlak, J., Zygmunt, A.: A Proposition of knowledge management methodology for the purpose of reasoning with the use of an upper-ontology. Knowl. Creation Diffus. Utilization **8**, 117–133 (2007)
11. Scharffe, F., Euzenat, J., Fensel, D.: Towards design patterns for ontology alignment. In: Proceedings of the 2008 ACM symposium on Applied computing, pp. 2321–2325. ACM, March 2008
12. Jeong, K.C., Kim, Y.D.: Performance analysis of assembly/disassembly systems with unreliable machines and random processing times. IIE Trans. **30**(1), 41–53 (1997)

13. Balbo, G.: Introduction to generalized stochastic Petri Nets. In: Bernardo, M., Hillston, J. (eds.) SFM 2007. LNCS, vol. 4486, pp. 83–131. Springer, Heidelberg (2007). https://doi.org/10.1007/978-3-540-72522-0_3

14. Wang, J.: Petri Nets for dynamic event-driven system modeling. In: Fishwick, P. (ed.) Handbook of Dynamic System Modeling, pp. 1–17 (2006)

Engineering Knowledge Extraction for Semantic Interoperability Between CAD, KBE and PLM Systems

Jullius Cho[1(✉)], Thomas Vosgien[2], and Detlef Gerhard[1]

[1] TU Wien, Vienna, Austria
{jullius.cho,detlef.gerhard}@tuwien.ac.at
[2] V-Research GmbH, Dornbirn, Austria
thomas.vosgien@v-research.at

Abstract. For the deployment of both Product Lifecycle Management (PLM) and Knowledge-Based Engineering (KBE) approaches, product and process engineering knowledge needs to be identified, acquired, formalized, processed and reused. While knowledge acquisition is still a bottleneck process, the formalized engineering knowledge is still too often encapsulated in CAD models and in KBE systems developed in vendor-specific environments. To address this issue, this paper introduces a possible solution enabling the enrichment of a CAD-KBE-PLM integration schema that provides a standardized and neutral representation of engineering knowledge for further reuse across heterogeneous CAD, KBE and PLM systems. To enrich this schema, the proposed solution combines the use of a Multi-CAD API library – which allows platform-independent and automatic extraction of engineering knowledge from CAD models into an XML-based representation – and a Knowledge Acquisition and Formalization Assistant (KAFA) which assist domain experts to formalize their procedural knowledge.

Keywords: Knowledge acquisition · Semantic interoperability
Computer-Aided Design · KBE-PLM integration

1 Introduction

The Product Lifecycle Management (PLM) concept aims at integrating all information produced throughout a product's lifecycle [1]. However, the multiplicity and diversity of PLM and automation enabling technologies such as Computer-Aided Design (CAD), Knowledge-Based Engineering (KBE) and IT systems do generate and consume engineering knowledge chunks which are isolated and/or locked down in various vendor proprietary applications. To support an efficient PLM approach, the isolated chunks of engineering knowledge need to be made accessible for reuse across these applications and all along the product lifecycle. In product development, CAD systems are the most widely used authoring applications. The CAD model is a container of engineering knowledge [2] holding much information that could be used to describe the structure, the functional and behavioral aspects of artifacts they represent. Moreover, for many design applications, the CAD model of a product is the basis on which many downstream

© IFIP International Federation for Information Processing 2017
Published by Springer International Publishing AG 2017. All Rights Reserved
J. Ríos et al. (Eds.): PLM 2017, IFIP AICT 517, pp. 568–579, 2017.
https://doi.org/10.1007/978-3-319-72905-3_50

virtual analyses are performed such as finite element analysis and computer-aided manufacturing [3]. In designing product artifacts using CAD systems, experts also need to complement their design with an understanding of their product behavior as well with their design intent. Manufacturing companies tend more and more to hoard engineering knowledge (the know-what, know-why and know-how of product designs) for partial or total reuse in different contexts and projects. However, identifying, extracting, storing, transmitting and reusing engineering knowledge is still an on-going challenge when heterogeneous applications are used [4]. This is mostly because engineering knowledge is embedded into CAD models and the know-how is locked down in the minds of domain experts, making it rather difficult to extract and reuse. These barriers can be summarized as follows:

- Technological differences in CAD applications and CAD models;
- The lack of implementations of existing open standards defining the representation and exchange protocols of engineering knowledge;
- Subjective nature of experience garnered by domain experts.

These barriers warrant research in the area of data and system interoperability amongst PLM enabling technologies. There are various approaches for deploying platform-independent authoring and IT applications and for making engineering knowledge reusable. Some of these include Model-Driven Engineering (MDE), Model-Based Definition (MBD) and the use of product data standards such as ISO 10303 [5]. While the implementations of such approaches or solutions can solve some interoperability issues, they generally lack the capability to serve up all required information ensuring cohesion and traceability of product data across various domains and downstream applications. In this paper, we analyze the semantic interoperability problem and propose a possible solution to generate a common and neutral dataset to be reused across CAD, KBE and other PLM systems. To address this challenge, we propose a solution enabling the enrichment of the CAD-KBE-PLM integration schema introduced in [6] which provides a standardized and neutral representation of engineering knowledge for re-use across heterogeneous CAD, KBE and PLM systems. To enrich this schema, the proposed solution combines the use of a Multi-CAD API library (Sect. 3.3) – which allows platform-independent and automatic extraction of engineering knowledge from CAD models into an XML-based representation – and a Knowledge Acquisition and Formalization Assistant (KAFA) introduced by [7] which assists domain experts to formalize their procedural knowledge (Sect. 3.4). In a nutshell, the proposed solution is intended to capture geometric features and parameters, assembly structures and configuration rules, design intent and rationale from CAD models and domain experts and to enable the semantic interoperability of CAD, KBE and PLM enabling systems.

2   Related Work

PLM enabling technologies such as Product Data Management (PDM) are widely used as a means to store engineering data, especially CAD models and metadata. Products such as Teamcenter, ENOVIA, Windchill, etc. come to light as vendor solutions to the concept of PLM as a global repository for complete product definition. These solutions are however, locked down in vendor environments with restrictions to interoperability with other out-of-environment solutions. Some other efforts that attempted to address this challenge include the Methodology for Knowledge Based Engineering Applications (MOKA) project [8] which provides a methodology to manage engineering data, information and knowledge as well as the Model Driven Architecture (MDA) introduced by the Object Management Group (OMG) [9]. These however, have not solved the data inconsistency gap [10, 11]. Generally, engineering knowledge represents all pieces of data, information and knowledge which define the composition of a product, the intended functionality as well as the processes required to build the complete product. In [1], the authors provide various classifications of engineering knowledge such as Product Knowledge vs. Process Knowledge. While product knowledge describes what to design in a product, the process knowledge defines how to design the product. This knowledge could be found is various documents, embedded in CAD models in the form of geometry, parameters, structure or as experience garnered by domain experts such as modeling rules and logic. This paper focuses on CAD data extraction and domain expert procedural knowledge elicitation as well as their design intent.

Most CAD vendors do offer an application programming interface (API); a gateway to programmatically gain access to the functionality of their application. In extracting information from CAD models, their APIs do offer access to the internals of the respective CAD application but with varying degrees of access as seen for example in [12, 13]. There is however, no convention for generating API's and for defining which parts of the CAD application functionality they expose. Some researches such as [14] have proposed a method of extracting valuable engineering knowledge from engineering drawings. Vendor applications such as RuleStreams, Knowledge Fusion and TactonWorks are designed to aid in the extraction, management and reuse of engineering knowledge. These are however, closed systems providing no access to out-of-environment applications.

There are a good number of methods for eliciting knowledge from design experts [15]. In [16], the authors provide a comprehensive range of tools employed to elicit engineering knowledge. From experience, the most used method is the interview in its various forms. However, knowledge elicitation from experts could be flawed due to subjectivity, bias, beliefs, etc. on both domain expert and the design engineer who may be participating in the elicitation process. To solve these problems, the KAFA offers an intuitive user interface to systematically define the relationships between parts in the assembly model. This is also enhanced by the Multi-CAD API which automatically extracts some information from CAD models, providing some kind of semi-automation.

No discussion on neutral product data formats is worthy without mention of the initiative of ISO 10303 known as STEP standard. STEP has been particularly successful in its use to exchange geometry and CAD meta-data between CAD applications as well as basic PDM meta-data and assembly product structures through its Application Protocol AP242 which is a merge of AP203 and AP214. Even though many other aspects of engineering knowledge are defined in the various STEP parts and protocols, they have not yet been implemented by vendors. Making use of the groundwork set in STEP, in [6], we have proposed a PLM-KBE integration schema combining several STEP parts and other neutral product data models. This schema depicts a concept for representing in a neutral way a configured product definition, the explicit knowledge encapsulated in parameterized CAD models and the implicit knowledge related to the design intent and rationale of these models. In [4], the authors provide a study for a neutral format to exchange and reuse rule-based procedural knowledge across different KBE applications: the Rules Interchange Format (RIF). However, there is still a lack of standardized methods to extract and neutrally formalize knowledge from CAD and KBE models. By introducing the Multi-CAD API, this work aims at finding an integrated solution which will cover major CAD applications thereby providing users a bigger solution space.

3 Extracting, Formalizing and Reusing Design Knowledge for Design Automation Applications

In this section, we describe a method to capture explicit and tacit engineering knowledge for reuse in product development. To set the stage for this, we first define an integrated use case scenario, positioning our proposed solutions and defining what actually is meant by "engineering knowledge". We then delve into extracting, formalizing and representing engineering knowledge for reuse across PLM enabling technologies.

3.1 Integrated Use Case Scenario

Figure 1 illustrates an integrated use case scenario portraying the identification, acquisition/extraction, formalization, storage and reuse of engineering knowledge. The aim is to extract engineering knowledge from parametric CAD models and reuse this knowledge in generating a configuration model. In the addressed example, the used CAD system is SolidWorks and the used KBE configurator is TactonWorks which is a SolidWorks add-on. The idea is to be able to reproduce the same scenario and/or reuse the same mechanisms and the extracted knowledge with other CAD, KBE and PLM systems.

The Multi-CAD API manager parses a CAD model and extracts engineering knowledge from it. This knowledge is used to generate the KAFA matrix. The KAFA then provides an intuitive GUI for the design engineer and the domain expert to systematically define the parameters, relationships and rules which are beyond a CAD configuration model. The output of the Multi-CAD API manager and the KAFA are then used to enrich the KBE-PLM integration schema proposed in [6] and which provides a structured and neutral data set for semantic interoperability between PLM enabling applications. This schema can then be parsed and a configuration model generated. Particularly important for the configuration model is the general structure of the model, the relationship between the parts, the parameters and the functions that drive the parameters leading to different configurations.

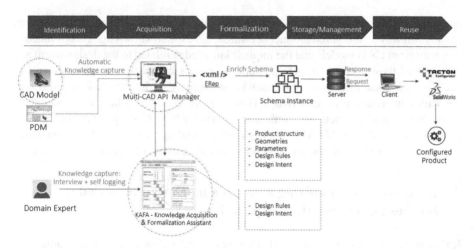

Fig. 1. Use-case scenario: acquiring, formalizing and re-using knowledge for 3D configurators

3.2 CAD Data Representation

Figure 2 shows a simple tree structure portraying the type of information – structure, geometry, and topology, rules etc. – conveyed through CAD models. For this data or knowledge to be reused in other parts or processes of the product's lifecycle, it needs to be identified, extracted and harnessed for seamless access.

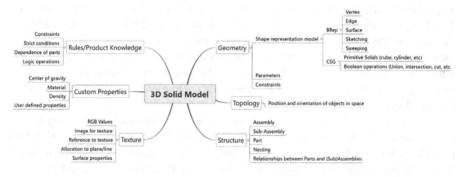

Fig. 2. Type of information embedded in CAD models

In order to generically represent the structure, geometry, parameters and other information pertaining to CAD models without a commitment to an underlying core modeler, we adapt the Editable Representation (ERep) proposed by [17]. An excerpt of the Domain Specific Language (DSL) for this representation is shown in Fig. 3.

```
 1  <assembly>          ::= ASSEMBLY
 2                          <name>
 3                          <stamp>
 4                          <global_info>
 5                          <parts_list>
 6                          END_ASSEMBLY
 7
 8  <global_info>       ::= GLOBAL UNITS
 9                          <unit>
10
11  <stamp>             ::= integer
12
13  <unit>              ::= mm | cm | m | in | ft
14
15  <matching_rules>::= <rule>
16                          | <matching_rules>; <rule>
17
18  <rule>              ::= <mating>; <aligningn>
19
20  <mating>            ::= MATE <geo_pair>
21                          | MATE OFFSETv<exp><geo_pair>
22                          | ALIGN <geo_pair>
23                          | ALIGN OFFSET <exp><geo_pair>
24
25  <geo_pair>          ::= <point> <axis> <stamp>
26
27  <part>              ::= PART <name> <stamp>
28                          <global_info>
29                          <feature_list>
30                          END_PART
31
```

Fig. 3. Excerpt of domain specific language for CAD data representation adapted from [17]

3.3 Multi-CAD API for Automatic Knowledge Extraction

The main idea behind the Multi-CAD API is to use the object-oriented programming paradigm (OOP) and build a core abstraction layer which would be implemented by different CAD applications using their respective API's as shown in Fig. 4. The core application or core abstraction layer defines functionality through interfaces [18], applying the principle of loose coupling [19] where the implementation of any of the interface classes could be changed without having to change the core interface class itself. These interfaces are implemented by requesting data from selected CAD applications using the respective API's that they expose, but the domain logic is retained by the core abstraction layer.

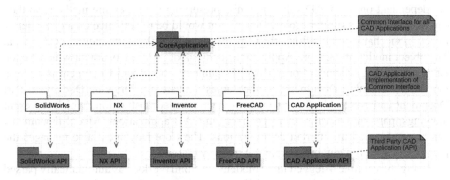

Fig. 4. Modular architecture for Multi-CAD API

Figure 5 shows a simplified implementation of the Core Application with Solid-Works.

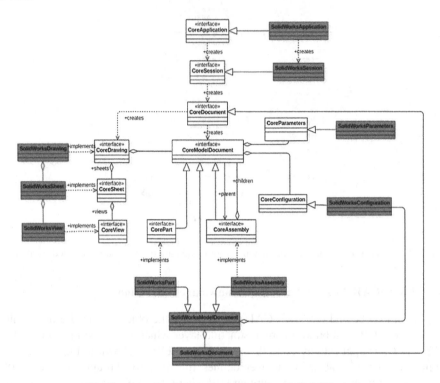

Fig. 5. Core Application implementation in SolidWorks

The core system will therefore not know which CAD application is actually in use. In this way the Multi-CAD API is independent of any CAD application for its logic and functionality. An objective of the Core Application is to make it completely generic and not dependent on any CAD solution, while preserving the accessing methods so they can be used for any similar project. The caveat would be the reliance on a dependency injection mechanism that allows the Core Application to load the required CAD data. The object model of the Core Applications consists of a Core Document which can be either a Drawing Document or a Model Document. The Model Document is either a Part or an Assembly Document. As the names indicate, the Drawing Document, Part Document and Assembly Document are object oriented abstractions which represent drawings, parts and assemblies respectively in CAD applications. Model Documents can be represented in different configurations. The Core Document also manages the parameters used in Drawing, Part and Assembly classes.

In Fig. 6, a simple 4-legged table modeled in SolidWorks was automatically parsed by the Multi-CAD API and relevant information extracted. The result is a well formed XML document containing information pertaining to the parts and assemblies. This includes the structure, the parameters at part and assembly levels, the mates and relationships between the parts in the assembly structure, etc. This XML document can now be parsed and the results used to generate an extended DSM (see Fig. 7) for eliciting more and relevant design intent and design rationale from a domain expert. The knowledge then has to be prepared or formalized for re-use.

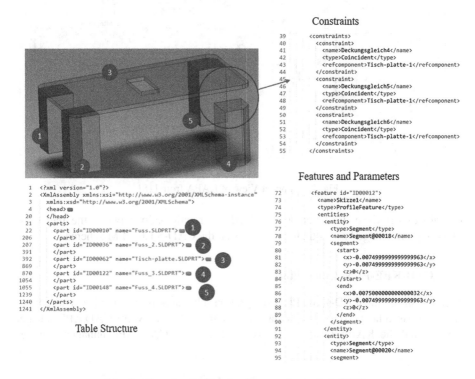

Fig. 6. Core Application implementation in SolidWorks

3.4 Knowledge Acquisition and Formalization Assistant

The main aim of the Knowledge Acquisition and Formalization Assistant as introduced by [7] is to help in capturing engineering knowledge from domain experts. One component of KAFA is a component-component parameters relationship matrix which graphically projects the parts and parameters of an assembly model in relationship to each other. The domain expert and the engineer then have an intuitive interface – a design structure matrix – to systematically define the relationships between parts in the assembly model. While the generation of the KAFA was more of a manual process, we have automated the generation process with the support of the Multi-CAD API. All components and parameters are automatically extracted from a CAD model dataset and the KAFA interface is automatically built. Moreover, KAFA has been extended with a Component-Parameter/Requirement-Function matrix to capture the design intent in a set of functional and non-functional requirements. After the design engineer and the

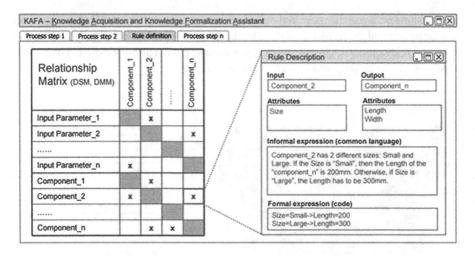

Fig. 7. Concept View of KAFA from [18]

domain expert have discussed and defined the relationship between the parts, the resulting knowledge base is then used to enrich the CAD-KBE-PLM schema.

3.5 CAD-KBE-PLM Integration

Figure 8 shows the CAD-KBE-PLM integration schema introduced in [6]. These highlighted areas indicate some classes that will be enriched by the Multi-CAD API manager (green) and the KAFA (blue) respectively. The Multi-CAD API manager provides

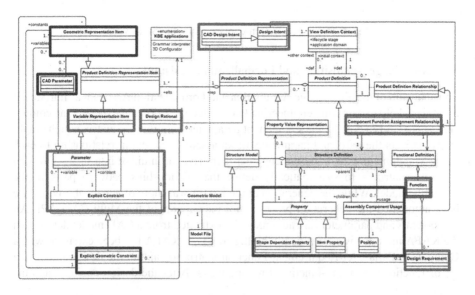

Fig. 8. CAD-KBE-PLM Integration Schema from [6] (Color figure online)

general information describing the structure. While the component-component matrix of the KAFA provides information about the relationships between the components, the design intent can be captured using the component/parameter – requirement matrix.

4 Discussion

The goal of this research work is to demonstrate the feasibility of extracting relevant engineering knowledge from CAD models as well as the design intent of the engineer on the one hand, and to enable the exchange and re-use of this knowledge across heterogeneous CAD, KBE and PLM systems on the other hand.

Using OOP principles, the Multi-CAD API manager automatically extracts relevant knowledge embedded in CAD models. While the Multi-CAD API is dependent on CAD applications for data structures but is independent of any CAD application for its logic and functionality. The full capability of such a Multi-CAD API can however, only be achieved if the CAD vendors expose the required functions in their API's. As mentioned in [6], another limitation of the Multi-CAD API manager approach is the need to develop different interfaces for the different systems to be integrated. Moreover, current CAD systems provide knowledge-based capabilities where modeling rules can be defined and re-used by the user. Such objects are part of the data structure of the commercial systems which is considered as strategic intellectual property of their solutions. Although the solution and schema proposed in this paper aim at overcoming this barrier, the potential implementation of such a solution in industrial environments will depend on the willingness of these software vendors to implement and maintain the required interfaces.

For the elicitation and formalization of design intent and rationale from domain experts, the proposed KAFA proposes a formalization of component-parameters relationships (modeling rules and constraints) on the one hand and Component-Parameter/ Functional Requirements relationships on the other hand. The rules defining these relationships are expressed in a natural language and transformed in executable code. One limitation is that, depending on the complexity of the product knowledge to formalize, the dataset could be very large and lead to conflicting rules. A mechanism has to be put in place to check redundancy and inconsistency thereby supporting the elicitation and formalization of procedural knowledge from the domain expert.

5 Conclusion

The investigations reported in this paper comprise an attempt at developing a solution to generate a common and neutral dataset aiming at tackling the semantic interoperability issue that prevents the efficient exchange of engineering data between CAD, KBE and PLM systems. The target source of product knowledge is the CAD model on the one hand, and the domain experts' know-how on the other hand. The ideas, results and related works presented in this paper lead to the general conclusion that the reuse of engineering data, information and knowledge across CAD, KBE and PLM enabling applications is still a major challenge and open issue in engineering design. This is mainly due to the inexistence of established standardized methods or approaches for automatically extracting and formalizing this engineering knowledge in a platform-independent and neutral standardized way. The main identified shortcomings are the lack of a suitable neutral knowledge representations with well-defined syntax, axioms, and semantics to be shared across multiple platforms and to enable interoperability [20]. This paper argues that when a structured approach towards integrating CAD, KBE and PLM enabling applications with product development is considered, consistent representations of CAD geometric features, modeling parameters, rules and constraints as well the related design intent and rationale are needed. The challenges addressed in this research work is first to be able to extract and formalized all this information from the available sources of knowledge (CAD models and domain experts) and to be able to exchange and re-use it across heterogeneous CAD, KBE and PLM applications. The Multi-CAD API demonstrates a possibility of unlocking engineering knowledge embedded in CAD models independently from the used CAD system. The extracted CAD features are then used by domain experts in order to formalize the above mentioned design intent and rationale with the support of the proposed KAFA.

The next step will be first to effectively use the output of the Multi-CAD API manager and the KAFA to enrich the CAD, KBE, PLM integration schema previously introduced in [6]. This should also be accompanied by an appropriate GUI to ease the interaction with user. The use case scenario introduced in this paper will have to be extended to include KBE and PLM data exchange steps as well as automatic validation and reporting mechanisms for checking the compliance of the extracted and formalized knowledge to the PLM-KBE integration schema.

Acknowledgments. This work was supported by the K-Project 'Advanced Engineering Design Automation' (AEDA) that is financed under the COMET (COMpetence centers for Excellent Technologies) funding scheme of the Austrian Research Promotion Agency.

References

1. Chandrasegaran, S.K., Ramani, K., Sriram, R.D., et al.: The evolution, challenges, and future of knowledge representation in product design systems. Comput. Aided Des. **45**, 204–228 (2013)
2. Badin, J., Chamoret, D., Gomes, S., Monticolo, D.: Knowledge configuration management for product design and numerical simulation. In: Proceedings of 18th International Conference on Engineering Design, ICED 2011, Impacting Society through Engineering Design, vol. 6 (2011)
3. Gerbino, S., Brondi, A., et al.: Interoperability issues among CAD systems: a benchmarking study of 7 commercial MCAD software. In: 32 Proceedings of Design 2004 8th International Design Conference, Dubrov, Croat (2004)
4. Colombo, G., Pugliese, D., Klein, P., Lutzemnberger, J.: A study for neutral format to exchange and reuse engineering knowledge in KBE applications. In: International ICE Conference on Engineering, Technology and Innovation, ICE 2014, pp. 1–10. IEEE (2014)
5. Bondar, S., Shammaa, A., Stjepandić, J., Tashiro, K.: Advances in parameterized CAD feature translation. In: ISPE CE, pp. 615–624 (2015)

6. Cho, J., Vosgien, T., Prante, T., Gerhard, D.: KBE-PLM integration schema for engineering knowledge re-use and design automation. In: Harik, R., Rivest, L., Bernard, A., Eynard, B., Bouras, A. (eds.) PLM 2016. IFIP AICT, vol. 492, pp. 43–55. Springer, Cham (2016). https://doi.org/10.1007/978-3-319-54660-5_5

7. Gerhard, D., Christoph, L.: IT-based configuration and dimensioning of customer specific products–towards a framework for implementing knowledge based design assistant systems. In: 68-6 Proceedings of 18th International Conference on Engineering Design, ICED 2011, Impacting Society through Engineering Design, vol. 6 (2011)

8. Stokes, M., MOKA Consortium: Managing Engineering Knowledge: MOKA: Methodology for Knowledge based Engineering Applications. Professional Engineering Publishing (2001)

9. OMG: KBE Services for PLM (2006)

10. Barbau, R., Krima, S., Rachuri, S., et al.: OntoSTEP: enriching product model data using ontologies. Comput. Aided Des. **44**, 575–590 (2012)

11. Fowler, J.: STEP for Data Management, Exchange and Sharing. Technology Appraisals Ltd., Twickenham (1995)

12. Liu, M., Ma, J., Lin, L., et al.: Intelligent assembly system for mechanical products and key technology based on internet of things. J. Intell. Manuf. **28**, 1–29 (2014)

13. Mathew, A., Rao, C.S.P.: A CAD system for extraction of mating features in an assembly. Assem. Autom. **30**, 142–146 (2010)

14. Amran, M.F.M., Sulaiman, R., Kahar, S., et al.: A proposed information extraction technique in engineering drawing for reuse design. World Acad. Sci. Eng. Technol. Int. J. Mech. Aerosp. Ind. Mechatron. Manuf. Eng. **6**, 441–445 (2012)

15. Verhagen, W.J.C., Bermell-Garcia, P., van Dijk, R.E.C., Curran, R.: A critical review of knowledge-based engineering: an identification of research challenges. Adv. Eng. Inform. **26**, 5–15 (2012)

16. Burge, J.E.: Knowledge elicitation tool classification. Artificial Intelligence Research Group, Worcester Polytechnic Institute (2001)

17. Hoffmann, C.M., Juan, R.: EREP An editable high-level representation for geometric design and analysis (1992)

18. Goyal, G., Sachin, P.: Importance of inheritance and interface in OOP paradigm measure through coupling metrics. Int. J. Appl. Inf. **4**, 14–20 (2012)

19. Leymann, F.: Loose Coupling and Architectural Implications [Powerpoint slides] (2016). http://esocc2016.eu/wp-content/uploads/2016/04/Leymann-Keynote-ESOCC-2016.pdf

20. Trehan, V., Chapman, C., Raju, P.: Informal and formal modelling of engineering processes for design automation using knowledge based engineering. J. Zhejiang Univ. Sci. A **16**, 706–723 (2015)

Towards a Proactive Interoperability Solution in Systems of Information Systems: A PLM Perspective

Zoubida Afoutni[1,2], Julien Le-Duigou[1(✉)], Marie-Hélène Abel[2], and Benoit Eynard[1]

[1] Sorbonne Universités, Université de Technologie de Compiègne,
UMR CNRS 7337 Roberval, CS 60319, 60203 Compiègne Cedex, France
{zoubida.afoutni,julien.le-duigou,
benoit.eynard}@utc.fr
[2] Sorbonne Universités, Université de Technologie de Compiègne,
UMR CNR 7253 Heudiasyc, CS 60319, 60203 Compiègne Cedex, France
marie-helene.abel@hds.utc.fr

Abstract. PLM is an approach which aims to manage a product throughout its life cycle. Today, there are powerful and well-adapted tools for each phase of the product lifecycle, such as CAD (Computer Aided Design), SDM (Simulation Data Management), Enterprise Resource Planning (ERP) etc. However, their complete integration and more particularly the linkage from one phase to another are not yet fully operational and effective. To reach the PLM goal, it is necessary to guarantee the interoperability between the information systems (IS) supported by the business applications throughout the product lifecycle. Also, in the extended enterprise, from one project to another, the applications used for the product development process can change as business partners may change as well. An interoperability solution should be designed taking into account the potentially changing contexts of enterprise cooperation. A possible solution consists in designing the interoperability solution of the PLM systems by adopting the principles of the system of systems (SoS) concept. This work proposes a system of systems of PLM based on multi-agent systems to treat the interoperability, as well as knowledge capitalization issues.

Keywords: Interoperability · System of systems · Multi-agent system
Ontologies · Knowledge capitalization · MEMORAe

1 Introduction

PLM is *"a product centric – lifecycle-oriented business model, supported by ICT, in which product data are shared among actors, processes and organisations in the different phases of the product lifecycle for achieving desired performances and sustainability for the product and related services"* [1]. Nowadays, there are many effective tools for each phase of products lifecycle such as CAD (Computing Aided Design), SDM (Simulation Data Management), ERP (Enterprise Resource Planning), etc. The PLM approach requires the ability to jointly use all of these systems. However

© IFIP International Federation for Information Processing 2017
Published by Springer International Publishing AG 2017. All Rights Reserved
J. Ríos et al. (Eds.): PLM 2017, IFIP AICT 517, pp. 580–589, 2017.
https://doi.org/10.1007/978-3-319-72905-3_51

these tools had been conceived independently. To reach the PLM goal, it is necessary to guarantee the interoperability between the information systems (IS) supported by the business applications throughout the product lifecycle. So, in the current industrial context, several companies collaborate during a project to develop a new product. This is known as the "extended enterprise". From one project to another, all applications used for the product development process can change as business partners may change as well. An interoperability solution should be designed taking into account the potentially changing contexts of enterprise cooperation, which leads us to study the concept of a "system of systems" (SoS). A SoS is a set of heterogeneous and existing subsystems assembled together to achieve a global, mission that a system alone cannot fulfil, a SoS has five key features [2]: (i) Operational independence of elements (ii) managerial independence of elements (iii) evolutionary development (iv) emergent behavior (v) geographical distribution. In the PLM context, all the business applications involved in product management have the characteristics of being heterogeneous, autonomous, each having its own functions and objectives; all of their functionalities contribute in achieving the goal of the PLM strategy. PLM can be seen therefore as a SoS, or at least promoting the interoperability solution between different PLM applications can be thought by adopting the concept of SoS. According to [3], the architecture of a SoS must be designed according to the following principles: (i) the complexity of the SoS framework does not grow as constituent systems are added, removed, or replaced (ii) the constituent systems do not need to be re-engineered as other constituent systems are added, removed, or replaced.

Furthermore, PLM systems generate a large amount of information that may contain explicit knowledge. This knowledge constitutes the enterprises' immaterial heritage that it is necessary to capitalize, share and maintain.

In this work we are interested in the problem of interoperability of IS PLM systems and the capitalization of PLM knowledge by adopting the SoS concept. To do this, we use the collaborative MEMORAe platform for knowledge management (KM), ontologies to be used both for KM and semantic interoperability between the different PLM systems, the multi-agent system (MAS) to design a SoS PLM that respect the key features of a SoS. It should be noted that this work is under development. In Sect. 2, we discuss the problem of interoperability. Section 3 presents our solution for interoperability and knowledge capitalization. In Sect. 4, we present a first prototype of technical interoperability between ARAS and MEMORAe platform.

2   Research Review

2.1   Interoperability

Wegner [4] defines interoperability as "*the ability of two or more software components to co-operate with differences in language, interface, and execution platform*". EIF [5] defines three levels of interoperability: the technical level, the semantic level and the organizational level. The technical level should ensure the continuity of the digital flow between the different business applications. The semantic level treats the sustainability of the semantic flow. The organizational level addresses the processes, users and people participating in the system operation. Thus, three solutions to deal with semantic interoperability are possible [6]: integration, unification and federation. Integration approach means to define a standard data model shared between all systems. Unification approach is based on a high level common format used to establish the semantic mapping between the information of the different IS. To ensure interoperability by unification, two solutions are possible [7]: the first one consists in defining an *ad hoc* model specific to the needs. The second solution consists in using a standardized model such as STEP [8]. Regarding the federative approach, the mapping between the different information coming from the different systems is established in a dynamic and *ad hoc* way.

Among the approaches that are used to treat interoperability and knowledge management in PLM field, we find web services (WS), ontologies and MAS. WS and ontologies deal with the technical and semantic interoperability. MAS is generally used to ensure the knowledge management or to exploit autonomously information scattered across the PLM systems.

Ontology. Ontologies are considered as a relevant solution to ensure interoperability and knowledge capitalization throughout the product lifecycle. Indeed, since ontology is a formal specification of a shared conceptualization, it allows data exchange between business applications while preserving the semantic of the information exchanged. In the PLM context, several ontologies have been proposed. For example, in [9] the authors proposed a product-centric ontology called ONTO-PDM based on STEP ISO 10303 and IEC 62264 standards to allow interoperability between CAD data, PDM, MES and ERP. In [10], the authors proposed CPM (Core Product Model) to represent the product in design phase. In [11] an ontology-based methodology for exchanging information between PLM systems based on semantic web and the I-Semantic platform called SPIKE was proposed. In [12], PARO (Product Activity Resource Organization) ontology based on PLM requirements to ensure the linkage at meta-level between the concepts of the different companies for product development was proposed. PARO was enriched with recent works on mechanical ontologies. The early and detailed design phases are support by classical data model, as STEP AP239 PLCS or CPM integrating an interface model especially designs for multidisciplinary integration [13]. The simulation step is based on [14] where an ontology based on STEP AP209ed2 is proposed. In [15], an ontology called OntoSTEP-NC which represents information of the manufacturing phase was proposed.

Web services. Provide a robust framework for interoperability between heterogeneous applications, allowing them to create flexible and reactive links without imposing any restrictions on their technical features. In the PLM domain, several solutions based on WS have been proposed. For example, "PDMs Enablers" based on middleware technologies and "PLM Services" are web technologies developed to facilitate communication between PLM systems [16]. PDMs Enablers make PDM services accessible to applications in a Common Object Request Broker Architecture [17]. In [18] a technical framework exploiting predefined WS to ensure interoperability between the knowledge management platform developed within the ADN (Digital Data Alliance) project and PLM systems was proposed. This framework was implemented through a connector tested between Windchill and the ADN system. So, in the industrial world, commercial PLM companies have also adopted WS technologies as a solution for interoperability. For example, ARAS Innovator offers a full panel of open WS. An external application can interface directly with ARAS via XML/SOAP. Windchill offers several WS such as REST to ensure integration with other systems.

Multi Agents system. Is one of the most appropriate technologies to develop complex distributed systems. Indeed, agent paradigm offers the ability to model distributed activities and information exchange between heterogeneous applications. In the PLM field, several works based on MAS have been proposed. For example, [19] proposed a product-centric modeling framework for PLM systems based on agent approach, including a business process model and a product information model. The main idea is to consider the product as a proactive entity capable of identifying the opportunities to be exploited and helping business actors in their decision-making process. The product is then represented by the "Product Agent" which acts as an automated expert connected to all applications supporting PLM activities, able to identify events occurring in its environment and act accordingly. Concerning semantic interoperability, the authors proposed an extension of the CPM ontology [10] as a standard data model common to all systems. In [20] a collaborative system architecture based on MAS, virtual reality and RIOCK (Role, Interaction, Organization, Competence, and Knowledge) formalism to help designing industrial processes as well as the analysis and the simulation of these processes was proposed. Knowledge management is ensured by an agent-based system called KATRAS that interacts with business stakeholders in order to identify, validate and evaluate the knowledge to capitalize.

2.2 Synthesis

We have presented briefly three approaches to treat interoperability and KM in PLM field. Thanks to web services the different systems used to manage product along its lifecycle moves from isolated automation system towards a set of systems that can communicates and exchange information and services. It allow thus to guarantees the continuity of the digital flow. Regarding semantic interoperability, the integration approach is not appropriate for addressing the interoperability in the context of SoS of existing systems. Indeed, integration approach requires the use of a common format for all information models. So, there are no problems of interoperability within a single PLM system. But the problems appear when we aim for add or change a system in the SoS. In the unification approach each system maintains its own data model. However, this standards-based approach also has limitations as the lack of sharing a common semantics that limits mutual understanding of the information contained in the models. The federative approach, advocates establishing automatic connection between models based on logic. The ontologies are seen as the adequate tools to realize this dynamic exchange, because ontological models are based on logic and can reason. Federative approach seems to be the appropriate approach to ensure semantic interoperability in the context of SoS. As we have indicated previously this work is in progress, we aim later to explore the federation approach by using the PARO ontology to ensure the semantic interoperability in the SoS PLM. MAS in PLM field allow introducing reactivity and pro-activity, exploiting autonomously information that are distributed across PLM systems, integrate the business actor in the process of knowledge validation. MAS, a computing paradigm for developing intelligent systems, can be a credible approach to design SoS of PLM systems. Indeed, SoS features specified in the introduction are consistent with the notions of autonomous agents and of MAS. Loose coupling, unified interfaces and protocols in agent systems' architecture allows build a SoS PLM systems that respect the principles of SoS presented in the introduction.

3   Proposed PLM SoS Approach

This paper aims to provide a SoS of PLM systems to handle interoperability and knowledge capitalization of existing information systems having the following features: (i) not intrusive interoperability, that is the participating systems are not modified in their usual features (ii) the addition of a system should not cause important developments (iii) enable user to seamlessly access heterogeneous and distributed resources of PLM. Figure 1 shows the architecture of our proposal. We defined four groups of agents: knowledge agents, interface agents, observer and mediator agents.

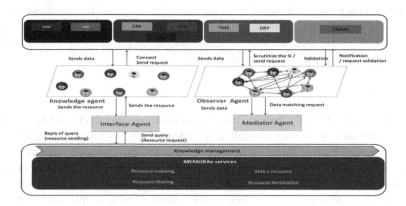

Fig. 1. SoS of PLM systems.

3.1   MAS for Interoperability

PLM data volume and the associated evolution require the control of their consistency throughout the product life cycle. For example, product bill of material (MBOM) generation is based on design nomenclature (EBOM). This is generated by PLM application while the MBOM is generated by ERP application. These two nomenclature are strongly linked and without communication between ERP and PLM, the company has to manage the mapping manually between these BOM. This may lead to errors and a loss of time for the business actors. It is necessary thus to be able to automatically generate the MBOM from the EBOM. Also, in concurrent engineering the different phases of the PLM may occur simultaneously. It is possible to generate the

MBOM while its corresponding EBOM may be further modified. Therefore, it is not enough to be able to automatically generate the MBOM from the EBOM, but also to be able to reconcile these two BOM dynamically.

Our goal is firstly to ensure interoperability at technical and semantic level between PLM business applications and secondly to propagate any data updates between different PLM applications transparently to the user. For that we have defined what we call "observer agent". Each system (PDM, ERP, SDM …) is associated with an observer agent whose role is to scrutinize the IS of its application and to notify the other agents of the system at a modification, addition/deletion of data of It IS. Agents are organized in networks of acquaintances; each agent interacts by direct communication with the other agents of its environment. Thus, when an agent receives notification from another agent, it notifies in turn the user of its business application. The user will be thus informed of changes undergone by information concerned by its business application. However, user should be able to evaluate changes' impact on his own activities and data to make modification if necessary; he should access details of changes. For this, each observer agent also interacts with the mediator agent. This latter is responsible for translating information to a format usable by the application of the target agent, allowing user to access details about changes and to evaluate them. For example, the PDM agent observes a change in the EBOM, it will forward the modified EBOM to the mediator agent that will generate a MBOM conform to the target application data model. The PDM agent alerts the ERP agent of the change by sending it the new MBOM. The ERP agent in turn notifies the user with the new MBOM. The user will have the choice to validate the modification or not. If the change is enabled, the new MBOM will replace the previous MBOM; otherwise, the user can put a note of the reason for rejecting the change. The ERP agent will notify the PDM agent of the user's choice, which will in turn notify the user.

3.2 Mas for Knowledge Management

One of the enterprise challenges is to capitalize the knowledge generated by the PLM systems. In this work, we have chosen MEMORAe[1] to ensure knowledge capitalization of PLM systems.

MEMORAe. Is the combination of a model and a web platform to manage heterogeneous knowledge in an organization based on OWL languages and semantic web standards [21]. Regarding the purpose of this work, MEMORAe allow business actors to capitalize their relevant information based on a semantic map. Capitalization is done through the process of indexing the various resources coming from the PLM systems according to the map concepts. MEMORAe gives thus the actors the possibility to "classify" the resources according to different points of view expressed by the semantic map, which has the advantage of delimiting the context and giving a common understanding to the different concepts and consequently to the different resources indexed by these concepts. A resource can be a BOM, a CAD document, a note, etc.

---

[1] http://memorae.hds.utc.fr/.

The set of resources is therefore made visible in MEMORAe through the semantic map. Each resource is accompanied by a description and a link allowing to directly accessing the resource in its original application. The first step in the knowledge capitalization process is to define the semantic map that will be shared by the experts in MEMORAe. The second step consists in making accessible the different PLM resources in MEMORAe so that they can be indexed. It is therefore a question of being able to query the IS of PLM systems. A user of MEMORAe may have to capitalize information about a product/project that are distributed in different SI. The necessary work consists in being able to: (i) formalize requests made by users (ii) decompose this requests into sub-queries (iii) formulate these requests in a format consistent with the target IS (iv) transcribe the answers into a format that can be used by MEMORAe. To do so, we define two groups of agents: interface and knowledge agents.

Interface Agent. Its role is to interact on the one hand with the user of the platform MEMORAe in order to acquire his requests and on the other hand with the knowledge agents to collect the resources requested by the user. A query from the user is then reformulated by the interface agent into a query language (e.g. XQuery, SQL). Once formalized, the interface agent decomposes the query into a set of basic queries that will then be sent to the knowledge agents. Upon receipt of the results sent by the knowledge agents, the interface agent translates them into a format that can be indexed by the user in MEMORAe (e.g. JSON).

Knowledge Agent. The knowledge agent interacts on the one hand with the interface agent and on the other hand with its business application. In fact, there are as many knowledge agents as there are business applications. Each agent requires the development of a specific interface that allows communication with the business application and this according to the communication protocol. The knowledge agent is responsible for transforming the request (s) received from the interface agent into the language used by its business application so that it can query its application.

The interface and knowledge agent ensure technical interoperability between MEMORAe and the different IS PLM, the semantics of PLM resources accessible in MEMORAe is defined by the users through the process of indexing by the concepts of the map. MEMORAe creates an environment allowing the emergence and sharing of knowledge trough the services they offer such as annotation, forums etc.

4 Prototype

The technical level is the first step to guarantee the interoperability between PLM systems. We carried out a first implementation to test the feasibility of the connection between Aras[2] and MEMORAe by using Jade[3] multi-agent platform. The objective is to test requests on our Aras server in order to retrieve information about the resources and make them accessible in MEMORAe. We have developed two simple agents that

---

[2] http://www.aras.com/.

[3] http://jade.tilab.com/.

extend jade.core.Agent class: Interface Agent and Kowledge Agent. The behavior of Kowledge Agent consists in querying the Aras server through AML queries. Queries are currently manually defined before being encoded. The user specifies trough the MEMORAe platform the resource to visualize, for example, Part, BOM, workflow, etc. (Fig. 2). These keywords are sent by the Interface Agent that is connected to MEM-ORAe to the Kowledge Agent to retrieve the requested resource. Upon receiving the data, the Agent Interface converts them into JSON format so that they can be made visible and thus indexed in MEMORA. Figure 2 shows an example of the description of the "Part" entity in Aras while Fig. 3 shows its description in MEMORAe.

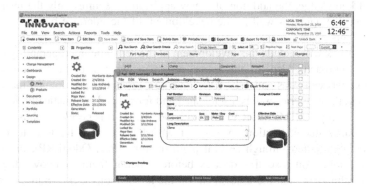

Fig. 2. Part in Aras Innovator

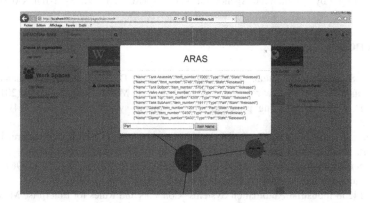

Fig. 3. Description of the "Part" resource of Aras Innovator in MEMORAe

5 Conclusion

We have described our architecture for the interoperability of information systems PLM and the capitalization of knowledge. To do so, we proposed to interoperate PLM application with MEMORAe platform; the knowledge distributed through the business applications used in PLM field can now be capitalized in MEMORAe platform while constructing a shared understanding of these knowledge. Also, we have postulated that an interoperability solution adapted in the context of extended enterprises should be thought in accordance with the principles of a SoS. Adding a new system should not require much development. For this, we have separated the agent responsible for the semantic translation of the information between the different applications from the agents in charge of maintaining the consistency of the information in the PLM systems. The addition of a new business application therefore requires instantiating an observer agent as well as developing the interface that binds the business application to its agent without worrying about the overall functioning of the SoS. Concerning the capitalization of knowledge, the addition of a new application requires only the instantiation of a knowledge agent as well as the development of the interface between the application and this agent.

Future work will include the development of the semantic interoperability based on federative approach. Also, in the actual prototype we tested the feasibility of the connection between Aras and MEMORAe using queries that are defined manually. In future work, these queries will be established and formalized automatically; in addition, we aim to interoperate MEMORAe also with OdooERP. It is necessary thus to treat the issue of query decomposition. A user of MEMORAe may be lead to capitalize knowledge distributed through several platform (ex. Aras, OdooERP), the interface agent have to decompose this queries before sending them to knowledge agents. Finally, a refinement and the assessment on the applications architecture are needed.

Acknowledgement. This work was carried out and funded in the framework of the Labex MS2T. It was supported by the French Government, through the program "Investments for the future" managed by the National Agency for Research (Reference ANR-11-IDEX-0004-02).

References

1. Terzi, S., Bouras, A., Dutta, D., Garetti, M., Kiritsis, D.: Product lifecycle management–from its history to its new role. Int. J. Prod. Lifecycle Manag. 4(4), 360–389 (2010)
2. Maier, M.W.: Architecting principles for systems-of-systems. Syst. Eng. 1(4), 267–284 (1998)
3. Selberg, S., Austin, M.A.: Toward an evolutionary system of systems architecture. Technical report, Institute for Systems Research, University of Maryland, USA (2012)
4. Wegner, P.: Interoperability. ACM Comput. Surv. CSUR 28(1), 285–287 (1996)
5. EIF European Interoperability Framework, White Pages, pp. 1–40 (2004)
6. ISO 14258 Industrial Automation Systems- Concepts and Rules for Enterprise Models, ISO TC184/SC5/WG1 (1994)
7. Paviot, T., Lamouri, S., Cheutet, V.: A generic multiCAD/multiPDM interoperability framework. Int. J. Serv. Oper. Inform. 6(1–2), 124–137 (2011)
8. Lee, S.-H., Jeong, Y.-S.: A system integration framework through development of ISO 10303-based product model for steel bridges. Autom. Constr. 15(2), 212–228 (2006)
9. Panetto, H., Dassisti, M., Tursi, A.: ONTO-PDM: product driven ontology for product data management interoperability within manufacturing process environment. Adv. Eng. Inform. 26(2), 334–348 (2012)

10. Fenves, S., Foufou, S., Bock, C., Sriram, R.: CPM: a core product model for representing design information. Technical report, Manufacturing Systems, Integration, Division, National Institute of Standards and Technology, Gaithersburg, USA (2007)
11. Sriti, M.F., Assouroko, I., Ducellier, G., Boutinaud, Ph, Eynard, B.: Ontology-based approach for product information exchange. Int. J. Prod. Lifecycle Manag. 8(1), 1–23 (2015)
12. Le Duigou, J., Bernard, A., Perry, N., Delplace, J.C.: Generic PLM system for SMEs: application to an equipment manufacturer. Int. J. Prod. Lifecycle Manag. 6(1), 51–64 (2012)
13. Zheng, C., Bricogne, M., Le Duigou, J., Eynard, B.: Survey on mechatronic engineering: a focus on design methods and product models. Adv. Eng. Inform. 28(3), 241–257 (2014)
14. Blondet, G., Belkadi, F., Le Duigou, J., Bernard, A., Boudaoud, N.: Towards a knowledge based framework for numerical design of experiment optimization and management. Comput. Aided Des. Appl. 13(6), 872–884 (2016)
15. Danjou, C., Le Duigou, J., Eynard, B.: Closed-loop manufacturing process based on STEP-NC. Int. J. Interact. Des. Manuf. 1(1), 1–13 (2015)
16. OMG Manufacturing Domain Task Force RFP 1, "PDM Enablers V2.0", Request for Proposal, OMG Document: mfg/2000-01-02, Fig. 14. Translation of Airvane part to PLM Services standard. Gunpinar, E., Han, S.: Advanced Engineering Informatics 22 (2008) 307–316 315 Submissions due: May 22, 2000 (2000)
17. CORBA Specification, The Common Object Request Broker: Architecture and Specification, Revision 1.1. Object Management Group (1992)
18. Penciuc, D., Durupt, A., Belkadi, F., Eynard, B., Rowson, H.: Towards a PLM interoperability for a collaborative design support system. Procedia CIRP 25, 369–376 (2014)
19. Marchetta, M.G., Mayer, F., Forradellas, R.Q.: A reference framework following a proactive approach for product lifecycle management. Comput. Ind. 62(7), 672–683 (2011)
20. Mahdjoub, M., Monticolo, D., Gomes, S., Sagot, J.C.: A collaborative design for usability approach supported by virtual reality and a multi- agent system embedded in a PLM environment. Comput. Aided Des. 42(5), 402–413 (2010)
21. Abel, M.-H.: Competencies management and learning organizational memory. J. Knowl. Manag. 12, 15–30 (2008). special issue on competencies management: Integrating Semantic Web and Technology Enhanced Learning Approaches for Effective Knowledge Management

Design and Implementation of a Prototype for Information Exchange in Digital Manufacturing Processes in Aerospace Industry

Andrés Padillo[1(✉)], Jesús Racero[1], Manuel Oliva[2], and Fernando Mas[2]

[1] Fundación para la Investigación de las Tecnologías de la Información en Andalucía,
Sevilla, Spain
andres.padillo@p2lm.org, jrm@us.es
[2] PLM Methods, Process and Tools, Airbus, Sevilla, Spain
{manuel.oliva,fernando.mas}@airbus.com

Abstract. Aerospace companies have a wide range of information systems with different functionalities that are used along the aircraft lifecycle; this causes problems in terms of integration, information exchange and long term archiving of data. Ongoing standardization efforts, mainly under the standard ISO 10303 and the LOTAR initiative are addressing such problems. This communication shows a starting work dealing with the exchange of aircraft industrialization information. It proposes a simplified data structure to illustrate and validate an exchange approach based on combining ISO 10303 EXPRESS-G, UML class diagram and ISO 10303 EXPRESS-I. The PLM software Aras Innovator was used to make the implementation and validate the approach.

Keywords: Interoperability · iDMU · ISO 10303 · STEP · Express-G · UML

1 Introduction

Since the beginnings of the 90s, the development of an aircraft program is performed using methods based on concurrent engineering, with multidisciplinary work teams, and with the support of PDM/PLM/CAX (Product Data Management/Product Lifecycle Management/Computed Aided apps) [1–4].

The life cycle extension of an aircraft has a relevant impact on the volume of data generated, its management, as well as its long-term storage and access [4]. The integration of product data and industrialization data leads to an evolution from a digital mock-up (DMU) based on product data to an industrial digital mock-up (iDMU), which integrates both [3]. When limiting the industrialization to the product assembly, the industrial context contains the entire product structure, the assembly processes and the assembly resources, all of them integrated within a virtual definition of an assembly process structure. In the aerospace sector, the creation of the iDMU involves several organizations (OEM, suppliers), lasts several years and evolves over time [3]. This

J. Ríos et al. (Eds.): PLM 2017, IFIP AICT 517, pp. 590–600, 2017.
https://doi.org/10.1007/978-3-319-72905-3_52

situation makes particularly relevant the exchange of information and its long-term storage.

There is extensive literature addressing the issues of integration and interoperability of information systems, and the standardization of information exchange as a way to address those issues [5–8]. The different information systems, used by aerospace companies over time, leads to a dependency situation where the aerospace company owns the data and information IP (Intellectual Property), but does not have full control of access to such intellectual property (knowledge) throughout the entire aircraft life-cycle [8].

When looking at the current trends in collaborative engineering practices, the implementation of Model-Based System Engineering (MBSE) practices, where domain models are used as means of information exchange, prompts a higher relevance of the interoperability issues. Facilitate the exchange of information independently of the software systems acquires greater relevance. Eventually, the aim is the complete implementation of the collaborative engineering based on models, from the early design stages to the operation services. The key element to facilitate such a MBSE practices is ontology [9]. Therefore, the development of ontologies becomes the fundamental support element for the interoperability of software systems used in design, manufacture, certification, operation, support services and disposal of the aircraft.

Focused on the assembly processes, this work shows a starting approach to facilitate the information exchange within an iDMU context. The method used was structure into three main steps:

- Definition of a data model to support the iDMU concept. The developed data model is a simplified attempt to integrate the three main structures that comprises an iDMU: product, processes and resources. The data model was created using UML (Unified Modeling Language).
- To follow the STEP methodology, the data model must be specified in the EXPRESS language. Current UML based modeling and design tools, such as Enterprise Architect (EA), allow creating templates to transform existing UML class diagrams into different notations. This feature was used to create an EXPRESS-G schema from the proposed iDMU UML data model. EA macros were also developed to populate and validate the data model by creating instances and their persistent storage using EXPRESS-I notation.
- Implementation of the proposed iDMU data model in ARAS Innovator, a commercial open-access PLM software.

The paper is structured into several parts. Section 2 provides a description of the iDMU concept. Section 3 provides a brief description of the standard for product data exchange ISO 10303 (STEP) and the graphical modeling notation EXPRESS-G. Section 4 shows the proposed simplified data model and its implementation in a first prototype. Section 5 shows the results obtained. Finally, the conclusions of this work are presented.

2   Components of the Industrial Digital Mock-up (iDMU)

The iDMU concept is an approach defined in Airbus to facilitate the integration of information along the collaborative development of an aircraft [3].

An iDMU aims integrating all the industrialization information, in particular, Product, Processes and Resources to model a virtual assembly line [3, 10].

The model establishes the links and assignments between the different elements that compose it. That is, between Assembly Processes, Products and Resources. These relationships and assignments are established with the aim of designing and validating an industrialization context. Figure 1 shows a generic example.

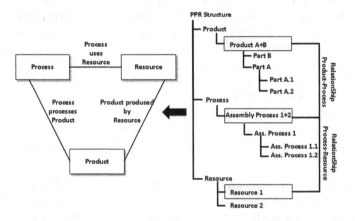

Fig. 1. Example of Product, Process and Resource relationship structure.

3   Information Exchange: ISO 10303 STEP

STEP, the Standard for the Exchange of Product Model Data, is a comprehensive ISO standard (ISO 10303) that describes how to represent and exchange digital product information. STEP is the main reference in the neutral specification of product data for the integration and interoperability between computer applications over the product life cycle [11–13].

EXPRESS is a standard data modeling language defined in the part ISO 10303-11. A data model can be defined in two ways, textually (EXPRESS) and graphically (EXPRESS-G). EXPRESS-I can be used to create instances of the entities defined in the model. Although the persistent storage of instances is specified in the EXPRESS file format specified in the ISO 10303-21 [13].

EXPRESS-G is a useful notation, for visual interpretation of the static part of a data model, type of entities and attributes, relationships and cardinality. The capabilities of EXPRESS-G can be easily map into UML Class diagrams or vice versa [14, 15].

According to the STEP standard, the specification of the information or data exchange within a specific context requires the definition of an Application Protocol

(AP). Three models compose an AP: Application Activity Model (AAM), Application Reference Model (ARM) and Application Interpreted Model (AIM) [12].

- The AAM model contains a description of the context in terms of functions and processes involved in the industrial application. This model is basically documented using the IDEF0 technique, is an informative part of the AP and is not a standard part [12].
- The ARM model contains a specification of the information/data of the application context. It is also an informative part of the AP and is not a standard part [12].
- The AIM model contains the interpretation and mapping between the concepts of the ARM model and the concepts defined by the STEP standard itself in the different resource parts. This model is documented in EXPRESS and is the standard part of the AP [12].

STEP APs cover a wide variety of contexts, some of them are specific to some industrial sectors (e.g. AP 214 is focused on Automotive Industry), but other ones are generic (e.g. AP203 applies to mechanical 3D CAD in general). Several APs are relevant to the aerospace sector, for instance, for 3D CAD with product manufacturing information (AP203 and AP214), for engineering analysis and simulation (AP209 and AP242).

The application of STEP APs goes beyond data exchange and has become a key element in the aerospace long term archiving of data. The project LOTAR (Long Term Archiving and Retrieval), focused on product and technical documentation in digital format, is a project initially promoted by the ASD (AeroSpace and Defense – Industry Association of Europe), and whose outcomes are published as European standards by the European Committee for Normalization (CEN). Whenever possible, the LOTAR standards are based on STEP, and the LOTAR WGs participates actively in the development of STEP [16, 17].

4 Proposed iDMU Data Model: Structure and Implementation

4.1 Structure of the Proposed iDMU Data Model

The Unified Modeling Language (UML) is especially suited for the modelling of complex, distributed and concurrent systems [18, 19].

Class diagrams are a type of static structure diagram where the entities are represented and defined in the data model. A class is formed by attributes and operations, and may have associations with other classes. By means of a compiler or code generation utility, it is possible to generate source code in an object oriented programing language from a class diagram. Although, there are a few compilers to generate source code from an STEP EXPRESS schema, an interesting alternative is to map an EXPRESS-G schema into an UML class diagram, and then compile such a class diagram to generate source code in an object oriented programming language [18, 19]. This approach was adopted in this work.

When considering a possible structure of an iDMU data model, the work Mas [10] is a reference to be considered. Taking that work as basis, an iDMU simplified model was created to demonstrate and validate a possible industrialization data exchange between software systems. Figure 2 shows the simplified model used in this work.

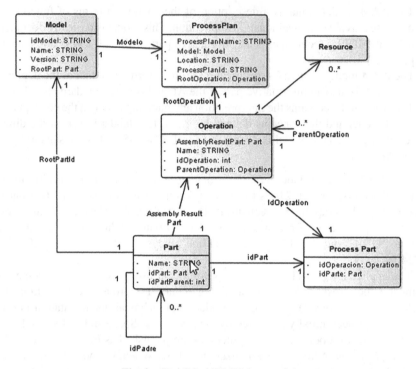

Fig. 2. Simplified iDMU data model

The following entities or classes represent the different elements of the iDMU structure:

- **Process Plan:** represents the root node in a manufacturing structure, responsible for the description and sequencing of operations necessary for the transformation of different parts into a finished product.
- **Model:** represents an entity to specify the graphical representation of a specific product.
- **Operation:** represents an action of transformation collected in a process plan.
- **Part:** represents the lower level unit that results from decomposing a product.
- **Process Part:** represents the entity resulting from the transformation of different parts collected in a process plan.
- **Resource:** represents the sources or supplies used in any transformation action included in a Process Plan.

One of the main features of existing tools in relation to diagrams based on UML notation is the ability to generate source code in an explicit object oriented programming language. Among UML-based code generation tools Enterprise Architect allows a complete parameterization offering the opportunity to analyze the feasibility of developing templates for the generation of "Schemas" using EXPRESS-G based on UML class diagrams. In addition to a macro language for the generation of code in EXPRESS-I format and transformation code in different languages based on the schema.

4.2 Implementation of the iDMU Data Model

The functional model has been structured in two parts. The first one defines the iDMU data model structure using a class diagram (Fig. 3 iDMU Definition). The second one, the code generation of data model in EXPRESS-I as well as the transformation functions for systems and whose interoperability to be implemented.

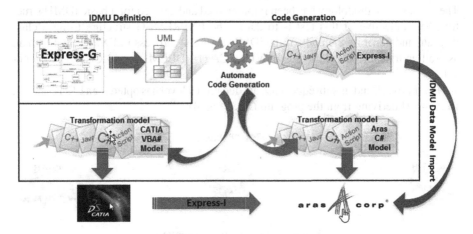

Fig. 3. Functional model

This paper reflects the feasibility and interoperability between PLM systems. Throught out an EXPRESS-I file to implement it in PLM software ARAS INNOVATOR [16] to allow importing the iDMU data model structure from CATIA/DELMIA V5.

DELMIA's V5 DPM Assembly (commercial software, which integrates CATIA design with assembly process definition) is a CAM developed by Dassault Systèmes to optimize process engineering and the assembly manufacturing, enabling to users simulate and validate a manufacturing process plan.

ARAS Innovator is an Open Source software that offers PLM and PDM solution integration services on a single platform, and allows the user to manage the entire product life cycle. The programming code is open so the software can be distributed, developed and modified freely without restrictions of licenses.

To achieve flexibility, ARAS has focused on the creation of a run-time web application that runs a set of services coupled, that is, forming a service-oriented architecture (SOA).

The development of applications associated with the ARAS Innovator system can be done either from the system or from the Visual Studio .NET programming environment and they can be executed in the client or server environment. This work has been developed in applications server because imply a customization of the system with new types of data.

To demonstrate the interoperability study, it will be necessary to update ARAS for reading based on ISO 10303 through a C# reconciliation interface between the Express schema and the data import from the iDMU to ARAS. It will read the schema file with the entities, relations and attributes besides creating the own data types in ARAS, in order to introduce the product data and the scheme both in ARAS and define automatically an assembly structure based on the iDMU. (Fig. 3)

5   Results

The proposed methodology has been implemented and applied for a basic iDMU structure. The objective of this test is to define the EXPRESS-G structure using a class diagram and generate the code of the iDMU assembly process in EXPRESS-I format, as well as transformation models in VBA (CATIA/DELMIA) and C# (ARAS Innovator).

For this work and its subsequent use at educational level has opted for a LEGO model, the 6745-H deriving from the program 6745 (Fig. 4).

Fig. 4. Define program and projects

The helicopter has a total of 247 pieces and the purpose of this test is to define the assembly process in format.

The steps for designing the manufacturing structure model have been:

- Definition of EBOM structure (Engineering Bill Of Material), to describe the groupings and different parts of the model with the aim of making a more coherent the manufacturing process.
- Definition of the MBOM structure (Manufacturing Bill Of Material), to describe how the product is manufactured and to facilitate a rapid relationship between the manufacturing process and the assembly product obtained.

The data model defined for transformations between systems includes entities and attributes, schemas, and relationships between entities (Class diagram and Activity diagram). This data model is the base for generation code in the transformation models, because generates the source code automatically for the import and generation of data types (Fig. 5).

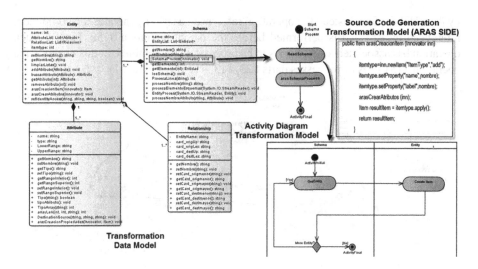

Fig. 5. Definition of Transformation Model structure for code generation (from UML to EXPRESS)

The EXPRESS-I generated code for schema is show below, the file begins with the header where it is provided information of the characteristics of the data.

```
ISO-10303-21;
HEADER;
FILE_DESCRIPTION(/* descripcion */ ('Definicion de una
estructura de fabricación minima'),/* implem */ '2;1');
FILE_NAME(/* name */ 'demo',/* time_stamp */ '2016-09-
107T11:57:53',/* author */ ('Andres Padillo'),
/* organization */ ('ETSI'),/* preprocessor_version */ '
',/* originating_system */ 'IDA-STEP',/* author */ ' ');
FILE_SCHEMA (('PPR MANUFACTURING {1 0 10303 214 2 1
1}'));
ENDSEC;
DATA;
```

After the header section the data is displayed. Each data is identified by a number on the left and preceded by a #. This identification is fundamental to reference information between entities. The first four data lines describe the process plan, the model and the parts/components/subproducts of the manufacturing structure. the process plan 6745H-PPR has associated a model whose definition is in #11. The model has a part or final product whose definition is in #12. It is important to emphasize that the parts do not have associated subcomponents, but each part specifies the part to which it is united to form a superior set, except the first one that does not have father (Specified with a $).

The operation entity is defined by name, the part/product or resulting component or result of the operation and the parent operation that needs this operation to be performed. For example, reference #150 defines the root operation used to obtain the part referenced by #12 (Helicopter). Instead the operation referenced as #151 generates the component referenced by #13 and is performed before the parent operation #150. Finally, each operation has associated a set of parts to be processed or assembled, in this example the operation #151 uses or processes parts #23, #13, #17 (Figs. 6 and 7).

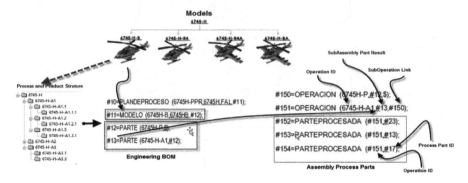

Fig. 6. Interoperability data between software platforms (Express Based)

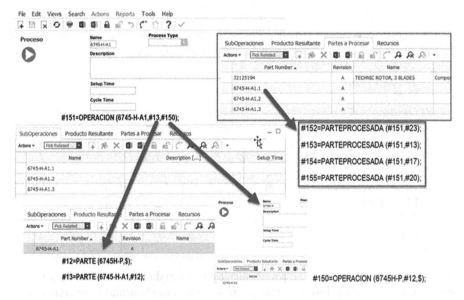

Fig. 7. ARAS Innovator, process plan interoperability.

6   Conclusions

Interoperability among engineering software systems, mainly CAX and PLM, is one of the main concerns of the ISO TC184 SC4, which is in charge of developing standards such as the ISO 10303 STEP. The currently available data translators, implementing STEP application protocols, deal mainly with 3D geometric data, tolerancing and dimensioning data and basic management data. Those data are particularly relevant for a product DMU, when considering an industrial DMU (iDMU), and in particular, assembly processes, it seems to be a gap. This work shows a very basic study dealing with that gap and with its application in an aerospace context.

In particular, the outcomes of this work come in two ways. Firstly, with a development of a tool to map EXPRESS-G and UML class diagrams. Secondly, with the proposal of a basic iDMU data model used to implement a data exchange between CATIA/DELMIA V5 and ARAS Innovator. Industrialization data are created in the CATIA/DELMIA V5 software system; it is exported into an STEP file, and then imported into ARAS Innovator. The data exchange comprises iDMU management data. It is an initial work aiming to understand the development implications of this kind of information exchange in a PLM context.

References

1. Altfeld, H.-H.: Commercial Aircraft Projects: Managing the Development of Highly Complex Products. Ashgate Publishing Limited, Farnham (2010)
2. Mas, F., Menéndez, J.L., Oliva, M., Gómez, A., Ríos, J.: Collaborative engineering paradigm applied to the aerospace industry. In: Bernard, A., Rivest, L., Dutta, D. (eds.) Product Lifecycle Management for Society, PLM 2013, IFIP Advances in Information and Communication Technology, vol. 409, pp. 675–684. Springer, Heidelberg (2013). https://doi.org/10.1007/978-3-642-41501-2_66
3. Mas, F., Menéndez, J.L., Oliva, M., Ríos, J., Gómez, A., Olmos, V.: iDMU as the collaborative engineering engine: Research experiences in Airbus. In: 2014 International ICE Conference on Engineering, Technology and Innovation (ICE), pp. 1–7. IEEE, June 2014
4. Pardessus, T.: The multi-site extended enterprise concept in the aeronautical industry. Air Space Europe **3**, 46–48 (2001)
5. Kern, V.M., Bøhn, J.H.: STEP databases for product data exchange. In: Proceedings of I International Congress of Industrial Engineering, vol. 3, pp. 1337–1341 (1995)
6. Subrahmanian, E., Rachuri, S., Fenves, S.J., Foufou, S., Sriram, R.D.: Product lifecycle management support: a challenge in supporting product design and manufacturing in a networked economy. Int. J. Prod. Lifecycle Manage. **1**(1), 4–25 (2005)
7. Rachuri, S., Subrahmanian, E., Bouras, A., Fenves, S.J., Foufou, S., Sriram, R.D.: Information sharing and exchange in the context of product lifecycle management: Role of standards. Comput. Aided Des. **40**(7), 789–800 (2008)
8. AeroSpace and Defence Strategic Standardization Group (ASD SSG). Through Life Cycle Interoperability: a critical strategic lever for competitiveness (2014). http://www.asd-ssg.org
9. Van Ruijven, L.C.: Ontology and model-based systems engineering. Procedia Comput. Sci. **8**, 194–200 (2012)
10. Mas, F.: Desarrollo de un sistema basado en el conocimiento para la definición de líneas de montaje aeronáuticas en la fase conceptual: Aplicación a una aeroestructura aeronáutica. (Doctoral thesis, Universidad Politécnica de Madrid, Spain) (2014). http://oa.upm.es/28993/
11. Mason, H.: 'ISO 10303 – STEP. A key standard for the global market', ISO Bulletin, pp. 9–13, January 2002
12. ISO 10303-1:1994 Industrial automation systems and integration – Product data representation and exchange – Part 1: Overview and fundamental principles, ISO (1994)

13. ISO 10303-21:1994. Industrial automation systems and integration – Product data representation and exchange – Part 21: Implementation methods: Clear text encoding of the exchange structure, ISO (1994)

14. Arnold, F., Podehl, G.: Best of both worlds – a mapping from EXPRESS-G to UML. In: Bézivin, J., Muller, P.-A. (eds.) UML 1998. LNCS, vol. 1618, pp. 49–63. Springer, Heidelberg (1999). https://doi.org/10.1007/978-3-540-48480-6_5

15. CSN EN 9300-003. Aerospace series - LOTAR – Long term archiving and retrieval of digital technical product documentation such as 3D, CAD and PDM data - Part 003: Fundamentals and concepts, CSN (2012)

16. Delaunay, J.Y.: Long term archiving and retrieval of PLM information in the aerospace and defence industries. In: ProSTEP iViP Symposium, May 2012 (2012)

17. Object Management Group. Reference Metamodel for the Express Information Modeling Language V1.1 (2015). http://www.omg.org/spec/EXPRESS/1.1/. Accessed 02 Mar 2017

18. Florian, A., Gerd, P.: Best of both worlds -a mapping from EXPRESS-G to UML. In: International Conference on the Unified Modeling Language UML 1998: The Unified Modeling Language. «UML» 1998: Beyond the Notation, pp. 49–63 (1998)

19. Aras Corportation. Making the Case for resilient PLM (2015). http://www.aras.com/. Accessed 02 Mar 2017

20. Dassault Systemes. Delmia V5 DPM Assembly. https://www.3ds.com/fileadmin/PRODUCTS/DELMIA/PDF/Brochures/delmia-dpm-assembly.pdf/. Accessed 02 Mar 2017

Study of Data Structures and Tools for the Concurrent Conceptual Design of Complex Space Systems

Clément Fortin[1]([⊠]), Grant McSorley[2], Dominik Knoll[1], Alessandro Golkar[1], and Ralina Tsykunova[1]

[1] Skolkovo Institute of Science and Technology, Moscow, Russia
{c.fortin,d.knoll,a.golkar}@skoltech.ru,
ralina.tsykunova@skolkovotech.ru
[2] University of Prince Edward Island, Charlottetown, Canada
gmcsorley@upei.ca

Abstract. Concurrent design facilities are used by space agencies and private organizations to conduct preliminary design activities in the development of space systems. Concurrent conceptual design is characterized by dynamic exchanges between a limited team of experts, defining the operational requirements, the systems architecture, the baseline design, and budgets for different resources. The results are a preliminary system baseline and product requirements that are used as inputs to the subsequent product development phases.

A study of the input and output of this early phase of product development has confirmed that data generated in concurrent design studies essentially describes behavior with a limited set of information about the geometry. The geometry at this stage is mainly composed of functional configurations with geometric envelopes.

Based on this behavioral information content, the authors have looked at the SAPPhIRE model of causality, initially developed by Chakrabarti, as a potential data structure to support this early phase of system development and possibly all phases of the product lifecycle.

In this current work, we present two concrete examples of concurrent conceptual design data structures for space applications and show how such data structures could be represented within the extended SAPPhIRE model.

When compared to current PLM data structures, the use of the extended SAPPhIRE model represents an alternative means of structuring information and communicating this information between stakeholders, providing better understanding of the relation between a system's structure, function and behavior. It also explicitly represents the links between subsystems and the iterative nature of the design process.

Keywords: Conceptual design · Functional system model
Behavioral system model · Concurrent engineering · Space systems
Product lifecycle management · Product data management
Concurrent data exchange

© IFIP International Federation for Information Processing 2017
Published by Springer International Publishing AG 2017. All Rights Reserved
J. Ríos et al. (Eds.): PLM 2017, IFIP AICT 517, pp. 601–611, 2017.
https://doi.org/10.1007/978-3-319-72905-3_53

1 Introduction

For most systems and products, the conceptual design phase is generally carried out by a small group of individuals working closely together with computer-based models of their subsystem of competence. In recent years for space systems, this phase is being carried-out in concurrent design facilities, which have been developed by space agencies and private organizations. The concurrent conceptual design is characterized by dynamic exchanges between a limited team of experts that study the operational requirements, evaluate different options of systems architecture, a baseline design, and budgets for the system-level spacecraft resources (e.g. mass, power, and link budgets). The typical result of a concurrent design study is made of a preliminary system baseline and product requirements, which are used as inputs to subsequent phases of the product development process.

To appropriately support this effort and to better integrate its results with the subsequent phases of the system and product development, it is important to analyze the types of information that are required at the conceptual phase. The aim of this work is to present such an analysis for satellite systems and the preliminary results. Based on these results, we propose a data model that is well suited to support this early phase of the system design and the subsequent phases through to the system delivery and operation phases.

The paper is structured as follows: In Sect. 2 we set the context of our work on concurrent conceptual design of complex space systems. Section 3 contains the analysis of information used in the conceptual design of two satellite case studies: CubeSat and LaserNaut. We explain the extended SAPPhIRE model in Sect. 4, and the application of this model to the concurrent data exchange tool CEDESK in Sect. 5. This application is demonstrated through modelling of the thermal subsystem of the CubeSat analysed in Sect. 2. Finally we sum up our work and give an outlook on future work.

2 Concurrent Design and Engineering

The conceptual or preliminary design of complex engineering products (such as space missions) requires contributions from multiple disciplines, including engineers focused on specific subsystems as well as programmatic, manufacturers and operation experts. In the space field, concurrent design is defined as an engineering design methodology that brings people with expertise in different fields together in a collaborative physical workspace to design in parallel and closely coordinated to effectively achieve cohesive and feasible product or system designs [1]. Space agencies adopting the concurrent engineering approach have been able to reduce the duration of a preliminary design analysis to between 3 and 6 weeks against 6–9 months [2].

Among other things, the tool for enabling collaboration and exchange of data among experts of different disciplines on a common system model plays an important role. Such a data exchange tool acts as a data repository for the shared system model and allows engineers participating in the design study to connect their domain specific models. Figure 1 shows the architecture of the data exchange and its linkages to domain specific models.

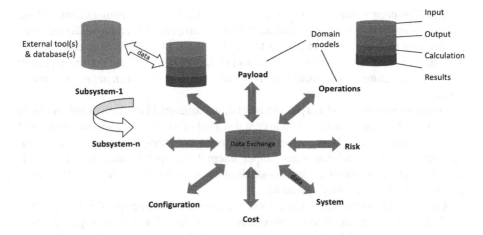

Fig. 1. A central data exchange connecting all domain models, adapted from [1]

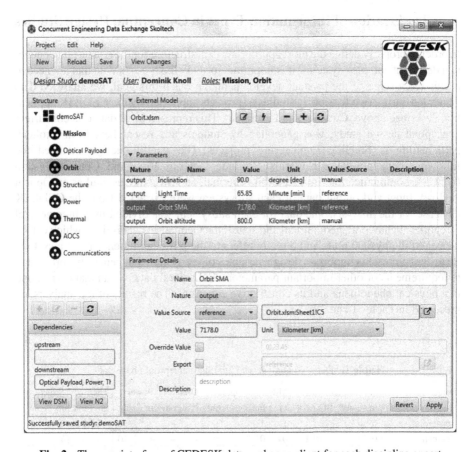

Fig. 2. The user interface of CEDESK data exchange client for each discipline expert

The European space community has published a technical memorandum [3] for standardizing the data exchange in order to foster interoperability among different tools. An instance of such a data exchange tool is CEDESK [4]. This tool is able to store parametric system models in accordance to [3]. In CEDESK, model entities represent the system structure, its parameters, units of measures, links between parameters, users, and roles.

A system is represented as a product breakdown structure in the form of a hierarchical tree of model nodes. Each model node contains a list of parameters and a list of external models. External models represent models made by third-party engineering tools. Parameters can be of different nature: input, internal or output. Parameters can get their value from other parameters, external models or it is set manually by the user. Parameters can be associated to a unit of measure.

CEDESK allows multiple users to work concurrently on the design of a system, while distributing design authority over subsystems among discipline experts. Figure 2 shows the user interface used by discipline experts to collaborate on a system model, here a satellite with its subsystems and disciplines, such as 'Orbit' with its design parameters.

3   Classification of Information Types in Conceptual Design Studies

In order to properly define the most appropriate data structure for the concurrent conceptual design of complex systems, it is important to study the types of data that are needed at this early stage of the product development. To reach this goal, we analyzed data generated during two feasibility studies of projects supported by the CEDESK application described above: CubeSat and LaserNaut. This representative data of a concurrent conceptual design study, was generated by students and researchers from Skoltech participating in Satellite Engineering projects. The satellite design included the following conventional subsystems: Attitude Determination and Control System (ADCS), Communication, Power, Orbit, Thermal, and Structure as well as an Optical payload. Input and output data of each subsystem were extracted from the CEDESK database for the analysis. The data for each subsystem was divided into three general categories: behavioral, geometrical and state data. Geometric data is data, which can be measured in physical units and directly refers to the physical dimensions of a system. State data represents important design variables of the system that generally correspond to requirements or other important parameters. Behavioral data is data that correspond to a physical phenomena and its constitutive equations. The results of the analysis are presented in Tables 1 and 2 below.

Table 1. Detailed analysis of CubeSat conceptual phase data

Data	AOCS		Com		M&P		Optical		Orbit		Power		Thermal		Structure	
	in	out	in	out	in	out	in	out	in	out	in	out	in	out	in	out
Behavioral	6	20	16	1	17	17	–	3	–	–	3	6	2	2	1	9
Geometric	0	0	1	1	0	0	–	5	–	–	–	10	7	–	7	7
State	6	–	11	–	–	–	14	1	3	4	6	1	10	–	4	–

Table 2. Classification of conceptual phase data from CubeSat and LaserNaut studies

Data Type	CubeSat			LaserNaut		
	Input	Output	Total	Input	Output	Total
Behavioral	39%	67%	53%	76%	76%	76%
Geometric	13%	26%	20%	22%	21%	22%
State	47%	7%	27%	2%	3%	3%

Table 1 presents the detailed results obtained from the analysis of the results of the CubeSat feasibility study. The results show that the amount of behavioral data, for both inputs and outputs, is greater than or equal to the amount of geometric data in 6 out of 8 system models. Table 2 presents a summary of the CubeSat analysis as well that of the LaserNaut system. In each case, the overall amount of behavioral data is greater than the amount of geometric data. The results confirm our hypothesis, which means that we need to predominantly operate with non-geometric data during the initial phases of product development. It should be noted that there are significant differences in the proportion of state data between the two studies. The reasons for this discrepancy will be a topic of future work.

4   Extended SAPPhIRE Model for Supporting Concurrent Conceptual Design

The SAPPhIRE (State-Action-Parts-physical Phenomenon-Inputs-oRgan-physical Effect) causality model developed by Chakrabarti et al. [5], shown in Fig. 3a, provides a visual representation of how the behavior and function of the system are brought about

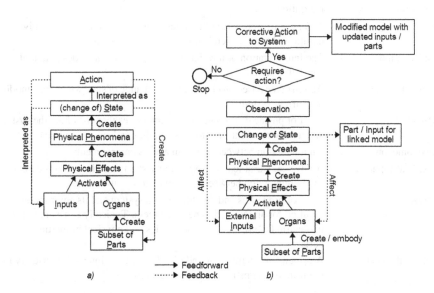

Fig. 3. (a) Original SAPPhIRE Model (based on [9]) (b) Extended SAPPhIRE Model [11]

through one or multiple changes of state which occur due to the physical laws acting upon the system. This model provides a richer representation, at various levels of granularity, of the relationships between the function, behavior and structure of a system, than previous function-behavior-structure models, such as those of [6–8].

The significant proportion of behavioral information found to be present during the conceptual design of satellite systems suggests that such a system representation using causal chains would be particularly useful at this stage of the design process. Indeed, the original application of the SAPPhIRE model [5] was to support the synthesis of innovative solutions at the conceptual design stage. A structured database was created containing representations of both natural and artificial systems using the SAPPhIRE model, allowing designers to browse or search based on the model constructs. In further work, it was demonstrated how the model could also be used for the analysis of design problems [9]. In both cases, the objective was to aid designers in exploring the design space. Subsequently, the SAPPhIRE model has been modified for the representation of in-service [10], test [11] and conceptual design data [12], and proposed as a framework for product lifecycle management [11].

The current work proposes a data model appropriate for not only the conceptual design phase, but for subsequent lifecycle phases as well, and as such, the extended SAPPhIRE model (Fig. 3b), proposed by two of the co-authors in [11], will be adopted. This adaptation of the SAPPhIRE model more closely reflects the evolution of a product throughout its lifecycle than the original SAPPhIRE model, and reframes certain elements of the model to be more directly applicable to the typical product lifecycle stages. Table 3 presents the elements of the extended SAPPhIRE model and a more detailed comparison with the original SAPPhIRE model is presented in [11].

Table 3. Constructs of the extended SAPPhIRE model – Based on [9] and [11]

Construct	Definition
Change of State	A change in a property of a system (and environment) over a given duration of time, which is involved in an interaction
Observation	The interpretation of the change of state which precedes potential corrective action
Corrective Action	Action taken based on observation of change of state which may modify the current system
Parts	A set of physical components and interfaces that constitute the system and its environment. Includes assemblies and sub-assemblies
Phenomenon	An interaction between a system and its environment
External Input	A physical variable that crosses the system boundary, and is essential for an interaction between a system and its environment
Organ	A set of properties and conditions of a system and its environment required for an interaction between them. Typically consisting of the geometric features, key characteristics and physical properties of the parts
Physical Effect	A principle of nature that underlies/governs an interaction, usually in the form of a constitutive or physical law

As indicated by the arrows linking the model elements in Fig. 3, both models provide a logical process for understanding a causal chain within a system. Of particular importance in Fig. 3b are the connections from the change of state to the current subset of parts and the external inputs, and from corrective action to the modified model. These arrows indicate that the results from the change of state or corrective action can modify the configuration of a system, giving rise to physical, behavioral and functional changes over time. The concept of linked models is also made explicit in the extended model, indicating that the result of a state change can act as a part or input to a linked system.

In order to effectively collaborate during the conceptual design phase, engineers require the means to share information regarding partially developed systems in a structured fashion. It is proposed that the extended SAPPhIRE model can be used to not only allow the querying of previously documented systems, but if combined with a collaborative design tool such as CEDESK, can enable the efficient communication and sharing of conceptual design data as it is created. By associating the appropriate elements of the CEDESK system models with the appropriate SAPPhIRE constructs, this conceptual design data can be stored and reused in future projects. It is believed that this combination of a generic model of causality with domain specific system models will allow for efficient reuse of the data created, increasing its value to the organization. In the following section, a case study will be presented for an initial integration of CEDESK and the extended SAPPhIRE model.

5   Mapping of CEDESK Data Structure to the SAPPhIRE Model

As previously stated, the primary model entities in CEDESK represent the system structure, its parameters, units of measures, links between parameters, users, and roles [4].

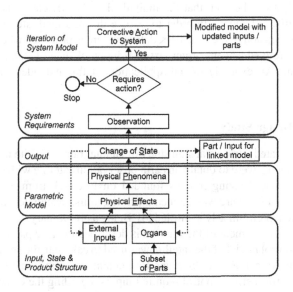

Fig. 4. Mapping of CEDESK elements to extended SAPPhIRE model

The parameters can be of type input, output or state. In order to explore the behavior and evaluate the functionality of the system model (represented by output parameters), the input and state parameters are used to resolve the parametric models composing the system. Viewed in this way, these elements of the CEDESK data structure can be mapped to the extended SAPPhIRE model as shown in Fig. 4. In examining the use of CEDESK for a design study, three additional observations were made regarding system requirements, the product structure, and iterations of the system model.

System Requirements. Requirements are defined before beginning the conceptual design study, and are not considered explicit inputs unless used to resolve a system model. However, it was found that designers did record requirements within CEDESK, for example in spreadsheets used for calculating system model results. It is suggested that a new requirements parameter be defined to reflect this. This parameter would be directly related to requirements for evaluating whether the outputs of a model iteration are acceptable.

Product Structure. While the product structure remains high level at the conceptual design stage, certain decisions are made and recorded within CEDESK in terms of component type, shape and material, which are not treated as inputs to system models. It is suggested that this type of data be classified as part or organ parameters.

Modelling Iterations. The extended SAPPhIRE model also explicitly represents the evolution of the system through iteration. This is part of the generic concurrent design process developed by [4], and covered in CEDESK data structure by keeping track of the change history of the parameters. This allows to reconstruct the evolution of design parameters over design iterations. Since at the conceptual design phase the emphasis is on exploration, there is no approval enforced. The appropriate balance of control and design freedom is an area for future work.

From Fig. 4, it can be seen that the individual CEDESK elements are mapped to multiple SAPPhIRE elements. In order to resolve this and facilitate the integration of the models, an extension of the CEDESK data structure is proposed where these parameters are further refined as part, organ, external input, change of state, physical effect, and requirement. An example of the application of this extended data structure is presented next.

5.1   Cubesat Design Study

We use data generated during a design study of an integrated satellite model, where the mission requirements were to obtain an earth observation satellite with optical payload, and using Excel-based sizing models founded on FireSAT from SMAD [13]. The systems breakdown structure was defined a-priori and the design dependencies among parts of the system preliminarily identified [4]. Being a preliminary design each physical subsystem or logical element of the mission is described in basic parametric models.

A thermal control model of the satellite was used to calculate the surface heating due to the radiation from the sun. In order to calculate equilibrium temperatures, the CEDESK model for thermal control required inputs regarding the CubeSat mission as well as its configuration and thermal properties. These inputs and outputs are presented in Table 4. These elements are further defined based on the proposed extension to the CEDESK data structure. It can be seen that from the temperature requirements equipment list it is possible to derive information regarding the initial structure of the system, as it relates to the thermal subsystem model (e.g. avionics baseplates, batteries, solar arrays, etc....). Furthermore, the material of the CubeSat shell, considered an organ, as well as the parametric model of the satellite's thermal behavior, considered the physical effect, were extracted from data within the thermal control model.

Table 4. Corresponding CEDESK and SAPPhIRE model elements from CubeSat study (sample)

CEDESK Element					SAPPhIRE Element
	Temperature	*Equipment*	*Operational*	*Survival*	
	requirements	Avionics baseplates	-20-60	-40-75	Requirement
	(deg Celsius)	Batteries	10 - 30	0-40	Requirement
	Mission	Orbit altitude	620 km		External Input
		Orbit inclination	21.5 deg		External Input
Thermal		Internal power dissipation	126 W		Organ
Inputs		Power dissipation spike	139 W		Organ
	Satellite	Bus geometry	Octogonal		Organ
	configuration	Main Diameter	0.6 m		Organ
	and thermal	Height	0.7 m		Organ
	properties	Absorbing area	1.5 m2		Organ
		Radiating area	1.5 m2		Organ
Thermal Outputs		Equilibrium Temperature Hot conditions	-8.173 deg C		Change of State
		Equilibrium Temperature Cold conditions	-23.763 deg C		Change of State
Extracted Elements		Avionics baseplates			Part
		Batteries			Part
		Parmetric model of thermal behavior			Physical Effect
		AL7075-T6			Organ

Once the elements from CEDESK are mapped to the SAPPhIRE model elements, a graphical representation can be created describing the thermal behavior of the satellite (Fig. 5). While the elements included in the model are high-level summaries of the data presented in Table 4, it nonetheless provides a clear representation of the thermal behavior of the overall CubeSat. In future work, the graphical representation will be developed into an interactive model which can be used to retrieve the data to which the elements are linked. It is important that this related data be as specific and detailed as possible as it will allow reviewing the design rationale for the system. It also facilitates verification that all relevant information is considered when analyzing a particular module. Moreover, access to detailed data would increase the effectiveness of keyword searches completed on a behavioral database.

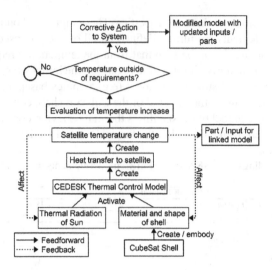

Fig. 5. Extended SAPPhIRE model applied to CubeSat thermal model

6   Conclusion

In this project, we analyzed typical concurrent design data structures based on the CEDESK data exchange tool, which has been developed to support conceptual design activity for space systems. The results of this analysis indicate that the extended SAPPhIRE model is a viable representation of the essential elements in a concurrent design study and that it can facilitate the representation, data exchange and reuse of information generated in such studies. This approach can also potentially contribute to the creation of a library of concurrent design models.

The extended SAPPhIRE model represents an alternative means of structuring system information and communicating this information between various stakeholders and provides a better understanding of the relation between structure, function and behavior of a system. It also explicitly represents the linking of input and output parameters to other subsystems, the decision making process necessary for evaluating the current design, and the iterative nature of the design process.

The extended SAPPhIRE model could also be used as a support data structure for the complete product lifecycle where the product structure, the system behavior and process information are all important. The integration of concurrent design studies to further phases of system and product development, which is an ongoing challenge in product lifecycle management, could then be greatly simplified.

Although it is too early to say that our results can be generalized to all space system development studies as well as those of other fields of design, this preliminary research clearly demonstrates the potential of this approach. We certainly consider our results as preliminary observations based on two pilot studies, but intend to extend this approach to multiple mission studies in our future work.

References

1. Bandecchi, M., Melton, B., Gardini, B., et al.: The ESA/ESTEC concurrent design facility. In: Negele, H., Fricke, E., Schulz, A. (eds.) 2nd European Systems Engineering Conference, p. 329, EuSec, Munich, 13–15 September 2000. Herbert Urtz Verlag, Munich (2000)
2. Di Domizio, D., Gaudenzi, P.: A model for preliminary design procedures of satellite systems. Concurrent Eng. **16**(2), 149–159 (2008). https://doi.org/10.1177/1063293X08092488
3. ESA European Coorporation for Space Standardization. ECSS-E-TM-10-25A, Space engineering - Engineering design model data exchange (CDF) (2010)
4. Knoll, D., Golkar, A.: A coordination method for concurrent design and a collaboration tool for parametric system models. In: 7th International Systems and Concurrent Engineering for Space Applications Conference, Madrid, Spain, 5–7 October 2016 (2016). https://doi.org/10.1177/1063293X17732374
5. Chakrabarti, A., Sarkar, P., Leelavathamma, B., et al.: A functional representation for aiding biomimetic and artificial inspiration of new ideas. AI EDAM **19**(2), 113–132 (2005). https://doi.org/10.1017/S0890060405050109
6. Hubka, V.: Principles of engineering design. Butterworth Scientific, London (1982)
7. Gero, J.S., Kannengiesser, U.: The situated function–behaviour–structure framework. Des. Stud. **25**(4), 373–391 (2004). https://doi.org/10.1016/j.destud.2003.10.010
8. Umeda, Y., Ishii, M., Yoshioka, M., et al.: Supporting conceptual design based on the function-behavior-state modeler. AI EDAM **10**(4), 275–288 (1996). https://doi.org/10.1017/S0890060400001621
9. Chakrabarti, A., Srinivasan, V.: Sapphire–an approach to analysis and synthesis. In: Norell Bergendahl, M., Grimheden, M., Leifer, L., et al. (eds.) ICED09: 17th International Conference on Engineering Design, p. 417, California, 24–27 August 2009. The Design Society, Paolo Alto, California (2009)
10. Jagtap, S.: Capture and structure of in-service information for engineering designers. Dissertation. University of Cambridge (2008)
11. McSorley, G., Fortin, C., Huet, G.: Modified SAPPhIRE model as a framework for product lifecycle management. In: Marjanovic, D., Storga, M., Pavkovic, N., et al. (eds.) DS 77: DESIGN 2014 13th International Design Conference, p. 1843, Dubrovnik, 19–22 May 2014. The Design Society, Glasgow, UK (2014)
12. Tsykunova, R.: Study of data structures, tools and processes to support concurrent conceptual design of space products. Thesis, Skolkovo Institute of Science and Technology (2016)
13. Wertz, J.R., Everett, D.F., Puschell, J.J., (eds.): Space Mission Engineering: The New SMAD, 3rd edn. Microcosm Press, El Segundo (2011)

Data Model in PLM System to Support Product Traceability

Dharmendra Kumar Mishra[1], Aicha Sekhari[1(✉)],
Sebastien Henry[2(✉)], and Yacine Ouzrout[1(✉)]

[1] DISP Laboratory, University Lumiere, Lyon 2, Lyon, France
{dharmendra-kumar.mishra,aicha.sekhari,
yacine.ouzrout}@univ-lyon2.fr
[2] DISP Laboratory, University Claude Bernard Lyon 1, Villeurbanne, France
Sebastien.henry@univ-lyon1.fr

Abstract. The demand of oxygen gas in Nepal is increasing. The gas companies manufacture the gas and supply to various hospitals and glass companies across the country. All the information management is done in manual basis and there is no any tracking mechanism. During some emergency, the gas companies immediately supply the gas to some customers without any record. This results the loss of cylinders in the network. The gas supply chain is complex network as a gas company has many customers which in turn takes gas from various distributers. In this paper, a trace algorithm is developed to implement data model to trace the product using a use case study in Oxygen gas supply chain in Nepal. Each cylinder has certain life span, so PLM system is used to record the information related with cylinders to check the quality issue of cylinders. The concept of SaaS (Software as a Service) of Cloud Computing is used to keep the traceability system in the cloud. A user friendly framework is conceptualized which facilitates the easy access of required information.

Keywords: Traceability · PLM · SaaS · Data model

1 Introduction

High customers demand and competition among the manufacturers require safe and timely delivery of product at customer's doorsteps. Increased awareness of customers towards high quality product draws keen interest in developing traceability system in product supply chain. Many countries have legislative requirement to have traceability system across the supply chain especially in food and medical sectors. But, the requirement of such system in other supply chain network cannot be ignored. Meeting production plans and cost, fighting with counterfeit threats, achieving product safety, meeting regulatory compliance and enhancing the product quality make the traceability system important [1]. Traceability system reduces the overall production cost of companies which is another reason of making it important tool. In this way, it is now well known that the supply chain actors have to implement their traceability system not only to meet

© IFIP International Federation for Information Processing 2017
Published by Springer International Publishing AG 2017. All Rights Reserved
J. Ríos et al. (Eds.): PLM 2017, IFIP AICT 517, pp. 612–622, 2017.
https://doi.org/10.1007/978-3-319-72905-3_54

the legislative obligation but also to enhance their overall production plan. Considerable researches are being done to trace the product at any point from the academia. The summary of these research works are explained in Sect. 2.

In Nepal, there is considerable number of manufacturers and distributers of Oxygen gas. Gas manufacturers refill the empty cylinders and despatch these to distributers as per the order. There exists no computerized system to trace the cylinders after these are despatched from the companies. The author visited the gas companies based on Kathmandu, the capital city of Nepal and asked the owner to know whether they are facing any problem in supply chain network. It is found that some of time they lose their cylinder in the market when it goes to customers as some customer do not return the empty cylinders and they have no idea of where their cylinder is. This results the companies to face ample amount of financial loss. There is chance of misuse of these cylinders resulting big threats to the patients and this also affect the company's brand. Product tracing in complex network is a challenge. There exists traceability systems in literature to cope with this challenge. Among them, many have proposed to use RFID tagging in the product that records the data associated with the product form its production till use. A web based application access these data.

The products have their lifecycle from conception to end. In case of Oxygen gas cylinders, the gas is consumed but the cylinders have limited life span. There are two categories of cylinders: Small and large. Small cylinders are used for personal purpose and the large ones are being used by hospitals. Lifespan of small cylinders is up to 12 years and for the larger ones it ranges from 17 to 20 years. Lifespan also depends on how the cylinders are handled by the persons who fill, transport, and store and use it. There is chances of rust formation when cylinders come to contact with air during refilling. This affects the gas quality. A PLM system will be used to manage and store the cylinder's refilling information throughout its life cycle to check the quality issues by connecting the PLM system with traceability system. The purpose of this work is to implement a traceability data model considering the use case of oxygen gas supply chain. In previous work by these authors, a bi-graph model was proposed to trace the product in global supply chain based on which a data model is presented [2]. In this work, model is enhanced by developing trace algorithm and a trace framework is proposed by connecting the traceability system with PLM system.

1.1 Traceability Data Model

Some researcher works in the field of traceability data model. Thierno et al. develop a data model to handle unitary traceability based on IEC 62264 and GS1 global standard [15]. The author aims to represent the internal traceability data to find the root cause and facilitate data exchange [2]. A data model is proposed to support the traceability process in the food supply chain [16]. Similarly, M. khabbaji et al. propose data model to manage the lot traceability on the basis of make order [17]. The model is said to support to control the material flow in all quality and production process. Some other works [17, 18], develop internal traceability data model in terms of materials and process data registration. We propose global traceability data model tracing each data at each point from production till the use of the product [2]. There is many to many relationship between the actors sharing the data. The data generated at each point of the supply chain are company name, product s.n, date of order received, product received information, distributer id, order delivery report etc. It is mandatory for the actors to enter all the necessary information in the system.

1.2 Oxygen Gas Supply Chain Nepal

In this work, the authors implements the supply chain process of Sagarmatha Oxygen Gas Company based on Kathmandu, Nepal. This Company manufactures Oxygen and Nitrogen gas and supplies to various hospitals and glass industries through various distributers throughout Nepal. Authors consider oxygen gas network only as a case study to implement the trace algorithm. It has around 27 hospitals and 200 glass product manufacturers as customers. Hospital use the oxygen gas for patient's treatments and the glass manufacturers use it to cut the glass. The gas company has 23 distributers through which it supplies the product to its various customers. Considering the use of Oxygen in the hospitals, the company undergoes through continuous manufacturing process. It does not wait for order from the customers to satisfy timely delivery of gas cylinders. It is found that the company pay proper attention in quality checking process. When the gas is manufactured a continuous quality checking process is adopted by purity operator before refilling the cylinders.

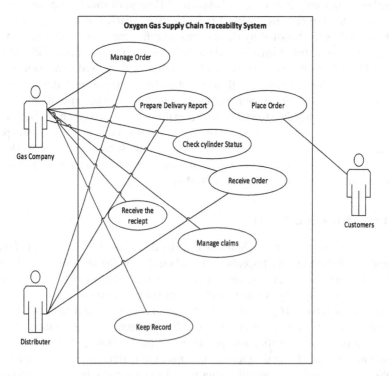

Fig. 1. Use case diagram of oxygen gas supply chain traceability system

The company has many distributers which supplies the gas cylinder to customers, in turn, the customers have also many suppliers of the gas cylinder. As shown in the Fig. 1 the gas company manufactures and supplies the gas upon receipt of order from its distributers. Distributers receives order from the customers and supplies to them. All the order management process is done manually.

Though it is mentioned in the previous paragraph there are 27 distributers and more than 200 customers the company has, authors took only three to show the representations. In the next section, the overall of tracing system is described.

1.3 Traceability System

Enhancing the product quality, delivering the product on right time in the market, fighting product counterfeiting to protect the brand are the key challenges companies must have to cope with [2]. A proper trace and track mechanism is quite helpful and essential to cope with these challenges. There are many actors in supply chain scattered around the globe having multiple roles and objectives, make the modern day supply chain: a complex system [2]. Tracing all the information at each point is still a challenge. Many works are found in literature in this area. The concept of traceability first used by the field related with space, health and military [3]. Growing competitive environment, consumer's awareness about the product usage, customer's safety from the contaminated product and legislative requirement cause manufacturers to have their product traceability system in last 2 decades.

There are two terms "tracking" and "tracing" mostly used in traceability literature. Tracking is the process of going forward in upstream to follow the product while tracing is going backward in downstream to find the origin of the product. Product's visibility across the entire supply chain network is essential which is achieved by these two process. A good traceability system must have to implement these two process efficiently [1].

The traceability system consists of identifying the product location, storing the data, capturing the products related information and disseminating the information across the global network. Use of RFID is common tool being used in product identification using some standards. GS1 is a global standard organization very popular among the general traceability standards. Apart from RFID and GS1 global standards there have been some common techniques being used to implement the traceability system. GPS (Global positioning System), use of Cloud model and bar codes are to name few among them.

2 Research Problem

Many works have been found in the traceability literature that includes the development of a traceability model or a framework towards tracing the product's information in supply chain. In 2007, A. Reggattieri et al. studied the need and importance of traceability in food supply chain performing a case study of traceability solution used by Parmigiano Reggiano cheese, a famous Italian Cheese [5]. The Italian Pizza uses the RFID tag in the whole cheese and alphanumeric code in the partitioned one. The RFID tag and the code store all the related information from processing of bovine milk in dairy to making of cheese to warehousing and packaging. The traced data are stored in a central server from where they can be accessible using a dedicated website by entering the alphanumeric code. In their work "a secure RFID-based Track and Trace solution in Supply Chains" in 2008 W. He et al. proposed use of RFID based on EPC global standard to identify products in the whole supply chain [6]. The important aspect of this work is that the authors proposed two levels of trust model for data security. Any web based services can be used to trace the data from the EPCIS server through this two level of trust model. In 2009 W. He, N. Jhang et al. studied the use of RFID, GPS and EPC to trace the products [7]. The authors implemented an integrated model which contains RFID tag, EPC global standard and GPS receiver. A web based application can be used to access the information from the central server. Use of RFID, EPCIS and GIS has been studied in 2010 by R. Shougang. Here the authors proposed that every meat product have RFID tag with EPC on it. At each point of supply chain the information are updated by EPCIS system that are integrated with corresponding geographic information of each distribution point and users get these data by inputting the EPC on given traceability system [8]. A cloud platform for the traceability was proposed in 2011 by the authors Cao et al. [9].

Next, in 2012, a service oriented Livestock management system using mobile cloud architecture was proposed by Teng et al. [10]. In this work, the RFID tag is attached in the ear of the animal. Microsoft azure and service oriented architecture is used for the information management. The mobile client application interfaces with the RFID reader to get the unique ID from the tag. Farmers use web based application to access the information. Similarly, an innovative cloud based traceability architecture and service was proposed by N. Madhoun, F. Amine et al. in the same year [11].

Use of wireless sensor networks (WSN) was studied by I. Exposito, I. Cuinas et al. in 2013 to develop traceability solution for wine production company [12]. The authors proposed to use RFID which holds all the required information from grapes harvesting to bottling. Sensors are put on six different points across the wine production lines to measure ambient and soil temperature and humidity and leaf wetness. The information are stored on the central server and accessed by a customized desktop application through API. In another work by A. Kassahun, R. Hartog et al. in 2014 proposed to keep EPCIS on the cloud to maintain transparency in meat supply chain [13].

A case study method is adopted to develop a traceability framework to maintain transparency and to achieve security in dairy supply chain network in India [19]. Event driven process chains (EPCs), E-R model and activity based costing (ABC) are used to develop a framework that define and analyse the current supply chain [20]. Authors develop business process reengineering for fourth range vegetable product supply chain and set up computerized system to manage product traceability. A multifunctional database model is developed to manage internal traceability of grain elevator [21]. The model stores product and quality information related to individual grain lots. A UML model to develop and implement internal traceability system of vegetable supply chain is designed [22]. Authors develop UML class diagram of traceability data model. RFID is considered to identify the products information at every point. GS1 standard has been used for web based implementation of the model to manage internal as well as chain traceability.

The conclusion of all the above works is to propose a traceability system with basic information. There is lack of common standards between the actors which result loss of information. No works explain the need of PLM system with the traceability system. As the every product has its life span, the products information from its conception to use in the PLM system helps proper data management. Interfacing the PLM system with the traceability system will add the extra value in the traceability literature.

This work solves the issue by implementing the traceability data model using a case study.

3   Implementation

3.1   Traceability System Requirements

A proper traceability system must be able to store and communicate with actors about product's location, quality, user's safety, actors and process involved in product's manufacturing, handling, transportation and storage [4]. To achieve this, the identification of usage requirements is the first task to be accomplished. UML use case diagram is used to identify the traceability system requirements in this work. Figure 1 shows the diagram.

As shown in the diagram, the system has following use cases associated with each actors:

- *Mange Order:* Distributer receives order form the customer and accordingly it places the order to the gas company. Management of order includes date and time of orders received and placed, quantity of gas cylinder demanded and delivery order given to the production team.
- *Prepare Delivery report:* The production team prepares delivery report for the distributer when the cylinders are ready for despatch. Accordingly, distributers prepare delivery report for the customers as per their order.
- *Check Cylinder status:* Gas Company checks the status of cylinder which includes quality testing and location identification of the cylinder. The cylinder has been given unique identification as per GS1 standard, GTIN. GTIN is a 14 digit (EAN.UCC) data structure which is encoded in various type of carrier. In this work, RFID tagging is used on each cylinder. This uniquely identify the cylinder at each point of gas supply chain.
- *Receive receipt:* When the gas cylinders are delivered to either distributer or the customers each actors must authenticate that the cylinders are properly received as per their order.
- *Place Order:* Customers place order to the distributers as per their requirements and distributers place order to the gas company.
- *Receive Order:* Gas Company receive order from Distributers and Distributers receive order from Customers.

- *Keep record:* Each actor keeps record of the date of placing or receiving order, date and no. of cylinders despatched and received. The gas company despatches the filled cylinders after receiving the empty cylinders only. So, gas company must keep record whether it receives the empty cylinders from the distributer or not. Similarly, distributer also note the acceptance of such cylinders from customers.
- *Manage Claims:* The system users manage claims as per the data stored in the system. For example, if a cylinder is lost after being despatched, the users must know where it has gone.

3.2 OGtrace Algorithm

The main problem the gas company faces is the loss of empty cylinder sometimes. The cylinders given to some customers are not returned and the company does not have proper information to which customers the cylinders have.

To overcome this problem we have developed our OGCtrace (Oxygen Gas Cylinder trace) algorithm using bi-graph model.

In graph theory, bi-graph (Short form of bipartite graph) is a graph, whose vertices are divided into two disjoint independent sets U and V of which there is an edge from every vertices in U to that of in V, such that U ∪ V = All the vertices in the set and U ∩ V = φ that is null [13].

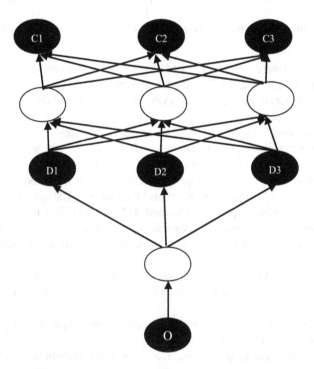

Fig. 2. bi-graph model of oxygen gas supply chain

Figure 2 shows the bi-graph model of gas supply chain. In the model, the actors belong to one set of vertices while the cylinders (Empty or Filled) to other. The filled circles in the Fig. 3 shows the actors and other circle denotes either filled or empty cylinders. O denotes the oxygen gas company, D is for the distributer and C is for the customer. We model the graph as G(A, B, E) where A represents the actors (Gas Company, Distributers and Customers), B represents filled or empty cylinders and E represents the edge connects one vertex from other.

Further we assign the weight to the edges as follow:

$$W(E) = \begin{cases} = 0, \ if \ B \to A, \ if \ B \to A \\ = 1, \ if \ A \to B, \ if \ A \to B \end{cases}$$

Since the nodes are different in 2 sets, the differences are shown as follow [14]: Let $\phi(A)$ be a function representing the various actors then

$$\phi(A) = \begin{cases} \theta 1, \ if \ A \ is \ Gas \ Company \\ \theta 2, \ if \ A \ is \ Distributer \\ \theta 3, \ if \ A \ is \ Customer \end{cases}$$

And let $\varphi(B)$ be the function representing cylinders then we represent it as follow:

$$\varphi(B) = \begin{cases} \lambda 1, \ if \ B \ is \ empty \ cylinder \\ \lambda 2, \ if \ B \ is \ filled \ cylinder \end{cases}$$

Now we model our graph as $G(A, \phi(A), B, \varphi(B), E, W(E))$. Based on these parameters the OGCtrace algorithm below trace a lost cylinder at any point in the supply chain. We start from a vertex in the graph and start searching the graph using breadth first search algorithm. Given below is the pseudocode of the algorithm.

1. Set a vertex 'V' as a point of interest in SC;
2. Initialize the graph $G(A, \phi(A), B, \varphi(B), E, W(E))$;
3. Initialize the traced_data=0;
4. Add 'V' to queue;
5. While Queue is not empty {
    Delete V from queue;
    Let 'u' be a vertex adjacent to V;
    While u{
    Add u to queue;
    Store the information in traced_data;
    Update G();
    }
    U= next vertex that is adjacent from V;
    Return traced_data;
    Return G();}

The algorithm is based on queue data structure, in which the nodes are being added in the queue until a faulty node is found. The faulty node is a point in supply chain where a problem is encountered. The traced_data in algorithm, has the information of lost cylinder. Upon receiving the location of the cylinder, the gas manufacturer checks the quality issue of the cylinder.

3.3 Proposed Oxygen Gas Traceability System (OGTS) Framework

The gas company imports the cylinder from other countries. There is no company that manufactures the oxygen gas cylinder in Nepal.

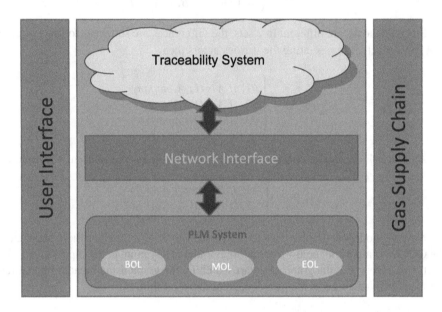

Fig. 3. Proposed traceability system architecture

Figure 3 shows the proposed traceability system architecture. Every cylinder has its life span. As per the conversation with concerned authorities of the company, a cylinder has 17 to 20 years life span. We use the concept of PLM (product life cycle management) to develop the system. All the required information of cylinders like date of purchase of new cylinders, date of refilling, no. of times of refilling etc. are put into the PLM system. The empty cylinders are refilled three times per month in average. The cylinders has to go through hydraulic testing to check whether there is formation of rust or not. During refilling, if the cylinders get in contact with air, rust is formed on the surface of cylinders, which detoriates the gas quality. Refilling information in the PLM system helps to check the quality issue of the cylinders when a problem is encountered.

To uniquely identify the cylinders, GS1's GTIN standard is used, which is encoded in RFID tag attached with every cylinders. RFID allows automatic identification of data encoded with it [23]. Reading and writing is done in the RFID tag through radio waves without physical contact of reader and tag. Active and passive are two categories of RFID tag. Active tag takes power from internal storage (battery) whereas passive tag uses power gained from radio frequency through reader. RFID works on various frequencies level: UHF (Ultra high frequency: 860 MHz to 960 MHz), HF (High Frequency: 13.56 MHz) and LF (Low Frequency: 125 kHz to 134 kHz) [23]. We use the SaaS concept of Cloud Computing and put the traceability system on to it. A web based system will be developed based on the architecture shown in Fig. 3, which connects the traceability system with PLM system. This system will be used by every stakeholders of the gas supply chain and disseminate all the required information when needed.

4   Conclusion

The on time delivery of oxygen gas in the hospitals is essential. To achieve this, the gas companies must have the proper production plan so as to manage the production as per the need of customers. A traceability system in the gas supply chain not only helps the manufacturers to properly manage the order but also it helps them to track their filled or empty cylinders in the network. In this work, a traceability framework is proposed to trace the cylinders in the gas supply chain using the concept of PLM and Cloud Computing. A trace algorithm is developed based on bi-graph model of previous work of authors. The OGTS framework proposed in the work, ensures the required exchange of information between the actors to achieve a proper traceability system. The main aim of the framework is to supply the necessary information of the cylinders when it is lost or a quality issue is encountered at any point of supply chain.

References

1. Thakur, M., Hurburgh, C.R.: Framework for implementing traceability system in bulk grain supply chain. J. Food Eng. **95**, 617–626 (2009)
2. Mishra, D., Sekhari, A., Henry, S., Ouzrout, Y.: Traceability in product supply chain: a global model. In: International Conference on Product Life Cycle Management. University of South Carolina, Columbia (2016)
3. Ene, C.: The relevance of traceability in the food chain, Economics of agriculture 2/2013, UDC: 005.6.338.439 (2013)
4. Folinas, D., Manikas, I., Manos, B.: Traceability data management for food chain. Br. Food J. **108**(8), 622–633 (2006)
5. Regattieri, A., Gamberi, M., Manxini, R.: Traceability of food products: general framework and experimental evidence. J. Food Eng. **81**, 347–356 (2007)
6. He, W., Zhang, N., Tan, P.S., et al.: A secure RFID-based track and trace solution in supply chains. IEEE (2008)
7. He, W., Tan, L., et al.: A solution for integrated track and trace in supply chain based on RFID and GPS. IEEE (2009)
8. Shougang, R., Huanliang, X., et al.: Research on RFID-based meat product track and traceability system. IEEE (2010)
9. Cao, R.Z., He, X.Y., et al.: Establish trust from whole chain traceability. IEEE (2011)

10. Teng, C., Brown, K., et al.: A service oriented livestock management system using mobile cloud architecture. IEEE (2012)
11. Madhoun, N., Amine, F., et al.: An innovative cloud based traceability architecture and service (2014)
12. Exposito, I., Cuinas, I., et al.: Efficient traceability solutions in the wine production by RFID and WSN. In: Seventh European Conference on Antennas and Propagation. IEEE (2013)
13. Barchetti, U., Bucciero, A., et al.: Impact of RFID, EPC and B2B on traceability management of the pharmaceutical supply chain. Department of Innovation Engineering, University of Salento, Italy (2010)
14. Li, X., Liu, X., et al.: Bigraph-based modeling and tracing for the food chain system. In: IEEE International Conference on Information Science and Cloud Computing Companion (2013)
15. Diallo, T.M.L., Henry, S., Ouzrout, Y.: Using unitary traceability for an optimal product recall. In: Grabot, B., Vallespir, B., Gomes, S., Bouras, A., Kiritsis, D. (eds.) APMS 2014. IAICT, vol. 438, pp. 159–166. Springer, Heidelberg (2014). https://doi.org/10.1007/978-3-662-44739-0_20
16. Pizzuti, T., Mirabelli, G.: The global track & trace system for food: general framework and functioning principles. J. Food Eng. 159, 16–35 (2015)
17. Khabbazi, M.R., Ismail, N., Ismail, Y.: Data modelling of traceability information for manufacturing control system. IEEE (2009)
18. Jansen-Vullers, M.H., Van Drop, C.A., et al.: Managing traceability information in manufacture. Int. J. Manage. 23, 395–413 (2003)
19. Pant, R.R., Prakash, G.: A framework for traceability and transparency in the dairy supply chain networks. Procedia Soc. Behav. Sci. 189, 385–394 (2015)
20. Bevilacqua, M., Ciarapica, F.E., et al.: Business process reengineering of supply chain and traceability system: a case study. J. Food Eng. 93, 13–22 (2009)
21. Thakur, M., Martens, B.J., et al.: Data model to facilitate internal traceability at a grain elevator. Comput. Electron. Agric. 75, 327–336 (2011)
22. Hu, J., Zhang, X., et al.: Modelling and implementation of the vegetable supply chain. Food Control 30, 341–353 (2013)
23. Madhoun, N.E., Guenane, F.A.: A Novel Cloud-based RFID Traceability Architecture and Service. Sorbonne Universite UPMC Univ Paris 06, UMR 7606, LIP6, F-75005, Paris, France

Deriving Information from Sensor Data

A General Approach for the Introduction of IoT Technologies for Field Data Analysis in Complex Technical Systems

Marco Lewandowski[1(✉)] and Klaus-Dieter Thoben[2]

[1] BIBA – Bremer Institut für Produktion und Logistik GmbH, University of Bremen,
Bremen, Germany
lew@biba.uni-bremen.de
[2] Institute for Integrated Product Development, University of Bremen, Bremen, Germany
tho@biba.uni-bremen.de

Abstract. Not least because of the triumph of different IoT technologies, the uptake of sensor data during the use phase of complex technical systems has become mandatory. These data, especially in combination with additional field data, promise to improve the technical management of systems. Various concepts have also been developed to determine the usefulness of returning the data to product development. Regardless of whether the use of the field data analysis is carried out within the utilisation phase or over phase boundaries, it is also a great challenge to process the data in such a way that information and action-oriented knowledge are generated. The consolidation of results from different analyses to uniform priorities of systems and system components is crucial for the management of systems, for example with regard to decision support. Therefore, an approach is presented and discussed in order to support the systematic combination of methods for sensor field data evaluation. This includes both a general approach model and a corresponding system architecture both on a methodology level. This approach is illustrated by an example and leads to the conclusion that multiple analyses of sensor series using different methods together lead to more reliable information on system components. With regard to the summary of the contribution, the approach shows great potential for the faster introduction of field data analyses in companies, but further developments are required for the selection of the individual methods as well as for the data compaction itself.

Keywords: IoT · Sensor data · Field data · Data analytics
Design methodology

1 Introduction

So-called field data arises along the complete lifecycle of products essentially in the usage phase [1]. Besides traditional data sources that take into account maintenance reports, complaints, warranty cases, field service reports, etc. automatic data acquisition

J. Ríos et al. (Eds.): PLM 2017, IFIP AICT 517, pp. 623–631, 2017.
https://doi.org/10.1007/978-3-319-72905-3_55

units by means of Internet of Things technology open up a huge potential for the target-oriented analysis of field data [2]. The amount of raw data that can be processed in order to gain action-oriented information for all kinds of business-related decisions is growing according to the growth of embedded IoT technology in products [3].

The challenge in dealing with field data consists in the systematic and efficient acquisition and then in the return of the field data for use in the first phases of the product lifecycle for instance when considering the development of a next product generation or the creation of product-related services [4]. Under the terms Big Data, Data Analytics, Predictive Analytics and similar ones, research and industry try to investigate in IT-based solutions encompassing advanced mathematical concepts to find "truths" that lay somewhere in the massive datasets of companies [5].

It is widely spread that algorithms for that purpose are more or less of general type, i.e. not dedicated to a particular problem or application domain. Actually, most of the recent developments in this field arise from the artificial intelligence domain, thus applying neural networks and deep learning to field data analysis [6]. While these approaches facilitate very powerful analytics tools, the generalissimo might be problematic from case to case as technical knowledge is required to understand and model cause-effect-relations within the analytical calculations. Otherwise, there is a not slight chance of detecting obvious correlations.

This leads to the requirement of defining approaches and concepts that explicitly take into account the "analytics engineering process" that will be performed as a creative process involving engineers, data scientists and IT specialists. In general no scientific work has been found on this issue, however, embedding data analytics as part of an operational management process is of great concern in enterprises.

In the remaining paper, we will sketch a possible approach on a methodology level which aims at the effective introduction of supporting technologies like Internet of Things (IoT), Big Data acquisition by means of Field Data acquisition and predictive analytics by means of modern algorithms from the field of artificial intelligence and deep learning. This concept takes into account the usage of data and the derived information for efficient operation and maintenance of complex technical systems as well as the backflow of information to research and design processes thus exploiting the complete lifecycle of individual products (at present excluding disposal, reuse or recycling at the end of life for the further discussion in this paper). Followed by a so-called experiment we will outline the effect of technology usage in order to derive information from data by an example. Finally, results and possible following research issues are given.

2   General Concept

The introduction of technical support systems to implement condition-based operation and maintenance concepts, as well as the return of field data, technically requires an implementation project based on a methodological and application-specific system-analytical approach. This initially supports the development and integration of technical systems, such as Internet-of-Things technologies and so-called condition monitoring technologies. The collection of technical data on complex systems leads to the overall

operational use of the system during the operating and maintenance phase and to opti-
mise new product generations from the derived information [7].

As an overarching model for solving these challenges, different aspects must be taken
into account in project development. Figure 1 illustrates the systematics of the model.
The basis is a modified approach model, which supports the project engineer during
strategy adaptation, including the necessary technical structures. As part of the basic
analysis phase, a functional and procedural model of the technical system under consideration is crucial in order to develop appropriate solutions from the outset.

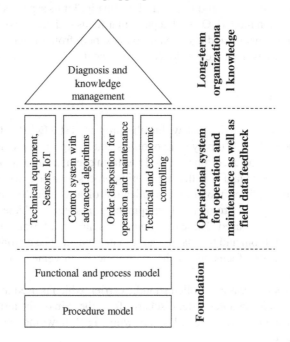

Fig. 1. Overarching model for the introduction of technical system to support operation and
maintenance as well as field data feedback

On the further level is the actual detection system for the condition of the complex
technical systems, which in the broader sense solves the essential challenges with regard
to the data collection and evaluation and thus supports the operational tasks and measures
within the framework of field data processing. It is subdivided into other self-contained
but linked aspects (shown as vertical columns in Fig. 1):

First of all, this is the technical equipment of the technical system to be monitored,
for example with sensors and IoT devices. In addition, the enrichment of information
and knowledge should be designed as a rule-based framework in terms of decision-
making encompassing domain-specific algorithms. With respect to the overall condition
assessment of the entire complex technical system, the ambivalent outcome of different
assessment algorithms should be brought together into a single indicator. The result,
which describes, for instance, the perspective necessity of maintenance measures (i.e.
inspection, maintenance and repair), are then to be used in the planning and control level,

and are therefore decisive for the order disposition as an essential aspect of the planning and control. The final pillar, however, also includes the technical and economic controlling of the plants and the processes, the possibilities of which are to be brought more strongly into the focus due to the expected improved data situation in condition monitoring. This is used to address the return of field data as a further target.

With the transition from the operational area into the tactical and strategic planning horizon, a long-term organizational knowledge based on information from the field data is to be developed and to be used both during operation and maintenance as well as in the early stages of life of new product generations (in Fig. 1, this aspect is the overarching roof of the integration model). Overall, a particular focus is therefore on the integration of the different information and knowledge sources, both from the technical sensor and IoT systems as well as from the employee environment.

3   Experiment

Based on a case study carried out within the project "ISETEC II - Instandhaltung" supported by the Federal Ministry of Economics and Energy in Germany, the concept of the overarching model according to Fig. 1 has been exemplarily tested. The presented model is intended to explain how the engineering process can be carried out in order to achieve a useful condition monitoring application of a technically complex system. During the case study, a prototypical equipment of a special vehicle with condition monitoring systems was used. These were integrated into an information system for the operational control room and the maintenance management. The continuous documentation of the data also focussed on the systematic improvement of the technically complex system.

The special vehicle was a so-called straddle carrier, which is used in the port area to process standard ISO containers after discharge from the ship on the terminal ground or to place them on other traffic carriers. The following Fig. 2 shows the schematic structure of a straddle carrier.

The overriding task is to integrate a condition monitoring system based on sensors to be installed, which in conjunction with further field data from the utilisation phase provides a digital image of the system that is as continuous as possible. In the following, we briefly describe the application of the previously described model to the presented case. The focus lies on the explanation of possible contents in each element, providing an overarching description of the engineering tasks.

3.1   Procedure Model

Based on the proposed engineering model, the first step is the coordination of a specific procedure model. In the experimental application, the system is already existent in its main features and is also in use. Field data in the form of reports are available and acquired with the help of mobile technology. In order to assist the operation and maintenance phase as well as for the rebuild of the product life cycles in a digital record, it

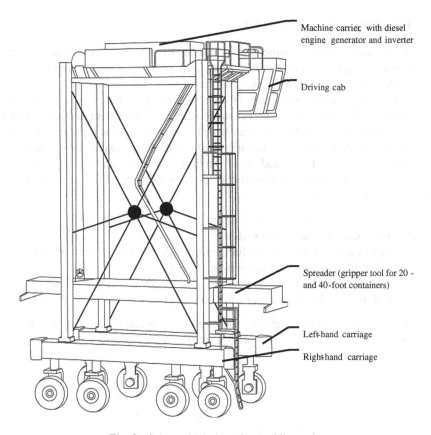

Fig. 2. Schematic design of a straddle carrier

is intended to apply further sensor systems and condition monitoring technologies on the straddle carrier.

The procedure model accordingly has to take into account this aspect and could form a linear process consisting of the phases drafting of the supplement technology, development of the technology, integration into the decision support, commissioning and operation. The following Fig. 3 illustrates an appropriate procedure for the described case and gives some keywords about typical tasks in each phase of a project.

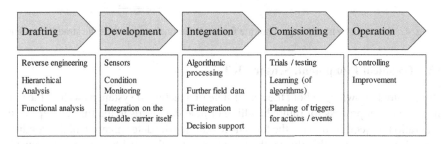

Drafting	Development	Integration	Comissioning	Operation
Reverse engineering	Sensors	Algorithmic processing	Trials / testing	Controlling
Hierarchical Analysis	Condition Monitoring	Further field data	Learning (of algorithms)	Improvement
Functional analysis	Integration on the straddle carrier itself	IT-integration	Planning of triggers for actions / events	
		Decision support		

Fig. 3. Specific procedure model based on the straddle carrier

3.2 Functional and Process Model

Both in the case of the development of completely new products as well as in the case of supplement equipping as described here, the functional model should be clear to identify the opportunities of field data analytics.

The first step in the introduction of IT-based technologies in the field thus comprises a detailed recording and analysis of the current state. It is fundamentally different in the available data sources whether the actual state is based on existing technical systems or whether the system is under consideration (still in the design and construction phase). With respect to the least mentioned, data from the real operation cannot yet be accessed. The functional and procedural model for the ascertainment of the actual as-is-state comprises five sub-areas:

A. The hierarchical structure of the system;
B. The functional structure of the system;
C. Key figures and characteristic values for the collection and documentation of the technical reliability based on the system structure;
D. The assessment of the technical reliability of individual system components;
E. The analysis and classification of additional existing maintenance-relevant data.

For each of the subareas, methods can support the process; the following Fig. 4 just gives an excerpt of a modelling technique for the functional structure of the straddle carrier.

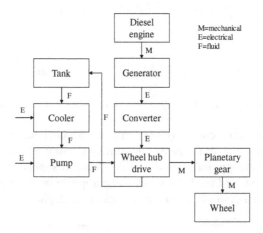

Fig. 4. Excerpt of a modelling technique for the functional structure of the straddle carrier

3.3 Technical Equipment, Sensors, IoT

The acquired knowledge about the actual state of a technical system as well as the planning of a target process for future handling of field data leads to the further steps of the integration project. Above all, the tools necessary for the determination of the condition as well as, subsequently, the methods required for the evaluation of data must be designed and dimensioned. This task is followed by a three-step process by first examining the appropriateness of a technology for the automated recovery of the condition. Based on this, the selection of a specific technique or a tool for determining the state is made by means of relevant technical parameters or other field data sources. Sometimes a combination of techniques and data sources is required. Finally, methods should be defined with which the measured data can be transferred into information about the state of the technical object under consideration.

3.4   Control System with Advanced Algorithms

The definition of the technical systems for recording physical parameters, which are intended to provide information on the state of a technical system, is followed by the requirement of a diagnostic system for detecting technical malfunctions. The integration of additional field data sources must be taken into account. If this system is initially considered superior, it consists of the following three modules:

A. Input the data from different sources and from the techniques of the recovery of the state,
B. Processing the input data with regard to abnormalities using the appropriate methods and methods
C. Derivation of a decision template as the output of the system.

While (a) and (b) have been dealt with in the previous sections, the concrete rule system has to be specified below. The known methods for compaction of raw data, for example from time series to corresponding information, are manifold and differ in terms of their output expenditure. Typical output forms of the methods are (a) time series with a trend extrapolation, (b) classification or categorization, (c) statistical distributions or representations (e.g., histogram, Weibull distribution, etc.), (d) key figure (e.g., MTBF, MTTR, etc.), etc.

In addition, the outputs or results of the different methods can also serve as input to a further method, which leads to cascaded calculations. From an application-oriented viewpoint, the exact configuration of accounting runs is to be provided in the course of the selection of the appropriate methods. Corresponding to this task, therefore, respective instances are to be generated and defined which, correspondingly parameterized, analyse one or more input data series. The combination of several simple procedures, as well as the use of more complex calculation algorithms in a single system, is made possible. As a prerequisite, a collection of methods is required, as well as a platform for their use and configuration with regard to the available data. Figure 5 below illustrates the basic process.

3.5   Order Disposition for Operation and Maintenance

The processual and system-wide interconnection of the findings from the individual field data analysis increases the potential of the project. The objectives can be quite different.

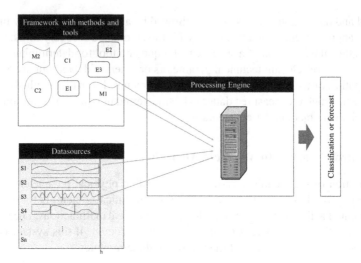

Fig. 5. Universal architecture for field data acquisition and analysis from sensors

In this context, it must be taken into account, in particular, that a direct information advance for the operation management and the maintenance management is created within the life phase. The focus here is primarily on people. It can also be checked whether evaluations can be directly linked from machine to machine.

3.6 Technical and Economic Controlling

The relatively long operating phase within the life cycle allows the continuous acquisition of data, which should be stored and archived for various purposes. This includes the documentation of performed activities for billing purposes and the fulfilment of regulated requirements, as well as the collection of data, information and knowledge about the technical system, in order to be able to plan and control operational optimisation projects based on a well-founded information basis. The goal here is the archiving of often implicitly existing knowledge from the company in an explicit database, in order to be able to access this knowledge more easily in the future as well as to prevent the danger of the loss of knowledge, for example by employee fluctuation.

3.7 Diagnosis and Knowledge Management

In the short and medium-term oriented controlling of maintenance measures the improvement of the processes and technical systems will follow themselves by the data-oriented consideration of the maintenance. This can be done, among other things, by incorporating maintenance data into the entire lifecycle view of technical systems. Life cycle management is to be understood as a holistic approach in which operational and operational optimisation efforts embrace the entire lifecycle of a product. The concept of closed-loop lifecycle management is understood as the concept of closed information circuits [8].

In addition to the use of data within the phase of operation and maintenance, the provision of information about the phase borders is also a means of establishing long-term organisational knowledge.

4 Summary and Outlook

This contribution made clear that the continuous use of field data, including the use of corresponding technical condition monitoring systems, requires a customised individual approach, which has been developed and proposed at this point in a generalized methodological form and detailed using a case. This allows interdisciplinary aspects of a project to be individually taken into account so that this paper provides a basic discussion about an acquisition, prioritisation and evaluation method for components of complex technical systems.

Furthermore, there is a concept for an information system which supports the transfer of the planning phase into the actual operating phase. With particular attention to different data sources, their evaluation and presentation, all the technologically relevant challenges of an integrated information system for field data have been taken up and designed in detail. Proposals for methodology have been developed and are only given as an example in this paper.

Clearly, above all, the basic necessity of a procedural model has been discussed. The further development of the framework with concrete methods and tools is to be continually developed further by means of further case studies.

References

1. David, M., Rowe, F.: What does PLMS (product lifecycle management systems) manage: data or documents? complementarity and contingency for SMEs. Comput. Ind. **75**, 140–150 (2016)
2. Främling, K., Holmström, J., Loukkola, J., et al.: Sustainable PLM through intelligent products. Eng. Appl. Artif. Intell. **26**(2), 789–799 (2013)
3. Zhang, Y., Ren, S., Liu, Y., et al.: A big data analytics architecture for cleaner manufacturing and maintenance processes of complex products. J. Clean. Prod. **142**, 626–641 (2017)
4. Sakao, T., Lindahl, M. (eds.): Introduction to Product/Service-System Design. Springer, London (2009)
5. Zhong, R.Y., Newman, S.T., Huang, G.Q., et al.: Big Data for supply chain management in the service and manufacturing sectors: challenges, opportunities, and future perspectives. Comput. Ind. Eng. **101**, 572–591 (2016)
6. Wuest, T., Weimer, D., Irgens, C., et al.: Machine learning in manufacturing: advantages, challenges, and applications. Prod. Manuf. Res. **4**(1), 23–45 (2016)
7. Lützenberger, J., Klein, P., Hribernik, K., et al.: Improving product-service systems by exploiting information from the usage phase. A Case Study. Procedia CIRP **47**, 376–381 (2016)
8. Kiritsis, D.: Closed-loop PLM for intelligent products in the era of the internet of things. Comput. Aided Des. **43**(5), 479–501 (2011)

Context of Text: Concepts for Recognizing Context of Acquired Knowledge from Documents

N. Madhusudanan$^{(\boxtimes)}$, B. Gurumoorthy, and Amaresh Chakrabarti

Technological Data Analytics Laboratory for Smart Network
Enabled Manufacturing, Centre for Product Design and Manufacturing,
Indian Institute of Science, Bengaluru, India
{madhusudanan, bgm, acl23}@iisc.ac.in

Abstract. Documents contain expert knowledge that can be potentially reused across products and lifecycles. In this research, the aim is to reuse diagnostic knowledge from the assembly phase in the next design/planning stage, by acquiring knowledge from documents. While the acquisition itself is a separate research problem, an important part of the acquired knowledge is the context in which it is expressed in the documents. This context dictates the set of situations to which the knowledge applies. In this paper we study various methods from literature that address this challenge in different domains. We highlight current challenges faced in this work. Two possible means to identify sources of context that are built upon previous work are then discussed. Based on one of them, a method for understanding the context of issues in documents is then proposed. The implementation and evaluation of the method are ongoing.

Keywords: Context · Knowledge acquisition · Assembly situation
Assemblability factors

1 Introduction

Knowledge is a core resource of an organization. Its capture, storage and reuse are perceived to be useful in the current day product development [1]. Product Lifecycle Management (PLM) systems do enable accessibility of information across the entire product lifecycle. However, there is also a need to enable PLM systems for connecting pieces of knowledge across the lifecycle [2]. In particular, extracting knowledge created during one product lifecyle to be used in the lifecycle of subsequent products is of considerable interest and an open problem. This paper is part of on-going research on reuse of diagnostic knowledge of assembly and manufacturing issues across the product lifecycle. The objective is to acquire knowledge about problems in assembly, from documents that are typically generated during the lifecycle of a product, that contain the knowledge. This knowledge is intended to be reused during subsequent assembly design/planning stages. It is hoped that such a reuse will prevent repetition of similar issues, leading to products that are less difficult to assemble. The proposed method of knowledge acquisition is shown in Fig. 1; it can be noted that there is a gap between

© IFIP International Federation for Information Processing 2017
Published by Springer International Publishing AG 2017. All Rights Reserved
J. Ríos et al. (Eds.): PLM 2017, IFIP AICT 517, pp. 632–641, 2017.
https://doi.org/10.1007/978-3-319-72905-3_56

the acquired knowledge and the knowledge to be applied. The knowledge is acquired in the context of the document, but is applied in the context of a current assembly plan. These two processes – acquisition and application – have to be matched in terms of the right context; this is elaborated further in the following sections.

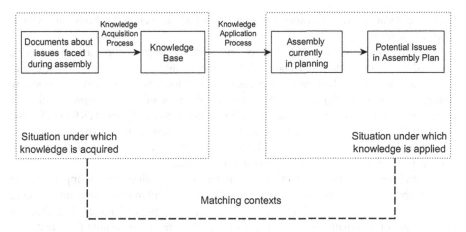

Fig. 1. The two sides of knowledge – acquisition and application; the need to match contexts arises from the two situations on either sides

2   Context

Many different definitions exist for context. As noted in Brézillon [3], literature struggles to agree on a singular definition, since it varies with usage. For the purposes of this work, we find at least two of these useful for our purpose: '*a set of preferences or beliefs*', and '*assumptions under which a statement is true or false*'. From a computing perspective, Henricksen *et al.* [4] defined it as '*Circumstances or situation in which a computing task takes place*'. In our research, knowledge about issues are assumed to be true only in the presence of a set of assumptions or conditions. The latter definition about circumstances dictates that a given chunk of knowledge is usable in a specific situation only.

For example, consider the following issue description from an assembly related text – "*Another disadvantage, pop rivets, being hollow, also introduced the need for sealing each of the holes in the installed rivet heads*". In this case, the knowledge acquired is there could be a need to seal the holes in installed rivet heads, if one type of rivets are used. This knowledge is useful only in the context of assembly operations where 'rivet' is used, and in particular, the 'pop rivet' is used.

Need to recognize context
In particular, the need of this paper is to ensure that knowledge acquired in one context can be applied in the right context. Brézillon [3] clearly stated that context of use must be elicited for a Knowledge Based system. Hence a channel is needed for ensuring that

the context of knowledge during acquisition matches the context while using it, as shown in Fig. 1.

3 Literature

Literature discusses various aspects of context in text, as well as methods and tools to represent context.

Pomerol and Brézillon [5] discuss and identify relationships among context, knowledge and contextualized knowledge. A theory that retains the context structure while mapping natural language sentences to logical form has also been developed by Kamp (mentioned in [5]). It is understood that the lack of explicit representation of context is a factor leading to the failure of Knowledge-Based Systems (KBSs) [3]. The contextual component of knowledge to be acquired from human experts cannot be missed, and the context of use should be acquired. Held et al. [6] stress on the need for context to have a good common representation format.

Henricksen et al. [4] say that context is temporally influenced, is imperfect, has various abstraction levels, and is interrelated amongst different context information. They define a classification, and discuss structural constraints of associations that can be modeled for a domain. But these cannot be used for realising context from text. The domain of pervasive computing, from the previous decade, has a large corpus of work with regard to context. For example, Dey and Abowd [7] have developed a Context toolkit. They highlight distinctions between context-aware and traditional desktop applications such as multi-source input, requirement of additional levels of abstraction, and independence of the context system from a single application. The toolkit itself consists of widgets, aggregators, and interpreters following the above distinctions. Bouzeghoub et al. [8] combine process-oriented and ontology based context management systems to identify situations from data. Categorical data such as "User, Activity, Environment (computing/physical), Device, Location and Time" are used in the work to recognise context of situations in real time. However, this may be more useful at the situation of the application, rather than being used on text sources.

The field of natural language processing has also addressed context for its own purposes. For example, context-vectors [9] have been used to measure similarity in text. Concepts such as Vector Space Models (VSM) represent text using vectors [10]. The bases for using these representations are hypotheses such as statistical semantics hypothesis, bag-of-words hypothesis, distributional hypothesis, etc. For example, distributional hypothesis predicts that similar words occur in similar contexts. Among many other applications, document retrieval is a popular one. Although VSMs form a basis for representation of context, it is still very low level – at words and pairs of words and is not organized with respect to meaning. It is still unclear as to how to use these representations as context for knowledge. Also, we have text documents only at one end of the comparison. On the other side, it is not exactly a text document being used, but a mixed set of not-so-detailed text and numerical information. This mismatch makes it all the more challenging to use the above set of methods, without further extensive study. Finally, the context is about issues, whose sizes are, by nature, very small compared to those of the entire text documents.

4   Possible Indicators for Context

As mentioned in the previous section, the need to define context of knowledge is influenced by its use. The common representation format mentioned by Held *et al.* [6] plays an important role in this activity. Hence, for the purposes of defining context for knowledge, we explore two concepts from previous research that may be potentially useful - the assembly situation model and the five important factors in assembly operations. A comparison of these two methods to choose the more suitable method is then presented in Sect. 5.

4.1   Assembly Situation Model

As shown in Fig. 1, situations are the means for describing knowledge, at the acquisition and application stages. Ye *et al.* (referred in [8]) define situations for a mobile computing environment as "external semantic interpretations of low-level context, permitting a higher-level specification of human behaviour in the scene and the corresponding system services". As part of earlier research by the same research group, an information model for representing assembly situations was developed [11]. It is called the assembly situation model (ASM), and is shown in Fig. 2. In its elementary form, an assembly task is represented as transitioning from an initial state of unassembled parts to a final assembled state of parts, via an assembly process. The dotted box around the first assembly process (Parts A, B; Process 1; Subassembly AB) shows such an elementary ASM. This model for a single task can be extended to the assembly of an entire assembly tree. As shown in Fig. 2, Process 2 combines Part C, Part D and Part E, and Process 3 combines Subassembly AB, Subassembly CDE and Part F, resulting in the assembled product ABCDEF.

The model simplifies the representation of information related to an assembly process. Information about all the parts prior and post their integration into the

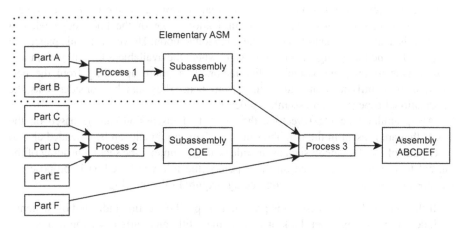

Fig. 2. Example of an assembly situation model for a six part assembly. The dotted portion shows an elementary ASM

assembly is available (including geometric and non-geometric information from CAD). Information of possible assembly sequences as well as information about the processes (such as pre-processes, process parameters and description of steps) can also be represented.

With the above representation, the ASM ensures that it is possible to attribute a piece of knowledge to a particular step in the assembly. Otherwise, the only representation of an assembly would have been the final assembled product, that is typically represented by CAD models at the design/planning stage.

4.2   Factors Affecting Assemblability

In order to understand what information is available at the usage stage of knowledge, a universal set of all necessary information is needed. However, there is currently neither a classification nor a master-list of such information. In order to overcome this disorganized status, the work of Santhi *et al.* [12] is used. They propose that there are five factors that affect assemblability, namely part, person, process, tool and environment.

Note that these factors may be interpreted as representing

(a)   The different parts of an assembly process that interact together, and
(b)   A classification scheme for information related to the assembly process.

Hence, it is possible to use the above set of factors themselves, in combination with the assembly situation model, to identify the location of a specific piece of knowledge in the assembly process.

5   Proposed Method to Recognise Context

In the previous sections, two primary means for capturing assembly related information have been proposed - namely the assembly situation model and the assemblability factors. The ASM is associated with an existing assembly situation and its purpose is to construct a usable information model of a situation from available CAD and process data. This makes it more useful at the utilization stage of the knowledge when a situation is available at hand to apply the knowledge upon. However, in this paper, we are placed in the knowledge acquisition stage, where the available information is in text format. Due to this, the assemblability factors look more appealing from the perspective of identifying contextual clues from text. They can be considered as the informational aspects of an assembly process.

Also, similar to context vectors, the context of discussion can be based on the words that are present in the neighbouring text. This argument can be extended also to other parts of the document, such as the title of the document, the section heading of the current text, and so on. Based on these points, the following method is proposed to capture the context of the knowledge being acquired (also see Fig. 3):

– If the knowledge about issues is present at a specific location indicated by sentence index S_i in the text, then look at its document title and current section heading.

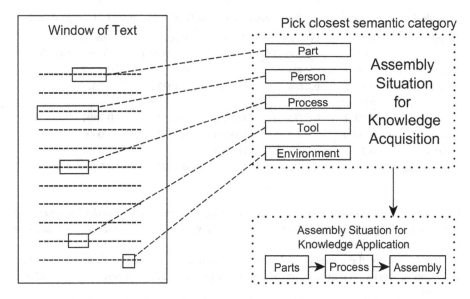

Fig. 3. Proposed method and scheme for identifying context of situation

- Also, store the surrounding text of S_i within a window of predefined distance, say, for example, a 10-sentence window on either sides.
- List all the nouns and verbs in the text window, as well as in the document and section titles.
- Classify these words into the five context containers i.e. assemblability factors. For this, the closest of the categories to which each entity from the previous step relates to, must be identified. Hence, words such as 'rivet', 'glue' etc. would be closer to process and tool; 'temperature', 'humidity' etc. are closer to environment; and 'shoulder' and 'head' would be closer to operator.
- The above values for the context containers constitute a signature of context for the issue-related knowledge under consideration.

To illustrate the fourth point above, words intended for each factor are evaluated for similarity with the title of the factors. This is shown in Table 1. WordNet-based 'lin' similarity measures have been evaluated using the WS4 J web-interface (http://ws4jdemo.appspot.com). The closest appropriate synsets (word sense) have been chosen by the tool itself for the highest score, and not by researcher.

It is observed that for the words 'wing', 'machine', 'rivet', and 'sealing', the decision to categorize them is straightforward. However, with the word 'hand', the initial category of choice is 'part'. Due to the word-sense being automatically chosen on the basis of the highest score, the word-sense chosen for 'part' was 'part#n#3' ('*Portion of natural object*'). When it was evaluated with the more appropriate sense of 'part' (part#n#2: '*Something less than the whole of a human artifact*'), the similarity with 'hand' was 0.1561. Similarly, similarity of 'hand' with 'process' (process#n#5: '*a natural prolongation/projection from a part of an organism*') was initially 0.4972.

Table 1. Lin similarity values for example words, with highest values being highlighted.

Word	Part ('part')	Person ('person')	Tool ('tool')	Process ('process)	Environment ('environment')
'wing'	**0.7073**	0.2004	0.2594	0.4321	0.1274
'hand'	0.7472 (0.1561)	**0.4466**	0.3578	0.4972 (0.3639)	0.3047
'machine'	0.1912	0.3075	**0.4754**	0.1107	0.1491
'rivet'	0.0000	0.0000	0.0000	**0.3337**	0.0000
'sealing'	0.3655	0.0683	0.2524	**0.3780**	0.0851
'temperature'	0.3510	0.0833	0.1880	**0.6697**	0.3380

But after changing to the more appropriate sense (process#n#1: *'particular course of action intended to achieve a desired result'*), it was 0.3639. These are indicated in parentheses in the table.

Hence, use of the correct word sense is a minor yet influential factor in the classification of words. We now describe a more detailed example of how this method can be used.

5.1   Example

In Fig. 4, we illustrate the steps of the proposed method using an example. All the steps were carried out manually (except Part Of Speech tagging), since a computer based implementation is yet to be carried out. The input text is shown, and the location of the assembly issue is indicated using a box. A window of 8 sentences has been selected on either side of the text. For this example we have not considered the document and section titles. A list of nouns is extracted from the text, though it is also possible to extract verbs and other parts of speech. The nouns are compared with the words indicating factors, and classified into one of the five context containers, using similarity measures described above. These labels can then be used as indicators of context while matching context during knowledge application. Note that not all the containers are uniform in terms of number of words. The classifications are also not perfect, due to reasons such as ambiguity, domain specific terms and noun-phrases.

5.2   Using Context

Once these context-containers are available at the stage of application of a piece of knowledge, they can be matched against the situation in which the knowledge is to be applied. Based on the extent to which it matches, a mathematical score can be assigned to indicate the extent of relevance of the piece of knowledge, as shown in Fig. 3. In the figure, the matching between the application situation and the context containers would have to be employed in a manner similar to the similarity measures that are used in Table 1.

To illustrate, consider an example based on the knowledge indicated in Fig. 4. It is possible that, for an application situation, an assembly operation may involve the process of *gluing*. The ASM for this application situation would contain information

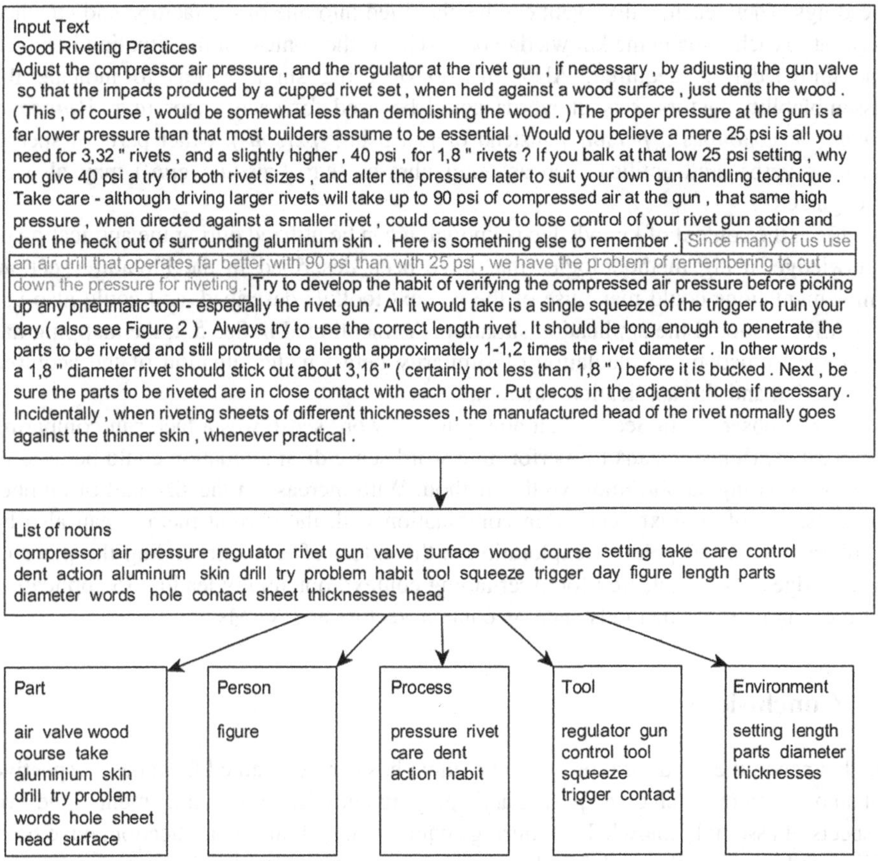

Input Text
Good Riveting Practices
Adjust the compressor air pressure , and the regulator at the rivet gun , if necessary , by adjusting the gun valve so that the impacts produced by a cupped rivet set , when held against a wood surface , just dents the wood . (This , of course , would be somewhat less than demolishing the wood .) The proper pressure at the gun is a far lower pressure than that most builders assume to be essential . Would you believe a mere 25 psi is all you need for 3,32 " rivets , and a slightly higher , 40 psi , for 1,8 " rivets ? If you balk at that low 25 psi setting , why not give 40 psi a try for both rivet sizes , and alter the pressure later to suit your own gun handling technique . Take care - although driving larger rivets will take up to 90 psi of compressed air at the gun , that same high pressure , when directed against a smaller rivet , could cause you to lose control of your rivet gun action and dent the heck out of surrounding aluminum skin . Here is something else to remember . Since many of us use an air drill that operates far better with 90 psi than with 25 psi , we have the problem of remembering to cut down the pressure for riveting . Try to develop the habit of verifying the compressed air pressure before picking up any pneumatic tool - especially the rivet gun . All it would take is a single squeeze of the trigger to ruin your day (also see Figure 2) . Always try to use the correct length rivet . It should be long enough to penetrate the parts to be riveted and still protrude to a length approximately 1-1,2 times the rivet diameter . In other words , a 1,8 " diameter rivet should stick out about 3,16 " (certainly not less than 1,8 ") before it is bucked . Next , be sure the parts to be riveted are in close contact with each other . Put clecos in the adjacent holes if necessary . Incidentally , when riveting sheets of different thicknesses , the manufactured head of the rivet normally goes against the thinner skin , whenever practical .

List of nouns
compressor air pressure regulator rivet gun valve surface wood course setting take care control dent action aluminum skin drill try problem habit tool squeeze trigger day figure length parts diameter words hole contact sheet thicknesses head

Part	Person	Process	Tool	Environment
air valve wood course take aluminium skin drill try problem words hole sheet head surface	figure	pressure rivet care dent action habit	regulator gun control tool squeeze trigger contact	setting length parts diameter thicknesses

Fig. 4. Example of the working of the proposed method.

about gluing. This would have to be compared with the context containers of the acquired knowledge. Most terms (except for a few for the tool e.g. 'gun' and 'squeeze') are semantically far away from the application situation. However, if the ASM of the application situation had a riveting operation, then the context containers are more likely to be semantically closer, hence more relevant. The similarity between the context containers of acquired knowledge and application situation would not be an exact match, but rather, a number that represents the distance between these two sets of context containers.

6   Future Work

Based on the proposed method discussed in the previous section, the immediate step is to implement it, by capturing the text around the issues, recognizing the entities and events in the surrounding text and other indicators such as the section and document headings. Then, each entity/event can be classified into one of the factors, and attached as a set to each issue in the knowledge base. This is the context of the situation in which the knowledge is acquired. Also, instead of using single words to indicate the assemblability factors, sets of words could be used for each factor (e.g. {'*human*', '*man*', '*ergonomics*', '*person*'} instead of just using '*person*'). Other parts of speech such as verbs, and entities such as noun phrases (e.g. '*riveting gun*') may also be recognized.

Once the context of knowledge is known, it can be utilized during the application of knowledge, using methodologies that have been described in the literature section. Implementations could make use of the context toolkits described, and could also use the ASM to model the application situation. As mentioned in Sec 5.2, the mapping has to be performed by a calculation of similarity between the situation of the acquired knowledge and the application situation.

It was observed in Sect. 5 that ambiguity of word sense was a factor in comparing similarities. Hence, means for performing word sense disambiguation could be used as a pre-processing step to improve the method. With increase in the size and of number of texts, use of context vectors, in combination with the current method can also be explored. A further point of exploration is the extent of text surrounding the piece of knowledge to be considered for ascertaining context, potentially leading to application of more large-scale methods such as context vectors and VSMs.

7 Conclusions

In this paper, the need for representing context has been explained from the perspective of an ongoing research on acquiring and applying knowledge from documents. The two aspects of assembly knowledge – during acquisition, and during application, have been discussed. Potentially useful indicators, such as an assembly situation model and assemblability factors, have been described for the application and acquisition situations respectively.

The core contribution of this paper is the proposed method for identifying indicators of context during knowledge acquisition. This method uses assemblability factors as context containers, into which the words surrounding a piece of assembly knowledge can be classified. It is proposed that these words represent the context in which this piece of knowledge was expressed in the document. The next step is to implement this method, and to use the context in the knowledge application stage.

Acknowledgements. The research work described in this paper was carried out with funding from Robert Bosch Centre for Cyber Physical Systems, IISc, under Project RBCO0015.

References

1. Regli, W.C., Szykman, S., Sriram, R.D.: The role of knowledge in next-generation product development systems. J. Comput. Inf. Sci. Eng. **1**, 3–11 (2001)
2. Ameri, F., Dutta, D.: Product lifecycle management: closing the knowledge loops. Comput. Aided Des. Appl. **2**(5), 577–590 (2005)
3. Brézillon, P.: Context in human-machine problem solving: a survey. LIP **6**, 029 (1996)
4. Henricksen, K., Indulska, J., Rakotonirainy, A.: Modeling context information in pervasive computing systems. In: Mattern, F., Naghshineh, M. (eds.) Pervasive 2002. LNCS, vol. 2414, pp. 167–180. Springer, Heidelberg (2002). https://doi.org/10.1007/3-540-45866-2_14
5. Pomerol, J.-C., Brézillon, P.: About some relationships between knowledge and context. In: Akman, V., Bouquet, P., Thomason, R., Young, R. (eds.) CONTEXT 2001. LNCS (LNAI), vol. 2116, pp. 461–464. Springer, Heidelberg (2001). https://doi.org/10.1007/3-540-44607-9_44
6. Held, A., Buchholz, S., Schill, A.: Modeling of context information for pervasive computing applications. In: Proceedings of SCI, pp. 167–180 (2002)
7. Dey, A.K., Abowd, G.D.: The context toolkit: aiding the development of context-aware applications. In: Workshop on Software Engineering for Wearable and Pervasive Computing, pp. 431–441 (2000)
8. Bouzeghoub, A., Taconet, C., Jarraya, A., Kien Do, N., Conan, D.: Complementarity of process-oriented and ontology-based context managers to identify situations. In: 2010 Fifth International Conference on Digital Information Management (ICDIM), pp. 222–229. IEEE (2010)
9. Patwardhan, S., Pedersen, T.: Using WordNet-based context vectors to estimate the semantic relatedness of concepts. In: Proceedings of the EACL 2006 workshop Making Sense of Sense-Bringing Computational Linguistics and Psycholinguistics Together, vol. 1501, Trento, pp. 1–8 (2006)
10. Turney, P.D., Pantel, P.: From frequency to meaning: vector space models of semantics. J. Artif. Intell. Res. **37**, 141–188 (2010)
11. Madhusudanan, N., Chakrabarti, A.: A model for visualizing mechanical assembly situations. In: ICORD 2011: Proceedings of the 3rd International Conference on Research into Design Engineering, Bangalore, India, 10.-12.01. 2011 (2011)
12. Santhi, B., Gurumoorthy, B., Chakrabarti, A.: A new approach for assemblability assessment using time and postural analysis—a case study. In: ICORD 09: Proceedings of the 2nd International Conference on Research into Design, Bangalore, India 07.-09.01. 2009 (2009)

Knowledge Modelling for an Electrical PLM System in Aeronautics

Christophe Merlo[1,2(✉)], Éric Villeneuve[1], Sébastien Bottecchia[1], and Pierre Diaz[1]

[1] ESTIA, ESTIA Research, Bidart, France
c.merlo@estia.fr
[2] IMS, UMR5218, Univ. de Bordeaux, Bordeaux, France

Abstract. Management of the whole product lifecycle is a major stake that most companies have now integrated into their strategies. Research works have been focused on this asset but mainly for mechanical products. In previous work proposes a knowledge modelling approach in a mechanical context, centred on expert users' collaboration. In this paper, we worked with an aeronautical company in charge of electrical maintenance. Its objective was to improve its business processes, from design phase to production phase, by developing a new PLM system, integrated to its electrical CAD software. Our research aim is to evaluate the genericity of previous knowledge modelling approach in this electrical context. We propose then an integrated knowledge model based on three dimensions: (electric) product modelling, (aeronautics retrofitting) process/project modelling and organization/collaboration modelling. We show how this model identifies generic vs expert knowledge and how 'business rules' can be defined to support collaboration and to reduce time of development process. Finally, we propose a global PLM system and we detail the impact on the collaborations and on the whole 'product' lifecycle. This PLM system is actually developed by an electrical CAD editor, ensuring the integration between CAD data and PLM database. We conclude on future work extending this first PLM system: a generic problem-solving approach for capitalizing and reusing knowledge then an augmented reality environment for using PLM product data during installation phase.

Keywords: PLM system · Knowledge modelling
Collaborative life cycle management · Knowledge reuse

1 Introduction

Manufacturing industries and product development process have strongly evolved for almost twenty years. Many approaches, methods and tools have been implemented to improve the performance of design projects. These approaches and methods can be focused, for example, on multidisciplinary design teams' coordination [1], concurrent engineering [2], or products complexity management [3].

One of the key success factors is the efficiency of collaboration between team members and the relevancy of available design support environments [4]. "To survive

J. Ríos et al. (Eds.): PLM 2017, IFIP AICT 517, pp. 642–654, 2017.
https://doi.org/10.1007/978-3-319-72905-3_57

in global competitive markets, says [5], the Product Lifecycle Management (PLM) is an emerging philosophy to improve strategic engineering for managing information, processes and resources to support the life cycle of a product".

Actual trends for the industry 4.0 focus on collaborative companies that design, manufacture, produce and deliver complex products and services. Such large companies use generally PLM systems [6] but need to be supported by more relevant knowledge-centred information systems designed for the different phases of the product life-cycle. Therefore, major PLM challenges are based at least on the following key axes [7]:

- an efficient and effective access to the right information, for every stakeholder involved in product development projects, everywhere in the world and when he/she requires this access;
- the definition of an effective information management strategy coupled with a knowledge modelling approach to support the activities of each actor, according to his/her business profile.

In this context, knowledge modelling may be studied through several viewpoints: the modelling of adequate product knowledge, the reengineering of the product development process and the coordination of design-manufacture-maintenance activities as part of the product lifecycle management [8].

By knowledge modelling, it is referred to explicit and implicit knowledge as mentioned in [9] with the aim of structuring knowledge and of proposing a support for team's communication and traceability, through a new generation of PLM system.

In this paper, we study how knowledge modelling helps in defining solutions that will be implemented into a PLM system, allowing the company to become a collaborative company through the whole product lifecycle and to be more competitive. In Sect. 2 we introduce the case study and describe the initial situation of the company and its main process for a specific business activity. Section 3 describes the proposed integrated knowledge model and we show how collaboration between actors is fostered by using the structured knowledge model. Finally, we discuss our proposal and introduce future work that will introduce augmented reality in the production phase of the product life-cycle.

2   Case Study

Our case study has been implemented throughout the 2π-MCO project (PPIMCO: Productivité des PME en Ingénierie électrique pour une Maintenance et une Conception Optimisées/Productivity of SMEs in Electrical Engineering for Optimised Design and Maintenance). This project (2013–2016) was funded by French agency BPI France and the Aquitaine Region, and received Aerospace Valley competitivity pole support. The project leader was an editor of electrical CAD solutions, and the consortium was composed of two "user companies", two research laboratories, two education partners and one "e-learning" company.

2.1 Airplane Retrofit Case Study

The 2π-MCO project aims to implement prototype tools and methods for increasing the productivity of SMEs and Midsize Business companies working in the field of automation and wiring either in maintenance or design (retrofitting). It helps them to remain competitive by reducing design time studies and reducing errors in information transmission.

For that, we focused on industrial processes improvement and capitalizing knowhow. First analysis lead to work on:

- Reliable deliverables.
- Greater collaboration between businesses: design, manufacture, installation, testing, documentation, by lower information redundancy; controls automation and document generation; the centralized and shared access to information, etc.
- Implementation of a new PLM environment suitable for this type of business.

The studied company, that we will name "Airplane retrofit" company, is specialist of airplanes maintenance. Its market corresponds to airplanes used for public activities (commercial flights, scientific/public missions or governmental flights). Its main business activities can be divided into two main activities: direct maintenance tasks, or complete airplane retrofitting that implies to redesign internal infrastructures and equipment then install them into the planes. The case study is based on the retrofit activity so we consider the redesigned infrastructure and equipment as the "product" and their installation (assembly) as the production phase.

ESTIA was mandated to support this company to highlight its needs and recommend models, features and software MMI (Man/Machine Interface) proposals, which will be implemented via a new PLM tool. This development will be provided by the software editor, already a supplier of CAD wiring solution.

2.2 Airplane Retrofit Business Process

Our approach relied in this case study on interviews and observations. We met several actors to be able to analyse all phases of the product life-cycle. We aim to define with them what were their activities, what kind of information they need, they produce and they send and finally what tools do they use.

As shown in Fig. 1, the product development process of an airplane retrofit can be split into four phases: Customer Specifications, Preliminary Design, Detailed Design and Manufacture before Assembly. A fifth phase that we call the installation/production phase corresponds to all the operations of disassembly of old equipment and assembly of new ones into the airplane.

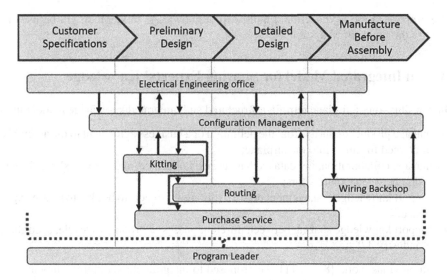

Fig. 1. The studied collaborative product development process

During all phases, several expert actors are involved and need to work together, collaboratively and simultaneously, for a successful outcome of the business agreement with the shortest time. The Program Leader oversees the ongoing project and validates technical design choices with the customer. He is the interface between customer and technical teams. The Electrical Engineering Office performs four types of plans during the entire process to answer to customer specifications, from the most general to the most detailed (Layout Diagram, Block Diagram, Schematic Diagram, Wiring Diagram). Each diagram and document is evaluated then published: the Configuration Management team retrieves these plans and documents, checks the parent-child links to validate the product structure and makes them available to other teams. The Kitting team oversees two documents (Preliminary Equipment List and Kit List) built by using product structure and makes the connection with the Purchase Service. Routing team retrieves the plans made by the Electrical Engineering Office, designs pathways and calculates the lengths of cables that will be installed on the aircraft. Its work is also used by the Kitting. Finally, the Wiring Backshop manufactures cables and pre-assembles equipment for later assembly operations in the aircraft, during the production phase.

The whole process is strongly collaborative, nevertheless, there is no collaborative tool for managing all data produced. The Electrical Engineering Office uses a wiring CAD system for design. The Configuration Management team uses a specific product structure manager tool. Validated diagrams from the CAD system are stored into a specific database to be viewed by Purchase Service and Production Department through the company ERP tool (SAP®). Other teams use Excel® files to work and to exchange with other teams.

Our challenge is to propose models then tools that will improve collaboration between all actors involved during the whole product life-cycle for the retrofit activity.

We propose in the next section a multi-expert knowledge model that will be used to specify the future PLM system.

3   An Integrated Model for Sharing Experts' Knowledge

In this situation of airplane retrofit, a structured and integrated knowledge model must:

- manage product maturity from the definition of a business agreement to the assembly of defined furniture into the airplane;
- manage collaboration, i.e. data exchanges and coherence, and activities' synchronisation between expert actors;
- support knowledge management between different projects to be able to re-use experience;
- support knowledge sharing between different phases of product lifecycle, according to industry 4.0 approach.

In previous work, [8, 10, 11], we proposed to integrate three different dimensions, product, process and organisation/collaboration, to structure an integrated knowledge model, called the PPO model. The objective of integrating such three dimensions is to support the management of the expert know-how during product development process and to enable the efficient coordination of product lifecycle. This knowledge model was studied in a mechanical context but this work had similar objectives with the airplane retrofit case study.

3.1   Product Modelling

Product knowledge is a major issue, generally based on a breakdown into several levels of abstraction such as in the FBS model (Function-Behaviour-Structure) proposed by [12]. It must support the possibility for design experts to define specific concepts and to share them in a simple way. But it must support also the management of product maturity in order that other expert actors may use the relevant information for their own activities.

In this specific domain of electrical engineering for aeronautics, the 'product' has not the same meaning as in mechanics. The product is a set of technical elements (wires, connectors, electrical systems, etc. but also assembled or bought systems), linked together. They are defined through several sets of drawings corresponding at different levels of maturity of the design process. For example, an assembled system may be a furniture, containing different bought systems connected with wires, connectors, etc. A bought system can be a power supply system, a routing system, a television or a phone.

We must consider this very specific aspect of electrical design: a technical element cannot be defined on a single drawing. One drawing will define several elements with heir connecting characteristics and an element is defined through several drawings. This set of elements and systems corresponds to a graph structure, and its complexity is very high due to their numerous occurrence: several thousands of items. To control this complexity actors generate different kind of diagrams but the validation is mainly manual for different experts. The knowledge model to be proposed must allow more automated control by integrating knowledge rules from experts.

As we can see in Fig. 2, product knowledge is then structured into the product dimension by two main concepts that are generic for all experts: the 'document' concept and the 'functional component' concept. As in [13], a PLM system manages product data and related documents even if some PLM systems are document-based systems, and others are clearly product structure-centred. A PLM dedicated to electrical engineering clearly needs to integrate both concepts to facilitate the management of data by the experts. The 'functional component' is always associated to a 'part' which represents its physical instantiation through a unique identification number. As a system, a 'functional component' can be self-decomposed. It is always 'connected' to other 'functional components'.

The 'Diagram' is the generic document designed or used by all experts, that can be decomposed into himself to detail the solutions, and that is associated to other 'diagrams' to manage the evolution of the solution according to FBS approach. Thus, an implemented diagram can be a layout diagram, then a block diagram, a schematic diagram, and finally a wiring diagram, according to the design progress from first customer specifications analysis to detailed design phase.

As many PLM systems [14], previous concepts are managed using 'lifecycle' concepts to control their maturity level. This is not represented in Fig. 1.

Then several expert concepts have been defined to enrich generic concepts. For example:

- 'Kitting' experts will define how a 'functional component' will be furnished using a 'supply type' concept.
- 'Routing' experts need a 'cable' concept to define the characteristics of the wires (sub-concept of the 'functional component' concept) that have been identified by electrical designers.
- 'Kitting' experts then add the manufacturing characteristics of this specific kind of 'functional component'/'part', then define the 'cable reel' i.e. the initial raw material used for producing the required 'cables'.
- Then 'Wiring backshop' experts generate 'cutting program' which is a specific 'document' that allows to produce all 'cables' from the 'cable reel'.
- These concepts are used again by the 'kitting' experts to prepare the 'cable reel' purchase by defining a 'supply scheduling' concept.

Such product dimension allows the different experts to achieve their specific business activities by formalising expert knowledge and sharing it throughout few shared concepts.

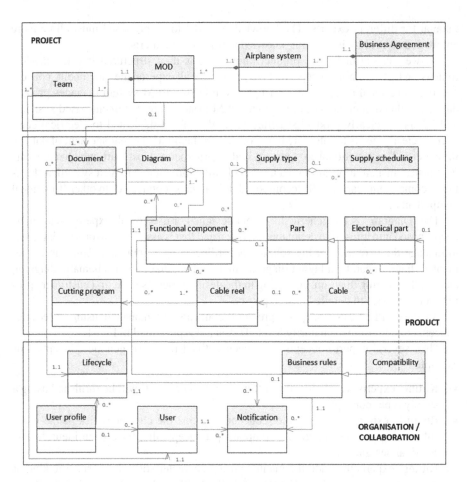

Fig. 2. An integrated knowledge model for electrical engineering in aeronautics

3.2 Process and Organisation/Collaboration Modelling

The process dimension is generally associated to project management concepts by characterising activity sequences [15]. In the case study, and due to the low maturity of the company, we have focused on the project structuring without implementing a formal process dimension. The project is then modelled through the 'business agreement' concept, and is decomposed into 'airplane system' concept which corresponds to a standard decomposition of an airplane into sub-systems impacted by customer specifications. Then each 'airplane system' is divided into 'MOD' concept which corresponds to a set of functional MODifications, according to customer specifications. This decomposition helps managing human resources by allocating experts ('team' concept) to specific 'MODs'. It helps also experts to search information by filtering on a single 'MOD'.

The organisation dimension must allow defining the different stakeholders and their expertise and facilitate collaboration between them all along the product lifecycle, as studied by [16]. Main concept is then 'user profile', which characterizes the different experts, their skills and their access rights to product information according to the phases of the 'product lifecycle', the status of product data and the 'MODs' they have in charge.

The aim of the proposed model is to improve the collective performance of the whole lifecycle. In the product dimension, we already formalise expert knowledge but we only consider knowledge corresponding to information produced by an expert. In order to improve collaboration, we propose now to formalise also rules and methods that can be captured from expert experience and that will automate activities with low added-value. We define an 'expert rule' concept that will formalise links between generic and expert concepts from product, project and organisation dimensions. A 'business rule' is used to detect specific and predefined events such as a change of maturity level of a 'document' and/or a 'functional component' then to start impacting actions to relevant experts. These events are described through a 'notification' action.

For example, when a schematic 'diagram' reaches the state "Released", a specific 'business rule' is activated first. Second the expert/'user' associated to the document is identified: here the 'kitting' user. Third it sends a notification to the 'kitting' user to inform that the document is available. Finally, the 'kitting' user edits the Preliminary Kit List and achieves its activities. This example is the most common way of using 'business rules'.

More generally, the 'business rules' mechanism allows automating the communication flows and the impacts of the solution maturity evolution for the different experts, as already studied in [17]. Some rules require additional concepts to manage more complex links such as in Fig. 1 an electronic part with a specific 'compatibility' rule.

4 Towards an Electrical Engineering PLM System

4.1 PLM Implementation

Actually, the PLM system is under development. Both architecture and business oriented Man-Machine Interfaces are defined. Generic and expert concepts are implemented. Automated business rules are implemented through the definition of new functions and they are integrated to existing functions in a transparent way: for example for automated evolution controls, coherency evaluation or impact evaluation. The implemented architecture is described in Fig. 3 and proposes an access through the CAD system (functions in white boxes) or through a Web-based interface (grey boxes). White-to-grey boxes designate functions that are available on both interfaces.

CAD interface is built for electrical design department, wiring and kitting whom tasks require a direct use of electrical diagrams. Web-based interface is dedicated to collaboration and proposes a dashboard customised for each expert profile. Standard viewer function, versioning and maturity management functions are implemented. Expert functions are available, as for example extraction of manufacturing diagrams by 'wiring backshop' experts. Specific standards management (e.g. libraries) and other business rules are also implemented.

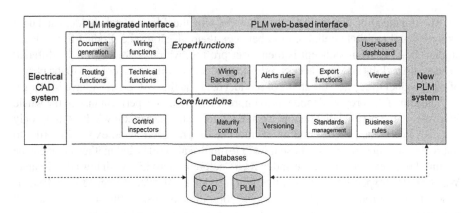

Fig. 3. Architecture of the implemented electrical PLM system

Figure 4 shows the integration of a new PLM function into the CAD system: on the top-right of the figure, four tabs correspond to the four types of diagram. For each tab, the different functions are listed below. Finally, on the bottom-right are indicated tasks depending on the context: here the expert (designer) has the possibility to change the maturity of the schematic diagram from 'work in progress' to 'frozen'. A specific business rule will then send a message to configuration management expert for diagram evaluation.

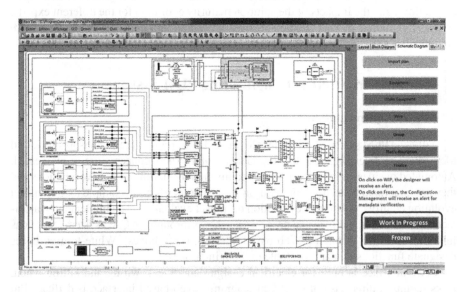

Fig. 4. CAD interface proposal for integrating Diagram generation and evolution

Web-based interface integrates a dashboard of the configuration management expert, where previous message is active. This interface integrates notifications, global overview of projects progress and available functions.

4.2 Synthesis

This integrated model provides the core data for developing a new PLM system, coupled with the used electrical CAD system. Product dimension allows managing generic product data and documents, controlling their evolution and the users' access. Expert data extends PLM functions by defining specific business data and associating it to generic product data.

This mechanism supports the definition of automated and parametric 'business rules', defined in the organisation/collaboration dimension. Rules are based on links analysis and cross-referencing between several types of data. Such rules introduce automated communication between experts and flexibility to the system. It improves collaboration between experts in a pro-active way by anticipating the expert tasks during the whole development process.

A generic retrofit project generates several thousands of wires and connectors. The coherency of the design, the liability of the solutions and the adequacy with customer specifications were made manually by different experts. Therefore, less errors and reduced development process time are expected with the implementation of the proposed knowledge model.

Nevertheless the complete system still has be evaluated in real situations. Actually, functions integrated to the CAD system have been recently delivered to the company. First results show that all expert rules associated to automated controls generates a qualitative time saving but no quantitative or qualitative study is available. PLM Web interface is still not implemented into the company.

4.3 Future Work

In this paper we have stated on the first results of our research. Proposing an integrated knowledge model then implementing it through a new PLM system dedicated to electrical engineering builds a strong basis for further research advances.

First work axis relies on the integration of knowledge capitalisation and re-use mechanisms (e.g. experience feedback [18, 19]). One of the most performant methods to implement industrial experience feedback is based on the instrumentation of problem solving methodologies to formalize experiences in the knowledge base [20]. Experience feedback is a useful tool which fits perfectly with the continuous improvement programs implemented in almost all the industrial companies. Indeed, it allows to identify progression tracks by analysing past experiences and to propagate the benefits to similar situations. In a future paper we will propose how project experience can be modelled, implemented and re-used.

We also focused on the product development phases and we do not consider the final phase of installation/production. We have to consider first that the development phases, from the design to the preparation of all components to be assembled, is done without the physical plane. Everything must be ready when the airplane comes to be retrofitted. Operators often discover the real situation of the plane at this moment and modifications are required on the design, and on the furniture. The evaluation of the plane situation by the operators is a long and manual phase that can be improved and time-reduced.

Moreover, when operators assemble on the plane the new systems, they spend a lot of time to identify the different locations where the systems, wires, connectors... have to be installed. They can be helped to do these tasks better. Since middle 90', such pre-industrial systems where develop, introducing augmented reality technology on them [21, 22, 23], but technological environment was not ready. Today it is, and new projects, like SUMATRA project, started in 2016 with same CAD editor, can help improving operators' tasks. The aim of this project is to support industrial maintenance operators in their work around three main principles; having contextual information from multiple Information Systems, visualise and manipulate them thanks to modern technologies like augmented reality, and be able to interact with a remote expert thanks to NICT.

Our work will be to adapt such techniques to "mobile terminals" in order to have a new way of interacting and to visualise both the "real view" of the operators, looking at specific elements and systems directly in the plane, and the "virtual view" of the corresponding elements and systems as known by the PLM system. This work will completely integrate the production phase as an operational phase of the product lifecycle management strategy of the company. Moreover, it applies several technologies and methods fostered by Industry 4.0 approach to transform step by step the studied company towards a more digital company.

5   Conclusion

In this paper we study how knowledge modelling and computer-supported collaboration participate to the industry 4.0. Our work is based on aeronautical context, for electrical companies. We have proposed an integrated knowledge model composed of three dimensions: product modelling, project modelling and organization/collaboration modelling. We identify generic and expert knowledge and automated mechanisms modelled through 'business rules' in order to support pro-active collaboration. This model is actually used by the CAD editor to implement its corresponding PLM systems. We will be involved in the experiments. Further work will concern the generalisation of such model to be applicable in non-aeronautical contexts.

Acknowledgments. This work was supported by French Interministerial Unique Funding. We thank all partners from 2π-MCO project, and especially Jean-Jacques Péré-Laperne, as project leader, Eric Zago, manager of the Electrical Design department, with whom we worked deeply and friendly, and Anthony Cianni who made a great job in our team.

References

1. Chen, L.: Development of a multidisciplinary collaborative design system. Mater. Sci. Forum **628–629**, 31–36 (2009)
2. Bouikni, N., Desrochers, A., Rivest, L.: A product feature evolution validation model for engineering change management. J. Comput. Inf. Sci. Eng. **6**, 188–196 (2006)

3. Abramovic, M., Bellalouna, F.: Integration and complexity management within the mechatronics product development. In: Takata, S., Umeda, Y. (eds.) Advances in Life Cycle Engineering for Sustainable Manufacturing Businesses, pp. 113–118. Springer, London (2007). https://doi.org/10.1007/978-1-84628-935-4_20

4. Girard, P., Robin, V.: Analysis of collaboration for project design management. Comput. Ind. **57**(8–9), 817–826 (2006)

5. Nosenzo, V., Tornincasa, S., Bonisoli, E., Brino, M.: Open questions on Product Lifecycle Management (PLM) with CAD/CAE integration. Int. J. Interact. Design Manuf. (IJIDeM). **8**(2), 91–107 (2014). https://doi.org/10.1007/s12008-013-0184-1, Springer, Paris

6. Pinquie, R., Rivest, L., Segonds, F., Veron, P.: An illustrated glossary of ambiguous PLM terms used in discrete manufacturing. Int. J. Product Lifecycle Manag. **8**(2), 142–171 (2015)

7. Jones, D., Chanchevrier, N., McMahon, C., Hicks, B.: A strategy for artefact-based information navigation in large engineering organisations. In: DS 80-10 Proceedings of the 20th International Conference on Engineering Design (ICED 2015). Design Information and Knowledge Management, Milan, vol. 10, pp. 143–152 (2015)

8. Robin, V., Merlo, C., Pol, G., Girard, P.: Management of a design system in a collaborative design environment using PEGASE. In: Heisig, P., Clarkson, P.J., Vajna, S. (eds.) Modelling and Management of Engineering Processes, 189-200. Springer, London (2010)

9. McMahon, C., Lowe, A., Culley, S.: Knowledge management in engineering design: personalization and codification. J. Eng. Des. **15**(4), 307–325 (2004)

10. Noel, F., Roucoules, L.: The PPO design model with respect to digital enterprise technologies among product life cycle. Int. J. Comput. Integr. Manuf. **21**(2), 139–145 (2008)

11. Yesilbas, L.G., Rose, B., Lombard, M.: Specification of a repository to support collaborative knowledge exchanges in IPPOP project. Comput. Ind. **57**(8–9), 690–710 (2006)

12. Umeda, Y., Takeda, H., Tomiyama, T., Yoshikawa, H.: Function, behaviour and structure. In: Applications of Artificial Intelligent in Engineering. Springer, Berlin (1990)

13. Mickaël, D., Frantz, R.: What does PLMS (product lifecycle management systems) manage: data or documents? complementarity and contingency for SMEs. Comput. Industry **75**, 140–150 (2016). ISSN 0166-3615

14. Terzi, S., Bouras, A., Dutta, D., Garetti, M., Kiritsis, D.: Product lifecycle management – from its history to its new role. Int. J. Product Lifecycle Manag. **4**(4), 360–389 (2010)

15. Ullman, D.G.: The Mechanical Design Process. McGraw-Hill, New-York (2009)

16. Belkadi, F., Troussier, N., Eynard, B., Bonjour, E.: Collaboration based on Product Lifecycles Interoperability for Extended Enterprise. Int. J. Interact. Des. Manuf. **4**(3), 169–179 (2010)

17. Wehbe, A., Merlo, C., Pilnière, V.: Integrating competence management into a coupled project-system design management. In: Emmanouilidis, C., Taisch, M., Kiritsis, D. (eds.) APMS 2012. IFIP AICT, vol. 397, pp. 630–637. Springer, Heidelberg (2013). https://doi.org/10.1007/978-3-642-40352-1_79

18. Rakoto, H., Hermosillo, J., Ruet, M.: Integration of experience based decision support in industrial processes. In: IEEE International Conference on Systems, Man and Cybernetics, vol. 7 (2002)

19. Villeneuve, E., Béler, C., Pérès, F., Geneste, L.: Hybridization of statistical and cognitive experience feedbacks to perform risk assessment. In: IEEE International Conference on Industrial Engineering and Engineering Management (IEEM), Hong-Kong, China, pp. 10–13 (2012)

20. Bejarano, R., Camilo, J. Coudert, T., Vareilles, E., Geneste, L., Aldanondo, M., Abeille, J.: Case-based reasoning and system design: an integrated approach based on ontology and preference modeling. Artif. Intell. Eng. Design Anal. Manuf. **28**(1), 49–69 (2014). ISSN 0890-0604

21. Caudell, T.P., Mizell, D.W.: Augmented reality: an application of heads-up display technology to manual manufacturing processes. In: Proceedings of the Twenty-Fifth Hawaii International Conference on System Sciences, vol. 2, pp. 659–669 (1992)
22. ARVIKA: Augmented reality for development, production, servicing (1999). http://www.arvika.de
23. ARMAR: Augmented Reality for Maintenance and Repair (2007). http://graphics.cs.columbia.edu/projects/armar/

Development of a Smart Assembly Data Model

Luiz Fernando C. S. Durão[1], Sebastian Haag[2], Reiner Anderl[2], Klaus Schützer[3],
and Eduardo Zancul[1(✉)]

[1] University of São Paulo, São Paulo, Brazil
{luiz.durao,ezancul}@usp.br
[2] Technische Universität Darmstadt, Darmstadt, Germany
{haag,anderl}@dik.tu-darmstadt.de
[3] Methodist University of Piracicaba, Piracicaba, Brazil
schuetzer@scpm.unimep.br

Abstract. Current technological advances pave the way for highly flexible production processes within Cyber-Physical Production Systems (CPPS). In a CPPS, every component being produced may be represented by a virtual data model containing its own unique information. Components are also information carriers with communication features enabled by an Internet-based exchange of information. The exchange of information between components and with the production system may happen over the whole manufacturing process. The availability of detailed information about every component supports the implementation of optimized assembly processes, called Smart Assembly of smart components. Smart Assembly is an approach to assembling different components according to unique specifications of every product variant, and considering the most efficient combination of components for each assembly. Therefore, a structured component data model considering data storage and data access is needed. However, for the Smart Assembly of smart components, the underlying data structure and processes have to be developed. The objective of this paper is to propose a data structure to enable the Smart Assembly of components in an assemble-to-order production scenario. To achieve the proposed objective, two use cases have been developed to simulate the Smart Assembly of smart components.

Keywords: Smart Assembly · Smart components · Industrie 4.0

1 Introduction

Current market trends indicate increasing demand for tailor-made products and solutions, with reduced delivery times [1]. The manufacturing process in this scenario involves dealing with a great variety of products [2]. Each client provides unique information so that the product can be tailored to its requirements, challenging the assumptions of traditional mass production [3, 4]. The increase in product variety, provided by the individualized products, may decrease internal operation performance [2, 5]. A major issue for the industry is to offer customized products without substantial impact on final

© IFIP International Federation for Information Processing 2017
Published by Springer International Publishing AG 2017. All Rights Reserved
J. Ríos et al. (Eds.): PLM 2017, IFIP AICT 517, pp. 655–666, 2017.
https://doi.org/10.1007/978-3-319-72905-3_58

costs both at the manufacturing and distribution of the products [2]. Therefore, new approaches and solutions are required for manufacturing and assembly.

The assembly process is one of the most relevant steps to high product variety [6, 7]. Several approaches, methodologies and techniques have been researched and developed over the years for manufacturing assembly process planning. The historical development of assembly can be organized into three main phases: (i) manual assembly; (ii) line assembly, introduced by Ford; (iii) flexible, semi-automated assembly. More recently, the assembly process has been impacted by new technologies related to process control, information technology, and networking – leading to what can be called Smart Assembly. A more agile and responsive assembly process strategy has to be developed to increase the efficiency of the process [7].

Internet technologies, information exchange and communication between people, products, machines, and resources are applied to a networked environment of physical objects and their virtual representation, resulting in an Internet of Things [8] – as considered by the initiative *Industrie 4.0*. These technologies and elements may be the key to create a Smart Assembly process. However, the amount of data generated during production and assembly in a connected environment requires a proper data structure to collect and process the information correctly.

The objective of this paper is to propose an initial data structure to enable the Smart Assembly of components in a manufacturing scenario. The scenario has been implemented in two use cases representing a regular assembly process, and a Smart Assembly process. These use cases simulate an Internet-based collaboration between the central factory and a distributed production site located respectively in Germany and Brazil.

The paper is structured in five sections. After the introduction of the research topic in Sect. 1, Sect. 2 provides a state of the art literature review. In Sect. 3, the research approach is presented. Section 4 contains a detailed scenario description, discussing the most important technical aspects and testing procedures. The conclusion and an outlook on further research needs are discussed in Sect. 5.

2   Data Model Requirements – Literature Review

In this section, the state of the art concerning Industrie 4.0 (Sect. 2.1), assembly process (Sect. 2.2), and Smart Assembly (Sect. 2.3) are presented.

2.1   Industrie 4.0

The term "Industrial Revolution" refers to a profound change not only in the manufacturing methods and tools, but also on the way that society interacts with the manufacturing systems [9].

In the first industrial revolution, manufacturing was mechanized by steam power. In the second, production was marked by electrification and division of labor. Starting from the 1970s up to now, the third industrial revolution has been characterized by rapid advancements in Information Technology (IT), including automated manufacturing processes [8]. The adoption of Advanced Manufacturing Technology in connected environments, creating smart factories, is currently triggering a new industrial revolution (called fourth industrial revolution or *Industrie 4.0*) enabling the integration of information from various sources, and the production of items that are more complex, in reduced time [8].

Advanced Manufacturing Technologies (AMT) are computer assisted technologies used by industrial companies to produce their products [10, 11]. The term AMT can be described as a group of technologies used to monitor and control manufacturing activities (e.g. storing and handling data). Considering that the assembly process may represent up to 50% of total production time, the adoption of AMT in the assembly may considerable increase efficiency and efficacy [7, 12, 13].

Modern and reconfigurable manufacturing systems, as proposed by *Industrie 4.0*, facilitate complex assembly processes, enabling the communication and matching of components in a smart environment [14].

2.2 Assembly Process

Assembly process is the process of connecting components or subsets of components to form a more complex end-product [7].

A proper assembly process can increase product quality, decrease the costs and time to market [15]. These characteristics are particularly important in a scenario in which the client requires different variants of products, tailored to its specific needs [1, 16].

One of the biggest challenges regarding the assembly process is the optimized matching between components to be assembled. In manufacturing environments, the components are produced based on nominal dimensions with an additional tolerance range according to the product specification. As result of the manufacturing process, the produced components have real dimensions [17], that may be optimally combined for assembly.

That situation is caused by dimensional variability propagation in every manufacturing process within the production system. It may create compliance difficulties such as slack differences involving the assembly of different components [18].

These differences include imperfections in the measurement instruments and machines, material deformation and operation flaws. Thus, it is necessary to determine and establish deviations within which the parts produced can still operate and function properly.

Those deviations constitute the upper and lower mechanical tolerance of a measurement or dimension. It is expected that, given a statistical margin, the parts produced have dimensions according to their nominal size considering the tolerance interval [19]. However, the tolerance interval is not the only factor to be considered for the best matching of components [1].

The material analysis may also be considered when treating the tolerance domains. Different methods of production and assembly of components must take the material's behavior into consideration. Stress and strength analyses can be used to observe effects of geometry, orientation, and thickness, so that it may be possible to determine types of adjustment and tolerance intervals [20].

To provide an optimal global tolerance of the assembly components, selective assembly selects a better mating pair by measuring, marking, and pairing the components accordingly [21]. However, the selective assembly continues to be a manual process. In this case, the automation of the assembly line is related to assembly itself, not to the selection of components.

As product variety increases in more customizable production systems, assembly methods and systems should be designed to handle such variety [6]. The complexity of those assembly processes increases with the demand of different variants, since the matching of components depends not only on tolerance intervals, but also on the part characteristics and specification.

Nerakae, Uangpairoj, and Chamniprasart [21] propose the use of machine vision to for selecting different components on an assembly line, representing initial efforts on automatic selection of different parts. However, it does not considers the best pairing between the components. Smart Assembly is being considered to promote an automatic selective assembly in the context of *industrie 4.0* [22].

2.3 Smart Assembly

"Smart Assembly is the incorporation of learning, reconfigurability, human-machine collaboration, and model-based techniques into assembly systems to improve productivity, cost, flexibility, responsiveness and quality" [23].

The development of "Smart Assembly" (SA) brings changes to the current assembly processes by re-inventing both its engineering and operations, considering the new technological and information environments of the manufacturers. In recent years, the further development of *Industrie 4.0* promoted the technology required for Smart Assembly.

SA goes far beyond traditional mechanization and automation to exploit the effective collaboration of man and machine in engineering and operations. It integrates highly skilled, multidisciplinary work teams with self-integrating and adaptive assembly processes. It unifies "virtual" and "real-time" information to achieve dramatic improvements in productivity, lead-time, agility, and quality. The vision for Smart Assembly is a system consisting of the optimal balance of people and automation interacting effectively, efficiently, and safely [24].

Therefore, a Smart Assembly system relies on its following characteristics [24]:

- Empowered, and knowledgeable people: skilled and enabled workforce to take the best overall decisions;
- Collaboration: between people and automation;
- Configurable: easy to reconfigure and reprogram the system due to changes in products, equipment, and software;
- Model and data driven: feasibility of modeling and simulating changes and actions virtually to evaluate, optimize and validate before definitive/costly implementations;
- Capable of learning: prevent repeated mistakes and avoid new ones.

Linked to the previous characteristics, there are some technological requirements to enable a successful Smart Assembly system: intelligent flexible assembly processes, equipment, and tools; an accurate, easy-to-use, persuasive, and persistent virtual capability; real-time actionable information for man and machine. In other words, these requirements focus mainly on multi-functionality, effectiveness, and reliability of the new technologies. Furthermore, the main challenge of the development of Smart Assembly is not the required enabling technologies themselves, but rather the integration of technologies.

The design of Smart Assembly processes, from the equipment and tools perspective, is simplified by adopting modular and multifunctional assembly components, i.e. components that have a specific or a combined set of functionalities that can be easily attached or detached to the project, with quick identification of consequences of the modifications on the other modules. The modularity grants to the Smart Assembly process flexibility and possibility of incremental and regular upgrades and updates (modularity is needed, given the common changes to manufacturing due to *Industrie 4.0*). It appeals to iterations of enhancement, learning, and adaptations, providing substantial and constant benefits related to the quality, effectiveness, and efficiency of products and processes.

Strang and Anderl [25] propose an Assembly Data Model to manage the large amount of data that is generated during the Smart Assembly. This model is composed of five work packages: Assembly Process Data, Product Data, Resources Data, Organization Data, and Deviation Management. It proposes the exchange of information between the assembly station and one component to be assembled, and clusters the information based on activities.

Therefore, the Assembly Data Model is associated with the Component Data Model and a new combination of information is stored for the assembly process [25].

The model proposed by Strang and Anderl [25] does not consider the best mating components, leaving space for improvements at the clustering of information and mating analysis.

3   Methodology

The applied research approach is based on designing, implementing, and testing a Smart Assembly scenario. Besides, a literature review was conducted to define the preliminary requirements for Smart Assembly. The scenario simulates the application of *Industrie 4.0* concepts and technologies for communication. The focus of the broad research is in the data model requirements for Smart Assembly. This paper focuses on the creation of a preliminary data model for Smart Assembly. Two different scenarios were implemented and simulated: a regular assembly process; and a Smart Assembly process.

The scenario was implemented at the Technical University of Darmstadt (TUD), Germany, the University of São Paulo (USP) and the Methodist University of Piracicaba (UNIMEP), Brazil. The scenario implementation is part of a broader research project within the research collaboration framework in manufacturing called BRAGECRIM (Brazilian-German Collaborative Research Initiative in Manufacturing).

The scenario focuses on the production of a pneumatic cylinder. The pneumatic cylinder is composed of two parts, produced separately. This part is a standard item already used at the Center for Industrial Productivity (CiP) located at TUD. Simplifications were made to the model to facilitate production with the equipment available and to cope with intellectual property requirements, as the part used at CiP is real.

Through those scenarios, it is possible to gather the advantages and disadvantages of each assembly alternative. The comparison is made between the "regular assembly" model, which refers to a system that would be utilized nowadays and the "Smart Assembly" model, which would be theoretically implemented in a smart factory that follows the vision of *Industrie 4.0*.

In the first scenario (Fig. 1), the central factory located at TUD in Germany sends the production order to both factories in Brazil (Site 1 and Site 2). The manufacturing process begins and is monitored by the central factory. After the parts are produced, they go through quality control, which indicates if the part is suitable for use. It is important to notice that in this model, the central factory has no control over the quality inspection.

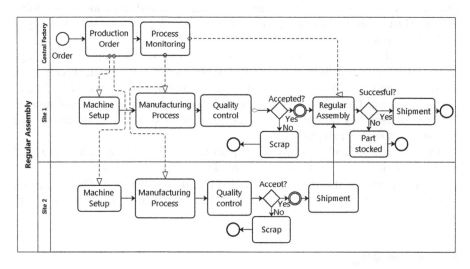

Fig. 1. Scenario 1 – Regular Assembly

Afterwards, the parts from Site 2 are shipped to Site 1, where the assembly is held and feedback is sent to Germany. When successful, the assembled product may be forwarded and shipped to customers.

In the second scenario (Fig. 2), the German central factory sends the production order to the factories in Brazil. Then the manufacturing processes is triggered (Site 1 and Site 2). After parts are produced, they go through a precise measurement and registration system, which send all the information to the central factory. The relevant aspect here is that the quality control fulfillment is held remotely in the central factory (in Germany), giving full control to the central factory over which parts should be accepted and which should be discarded or remanufactured.

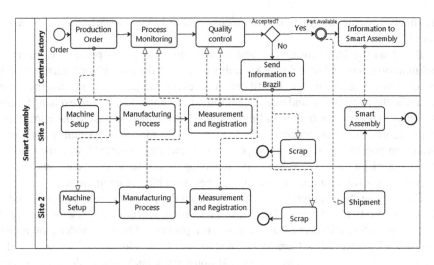

Fig. 2. Scenario 2 – Smart Assembly

After the quality inspection, the information is sent back to Brazil, indicating which parts should be forwarded to the assembly process. The parts from Site 2 are then shipped to Site 1 where the Smart Assembly takes place. Finally, the assembled products are shipped to the customers.

The development of those scenarios provided context and requirements for the development of a preliminary data model for Smart Assembly.

4 Preliminary Data Model

Based on the literature review, requirements for Smart Assembly were identified. Table 1 presents the requirements, the type of the requirement, and the requirement's source.

Table 1. Requirements for Smart Assembly

Requirement	Type	Source
Material information	Specification	[18]
Equipments and machines	Specification	[18]
Tolerance	Specification	[19]
Variant information	Order	[1]
Unique identification	Order	[26]
Real-time information	Process	[24]
Flexibility	Process	[22]
Capable of learning	Process	[24]

Requirement types are: Specification - related to the nominal characteristics of the product as nominal dimensions, material, equipments and machines; Order - related to the clients' specific information; and Process - related to the manufacturing characteristics [1].

Based on the literature review and on the simulation, it is possible to design a preliminary data model for a Smart Assembly process. A data model for Smart Assembly process must contain a unique identification for every component, the geometric information of the component, and tolerance information. It must be able to exchange information with other components and process this information to ensure the correct and best matching of the components. Thus, a data model for Smart Assembly is an integrated component data model, as proposed by Picard and Anderl [1], with the addition of a new work package for exchange and receiving data from different components, and processing this information for ensuring the best matching of components.

Considering the requirements gathered, the model proposed by Picard and Anderl [1] is extended to a preliminary Data Model for Smart Assembly as presented in Fig. 3. Combining different information on a new work package. The data model is organized into six work packages: the Core Model, that handles basic administrative tasks and also provides an extension interface for the additional work packages: Order-related Data, Rights Management Data, Production Data, Identification & Specifications Data, and Assembly Data.

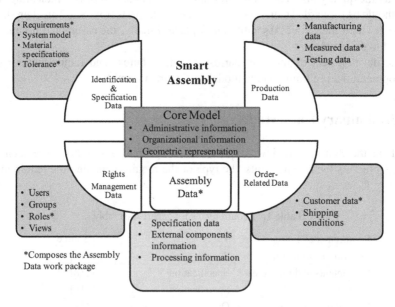

Fig. 3. Data Model - Smart Assembly - Adapted from [1]

Thus, a Smart Assembly data model is composed by its Identification and Specifications Data, Production Data, Rights Management Data, Order-Related Data, and Assembly Data. All work packages are connected by an identification number as a primary key (core) to connect information over the assembly model.

Identification and Specification carries the requirements of the components itself and of the whole product, leading to the next steps of the assembly process. This enables traceability of the component's production history and allows the optimization of future products and production processes [27]. Besides, it carries the tolerance information, used for a mating analysis.

The Order-Related Data captures customer-specific requests and, therefore, enables customized production of components within a smart production environment. For a smart assembly process, the Order-Related Data is important for providing different combinations of components, according to customer request. It becomes the primary assembly criteria, matching the different components of the same customer. Besides, it provides the shipping information.

The information contained at this two proposed work packages (Identification & Specification Data and Order-Related Data) are inserted both at Product Data and Process Data in the model suggested by Strang and Anderl [25], which clusters the data by the type of activity (assembly or manufacturing, for example). This type of clustering increases the complexity of data storage once that the activity becomes a primary key over the type of information.

Production Data capture the characteristics of the specific component with data originating from manufacturing execution systems (MES). Process data such as responsible worker, utilized machines, workstations, and tools together with testing data, such as measurements, are captured to constitute actual production activities. This information is associated with the Resources Data suggested by Strang and Anderl [25], once they carry the machines and workforce that are required for the assembly process.

To ensure that only authorized parties can access and modify the data, the Rights Management Data tracks all user (human users and smart systems) and user groups (departments, organizations, etc.) of component data together with their respective privileges, what is directly associated with Organization Data suggested by Strang and Anderl [25].

Finally, the Assembly Data work package is responsible for the communication between the component that is to be assembled and the component that is to be received. It is responsible for indicating the best match between two different components considering the product tolerance, the product material, the client specification, and the needed assembly. This work package improves the model proposed by Strang and Anderl [25], as it enables an intelligent matching process.

The Assembly Data work package collects the ID information from the part to be assembled via RFID or QRCode. This information is a primary key and it is used to track the part. Afterwards, the system searches for the specifications of that part, storing the actual dimension and the mating component. Once it is known which part to search for, both for the Order-Related Data and for Identification & Specification Data, the system searches for different parts of the required type. Each part is submitted to a 360° image analysis, allowing the part to be compared with the customer data and requirements, producing a best matching according to two criteria: first, Order-Related data, and second, an automatic selective assembly process. The Assembly Model compares the optimized matching sending this information back to the component data model, providing the best fit in an efficient way. Besides, considering that the model possess all different measures from the mating components, the best combination is automatically calculated during the process, decreasing re-manufacturing needs, once that the remaining measures are known.

Figure 4 brings in detail the Assembly Data work package represented by an UML diagram. UML models provide stereotypes and constraints, together with syntax and semantics of the elements [28].

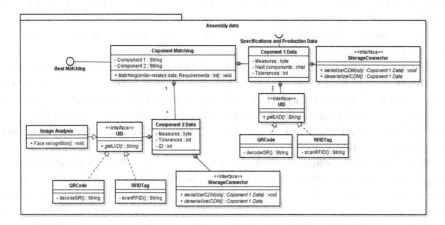

Fig. 4. Smart Assembly

It is important to highlight that the Assembly Data work package is fast responsive and provides real-time information indicating the part to be assembled and the best mating components, automating a selective assembly process. Besides, it can be adapted according to clients' specification, considering that the Order-Related Data is one of the prior matching characteristic. Therefore, instead of having an assembly model containing a Component Data Model, the proposed model is a combination of the Component Data Model and the assembly specific data, clustering the data based on the type of information. This supports a more accurate traceability, going from the type of information to the activity, not the other way around. Also, it improves the global tolerance by automatically selecting the best mating components.

5 Conclusions

The research initiative *Industrie 4.0* aims to be a driving force of the 4th Industrial Revolution. Its purpose is to create an intelligent production chain connecting the physical product with data collected over the product lifecycle and turning this data into information. Each client provides unique information so that the product can be tailored to its requirements, challenging the assumptions of traditional mass production. A major issue for industry is to offer customized products without substantial impact on final costs at both the manufacturing and distribution of the products [2]. Therefore, new approaches and solutions are required for manufacturing and assembly.

The assembly process is one of the most relevant steps to high product variety. A Smart Assembly Data Model aims to create a representation of the communication between the component and its surrounding environment over its entire lifecycle. It contains a unique identification for every component, the geometric information of the component, tolerance information. It must also be able to exchange information with other components and process this information to ensure the correct and best matching of the components.

This paper represents the initial effort on the development of a Smart Assembly Data Model within the collaborative research project "Smart Components within Smart Production Processes and Environments - SCoPE" supported by the BRAGECRIM Program. It improves previous assembly models by considering an automatic selection of the best mating pairs and clustering data by the type of information. Next steps in this research stream include further development of the Smart Assembly Data Model, prototypical implementation, and advanced scenario testing.

Acknowledgments. The authors thank the Coordination for the Improvement of Higher Education Personnel (Capes), the Brazilian National Council for Scientific and Technological Development (CNPq), and the German Research Foundation (DFG) for supporting related projects. The authors also thank the companies involved for providing real case applications.

References

1. Piccard, A., Anderl, R.: Integrated component data model for smart production planning. In: 19° Seminário Internacional de Alta Tecnologia (2014)
2. ElMaraghy, H., Schuh, G., Elmaraghy, W., Piller, F., Schönsleben, P., Tseng, M., Bernard, A.: Product variety management. CIRP Ann. - Manuf. Technol. **62**, 629–652 (2013)
3. Salvador, F., De Holan, P.M., Piller, F.: Cracking the code of mass customization. MIT Sloan Manag. Rev. **50**(3), 71 (2009)
4. Zipkin, P.: The limits of mass customization. MIT Sloan Manag. Rev. **42**, 1–7 (2001)
5. Salvador, F., Forza, C., Rungtusanatham, M.: Modularity, product variety, production volume, and component sourcing: theorizing beyond generic prescriptions. J. Oper. Manag. **20**, 549–575 (2002)
6. Hu, S.J., Ko, J., Weyand, L., Elmaraghy, H.A., Lien, T.K., Koren, Y., Bley, H., Chryssolouris, G., Nasr, N., Shpitalni, M.: Assembly system design and operations for product variety. CIRP Ann. Manuf. Technol. **60**(2), 715–733 (2011)
7. ElMaraghy, H., ElMaraghy, W.: Smart adaptable assembly systems. Procedia CIRP **44**, 4–13 (2016)
8. Kagermann, H., Wahlster, W., Helbig, J.: Recommendations for implementing the strategic initiative INDUSTRIE 4.0. Final Rep. Ind. 4.0 WG, no, p. 82, April 2013
9. Hobsbawn, E.: The Age of Revolution, vol. 39 (1961)
10. Ariss, S., Raghunathan, T., Kunnathar, A.: Factors affecting the adoption of advanced manufacturing technology in small firms. S.A.M. Adv. Manag. J. **65**, 14 (2000)
11. Sun, H.: Current and future patterns of using advanced manufacturing technologies. Technovation **11**, 631–641 (2000)
12. Boyer, K., Pagell, M.: Measurement issues in empirical research: improving methods of operations strategy and advanced manufacturing technology. J. Oper. Manag. **18**, 361–374 (2000)

13. Kotha, S.: Strategy, manufacturing structure and advanced manufacturing technology. In: National Conference of the Academy of Management (1991)
14. Koren, Y., Shpitalni, M.: Design of reconfigurable manufacturing systems. J. Manuf. Syst. 29(4), 130–141 (2010)
15. Wang, H.P., Li, J.K.: Computer-Aided Process Planning. Elsevier, North Holland (1991)
16. Mourtzis, D., Doukas, M.: Design and planning of manufacturing networks for mass customisation and personalisation: challenges and outlook. Procedia CIRP 19, 1–13 (2014). https://doi.org/10.1016/j.procir.2014.05.004
17. Rajput, R.K.: A Textbook of Manufacturing Technology (Manufacturing Processes). Laxmi Publications, New Delhi (2007)
18. Camelio, J., Hu, S.J., Ceglarek, D.: Modeling variation propagation of multi-station assembly systems with compliant parts. J. Mech. Des. 125, 673–681 (2003)
19. Seo, H.S., Kwak, B.M.: Efficient statistical tolerance analysis for general distributions using three-point information. Int. J. Prod. Res. 40(4), 931–944 (2002)
20. Camanho, P.P., Matthews, F.L.: Stress analysis and strength prediction of mechanically fastened joints in FRP: a review. Compos. Part A Appl. Sci. Manuf. 28(6), 529–547 (1997)
21. Zhang, Y., Yin, Y., Yang, M.: A new selective assembly approach for remanufacturing of mating parts. In: 40th International Conference on Computers and Industrial Engineering: Soft Computing Techniques for. Advanced Manufacturing and Service Systems, CIE40 2010 (2010)
22. Liu, M., Ma, J., Lin, L., Ge, M., Wang, Q., Liu, C.: Intelligent assembly system for mechanical products and key technology based on internet of things. J. Intell. Manuf. 28(2), 271–299 (2014)
23. IMTI - NIST, A Report on Smart Assembly (2006)
24. Slotwinski, J.A., Tilove, R.B.: Smart assembly: Industry needs and challenges. In: Workshop on Performance Metrics for Intelligent Systems, pp. 271–276 (2007)
25. Strang, D., Anderl, R.: Assembly process driven component data model in cyber-physical production systems. In: World Congress on Engineering and Computer Science, vol. II, pp. 22–24 (2014)
26. Takata, S., Kimura, F., Van Houten, F.J.A.M., Westkämper, E.: Maintenance: changing role in life cycle management. CIRP Ann. Manuf. Technol. 53(2), 643–655 (2004)
27. Durão, L.F.C.S., Eichhorn, H., Anderl, R., Schützer, K., de Senzi Zancul, E.: Integrated component data model based on UML for smart components lifecycle management: a conceptual approach. In: Bouras, A., Eynard, B., Foufou, S., Thoben, K.-D. (eds.) PLM 2015. IFIP AICT, vol. 467, pp. 13–22. Springer, Cham (2016). https://doi.org/10.1007/978-3-319-33111-9_2
28. Tang, X., Yun, H.: Data model for quality in product lifecycle. Comput. Ind. 59(2–3), 167–179 (2008)

Managing Maturity States in a Collaborative Platform for the iDMU of Aeronautical Assembly Lines

Domingo Morales-Palma[1(✉)], Ignacio Eguía[2], Manuel Oliva[3], Fernando Mas[3], and Carpóforo Vallellano[1]

[1] Department of Mechanical Engineering and Manufacturing, University of Seville, Seville, Spain
{dmpalma,carpofor}@us.es
[2] Department of Industrial Management, University of Seville, Seville, Spain
ies@us.es
[3] PLM Methods, Process and Tools, Airbus, Sevilla, Spain
{manuel.oliva,fernando.mas}@airbus.com

Abstract. Collaborative Engineering aims to integrate both functional and industrial design. This goal requires integrating the design processes, the design teams and using a single common software platform to hold all the stakeholders contributions. Airbus company coined the concept of the industrial Digital Mock Up (iDMU) as the necessary unique deliverable to perform the design process with a unique team. Previous virtual manufacturing projects confirmed the potential of the iDMU to improve the industrial design process in a collaborative engineering environment. This paper presents the methodology and preliminary results for the management of the maturity states of the iDMU with all product, process and resource information associated with the assembly of an aeronautical component. The methodology aims to evaluate the suitability of a PLM platform to implement the iDMU in the creation of a control mechanism that allows a collaborative work.

Keywords: Product and process maturity · industrial Digital Mock-Up (iDMU) Digital manufacturing · Digital factory · PLM

1 Introduction

Reducing product development time, costs and quality problems can be achieve through effective collaboration across distributed and multidisciplinary design teams. This collaboration requires a computational framework which effectively enables capture, representation, retrieval and reuse of product knowledge. Product Lifecycle Management (PLM) refers to this enabling framework to help connect, organize, control, manage, track, consolidate and centralize all the mission-critical information that affects a product and the associate processes and resources. PLM offers a process to streamline collaboration and communication between product stakeholders, engineering, design, manufacturing, quality and other key disciplines.

© IFIP International Federation for Information Processing 2017
Published by Springer International Publishing AG 2017. All Rights Reserved
J. Ríos et al. (Eds.): PLM 2017, IFIP AICT 517, pp. 667–676, 2017.
https://doi.org/10.1007/978-3-319-72905-3_59

Collaboration between product and process design teams has the following advantages for the company: reduction of time required to perform tasks; improvement of the ability to solve complex problems; increase of the ability to generate creative alternatives; discussion of each alternative to select as viable and to make decisions; communication improvement; learning; personal satisfaction; and encouraging innovation [1]. However, collaboration processes need to be explicitly designed and managed to maximize the positive results of such an effort.

Group interaction and cooperation requires four aspects to be considered: people have to exchange information (communication), organize the work (coordination), operate together in a collective workspace (group memory) and be informed about what is happening and get the necessary information (awareness).

Maturity models have been designed to assess the maturity of a selected domain based on a comprehensive set of criteria [2]. These models have progressive maturity levels, allowing the organization to plan how to reach higher maturity levels and to evaluate their outcomes on achieving that.

A maturity model is a framework that describes, for a specific area of interest, a set of levels of sophistication at which activities in this area can be carried out [1]. Essentially, maturity models can be used: to evaluate and compare organizations' current situation, identifying opportunities for optimization; to establish goals and recommend actions for increasing the capability of a specific area within an organization; and as an instrument for controlling and measuring the success of an action [3].

Product lifecycle mainly comprises several phases, e.g. research, development, production and operation/product support [4]. The development phase comprises the sub phases shown in Fig. 1: feasibility, concept, definition, development and series, which involve improvement and modifications. Product collaborative design encompasses all the processes before the production phase, and the information management strategy of products achieve internal information sharing and collaborative design by integrating data and knowledge throughout the whole product lifecycle and managing the completeness of the information in each stage of product design.

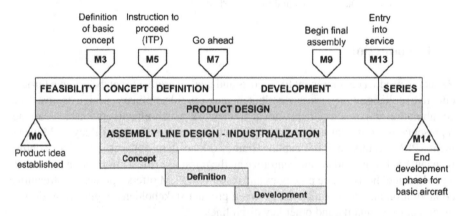

Fig. 1. Airbus product lifecycle and milestones development.

Researches on the product maturity are mainly about project management maturity which are used to evaluate and improve the project management capabilities of enterprises. A smaller part of the researches have discussed the concept of product maturity, and the number of works devoted to studying maturity of related processes and resources is insignificant. Wang et al. [5] proposed the concept of space product maturity and established a management model of product maturity, but it lacks the research about product maturity promoting the product development process. Tao and Fan [6] discussed the concept of maturity and management control method in the process of integration, but the division of the maturity level is not intuitive, and discussed little about application of product maturity in collaborative R&D platform. Chen and Liu [7] provided the application of a strategy of product maturity for collaborative design on the collaborative development platform Teamcenter to verify the effectiveness and the controllability of the strategy. Wuest et al. [8] adapted the state gate model, a well-established methodology for product and software development, to production domain and indicated that it may provide valuable support for product and process quality improvement although the success is strongly dependent of the right adaptation.

The main objective of this paper is the design of a maturity management model for controlling the functional and industrial design phase of an aeronautical assembly line in the Airbus company (Fig. 1), and explores the development of this model in 3DExperience, a collaborative software platform by Dassault Systèmes [9].

2   Antecedents and iDMU Concept

The industrial Digital Mock-Up (iDMU) is the Airbus proposal to perform the design process with a unique team with a unique deliverable. The iDMU is defined by Airbus to facilitate the integration of the processes of the aircraft development on a common platform throughout all their service life. It is a way to help in making the functional and the industrial designs evolving jointly and collaboratively. An iDMU gathers all the product, processes and resources information to model and validate a virtual assembly line, and finally to generate the shopfloor documentation needed to execute the manufacturing processes [10, 11].

Airbus promoted the Collaborative Engineering in the research project "Advanced Aeronautical Solutions Using PLM Processes and Tools" (CALIPSOneo) by implementing the iDMU concept [12–14]. The iDMU implementation was made for the industrialization of the A320neo Fan Cowl, a mid-size aerostructure. It was built by customizing CATIA/DELMIA V5 [9] by means of the PPR model concept. The PPR model of this commercial software provided a generic data structure that had to be adapted for the products, processes and resources of each particular implementation. In this case, a specific data structure was defined to support the Airbus products, the industrial design process, the process structure nodes, the resources structure nodes and their associated technological information, 3D geometry and metadata.

The process followed by Airbus to execute a pilot implementation of the iDMU is briefly described as follows. The previously existing Product structure was used and an ad-hoc application was developed that periodically updated all the modifications released by functional design. The Process and Resources structures were populated directly in the PPR context. The Process structure comprised four levels represented by four concepts: assembly line, station, assembly operation and task. Each concept has its corresponding constraints (precedence, hierarchy), its attributes and its allocation of products to be assembled and resources to be used. Once the PPR structures were defined, the system calculated the product digital mock-up and the resources digital mock-up that relate to each process node. As a result, the designer created simulations in the 3D graphical environment to analyse and validate the defined manufacturing solution. This validation of the process, product and resource design, by means of Virtual Manufacturing utilities in a common context, is a key feature in the Collaborative Engineering deployment.

The iDMU supports the collaborative approach through 3 main elements. First, it allows sharing different design perspectives, to reveal solutions that while valid for a perspective (e.g. resources design) cause problems in other perspectives (e.g. industrialization design), and to solve such issues. Second, it enables checking and validation of a high number of alternatives, allowing improving the harmonization and optimization of the design as a whole. And third, it is possible to reuse information contained in the iDMU by other software systems used in later stages of the lifecycle, facilitating the integration and avoiding problems with translation of models into intermediate formats, and making easier the use of new technologies such as augmented reality.

The CALIPSOneo project, with a scope limited to the A320neo fan cowl, allowed confirming that the iDMU provides a suitable platform to develop the sociotechnical process needed by the collaborative engineering. However, the project also revealed that the general functionalities provided by the adopted PLM commercial solution required an important research and development work to implement the data structures and functions needed to support the iDMU.

An important factor in the implementation of an iDMU is the need for a PLM tool capable of coordinating the workflow of all participants by means the definition and control of the lifecycle of allocated elements of the PPR structure, i.e. to manage its maturity states. At present, this issue is being addressed in the research project "Value Chain: from iDMU to Lean documentation for assembly" (ARIADNE).

3   Methodology

As said before, one of the studies carried out within the scope of the ARIADNE project was the analysis of capabilities that a PLM tool requires to manage the maturity states of the iDMU. Such a PLM tool aims the following objectives:

- To define independent and different maturity states sets for Product, Process and Resource revisions.
- To define precedence constraints between the maturity states of a Process revision, and the maturity states of its related Products and Resources.
- To define, for each Process revision maturity state, other conditions (e.g. attribute values) that are to be met prior to evolving a Process revision to the maturity state.

- To define, for each Process revision maturity state, that some process data or relations are not modifiable from this maturity state onwards.
- To display online, in the process revision iDMU, the Products and Resources evolved through maturities from the last time it was vaulted.
- To display online, in the process revision iDMU, the impact of the evolved Products and Resources and how easy these issues can be fixed.

In order to prove the capabilities of a new PLM tool to meet these objectives, a simple lifecycle model is proposed. The model has only three possible maturity states for every element of the PPR structure: In Work, Frozen and Released. However, the importance of the proposed model lies in a set of constraints that prevent the promotion between maturity states, as described below. This simple model aims to be a preliminary test to evaluate a new PLM tool, so that it can be improved and extended with new states, relationships, constraints, rules, etc.

The *In Work* state is used for a new version of a product, process or resource element in the PPR structure. *In Work* data are fully modifiable and can be switched to *Frozen* by the owner, or to *Released* by the project leader. *Frozen* is an intermediate state between *In Work* and *Released*. It can be used, for example, for data waiting for approval. *Frozen* data are partially modifiable (for minor version changes) and can be switched back and forth between *In Work* and *Frozen* by the owner, or to *Released* by the project leader. *Released* is the final state of a PPR element, e.g. when a product is ready for production, a process is accepted for industrialization, or a resource is fully configured for its use. *Released* data cannot be deleted and cannot switched back to previous states.

Figure 2 shows a schema of the proposed model. At the beginning of the lifecycle, since Design Engineering starts the product design, usually Manufacturing Engineering can begin to plan the process, set up the layout and define the necessary resources. In this situation, all product, process and resource elements in the PPR structure are *In Work*. The collaborative environment must allow the visualization and query of information under development to the different actors of the system, based on roles and permissions, so that it helps to detect design errors and make right decisions.

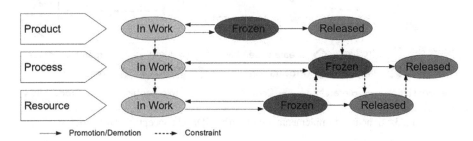

Fig. 2. Proposed simple model for the lifecycle of the PPR structure.

The new PLM tool must provide a set of rules or constraints that allow to control and alert the designer about non-coherent situations. Figure 2 schematically presents some constraints to promote a PPR element. For instance, it is not possible to assign to a process node a maturity state of *Frozen* until the related product node has a maturity state of *Released* and the allocated resource has a maturity state of *Frozen*. In a similar way, to promote a process to *Released*, the allocated resource must be in *Released*. On the other hand, the resource element can only reach the maturity state of *Released* when the process element has been *Frozen* previously.

In addition to define constraints between elements of different types (product, process and resource), it is necessary to establish rules between elements of the same type to control the change of maturity states of their interconnected elements. For instance, the following constraint inside the Product structure could be established: the designer of a product consisting of several parts can change the state of the product element to *Frozen/Released* when all its parts already have that same state, so that a part still unfinished (*In Work*) alerts him that the product cannot be promoted yet.

4   Practical Application

The proposed model for managing the maturity states of an iDMU was implemented and tested in a PLM commercial software, within the frame of the ARIADNE project. The implementation was carried out with the 3DExperience software solution by Dassault Systèmes.

The PPR structure in 3DExperience differs slightly from CATIA/DELMIA V5 so that the process of building the iDMU is different from those developed in previous projects. A significant difference is that the previous 3-elements PPR structure is replaced by a 4-elements structure, as represented schematically in Fig. 3:

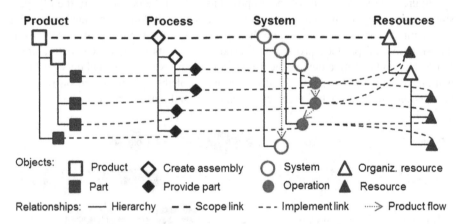

Fig. 3. Schema of implementation of Airbus iDMU concept in 3DExperience.

- Product: it presents the functional zone breakdown in an engineering oriented organization. It is modelled by Design Engineering to define the functional view for structure and system installation.
- Process: it is focused to model the process plan from a functional point of view. It is indeed a product structure composed of a cascade of components identified by part

numbers that presents how the product is built and assembled. Thus, both product and process elements of the PPR structure are directly correlated.

- System: it defines the work flow operation. It contains a set of system/operations that corresponds to the steps necessary to correlate with the Process structure. It contains the information necessary to perform operations such as balancing the assembly lines.
- Resource: it represents the layout design for a manufacturing plant. Resources can be classified as working (e.g. robot, worker, conveyor), non-working (e.g. tool device) or organizational (e.g. station, line). The required resources are attached to operations in the System structure, as shown in Fig. 3.

The adopted PLM software integrates a default lifecycle model to any created object that controls the various transitions in the life of the object. This model includes elements such as user roles, permissions, states and available state changes. To facilitate the collaborative work, 3DExperience also provides a lifecycle model to manage Engineering Changes, which has links to PPR objects, and a transfer ownership functionality that can be used to pass an object along to another authorized user to promote it. Both PPR and Engineering Changes lifecycle models can be customized. These characteristics made 3DExperience an adequate collaborative platform for the purpose of this work.

The objectives that a PLM tool must satisfy for managing the maturity states, described in the previous section, were analysed to fit the 4-element PPR structure of the 3DExperience software. Accordingly, the proposed model was redefined as shown in Fig. 4(a). As can be seen, the set of constraints for the System lifecycle is equivalent to the previous set of constraints for the Process lifecycle, whereas that Process elements are the bridge between Products and Systems.

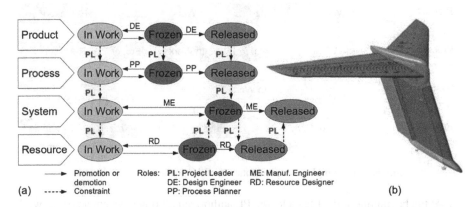

Fig. 4. (a) Extension of proposed model and (b) Airbus A400M empennage.

A series of roles has been defined (see Fig. 4(a)) to implement the proposed model of maturity states in 3DExperience, such as the Project Leader (PL) and a different type of user to design each of the PPR structures: a Designer Engineer (DE), a Process Planner (PP), a Manufacturing Engineer (ME) and a Resources Designer (RD). Each system user is responsible for designing and promoting/demoting each node of its structure to the three possible states, as shown in Fig. 4(a). The PL coordinates all maturity state changes: he checks that there are no inconsistencies and gives the other users permission to make the changes.

Designers have several possibilities for building the iDMU using the 3DExperience graphical interface. Briefly, the maturity state is stored as an attribute of each PPR element, so it can be accessible from the query tool "Properties". The software also provides the "Team Maturity" utility to display information in the graphical environment about the maturity states. This utility displays a coloured flag in each element of the model tree that indicates its maturity state; however, it applies just for Product and Resource elements, i.e. elements that have associated geometry. Another utility allows displaying graphical information about the related elements of an allocated iDMU element. Both graphical utilities, for maturity states and related elements, were used to search and filter information before changing an object state. To promote or demote the maturity state of an iDMU element, the "Change Maturity" utility presents different fields with the available changing states and related information according to the life-cycle model, roles and permissions.

The Airbus A400M empennage (about 34000 parts, see Fig. 4(b)) and its assembly processes were selected to develop the iDMU in 3DExperience. The empennage model developed in CATIA V5 was used as the Product structure. Process, System and Resource structures were modelled from scratch. Different use cases were evaluated by choosing small and more manageable parts of the iDMU to change their maturity states in the collaborative platform. The following is a summary of the implementation process carried out. An example is shown in Fig. 5.

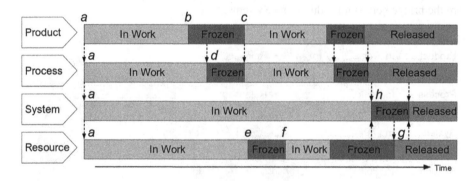

Fig. 5. An example of implementation of the proposed simple model.

At the beginning of the lifecycle, the PL authorized all other system actors to work together in the iDMU at the same time in the collaborative platform (label *a* in Fig. 5). The main PPR structures were created and scope links were established between them. In this situation, all PPR nodes were *In Work* while the iDMU was designed in a collaborative and coordinated way.

One of the first state changes in the iDMU is made by the DE when it promotes a component or subproduct to *Frozen* (*b*). In this situation, only minor design changes could be made to the frozen component, which will have no impact on the rest of the iDMU (including other components of the product). Demoting the component to an *In*

Work state (*c*) would indicate that major changes are required as a result of the current design state in other areas of the iDMU. In general, the promotion to *Released* of every PPR structure will be carried out in an advanced state of the whole iDMU. This means that their design has been considered as stable and that no significant changes will occur that affect other parts of the iDMU.

Maturity state changes in the Process structure are conditioned by the state of related components in the Product structure. Thus, before promoting a Process element (*d*), the PP must check the status of related components with the aforementioned 3DExperience utilities to search and analyse the related elements and their states of maturity. If the related product is *Frozen/Released*, the PP can request authorization to the PL to promote the Process element.

Another of the first state changes of maturity that occurs in the iDMU is that of resources. Thus, the RD promotes a resource to *Frozen* (*e*) or demotes it to *In Work* (*f*) following the same guidelines as the DE with the products. Instead, the promotion of a resource to *Released* (*g*) can only be authorized by the PL when the related assembly system is *Frozen*, indicating that the assembly line has been designed except for possible minor changes that would not affect the definition of the resources.

The ME is the last actor to promote the state of his work in the iDMU: the design of the assembly system/line. In order to freeze his work (*h*), the ME needs to know in advance the final design of the product assembly process and also the definition of the necessary resources. Any changes in product or process structures, even if they are minor, could have a relevant impact on the definition of the assembly line. Therefore, the ME must previously verify that related assembly processes are *Released* and required resources are *Frozen*. Since resource nodes are linked to the System structure through operation nodes, the ME extensively uses the 3DExperience utilities to trace all affected nodes and check their maturity states. As discussed above, the promotion to *Released* of all PPR structures occurs in an advanced development of the iDMU, being the last two steps those relating to Resource and System structures.

5   Conclusions

This paper presents the methodology and preliminary results for the management in a collaborative environment of the maturity states of PPR elements with all product, process and resource information associated with the assembly of an aeronautical component. The methodology aims to evaluate the suitability of PLM tools to implement the Airbus methodology in the creation of a control mechanism that allows a collaborative work.

The proposed model shows in a simple way the importance of the flow of information among the different participants of a unique team to build an iDMU as the unique deliverable in a collaborative platform. An outstanding feature of the lifecycle model is its ability to authorize or restrict the promotion of a product, process or resource element depending on the states of the related elements. Different use cases with coherent and non-coherent situations have been successfully analysed using 3DExperience to implement an iDMU for the Airbus A400M empennage.

In this work, the change management of maturity states has been coordinated by a Project Leader. The next step will be to customize 3DExperience to automate the maturity state changes, so that the system is responsible for evaluating the information of related elements, allowing or preventing the designer from promoting an iDMU element.

Acknowledgements. The authors wish to thank the Andalusian Regional Government and the Spanish Government for its financial support through the research project "Value Chain: from iDMU to Lean documentation for assembly" (ARIADNE). The work of master thesis students, Gonzalo Monguió and Andrés Soto, is also greatly acknowledged.

References

1. Alonso, J., Martinez de Soria, I., Orue-Echevarria, L., Vergara, M.: Enterprise Collaboration Maturity Model (ECMM): preliminary definition and future challenges. In: Popplewell, K., Harding, J., Poler, R., Chalmeta, R. (eds.) Enterprise Interoperability IV, pp. 429–438. Springer, London (2010). https://doi.org/10.1007/978-1-84996-257-5_40
2. De Bruin, T., Freeze, R., Kaulkarni, U., Rosemann, M.: Understanding the main phases of developing a maturity assessment model. In: Australasian Conference on Information Systems (ACIS), Sydney, Australia, pp. 1–11 (2005)
3. Hain, S.: Developing a Situational Maturity Model for Collaboration (SiMMCo) – Measuring Organizational Readiness, St. Gallen, Switzerland, pp 1–6 (2010)
4. Wellsandt, S., Nabati, E., Wuest, T., Hribernik, K., Thoben, K.-D.: A survey of product lifecycle models: towards complex products and service offers. Int. J. PLM **9**(4), 353–390 (2016)
5. Wang, W., Zhu, X., Li, Y.: Research on space product maturity and application. Aerosp. Ind. Manag. **7**, 26–31 (2007)
6. Tao, J., Fan, Y.: Application of maturity in development of aircraft integrated process. J. Beijing Univ. Aeronaut. Astronaut. **32**, 1117–1120 (2006)
7. Chen, M., Liu, J.: Maturity management strategy for product collaborative design. Adv. Mater. Res. **712–715**, 2856–2860 (2013)
8. Wuest, T., Liu, A., Lu, S.C.-Y., Thoben, K.-D.: Application of the stage gate model in production supporting quality management. Proc. CIRP **17**, 32–37 (2014)
9. Dassault Systèmes. https://www.3ds.com
10. Menéndez, J.L., Mas, F., Serván, J., Ríos, J.: Virtual verification of the AIRBUS A400M final assembly line industrialization. AIP Conf. Proc. **1431**(1), 641–648 (2012)
11. Mas, F., Menéndez, J.L., Oliva, M., Ríos, J.: Collaborative engineering: an airbus case study. Proc. Eng. **63**, 336–345 (2013)
12. Mas, F., Menéndez, J.L., Oliva, M., Gómez, A., Ríos, J.: Collaborative engineering paradigm applied to the aerospace industry. In: Bernard, A., Rivest, L., Dutta, D. (eds.) PLM 2013. IAICT, vol. 409, pp. 675–684. Springer, Heidelberg (2013). https://doi.org/10.1007/978-3-642-41501-2_66
13. Mas, F., Menéndez, J.L., Oliva, M., Ríos, J., Gómez, A., Olmos, V.: iDMU as the collaborative engineering engine: research experiences in airbus. In: 2014 International Conference on Engineering, Technology and Innovation (ICE), pp 1–7 (2014)
14. Mas, F., Oliva, M., Ríos, J., Gómez, A., Olmos, V., García, J.A.: PLM based approach to the industrialization of aeronautical assemblies. Proc. Eng. **132**, 1045–1052 (2015)

Product, Service, Systems (PSS)

The Design for Product Service Supportability (DfPSSu) Methodology: Generating Sector-Specific Guidelines and Rules to Improve Product Service Systems (PSSs)

Claudio Sassanelli[1,2(✉)], Giuditta Pezzotta[2], Roberto Sala[2],
Angelos Koutopes[3], and Sergio Terzi[1]

[1] Department of Economics, Management and Industrial Engineering, Politecnico di Milano,
Via R. Lambruschini 4/b, 20156 Milan, Italy
{claudio.sassanelli,sergio.terzi}@polimi.it

[2] Department of Management, Information and Production Engineering, University of Bergamo,
Viale Marconi, 5, 24044 Dalmine, BG, Italy
{claudio.sassanelli,giuditta.pezzotta,roberto.sala}@unibg.it

[3] N. Bazigos S.A. Design and Manufacturing of Moulds,
26th Km Old National Road - Athens - Thiva, 19600 Mandra, Attikis, Greece
akoutoupes@bazigosmolds.com

Abstract. Nowadays manufacturers' need to systematically develop innovative integrated solutions is increasingly pushed by new technologies, a multiple functionalities demand and a change in the customer value perception. For these reasons, it is very complex for Product Service Systems (PSS) providers to fulfil all the design requirements: designers must consider all the objectives the PSS wants to achieve during its whole lifecycle according to different criteria, which are often to be considered according to a trade-off balance. At present, Design for X (DfX) design methods represent the most important attempt to enhance product development according to certain characteristics or lifecycle phases: authors believe they can also support the PSS design, redesigning or enhancing products in certain X-dimensions, in particular those ones related to "service supportability". On this basis, a methodology generating new Design for X (DfX) guidelines has been proposed: in this paper an application case in the mold industry shows how a physical product can be improved when a service has to be added and integrated. At the same time, new industry-specific PSS design guidelines and rules are proposed.

Keywords: Product Service System (PSS) · PSS design · Design for X (DfX)
Design for Product Service Supportability (DfPSSu) · Design guideline

© IFIP International Federation for Information Processing 2017
Published by Springer International Publishing AG 2017. All Rights Reserved
J. Ríos et al. (Eds.): PLM 2017, IFIP AICT 517, pp. 679–689, 2017.
https://doi.org/10.1007/978-3-319-72905-3_60

1 Introduction

Nowadays manufacturers are always more absorbed by Service Economy. To boost their performance the paradigm of Product-Service System (PSS) has been presented to the market. PSSs are characterized by the integration of Products and Services bundled into unique solutions fulfilling the user's needs [1]. However, companies are not fully actually aided by consistent PSS design methodologies, and supporting tools, which could enable them to focus on both customer's perspective and company's internal performance but also to integrate service and product components along their whole lifecycle [2]. Some traditional PSS methodologies (e.g. [3–5]) tried to continue going down the river of traditional product design approaches to attempt to fill this gap. Moreover, [6] proposed some more conceptual strategies to move in that direction: the idea was that starting from the physical product properties and features, service design can be properly integrated in it, without neglecting a lifecycle perspective on the entire integrated solution. In such a competitive and fast changing environment, concurrent engineering approaches, such as Design for X (DfX), have been proposed in literature, being more able to cope with different simultaneous issues dealing with products, processes and systems design. Overcoming the typical issues of the traditional sequential engineering, this kind of approaches can indeed adapt the physical products in various ways according to the PSS lifecycle, also addressing designers' lack of knowledge in important product and service lifecycle areas [7]. A methodology generating Design Guidelines and Rules, fostering the adoption of the Design for Product Service Supportability (DfPSSu) approach [8], aims at integrating product and services with a lifecycle view. With this objective, Sect. 2 describes the research methodology adopted and Sect. 3 the application case characteristics. Finally, Sect. 4 presents the validation results and Sect. 5 introduces the future research developments.

2 The Methodology for Generating DfPSSu Guidelines/Rules

Figure 1 summarizes the methodology mentioned above: it has the aim of creating Design Guidelines and Rules to enhance the design of the product features enabling and supporting the delivery of excellent services. Guidelines provide a proper basis for considering generic, non-company-specific, lifecycle oriented information to be followed during the design phases. Rules become concrete and quantitative instructions for PSS developers to be followed during their daily specific design activities, representing the characterizing knowledge belonging to the company. The methodology, and its supporting tool to manage the generated Guidelines and Rules in a consistent repository, have been developed according to different research traditions [9]. The methodology is composed of 6 phases clustered in 4 main sections.

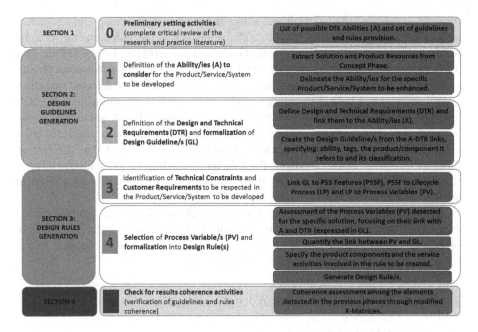

Fig. 1. The PSS design guideline/rule methodology (adapted by [9])

Section 1: before starting with the content guideline and rule creation procedure, preliminary activities need to be performed in order to collect the basic information to be used through the adoption of the methodology. All the Design for X approaches that could be involved during the PSS design are collected: they represent the possible Abilities (A) the PSS under design could achieve and represent the starting point for the guidelines/rules definition. The DfX Ability concept is based on the "function" concept defined by [10]: they are those principles through which the PSS functions can be explicated and explained and represents what exactly the guideline addresses.

Section 2: The design process can start when a PSS concept is already available. Once defined in Phase 1 the Ability/ies (A) the product under design has to achieve, an analysis must be conducted in order to create, if not existing, new suitable content guideline/s. Thus, Design and Technical Requirements (DTR) are defined: they represent the practical and technical recommendations to be followed by designers and engineers, through which abilities could be achieved. Therefore, the new DTR has to be linked to the Ability/ies, also specifying the importance degree of the relationships. Based on the identified links between A and DTR, guidelines able to guide the designer/engineer activities in the Product/Service/System development must be formalized in text and made available as company knowledge.

Section 3: in this section design rules are created. Here, the methodology must lead the designer/engineer to focus on the specific company context. In order to create a bridge between the functionalities of the PSS to be achieved and the related lifecycle variables that need to be managed, an extended version of the Function Transformation Matrices (FTM) methodology [10] is used. A series of them, all based on the same structure, is adopted to document and gauge the relationships among various factors such as: (a) PSS Features (PSSF), those characteristics of the PSS components to be considered to act on DTR expressed in the Guidelines (GL); (b) PSS Lifecycle Processes (LP) represent all those activities of the PSS lifecycle (from the design to disposal phase); (c) PSS Process Variables (PV) are those variables which need to be detected since they affect LP. They can belong to any process of the several phases composing the PSS lifecycle. Finally, Design Rules are systematically developed based on the links found in the previous steps: their aim is the ability-driven control of lifecycle variables in order to better manage the design activities to improve the physical product of a PSS. Design Rules are indeed developed to provide the links for controlling the variables that directly affect the PSS Ability/ies enabled by the introduction of a new service on a physical product.

Section 4: In this last section, the coherence of all the elements considered during the design process is verified, supporting designers and engineers in finding the right connections between the obtained high level Guidelines and the more operative Rules. For this aim, two modified X-Matrices [11] are used.

3 Research Methodology and Application Case

3.1 Research Methodology

The application case has been conducted with the aim of testing the suitability of the presented methodology generating DfPSSu Guidelines and Rules. The paper also evidences the related benefits for companies and the increased efficiency, deriving from its application, in solving issues in the detailed design phase of PSS. The application case was conducted in two steps. First of all, a video has been shared with participants to train them about the methodology. Thus, the face-to-face workshop has been organized to apply the methodology in the industrial context. This interactive session was led by two academics and involved two additional academics with which the company has long term relationship, in addition to the production monitoring employee and one product designer. After realizing the actual DfX methods level of use in the company, DfPSSu approach was presented. Hence, a solution, the mold digital history of repairs, has been detected through a concept design brainstorming, in order to enhance the company business. The methodology has been performed and design guidelines and rules supporting the design of this new PSS were obtained. Moreover, useful feedbacks on the suitability of the approach were given.

3.2 The Application Case: N. BAZIGOS SA

The application case has been conducted in N. BAZIGOS SA, a B2B Greek company designing and manufacturing molds. Design methodologies for the product itself are long established using PLM, CAD and other software tools and methods, supported by a strong and experienced design and engineering division. Going through the servitization process, their actual intent is to: reduce their environmental impact, wastes in material, energy consumption, design and machining time, time to market, frequency of failure; improve customer involvement in the design and customer satisfaction; increase competitiveness and income; access to new market sectors. Indeed, in the company, PSS offerings are in early stages of adoption. The provided services are offered in isolation from the product, which is the mold, without considering a combined PSS eco-system. However, the nature of this manufacturing sector dictated up to now that the services aspect is indirectly treated. Given this lack of service-oriented approaches in the industry, the company is thus considering new PSS projects like mold delivery time estimation as a service, maintenance history per customer, joint provider-customer proactive production planning for mold modifications or opinion mining offered to customers as a service. This would enhance the monitoring and control of mold lifecycle and shorten mold downtime.

The methodology was applied in N. BAZIGOS SA, starting with Sect. 1, where some preliminary setting activities consisted in assessing the AS-IS of its design procedures. The company does not adopt a really structured approach to design mold. They follow some basic principles, e.g. optimize mold cycle time (to inject, cool and eject a part). Moreover, the design guidelines and rules, that represents the company knowhow needed to implement these approaches, are not codified and written down and reside only in designers' background. Furthermore, customers' requirements are almost connected to production optimization, from either a quantity or quality point of view. Therefore, designers are committed to add on the basic mold some extras and to focus on certain precise aspects of the product lifecycle in a concurrent way. Most of the time the main target for the design team is to optimize, also through a consistent choice of the steel adopted, the expected number of pieces produced with the mold, minimizing downtimes. Thus, when steel hardening can be avoided, the company costs are lower, the price for the customer is lower but it will soon present more problems in maintenance. To manage this issue, principles belonging to Design for Modularity and Customizability, adding changeable cups and bases, are directly linked to Maintainability. On the contrary, using thicker plates or considering other suitable solutions, the mold can become more reliable. However, it requires a more complex design and principles as Maintainability cannot be neglected. Therefore, through the DfPSSu Methodology, it is useful to reconsider the design of an already existing mold in order to improve its functionalities (especially from a Maintainability point of view) and understand what would change. A new solution, able to meet N. BAZIGOS SA's needs, was identified: the digital history of repairs of the mold. Thus, a product to be redesigned, referring to a customer operating in the plastic industry, was detected: a "2 cavity, 1 L Seal Lid" mold. The description of the main components (shown in Fig. 2) and the main issues with them are shown in Table 1:

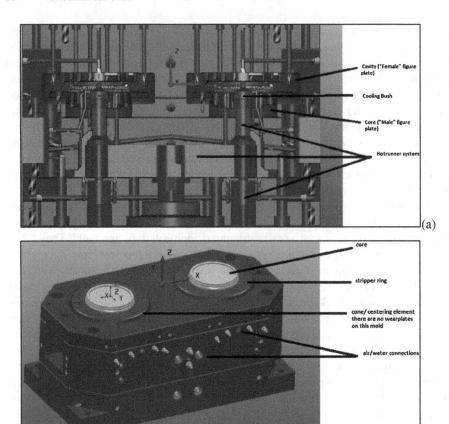

Fig. 2. "2 cavity, 1 L Seal Lid" mold: General section (a) and fixed side (b)

Table 1. "2 cavity, 1 L Seal Lid" mold: component and issues description

Component	Description	Issue
1. Core & Cavity	The two halves of the mold that create the plastic product geometry	They usually carry the centering elements: these are the two parts that need to be aligned properly
2. Cooling bush	An insert, that carries the injection point (hole) from which the plastic flows, also carries cooling circuit)	The hole is damaged by material flow. They are designed as inserts for manufacturability reason, and thus they are also replaceable
3. Hotrunner system	Provided by specialized suppliers, distributes the plastic material to multiple cavities	Nozzle tips (and other contact points with accurate fitting are often damaged by material flow
4. Stripper ring	The component that moves relatively to the core, in order to eject the plastic part from the mold)	Accurate fitting is required and, due to natural wear, it needs repair or replacement

3.3 Guidelines and Rules Generation in N. BAZIGOS SA

Having analyzed the current design approach of the company, according to the methodology procedure in Sect. 1, and detected the solution to be developed, DfPSSu Guidelines and Rules were developed following the steps described from Sects. 2, 3 and 4. Besides the aim of guiding the creation of a product consistent with the customer's needs, the Design Guidelines and Rules are useful to limit the reworks, since they are thought to give precise information on how to design the product.

Figure 3 (from solutions in the bottom part of the figure following a clockwise direction) summarizes the results obtained through the application of Sect. 2: it begins with Phase 1, focused on Abilities definition, the five most important abilities to develop the solution desired have been identified. They were related to the physical product properties needed for the PSS provision: Modularity, Maintainability, Inspectability, Easy Assembly/Disassembly operations, ID Coding & Traceability.

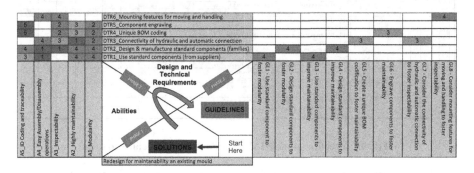

Fig. 3. A section of the FTM - X Matrix from solution to guidelines

In Phase 2, six DTRs were defined to fulfill the previous Abilities: use standard components from suppliers, design and manufacture standard components for product families, connectivity of hydraulic and automatic connection, unique BOM coding, component engraving, mounting features for moving and handling. Then, the relationship grade between each Ability and DTR was defined. As a result, fourteen Guidelines (GL) were obtained since only the relationships with a weight equal or higher than "3" were considered significant and thus investigated and translated in operational guideline for the designer.

Later, Sect. 3, summarized in Fig. 4 (from guidelines in the bottom part of the figure following a clockwise direction), was carried out in order to create detailed rules. In Phase 3 the PSS Feature were defined. They were aimed at improving the Abilities, defined in the previous steps, of some critical components, such as: hotrunner, guiding components, cooling bush, sockets, centering elements, water manifold, mounting holes, centering cone. Then, the team brainstormed once again to define the relationship between the Guidelines and the PSSF. In Phase 4, the designers' attention moved on the Lifecycle Process (LP) steps identification, in particular seven phases were identified (Concept & Design, Manufacturing, Assembly, Validation, Use, Maintenance, Disposal). The definition of the relationships between the PSSF and the LP, aided engineers in understanding the value of the PSSF in all the phases of the solution life-cycle. Once again, the resulting links fostered the creation of the Design Rules to be followed by the designers. 53 specific new Rules have been created (listed in part in Fig. 4).

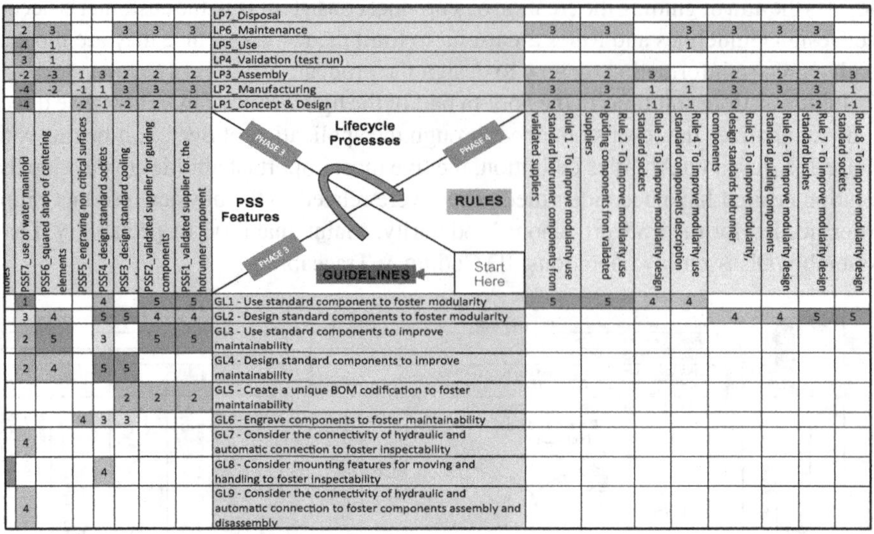

Fig. 4. A section of the FTM - X Matrix from guidelines to rules

Finally, in Phase 5, the team checked the coherence between all the information created along the methodology thanks to the analysis of the X-Matrices. No strong contradictions emerged. Only one Guideline (GL5), not being linked to any PSSF, wasn't explicited in specific Rules. Moreover, Rules related to PSSF6 (squared shape of centering element) and PSSF7 (use of water manifold) were characterized by a very negative weight at the beginning of PSS lifecycle, resulting in the need of a strong effort for the company: designers should consider, with a further trade-off brainstorming, if it's worth to follow them. However, many benefits could be obtained also by their achievement. For example, in order to achieve A3, Inspectability, DTR3, Connectivity of hydraulic and automatic connection, and DTR6, Mounting features for moving and handling, were considered. In particular, the relation A3-DTR3 was explicited in GL7 ("Consider the connectivity of hydraulic and automatic connection to foster inspecta-bility"). To act on this, PSSF7, Use of water manifold, was considered: this feature requires a very important effort in the beginning of the PSS lifecycle (Concept & Design and Manufacturing and less in Assembly) but makes the validation test run easier, giving also a huge improvement in the Use and Maintenance phases. Indeed, Rule 30, "To improve Inspectability, use water manifold while designing the connectivity of hydraulic and automatic connection", contributes to GL7's aim.

4   Discussion

Several and different results have been obtained through this application case. The main evidence is that the proposed methodology is able to solve product engineering issues, fostering the product and service features integration in the detailed PSS design [9]. In particular, following the methodology, 14 new Guidelines (Fig. 3) and 53 connected Rules (Fig. 4) were obtained and checked. Feedbacks collected during the methodology application in N. BAZIGOS SA could be considered as an additional result: the difference between "Guidelines" and "Rules" could be strengthened through the way they are written (e.g. considering the use of the passive tense for the Guidelines) and the X-Matrix visualization could be enhanced (to automatically better explain its outcomes). Their main concern with the methodology regarded the effort needed to apply it, if compared to their standard procedures. N. BAZIGOS SA is a SME: designers are free to design as they want, always keeping in mind the mold manufacturability but without the need of always designing something really innovative. The mold, a B2B industrial product, should only satisfy the customer's requirements: its innovation could be considered strategic only from the service point of view, confirming the importance of the DfPSSu concept. Indeed the methodology adoption would require designers an additional amount of time to get used to the different concepts introduced (even if it resulted to be very easy to follow) and to structure the obtained knowledge in the tool repository. In companies it is difficult to change routines and to work with a new tool: experienced designers could state they don't need to use the proposed methodology because they already know the design rules. Finally, the methodology appeared to be pretty much useful to capture brainstorming during the design phase but at the same moment it represents a very structured way to govern it, decreasing a bit the sense of relax supposed to obtain new ideas. However, according to N. BAZIGOS SA employees, this methodology can improve in an important way the PSS design phase mainly if applied in big multinational companies. Big companies indeed typically are more involved in the continuous process of innovation of their solutions, follow very strict requirements and have a stronger structure of resources able to exploit this procedure in a deeper way. Furthermore, with its adoption, the problem-solving process could be simplified and speeded up also along the space, in different industrial plants scattered in diverse places, and the time, among different designers generations, and can foster collaboration among companies' divisions and networks.

5   Conclusions and Further Developments

This paper investigates how to support companies in the integration of service features already in the product design of the PSS. In order to do it and to have an empirical feedback in the industrial context, the methodology generating DfPSSu guidelines and rules proposed in [9] has been adopted in an application case. This has been thus conducted in a SME producing mold for B2B market, willing to go through servitization. Thus, among the already existing products belonging to the company portfolio, the solution to be designed and provided to the customer as a PSS has been hence detected:

the injection mold (for plastic industry) maintenance, based on the digital history of repairs. Through this application case, the physical product was enhanced and service features were integrated in it: indeed the methodology confirmed to be strongly engineering based, being aimed at the development of a new DfX-driven approach for PSS development and at easing the problem solving process, typical of the design phase, also balancing in a trade-off the different abilities to be satisfied. The case was conducted allowing designers/engineers to freely use the methodology. According to them, the proposed methodology would yield more benefits to a large company, where designers might be based even in different countries - but required to maintain consistency in their designs. In smaller companies, where experienced designers train junior designers, day by day - working next to each other - knowledge, although valuable, remains tacit. Based on this, a further test could be conducted in future in a multinational company in order to evaluate the design methodology effectiveness not only in SMEs but also in such a different context. Finally, new sector-specific DfPSSu Guidelines and Rules were obtained: in this sense, the provision of a tool, used as a repository for both the generic Guidelines and the more specific Rules, can ease designers' activities in protocolling the design knowledge obtained during the design phase. This knowledge can be linked, through the use of tags, either to the design project or to PSS Abilities or to other kind of concepts. Furthermore, this knowledge, consistently filtered, can also be reused for future design projects. Based on this, a tool, already used in the application case in its prototype version, is going to be developed and provided to practitioners.

Acknowledgments. This work was funded by the European Commission through Diversity Project, GA 636692, under the H2020 program.

References

1. Goedkoop, M., Van Halen, C.J.G., te Riele, H.R.M., Rommens, P.J.M.: Product Service systems, Ecological and Economic Basics, vol. 36, March 1999
2. Pezzotta, G., Pirola, F., Rondini, A., Pinto, R., Ouertani, M.-Z.: Towards a methodology to engineer industrial product-service system – evidence from power and automation industry. CIRP J. Manuf. Sci. Technol. **15**, 19–32 (2016)
3. Aurich, C., Fuchs, C., Wagenknecht, C.: Modular design of technical product-service systems. In: Brissaud, D., Tichkiewitch, S., Zwolinski, P. (eds.) Innovation in Life Cycle Engineering and Sustainable Development, pp. 303–320. Springer, Dordrecht (2006). https://doi.org/10.1007/1-4020-4617-0_21
4. Maussang, N., Zwolinski, P., Brissaud, D.: Product-service system design methodology: from the PSS architecture design to the products specifications. J. Eng. Des. **20**(4), 349–366 (2009)
5. Hara, T., Arai, T., Shimomura, Y., Sakao, T.: Service CAD system to integrate product and human activity for total value. CIRP J. Manuf. Sci. Technol. **1**(4), 262–271 (2009)
6. Tan, A.R., Matzen, D., McAloone, T.C., Evans, S.: Strategies for designing and developing services for manufacturing firms. CIRP J. Manuf. Sci. Technol. **3**(2), 90–97 (2010)
7. Sundin, E.: Life-cycle perspectives of product/service-systems: in design theory. In: Sakao, T., Lindahl, M. (eds.) Introduction to Product/Service-System Design, pp. 31–49. Springer, London (2009). https://doi.org/10.1007/978-1-84882-909-1_2

8. C. Sassanelli, G. Pezzotta, F. Pirola, S. Terzi, M. Rossi: Design for Product Service Supportability (DfPSS) approach: a state of the art to foster Product Service System (PSS) design. In: 8th CIRP IPSS 2016, vol. 47, pp. 192–197 (2016)
9. Sassanelli, C., Pezzotta, G., Sala, R., Correia, A., Terzi, S.: Testing the methodology to generate Design for Product Service Supportability (DfPSS) guidelines and rules: an application case. In: Procedia CIRP, pp. 265–270 (2017)
10. Mital, A., Desai, A., Subramanian, A., Mital, A.: Product Development. Elsevier (2008)
11. Jackson, T.L.: Hoshin Kanri for the Lean Enterprise: Developing Competitive Capabilities and Managing Profit (2006)

Secure Concept for Online Trading of Technology Data in Global Manufacturing Market

Ghaidaa Shaabany$^{(\boxtimes)}$, Simon Frisch, and Reiner Anderl

The Department of Computer Integrated Design, Technical University of Darmstadt,
Otto-Berndt Strasse 2, 64287 Darmstadt, Germany
shaabany@dik.tu-darmstadt.de

Abstract. The high-tech strategy of the German government aims to expand the networking and intelligence capabilities of machines, products and services. Thereby it is essential to apply extensive utilization of information and communication technologies (ICT). The goal of the German term "Industrie 4.0" is to merge the physical world with the virtual world [1]. This interconnected digital world enables various opportunities for creating new business models and increasing companies' revenues at the same time. Online trading of goods increased extensively in the last years, especially online trading of digital goods like music, films and e-books. Various license models and usage control policies are developed for a secure utilization of these goods by customers. Indeed there are still challenges regarding IT security issues that hinder the expansion of digital trading in the industry. This paper demonstrates a new business model for online trading in the automation and manufacturing industry. This model is based on existing resources in companies and hence improves the added-value-chain in companies. Thereby technology data that is required for machine operation in manufacturing processes will be traded. The main concept and workflow of trading processes will be presented. Furthermore various needed license models for usage control of Technology Data (TD) after trading are demonstrated.

Keywords: Industrie 4.0 · License models · IT security · Online trading
Technology data · Usage control · DRM

1 Introduction

One of the main goals of the high-tech strategy in Germany is to support small and medium-sized enterprises (SMEs) with the development of innovative services and products and enabling them to lead the future market [2]. Within this scope the fourth generation of industry, known as Industrie 4.0 (I 4.0) in Germany was called into life.

The essential idea of I 4.0 is to apply digitization widely in different perspectives, industries, corporate functions, technologies and various fields of study. A recent survey published in 2016 aimed to find a general understanding of I 4.0 in the global market, which considered six different countries including Germany, US, UK, Japan, South Korea and China. There are five fields of interest which I 4.0 is focusing on, according to that survey. These fields are: increasing networking and digitization in economy

© IFIP International Federation for Information Processing 2017
Published by Springer International Publishing AG 2017. All Rights Reserved
J. Ríos et al. (Eds.): PLM 2017, IFIP AICT 517, pp. 690–700, 2017.
https://doi.org/10.1007/978-3-319-72905-3_61

(26%), development of smart products, (20%), optimization of production processes (20%), automation (18%) and creation of new business models (16%). [3] In consequence of these changes, new chances and innovative business models are being developed that are mainly based on digital data. However, there are many challenges that SMEs face through implementing I 4.0 use cases that are characterized by intensive networking and digitization especially in the manufacturing sector [4] – primarily challenges regarding IT security issues. New threats and wide attack areas may be figured out by hackers easier. Possible goals of these hackers are manipulation of data and sabotage. Moreover, theft of competitors' know-how and getting financial benefits can be a motivation for hacking. Thus many new security measures regarding sensitive data, know-how and workflow in enterprises should be developed. Many studies and research projects with respect to security issues are carried out currently in the industrial field, especially in the manufacturing sector.

This paper demonstrates a concept of one innovative business model that considers online trading of technology data (TD) that is called technology data market place (TDMP). TD are various sets of data that are needed to calibrate a machine for a manufacturing process in order to ensure a smooth operation of machines under different circumstances e.g. cutting speed and movement and tools features. These sets of data represent the digital goods that will be traded on TDMP. We will use the expression technology data (TD) in this paper to illustrate these machine's functioning parameters. In the first section an introduction of e-commerce concepts and many examples of similar existing market places is given. Then, the concept, the requirements, the scenarios and activities of TDMP during online trading of TD will be illustrated. Moreover different license models for offering TD at TDMP are presented.

2   State of the Art

In this section we have a look on existing online trading concepts before we will present our TDMP concept. E-commerce has seen tremendous growth over the past few decades. It has evolved into several types of online businesses like online marketplaces, online stores, storefronts, virtual communities etc. Online marketplaces are the digital version of the trade fairs of the past, where buyers can discover and do business with sellers and vice versa.

There are several different kinds of e-commerce marketplaces. These are characterized as business-to-business (B2B), business-to-customer (B2C) or customer-to-customer (C2C). Our area of focus is B2B; the marketplaces that involve trading between different companies or businesses, for example between a supplier and distributor. B2B marketplaces are internet-based interorganizational trading platforms that facilitate and foster the exchange of information, products and services, and other business transactions among many buyers and sellers [5]. B2B transaction is a rapidly growing sector within e-commerce. However, despite the increase in the number of B2B transactions, only a few e-marketplaces have successfully attracted a large number of buyers and sellers. There are several factors that are very important in determining the success of a B2B marketplace. The most important, most researched and most documented factor in this context is trust. Nearly every study about marketplaces in general, mentions the role of trust for success of the marketplace [6–8]. The design of the website and its ease of use has an impact on a user's trust in the marketplace. Furthermore security level of the website play a major role with trust in marketplaces. *Niranjamurthy* provides an overview of e-commerce security issues and threats in [9] that shows the common security threats in online trading. These threats are denial of service (DoS), unauthorized access, theft and fraud. We think, that trust depends mainly on the character of marketplaces and their design that enable an acceptable level of security without affecting the availability of trading processes.

The idea of a platform for trading technology data over the internet is a fairly new concept. There isn't any known work taking a comparable approach in the field of automation and manufacturing. Online marketplaces with certain similarities are, however, established in the fields of consumer electronics and multimedia. Mobile apps for smart phone operating systems such as Android and iOS serve a similar purpose as TD do on machine tools: both are digital goods used to expand the range of functions on a device [10]. Google Play and Apple App Store – digital platforms for trading mobile apps – address issues of maintaining a trustful trade environment. This includes mechanisms to protect the know-how of app providers as well as measures to protect the customers against malicious apps. [11–14] discuss the security mechanisms implemented by the above mentioned platforms and the related operating systems. Microsoft and Amazon run marketplaces comparable to Google's and Apple's platforms for their own mobile. Further information to mobile app marketplaces in general is provided by [15].

One key element of TDMP's concept is the usage control of purchased and licensed TD. Whereas this as well is a new topic in the automation and manufacturing sector, there are several established solutions dealing with this issue in the area of multimedia. These can be subsumed under the term digital rights management (DRM). One of the main design philosophies of a DRM system is to offer a content with different usage policies. This allows the content to be distributed or downloaded freely. However, it cannot be consumed without a valid license, which has a proper rights object [16].

For instance, both Amazon and Adobe use DRM technology for their e-book formats [17]. Furthermore DRM solutions are provided by Microsoft (Windows Media Audio), Apple (Fairplay) and others for controlling the use of digital audio content [18].

3   Concept of TDMP

Commonly various sets of data are needed to calibrate a machine for a clean manufacturing process for different conditions. For example under different ambient pressure, temperature or when working up different materials it is necessary to adjust one or many of machine's functioning parameters like cutting speed and movement and tool features. When a machine is purchased from a machine manufacturer, some sets of TD are provided for basic functions and processes. In some cases, the machine might need to be operated under new conditions for which there are no manufacturer recommendations available. Thus manufacturer have to experiment on the machine in order to derive these new needed parameter. For a company that only uses such a machine to manufacture products, it is mainly concerned with productivity and delivering the orders on time. If manufacturers have to figure out the needed parameters by using their own resources and expertise first, the productivity is diminished because of these extensive effort. It would be much more beneficial for the enterprise to get these parameters from someone else who could be another company making similar products on similar machines. At the same time the other company can improve its added-value-chain by offering the already existing data. To meet such needs of manufacturers we developed the concept of TDMP. The main goal is to design a platform that enables involving those both parties, TD provider and TD customer in an online trading process of requested TD. Moreover it enables a highly interconnected and dynamic industry in the global market and at the same time it improves the added-value-chain in enterprises by generating new business models based on existing resources [19].

However various threats and risks regarding protection of traded digital goods, namely TD can affect the smooth operation of TDMP. Therefore many requirements should be met in order to operate the TDMP successfully:

- Protecting of manufacturing know-how through encryption of TD as well as secured communication between parties
- Access on TDMP only for authenticated users
- Integrity check of traded TD
- Enabling a usage control policies for TD
- Equipping concerned machines for a controlled handling of TD
- Reliability of TDMP
- Availability of TDMP

This paper focuses on the first five requirements of TDMP concept. The last two points are primary requirements for every marketplace and are adequately discussed in many studies.

3.1   License Models

Digital data has a lot of special characteristics when it comes to ownership, reuse and licensing compared to physical goods. The license file of the presented concept contains the rights object which incorporates the terms and conditions applied for usage of the licensed content. A rights object specifies the permissions for various ways of use of associated content by a consumer or a device. In case the content is encrypted, the license contains the key for decrypting it. Due to license files, the same content can be associated with different usage rights to specify different modes of content consumption. This attempt provides flexibility and ease of management. In our concept, the licensed consists of TD.

Customers can purchase the right to use one or several specific TD sets offered on TDMP. This process is referred to as *purchasing* or *licensing* in this paper. That means that the purchased TD sets can be used under the terms and conditions of license models only. The terms of use for TD sets are defined via a license file. These terms are enforced by trusted software on the customer's machine while processing the TD set. The tangible license file for a TD set is generated during the purchasing process described in Sect. 3.3. It is individual for every purchasing process. Thus, it includes the following information: TDMP code, purchasing ID, machines ID, customer ID, license features and a time stamp of generating process. The license file is derived from a license model selected by a TD provider when publishing a new offer on TDMP. From one time usage, pay-per-use to fixed price packages or long term subscriptions, TDMP enables a variety of different license models:

- Pay-per-use model: the customer can use a TD set only in a certain amount of manu-facturing processes. To enforce this, each use of a TD set is registered on the machine and a counter is increased until the maximum of permitted uses times is reached.
- Time-based model: the customer can use a TD set only within a certain period of time. It can be defined either by a fix date of expiry or by a specific time span since the first use of the TD set. The enforcement of license files based on this model requires a trusted clock on the target machine. Manipulating this clock is prevented by technical means.
- Unlimited use model: the customer is allowed to use the TD set on all licensed machine without further limitations. He is, however, not able to copy or to read the TD set in clear text.

The above-mentioned license models form a basis for other models such as trial licenses which can be understood as special forms of one of the three basic license models.

3.2 Scenarios for Trading Processes on TDMP

The required scenarios for a clean functionality of TDMP will be demonstrated as follows:

(a) **Administrating market place.** To ensure the smooth running of trading processes on the marketplace, it is necessary to administer the infrastructure of TDMP by a marketplace system. The system ensures that there are no problems with registration of market place users, the data provided is of the correct format and adheres to marketplace policies, as well as security of technology data sets while being stored at the marketplace or when being uploaded or downloaded from the marketplace. Furthermore users' data like needed accounts details and personal data should be managed.
(b) **Participation at market place.** In order to participate on the marketplace either as a buyer or a seller, a user has to be registered with the marketplace according to specific credentials. User business and personal data have to be verified and approved by the administrator of the TDMP.
(c) **Developing technology data.** In order to be able to sell TD at the TDMP, TD providers first have to develop this TD for a specific material on a specific machine. During operating the machine for producing certain products the provider replicates cutting processes many times trying different parameters every time until reaching the desired cutting quality of these products. Then the provider writes a description of TD including operating conditions and quality. This description will then be

verified by the system to make sure that it abides by the TDMP policy. Then TD is exported from the machine and has to be signed digitally by the provider to ensure authenticity before being uploaded to the marketplace for starting trading process.

(d) **Requesting technology data.** Once a buyer is an approved, registered member of the technology data marketplace (TDMP), he can then search for the TD that he needs. If needed data is not found, a request for needed TD can be written by the buyer with the required TD properties e.g. machine type and performance, material, use time or duration and desired quality and then the request can be published on TDMP. After that, TD provider can respond to this request and offer TD that is appropriate to this request if it is existing or can be developed by him. After that, the process for purchasing of this data can be initiated, if the offer suits the request conditions.

(e) **Administration of technology data.** TD providers can open their own profiles after a successful log-in on the marketplace (frontend), to get an overview about previous actions they did. TD offers can be administrated for example updates of TD characteristics, prices and handle conditions can be conducted. Moreover existing TD offers can be deleted and, at the same time, new offers can be uploaded and activated by providers.

(f) **Processing of technology data.** The purchased TD that are already saved on TDMP's server are available to be used by an authorized operator. Thus TD can be downloaded to be processed on the machine only if the license is still valid. Thus by every use of TD the license should be checked for its validity and then synchronized with the TDMP. This machine should be capable of using TD according to the provided license.

3.3 Workflow of Trading Process on TDMP

In the following section the workflow of trading processes on TDMP will be presented. These processes are demonstrated by means of two activity diagrams that present the offering as well as the purchasing processes.

TD Offering

Similar to traditional marketplaces, TDMP acts as a mediating platform where prospective buyers and different providers of goods make contact. Because TDMP doesn't act as a creator and a vendor of its own TD, TDMP provides a simple workflow that enables every verified participant to offer TD sets securely on the marketplace.

Figure 1 provides an overview over the activities of this workflow. It starts with the actual generation of TD. In the majority of cases, this activity is conducted on a standard machine tool by manually elaborating machine parameters. The newly generated TD set then needs to be exported.

In order to meet the security objectives integrity and non-repudiation, the provider has to sign the exported TD set with his private key subsequently. The following activities are directly processed on TDMP's website. After having accessed the website, the TD provider has to be authenticated by entering his log-in data. In case he is not already registered, a registration process is initiated instead. During this process several steps are necessary in order to create a valid profile. The most important step is to verify the identity of the new TDMP participant and his business contact data. Also, it's checked if the registrant meets all defined participation conditions. By that, it's made sure that only trustful participants will be able to offer technology data sets on TDMP. The verification of the registrant's identity and stated information can be conducted via a call, a mail, postal letters and submission of official identification documents. Having passed the verification process, the registrant sets his log-in information and provides his public key for later authentication checks. Then he is able to log-in regularly on the TDMP website. After having logged-in, the provider is able to access the TD offering section of TDMP's website. On the offering section a new offer for generated TD set can be created. By doing so, he has to give a description of the TD set as a text, to define machine types and materials that are compatible with the offered TD set and to defines the desired license models for later purchasing processes. As presented in Sect. 3.1, license models specify in which manner the TD set is allowed to be used on a customer's machine. In a final step, the provider uploads the signed TD set to TDMP. It is necessary to check the uploaded TD set integrity by verifying the digital signature with the provider's public key before storing these data in a database on the server and eventually publishing the offer on TDMP's website.

TD Purchasing

When receiving an order for producing a specific product with particular characteristics for example material, quality, etc. machine's operator has two possibilities, to develop the needed TD or to search and buy them from TDMP. Figure 2 shows the activities that should be done by a purchasing process that starts with the action *"access TDMP Website"*. Before beginning trading process on TDMP, a customer should be authenticated by system. This step is important to manage customer's identities and related actions on marketplace. With action *"Enter log-in data"* the customer should enter his username and password to log-in into his own profile. As mentioned by offering TD, new participants should register on TDMP. That is important to ensure the reliability and enables a clean workflow of trading process on TDMP. As soon as this action is done successfully, the customer's participation is confirmed and further actions like purchasing or providing on marketplace can begin. A customer starts the purchasing process with searching for required TD on the marketplace using some search criteria as material type, machine model/serial number, needed quality, etc. After finding the suitable TD, it is also important to specify a license model according to the use case of order and budget requirements. For example, if the buyer only needs to use this data for one week, it might not be suitable or economic to buy a data set that has a one year license model available. Then, the purchased TD is encrypted with the key that is generated from license information for the machine, which uses TD set.

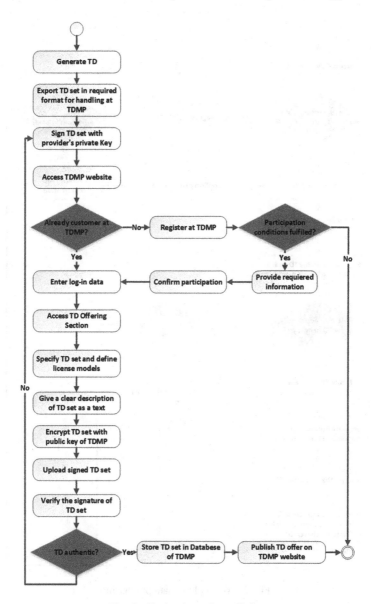

Fig. 1. Technology data offering

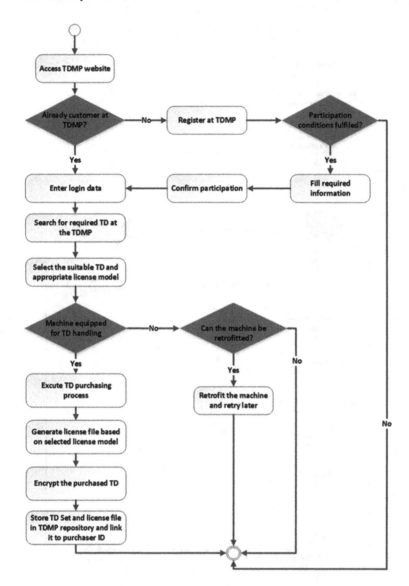

Fig. 2. Technology data purchasing

Once a suitable TD set and an acceptable license model is selected, the customer will be asked about the capability of the machine that will process this TD and if it is equipped for this process. The machine should ensure a secure and clean handling of TD and at the same time it should enable to use TD only according to selected license models. This includes being able to verify the availability of using TD by checking the license information and synchronizing them with TDMP server.

It is also necessary that the machine can use the acquired data set in accordance with the license associated with it. The machine must support the licensing system and be able to properly interpret the usage rights specified in the license file. Meaning that the machine must be able to read, understand and abide by the terms provided by the license file. Otherwise the customer should retrofit the machine to be able to handle TD and try again later. If the machine is not able to be retrofitted, a trading process should be ended.

Once all these conditions are met, the TD set can be purchased and then a license file based on the selected license model is generated by the system. After that, the selected TD set and the generated license file are stored in TD repository with a link to the purchaser's identity. This TD set will be stored on server and is available for use until a buyer accesses the website to download data for operating the machine according to the terms of the license model. Once the license validity period is over, the key that can decrypt the TD set expires and the machine can no longer use this data. As an alternative, the buyer has the option to extend or to buy another license model if the TD is still needed.

4 Conclusion

A new concept for online trading of TD on a technology data marketplace in the sector of automation und manufacturing is presented in this paper. This concept illustrates that existing data are the digital goods of the future. This industry enables to raise enterprises' revenues by facilitating innovative business models that handle with existing resources, namely needed TD for machine operation. However, suitable security means that protect this data overall trading processes are required. Furthermore it is essential to develop appropriate license models that manage usage policies of executing these data. Otherwise it will be ineffective to develop and operate this marketplace. In order to establish TDMP the workflow of offering and purchasing processes are then demonstrated. We focused on these two main scenarios to analyze the requirements that are needed and specified essential protection means.

Acknowledgements. This work has been funded by the German Federal Ministry of Education and Research (BMBF) in the project IUNO – National reference project on IT-Security in Industrie 4.0 (project number 16KIS0328).

References

1. MacDougall, W.: Marketing and Communications Germany Trade & Invest. Industrie 4.0 Smart Manufacturing for the future. Germany Trade and Invest, Gesellschaft für Außenwirtschaft und Standortmarketing mbH (2014)
2. Federal Ministry of Education and Research (BMBF). The New High-Tech Strategy Innovations for Germany, Berlin, August 2014
3. Kagermann, H., Wahlster, W., Helbig, J.: Umsetzungsempfehlungen für das Zukunftsprojekt Industrie 4.0: Deutschlands Zukunft als Produktionsstandort sichern: Abschlussbericht des Arbeitskreises Industrie 4.0 (2013)
4. Ludwig, T., et al.: Arbeiten im Mittelstand 4.0 – KMU im Spannungsfeld des digitalen Wandels. HMD Prax. Wirtsch. **53**(1), 71–86 (2016)

5. Thitimajshima, W., Esichaikul, V., Krairit, D.: Developing a conceptual framework to evaluate public B2B E-marketplaces. In: PACIS 2015 Proceedings (2015)
6. Chien, S.-H., Chen, Y.-H., Hsu, C.-Y.: Exploring the impact of trust and relational embeddedness in e-marketplaces: An empirical study in Taiwan. Ind. Mark. Manage. **41**(3), 460–468 (2012)
7. Beige, S.A.K., Abdi, F.: On the critical success factors for B2B e-marketplace. Decis. Sci. Lett. **4**(1), 77–86 (2015)
8. Kumar, B.A.: Cogniton based trust model for B2B E-Market. In: presented at the 2015 1st International Conference on Next Generation Computing Technologies (NGCT), Dehradun, India (2015)
9. Niranjanamurthy, M., Chahar, D.: The study of E-commerce security issues and solutions. Int. J. Adv. Res. Comput. Commun. Eng. **2**(7), 1–12 (2013)
10. comScore: The U.S. Mobile App Report (2014)
11. Google: Android for Work Security White Paper (2015)
12. Google: Google for Work Security and Compliance Whitepaper, 10 November 2016
13. Dai Zovi, D.A.: Apple iOS 4 Security Evaluation, vol. 24, p. 37. Black Hat, USA (2011)
14. Egners, A., Marschollek, B., Meyer, U.: Hackers in your pocket: a survey of smartphone security across platforms. RWTH Aachen Technical Report AIB-2012-07 (2012)
15. Holzer, A., Ondrus, J.: Mobile application market: A developer's perspective. Telematics Inform. **28**(1), 22–31 (2011)
16. Rosenblatt, W., Mooney, S., Trippe, W.: Digital Rights Management: Business and Technology. Wiley Inc., New York (2001)
17. Azad, M.M., Ahmed, A.H.S., Alam, A.: Digital rights management. Int. J. Comput. Sci. Netw. Secur. **10**(11), 24–33 (2010)
18. Hammersland, R., Strømstad, J.: Digital Rights Management (2008)
19. Shaabany, G., Grimm, M., Anderl, R.: Secure information model for data marketplaces enabling global distributed manufacturing. In: The Proceedings of the 26th CIRP Design Conference, June 2016

Changing Information Management in Product-Service System PLM: Customer-Oriented Strategy

Alexander Smirnov[1,2], Nikolay Shilov[1,2(✉)], Andreas Oroszi[3],
Mario Sinko[3], and Thorsten Krebs[4]

[1] SPIIRAS, St. Petersburg, Russia
{smir,nick}@iias.spb.su
[2] ITMO University, St. Petersburg, Russia
[3] Festo AG & Co., Esslingen, Germany
{oro,sni}@de.festo.com
[4] encoway GmbH, Bremen, Germany
krebs@encoway.de

Abstract. Increasing competition and appearance of new information and communication technologies makes companies to introduce new production and marketing models. The paper shares the experiences of improving PLM information management at an automation equipment manufacturer caused by implementation of product-service systems and their customer-driven configuration. Though the research results are based on the analysis of one company, the presented work can give significant input to achieve benefits for component manufacturers that tend to become system vendors in general.

Keywords: Customer-oriented view · Application view
Product-service-system · Strategy · Information management

1 Introduction

Saturation and globalization of modern commoditized markets requires companies to apply new models for production and marketing [1, 2]. The markets are shrinking and companies see service provision as a new path towards profits and growth. Automation equipment production is not an exception. The carried out analysis of the business and information management processes at different PLM stages related to an automation equipment producer shows that instead of offering separate products, the company now tends to offer complex products (which may consist of several other products), whole integrated systems and also software units using different services. Product-Service Systems (PSS) assume orientation on combination of products and services (often supporting the products) instead of focusing only on products. This paradigm fits well automation equipment producers, for which tight relationships with customers are of high importance. These tight relationships enable the possibility to get valuable equipment usage statistics at the PLM stages beyond the production and sales, i.e., analyse use cases and get direct user feedback.

J. Ríos et al. (Eds.): PLM 2017, IFIP AICT 517, pp. 701–709, 2017.
https://doi.org/10.1007/978-3-319-72905-3_62

Achievements in the area of artificial intelligence (AI) open new possibilities for increasing customer satisfaction from customer-driven design to reduced lead-time. The current wave of progress and enthusiasm for AI began around 2010, driven by three mutually reinforcing factors: (1) the availability of big data from sources including e-commerce, businesses, social media, science, and government, which provided raw material for (2) dramatically improved machine learning approaches and algorithms, which, in turn, relied on (3) the capabilities of more powerful computers [3]. Therefore, adaptation of information management in companies to the new trends is mandatory to succeed in the current situation.

This trend opens a whole new world of business models allowing companies to transform from product suppliers to service providers or even to virtual companies acting as brokers. For example, Rolls-Royce instead of selling aircraft engines now charges companies for hours that engines run and takes care of servicing the engines [4]. Another famous example is Uber, that does not only provides taxi services, but it does this without actually owning cars and acts just as a connecting link between the taxi drivers and passengers. Timely changed business model can provide for a significant competitive advantage (e.g., the capitalisation of Uber in 2015 was between $60 and $70 billion, which was higher than that of GM ($55 billion) [5]).

Automation equipment production is not an exception. The carried out analysis of the business and information management processes related to an automation equipment producer shows that instead of offering separate products, the company now tends to offer complex products (which may consist of several other products), whole integrated systems and also software units using different software services [6, 7]. Product-Service Systems (PSS) assume orientation on combination of products and services (often supporting the products) instead of focusing only on products. This paradigm fits well automation equipment producers, for which tight relationships with customers are of high importance. These tight relationships enable the possibility to get valuable equipment usage statistics, analyse use cases and get direct user feedback [8–10].

However, implementation of this paradigm requires significant changes in information management at nearly all stages of the lifecycle [11]. The paper investigates the problem of PSS information management at different PLM stages in a customer-oriented way and presents the way it has been solved.

2 Proposed Approach

The paper is based on the analysis and modification of the business and information management processes related to PSS configuration and engineering at the automation equipment producer Festo AG & Co KG. It produces pneumatic and electronic automation equipment and products for various process industries and has more than 300 000 customers in 176 countries supported by more than 52 companies worldwide with more than 250 branch offices and authorized agencies in further 36 countries. For companies with wide assortments of products (more than 30 000 – 40 000 products of approx. 700 types, with various configuration possibilities), it is very important to ensure that customers can easily navigate among them to define needed services.

The used "gap analysis"-driven methodology was implemented through the following steps. First, the analysis of the current organisation of the product information management was carried out. Then, the expert estimation of the company benchmark was done. Based on this, the comparison of the present and desirable business process and information management organisation was done resulting in creating corresponding process matrixes. This has made it possible to identify major gaps between the present and the desirable business organization, analyse these and define strategies to overcome these gaps.

Research efforts in the area of information management show that information and knowledge needs of a particular employee depend on his/her tasks and responsibilities [12, 13]. Different stages of PLM processes in the company are associated with different roles like product managers, sales personnel, and other including customers. The representatives of different roles have different needs when interacting with an application like a PSS configurator [e.g., 14]. A product manager, for example, knows about the products and is able to configure by deciding on technical facts. A customer, on the other hand, may not know about the technical details of the company's products or even what kind of product he/she may use to solve his/her application problem. This is the reason why technical product details should be hidden from the customer under the application layer. As a result, the overall concept of customer-centric view on the PSS has been formulated. It includes a new role of "system architect" responsible for the holistic view to PSS and its configuration, description of its functionality and applications, and designing a customer view to it.

3 Product Lifecycle Support for PSS

PLM encompasses the processes needed to launch new products, manage changes to existing products and retire products at the end of their life. In this sense, typical product life cycle stages are development, introduction, growth, maturity and decline [11]. The development stage is when new products are conceived and prepared for manufacturing. For variant-rich products, the stages introduction and growth as well as the maturity are typically supported with product configurators. The decline stage, in contrast to previous ones, is the latest stage at which either a considered product is completely phased out or well-suited successor products are sought.

The development stage is distinguished from the introduction and following stages in the sense that development deals with setting up product master data, structures and configuration rules. The stages from introduction to maturity use this data for effective sales supported by product configuration.

Product lifecycle support for PSS differs from that for products. Major differences arise from the point of view to the products.

The PSS view comes from the application side (Table 1). After defining of the application area, configuration rules and constraints to the system are defined. They are followed by characteristics and system structure definition. Finally, the apps (software applications and services) enriching the system functionality or improving its reliability and maintenance are defined. The same applies to the sales stage.

Table 1. Product information priority at different stages of PSS life cycle.

Market evaluation	Engineering	Production	Sales	Maintenance	Phase out
Application	Product structure	Characteristics	Application	Apps	Product structure
Constraints	Characteristics	Constraints	Constraints	Product structure	Characteristics
Characteristics	Constraints	Product Structure	Apps	Characteristics	
Product Structure		Apps	Characteristics	Constraints	
Apps			Product Structure		

As a result, implementing application-constraints-system mentioned above view addresses the problem of designing the customer view on system selection, configuration and processing (defining user experience, "talking in a customer-understandable language") [15].

4 Identified Goals and Related Strategies

The result of the carried out "gap analysis" has made it possible to identify two major gaps and strategies aimed at overcoming these:

1. Designing customer view on PSS selection, configuration and processing.

There are different types of information users at different PLM stages, like product managers, sales personnel, or customers. These users have different needs when interacting with an application like a PSS configurator. The "customer view" and the "company's internal view" describe two contrary views addressing the intersection between the company's product diversity and the customer's individuality with a common goal: being able to guide a customer in selecting and configuring the right system for his/her application problem. At first sight, diversity and individuality seem to have a lot in common, but the goal behind each is rather distinct. It is important to analyze the customer's context (especially for offering services): system usage, customer's industry, who does the maintenance, country-specific regulations, etc.

2. Increasing PSS modularity/reusability in the context of product combinations and systems.

The structure of product combinations and systems needs to modularized. "Comparable" modules have the key ability to be used in multiple configuration contexts. This concerns not only products and components, but also product combinations and whole PSSs assuming building a multilevel PSS engineering model. Thus, a general PSS model architecture needs to be set up.

Below, these issues are considered in detail.

4.1 Designing Customer View on PSS Selection, Configuration and Processing

The complex PSS view comes from the application side. After defining the application area, configuration rules and constraints to the system are defined. They are followed by characteristics and system structure definition. Finally, the apps (software applications) enriching the system functionality or improving its reliability and maintenance are defined. The same applies to the sales stage of the lifecycle.

As it was mentioned, different information needs of different roles (product managers, sales personnel, customers, etc.) are the reason to hide the technical product and service details under the application layer. In addition, the selection of the right system for solving the application problem can be based on a mapping between the application layer and a (hidden) technical layer. In the optimal case, a customer does not notice whether he/she is selecting a product or configuring a complex system.

As a result, the overall concept of customer-centric view on the products has been formulated as shown in Fig. 1. It includes the introduced above new role of "System architect" responsible for the development of the holistic view to the system, its configuration, description of its functionality and applications, and designing a customer-centric view to it.

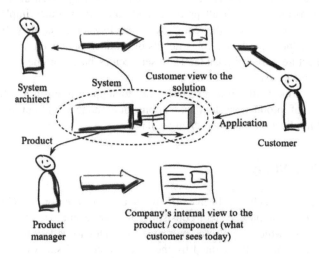

Fig. 1. Customer-centric application view

4.2 Increasing System Modularity/Reusability in the Context of Product Combinations and Systems

The changing requirements on business processes also induce changing requirements on information systems.

In today's world, most companies still do product specification with Microsoft Word documents or similar approaches. These documents are handed over to construction. Construction hands over other data, e.g. technical characteristics via PDM systems or CAD files, to manufacturing, and so on. At the time a sales channel is set up for the new product, the initial data from product specification is lost. Thus, a new requirement for effectively setting up sales configurators and after-sales support is a continuous database. Knowledge about the product's application domain should be formally acquired already in the early phases of new product development. In this case, the data is available whenever needed in later steps of the product lifecycle process.

Typically, the new product development process is structured in several milestones, such as design approval, technical approval or sales approval. During the entire life cycle, different roles work on product-centred data: product managers, engineers, controllers, marketing, sales personnel, and so on. Thus, either the relevant product data needs to be handed over – and potentially transformed – from a phase of the life cycle to later phases, or there is a single information system with which all the different roles carry out their daily work; every role on their specific view on a portion of the product data. In both cases, one of the major benefits for all concerned roles would be a seamless integration of all product life cycle phases within a comprehensive workflow.

A system modelling environment must be capable of designing modular system architecture. This means that using such an environment, it must be possible to reuse single product models in the scope of system configurations and assign product or system models to application knowledge. This requires the definition of well-formed system and product model interfaces to allow for modularity. Such interfaces enable a black-box approach, in which all products and software modules implementing this interface can be chosen for the complex product/system; i.e. they become inter-changeable. For the user, the complex details of product models on lower levels of the system architecture remain invisible. The user decides based on the visible character-istics of the "black box".

Finally yet importantly, it is also necessary to support multi-user activities on the different parts of product, system and application models without losing track of changes and implication that such changes have.

5   Pilot Case Study

The developed approach has been verified on a pilot case for the Control cabinet system. This is a complex system consisting of a large number of different control elements, some of which are also complex systems. Due to variety of components, its functionality is significantly defined by the software control subsystem. Control cab-inets are usually configured individually based on the customer requirements since their configurations are tightly related to the equipment used by the customer.

Before the change, the customer had to compile a large bill of materials by deciding individually for every single component, in order to get the control cabinet. Now, with a holistic view to the control cabinet as to a single complex PSS including corre-sponding apps and software services, it can be configured and ordered as one product.

At the first stage, based on the demand history, the main requirements and com-ponents are defined at the market evaluation stage.

Then, at the engineering stage the components, baseline configurations based on branch specific applications as well as possible constraints are defined. The result of this is a source data for creating a cabinet configurator tool that makes it possible for the customers to configure cabinets based on their requirements online. At this stage, such specific characteristics are taken into account as components used, characteristics and capabilities of the cabinet, as well as resulting lead time and price (Fig. 2).

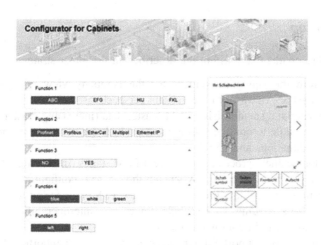

Fig. 2. Control cabinet configurator: an interface example

Based on the customer-defined configuration the engineering data is generated in an automatic (in certain cases – semi-automatic) way, which is used for the production stage. As a result, the centralized production of cabinets is based on the automatically generated engineering file (Fig. 3).

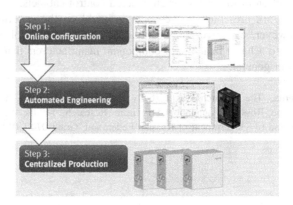

Fig. 3. Control cabinet: from online configuration to production

The new business process made it possible to reduce the time from configuration to delivery from several weeks to few days (depending on the required components). The product maintenance is also significantly simplified due to the system-based view. All the data about this product (not only separated components) is available and can be used for modification of its configuration on customer's demand.

6 Conclusion

The detailed steps identified within the described in the paper strategies include:

1. Change from the single convenient for the company view of products to the user-friendly PSS views from the various perspectives.
2. Homogenizing and standardizing PLM master data (increasing master data quality; e.g. for being able to compare components, which are necessary to build partially defined combinations and PSSs).
3. Aligning the business processes of different PLM stages (improving interoperability and avoiding redundant tasks). When building a new configurator platform, it is important to align business processes like new PSS engineering together with the desired outcome. Doing so can help improving interoperability and avoiding redundant tasks e.g. in data maintenance.
4. Implementing tool support for the changed processes (supporting the improved business processes).

Step 1 required an introduction of a new role of "system architect". Step 2 has mostly been achieved by defining the common ontology and forcing the use of globally defined attributes [16, 17]. Regarding steps 2 and 3, some tools for the current business organization have been implemented. The productive use of all these tools proves that the ideas behind the common ontology work well. The developed business process and supporting information systems made it possible to implement a pilot scenario of the automated production of the customer-engineered control cabinets.

Though the work presented in the paper is based on the experiences from one company, it however, can give significant input (for example, following strategies identified above) to achieve benefits for component manufacturers that tend to become system vendors in general.

Acknowledgements. The research was partially supported by projects funded by grants# 16-07-00375 of the Russian Foundation for Basic Research, by the State Research no. 0073-2014-0005, and by Government of Russian Federation, Grant 074-U01.

References

1. Zhang, M.-R., Yang, C.-C., Ho, S.-Y., Chang, C.H.: A study on enterprise under globalization competition knowledge management and creation overhead construction. J. Interdisc. Math. **17**(5–6), 423–433 (2014). https://doi.org/10.1080/09720502.2013.800299
2. Erdener, K., Hassan, S.: Globalization of Consumer Markets: Structures and Strategies. Routledge, London (2014)
3. Artificial Intelligence, Automation, and the Economy. Report of Executive Office of the President of the United States, December 2016. https://www.whitehouse.gov/blog/2016/12/20/artificial-intelligence-automation-and-economy
4. Bryson, J.R., Daniels, P.W. (eds.): Handbook of Service Business: Management, Marketing, Innovation and Internationalisation. Edward Elgar Publishing, Cheltenham (2015)
5. La Monica, P.R.: Is Uber really worth more than Ford and GM? CNN Money (2015). http://money.cnn.com/2015/10/27/investing/uber-ford-gm-70-billion-valuation/
6. Ceschin, F.: Product-service system innovation: a promising approach to sustainability. Sustainable Product-Service Systems. SAST, pp. 17–40. Springer, Cham (2014). https://doi.org/10.1007/978-3-319-03795-0_2
7. Wallin, J., Parida, V., Isaksson, O.: Understanding product-service system innovation capabilities development for manufacturing companies. J. Manuf. Technol. Manage. **26**(5), 763–787 (2015). https://doi.org/10.1108/JMTM-05-2013-0055
8. Baumeister, H.: Customer relationship management for SMEs. In: Proceedings of the 2nd Annual Conference eBusiness and eWork e2002, Prague, Czech Republic (2002)
9. Fjermestad, J., Romano Jr., N.C.: An integrative implementation framework for electronic customer relationship management: revisiting the general principles of usability and resistance. In: Proceedings of the 36th Hawaii International Conference on System Sciences (HICSS 2003), Big Island, HI, USA (2003)
10. Piller, F., Schaller, C.: Individualization based collaborative customer relationship management: motives, structures, and modes of collaboration for mass customization and CRM. In: Working Paper No. 29 of the Department of General and Industrial Management, Technische Universität München (2004)
11. Stark, J. (ed.): Product Lifecycle Management, 365 p. Springer, Heidelberg (2015)
12. Gao, S., Guo, Y., Chen, J.: The performance of knowledge collaboration in virtual teams: an empirical study. Int. J. Multimedia Ubiquit. Eng. **9**(8), 193–212 (2014)
13. Andersson, J.: Representing human-automation challenges. Chalmers University of Technology (2014)
14. Felic, A., König-Ries, B., Klein, M.: Process-oriented semantic knowledge management in product lifecycle management. Procedia CIRP **25**, 361–368 (2014)
15. Smirnov, A., Kashevnik, A., Shilov, N., Oroszi, A., Sinko, M., Krebs, T.: Changing business information systems for innovative configuration processes. In: Matulevičius, R., Maggi, F. M., Küngas, P. (eds.) Joint Proceedings of the BIR 2015 Workshops and Doctoral Consortium co-located with 14th International Conference on Perspectives in Business Informatics Research (BIR 2015), CEUR, vol. 1420, pp. 62–73 (2015)
16. Smirnov, A., Kashevnik, A., Teslya, N., Shilov, N., Oroszi, A., Sinko, M., Humpf, M., Arneving, J.: Knowledge Management for Complex Product Development. In: Bernard, A., Rivest, L., Dutta, D. (eds.) PLM 2013. IAICT, vol. 409, pp. 110–119. Springer, Heidelberg (2013). https://doi.org/10.1007/978-3-642-41501-2_12
17. Bruno, G., Korf, R., Lentes, J., Zimmermann, N.: Efficient management of product lifecycle information through a semantic platform. Int. J. Prod. Lifecycle Manage. (IJPLM) **9**(1), 45–64 (2016)

A Method for Lifecycle Design of Product/Service Systems Using PLM Software

Tomohiko Sakao[1(✉)], Yang Liu[1], Rolf Gustafsson[2], and Gabriel Thörnblad[2]

[1] Division of Environmental Technology and Management, Department of Management and Engineering, Linköping University, 581 83 Linköping, Sweden {tomohiko.sakao,yang.liu}@liu.se

[2] Maxiom AB, 413 28 Göteborg, Sweden {rolf,gabriel}@maxiom.se

Abstract. Environmental sustainability and resource scarcities are urgent issues, and innovative ways of providing products and services are needed. In light of a circular economy, manufacturers have yet to learn and implement innovative ways of design covering the entire product lifecycle and incorporating sustainability and resource issues based on system perspectives. This paper aims at proposing an innovative and practical method to support manufacturers in the design of a product/service system (PSS) for resource efficiency and sustainability. The intention is that the method be implemented as an add-on feature for commercial PLM (product lifecycle management) software, with a lifecycle focus, including calculation of lifecycle cost (LCC).

Keywords: Commercial PLM software · LCC (lifecycle cost)

1 Introduction

Environmental problems and resource scarcities are forcing rapid changes in manufacturing firms, and innovative ways of providing products and services are needed. In light of the circular economy [1], manufacturers acknowledge the importance of resource efficiency and technology to survive in global competition. To increase resource efficiency by circular flows of materials, the lifecycle perspective is critical, and design is the most influential activity on the lifecycle. In addition, services such as take-back, repair, and repurpose are often provided effectively with products by manufacturers, where such an offering is often called a product/service system (PSS) [2].

Despite academia's advances in scientific methods for lifecycle design of products and services, manufacturers, especially small and medium-sized enterprises (SMEs), have yet to learn and implement innovative ways of design covering the entire product lifecycle and incorporating resource issues. This is the challenge targeted by the paper

© IFIP International Federation for Information Processing 2017
Published by Springer International Publishing AG 2017. All Rights Reserved
J. Ríos et al. (Eds.): PLM 2017, IFIP AICT 517, pp. 710–718, 2017.
https://doi.org/10.1007/978-3-319-72905-3_63

because, according to a thorough review in the area [3], virtually no practical solution is available to fill this gap.

Manufacturing firms, even SMEs, often utilize CAD (computer-aided design) and/or PLM (product lifecycle management) software in their routines to design their products. The paper takes these tools as an excellent opportunity to build a practical solution. As a first step, the paper aims to propose an innovative and practical method to support manufacturers in their design of a PSS lifecycle from the environmental and economic perspectives. The intention is to implement the method as an add-on feature for a commercial PLM software package.

2   Related Works

2.1   Ecodesign Methods and Tools

For increasing resource efficiency, design is seen as a key activity because it has a high impact on the performance of a designed product and/or service [4]. There have been numerous methods and tools proposed over the last two decades to support design for resource efficiency (see e.g. a review by [3]). The most widely known are a checklist method, e.g. [5], and lifecycle assessment (LCA). Both of these are effective for assessing a product from an environmental viewpoint. Even a discussion of how to implement environmental assessment scientifically in CAD software is available; see e.g. [6]. Another type is a method with a specific purpose, e.g. Design for Disassembly (DfDA) [7, 8] and Design for Remanufacturing [9]. However, most of these methods/tools focus on the environmental aspect and fail to consider business issues [10]; in other words, they focus on "design for social virtue" [11]. This is a fundamental problem that creates barriers for companies to use those methods/tools. A method needs to be embedded in a "must do" process for designers in order to be used in industry [12]. This is an especially relevant issue for SMEs, who are often unable to afford to use a method/tool that does not directly address the economic aspect, with the exception of regulations [13].

In light of the circular economy, which emphasizes economic benefits for companies [14], one competitive edge that is economically attractive to manufacturing firms today, even to SMEs as reported in [15], is integrating services (e.g. upgrade, maintenance, repair, product reuse, part reuse, repurpose, take-back, and remanufacturing) with physical products in design [16]. This way of offering both product and service is a pragmatic approach to decrease environmental impacts in real business; in other words, it does not automatically mean reduced environmental impact, but it has high potential towards better environmental performance. This type of integration has been reported with offerings on the market in different sectors to have decreased environmental impacts (see e.g. [17, 18]). This is in line with the frequent dominance of the use phase impact on the total lifecycle environmental impact, as discussed by e.g. [19]. Therefore, to guide designers to integrate products with services through economic motivation towards circularity is promising, even in terms of resource efficiency. There exist a few methods to support designers in such a manner that have been verified with industrial cases (e.g. [20, 21]. However, virtually no practical and simple solution is available today, especially for SMEs to be able to implement, according to different thorough reviews [3, 22].

2.2 PLM Software

PLM software is designed to manage product-related information such as data, processes, business systems and people throughout the entire lifecycle of a product efficiently and cost-effectively, from ideation, to design and manufacture, to service and disposal [23]. There are many commercial PLM software applications. Some of the major diverse functions and technologies converge through PLM, including: product data management (PDM), computer-aided design (CAD), computer-aided manufacturing (CAM), computer-aided engineering (CAE) and simulation.

Among these, PDM uses software to manage product and process-related data and information, such as CAD data, models, parts information, manufacturing instructions, requirements, and notes and documents, all in a central system.

According to one of the major PDM software vendors [23], the ideal system is accessible by multiple applications and multiple teams across an organization and supports business-specific needs, and the right PDM software can provide a company in any industry with a solid foundation that can be easily expanded into a full PLM platform.

Among the currently available commercial PLM software applications, none was found that significantly addresses the economic impact of products or PSSs, especially in the design phase. We aim to bridge this gap by introducing a new software concept which integrates the lifecycle cost (LCC) and lifecycle revenue (LCR) analysis in the traditional PLM software so that designers can evaluate the economic impacts during the design phase. The related works were reviewed, and there were merely a few; G. EN.ESI (Integrated software platform for Green ENgineering dESIgn and product sustainability), an EU FP7 project led by Germani, is one of the few public projects relevant to our concept [24, 25], and his research group published a series of articles [26–28]. The new concept introduced in this paper is developed to ensure its academic novelty.

3 Proposed Method

3.1 Overview

Figure 1 depicts the proposed method from the procedure viewpoint, and the steps with iterations are outlined below. The method builds upon the basic functions of an existing PLM software package.

Step 1. Define a lifecycle of the target system – This definition includes the major function (functional unit in LCA), the length of the lifecycle and the boundary for the system to be designed and analysed.

Step 2. Give a pricing model for the system – A method user (i.e., a designer of the system) gives the pricing model by which the customer pays money to the provider from the predefined alternatives below.

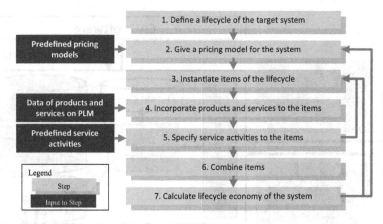

Fig. 1. Procedure with the proposed method

1. A price given to the product sold and prices given to additional services in a sub-system or a system
2. A price given to a sub-system or a system with a specific time period or an applicable condition (e.g., running hours)

Step 3. Instantiate items of the lifecycle – First, the user determines the level of granularity of the parts and processes described. Based on the outcome of Step 1 and the granularity, each of the parts and processes is instantiated as an item in a PLM software package.

Step 4. Incorporate products and services to the items – As an option, data from products and services on the PLM software is linked to the items from the outcome of Step 3.

Step 5. Specify service activities to the items – Service activities, i.e. take-back, reuse, remanufacturing, and recycle, are associated to each item of the parts only. When each of the service activities takes place and how much it costs for the provider and the customer are also specified.

Step 6. Combine items – As an option, items defined in Step 3 are assembled as another item on a higher level in the hierarchy of the system structure. This step is sensible because different payment models may be given to items in the same system.

Step 7. Calculate lifecycle economy – The PLM software calculates the cost and revenue for the given lifecycle of the system. According to the result, a user is given an opportunity to carry out iteration.

The overview of the software adopted in the proposed method as explained in the procedure above is depicted in Fig. 2. It involves basic functions of existing PLM applications as well as CAD software packages. Note that the new feature is shown with a shaded colour. The figure is explained in greater detail in the following sections.

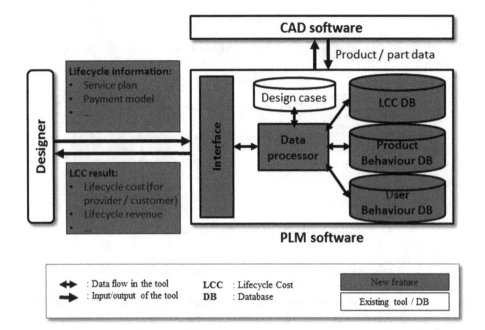

Fig. 2. Overview of the software adopted in the proposed method

3.2   Base PLM Software

Our method adopts existing commercial PLM software as a base, which is already widely in use for companies who want to organize their information. We build a new add-on feature based upon the current platform.

PLM is a system that spans several departments and areas of a business. The objective of PLM is a system that grows, evolves and changes so that it always supports the company's internal processes and procedures. The PLM system shall be able to be loosely integrated with other systems, e.g. CAD systems and business systems.

The base PLM software that is chosen by meeting the above requirements is called YaPdm. It is a PDM and PLM system with CAD integrations, workflows, a bill of materials (BoM) report, processes, etc. The system consists of a server and client. On the server side there is an SQL database and a vault, and the program itself is installed on the client's desktop. The system provides the following functions.

- Document Management
  All the documents and files can be structured and versioned. Templates, project structures and a set of attributes can easily be designed to answer all business needs.
- Integrations
  The CAD integrations ensure that the user is working with the right revisions of an assembly. The integrations to the Office programs synchronize the properties and attributes between the application and PLM.

- Item Management
  By creating items and item structures, documents such as drawings and instructions can be linked to the items.
- Projects
  To manage projects and related files, all documentation on a project is easily collected in one place. It is possible to control the project rights and status in the system.
- Revision Management
  To keep track of all documents and files, all revisions are saved and can be filtered by approval date.
- Workflows
  It is possible to create several approval flows and have control over what happens during the various steps in the process.

3.3 New Feature for Calculating LCC for PSS

As the main contribution of this paper, we aim to propose an innovative and practical method to support manufacturers in their design of PSS for resource efficiency and sustainability. This particularly requires addressing the economic and service aspects related to a lifecycle. Currently, there is no commercially available PLM software addressing such aspects when designing a lifecycle. The intention is that the proposed method be implemented as an add-on feature for existing commercial PLM software described in Sect. 3.1. The new added features mainly include a calculation of lifecycle cost for the manufacturer and customer, and lifecycle revenue for the manufacturer.

The purposes of the new feature

- To improve the economic aspect of a system in question from the lifecycle perspective.
- To support a user of the software design services, i.e. take-back, reuse, remanufacturing, and recycle, within the system.
- To share, reuse and modify cases of previous designs of systems in an efficient manner.
- To describe the system for carrying out LCA outside the software.

The functions of the add-on to be developed

- To receive information about services and the economic aspect of a system in question in an interactive manner with a user.
- To maintain links with the information on the base PLM software and the add-on.
- To calculate lifecycle costs of a system in question for the manufacturer.
- To calculate lifecycle revenues of a system in question for the manufacturer.
- To calculate lifecycle costs of a system in question for the customer.
- To report the result of the calculations as a text file.
- To save and show design cases of previous designs of systems.

The overall structure and key elements of the add-on

The overall structure of the software to be developed is depicted in Fig. 2.

Lifecycle information.

The lifecycle information is given to a specific system that is described on the software and includes:

- Service plan:
  - Which service activities are applicable, i.e. take-back, reuse, remanufacturing, and recycle
  - In which months to do a specific type of service of the system
  - Which hardware to do a specific type of service in which months
- LCC (lifecycle cost) and LCR (lifecycle revenue) hierarchies
  - Cost elements of a system
  - Revenue elements of a system

LCC database (DB).

The DB stores economic data for:

- Products included in the system
- Services included in the system

- Product behaviour DB:
  The DB stores a quantitative function to calculate the quality (to be degraded over time) of the product depending on the time from the start of the use and after maintenance.
- User behaviour DB:
  The DB stores a quantitative function to decide the customer's choice depending on the quality of the product from alternatives as follows:
  - Continue to use the product
  - Order maintenance of the product
  - Stop using the product

LCC result.

The LCC result depends on the lifecycle of the system and includes:

- Lifecycle cost (LCC) for manufacturer / customer
- Lifecycle revenue (LCR) for manufacturer

LCC and LCR are calculated as a summation based on the hierarchies defined in the software specification.

4   Concluding Discussion

The proposed software and method are expected to be used widely in the manufacturing industry because of its need, as described in Sect. 1. They could work as an innovative method for decision making in design and for follow-up in order to enhance resource efficiency from the lifecycle and system perspectives, because based on the literature surveyed [3, 22], no such method is available. As more information about things becomes available along the industrial megatrend of Internet of Things, it is expected to integrate information from sensors into the design phase. The software has a potential to function as an essential component to convey relevant lifecycle information to better design for e.g. reliability and remanufacturability. This paper presented an initial proposal of the method, and the method is yet to be validated.

5 Outlook

Future works include: 1. Implementation of the method as software, and 2. Evaluation of the method and the software with real cases from the manufacturing industry. The authors have been running a project with three manufacturing companies involved as lead users. Therefore, the plan is to apply the method and the software to cases from the three firms. Their systems are waste management systems, office furniture systems, and display systems at industrial fairs, which provide a substantial difference in terms of system lifetimes and thus opportunities to evaluate the method and the software in different circumstances. The reader is invited to contribute to the development of the method and the software, especially by offering an additional case from industry, as this development is under a pressing need from our societies transitioning towards a sustainable world.

Acknowledgements. This research is supported by the Circularis (Circular Economy through Innovating Design) project funded by VINNOVA, Sweden's Innovation Agency (No. 2016-03267).

References

1. European Commission: Towards a circular economy: a zero waste programme for Europe (2014)
2. Goedkoop, M.J., van Halen, C.J.G., Te Riele, H.R.M., Rommens, P.J.M.: Product Service systems, Ecological and Economic Basics (1999)
3. Umeda, Y., Takata, S., Kimura, F., Tomiyama, T., Sutherland, J.W., Kara, S., Herrmann, C., Duflou, J.R.: Toward integrated product and process life cycle planning—an environmental perspective. CIRP Ann. Manuf. Technol. **61**, 681–702 (2012)
4. Pahl, G., Beitz, W., Feldhusen, J., Grote, K.-H.: Engineering Design: A Systematic Approach. Springer, London (2007)
5. Wimmer, W., Züst, R.: ECODESIGN Pilot: Product Investigation, Learning and Optimization Tool for Sustainable Product Development. Kluwer Academic Publishers, Boston (2001)
6. Leibrecht, S.: Fundamental principles for CAD-based ecological assessments. Int. J. Life Cycle Assess. **10**, 436–444 (2005)
7. Harjula, T., Rapoza, B., Knight, W.A., Boothroyd, G.: Design for disassembly and the environment. CIRP Ann. Manuf. Technol. **45**, 109–114 (1996)
8. Chang, H.T., Lu, C.H.: Simultaneous evaluations of material toxicity and ease of disassembly during electronics design: integrating environmental assessments with commercial computer-aided design software. J. Ind. Ecol. **18**, 478–490 (2014)

9. Hatcher, G.D., Ijomah, W.L., Windmill, J.F.C.: Design for remanufacture: a literature review and future research needs. J. Clean. Prod. **19**, 2004–2014 (2011)

10. Sakao, T., Fargnoli, M.: Customization in ecodesign: a demand-side approach bringing new opportunities? J. Ind. Ecol. **14**, 529–532 (2010)

11. McAloone, T.C., Andreasen, M.M.: Design for utility, sustainability and societal virtues: developing product service systems. In: Proceedings of DESIGN 2004, the 8th International Design Conference, Dubrovnik, Croatia (2004)

12. Ernzer, M., Grüner, C., Birkhofer, H.: Implementation of DFE in the daily design work: an approach derived from surveys. In: 14th International Conference on Design Theory and Methodology, Integrated Systems Design, and Engineering Design and Culture, vol. 4, p. 345. ASME (2002)

13. Le Pochat, S., Bertoluci, G., Froelich, D.: Integrating ecodesign by conducting changes in SMEs. J. Clean. Prod. **15**, 671–680 (2007)

14. EMF: Towards the circular economy: an economic and business rationale for an accelerated transition, vol. 1. Ellen MacArthur Foundation (2012)

15. Hernandez-Pardo, R.J., Bhamra, T.A., Bhamra, R.S.: Designing sustainable product service systems in SMEs. Int. J. Des. Manag. Prof. Pract. **6**, 57–71 (2013)

16. Tukker, A.: Product services for a resource-efficient and circular economy - a review. J. Clean. Prod. **97**, 76–91 (2015)

17. Lelah, A., Mathieux, F., Brissaud, D.: Contributions to eco-design of machine-to-machine product service systems: the example of waste glass collection. J. Clean. Prod. **19**, 1033–1044 (2011)

18. Lindahl, M., Sundin, E., Sakao, T.: Environmental and economic benefits of Integrated product service offerings quantified with real business cases. J. Clean. Prod. **64**, 288–296 (2014)

19. Sanyé-Mengual, E., Pérez-López, P., González-García, S., Lozano, R.G., Feijoo, G., Moreira, M.T., Gabarrell, X., Rieradevall, J.: Eco-designing the use phase of products in sustainable manufacturing: the importance of maintenance and communication-to-user strategies. J. Ind. Ecol. **18**, 545–557 (2014)

20. Aurich, J.C., Fuchs, C., Wagenknecht, C.: Life cycle oriented design of technical Product-Service Systems. J. Clean. Prod. **14**, 1480–1494 (2006)

21. Sakao, T., Lindahl, M.: A method to improve integrated product service offerings based on life cycle costing. CIRP Ann. Manuf. Technol. **64**, 33–36 (2015)

22. Ramani, K., Ramanujan, D., Bernstein, W.Z., Zhao, F., Sutherland, J., Handwerker, C., Choi, J.-K., Kim, H., Thurston, D.: Integrated sustainable life cycle design: a review. J. Mech. Des. **132**, 91004–91015 (2010)

23. Siemens Product Lifecycle Management Software Inc.: What is PLM Software? https://www.plm.automation.siemens.com/en_us/plm/index.shtml

24. Germani, M.: G.EN.ESI Report Summary. http://cordis.europa.eu/result/rcn/171703_en.html

25. G.EN.ESI Consortium: G.EN.ESI Publications. http://genesi-fp7.eu/the-project/publications/

26. Germani, M., Mandolini, M., Marconi, M., Dufrene, M., Zwolinski, P.: A methodology and a software platform to implement an eco-design strategy in a manufacturing company. In: 18th Design for Manufacturing and the Life Cycle Conference; 2013 ASME/IEEE International Conference on Mechatronic and Embedded Systems and Applications, vol. 4. ASME (2013)

27. Favi, C., Germani, M., Marconi, M., Mengoni, M.: Innovative software platform for eco-design of efficient electric motors. J. Clean. Prod. **37**, 125–134 (2012)

28. Rossi, M., Germani, M., Zamagni, A.: Review of ecodesign methods and tools. Barriers and strategies for an effective implementation in industrial companies. J. Clean. Prod. **129**, 361–373 (2016)

Defining a PSS Lifecycle Management System: Main Characteristics and Architectural Impacts

Giuditta Pezzotta[1], Mariangela Lazoi[2,3(✉)], Roberto Sala[1], Fabiana Pirola[1], Antonio Margarito[2,3], and Lorenzo Quarta[3]

[1] CELS – Research Group on Industrial Engineering, Logistics and Service Operations, Università degli Studi di Bergamo, viale Marconi 5, 24044 Dalmine, BG, Italy
{giuditta.pezzotta,roberto.sala,fabiana.pirola}@unibg.it
[2] Dipartimento di Ingegneria dell'Innovazione, Università del Salento, Campus Ecotekne, via per Monteroni, 73100 Lecce, Italy
{mariangela.lazoi,antonio.margarito}@unisalento.it
[3] EKA Srl, via Garruba, 70122 Bari, Italy
lorenzo.quarta@eka-systems.com

Abstract. The global crisis and the fierce competition of emerging countries make companies struggling to stay ahead of competition. The number of companies that are enlarging their offer portfolio looking forward to new and increased sources of revenues is always increasing but the number of companies failing in successfully implementing servitization strategy is even more. One possible reason behind this is the lack of tools to support companies while dealing with services that by definition are characterized by high level of intangibility and perishability. In this context, the integration of product design in concurrent with the related service design is becoming very relevant in several industrial fields.

This process is very customer-centered and lead to the development of a product-service specific methodology. Specially, lean design methodologies can be used to foster and improve the integrated product-service design process. Based on this premise, the paper presents the PSS Lean Design methodology developed in the DIVERSITY project and its relations and impact on the data and information management of a product-service lifecycle system. A description of relations and modules customization for the development and diffusion of a PSS lifecycle management system is provided in the paper for an extension also in other contexts.

Keywords: PLMS · Product-Service System (PSS)
PSS Lean Design Methodology · PSS engineering environment

1 Introduction

In the globalised word, manufacturing companies are nowadays increasingly moving towards the adoption of business models based on the offering of a bundle of product and service [1–3]. This change in their offering is due to the modification of the customers' behaviours and their increasing interest in companies' services [4, 5]. Firms'

© IFIP International Federation for Information Processing 2017
Published by Springer International Publishing AG 2017. All Rights Reserved
J. Ríos et al. (Eds.): PLM 2017, IFIP AICT 517, pp. 719–728, 2017.
https://doi.org/10.1007/978-3-319-72905-3_64

response to this substantiated into the delivering of a 'Product–Service System' (PSS) through the transformative paradigm of servitization [3, 6]. Despite this proposal, many companies occur in the "service paradox" since the promised value of adding service to existing products is never realized in practice [7]. One of the reasons is related to the difficulty in merging products and services not originally designed to be sold together [7, 8]. In fact, the Product-Service engineering discipline suffers the absence of a methodology and a tool with an integrated vision on the products and services design, and able to take into account the requests and inquiries of all the stakeholders [9]. Namely, for a provider proposing a fully customer-oriented solution could imply the PSS's economic unsustainability, while, a provider-oriented solution could signify a failure in meeting the customers' demand [1].

With the scope of overcoming this problem, varied methodologies have been proposed in literature [10, 11]. Although, a comprehensive and holistic framework considering all the elements and actors involved in the PSS lifecycle is still missing [12–14]. In this context, the methodology proposed in the DIVERSITY project, the Product-Service System Lean Design Methodology (PSSLDM) [15, 16], aims at surmounting these gaps by defining a new methodology that starting from the needs of all the stakeholders allows the design of product and service features in an integrated way.

Despite this, since the application of a theoretical methodology could result not easily accessible for the companies, mining its day-by-day application, an engineering platform, namely DIVERSITY Platform, to convert the theory into practice has been developed in order to really allow companies in exploiting the expected benefits of PSS [17]. To enhance properly the adoption of a platform supporting the product and service integration a shift in the way product lifecycle data and information are managed is needed.

The adoption of DIVERSITY Platform for the PSS design drives towards a redefinition of the main component of the PLMS (product life cycle management system) traditionally implemented in the manufacturing companies: configuration management, product configurator, PLM workflow modeller, PLM data modeller and requirement management. The introduction of the design of product-service system in manufacturing companies leads to think the management of the information not any more in terms of pure product but in terms of solution structure.

This paper, structured as follows, provides a description of the DIVERSITY Platform, centring then the attention on the PSLM tool, discussing its functional and technological evolution and foreseeing its future developments:

Section 2 discusses the structure of the DIVERSITY Platform, addressing an introductory explanation of the methodology and illustrating its transformation into an engineering environment; Sect. 3 highlights the rationale behind the PSLM tool, introducing the most important functionalities. Section 4 describes the PSLM tool from a technical point of view. Section 5 concludes the paper summarizing the main results.

2 The DIVERSITY Platform

Figure 1 depicts the methodology developed in the DIVERSITY project, the PSS Lean Design Methodology (PSSLDM), which consists of four phases equally divided into customer-related (the first and the last one) and company-related (the second and the third one). Starting from the monitoring of the KPIs and customer sentiment of the company's offering, the PSSLDM uses the customers' opinion and feedback analysis to identify customer needs (phase 1: Customer Analysis) from which start the conceptualization of the new PSS (phase 2: Solution Concept Design) that, once assessed, is translated into the design of an integrated PSS (phase 3: Solution Final Design). In this phase, the Lean Content Design Rules [18], sets of qualitative DfX guidelines and rules supporting the product design developed in a PSS perspective, are used to support the knowledge management and the integrated design of both service and product features. Finally, the PSS is launched on the market and its performances are monitored in order to identify new possible PSS improvements and new PSS opportunities (phase 4: Offering Analysis). All along the PSS design process a list of Development Process Rules [19, 20], representing indications to be followed by the design team during the project to reduce the wastes in which they can incur are adopted.

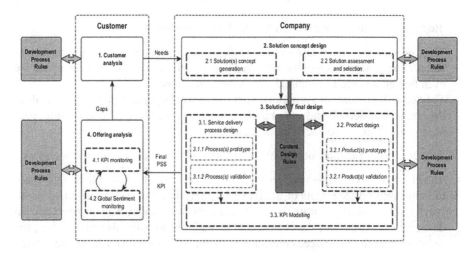

Fig. 1. Product-service system lean design methodology (PSSLDM)

The DIVERSITY Platform (Fig. 2) consists of a series of dedicated tools that have been developed after the definition of a list of specific industrial driven requirements.

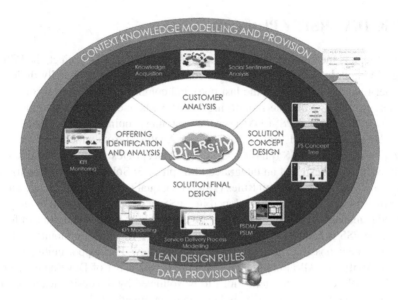

Fig. 2. Diversity platform

Regarding the first phase of the PSSLDM, the company actor uses

- The *Knowledge Acquisition tool* to store the information coming from the customers and the consumers, this tool has been developed with the scope of being a repository even though it could be modified to suit the firm's needs;
- The *Social Sentiment Analysis tool* with the scope of deeply and qualitatively analyse the opinions collected, and stored in the Knowledge Acquisition tool, and the feedback gathered from the social media platforms;

In the Solution Design Concept phase, the second one, the users are supported by

- The *Product-Service Concept Tree (PSCT) tool* [21], which allows the Design Team to brainstorm on the results of the feedback analysis (the Needs) performed in the previous phase and to identify the related elements to conceptualize the new PSS. To draw the PSCT, besides the Needs, it is essential to identify also the Wishes, the Solutions and the Resources connected to them. After the tree creation, the Design Team is called to evaluate the proposed solutions to identify the most suitable one for the customer Needs and the company exigencies;

The third phase (Solution Final Design) consists of the exploitation of four tools

- *Lean Design Rules tool*, based on the DfX approach this tool is used to support a proper exchange of knowledge and information through the definition of rules between the product and service design phases and to allow a coherent integration of the feature. In particular, the retrieve and definition of the Lean Content Design Rules to be followed by the Designer during the product design phase is made available;
- *PSLM tool* that supports the design starting from the product and service BOM management and, in the platform, constitutes the link between the company

proprietary engineering environment and the DIVERSITY one. The characteristics of this tool will be discussed in the next sessions;

- *Service Delivery Process Modelling tool*, used by the Design Team (in particular by the Service manager) to define (with the aid of the BPMN and the blueprinting technique) the service delivery process using the resource identified in the PSCT;
- The *KPI Modelling and Monitoring tool* used to define the list of KPIs to be monitored once the PSS is on the market;

Finally, in the fourth phase, the Design Team is supported by

- The *Social Sentiment Analysis tool*, used also in the first phase to monitor quantitatively the customers' sentiment and support therefore the identification of possible PSS gaps or opportunities which must be considered in the next phase;
- The *KPI Modelling and Monitoring tool*, in here used to monitor the PSS performance on the market and identify possible improvements.

Table 1 shows the correspondences between the DIVERSITY platform's section, the PSSLDM phases and the tools:

Table 1. Correspondence between the platform's sections, the PSSLDM phases and the tools

PSSLDM phase	Platform workflow	Tool
Development process phases	Make it leaner	Lean design rules tool
Customer analysis	Model KPI	KPI modelling and monitoring tool
	Model sentiment	Knowledge acquisition tool
		Social sentiment analysis tool
Solution concept design	Design concept	Product-service concept tree
	Associate design rules	Lean design rules tool
Solution final design	Design PSS	PSLM tool
	Design service	Service delivery process modelling tool
	Validate PSS	Lean design rules tool
Offering identification and analysis	Model KPI	KPI modelling and monitoring tool
	Model sentiment	Social sentiment analysis tool

It is possible to notice how some tools are used more than once with different scopes to cover all the aspects of the methodology, this, in order to support the design team during the whole design process. Moreover, this accent even more the flexibility of the DIVERSITY Platform.

In the following sections, the importance of PSLM tool will be stressed out, underlying its role in supporting the integration of product and service design and the integration between the external company proprietary engineering environment and the DIVERSITY Platform from a functional and technological point of view.

3   PSLM Tool Functional Rationale

The design of a PSS requires the involvement of a multi-disciplinary team that needs a system able to manage coherently the PSS configuration toward the development phases of the different components and involves also different methodologies. The definition and implementation of a valid set of authoring and management tool is the preliminary element for a PSS design that track and manage all the issues related to their lifecycle.

The design knowledge is contained on different ICT systems, in this view the PLM systems (PLMS) are the enabling technology for commonly managing the product life-cycle data and information [22] working as an effective authoring and management tool of technical data, information and workflows. PLMS serves as a central hub [23] for product data supporting the collaborative product design and development and the use and management of information in the whole network of actors (i.e. in an extended enterprise) involved in the realization of the product [24]. A PLMS allows to gather the information indirectly connected to the specific product knowledge (e.g. vendor application notes, catalogues, customer feedbacks, marketing plans, archived project schedules, etc.), to chronologically interrelate all the information and to track accesses and data. According to PLM Technology Guide [22], PLMS is very effective to support "innovation, new product development and introduction and product information management from ideation to end of life".

Based on these considerations, the need of development of a PSLM tool is led by: (1) the extension of PLMS through the concepts of PSS development introducing the elements of the PSSLDM methodology; (2) to create an interface between the DIVER-SITY Platform and the companies' tools used in the management of the engineering product data (PDM/PLM) that are external to the platform.

According to the first point, the PSLM tool supports the customization of PLMS with a main focalization on the data model extension. This includes the concepts linked with the PSS development that available on the DIVERSITY PSS ontology. Example of this it is the Product-Service System (PSS) concept where the BOM (Bill of Materials) has product and service items. In this context, another new concept is the definition of different service types managing the different characteristics in the attributes' definition. At the service concept is also linked the Service Delivery Model.

The PLMS data model is also enriched with other concepts. For each one of these, there are new item types, new relations among the new item types and new relations among these last ones and the existing item of a PLMS. The introduced item types have a direct association with new lifecycles. A "lifecycle" is a typical object treated in a PLM and used to check the evolution state of the different item types and the configuration rules related to the product structure.

The item types with their relations are part of an integrated Product-Service structure. The BOM generated by the product-service structure is managed in an integrated way and allows to maintain a right configuration along the development phases and to integrate all the linked aspects at the different lifecycles. Based on these assumptions, the validation workflows, which are commonly used to manage in a controlled way the transition between different states of a life cycle, are specified for each item type. It is possible thanks to a collaborative environment where the PSS configuration is guarantee and efficiently managed. A direct consequence is an impact also on requirements management that is extended to include also the requirements related to service development.

The second point leading the development of a PSLM tool is strictly related to the linkage of the DIVERSITY Platform with the companies PDM/PLM where are managed the product data. The PSLM tool has to verify that the external PLM system (i.e. external to the DIVERSITY Engineering Environment) has been modified for managing a PSS development. If this check is positive, the PSLM tool communicates with the external PLMS through a set of services. These last ones are used to share with the PSLM tool the data available on a PLM and vice versa, to save the change on products and services generated during the PSS design tasks. Everything is performed with particular attention to the right configuration structure to be managed.

4 PSLM Tool Technological Features

From a technological point of view, the PSLM tool, is a Java web application built according to Model-Control-View (MVC) design pattern, where the information exchange with the PDM/PLM enterprise systems external to the platform, is carried out through RESTful web services.

The PSLM Tool consists of five main modules, aimed to manage extensions presented above and to interface with these extended systems. These components are:

- *PSS Data Modeller*, which addresses the management of aspects related to the data model of the external PLM system and its extension to incorporate the PSS concepts;
- *PSS Workflow Modeller,* which deals with the management of workflow operating in the PLM system and their interaction with the DIVERSITY solution;
- *PSS Requirements Management*, which manages the product and service requirements;
- *PSS Configuration Management*, which manages the aspects of product and service configuration within the PSS design process;
- *PSS Configurator,* which supports conceptual design phase through the development of PSS configurations based on certain sets of selectable initial conditions.

The software architecture, as previous said, follows the Model-Control-View (MCV) pattern. In detail, the *Controller* has to be implemented specifically to the PDM/PLM interface of the solution available on the market. Through the use of a gateway, all the calls to the correct implementation of the various sub-components, based on the specific case, are assured.

The *Model* and *View* components are PDM/PLM-independent: the entities and the relations that model the enterprise knowledge are platform independent. Even the way to present the information is common, through a usable and independent user interface, hiding to user the complexity inherent the PLM systems.

To test the proper features of the tool, a first implementation was developed by interfacing with an instance of the PLM open source system ARAS Innovator v11, executed on an instance of IIS on a Windows Server 2012 R2. To access the ARAS Innovator and interact with the implemented extensions, custom REST endpoints have been developed using the .NET controls API made available by Aras. These functions, by REST services, allow the achievement of information from extended PLM through the passage of data according to the JSON standard. Those are generic and valid for each installation of ARAS Innovator v11 out-of-the-box to which the proposed modifications were applied, so they are widely reusable.

On request, the information is exposed to the other components of the DIVERSITY Platform through REST endpoints.

5 Conclusions

The paper presented the current gaps in the field of the PSS engineering methodologies, introducing the framework proposed in the DIVERSITY project – the PSSLDM – and the relative Engineering Environment. Besides the mere tools enumeration, when necessary, the information exchange between them has been explained. This led to the definition of the Platform's functioning, emphasising the concept of integrated design for the PSS, and pointing out the importance given to the customers' opinions and companies' necessities in defining market solutions suitable on the functionalities side (for the customers) and on the economic side (for the companies).

The central part of this work focused on the PSLM tool, which extended the conventional PLM tool to include the overall PSS design. In particular, this work outlined why and how this extension has been realized, addressing the main functional and technological points. The PSS Lean Design Methodology supports the PS requirements management definition and the design of the activities to define and later perform the service. Lean Rules are also provided in the methodology to orient the decision-making process suggesting task and check to be performed in the product design. In fact, generally, companies are familiar in the management of data and information of a product lifecycle through PLMS.

The adoption of the PSS Lean Design Methodology to foster an integrated PSS design requires a redefinition of the PLMS main components: configuration management, product configurator, PLM workflow modeller, PLM data modeller and requirement management. The introduction of the design of PSS in manufacturing companies needs to re-think the common management of the product structure including also service elements and also changing the structure to be adapted in the provision of service. A validation in three steps (one theoretical, and two practical with the platform's early and full prototype) in collaboration with the industrial partners will be performed to solve the issues resulting from the application of the new theoretical approach and the related tool and also to create implementation guidelines to support manufacturing companies along their transformation path to PSS providers.

Acknowledgements. This work was funded by the European Commission through Diversity Project (Cloud Manufacturing and Social Software Based Context Sensitive Product-Service Engineering Environment for Globally Distributed Enterprise), GA 636692. It is a European project funded under the H2020 program, started in February 2015 and planned to finish in January 2018.

References

1. Neely, A.: Exploring the financial consequences of the servitization of manufacturing. Oper. Manage. Res. **1**(2), 1–50 (2008)
2. Fang, E., Palmatier, R.W., Steenkamp, J.-B.E.: Effect of service transition strategies on firm value. J. Mark. **72**(5), 1–14 (2008)
3. Clegg, B., Little, P., Govette, S., Logue, J.: Transformation of a small-to-medium-sized enterprise to a multi-organisation product-service solution provider. Int. J. Prod. Econ. **192**, 81–91 (2017)
4. Rexfelt, O., Hiort af Ornäs, V.: Consumer acceptance of product-service systems. J. Manuf. Technol. Manage. **20**(5), 674–699 (2009)
5. Baines, T., Lightfoot, H.W., Smart, P., Fletcher, S.: Servitization of the manufacturing firm: exploring the operations practices and technologies that deliver advanced services. Int. J. Oper. Prod. Manage. **34**(1), 2–35 (2013)
6. Matzen, D., Tan, A.R., Andreasen, M.M.: Product/service-systems: proposal for models and terminology. In: 16th Symposium "Design for X", pp. 27–38 (2005)
7. Gebauer, H., Fleisch, E., Friedli, T.: Overcoming the service paradox in manufacturing companies. Eur. Manage. J. **23**(1), 14–26 (2005)
8. Suarez, F.F., Cusumano, M.A., Kahl, S.J.: Services and the business models of product firms: an empirical analysis of the software industry. Manage. Sci. **59**(2), 420–435 (2013)
9. Cavalieri, S., Pezzotta, G.: Product-service systems engineering: state of the art and research challenges. Comput. Ind. **63**(4), 278–288 (2012)
10. Qu, M., Yu, S., Chen, D., Chu, J., Tian, B.: State-of-the-art of design, evaluation, and operation methodologies in product service systems. Comput. Ind. **77**, 1–14 (2016)
11. Maussang, N., Zwolinski, P., Brissaud, D.: Product-service system design methodology: from the PSS architecture design to the products specifications. J. Eng. Des. **20**(4), 349–366 (2009)
12. Baines, T., Ziaee, A., Bustinza, O.F., Guang, V., Baldwin, J., Ridgway, K.: Servitization: revisiting the state-of-the-art and research priorities. Int. J. Oper. Prod. Manage. 1–28 (2016)
13. Qu, M., Yu, S., Chen, D., Chu, J., Tian, B.: State-of-the-art of design, evaluation, and operation methodologies in product service systems. Comput. Ind. **77**, 1–14 (2016)
14. Baines, T., et al.: State-of-the-art in product-service systems. Proc. Inst. Mech. Eng. Part B J. Eng. Manuf. **221**(10), 1543–1552 (2007)
15. Lazoi, M., Pezzotta, G., Pirola, F., Margarito, A.: Toward a PSS lifecycle management systems: considerations and architectural impacts. In: Enterprise Interoperability VII (2016)
16. Sassanelli, C., Pezzotta, G., Rossi, M., Terzi, S., Cavalieri, S.: Towards a lean product service systems (PSS) design: state of the art, opportunities and challenges. Procedia CIRP **30**, 191–196 (2015)
17. Pezzotta, G., Sala, R., Pirola, F., Campos, A.R., Margarito, A., Correia, A.T., Fotia, S., Mourtzis, D.: Definition of a PSS engineering environment: from the theoretical methodology to the platform implementation. In: XXI Summer School Francesco Turco 2016-SMART MANUFACTURING: NEW PARADIGMS FOR A SMARTER WORLD, pp. 97–101. AIDI-Italian Association of Industrial Operations Professors (2016)
18. Sassanelli, C., Terzi, S., Pezzotta, G., Rossi, M.: How lean thinking affects: Product service systems development process. In: 20th Summer School "Francesco Turco," (Industrial Systems Engineering), pp. 97–104 (2015)
19. Rossi, M., Kerga, E.T., Taisch, M., Terzi, S.: Proposal of a method to systematically identify wastes in New Product Development Process. In: 2011 17th International Conference on Concurrent Enterprising, ICE 2011, pp. 1–9 (2011)

20. Rossi, M., Taisch, M., Terzi, S.: Lean product development: a five-steps methodology for continuous improvement. In: 18th International Conference on Engineering, Technology and Innovation (2012)
21. Rondini, A., Pezzotta, G., Pirola, F., Rossi, M., Pina, P.: How to design and evaluate early PSS concepts: the Product Service Concept Tree. Procedia CIRP **50**, 366–371 (2016)
22. PLM Technology Guide (2008). http://plmtechnologyguide.com/site/
23. PLM Product Lifecycle Management (2009). http://productlifecyclemanagement.com/%0A
24. Garetti, M., Terzi, S.: Product Lifecycle Management: Definizione, Caratteristiche e Questioni Aperte, Milano (2003)

Author Index

Printed in the United States
By Bookmasters